The New Structural Social Work

Courage my friends . . . 'tis not too late to make a better world.
—*Tommy Douglas*

The New Structural Social Work

Third Edition

Bob Mullaly

OXFORD
UNIVERSITY PRESS

8 Sampson Mews, Suite 204, Don Mills, Ontario M3C 0H5
www.oup.com/ca

Oxford University Press is a department of the University of Oxford.
It furthers the University's objective of excellence in research, scholarship,
and education by publishing worldwide in

Oxford New York
Auckland Cape Town Dar es Salaam Hong Kong Karachi
Kuala Lumpur Madrid Melbourne Mexico City Nairobi
New Delhi Shanghai Taipei Toronto

With offices in
Argentina Austria Brazil Chile Czech Republic France Greece
Guatemala Hungary Italy Japan Poland Portugal Singapore
South Korea Switzerland Thailand Turkey Ukraine Vietnam

Oxford is a trade mark of Oxford University Press
in the UK and in certain other countries

Published in Canada
by Oxford University Press

Copyright © Oxford University Press Canada 2007

Library and Archives Canada Cataloguing in Publication

Mullaly, Robert P.
The new structural social work / Bob Mulally. — 3rd ed.

Prvious edition published under the title: Structural social work.
Includes bibliographical references and index.
ISBN-13: 978-0-19-541906-1 (pbk.)
ISBN-10: 0-19-541906-5 (pbk.)

1. Social service—Philosophy—Textbooks.   2. Social service—Textbooks.
3. Social case work—Textbooks.   I. Title.

HV40.M855 2006   361'.001   C2006-903602-0

19 20 − 18 17

Cover Design: Brett J. Miller

This book is printed on permanent (acid-free) paper ∞.
Printed in Canada.

MIX
Paper from
responsible sources
FSC® C004071

Contents

Acknowledgements

To write a book such as this, which calls for a social order and a social work approach different from those now dominant, requires a tremendous amount of angry energy. It is not enough to understand how our present set of social arrangements benefits a privileged minority (mainly white, bourgeois, entrepreneurial males) at the expense of the majority (mainly poor people, women, people of colour, immigrants, disabled persons, and the working class). One must be angry enough to want to do something about it. Paraphrasing Marx, it is not enough to understand the world, the task is to change it.

So, I wish to thank all those individuals and groups and organizations who have fuelled and sustained my sense of indignation and rage over attitudes and acts that unfairly and unnecessarily have denied so many people their essential human dignity and have blocked the realization of their human potential. Included among them are: conservative politicians of all stripes for pandering to the corporate agenda in exchange for monetary and political support, leaving millions of people to fend for themselves; business organizations such as the Canadian Manufacturers and Exporters, the Canadian Chamber of Commerce, and the Business Council on National Issues, who in their greed for higher and higher profits have created a social Darwinian culture in society that has swelled the ranks of the underclass; right-wing think-tanks that do not think at all but continue to recycle a 200 year old socially pernicious economic doctrine of laissez-faire that has never worked; the mainstream media that trivialize alternative social arrangements and economic policies and brainwash people into accepting a social system that victimizes and oppresses them; and all those social work academics and instructors who smugly and arrogantly dismiss progressive social work and continue to teach and write about recycled, conventional theories of social work that implicitly accept an inhumane social order and attempt to fit people into it; they should know better.

Of course, anger by itself is not enough to sustain one's writing. Support, encouragement, and help are also required. So I wish to thank the hundreds of people in Canada, Britain, the United States, and Australia—other progressive social work writers, instructors, students, and activists—who took the time to give me constructive feedback on the first two editions of *Structural Social Work*. I have been extremely fortunate in my career as I have met many, many progressive social work and social welfare writers who have shared with me their own ideas about progressive forms of social work. In particular, I want to thank a number of Australian colleagues and friends—Jan Fook, Bill Healy, and Mark Furlong from LaTrobe University; Jim Ife from Curtin University; Bob Pease,

Heather Fraser, Martin Mowbry, Linda Briskman, and June Allan from RMIT; Bill DeMaria from the University of Queensland; Phillip Mendes from Monash University; and the late Wendy Weeks from the University of Melbourne. And, of course, I want to thank my progressive Canadian brothers and sisters—Ben Carniol from Ryerson University; Peter Leonard and Eric Shragge from McGill University; Ernie Lightman from the University of Toronto; Donna Baines from McMaster University; Graham Riches from the University of British Columbia; the late Gordon Ternowetsky from the University of Northern British Columbia; Susan Strega and Leslie Brown from the University of Victoria; Allan Irving from Kings University College at the University of Western Ontario; and Amy Rossiter and Ramesh Mishra from York University. I am indebted to the excellent work of my editor, Richard Tallman. This is the third project on which we have worked together. He not only turns my rough manuscripts into polished form; he often challenges me and my ideas, and my work is better for it. Finally, I wish to pay tribute to the many, many social work practitioners all over the world who carry out emancipatory forms of social work practice on a daily basis. It is to them that I dedicate this book.

Preface

This book represents the third stage of the development of my thinking and writing with respect to 'structural social work'. The first edition, *Structural Social Work: Ideology, Theory, and Practice*, which was published in 1993, followed a period of relative quiet from the progressive or radical social work camp. The second edition, which was published in 1997, was one of many progressive social work books that appeared around this time. This new edition, which is called *The New Structural Social Work*, begs the question: what is new about structural social work? To answer this, a brief overview of the development of progressive social work in Anglo-democracies is presented here.

Although progressive forms of social work date back to the Settlement House movement of the late nineteenth and early twentieth centuries, the modern formulation of progressive social work began with the 1975 publications of Roy Bailey and Mike Brake's *Radical Social Work* in Britain, Jeffry Galper's *The Politics of Social Services* in the United States, and Harold Throssell's *Social Work: Radical Essays in Australia*. Despite being written independent from one another and in three different English-speaking continents, they contained a number of common themes (that had emerged in the radical sixties). Each criticized capitalism as a social and economic system that was antithetical to human need; each criticized mainstream social work for being an unwitting agent for capitalism; and each called for emancipatory/radical forms of social work practice that would contribute to the transformation of capitalism to some form of socialism.

A flood of progressive social work writings in the late 1970s and early 1980s focused mainly on class struggle (e.g., Bolger et al., 1981; Brake and Bailey, 1980; Carniol, 1979; Corrigan and Leonard, 1978; Galper, 1980; Jones, 1983; Longres, 1986; Moreau, 1979; Pritchard and Taylor, 1978; Wagner and Cohen, 1978). From these writings the progressive social work agenda was clear. The critical analysis of capitalism would be further developed to show not only its oppressive effects, but also its contradictions, which would provide the levers and latitude for the practice of radical social work. The critique of mainstream social work practices would also be further developed to show how they actually covered up many of the oppressive features of capitalism by helping people to cope with it, adjust to it, or fit back into it. These critical analyses of capitalism and mainstream social work would, in turn, be used to develop radical/progressive theories and practices of social work at both the personal and political levels. This would include raising the consciousness of social services users of how capitalism exploited them and encouraging them to organize and mobilize against it; joining with the trade union movement, which was seen as the major vehicle for overthrowing capitalism; building up the welfare state that had need rather than profit as its criterion for production and distribution; and electing social democratic political parties that were viewed as more committed to social justice than were bourgeois parties. Also, radical social work in the 1970s was responding to the criticism of feminist social workers that it was gender-blind and in the early 1980s to the criticism, mainly from black social workers, that it was colour-blind. In varying degrees, most social work educational programs incorporated some of these progressive ideas and analyses into parts of their curriculum, but for the most part, they occupied marginal or token positions alongside mainstream social work ideas and practices.

By the mid-1980s it was clear that the progressive project of radical social work was being undermined by the worldwide economic crisis and right-wing social policies brought about by the oil crisis in 1973 along with the inflation-fuelled Vietnam War. Led by 'big business' and bourgeois governments, economic restructuring occurred to address a worldwide recession and inflation (i.e., stagflation). Capitalism was transformed from its rigid and centralized post-war form to a flexible (for the capitalists at least) and global form (Harvey, 1989), thus making much of the earlier critical analyses of capitalism outdated and irrelevant. We witnessed, as Leonard (1997) pointed out, the ascendancy of neo-conservatism on a global scale and the virtual collapse of Left politics, a reduced welfare state, increasing disparities between rich and poor, national trade unions in disarray, and massive economic uncertainty. Given the irrelevance of much of its analysis of capitalism, the diminished political power of the trade union movement, continuous cutbacks in the welfare state, and the election of neo-conservative governments, the development of radical social work came to a halt and the whole radical social work movement seemed to have gone underground.

Though never dead, there was a period of inactivity and virtual invisibility (roughly during the 1980s) for radical social work before an important book was published in Britain in 1989. *Radical Social Work Today* contained articles from various radical writers and practitioners that reassessed the need for radical social work in its new socio-economic-political context. These authors identified what they believed to be the essential elements of a radical social work strategy in the 1990s. In my view, this book breathed new life into progressive social work. The title of its opening chapter, 'Whatever happened to radical social work?', addressed the questions that so many progressive social workers had. What *did* happen to radical social work? To what extent is it still relevant? Which aspects should be modified and/or rejected, given the events of the previous decade and the new realities facing social work? The editors of the book (Mary Langan and Phil Lee), who were also the authors of the first chapter, called attention to several factors that, in their view, would have to be considered and addressed before radical social work could move on. One of these factors, of course, was the changed practice context in which social work operated: dramatic increases in workloads of social workers; criticism and condemnation of social workers from conservative politicians and a mainstream media; the drive to push social workers into a more coercive and interventionist role in policing 'deviant' families; and a growing criticism from members of oppressed groups, such as women, people of colour, persons with disabilities, and older people, that their interests had not been adequately articulated by the radical social work movement. A major criticism of the 1970s radical social work was that it was strong on critique but short on practice. Although such objection seemed to underestimate how necessary this critical stance was, as well as the constructive role it played, by 1989 it was obvious that radical social work had to translate its critical analysis into practice if it were to move on. A few other books around this time furthered the critical analysis of social work and the social welfare state—Fiona Williams's 1989 book from Britain, *Social Policy: A Critical Introduction: Issues of Race, Gender, and Class*; Ben Carniol's second edition of *Case Critical* (1990) from Canada; and George Martin's *Social Policy in the Welfare State* (1990) from the US—but these did not really address the practice of radical social work.

It was shortly after the publication of *Radical Social Work Today* that I wrote the first edition of *Structural Social Work* (1993). In the first edition I attempted to address many of the criticisms made of radical social work in Langan and Lee's book, but in particular I focused on the inconsistent treatment that radical social work had received in the literature to that time and the criticism that it had not moved much beyond a critique of conventional social work. I sought to clarify the clutter of the existing radical social literature by providing a framework that integrated its ideological context, its theoretical base, and its political practice. As well, I tried to advance the existing theoretical and practice bases of radical social work beyond that which existed in the literature at that time by linking social work practice with individuals, families, and groups to contribute simultaneously to fundamental changes of structures in society. I chose critical social theory as my theoretical base and, as my framework, a particular school of radical social work pioneered in Canada by Maurice Moreau, which he termed 'structural social work'. I chose critical social theory because it, unlike mainstream social theory, goes beyond merely attempting to explain and understand social phenomena to a political purpose of changing social conditions and challenging oppression. I chose 'structural social work' for several reasons. First, the term 'structural' is descriptive of the nature of social problems in that they are an inherent part of our neo-conservative/liberal, capitalist society and do not reside in the individual. Second, the term is prescriptive, as it indicates that the focus for change is mainly on the structures of society and not on the personal characteristics of the individual. Third, structural social work has more potential for integrating various theoretical concepts and political practices because it does not establish hierarchies of oppression but is concerned with all oppressed groups. Fourth, it is a dialectical approach to social work practice and, therefore, does not get trapped within false dichotomies or binary opposites. Finally, most of the development of structural social work had occurred in Canada and it was increasingly becoming a major social work perspective.

Coincidentally, another radical social book was published in Australia in the same year as the first edition of *Structural Social Work*. Jan Fook's *Radical Casework* focused primarily on the practice (at the micro level) of radical social work and de-emphasized theory, whereas my *Structural Social Work* was stronger on theory than it was on practice.

Many radical social work instructors in Australia and Canada used the two books together as each supplemented the other. As well, these two books are credited by many as representing an important milestone in the development of radical forms of social work theory and practice, as evidenced by the plethora of progressive social work books published a few years after 1993. However, *Radical Casework* is still one of the best books written on the practice of radical social work.

The first edition of *Structural Social Work* proved immensely popular because, in my view, it filled a large gap in the literature. Many, many social work practitioners and academics were committed to fundamental social change and to social work practices that did not blame people experiencing social problems for their situations, and they were looking for workable progressive forms of social work. However, this first edition contained a number of limitations and, over time, required further development. For example, it did not contain a full analysis of the transformation of capitalism from its previous post-war, almost nation-by-nation basis to its global form. Thus, the book represented a reaction to the negative consequences of globalization without a full understanding of what was happening or how to challenge it. Although the first edition acknowledged other forms of oppression and furthered the analysis of social problems beyond those associated with class, it still did not emphasize enough other forms and sources of oppression, such as patriarchy, racism, and ageism, which not only existed in society but were also present in the post-war welfare state and in social work practice. As well, the first edition of *Structural Social Work* was conceptualized within a modernist framework, as postmodernism was just beginning to appear in the social work literature. Thus, it did not contain any of the insights of postmodernism and, in fact, was based on the emancipatory narrative of Western modernity, with certain claims to unqualified universalisms and essentialisms and with a linear view of history and progress.

In 1996, I began writing the second edition of *Structural Social Work*, which was published in late 1997. In that edition, among other changes, I attempted to address the limitations of the first edition and in doing so to further the development of structural social work theory and practice. I provided an overview of the transformation process from post-war capitalism to its global form (thanks to David Harvey, 1989) and outlined its negative consequences on vulnerable populations, the welfare state, and social work. Given this analysis, at least social work now knew what it was up against and who the beneficiaries and victims of globalization were. Without such understanding it is difficult to challenge or influence any such movement. I also included a chapter on oppression, which I presented as the primary focus of structural social work. In other words, it is not capitalism or class relations that constitute the major source of social problems and exclusion. Rather, it is the exploitation and oppression based on dominant–subordinate relations that result in social problems. Classism is one form and source of oppression, but not the only one. (It is interesting that today the Canadian Association of Schools of Social Work includes in its Standards of Accreditation that social work programs must demonstrate they have included oppression and anti-oppressive social work in their curricula.) I also included the postmodern critique of modernist thinking, which included earlier forms of radical (and mainstream) social work. I argued that it was not a case of modernist versus postmodernist thought; that both were necessary as each provided a corrective to and informed the other.

Several other books on progressive social work were published around the same time as the second edition of *Structural Social Work*. They included Jim Ife's *Rethinking Social Work: Towards Critical Practice* (1997) and *Human Rights and Social Work: Towards Rights-Based Practice* (2001); Peter Leonard's *Postmodern Welfare* (1997); Ben Carniol's third (1995) and fourth (2000) editions of *Case Critical*; David Gil's *Confronting Injustice and Oppression: Concepts and Strategies for Social Workers* (1998); Bob Pease and Jan Fook's *Transforming Social Work Practice: Postmodern Critical Perspectives* (1999); and Lena Dominelli's second edition of *Anti-Racist Social Work* (1997). By now there was a substantial body of literature on various schools of progressive social work.

In spite of attending to the limitations of the earlier edition of *Structural Social Work*, there were still gaps and weaknesses in the 1997 version. Although the analysis of the transformation of capitalism was included, there was no real plan or strategy of what to do about it beyond caring for its victims. In spite of arguing that postmodernism had to be a part of any progressive school of social work, the dominant paradigms that have played such an important part of my approach to structural social work were still steeped in modernist concepts and contained elements of universalism, essentialism, and linear progress with respect to the pursuit of social justice and equality. There was also criticism made that the chapters on practice were not sufficiently nuanced to address the complexities of real-world experience and that I did not address the micro-politics of practice sufficiently. In addition, little attention was given to issues of identity and subjectivity and to the structural social worker as a person, or to the social location of the worker and how this might impact on his or her practice.

In this new edition, I seek to address the criticisms made of the 1997 version of *Structural Social Work*. I have called this third edition *The New Structural Social Work* because it is sufficiently different from previous editions and because the context of social work is also different today from what it was 10 years ago. With respect to the latter point, many observers and commentators, such as Canada's John Ralston Saul, argue that globalization has run its course and is now on the decline. It has not delivered the goods that it promised and very few people expect that it will any longer; many countries have opted out of the globalization process and are reasserting their national autonomy over economic and social affairs; some of the leaders of the globalization movement have not only lost credibility because of their exorbitant salaries and benefits, but many of them are now before the courts answering to charges of corruption, fraud, and other white-collar crimes. In addition to the decline of globalization as an economic theology or religion, other hopeful signs today were not present 10 years ago. For example, in Canada at least, instead of being in a deficit situation as it was a decade ago, the federal government has had surpluses in each of the last eight years in the billions of dollars. Government deficit can no longer be used as the excuse for cutting social services. As well, the anti-globalization movement, once considered by the corporate and government elites to be a rag-tag group of extreme anarchists and radicals, showed that people can organize, can challenge the way that large corporations and governments do business, and can make changes in the face of formidable odds. What was made by an elite few can be unmade and remade.

In addition to a different economic and political context today, there is also a new intellectual context. When I wrote the 1997 version of *Structural Social Work*, there was a seemingly unalterable tension between modernist and postmodern ideas as they applied to ideas and ideals such as social justice, emancipation, and solidarity, all of which were crucial to the modernist notion of a progressive social work. Today, we have several versions of postmodernism, ranging from a nihilistic and individualistic form on one end of the continuum to a critical postmodernism on the other end, where writers and theorists are attempting to bridge the positive and liberating aspects of the critical social theory tradition with those of postmodernism. This developing epistemology calls for: work on the interstices of materialist philosophies and postmodernism; a retention of the ideals of social justice, emancipation, and equality in ways that respect difference, diversity, and inclusion; and an avoidance of totalizing belief systems and essentialisms, on the one hand, and politically disabling fragmentation and witless relativism, on the other hand. I believe that most of us who are writing in the area of progressive social work have moved beyond a modernist versus postmodernist dichotomy. This perspective is the one that guides the new structural social work. This is not to say that antagonisms do not exist between the two, but surely by now there is a healthy tension rather than a binary opposition or dualism.

When I wrote the first edition of *Structural Social Work*, only a few social work programs in Canada (and elsewhere) might have had a single course on radical social work. Today, entire social work programs advertise themselves as structural or anti-oppressive or some other variation of progressive social work. Times have changed and so has structural social work. I hope that *The New Structural Social Work* reflects and contributes to these changes.

Part I of the present work, 'In Search of a Paradigm', shows how and why current social work theory and practice are parts of the larger crisis of global capitalism and oppression, and what social work must do to contribute to the solution of social problems. Chapter 1 examines the transformation to global capitalism and the devastating effects that this shift and neo-conservative policies, more generally, have imposed on the labour market, the autonomy of communities, the social welfare state, the social work profession, and historically marginalized groups. To date, social work has been ineffective in dealing with the deleterious consequences of the 'fiscal crisis of the state' and, therefore, is itself in a state of crisis. This situation has resulted in considerable soul-searching within social work with respect to many of its comfortable assumptions about the nature of society, the nature of social problems, and the nature of social work practice. And although many social workers have fallen back on victim-blaming explanations for social problems, considerable criticisms have been made of our present set of social arrangements and our conventional social work practices, and there is a significant call for alternative models and practices. The concept of paradigm is presented in Chapter 1 as a means to explore alternative models of society more in keeping with human well-being, alternative explanations of social problems more in keeping with people's lived realities, and alternative theories of social work practice more in keeping with social emancipation than social control. Potentially, the hopeful signs today, which were not present a decade ago, could alleviate some of the devastation incurred since the mid-1970s by global capitalism and ease some of the pressure that social workers have experienced over the past three decades because of the fiscal crisis of the state.

Chapter 2 differentiates two major social work perspectives—the conventional view and the progressive view. The former accepts our current social system; the latter seeks to transform it. Structural social work is based on the progressive view: an alternative vision of society must exist in advance of practice as a necessary prerequisite to social transformation. An outline of such a vision based on a progressive view of social work values and principles is developed and articulated and a critique of the new Canadian Association of Social Workers' (CASW) 2005 *Code of Ethics* is provided. Chapters 3 to 6 examine the ideologies of four dominant societal paradigms—neo-conservatism, liberalism, social democracy, and Marxism—and consider how each paradigm views human nature, the nature of society, the role of the state, and the concepts of social justice and social change. Also presented is an explanation that each paradigm offers for the existence of social problems, the ideal social welfare system consistent with each paradigm's ideology and interpretation of social problems, and the nature and form of social work practice dictated by each paradigm. Chapter 7 presents three critiques of the four paradigms: the feminist critique (i.e., the paradigms are gender-blind), the anti-racist critique (i.e., the paradigms are colour-blind), and the postmodern critique (i.e., the paradigms are steeped in modernist thought where there is no respect for diversity and difference and oppressed groups are subjugated under working-class oppression). An argument is made that the progressive paradigms (social democracy and Marxism) must be reconstructed to accommodate these critiques. The Third Way, which some writers have heralded as a reconstituted social democracy and others as a modern version of conservatism, is assessed in Chapter 8 with respect to its potential to overcome the limitations and critiques of the four dominant paradigms.

Part II, 'Structural Social Work Theory and Oppression', presents the theoretical basis of structural social work, with oppression as its focus. Chapter 9 compares and contrasts the four paradigms with each other and with the elements of the progressive social work vision outlined in Chapter 2. Progressive social work is much more congruent with the socialist paradigms (social democracy and Marxism) than it is with the capitalist paradigms (neo-conservatism and liberalism). However, it must be a *revitalized socialism* and not the 'old' socialism of the twentieth century, which reflected a project of emancipation rooted in domination. This revitalized socialism must engage with postmodernism and with feminist, anti-racist, and other struggles against domination. As well, it needs to demand the acknowledgement and celebration of diversity in cultures, sexualities, races, ages, abilities, and other human characteristics that were excluded, suppressed, or discriminated against within an unreconstructed modernist version of socialism. The remainder of Chapter 9 discusses the fundamental components of structural social work theory—its socialist ideology, its radical social work heritage, its critical social theory base (including modernism and postmodernism), its conflict or change perspective, its dialectical analysis, its inclusion of all forms of oppression, and a conceptual framework that incorporates these components into transformative and emancipatory forms of social work practice. Chapter 10 argues that oppression is an issue of social justice and is the fundamental source of social problems. Rejected are the neo-conservative individual deficiency explanation and the liberal social disorganization explanation of social problems. Also examined here are the nature of oppression; its causes, sources, and forms; its production and reproduction; the three levels at which it occurs (personal, cultural, and institutional); its dynamics; its effects on oppressed groups, including its internalization; coping mechanisms used by oppressed persons; and the social functions it carries out in the interests of the dominant groups in society. A new section is added to this chapter where it is argued that the structural inequalities experienced by oppressed persons are socially sanctioned forms of physical and psychological violence, which over time leads to slow, agonizing, premature, and unpunished death.

Part III, 'Structural Social Work: Practice Elements', outlines several on-the-ground approaches of structural social work that are derived from its theoretical base. Chapter 11 focuses on structural social work practice within (and against) the system and Chapter 12 deals with structural social work practice outside (and against) the system. Chapter 11 discusses several structural social work practice elements to be used with service users that differentiate structural practice from conventional practice. This chapter looks also at how a structural social worker can survive in a workplace that she or he is attempting to politicize and democratize. Issues and strategies of protecting oneself from reprisal while trying to radicalize the workplace are discussed. Chapter 12 considers several arenas for struggle outside the workplace where structural social workers can contribute to social transformation, and presents a number of personal attributes that are essential in carrying out structural social work practice. It is argued in the final section of the chapter that structural social work is much more than a technique or a practice modality. It is a way of life.

PART 1

In Search of a Paradigm

Capitalism, Crises, and Paradigms

Subjects enter a social world they didn't make, but they are able to act upon it provided they can understand how it is made, and in so doing, develop a revolutionary praxis to free themselves.

— *Peter Leonard (1997), paraphrasing Karl Marx*

INTRODUCTION

This chapter presents an overview of the economic, social, and political crises that occurred over the last quarter of the twentieth century as capitalism transformed from its post-war (1945–73) welfare state form to a globalized version, which, as will be argued, peaked around 1995. Starting with the oil crisis and the Yom Kippur (October) War between Israel and its Arab neighbours in 1973, along with the inflation-fuelled Vietnam War, the chapter traces the latest mutation of capitalism, from when the nation-state was largely able to contain the worst excesses of capitalism by Keynesian interventions to the shift to a global economy. This process of economic globalization has reduced the autonomy of nation-states, limited the power of the trade union movement, resulted in a retrenched welfare state, and brought a crisis in confidence in social work among people both within and outside the profession. Some of the negative consequences of this new form of capitalism are presented. These consequences include vulnerability in the labour market, a re-emphasis of the subordinate positions of historically disadvantaged groups such as women and people of colour, draconian cuts in social services at a time of increased need, and an ineffective response by social work because it had no widely accepted theoretical analysis of the crises to respond to them. An overview of the 'globalization thesis' suggests that globalization is normal, natural, inevitable, and irreversible, and, therefore, should not be resisted.

Following a discussion of the various social, economic, and political crises that resulted from and/or were part of the globalizing of capitalism, we consider a number of hopeful signs that have emerged since 1995. Discussed are the successes of the anti-globalization movement, the 'collapse of globalism thesis', and the fact that the federal government, in Canada at least, went from a deficit to a surplus position in 1997 and has experienced eight successive budget surpluses in the billions of dollars. Government deficits can no longer be used as the reason or excuse for cutting back on social programs. The crises of the last quarter of the twentieth century have brought about considerable soul-searching in social work with respect to many of its comfortable assumptions about the nature of people, society, the state, and the relationship among them. And, although some social workers have fallen back on victim-blaming explanations for social problems and still others have clung tenaciously to old models of practice, such as ecological perspectives and systems theory, there has been a significant call for new or alternative social work theory and practice models that are relevant to today's economic, social, political, cultural, and intellectual reality.

The two concepts adopted here as a point of departure in response to this call for alternative theories and models of practice are those of 'ideology' and 'paradigm'. These are not new concepts and, in fact, their use has been criticized by many groups and writers as being part of the modernist tradition, which has inherent oppressive qualities (discussed in subsequent chapters). However, an attempt is made here to use postmodern and other forms of modernist critique to inform all analyses based on the concepts of ideology and paradigm. Behaviour, social organization, social movements, and so on are often influenced by ideology. Thus, ideological positions with respect to politics, political parties, and social attitudes, including those towards the state and social welfare, are examined in this chapter. Finally, the concept of 'paradigm' is explained in terms of how it helps to organize social thought in general and social work analysis and theory in particular.

THE CHANGING FACE OF CAPITALISM

Something significant has changed since the early 1970s in the way capitalism has been working, or not working. Although seldom steady and never free from tensions and conflicts, post-war capitalism managed to maintain an economic boom from 1945 until 1973. This long boom, to a certain extent, benefited unionized labour, raised material living standards for much of the population living in advanced capitalist countries, and provided a relatively stable environment for corporate profit-making. The particular set of labour control practices, consumption patterns, and configurations of political and economic power that characterized post-war capitalism depended on a series of compromises on the part of its key players: the corporate sector, the trade union movement, and the nation-state. In his celebrated book, *The Condition of Postmodernity* (1989), David Harvey outlines the nature of these compromises and the roles played by their major actors.

For its part, large corporate power was to assure steady increased investments that enhanced productivity, guaranteed economic growth, and raised living standards for the general populace. This involved a commitment to ongoing technological development, mass fixed capital investments in plants and equipment, increased managerial experience in production and marketing, and mobilization of economies of scale through standardization of products. Scientific management—in the form of Taylorism[1] and Fordism[2]—of all areas of corporate activity became the cornerstone of bureaucratic rationality, and the massing of workers in large-scale factories became the modus operandi of productive processes. This, in turn, required hierarchical work relations and a deskilled workforce.

The trade union movements in North America, like those in most other advanced capitalist regions, have never been marked by total solidarity or homogeneity. There have always been radical working-class movements, but they have been in the minority and, like the larger trade union movement, have been brought under strict legal discipline by way of state industrial relations and labour legislation. Although unions may have won considerable power in the area of collective bargaining, they have done so in return for adopting a collaborative stance with the corporate and state sectors. That is, the trade union movement would collaborate with capitalist ownership and bourgeois governments and not pursue radical social or economic reform. In exchange for real wage gains and job security from employers and for social insurance and minimum wage benefits from the state, trade union leaders undertook to control their membership and collaborate with business in plans to increase productivity using scientific management principles and techniques.

The state, for its part, assumed a variety of obligations to both the corporate sector and workers. It was to create relatively stable consumer demand conditions by curbing business cycles of 'boom and bust' through an appropriate mix of fiscal and monetary policies, that is, by applying Keynesian[3] economic principles. The state was to invest in areas such as transportation and public utilities, which are vital to mass production and mass consumption. Likewise, it was to ensure a certain level of social protection by providing programs of social insurance, health care, education, and housing.

In sum, 'the long postwar boom . . . was built upon a certain set of labour control practices, technological mixes, consumption habits, and configurations of political-economic power' (Harvey, 1989: 124). This model of capitalism can reasonably be called 'Keynesian capitalism', but is also known as 'welfare capitalism', as it reflected a belief that a welfare state could exist within capitalism (although there are competing explanations as to the real function of the welfare state, i.e., social care vs social control). These competing views will be explored in some detail in later chapters of this book. The major assumption of this model was that of infinite economic growth manifest by the production and consumption of more and more products, which in turn would be followed by more and more jobs, increased profits, higher wages, and more government revenue for an ever-expanding welfare state. Furthermore, as noted by Mishra (1999), Keynesian macroeconomic management presupposed a relatively closed national economy that could be regulated by the national government. Thus, although nation-states may have had close and co-operative relations with other nations in the post-war era, the nation-state itself was considered to be the basic unit of economic and political life (McBride, 2001).

Cracks were already appearing in the post-war Keynesian capitalist economy by the early 1970s. The Vietnam War fuelled inflation both in the United States and abroad. Subsequently, US President Richard Nixon announced in August 1971 that the US dollar would no longer be convertible to gold, and within a short time various national exchange rates were no longer fixed but were allowed to fluctuate, sometimes greatly. The sharp recession of 1973 that resulted from the OPEC oil crisis saw a quadrupling in the price of oil brought about by the 1973 Yom Kippur War between Israel and its Arab neighbours. These events set in motion a whole set of processes that shattered the 'grand corporate– labour–state accord' that underpinned Keynesian capitalism. Suddenly, the economy was no longer growing (Lightman, 2003). The corporate sector was the first to act and began a process whereby capitalism shifted away from its Keynesian form with national governments managing their respective economies to a global form where national governments have less control over their own national economies. In the face of unstable economic growth, inflation, and a worldwide recession, the corporate sector began to rationalize and restructure its operations. Technological change, automation, downsizing, mergers, acceleration of capital turnover, and moves to countries with cheaper and more manageable labour became the strategies for corporate survival (Harvey, 1989). These changes have re-emphasized the vulnerability of historically disadvantaged groups, particularly women, children, immigrants, visible minorities, and poor people. The changes in the organization of the labour market and industry have also weakened the trade union movement, which has lost core, full-time members in the face of the transition to a more flexible labour force (i.e., an increased reliance on part-time, casual, and subcontracted workers). The labour movement has also experienced some political repression through legislative curbs on union power and by the geographical relocation of many businesses to underdeveloped countries. And, of course, with a weakened and reduced trade union movement, class consciousness is reduced as well.

Governments also felt the effects of the transformation in capitalism. The 'stagflation' (a combination of high inflation and high unemployment) that occurred in the mid-seventies could not be explained by Keynesian economic theory and did not seem amenable to the usual practices of government intervention. Also, partly because of economic decline, governments began to receive less tax revenue than in the past but were confronted with growing numbers of people hurt by the recession and subsequent corporate restructuring who were in need of government-sponsored social programs. Critics of Keynesianism argued that governments that continue to provide services at a cost higher than a country's economic growth invite a serious fiscal crisis of overload. Faced with mounting deficits, governments could either raise taxes and extend the tax base (as some European countries did) or reduce government expenditures. Right-wing governments were elected in 1979 in Britain, in 1980 in the United States, and in 1984 in Canada. All three governments voiced similar priorities to deal with their respective economic crises. Thatcher's Conservatives stressed the values of 'self-reliance', Reagan's Republicans aimed 'to get big government off the backs of people', and Mulroney's Progressive Conservatives declared that 'Canada was open for business'. These governments chose to reduce expenditures rather than raise taxes, and all three targeted the welfare state as a major area of cost containment and/or cost reduction. Subsequent governments of nominally different political stripes in each of these countries have continued with cost-containment policies. Australia, under the Hawke and Keating Labour governments, although implementing such policies a little later and a little more slowly, went down the same road, but with the Howard Liberal government elected in 1996 that country has pursued the same course at a much more accelerated rate. As a result of these policy choices the welfare state in all four countries underwent (and continues to undergo) a 'crisis of legitimation'.[4] That is, it is seen as an unaffordable luxury by many people and organizations of the New Right. Survival in the global economy now seems to take precedence over meeting human and social needs. Many nations appear to measure success, not by the quality of life or social protection they provide for their citizens, but by how much they can cut costs to make them more attractive as investment sites for multinational corporations (Fisher and Karger, 1997).

THE GLOBALIZATION THESIS

There is by now a vast literature on globalization and no attempt will be made to summarize it. Instead, a critical view of the dominant explanation for the present course of globalization and its accompanying discourse of inevitability will be provided, along with some of the social and economic effects resulting from globalization. It should be noted here, however, that the concept of globalization and the explanation for the process that it has taken are contestable. For example, globalization is viewed by some (e.g., big business) as a positive phenomenon; others view it as a negative phenomenon (e.g., many persons who hold social programs dear); still others view it as neither inherently positive nor negative (e.g., Lightman, 2003; Mishra, 1999). An example of the latter view is provided by Lightman (2003), who argues that globalization processes can be positive or negative. He contends that the European Union (EU) is an example of positive economic integration as the participating nations built into their treaty social protections for workers. An example of negative economic integration, according to Lightman, is the North American Free Trade Agreement (NAFTA), which is based on free-market principles and does not include any direct social or political concerns. The position taken here concurs with that of Lightman (2003) and Mishra (1999), which is that globalization is neither inherently good nor evil. Rather, the problem is the dominant ideology underpinning the specific forms and processes of globalization. To date, globalization has been led by the United States and is based largely on that nation's dominant ideology of free markets, individualism, a minimal welfare state, and meeting corporate interests.

From the above, it is obvious that there is no single universal definition of globalization. Globalization may be viewed as primarily an economic process involving cross-border transactions in goods and services, international capital flows, and the rapid spread of technology. This view has been adopted by the International Monetary Fund (IMF) (Ferguson et al., 2002). Most social welfare and social work writers, however, view globalization as a much more complex phenomenon involving not only economic factors, but also cultural, political, and ideological processes (see, for example, Ferguson et al., 2002; George and Wilding, 2002; Mishra, 1999). It is nonetheless important to understand the dominant view of globalization because this view is used by corporations, governments, and others to rationalize reductions in social services spending. A critique of this dominant view will be presented in a subsequent section of this chapter. Box 1.1 summarizes the dominant explanation, or what Ferguson, Lavalette, and Mooney (2002) call the 'globalization thesis'.

BOX 1.1   THE GLOBALIZATION THESIS

- Globalization represents the triumph of capitalism over socialist alternatives.
- Neo-conservatism is the driving ideological force underpinning globalization.
- The dominant discourse of globalization assumes that globalization is normal, inevitable, and irreversible and, therefore, should not be resisted or interfered with.
- Nobody (or no group) is in charge of globalization; only the natural laws of the market regulate it.
- The spread of globalization will change dictatorships into democracies.
- Increased trade will spread prosperity across the globe; globalization benefits everyone.
- Nation-states must surrender much of their political and economic sovereignty to global markets.
- The welfare state is both unaffordable and the cause of many economic and social problems.
- The economy must be deregulated and labour unions regulated.

The first major component of the dominant explanation of globalization, as identified by Mishra (1999), is the collapse of communism and the retreat of the socialist alternative. The collapse of the Soviet Union in the last decade of the twentieth century signified for many the emergence of a new world order where capitalism had triumphed—we had reached what Fukuyama (1992) described as the end of history because there was no further basis for any ideological struggles against capitalism. 'Globalization and the triumph of the market would benefit us all' (Ferguson et al., 2002: 136).

A second major component of the current form and process of globalization is its ideological foundation—neo-conservatism or neo-liberalism. 'Contemporary globalization expresses, promotes and legitimates a particular ideology—neoliberalism [or neo-conservatism]—which has had . . . a profound effect on social policy' (George and Wilding, 2002: 56).[5] The values of economic growth and private gain are extolled at the expense of broader economic and social development (George and Wilding, 2002). There is broad consensus in the literature that neo-conservative or neo-liberal ideology has been driving the present course of globalization since the 1970s. Mishra (1999), for example, points out that what neo-liberalism (or neo-conservatism) presents as ideology, globalization makes into a virtue and a necessity. John Gray (1998) argues that the global economy did not emerge spontaneously, but that human agency played a critical role in engineering its development. Emphasizing the roles of Thatcher and Reagan, he argues that globalization was part of a deliberate (neo-conservative) ideological project to destroy the Keynesian state interventions that had dominated economic and social affairs at the national level during the post-war years.

An important component of globalization is that its logic and ideology are framed within a particular *discourse*[6] that justifies this new global capitalism—a discourse of economic determinism. The central message of this discourse is that global capitalism is a natural, normal, evolutionary, and inevitable process. Therefore, it should not be interfered with or resisted (especially by unions or governments), but instead should be embraced. Any form of Keynesian intervention is now dead because no one has control over the determining effects of global market forces, since they are the products of impersonal economic relations, new technologies, and new means of communication (Leonard, 1997)—or so we are told by neo-classical economists, the mainstream press, the corporate sector, and its government allies. The global economy is spoken about in terms of *economic laws* (e.g., the law of supply and demand, the laws of competition) and mystical market forces that presumably come from a higher source than humankind—perhaps nature or even Divine Providence. The dominant discourse of the new economy also speaks of the joys of entrepreneurial innovation and the economic necessity of worker adjustment. At the same time, it is made to appear imperative that any resistance to global economic changes must be overcome by whatever means are at hand (Head, 1996).

The discourse of globalization uses Hobbesian and Darwinian language[7] to urge us to accept that competitive life, although nasty and brutish, is necessary for survival in the global economy (Leonard, 1997). We are told that we must accept the negative consequences of the development of globalization on employment, wages, community, and class relations because the consequences would even be worse if we did not compete successfully in the global market. Growing poverty is deemed unsolvable because it is the product of an 'underclass' subculture (Fisher and Karger, 1997). Economic development is part of the discourse applied to exploitation of the developing world by global corporate capitalism, yet this latter world continues to provide cheap resources just as it did in the days of colonial rule. A significant part of the globalization discourse is to present the market and social investment as a contradiction. That is, how can a lean national economy that must compete in the global marketplace support a welfare state? The predictable answer, of course, is that it cannot. Leonard (1997: 113) comments on this position:

> The old ideas which ruled the modern welfare state—universality, full employment, increasing equality—are proclaimed to be a hindrance to survival. They are castigated as ideas which have outlived their usefulness: they are no longer appropriate to the conditions of a global capitalist economy . . . .

The discourse of inevitability or economic determinism perfectly suits neo-conservatism. It justifies free markets, unfettered competition, individualism, anti-unionism, and a reduced welfare state. (Neo-conservative ideology will be covered in some detail in Chapter 3.) Another part of the globalization discourse is that its proponents proclaim that free and prosperous markets will both increase the living standards of all participant nations and turn dictatorships into democracies. With respect to the latter claim, however, David McNally (2002) points out that none of the international economic accords, from the North American Free Trade Agreement (NAFTA) to the World Trade Organization (WTO), contain one clause that would establish a single addition to the civil or human rights of people. With respect to increased standards of living, the evidence suggests that free markets have led less to international prosperity than to increased international social inequality. Box 1.2 outlines the growing inequalities that have occurred because of globalization.

The globalization thesis tends to equate free markets with democracy. The belief is that increased prosperity coming from free markets will lift impoverished and oppressed people out of poverty and provide them with the means to convert dictatorships into democracies. Steger (2003) argues that globalization affirms the compatibility of these two concepts (i.e., free markets and democracy) and treats this compatibility as 'common sense', which precludes any challenge to it in public discourse, as evidenced by the following examples:

> The level of economic development resulting from globalization is conducive to the creation of complex civil societies with a powerful middle class. It is this class and societal structure that facilitates democracy.
>
> Francis Fukuyama, John Hopkins University, cited in Steger (2003: 110)

> The emergence of new businesses and shopping centers in former communist countries should be seen as the backbone of democracy.
>
> Hillary Rodham Clinton, US Senator from New York, cited in Steger (2003: 110)

A contention of the globalization thesis is that global markets, freed from narrow national interests and restrictive regulations, will bring forth waves of trade, which in turn will 'unleash a broad economic-social tide that would raise all ships, whether of our Western poor or for the developing world in general' (Saul, 2004: 34). Steger (2003: 104) quotes Alan Greenspan, the long-time head of the US Federal Reserve who finally stepped down in 2006, as representative of many 'globalists' who connect their arguments supporting globalization to the alleged economic benefits resulting from market liberalization: 'There can be little doubt that the extraordinary changes in global finance on balance have been beneficial in facilitating significant improvements in economic structures and living standards throughout the world.'

An important component of the globalization thesis is that the power of the nation-state was on its way out, to be replaced by that of global markets. Economics, not politics, would determine the course of human events. In other words, transnational corporations, not nation-states, would rightfully determine economic policies and markets, and they would do a better job of managing them with major rewards trickling down to the masses. The laws of the free market would necessarily supersede the laws of any particular nation-state.

Another component of the globalization thesis is that the welfare state on a national level is no longer sustainable. For almost the past hundred years, the state was considered to be the major provider of welfare and the key player in directing the economy. However, since the 1970s this view has come under constant attack from multinational capital and New Right governments, the argument being that interference in the economy by governments is the major cause of economic problems. The relationship between globalization and the welfare state is discussed in the next section of this chapter.

Ferguson et al. (2002: 136) summarize the final component (i.e., deregulation of the economy, accompanied by regulation of trade unions) of the globalization thesis:

> The globalization thesis is . . . part and parcel of neo-liberal [or neo-conservative] ideology. To expand and deepen capitalism, the free flow of capital, the 'opening up' of national economies and markets, the deregulation of economies and labour markets and the marginalization of illegitimate monopolies (such as trade unions) are seen as vital—they are the guiding principles of economic activity. These principles in turn require only minimal state 'interference' and where there has been state intervention this should be dismantled or 'rolled back'—markets represent the most efficient state distributive mechanism and any interference in markets brings disequilibrium into the system which, in turn, will increase the probability of breakdown and short-term economic crisis.

Given what we know of the globalization thesis, it may be asked, what have been the effects of globalization to date? A partial answer to this question is presented in Box 1.2.

BOX 1.2　THE OUTCOMES OF GLOBALIZATION: LOWER ECONOMIC GROWTH AND INCREASED GLOBAL INEQUALITIES

Lower Rates of Economic Growth
- Eighty countries in 2002 had lower per capita incomes than they did 30 years earlier.
- The number of countries with per capita incomes of $900 per year doubled between 1971 and 2000.
- Over the past 30 years, life expectancy has declined in 18 countries—10 in Africa and eight in Eastern Europe.

Increased Inequalities
- The richest 200 people in the world more than doubled their net worth between 1994 and 1998, to more than $1 trillion.

- A mere three billionaires have assets greater than the gross national product of the world's least developed nations and their 600 million inhabitants.
- The income gap between the one-fifth of the population living in the richest countries and the one-fifth living in the poorest countries went from 30:1 in 1960 to 60:1 in 1990 to 74:1 in 1997.
- In the developing world 1.2 billion people subsist on $1 a day or less; 2.4 billion lack basic sanitation, and 1 billion have no access to safe water.
- World trade has impoverished sub-Saharan Africa, where per capita incomes fell by 25 per cent between 1987 and 2000.
- Sub-Saharan Africa currently pays $337 million per day in debt payments to foreign banks and such lenders as the International Monetary Fund (IMF), which is more than the total amount of aid that comes to it from rich nations.

Source: From D. McNally (2002).

THE CRISIS OF THE WELFARE STATE IN AN AGE OF GLOBALIZATION

The economic, social, and political effects of global capitalism have had a profound effect on the welfare states of all Western democracies. The welfare states in Canada, the United Kingdom, Australia, and the United States, for example, have been in a state of crisis and restructuring for well over two decades. The growth that Western welfare states had experienced since World War II has been curtailed in some jurisdictions, halted in others, and even reversed in still others. Most writers on the subject pinpoint the mid-seventies as the starting point of the crisis of the welfare state, a result of the larger crisis of the slumping international economy brought on by sharp increases in oil prices, followed by stagflation and economic decline (Gough, 1979; Harvey, 1989; Lightman, 2003; Mishra, 1984, 1999; Riches, 1986). This combination undermined general confidence in the Keynesian-led economy and the welfare state.

BOX 1.3   THE WELFARE STATE IN CRISIS

Ferguson, Lavalette, and Mooney (2002) outline the elements of the welfare state in crisis in the UK. However, these same elements (and crisis) may be found in the welfare states of all Anglo democracies today.

- Pension benefits for elderly persons are under threat.
- Health services face a continuous crisis of underfunding.
- Educational provision is becoming increasingly fragmented because of privatization.
- Higher education continues to be associated with higher fees, leaving students with massive debts and reducing access.
- Workfare is becoming the primary means to social assistance.
- Homelessness continues to increase and is now a massive problem.
- Social workers are required to practise in more punitive ways and to handle ever-growing caseloads, and consequently are becoming more stressed.
- Privatization of social services, along with its deleterious consequences, continues to increase.

The rash of social legislation enacted after World War II via the Beveridge Report in Britain, the New Deal in the United States, the Whitlam reforms in Australia, and the Green Book proposals for Canadian post-war reconstruction marked for many the beginning of a new era, variously referred to as 'post-industrial society', the 'mixed economy', 'welfare capitalism', 'Fordist or Keynesian capitalism', or, more commonly, the 'welfare state'. The Great Depression had shown that, left on its own, a laissez-faire state with its free market could not function properly. The economic and social costs associated with cyclical recessions, the inefficiency and waste associated with unfettered monopoly development, and the political and social instability associated with civil unrest led to a profound transformation in the economy, in society, and in the role of the modern state. Indeed, World War II was viewed by many in Canada as a fight for a better society than that which existed under the free market economy prior to the war (Guest, 1997). From this historical context the welfare state represented a new deal or social consensus among government, capital, and labour whereby government would use public funds to provide a wide array of services and programs to protect citizens from many social hazards associated with a complex modern society. A history of Canada's welfare state is detailed elsewhere (Guest, 1997; McGilly, 1998; Chappel, 1997; Teeple, 2000).

As Mishra (1984) indicates in *The Welfare State in Crisis*, the post-war welfare state rested on two pillars: the Keynesian economic component and the Beveridge social component. Keynesian economic theory argued for 'state intervention' to ensure a high level of economic activity and full employment. Beveridge (1942) argued for 'state intervention' to protect people on a universal, comprehensive, and adequate basis against those contingencies that were part of a modern industrial society, and further argued that social welfare benefits were to be provided as a right to all and not as a form of charity to a few. Social welfare developed in most Western industrialized nations on the assumption that a harmonious relationship could exist between capitalism and the social welfare sector (thus the terms 'mixed economy' and 'welfare capitalism'). However, following the oil crisis of 1973, slower rates of economic growth, government deficits, excessive unemployment, inflation, and high interest rates brought this assumption into question and discredited Keynesianism.

The crisis of the welfare state can only be understood by seeing it within the larger international crisis in capitalism. Gough (1979: 32) notes that from the end of 1973 until 1975 the world capitalist economy experienced a slump greater than any since the Great Depression:

> The combined GNP of the OECD countries fell by 5 per cent, industrial output plummeted, and world trade declined by 14 per cent. Unemployment climbed to a staggering 15 million in all OECD countries combined. At the same time inflation accelerated and the advanced capitalist world experienced a growing collective trade deficit.

As Callaghan (2000) and other writers point out, the action of most (but not all) advanced capitalist governments has been to retreat from their post-war policies of state intervention and to return to the pre-war free market philosophy. Riches (1986: 105) writes:

> In response to this [international economic] crisis . . . rugged individualism, in the guise of neo-conservatism, fanned into life by Thatcher, in the United Kingdom, Reagan in the United States and the Fraser Institute and Premier Bennett in British Columbia, came to dominate economic and social policy thinking in Canada. . . . Neo-conservatism has been largely responsible for the collapse of the public safety net in Canada by rejecting Keynesianism and calling into question the legitimacy of the welfare state.

Demise of the American Welfare State

In a special issue of the *Journal of Sociology and Social Welfare* devoted to an examination of the effects of Ronald Reagan's policies and programs on the American welfare state, Midgely (1992) outlines some of the efforts made by the Reagan administration to disengage the state from welfare. In its first two years the Reagan administration imposed substantial budgetary cuts on social expenditures. By 1984 unemployment insurance had been reduced by 17.4 per cent, child nutrition programs by 28 per cent, food stamp expenditures by 13.8 per cent, and Aid to Families with Dependent Children (AFDC) by 14.3 per cent. In addition to these cuts, benefit levels were reduced and stringent eligibility requirements, which were put in place, prevented many needy people from receiving any form of aid. For example, nearly half a million families were eliminated from AFDC rolls, more than a quarter of a million had their benefits reduced, and more than 1 million people lost their eligibility for food stamps (Bawden and Palmer, 1984). Homelessness, the incidence of infant mortality, and hunger increased under Reagan as well. Among the conclusions presented in this special issue of the *Journal of Sociology and Social Welfare*

are that although the American welfare state remains intact it is more fragmented, its effectiveness has been impeded, and a reinforced popular antipathy to new revenues for human services was cultivated by the Reagan administration.

The attack on the American welfare state did not stop with the end of the Reagan administration. The first President George Bush's 'kinder, gentler nation' was anything but kinder and gentler on disadvantaged groups, and President Bill Clinton's promised social reform translated into further erosion of America's social safety net. For example, in August of 1996 Clinton signed welfare legislation that would: ban welfare to legal immigrants to the US; set a lifetime limit of five years of welfare per American family; give states block grants to run welfare programs and let them set many of the rules, such as terminating benefits sooner than five years; require an able-bodied adult to work after two years; and deny Medicaid coverage to adults who lost welfare by not going to work. George W. Bush, elected as President of the United States (the Florida electoral fiasco notwithstanding) in 2000, has continued the assault on the American social welfare state. He has carried out his campaign promise to expand private health care and resist any movement towards a public health-care system even though there are currently 40 million Americans without health-care coverage. He has continued the Reagan–Bush–Clinton policy of using police and prisons as the preferred way of dealing with the inevitable rise in poverty and homelessness that has resulted from the massive cuts in social programs (McNally, 2002). And, now in his second term, he is currently planning the ways and means to privatize social security that was initially put in place in 1935.

Demise of the British Welfare State

The Thatcher government came to power in Britain in 1979, a year and a half before Reagan assumed the US presidency. It was one of the earliest critics of the Keynesian–Beveridge welfare state and sought to retrench big government by reversing the advance of the welfare state and by giving market forces freer play in the allocation of resources and rewards. Like Reagan, Thatcher's anti-welfare rhetoric was greater than the actual welfare retrenchment effected by her government. However, as with Reagan, the negative impact on the welfare state was considerable. Public housing in Britain received the most retrenchment with completions falling to their lowest level in 50 years, rents more than doubling as subsidies were drastically cut, and over one million council houses (15 per cent of existing stock) being sold at an average discount of 44 per cent of their market value (Riddell, 1985; Taylor-Gooby, 1987). Minimum wages were deregulated and unemployment, caused by a recession along with the abandonment by Thatcher of a policy of full employment, rose from 4.5 per cent in 1979 to an estimated 13 per cent in 1985 (*Manchester Guardian Weekly*, 17 Mar. 1985). In the health field Thatcher increased user charges substantially, promoted privatization, and held down expenditures on health services as a means of stimulating the growth of private medicine (ibid., 31 Jan., 13 Mar. 1988). Commenting on the early days of the crisis of the welfare state in Great Britain, Gough (1979: x) stated:

Certainly the signs of crisis are everywhere to be seen . . . in the welfare field, social expenditure is being cut back whilst here and abroad a rising tide of criticism engulfs the major institutions of the welfare state. The goals of liberal education are questioned, social workers are vilified in the right-wing press, and a welfare backlash develops.

Ferguson, Lavalette, and Mooney (2002: 161) describe the grim outcome of the assault on the welfare state carried out by the Conservative governments under Margaret Thatcher and John Major over 18 years (1979–97):

when we cast our minds back to the period of Conservative rule in the 1980s and 1990s, among the most enduring memories will be of lengthening queues for NHS [National Health Service] treatment, school and hospital closures, long lines of the unemployed and other claimants at social security and other benefits offices and continual reports of others in need being refused benefits or being forced to live on the most meager state incomes. Lying behind these stark images is a story of increasing attacks on working class living standards and the degradation and casualisation of work—at a time when the rich saw their incomes rise dramatically.

In 1997, the Labour Party (calling itself New Labour) under the leadership of Tony Blair was elected to government on a wave of resentment against the 18 years of Conservative rule and social welfare cuts. However, Labour, the party of social reform and the party most clearly associated with the welfare state, continued with the previous Conservative government's economic policies of downsizing the public sector, extending privatization of public services, increasing the number of leading businessmen in key government posts, and committing itself to freeing up the market (Ferguson et al., 2002). New Labour has also deemed many of the post-war welfare reforms (brought about by previous Labour and Conservative governments) as failures. In fact, with respect to social policy, New Labour seems to have picked up where Thatcher left off. While New Labour has reduced the role of the state in some areas of social and economic life, it has extended the power of the state in other areas that can only be described as draconian. For example, the Blair government has increased law-and-order spending on such things as curfews, blaming society's social problems on the 'breakdown of the family unit' and implementing a policy of parenting classes for parents of 'delinquent' or 'anti-social' children. It has also expanded workfare programs, promoted non-statutory services, and espoused a shared view of globalization with the US (Ferguson et al., 2002). More will be said about New Labour and Blair's 'Third Way' in a subsequent chapter.

Demise of the Canadian Welfare State

Although Riches (1986) presented an impressive amount of evidence that led him to conclude that Canada's safety net (though never fully developed) had collapsed, several

Canadian writers have suggested that so far Canada has not followed the footsteps of Britain and the United States in attempting to dismantle the Canadian welfare state (Jenson, 1989; Lightman and Irving, 1991; Mishra, 1990). This suggestion loses all validity, however, when one examines those aspects of the 1990 budget of the Mulroney Progressive Conservative government and of the Chrétien Liberal government budget of 1995 that dealt with the Canadian welfare system. In 1990 alone the federal government of Mulroney ended its contribution to the Unemployment Insurance fund, increased the waiting period for unemployment benefits, and decreased the duration of benefits for many areas of the country; it reduced contributions to voluntary women's and Native groups; it cut funding for social housing by 15 per cent; it froze transfer payments to the provinces for health and education; it capped funding for social services for three provinces; it froze legal aid funds for two years at 1989 rates; and it 'clawed back' Family Allowance and Old Age Security payments from persons with annual incomes of more than $50,000 (Perception, 1991).

The federal election of 1993 saw the Liberals returned to office, with reduction of the federal deficit as its primary goal (Lightman, 2003). The 1995 budget of Finance Minister Paul Martin cut $7.5 billion from provincial transfer payments for social assistance, health care, and post-secondary education. The Liberals continued a systematic attack on Canada's Unemployment Insurance system, renaming it Employment Insurance and calling for a 10 per cent cut in expenditures, the fourth cut in the 1990s alone (Wiggins, 1996). The effects on the unemployed have been dramatic. In 1989, when the cuts to the program began, 83 per cent of unemployed workers qualified for benefits. This number dropped to 49.7 per cent who qualified in 1995 (CCPA Monitor, 1995). The federal government also announced the end of the Established Programs Financing Act under which it funded post-secondary education and health care. And, most draconian of all, it announced the end of the Canada Assistance Plan—the cornerstone of social assistance and social services in Canada for 30 years. In the place of these programs the Canada Health and Social Transfer, which lumps together into one block fund the federal transfer payments to the provinces for health, post-secondary education, and social assistance and social services, was enacted on 1 April 1996. By 1998 the federal government had eliminated its deficit, but at the direct expense of the provinces, which in turn downloaded their responsibilities to municipalities and the public at large. In 1999 the vastly downsized federal government introduced another social reform that many critics claim puts an end to its role as the dominant social welfare player in the federal state. Rather than another cut to social spending, the Social Union Framework Agreement (SUFA) was put in place. It focuses on process; that is, before the federal government can introduce a new social program, at least six provinces have to approve it. Lightman (2003) argues that this new program requirement ensures that Ottawa's hands are tied with respect to enacting any new federal social program, thereby ending its role as the major social policy player.

In 2005 a report was issued by the Canadian Feminist Alliance for International Action (FAFIA), which tracked the effects of federal government budgets over a 10-year (1995–2004) period. The report measured the federal government's performance against the explicit commitments it made to gender equality in 1995 when it adopted the Beijing Platform for Action that set out a detailed plan for addressing women's poverty, economic security, and health. The report looked at the budgets of the deficit era (1995–7) and those of the surplus era (1998–2004) and found that massive spending cuts unduly hurt women in the deficit era and that women's interests have been largely ignored since Ottawa began posting surpluses. Almost $12 billion a year was cut from Employment Insurance, the Child Tax Benefit, social housing, and the Canada Health and Social Transfer during the deficit era, and when the government began registering surpluses it allocated $152 billion to tax cuts, another $61 billion to pay down the debt, and $42 billion on new program spending on initiatives such as defence and innovation. The FAFIA report concluded that promises made to women were not kept.

The effects of governments reducing social expenditures in Canada are obvious to all who either depend on or work within social services. Between 1980 and 1995 poverty rates increased for all persons from 15.3 to 17.4 per cent; for families from 9.4 to 12.6 per cent; for unemployed persons from 7.5 to 9.5 per cent; and for children under 18 from 14.9 to 20.5 per cent (National Council of Welfare, 1997). The very nature of the welfare state itself has changed. 'Deregulation and privatization increased: costs were cut, but so were service levels in education, health, and welfare' (Lightman, 2003: 23). By reducing their involvement and by transferring much of their responsibility to the private sector, governments have relinquished their responsibility for assuring that many people's social rights are protected. Voluntarism, privatization, and self-help replaced many statutory programs, including the provision of basic, life-sustaining benefits and services. In other words, the welfare state has moved closer to a charity model such as existed in many countries before World War II.

In Canada, unemployment, social assistance, and child and family caseloads have increased while freezes on public-sector hirings have exacerbated the situation. Government retrenchment has led to the formation of Depression-type soup kitchens, food banks, and clothing depots, while the number of homeless people continues to increase. Churches and voluntary organizations have had to pick up the slack. This is the current situation facing those of us who thought that the 'fight for our daily bread' was over when the welfare state was put in place. The absurdity of soup kitchens and food banks should make us question an economic and political system that takes an enormous endowment of natural resources and immense human potential and converts them not into happiness, security, and abundance but into misery, want, and scarcity. The great irony of the welfare state crisis is that we seem to be returning to the very conditions that gave rise to the welfare state in the first place.

From a Needs-based Welfare State to a Privilege-based Welfare State

Although cuts to existing social programs are obvious, Mullaly (1994) contends that something more is happening. Using Richard Titmuss's (1963) seminal work on the 'social division of welfare', Mullaly extends the notion of social welfare beyond a simple collection of programs and services for disadvantaged and low-income groups. Titmuss described three class-based welfare systems that developed over time but independent from one another: (1) fiscal welfare that benefits mainly the capitalist class (i.e., the corporate sector); (2) occupational welfare that benefits mainly persons with good, full-time jobs; and (3) general welfare that is aimed primarily at unemployed and underemployed workers.

Fiscal welfare is the most lucrative welfare system and operates mainly through the Income Tax Act. Portions of corporate income are allowed to escape taxation by way of exemptions, deductions, deferrals, allowances, write-offs, and reduced taxation rates. Because there is no visible government spending involved, and because governments do not publish the amounts of money involved (i.e., not collected as tax revenues), it has been called Canada's 'hidden welfare system' (National Council of Welfare, 1976, 1979). It is estimated that for every $100 the federal government spends, it forgoes (does not collect) $30 to $50 in potential corporate tax revenue—which amounted to $30–$50 billion in 1985 alone (McKenna, 1985). Whereas the corporate sector generally views welfare programs for the poor as government handouts, it sees tax breaks as an unquestionable right and a mark of good business practice (National Council of Welfare, 1976). Although it claims that tax breaks represent investments in the economy, the evidence indicates that they are used to increase dividends of corporate owners, not investment (McKenna, 1985). While it is impossible to know its exact size because of its hidden nature, the fiscal welfare system continues to grow (National Council of Welfare, 1979). For example, it went from $6 billion in 1979 to $8 billion in 1980 (*Canadian Business*, Jan. 1985). By 1990 it was estimated to be around $16 billion. Esping-Andersen (1989) contends that countries governed by neo-conservative political parties emphasize fiscal welfare, given the electoral importance (and political contributions) of those who receive it.

Occupational welfare consists of occupational fringe benefits, such as health benefits and pensions, distributed through the workplace. Other forms are such 'perks' as housing allowances, interest-free loans, and company cars and expense accounts, which are usually given only to executives and other top-echelon workers. These benefits are based on one's position in the work organization and not on need. Businesses finance these fringe benefits by passing their costs on to the consumer of their goods or services and/or by deducting their costs as business expenses from their taxes. Thus, the costs of the occupational welfare system are paid by consumers and by the general public who must make up this lost money when they pay their own taxes. Occupational welfare fragments the working class as one sector has good pay and work-related fringe benefits and, therefore, does not feel the need to have an adequate general welfare system. The other sector does not have access to these fringe benefits and must rely on an ever-diminishing welfare system. Occupational welfare also creates in many workers, especially the professional and managerial groups, a sense of loyalty to the corporate sector and its call for reduced social expenditures. The whole tendency of occupational welfare is 'to divide loyalties, to nourish privilege, and to narrow the social conscience' (Titmuss, 1963: 52).

Titmuss's third welfare system is the one people generally think of when they hear the term 'social welfare'. It consists of modest universal transfers, means-tested programs, and minimal social insurance plans oriented mainly to low-income and other vulnerable populations. Its major aim is to relieve poverty by providing a safety net for those who cannot meet their basic needs in the market and who do not have access to private or occupational welfare benefits. It is the welfare system most oriented to people's basic needs. However, unlike the other two welfare systems, general welfare imposes a stigma on those who must rely on it. Whereas fiscal welfare, which serves principally the rich, has been thriving during the transformation from rigid Fordist capitalism to its new flexible form, and occupational welfare, which serves mostly the managerial and middle classes, has continued to grow, general welfare in Canada and other modern capitalist countries has been savaged (Mullaly, 1994).

Any true understanding of the current restructuring of the welfare state must take into account all of its components—that which caters to the rich, that which serves the well-paid middle and working classes with good permanent jobs, and that which is targeted at the growing number of the working class with low-paid, marginal jobs or no jobs at all. An awareness that there is more to this restructuring than simple cuts to general welfare and that, in fact, there has been a redistribution of money and resources away from the general welfare system to the other two systems opens up other possibilities for dealing with the fiscal crisis than the current 'slashing and burning' of social programs. Mishra (1990) makes this point by noting that although rising budget deficits, increasing inflation, economic stagnation, and high unemployment may constitute 'objective' phenomena, the analyses, explanations, and interpretations of these phenomena are 'subjective'. In other words, a crisis may be seen as an objective set of facts, but it includes a subjective interpretation. Such interpretations are usually based on particular ideologies and/or group interests.

A major theme of this book is that the welfare state is a social construction based on subjective and ideological grounds and not on objective and scientific grounds. Evidence of this is that not all countries affected by the international economic crisis have responded in the same way. Mishra (1990) notes two different ideological responses to it— one from the right and one from the left. Right-wing governments have called for a return to a pure form of capitalism—the rigour and discipline of the marketplace—including unemployment as natural and inevitable, privatization, a lean if not mean social welfare system, and reliance on non-governmental sectors for meeting social needs. Progressive governments have responded by attempting to maintain and consolidate the welfare component (high employment, progressive taxation, equity, adequate minimum wages, and a high level of social expenditures) of welfare capitalism. Each response 'represents a different cluster of values and a different pattern of the distribution of power and privilege in society' (Mishra, 1990: 12). Britain, the United States, Australia, and Canada fall within the first response. Sweden, Norway, and Austria are examples of countries that chose the second response.

The notion that interpretations of crises and problems are subjective phenomena defined in terms of ideology and group interests is crucial for students of social welfare and social work. Every Western industrial country has a social welfare state, but no two countries have identical welfare systems. There is tremendous variation in levels of expenditures, in goals, and in the form and administration of the welfare state of various countries. The welfare states of all countries exist to deal with social and economic problems. However, although the problems may constitute objective criteria, the interpretations and solutions of these problems are defined in ideological and subjective terms. In other words, welfare states represent socially constructed responses to social and economic problems.

SOCIAL WORK IN CRISIS

The responses by right-wing governments to the crisis in capitalism have also created a crisis in social work. The current restructuring of the welfare state means that the context for social work practice is changing. Commenting on the ideological and fiscal change occurring within the Canadian welfare state, Bracken and Walmsley (1992: 23) claim that 'A reduction in resources available for social work services places demands on social workers to provide "more with less".' In a 1983 special issue of the *Journal of Sociology and Social Welfare* devoted to Ronald Reagan's social policies during his first presidential term, Reisch and Wenocur (1983: 546) commented that 'The events of the last three years have shaken many social workers from the reverie of technique and forced them to face the harsh dawn of government cutbacks in programs for human welfare, accompanied by increasingly sharp attacks on the premises and goals of the unfinished United States welfare state.'

This changing context of social work practice poses many dilemmas and contradictions for social workers. The changes in the economic, political, and social environment are seen by many to be fundamentally in opposition to the values of the profession. Social workers often find themselves in unfriendly and hostile practice environments for people who sincerely believe that the role of social work is to make the world a better place for larger numbers of people and to further the cause of social justice by helping disadvantaged groups to empower themselves (Ife, 1996). The crisis in social work is manifest at all levels and in all areas of social work activity.

Jim Ife (1997) discusses the hostile context within which social workers are attempting to practise or, in many cases, simply survive. He outlines four interrelated components of this context: economic rationalism, managerialism, rationality, and competencies.

'Economic rationalism' is the Australian term for neo-conservatism, an ideology that gives primacy to the marketplace as the determinant of individual choice, freedom, and well-being. Government spending, especially on welfare, undermines the market, drains the economy, and reduces individual initiative. Social work services are not highly valued in such a policy environment as they are perceived to represent unnecessary costs and intrusions on people's fundamental rights and freedoms. For social workers who may have thought that their work was actually improving individual well-being and an overall quality of life for society, it is a cruel irony to be labelled as 'villains' or 'wimps' (Franklin, 1989, cited in Ife, 1997) rather than as heroes in the struggle for a just and fair society.

'Managerialism' is the belief that all that is needed to make organizations (including social services organizations) more effective and efficient is a generic set of business and entrepreneurial skills. Hence, social services managers do not need to know anything about social work practice or the nature of social services. This philosophy has resulted in:

- people with no background in social work assuming managerial responsibilities for social services organizations;
- managers with social work backgrounds identifying themselves more as professional managers than as professional social workers and de-emphasizing such social work values as human well-being, equity, and human rights in favour of managerial values of efficiency, effectiveness, and cost containment;
- many social work positions now defined as 'case managers', with top-down control and authority replacing notions of self-determination, empowerment, and democracy;
- a loss of autonomy with respect to creative, innovative, and empowering social work practice, especially within large governmental bureaucracies;
- a belief that social problems can be solved by technical means (e.g., organizational change) rather than these problems being seen as moral, political, and structural problems that are not amenable to managerial solutions.

'Modernist rationality' is the third component of the social work practice environment of the 1990s identified by Ife. It is similar to economic rationalism, but rather than believing in the primacy of economics as the determinant of policy-making it focuses on rationality itself, whether economic or otherwise. It assumes that organizational and policy decision-making ought to be based on the logical analysis of objective data only and not on value considerations. This technical approach to policy development and service delivery does not always fit the norms of social work practice, which historically has been a normative activity. The modernist rational approach is based on the belief that there is one best answer to any problem or question if the logical steps in deductive reasoning are applied. This one best answer is then imposed on the entire population. Of course, this approach minimizes or ignores the importance of cultural, regional, class, and other diversities that are important considerations for good social work practice.

The fourth component of the context for social work practice in the 1990s is that of 'competencies'. The competency movement is based on the notion that occupations should be defined according to the competencies required to perform them rather than on the formal requirements of the workers within the occupations. Jobs are advertised and filled in accordance with the required competencies rather than in terms of the qualifications or professional affiliations of persons applying for them. Jobs previously restricted to those possessing a social work degree are now being filled by those who can demonstrate the specified competencies. An example is that many income assistance positions previously occupied by social workers are now being filled by people without social work education or training. In effect, the competency movement has led to a deprofessionalization of many jobs previously designated as social work positions. These are now being called, for example, rehabilitation counsellor, youth worker, income assistance worker, child protection worker, and so on. In a competency-based job market there would be no need for extended professional education for social work students as they would not have to learn about the social and political context of their work, critical or social analysis, social and cultural diversity, innovative alternatives, and the like. Ife notes that 'social workers under this system readily become seen as cogs in the machine, to be controlled and regulated.'

The current crisis in social work is manifest at all levels and in all areas of social work activity (Fabricant and Burghardt, 1992). At the delivery level there have been cuts in social expenditure and decreased funding of programs (Herbert, 2003), increased categorization and targeting of programs, privatization of many public services, special investigations of welfare recipients (Mullaly, 1984), imposition of user fees, and cutbacks in public-sector social work employment. Along with these changes, social needs have increased because of demographic changes, changing social roles, increased unemployment and underemployment, and inequalities in earnings (Borland et al., 2001; Hunsley, 1987). The net effect is that it is now impossible to address the economic and social needs of increasing numbers of people in a meaningful way—particularly the poor, the disadvantaged, and the most exploited, which include women, immigrants, people of colour, and the unemployed. Not only does this situation make it more difficult for people in need; it also has made the job of social workers more frustrating as more time is spent on refusing clients' requests, as absurd systems of priorities are worked out, as better co-ordination is emphasized, as service delivery is increasingly defined from a managerial perspective emphasizing efficiency, cost containment, and worker control. The negative effects of these changes have been well documented by Rees and Rodley in Australia (1995), Dominelli (1996) in Britain, and Tudiver (1993) and the Canadian Association of Social Workers (CASW) (2004a, 2004b, 2005) in Canada, with many social workers reporting increasing levels of stress, burnout, and low morale.

As employees, social workers are being affected by the society's priorities, which lie in industrial enrichment and public order rather than in the well-being of the general population (Garrett, 1999; Simpkin, 1979). To meet these priorities social workers are asked not only to sacrifice their own living standards through wage control but to police the casualties of unemployment, inflation, economic neglect, and policies that place private profit above human need. Changes in the context of social work practice have meant larger (unmanageable) caseloads, declassification of professional social work jobs, increased use of part-time, casual, and contract social work positions, greater use of volunteers delivering services, and more decisions being made at the political level, which are passed down to social workers to implement. Some writers have termed this process the 'proletarianization of social work' (Fabricant and Burghardt, 1992), the 'deprofessionalization of social work' (Dominelli, 1996), and the 'deskilling of social work' (Fisher and Karger, 1997). Obviously, the deprofessionalization of social work results in many traditional social work tasks and functions being carried out by professionally untrained persons (Aronson and Sammon, 2000; Dominelli, 1996).

On a professional level social workers have experienced an increasing loss of autonomy in the workplace. Although never totally autonomous, social work has experienced a tendency towards increased bureaucracy in recent years. Neo-conservative policies made at the political level are passed down to social workers to implement, and often these policies violate our deeper impulses as human beings and contradict our professional beliefs and values. A study by Aronson and Sammon (2000) on social workers in the province of Ontario found that those within the child welfare and health areas often feel that they have to enforce decisions about entitlement that may contradict their own professional and political beliefs. Social workers are more and more today expected to use standardized organizational technology that is perceived to be cost-effective (Fisher and Karger, 1997; Harris, 1998). For example, the DSM (Diagnostic and Statistical Manual of Mental Disorders) in the US is mainly used to diagnose, catalogue, and treat service users on the basis of the symptoms described and defined in the manual. Leaning towards psychological variables, the DSM minimizes macro-contextual factors (e.g., poverty) and dismisses symptoms that defy categorization. Fisher and Karger (1997: 154) refer to this as an example of 'the dominance of [organizational] production over human need'. Another example is the increasing use of 'risk assessments'—a standardized instrument used by social workers to assess particular groups of people (e.g., parents in child welfare situations or persons in contact with the criminal justice system) according to 'risk factors' contained in the risk assessment. These risk factors, however, are directed towards pathological or dysfunctional characteristics of individuals, and larger structural factors are minimized or ignored. The key concern associated with risk assessments is for the social worker to make a 'defensible decision' (by following prescribed rules and procedures), not necessarily the correct decision (Parton, 1999). Fabricant and Burghardt (1992) argue that social workers today are being transformed from thinking, reflective problem-solvers to specialized, automatic, and mechanized technicians who are subordinated to inferior work roles. Often their prescribed activities are based on conservative notions of individual pathology or blaming-the-victim assumptions. Some employing agencies today do not understand social work roles or the complexity of social work practice (Herbert, 2003). Stephenson et al. (2000) found in their study of Canadian social work organizations and social workers that job performance has become quantified through the use of outcome measurement tools, with an increased focus on accountability and an expectation for social workers to rationalize their decisions consistent with these measurement tools.

A recent CASW (2004) review of the literature from 1994–2004 identified the following current working conditions for social workers and for social work practice, both in Canada and internationally: high caseloads, inadequate financial resources, increased complexity of the needs of service users, increased use of contract positions, supervision that is more administrative than professional, lack of opportunity for advancement. These conditions had several negative effects:

- job dissatisfaction, burnout, vicarious traumatization (i.e., a reaction to repeated exposure to the traumatic experience of service users);
- difficulty maintaining a work–life balance, physical and mental exhaustion, sleep disturbance, anxiety, dehumanizing service users;
- role conflict (i.e., a lack of a distinct identity for social workers);
- lack of opportunity to develop quality working relationships with service users;
- competing time demands that lead to increasingly crisis-oriented social work practice;
- feelings of increased isolation, of not being supported, and of vulnerability.

Although the precise nature of the crisis of the welfare state and its attendant crisis in social work are recognized by many social workers, what is less obvious is any theory or strategy to deal with these crises. Over 20 years ago, this prompted the president of the International Federation of Social Workers to ask, 'Faced with this state of affairs and these key issues—economic retrogression, governmental debilitation, and the economic/social development conflict—what is the role of the social work profession and what should be its strategies for dealing with the issues?' (Alexander, 1982: 63). Some writers see social work in its current state as under threat (Parton, 1994). Ife (1997: 9) describes the current situation in discussing social work's commitment to social justice and the worth of the individual:

> it is important to emphasize that social work has consistently been defined as a normative activity. It does not simply do what political leaders and managers tell it to do, but rather it works towards a better society, defined in its own terms. It is thus more than a technical activity, and is out of place in an environment of increasing bureaucratic and managerial control, where 'accountability' is defined as accountability to management rather than accountability to the community or the consumer. The current environment of practice does not readily allow for the kind of dissent, creativity and seeking of alternatives which are a natural consequence of social work's primary commitment to [its] value position.

Given the contradictions between social work values and its current work environment, what should social work do? How should it handle these contradictions and competing demands? To date, even though the neo-conservative ideology of welfare (or diswelfare) offends social work's traditional commitment to compassion, to social justice, and to preserving the dignity and autonomy of individuals (Mishra, 1989), social work has been, for the most part, ineffective in challenging the crisis confronting it. In the absence of a theory, strategy, or critical analysis, social work has tended to adjust to the retrenchment of the welfare state rather than look for (and fight for) alternative measures. Haynes and Mickelson (1992) present some examples of this adjustment in the United States, which are just as applicable in Canada. With the re-emergence of hunger and homelessness as issues, social workers have participated in establishing food banks, soup kitchens, and temporary emergency shelters rather than mounting large-scale campaigns to expand social assistance benefits and public housing. The effect of this action has been to institutionalize hunger, begging, and homelessness.

Several writers have presented reasons why social work has been unable to deal adequately with the present crises. Karger (1987) believes that the profession, before the crisis, thought that capitalism could be reformed and therefore was left unprepared to present any progressive alternatives to welfare capitalism. Similarly, others have cited its (supportive) relationship to the dominant ideology as the reason for social work's state of inertia in trying out new perspectives and roles. This ideology–social work nexus was well articulated in the 1970s (Dykema, 1977; Findlay, 1978; George and Wilding, 1976; Leonard, 1975; Pritchard and Taylor, 1978). Burghardt (1982) thinks that part of the problem is found within the methodologies and practice frameworks taught to social workers. Too many of them contain abstract propositions for action, such as 'link the social with the personal' or 'see the individual in his or her environment', and do not go beyond these declarations themselves. Jones (1975: 5–6) contends that the present crises are forcing social work to question some of its comfortable assumptions about the relationship between the individual and the state and the role of the state in securing the welfare of the individual, and that 'a process of soul-searching has begun in social work.' Others are more specific about the content of this 'soul-searching' and claim, as Corrigan and Leonard (1978: 90) do, that 'The inability of many social workers to act effectively derives in part from the fact that their analysis of the state and its welfare functions remains at a relatively undeveloped level.' Findlay (1978: 109) reinforces this claim, 'Unless social welfare workers comprehend the nature and role of the state . . . they cannot hope to be effective in the work of achieving a more humane society.' And Simpkin (1979: 25), writing on the deleterious effects of the welfare crisis on users and on social workers, concludes that 'In order to understand how this [crisis] comes about and what we can do to resist it, we must examine social work in relation to the state.' Other more recent writers have echoed these calls even in the face of the current neo-conservative discourse, which calls for smaller and less active governments (see. e.g., Fisher and Karger, 1997; Gil, 1998; Hugman, 1998; Leonard, 1997; Mullaly, 2001).

In the previous editions of this book I stated my agreement with such writers as Carniol (1984), De Maria (1982), Lowenberg (1984), and Pritchard and Taylor (1978), who argued that in order to deal with this crisis not only must social workers learn about the nature and role of the state and social work's relation to it, but there must also be a reformulation of social work theory. According to these writers this reformulation must include: (1) an explication of social work's ideology as a necessary step in building knowledge; (2) knowledge about the nature and role of the state and social work's rela- tion to the state; and (3) transformational knowledge of how social work practice can contribute to changing society from an entity that creates and perpetuates poverty, inequality, and humiliation to one that is more consistent with social work's fundamental values of humanism and egalitarianism. Although I still agree with this position, I now believe that, by itself, it is incomplete. In addition to being undermined by the massive and disruptive economic and social changes that have accompanied global capitalism, social work (particularly its progressive forms) has been challenged on another front as well. 'Postmodernism', with its ironic distrust of large theories and sweeping ideologies and its eclectically relativist view of the human condition, has challenged many of the ideals, concepts, and discourses that underpinned the notions of the welfare state as a progressive project (Leonard, 1997) and of social work as a progressive practice (Howe, 1994; McLaren and Leonard, 1993; Leonard, 1994; Pease and Fook, 1999).

HOPEFUL SIGNS

Before looking at the concepts of 'ideology' and 'paradigm' that help to frame my approach to progressive social work practice in general and to structural social work in particular, I want to present a few hopeful signs that I believe cut through some of the 'doom and gloom' messages that have been part of the globalization discourse and thesis over the past three decades. Specifically, I want to look at: (1) the anti-globalization movement; (2) the 'collapse of globalism' thesis of John Ralston Saul; and (3) the current economic situation of the government of Canada.

Anti-Globalization Movement

One of the characteristics of a paradigm and/or ideology is that although there may be a single dominant ideology or paradigm at any one particular point in history, it never enjoys absolute dominance. Gaps or differences between ideological claims (such as those of the globalization thesis) and people's experiences may give rise to competing paradigms or belief systems and to the organization of dissenting groups. As the twentieth century drew to a close, anti-globalization arguments began to receive more attention and credence in the public discourse on globalization—especially when it was becoming clear that globalization was producing extreme corporate profits that 'were leading to widening global disparities in wealth and well-being' (Steger, 2003: 113). Throughout the 1980s and much of the 1990s the resistance efforts by anti-globalization proponents were no match for the dominant globalization paradigm. The globalization discourse labelled them as groups of radicals who were out of touch with reality. However, since 1999 globalization has come under sustained attack by its opponents.

Cracks were already showing in the globalization thesis by 1999 (see Saul, 2005, for an overview of the decline of the globalization thesis) when the opponents of globalization began their concerted and well-orchestrated series of international demonstrations to protest meetings of those organizations and groups (e.g., the World Trade Organization [WTO], the International Monetary Fund [IMF], the World Bank, and the G-8 leaders)[8] that were leading the globalization movement. The first notable confrontation occurred on 18 June 1999 when various labour, environmental, and human rights groups organized international protests to coincide with the G-8 economic summit in Cologne, Germany.

The financial districts of major cities in Europe and North America were subjected to large street demonstrations along with more than 10,000 'cyber-attacks' perpetrated by sophisticated computer hackers against the computer systems of large corporations.

This protest was followed six months later by demonstrations against a WTO meeting by 40,000 to 50,000 people in the streets of Seattle. This eclectic alliance of anti-globalists comprised more than 700 organizations and groups that included student organizations, labour unions, environmental groups, human rights proponents, consumer activists, feminist organizations, anti-racist groups, animal rights organizations, church groups, advocates of Third World debt relief, and social justice groups. They protested the WTO's neo-conservative position on agriculture, multilateral investments, and intellectual property rights, as well as the massive wealth accumulation for the leaders of globalization that came at the expense of reduced health, education, social services, and decent jobs for many in both the developed and the developing worlds. The demonstrators made it difficult for delegates to access the conference centre where the WTO meetings were being held. In spite of a well-organized non-violent demonstration, the police over-reacted against the demonstrators with flailing batons, rubber bullets, and pepper spray.

Negotiations inside the conference centre did not proceed smoothly and began later than scheduled because of the demonstrations. Steger (2003: 126) articulates the significance of the Battle of Seattle with respect to social protest and the use of technology in the new millennium:

> Ironically, the Battle of Seattle proved that many of the new technologies hailed by the globalists as true hallmark of globalization could also be employed in the service of antiglobalist forces and their political agenda. For example, the Internet has enabled the organizers of events like the one in Seattle to arrange for new forms of protest such as a series of demonstrations held simultaneously in various cities around the globe. Individuals and groups can utilize the Internet to readily and rapidly recruit new members, establish dates, share experiences, arrange logistics, identify and publicize targets—activities that only 15 years ago would have demanded much more time and money. Other new technologies, like mobile phones, allow demonstrators not only to maintain close contact throughout the event, but also to react quickly and effectively to shifting police tactics. This enhanced ability to arrange and coordinate protests without the need of a central command, a clearly defined leadership, a large bureaucracy, and significant financial resources has added an entirely new dimension to the nature of street demonstrations.

Several large-scale demonstrations against globalization took place all over the world in rapid succession after the Seattle protest:

- Washington, DC (April 2000): Almost 30,000 opponents of globalization attempted to shut down the semi-annual meetings of the International Monetary Fund (IMF) and the World Bank.

- Prague, Czech Republic (September 2000): 10,000 protestors attempted to disrupt the annual meetings of the IMF and the World Bank.
- Davos, Switzerland (January 2001): Anti-globalization groups demonstrated at the World Economic Forum's annual meeting held in the Swiss resort of Davos. Thousands of police and military units were placed on high alert, and the harsh treatment of peaceful demonstrators was criticized within Switzerland and abroad.
- Quebec City, Canada (April 2001): Over 30,000 anti-globalization protestors marched at the Summit of the Americas.
- London, England (May 2001): Thousands of globalization opponents marched London's main shopping district. Unlike the other protests, disciplined police units and peaceful demonstrators avoided serious violent clashes.
- Gothenburg, Sweden (June 2001): Thousands of people demonstrated against globalization at the European Union summit. Three protestors were shot with live ammunition.
- Genoa, Italy (July 2001): 100,000 protestors demonstrated at the G-8 Summit.

These and other demonstrations stunned the architects of and true believers in globalization—they could be publicly humiliated by non-professionals (Steger, 2003). The demonstrations also changed the discourse of the proponents of globalization from one of enthusiastic optimism and inevitability to one of negativity and defensiveness (Saul, 2005). Leaders of the IMF were suddenly astonished to find themselves and their ideology being blamed for the myriad social problems that accompanied the globalization process. The president of the German Bundesbank began calling for a G-8 committee to watch the global economy and develop policy to deal with negative social outcomes. And Koffi Annan, Secretary-General of the United Nations, called on transnational corporations to meet standards on human rights. These events were the results of the anti-globalists convincing people that the impact of corporations on different societies could not be taken for granted. The protestors were no longer seen as disconnected from reality. In fact, Jim Wolfensohn, president of the World Bank, publicly expressed his concern for those left behind by globalization and noted that the Seattle protestors were not just a 'group of radicals', as they spoke for some 'very legitimate views' (*Financial Times*, 4 Feb. 2000, cited in Saul, 2005: 168). In sum, the anti-globalization movement successfully challenged many aspects of both the ideology and the laissez-faire process of globalization.

Plans were underway for similar large-scale demonstrations against the autumn 2001 meetings of the IMF and the World Bank when the World Trade Center in New York and the Pentagon in Washington were attacked by hijacked planes on 11 September 2001. Over 3,000 people died in less than two hours. We now know that Osama bin Laden ordered these attacks in response to various manifestations of globalization and that this event gave an unexpected jolt to the struggle over the meaning and direction of globalization (see Steger, 2003, for an elaboration of these points).

The 'Collapse of Globalism Thesis'

In his recent book, *The Collapse of Globalism: And the Reinvention of the World* (2005), the Canadian historian and philosopher, John Ralston Saul, makes a compelling case that although many of its effects (both positive and negative) are still with us, globalization as it was originally conceived and predicted by its supporters is now dead. Another Canadian writer, Adam Harmes, makes many of the same arguments in his 2004 book, *The Return of the State*. This does not mean, as Saul (2005: 204) points out, that the global economy is coming to an end. 'What it does mean is that the Globalization model of the 1970s and 80s has faded away. It is now, at best, a regional project—that region being the West. But even there, the moves to reregulation and the return of nationalism are carrying the twenty or so old democracies in quite unexpected directions.' Saul argues that after a long period of twitching, it finally died in January 2003 when the US Secretary of State, Colin Powell, announced to the economic forum at Davos, Switzerland, that the US would invade Iraq even if other countries would not join with it. In other words, the United States, the leader of the globalization movement, declared that it would go it alone if need be, and other countries were free to act in their own self-determined interests. Contrary to the globalization thesis, this declaration signalled that nation-states rule; economics do not. And so the economic system that once had the status of a religion (Saul calls it 'crucifixion economic theory') died at the age of 30 years, after a nasty, brutish, and short life. Saul bases his arguments on numerous events and occurrences that contradict and negate the globalization orthodoxy or globalization thesis. Some of these are outlined here.

(1) One of the tenets of globalization was that nation-states would lose power to global economic inevitability and the international institutions (WTO, World Bank, IMF) that were set up to regulate international trade and other global forces. However, by the turn of the century, it was obvious that nationalism and the nation-state were stronger in both democratic and non-democratic countries than they had been when globalization began. For example, Scotland voted in 1996 to create its own Parliament after being integrated for 290 years into one of the world's most centralized states. The global economic leadership could not deter the catastrophe that occurred in 1991 when Yugoslavia attempted to stop Slovenia and Croatia from leaving its federation, and thousands were killed to facilitate the creation of even more (not fewer) nation-states. Likewise, the genocides in Rwanda and the Congo were beyond the reach of this leadership. Saul claims that while the true believers continue to speak of globalization, we are in the middle of a political meltdown marked by astonishing levels of nationalist violence.

(2) The experience of Latin America contradicts the neo-conservative economic theory and prescriptions that underpin the international lending institutions and debt mechanisms. In the year 2000 the social and economic problems in Latin America multiplied. For more than 12 years most Latin American governments tried to follow the instructions laid down by the IMF, Western governments, and private banks. The 'crucifixion economics' eventually produced some solid growth, but the divide between rich

and poor grew even larger. Eventually, the recovery in each case was followed, a few years later, by even greater economic collapse. 'So after all of the liberalizations, privatizations, and inflation-stabilization programs, growth in Latin America in the late nineties was a little over half what it had been before the reforms' (Saul, 2004: 40). Latin American countries such as Argentina, Chile, and Brazil are now designing their own economic solutions. Latin America no longer believes in globalization.

(3) Two gigantic developing countries—India (a socialist and bureaucratic country) and China (a communist country)—are benefiting from global trade as their exports are exploding, high-tech jobs are flowing their way, poverty is shrinking, and the middle class is growing. However, Saul argues that the world's two most populous countries have done well by *not* following the economic principles of globalization. They had controls on capital and various limitations on movements and investments. Whatever market reforms they have employed have come in the context of nation-state interests. The Chinese government controls over half the country's industrial assets, invests heavily in infrastructure, and shapes economic and social development. The Indian government does the same, but to a lesser extent. Both countries view economic development as the means to deal with social problems rather than accepting the globalization approach of achieving economic development as an end in itself. In other words, India and China focus on national concerns (unemployment, poverty, homelessness) as the raison d'être for their economic policies. Contrary to globalization dogma, China does not perceive any relationship between democracy and an efficient, liberalized industrial market. Whereas Latin America no longer believes in globalization, India and China never believed in it (save for a few years in the early 2000s in India before the rural poor threw the government out of office in the election of 2004).

(4) In 1999 the electorate in New Zealand, which had formally embraced the full ideology of globalization in 1984, voted to change direction by electing a strong interventionist government devoted to a mix of national social policies, enforceable economic regulations, and a stable private sector. After 15 years of following the economic doctrine of globalization, New Zealanders concluded that it was a failure. Its national industries had been sold off to foreigners, which created a drain of money abroad. The economy was in decline and its standard of living had been stagnant throughout the 15-year experiment. Young people were emigrating so fast that the national population was in decline. The divide between rich and poor took on dramatic proportions, and New Zealand had accumulated one of the highest levels of national debt in the developed world. By abandoning the globalization project, a small country had actually reversed the global inevitability claim. Since 1999 there has been a net growth of population and unemployment has been cut in half, to its lowest level in 16 years. More importantly, New Zealand has reasserted that 'economics is an important servant, not the purpose, of society' (Saul, 2005: 214).

(5) In 1998, in the face of an economic meltdown in Asia, the leaders of Malaysia refused to continue down the masochistic road of globalization. The Prime Minister, Mahathir Mohamad, went about breaking most of the rules of globalization. He pulled the Malaysian currency off the world market, made it unconvertible, and pegged it low

enough to favour exports. He stabilized the country's economy by blocking the export of foreign capital and he raised tariffs. He adjusted regulations and strengthened and weakened controls as needed in a manner consistent with Keynesianism. All sorts of globalization proponents wrote off Malaysia as an economic basket case, declared Mohamad to be mentally unstable, and waited for the inevitable collapse of its economy. It never came. Mohamad thumbed his nose at the West's need for simple economic truths as the economic crisis in his country eased. Investments grew and production and exports increased. The Malaysian case showed that economic determinism was only wishful thinking and that nation-states were capable of making their own choices and succeeding through unconventional actions. It also contributed to some changing institutional attitudes about a global financial system on the part of sensible bankers, brighter business leaders, reserve bank governors, deputy ministers of finance, and some ministers of finance.

(6) One of the correlates of globalization has been the rise of a culture of corporate greed, especially among the executives of the largest corporations. Deregulation and the establishment of self-serving corporate regulations have been used to normalize the most basic forms of corruption. There has been an explosion in the use of share options by executives, along with executive salaries and benefits that have swelled way beyond any services rendered. Surveys of public opinion in many Western democracies report that private-sector leaders and elected officials compete for the two bottom spots with respect to trust, respect, and contributions to the public good. This is a relatively new phenomenon and is tied to a marginalization of ethics that has been part of the globalization process. At one time we would not question the integrity of our corporate masters. However, today, there has been a backlash that began in the mid-1990s. In recent years there has been constant public criticism of the failures of corporate leadership and resentment of such things as the fact that two-thirds of American corporations paid no federal income tax in spite of record profits. Not surprisingly, this atmosphere of greed spilled over into fraud, as in the Enron case or with the accusations against Conrad Black and his management of the Hollinger newspaper empire. Black and his CEO have been charged with 'helping themselves to some $400 million of Hollinger funds from 1996 to 2003. That's roughly 95 percent of the company's net income for the period' (*New York Times*, 2 Sept. 2004, A22, cited in Saul, 2005: 186). The fall of many corporate leaders from public trust and respect has cast doubt on the globalization project itself.

From Deficit to Surplus

As discussed earlier, a major reason for retrenchment of the welfare state has been rising government deficits that originated in the mid-1970s. In the case of Canada, the Liberal government of Jean Chrétien inherited a deficit of $28 billion in 1993, which grew to $42 billion in 1996. Although successive Canadian governments talked about deficit reduction, it was not until Finance Minister Paul Martin's infamous deficit-slashing budget of 1995 with its major cuts to social programs that the fiscal house of Canada was finally brought under control (Lightman, 2003). Since 1997 the federal government has had eight successive surplus budgets, with a surplus in 2000–1 of $20 billion. At the time of writing (2005–6) the surplus is projected to be $8.2 billion, rising to $11.3 billion by 2010–11, with the total amount of surpluses over this period projected to be $54.5 billion (Government of Canada, 14 Nov. 2005). Given the new Conservative minority government's Throne Speech and stated priorities, it is unlikely that these projected surpluses will change very much. What it gives away in the form of tax relief (e.g., 1 per cent drop in the GST), it will make up in program cuts (e.g., its less expensive daycare plan).

This surplus position is substantial. More important, however, is the fact that it represents a totally different context with respect to the Canadian welfare state from what existed from the mid-1970s to the mid-1990s. For decades, cuts to social programs had been rationalized as a necessary evil to deal with government deficits, but the federal government is now faced with the situation of what to do with its large surpluses. During the 2005–6 Canadian federal election campaign all political parties, in varying degrees, promised new social programs or extensions to existing social programs. None of the parties proposed cutbacks, because there is no economic reason for doing so any longer. Some parties, notably the governing Liberals and the victorious Conservatives, promised tax relief for various groups of the electorate, but these proposals were more attempts to gain favour with voters than efforts to contribute to the development of an overall tax system based on equity rather than political considerations. Other nation-states, such as the United Kingdom and the United States, are also in better economic situations than they were before 1995 (costs of the Iraq War notwithstanding). The main point here is that a surplus situation is more hopeful than a deficit situation with respect to devising and/or developing health, education, income maintenance, housing, and other systems that are responsive to human need.

THE CONCEPTS OF IDEOLOGY AND PARADIGM

A significant literature focuses on ideology as a point of departure when discussing the state, social welfare, and social work. Armitage (2003), Djao (1983), Drover and Woodsworth (1978), George and Wilding (1985, 1994), Williams (1989), Mendes (2003), and Mishra (1984) have presented comparative analyses of ideological perspectives on the welfare state. Finn and Jacobson (2003), Pritchard and Taylor (1978), Galper (1975, 1980), De Maria (1982), Carniol (1984), and Kerans (1978) have presented comparative analyses of ideological perspectives in social work. Lowenberg (1984) and Carniol (1979) point out that, to date, social work has not been successful in reducing the social problems with which it deals. Part of the reason, according to Lowenberg, is the eclectic theory base of social work; Carniol cites the 'jumble of confusion' taught to social work students when it comes to ideological analysis. Finn and Jacobson (2003) argue that the predominant theories and perspectives that guide the practice of social work are inadequate for meeting the current issues we face. These issues include increasing economic globalization and inequality, social exclusion and dislocation, continued trends towards privatization and profitability in the social service sector, and the precarious position of basic human rights. They point out that social work scholars and practitioners are engaged in debates over epistemology, theory, priorities, and the general relevance of the profession. They call for a new social work paradigm to confront these challenges, tensions, and contradictions based on a 'fundamental rethinking of the nature and direction of social work practice as we come to grips with the rapidly changing environment in which we live and work' (Finn and Jacobson, 2003: 58).

The task of reformulating social work theory, then, is to bring some sense of order to the field of social work knowledge and to develop alternative theories and approaches that can respond to the challenges of the twenty-first century. This is not to say that social work's currently confused theory base can or ought to be unified, but that an attempt must be made to develop what De Maria (1982) terms 'meaningful patterns' from its present non-unified theory base. A number of theories and ideologies focus on the state. There are several models of social welfare and various explanations of social problems. A plethora of mid-range theories of social work intervention may be applied differently according to whether one subscribes (advertently or inadvertently) to a consensus or conflict view of society. A host of micro theories focus on human agency and various macro theories emphasize structural variables. How is the social worker to make sense out of this jungle of ideas, theories, perspectives, practices, and ideologies? We need to challenge our certainties, acknowledge our uncertainties, and open up new ways of looking at and thinking about social problems and how the structuring of individuals and institutions are time-specific and contextually embedded.

The point of departure taken here relies on the concept of 'paradigm'. Thomas Kuhn's *The Structure of Scientific Revolutions* (1962, 1970) attacked the idea that scientific knowledge develops in a linear accumulation of facts and insights about natural phenomena. Struck by the amount of disagreement among scientists over the nature of their work and methods, Kuhn (1970: viii) wrote that 'Attempting to discover the source of that difference led me to recognize the role in scientific research of what I call "paradigms". These I take to be universally recognized scientific achievements that for a time provide model problems and solutions to a community of practitioners.'

By his own admission, Kuhn provided only a loose definition of paradigm. Masterman (1970) found 21 different usages of the term in Kuhn's book. Consequently, the use of the term 'paradigm' has become almost faddish.[9] We speak of research paradigms, educational paradigms, paradigms of social welfare, sociological paradigms, and so on. In spite of the semantic conflict over the ambiguity of the term, the meaning ascribed to it by some writers would appear fruitful for the development of social work knowledge: a paradigm represents a 'taken-for-granted reality' (Ford, 1975) or world view that consists of the entire constellation of beliefs, values, and techniques shared by a scientific community (Tornebohm, 1977). This does not refer to the beliefs of an entire discipline, as Kuhn points out, but to those who are dominant within the discipline (or profession). In other words, a paradigm represents a specific type of cognitive framework from which a discipline or profession views the world and its place in it. This framework allows for an analysis of the relationship between the scientific thought of a discipline and the social context in which it arises. Paradigms are the 'taken-for-granted contexts, within which one locates facts and methods and ascribes meanings to them' (Bandopadhyay, 1971: 8).

A paradigm is not a fixed or rigid social category, but rather an abstraction—an 'ideal type' comprised of a reasonably consistent set of social, political, and economic ideas, beliefs, and values (in other words, an ideology) that provides an explanation of the world. Different paradigms will include different ideologies, which, in turn, will provide different interpretations of the world. 'Ideologies provide a link between the world of ideas and the concrete realm of political action—for example, political parties, interest groups, mass movements, and constitutional systems' (Sigurdson, 2002: 115). That is not to say that people neatly fall into a single paradigm or subscribe to a single ideology. But people do tend to favour or adhere to many (but not all) of the ideas, beliefs, and values of a particular ideology. A primary function of an ideology is to explain the key problems facing a society and to interpret important events. For example, who or what is responsible for poverty? Are poor people the architects of their own misfortune? Or, is poverty caused by social events that are largely beyond the control of individuals? Conservative ideology would promote the former explanation whereas social democratic ideology would promote the latter.

It is conventional to use the terms *right*, *left*, and *centre* to refer to the orientation of a person or group according to a continuum of ideological or political positions (see Figure 1.1).[10] The concept of a continuum helps us to understand that values and ideals overlap between adjacent positions on the continuum (e.g., between conservative and liberal), and that being on the left or the right ideologically is a matter of degree. While more than one set of measures can be used to locate persons or groups along the continuum, a popular measure is attitude towards social change, including both the degree and direction of change. The more conservative individuals and groups are located on the right. They desire the least radical change to the status quo. In contrast, the radicals on the left seek far-reaching and often revolutionary change while the moderates are in the centre. There is a range of radical beliefs, depending on the extent of the change desired and the means to achieve it. Thus, anarchists and communists are further to the left than socialists, and social democrats are closer to the centre than others in the radical group. Radicals (anarchists, communists, Marxists, social democrats) often refer to themselves as progressives, since the changes they seek are forward-looking, inclusive, and intended to improve the well-being of all people in society, particularly the poor and oppressed. This book is situated within the radical camp.

The centre of the political spectrum is occupied by politically moderate individuals and groups who fall within the generic name of liberalism. As with the left and right wings, liberals hold a variety of political views. On the left are reform-minded liberals who, like social democrats, favour progressive social change and believe that government should be used to improve the well-being of all people in society through various kinds of social intervention and regulation. They favour an extensive welfare state, a mixed

FIGURE 1.1   THE LEFT–RIGHT CONTINUUM

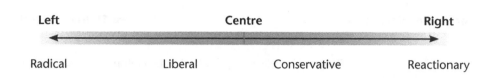

Left	Centre	Right

| Radical | Liberal | Conservative | Reactionary |

economy (private ownership along with some public corporations), and Keynesian fiscal policy (the use of public funds and regulations to prime the economy or slow it down). Reform liberals are also known as 'welfare liberals'. More to the right within the liberal range are 'classical' or 'market' liberals, who are concerned primarily with the right to private property and the protection of individual liberty against intrusive government interference. There is not much difference between classical liberals and contemporary neo-conservatives, as both wish to 'conserve' a free-market capitalist economic system. This overlap between a classical liberal and a neo-conservative is confusing, but is made even more confusing by use of the term 'neo-liberalism' for the re-emergence of classical liberal ideas and doctrines. These terms are discussed and differentiated more fully in Chapters 3 and 4.

The traditional conservative position believes in social inequality and aristocracy. Conservatives place order and authority above liberty in their hierarchy of values. They are relatively content with the way things are, and are skeptical of any attempts to change social institutions or to improve life through 'social engineering' (i.e., social intervention). They lament such progressive social movements as feminism, the trade union movement, same-sex marriages, multiculturalism, and so on. Conservatism is discussed more fully in Chapter 3. The political reactionary, on the other hand, is not content with the way things are, but wants to return to a day when things were better—real or imagined. Like the progressives, reactionaries seek widespread social change, but in the opposite direction. They would reduce equality and inclusiveness along with democracy. They usually favour government by an elite few, preferably by military leaders. This is the ideology of the far right and is usually characterized by racism, xenophobia, and ultra-nationalism (Sigurdson, 2002). The Nazis in Germany and the Fascists in Italy are examples of reactionary political parties. Skinheads, white supremacists, and paramilitary organizations are contemporary examples of reactionary groups.

An alternative continuum for distinguishing ideologies is the location of an individual's or group's attitude towards the state, that is, to what degree should government be involved in the affairs of individuals and society? Figure 1.2 depicts this continuum. Those on the left (Marxists and some social democrats) are more comfortable with the use of state power to promote social well-being than are those on the right. For example, they would support a well-developed welfare state and would call for total public ownership

FIGURE 1.2   ATTITUDE TOWARDS THE STATE

More State Intervention		Centre	Less State Intervention

Marxism	Reform Liberalism	Classical Liberalism	Anarchism
Fascism	Social Democracy	Conservatism	Libertarianism

and full state control of the economy. Those on the right (classical liberals and neo-conservatives but not anarchists), on the other hand, would oppose almost all government intervention and regulation, believing that a free market is the best instrument for regulating the economy and for distributing goods, services, and opportunities. Those towards the moderate centre (social democrats, reform liberals, and traditional conservatives) would support a considerable amount of government intervention and regulation, but for different reasons. Social democrats place their faith in a mixed economy as a strategy to move towards a socialist economy in an incremental manner. Traditional conservatives will allow a considerable amount of government control to ensure order and stability in society. Reform liberals will support a moderate amount of social reform in order to improve or refine present social arrangements rather than change them substantially. Fascists and anarchists are anomalies with respect to attitude towards the state. Fascists would use a strong state to promote their views, but these views are the polar opposite to those of Marxists and social democrats—fascist ideology promotes xenophobia, racial purity, and social hierarchy. Similarly, anarchism is on the right wing along with classical liberalism and neo-conservatism in its desire for less government, but it shares many of the values of Marxism and social democracy, including the wish to free people from the constraints of capitalism in order to promote the public good. Libertarianism also fits on the same side of the continuum as anarchism as it stands for the maximization of individual freedom and the absence of a coercive state. However, its motivations are different because it promotes minimal state intervention for capitalistic reasons, defending the inalienable right to acquire and own property without interference from the state. In this way, it is similar to the right-wing ideologies of conservatism and classical liberalism. President Ronald Reagan associated libertarianism with conservatism, but he would never associate anarchism with conservatism.

Figure 1.3 locates a number of political ideologies along the left–right ideological continuum. With the exceptions of anarchism and fascism, these ideologies will be discussed in subsequent chapters in regard to defining social problems, developing social welfare solutions to alleviate or eliminate these problems, and determining social work practices to deal with social problems and people who experience them.

A number of ideologies, as shown in Figure 1.3, do not comfortably fit on the left–right continuum. *Feminism*, for example, is found both within (e.g., liberal feminism, socialist

FIGURE 1.3   THE IDEOLOGICAL CONTINUUM

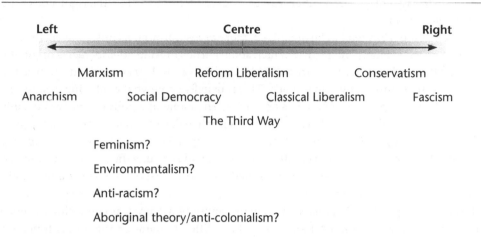

feminism) and outside (e.g., radical feminism) the traditional ideologies. Although all feminisms decry the subjugation of women, the various forms of feminism hold different views with respect to their analysis of the causes and remedies to gender inequality. However, even those branches of the broad feminist movement aligned with traditional ideologies have as their major concern gender inequality, which was omitted by the traditional ideologies. The feminist critique of traditional ideologies is contained in Chapter 7. *Anti-racist* or *black liberation ideology* also does not fall within the traditional ideologies since the latter were developed mainly in Europe at a time when the vast majority of the population was Caucasian (and where segments of the white population held almost total economic and political power). Thus, issues of race were not part of the social reality of European social, philosophical, and political thought that they are today. The anti-racist critique regarding the traditional ideologies being colour-blind is also considered in Chapter 7. Persons who subscribe to *environmentalism* as an ideology claim that it is not on the left, right, or centre and is the only ideology that does not advocate the domination of nature by humanity for purposes of humanity. In other words, environmentalists challenge the 'human-centred approach' of exploiting the environment, which all traditional ideologies hold, preferring instead an alternative, earth-centred philosophy.

The development of a distinct perspective based on a school of *Aboriginal* research and theory, which originated in the 1980s, is currently replacing many of the perspectives, analyses, and reports of mainstream writers who wrote from the traditional ideological foundations (Armitage, 2003). While contributions from liberal, socialist, feminist, environmental, and anti-racist ideologies or perspectives are part of the Aboriginal perspective, a distinct school of analysis of the Aboriginal reality based on their own experiences can be seen in Aboriginal writing and scholarship. Today, the traditional Eurocentric political ideologies are subordinate to Aboriginal perspectives.

Although none of these newer perspectives fit neatly on the left–right continuum, it is safe to say that, generally, they lean towards the left rather than the right side of the ideological divide.

Political parties tend to be organized, more or less, around a consistent set of ideological beliefs, values, and ideals. In fact, some parties in Anglo democracies originally named themselves after the particular ideology to which they subscribed, such as the Liberals and Conservatives in Canada. This is usually somewhat confusing to students unfamiliar with political ideologies or parties. The name of a political party is usually capitalized (e.g., the Liberal Party or the Conservative Party), whereas an ideology (e.g., liberalism, conservatism) is not. Over time, the original name of a political party may change. For example, the Conservative Party of Canada became the Progressive Conservative Party in 1942 because it championed some progressive measures and sought Manitoba Premier John Bracken, a Progressive, as its leader. Many years later, in 2003, the party dropped the 'Progressive' part of its name when it amalgamated with the much more right-wing Canadian Alliance Party. In addition to name changes over time, it is not uncommon for political parties to move away from their original respective sets of ideological beliefs. For example, the Liberal Party in Australia may have been based on liberal ideology at one time, but today it is a right-leaning neo-conservative party in spite of its name. During good economic times, when revenue is available for some social programs, most political parties will shift a little to the left on the political continuum and support popular social programs. As evidence of this, after eight years of successive large budget surpluses at the federal level, all Canadian federal political parties were promising to expand the welfare state in one way or another during the 2005–6 federal election campaign. When times are economically difficult, however, almost all political parties will shift slightly to the right by cutting back on social programs in an effort to bring public spending in line with shrinking revenues. Evidence of this is that most political parties in the Anglo democracies (United Kingdom, Canada, United States, Australia, and New Zealand) adopted policies to cut social services as a way of dealing with the deficit during the period from approximately 1975 to 1995. Given that a political party's name does not necessarily reflect its ideological beliefs, Figure 1.4 locates the major national political parties of Canada, the US, and Australia on the ideological continuum.

As with politics, so with the knowledge and scholarship within an academic discipline: although more than one paradigm can exist at the same time within a discipline or profession, usually one 'dominant paradigm' provides the discipline with a framework for viewing the world. This dominant paradigm also provides the criteria for selecting and defining problems for inquiry, guides scientific practice by providing laws and theories and models for their application, and is transmitted throughout the discipline or profession by practitioners and in the textbooks used for schooling new members of the discipline. Members of a discipline/profession often are not aware of the dominant paradigm as it tends to be viewed as the taken-for-granted reality. Because it is viewed as the only reality, phenomena that do not fit into the paradigm are often not perceived or are rejected as being metaphysical, as lying outside the boundaries of one's discipline, or as being too problematic to be worth the effort of considering (Tornebohm, 1977). In this way a paradigm can 'insulate the community [discipline] from those socially important problems that are not reducible to puzzle form [of the paradigm], because they cannot be stated in terms of the conceptual and instrumental tools the paradigm supplies' (Kuhn, 1962: 37). Thus, the person who brings any anomaly to the attention of the discipline or profession is to blame, not the reality (i.e., not the dominant paradigm).

How, then, do dominant paradigms change or become discarded? Kuhn contends that only when anomalies can no longer be explained away or when they become so numerically overwhelming does the discipline begin to explore the area of anomaly that has violated its 'paradigm-induced expectations' governing normal practice (Kuhn, 1962: 52–3). This exploration ends when the paradigm has been adjusted to accommodate the anomaly or when the dominant paradigm has been discarded in favour of another. And, Kuhn asserts, this adjustment or exchange of paradigms is generally preceded and followed by periods of resistance.

According to Kuhn (1962: 6) development of a new paradigm occurs 'when the profession can no longer evade anomalies that subvert the existing tradition of scientific practice. Then begin the extraordinary investigations that lead the profession at least to a new set of commitments, a new basis for practice.' Alternative interpretations are posed, which leads to a competition between the present dominant paradigm and the new revolutionary paradigm. 'Each revolution necessitates the rejection (not without resistance) of prior frameworks and rules in favour of new ones. The new paradigm is not simply grafted on to the old one: acceptance requires rejection of the old. When the transition is complete the profession will have changed its view of the field, its methods and its goals' (De Maria, 1982: 33). Shifts of paradigms bring members of a discipline/profession to see the world around them in a new light. To present an alternative paradigm is the ultimate revolutionary act.

The crisis of capitalism and the ensuing crises in social welfare and social work may be viewed in terms of paradigms. Prior to World War II the dominant paradigm in North America was conservatism, with its emphasis on an unfettered market economy, and charity, the Poor Laws, and voluntarism were the major means of addressing social need. The Great Depression of the 1930s brought this paradigm into disrepute, and after the war liberalism or welfare capitalism (see Chapter 4), complete with a modern welfare state, gradually became the dominant paradigm. In turn, the recession and oil crisis of the early 1970s brought about a questioning of welfare capitalism, and in the ensuing years a shift back to conservatism (i.e., neo-conservatism, see Chapter 3). However, this shift is by no means complete because we continue (thus far) to have significant government intervention into the economy and a welfare state (albeit reduced). There is consensus within social work that neo-conservatism is contradictory to social work values and beliefs. Is there a more compatible paradigm for social work? If so, what can we do to halt the present paradigmatic shift? What contributions can we make to transform our current society to one that is more sensitive to, and more capable of, meeting human need? These are a few of the questions addressed in this book.

FIGURE 1.4   POLITICAL PARTIES ALONG THE IDEOLOGICAL CONTINUUM

Left	Centre		Right

Marxism	Social Democracy	Reform Liberalism	Conservatism

Canada

Greens	NDP	Liberals	Conservatives	

United States

			Democrats	Republicans

Australia

Greens	Democrats	Labour	Liberals

Notes:

1. Individuals and groups tend to organize themselves politically based on particular shared ideologies.
2. Not all persons who belong to a particular political party will agree with all its values, ideals, policies, etc.
3. Political parties are not located at a particular point on the ideological continuum (as is shown above), but occupy a space on both sides of the point. There is a range of political positions within each party. For example, the Conservative Party of Canada comprises a group known as 'red Tories' who are socially progressive and a group of former Alliance members who are socially regressive.
4. Given that political parties occupy a space along the continuum, those adjacent spaces may even overlap with each other. For example, some progressive-minded Conservatives are more progressive than some Liberals on the right wing of their party. Thus it is not that uncommon to have some politicians switch political parties even after they have been elected. Examples are Belinda Stronach, a 'red Tory' who switched from the Conservative Party to the Liberal Party in 2005, and David Emerson, a cabinet minister in the Paul Martin Liberal government who switched to the victorious Conservatives almost immediately after the election to become a cabinet minister and was given the same portfolio (Industry) that he had in the Liberal cabinet.
5. The Green Party of Canada does not fit comfortably on the ideological continuum as its major issue is the environment, which attracts both progressive-minded and conservative-minded individuals.
6. The fact that the Liberal Party of Canada occupies the centre location on the political continuum makes it easier for it than for other parties to shift either left or right of centre, thus capitalizing on the mood of the electorate at any given time. Many political scientists attribute the electoral success that the Liberals enjoyed for most of the twentieth century to their central position on the continuum.

UTILITY OF THE PARADIGM CONCEPT FOR SOCIAL WORK

In view of the international economic crisis and the ensuing crises of the welfare state and social work, how does the concept of paradigm help social work deal with the problems it faces, including its own tangled web of ideological, political, and theoretical confusion? And how does it address the intellectual challenges that postmodernism presents to progressive forms of social work based on principles of social justice? It is my belief that the application of the paradigm concept can perform three major functions for social work in helping it to confront, understand, and deal with these crises.

First, as noted by Carniol (1984), ideological critiques and analyses at the level of social work methods abound in the literature. These critiques and analyses might be better appreciated, however, if they were presented within a framework that not only compares ideologies but also allows the student to compare and contrast the different views of the nature of social problems, of social welfare approaches, and of social work practices emanating from different ideologies. The concept of paradigm should help the student make the connection between ideology and social work practice, that is, how an ideology largely determines the nature and form of social work practice. In other words, it should help the student understand that there is no one universal approach to social work practice, nor is there only one explanation of social problems or one ideal type of social welfare system. Postmodernism teaches us that there are always multiple claims to truth. Using the concept of a paradigm helps us to compare and contrast different approaches to dealing with social problems and different claims as to what form both the welfare state and social work practice ought to take.

Second, one of the purposes of the above-mentioned comparison is to become aware of alternative ways of integrating economic and human welfare to that which is presently being offered by neo-conservatives (Mishra, 1989). A major theme of this book is that our present social order is not the natural and inevitable product of some evolutionary process; rather, there are alternatives. Sweden, for example, is representative of a different paradigm than that which exists in North America, and it has demonstrated that an efficient market economy does not have to be constructed at the expense of social welfare. Hopefully, an awareness of alternative world views—paradigms—will open everything to challenge and change, including our present social order, our present structure of social services, and the nature of our present social work practice. These things should not be predetermined by either present statistics or current power relationships. 'The shape of events is determined by people, all of us, and by our willingness to understand and seek to change the world for the better' (Burghardt, 1982: 20). Indeed, several writers have argued that an alternative vision is a prerequisite for meaningful social change (Berger and Luckmann, 1966; Ferguson and Lavalette, 2005; Mishra, 1989; Moreau and Leonard, 1997; Mullaly, 2001; Wineman, 1984). Such a vision, if consistent with social work ideals, values, and beliefs, could provide a goal and a direction for social work. An articulation of such a vision is presented in the next chapter.

The third function that the concept of paradigm may carry out for social work is to enhance our understanding of the dynamics of change, especially fundamental change. De Maria (1982: 34) informs us that 'The concept of paradigm, particularly the causal link between social context and knowledge, has a history in philosophy, sociology and political science.' For example, De Maria attempts to show how Kuhn's view of scientific development is similar to the Marxist view of social change. He states, 'Whether it be a social revolution in the Marxian sense or a scientific revolution in the Kuhnian sense, the dynamics appear to be the same, with the existing paradigm or the Marxist notion of epoch carrying within itself the potentiality for a new order' (p. 35). Three examples of characteristics of paradigms that have implications for understanding the dynamics of social change follow. First, the fact that one paradigm (e.g., neo-conservatism) usually is dominant over others means that it is the taken-for-granted reality of most people in society—including social workers. Second, only when the dominant paradigm can no longer explain away certain anomalies (such as decreasing levels of well-being for many in an expanding global economy) can a shift of paradigms begin to occur. And third, an acceptance of a new paradigm does not occur without resistance. Understanding these dynamics of change should help social work make a transition in its view of society, in its theory, and in its practice. These are a few of the tasks taken up here.

Two assumptions are made here. First, critical theory and ideological analysis in the modernist tradition can make important contributions in critiquing the dominant paradigm and in conceptualizing social work theory and practice so that these can adequately deal with the crises outlined in this chapter. Second, by themselves, modernist critical theory and ideological analysis are inadequate in carrying out these tasks. In fact, as many social work writers (e.g., Fook, 2000; Healy, 1999; Pease and Fook, 1999; Leonard, 1997) have argued and as many social movements have shown (e.g., trade union movement, socialist movement), modernist critical theories and progressive ideological analyses based on a singular idea of truth can be just as oppressive as social structures and social relations based on inequality and domination. They must be informed, supplemented, and complemented by the contributions of postmodernism, post-structuralism, feminism, and anti-racism, which by themselves are also insufficient for formulating emancipatory forms of social work theory and practice. Rather than viewing modernism and postmodernism as a dichotomy, the position adopted in this book is that each serves as a corrective for the weaknesses and limitations of the other. In other words, rather than an 'either-or' situation, they represent a dialectic,[11] a set of opposing forces that, taken together, help us to deconstruct and reconstruct social welfare and social work as emancipatory projects and activities within a progressive discourse. This position is similar to that of several other writers (Ife, 1997; P. Leonard, 1995, 1997; S. Leonard, 1990; Mullaly, 2001, 2002), and is discussed more fully in Chapter 9.

CONCLUSION

In this chapter an overview of the events surrounding the transformation of capitalism from its post-war form to a global form was presented, along with the deleterious effects that this new form of capitalism has imposed on so many social institutions (including the welfare state) and on so many social groups (including oppressed people and social work). The field of social work, generally, has been unprepared to confront social and economic change, and has lacked the analytical or theoretical framework to understand global capitalism and to deal with its negative consequences. Thus, there is a need to develop new and alternative forms of social work that reflect more closely the current social, economic, and political circumstances. A number of hopeful signs have emerged since the mid-1990s, and the concepts of ideology and paradigm offer potential for developing alternative forms of social work theory and practice, provided that this project is informed by the insights of postmodernism, post-structuralism, and other such epistemologies.

CRITICAL QUESTIONS

1. Is the main reason for globalization economic or ideological? Explain.
2. Why is it important that social workers be knowledgeable about globalization?
3. Instead of cutting back on social programs, what else could governments have done to deal with their economic problems? For example, why didn't they raise taxes on profitable corporations and wealthy individuals?
4. How do the concepts of ideology and paradigm help us to understand social policy and social welfare choices?
5. List the political parties that exist in Canada. What ideology is characteristic of each and what is the view of social welfare held by each party?
6. Although the welfare state in all Anglo democracies was under attack for more than two decades, it has in large measure survived. Why?

The Social Work Vision: A Progressive View

We do not anticipate the world with our dogmas but instead attempt to discover the new world through the critique of the old.

—Karl Marx (1818–83)

INTRODUCTION

The purpose of this chapter is twofold: (1) to present an argument that social work needs an alternative vision of society, one that is more in accordance with the social, emotional, cultural, physical, and spiritual well-being of all people (not just a privileged minority); and (2) to outline such a vision based on the espoused values of the social work profession. By itself, this twofold purpose is impossible to carry out because social work is not a unitary profession. There is no consensus within social work with respect to the ideal nature of society, or the nature and functions of the welfare state, or the nature and political consequences of social work practice. As the title of this chapter suggests, the analysis and discourse presented here are derived from the progressive wing of the social work profession as opposed to the conventional wing.

CONVENTIONAL AND PROGRESSIVE PERSPECTIVES WITHIN SOCIAL WORK

Modern-day social work has two traditions that date back to the latter part of the nineteenth century: the Charity Organization Society movement that began in 1877 in the United States and the Settlement House movement that began in 1884 in England (Chandler, 1995). Although both were products of industrialization and urbanization, each adopted a different view of and approach to the problem of poverty and those experiencing poverty.

The Charity Organization Society movement believed that a rational system of co-ordinated, private, and scientific philanthropy supplemented by an army of 'friendly visitors' would do much to diminish destitution, hardship, and begging. Co-ordination was seen as important because otherwise the poor might take advantage of a fragmented charity system and obtain duplicative goods and services. All decisions regarding this system were made by the 'right' people in the community (i.e., mainly white, middle-class businessmen) because the poor could not be trusted to make responsible decisions affecting their lives; their poverty, after all, was seen as evidence of this inability. (The United Way in Canada is the modern version of a Charity Organization Society.) The role of the friendly visitors (who were mainly volunteer women of high socio-economic status) was to visit the poor in their homes and teach them life skills, thrift, and moral behaviour. Obviously, the explanation for poverty was one of character defect and moral deficiency on the part of the poor, and the solution was to reform the individual. Out of this heritage came one of social work's primary methods (arguably, the primary method) of intervention, a type of casework with individuals and families that focused on coping, adjustment, and restoration of the poor rather than a change of social conditions.

The Settlement House movement's approach to the problem of poverty and to those experiencing it rested on a different assumption from that of the Charity Organization Society movement. Rather than seeing the poor as makers of their own misfortune, it believed that they were victims of an unjust social order that discriminated against large numbers of people so that a few might benefit. In other words, the capitalist system caused poverty, not poor people. People involved in the Settlement House movement established houses in slum neighbourhoods and worked directly with people in attempts to do something about poor sanitary conditions, slum housing, crime, poverty, sweatshop work conditions, and so on. Their focus was to reform society rather than to reform the person. Out of this heritage came another of social work's primary methods of intervention, a self-help model of community organization that focused on participation of the poor, community development, and social action.

BOX 2.1 BLEEDING HEARTS AND DO-GOODERS

Social workers are sometimes portrayed in negative stereotypes and called such names as 'bleeding hearts', 'busy bodies', and 'do-gooders'. In the early nineties I was teaching at St Thomas University in Fredericton, New Brunswick. Over the course of a few months there was a particular individual in the community who wrote a series of derogatory letters about social workers to the local newspaper, which were printed in the 'Letters to the Editor' page. Referring to social workers as 'do-gooders' was his major mantra. One day I had enough and wrote my own letter to the editor in response to his letters. The following is a modified version of my letter.

Dear Editor:

I wish to respond to the derogatory, uninformed, and prejudicial letters written by Mr Anti-Social Worker that have appeared in your paper over the past few months. In those letters he constantly refers to social workers and other community-minded people as 'do-gooders'. It seems to me that the label 'do-gooder' suggests there are three kinds of people in the world: those who do good, those who do bad, and those who do nothing. Since Mr Anti-Social Worker is obviously not in the do-good group, I wonder if he could tell us which of the other two groups he belongs to.

A reply from Mr Anti-Social Worker did not follow, and no more social worker-bashing letters appeared from this person.

When social work emerged in the 1940s in Canada as a profession requiring a university-based education, it was faced with the task of trying to reconcile these two different approaches to social problems and to integrate them into the curricula of Schools of Social Work. For a variety of reasons (i.e., the theories of Sigmund Freud and the medical model were the dominant scientific bases of knowledge at that time, and the Schools of Social Work were established mainly by social agencies that were part of the Charity Organization Society system) the casework 'reform-the-person' approach became dominant. One only has to look at the disproportionate share of faculty and resources allocated to direct practice courses in most Schools of Social Work today, or to the existing social work literature, or to the current practices employed in most social agencies, to see the dominance of casework with its individual reform-the-person approach.[1]

From the above two traditions modern social work has always had two major competing views of society, social welfare, and social work practice[2]—the conventional view and the progressive or critical view. The conventional view, which has always been held by the majority, is influenced by and reflective of popular beliefs and attitudes about the nature of the individual, of society, and of the relationship between the two. According to this perspective our present social order, although not perfect, is the best there is and it ought to be preserved. Society is viewed as comprising social institutions that serve the individual as long as she or he makes full use of available opportunities for personal success. This view acknowledges that social problems do exist but defines them in terms of personal difficulties or immediate environmental issues that require social work intervention either to help people cope with or adjust to existing institutions or to modify existing policies in a limited fashion. Carniol (1979), a progressive Canadian social work scholar, points out that the conventional approach is adopted by those who believe that our social institutions are responsive to and capable of meeting people's needs. Obviously, the political function of conventional social work practice is such that by conforming to established institutions, it reinforces, supports, and defends the status quo. This is not to say that there is no disagreement within the conventional view. Most of the political debate about social welfare has been conducted within a liberal-conservative framework, with the former seeing more services as a good thing and the latter seeing fewer services as a good thing (Galper, 1975). Neither liberalism nor conservatism questions the legitimacy of the present capitalist social order, however.

In contrast to the conventional view, the progressive or critical view does not believe that our present social institutions are capable of adequately meeting human need. Social workers with this view are quick to point out that in spite of a social welfare state and social work interventions that have existed for most of this century, social problems are not decreasing but, on the contrary, appear to be worsening. Twenty-five years ago there were no soup kitchens or food banks in Canada, nor were there emergency shelters to feed and house any other than derelict populations. Today these residual means of meeting basic needs have become institutionalized. Progressive social workers will also point to the growing gap between rich and poor, to the worsening plight of traditionally disadvantaged groups, to the resurrection of conservativism, and to the social control functions of welfare programs and social work practice as proof that the present set of social arrangements does not work for large numbers of people. Although there has always been a progressive or radical contingent within social work it has been a minority voice. However, in recent years and in the face of the fiscal crisis of the state, its numbers have been growing as have their challenges to the conventional view.

Carniol (2005) has termed the present situation of a society with increasing inequalities, of a welfare state that has failed to bring about a just society, and of the alienation of social workers from their work 'the social work crisis' and calls for a social transformation. This is the ultimate goal of progressive/critical social work, and the pursuit of this goal is a major theme of this book. This is not to say that there are no disagreements within the progressive camp. For example, although the elimination of oppression and inequality may be a common goal, feminists, Marxists, social democrats, visible minorities, and so on have often disagreed on the fundamental source of oppression and on the strategies to overcome oppression and inequality. This is further discussed in Chapters 9 and 10.

Historical overviews of social work perspectives and approaches that have been used in Canada have been discussed elsewhere (Hick, 2002; Lundy, 2004) and, therefore, will not be reproduced here. Instead, some of the major theories or approaches of social work are grouped in Table 2.1 according to the main focus or unit of analysis and change of each. There are two schools of conventional social work. One focuses on the individual or individuals as both the source of and the solutions for problems, and has as its goal to help the individual cope with, fit into, and/or adjust to society. The other focuses on the goodness of fit between the individual and his or her environment. This approach seeks change in either the individual or in the individual's limited environment (i.e., within the family, the community, the school, the workplace, etc.). No thought is given to the possibility that maybe the system itself (i.e., society) is unjust and unfixable and that the solution might be to transform it fundamentally to one based on a different set of values and social dynamics.

It is important to note here that although the conventional approaches outlined in Table 2.1 have historically reinforced the status quo, they can be used in progressive

**TABLE 2.1   SELECTED CONVENTIONAL AND PROGRESSIVE SOCIAL
WORK PERSPECTIVES/APPROACHES**

CONVENTIONAL (consensus-based)		PROGRESSIVE (conflict/change-based)
personal change	*person-in-environment* (personal change and/or limited social change)	*fundamental social change/transformation**
– psychodynamic	– general systems theory	– feminist social work
– behavioural	– ecosystems (ecological)	– Marxist
– client-centred	– life model	– radical
– psychosocial	– problem-solving	– structural
– clinical	– strengths perspective	– anti-racist
– family therapies		– anti-oppressive
– casework		– critical postmodern
		– post-colonial
		– indigenous (decolonization)
		– narrative therapy
		– just therapy

*   Progressive social work today recognizes that fundamental social change cannot occur without fundamental personal change also occurring. Earlier versions of progressive social work tended to emphasize structural changes and psychological preparation to participate in social change activities, but gave little or no consideration to the impact of oppressive structures on oppressed groups and how to respond to them in a way that was meaningful.

ways, as will be discussed in Chapter 9. In fact, widespread agreement exists that social work has responsibility for both individual and structural (social change) interventions (Trainor, 1996). Today, countless social work bodies and publications assert the need for social work to be involved in broader political action and social change (Schneider and Lester, 2001). Social work codes of ethics in Australia, the US, and to a lesser extent Canada (see below) all include strong statements in favour of social justice. Many social workers have become involved in political and social action within formal structures of political parties (for example, the current Minister of Finance in the Manitoba provincial government is a member of the Faculty of Social Work at the University of Manitoba), within professional social work organizations, and most of all at the local agency level (Gray et al., 2002; Mendes, 2003). However, many (perhaps most) social workers do not participate in social or political action and many workers believe that activism is incompatible with professional practice (Wharf, 1991). Haynes and Mickelson (2003: xi) contend that the social work profession is too often characterized by 'its dispassionate, objective and apolitical stance' and 'lack of interest in or even antagonism to social action'.

Unfortunately, systems theory and ecological perspectives (under the 'person-in-environment' subheading in Table 2.1), which have now been around for over 30 years, are still presented as core social work theory in many Schools of Social Work in North

America. Box 2.2 outlines a number of serious limitations and flaws with this perspective that have been cited in the progressive literature for over two decades (see, e.g., Pease, 2003; Finn and Jacobson, 2003). These and other limitations are discussed more fully in Chapter 9.

BOX 2.2 LIMITATIONS OF SYSTEMS AND ECOLOGICAL PERSPECTIVES

- They are not theories because they are descriptive only and have no explanatory or predictive capacities.
- They are so vague and general that they offer little specific guidance for practice.
- They do not deal with or explain power relationships (i.e., power differentials).
- They do not accommodate or deal with conflict. All social units (or subsystems) are viewed as interacting in harmony with each other and with the larger system (i.e., society). The whole purpose of a systems approach is to eliminate any conflict that disrupts the system.
- They operate to maintain the status quo since the goal is to restore the system to normal functioning.
- Social problems are believed to be a result of a breakdown between individuals and the subsystems (e.g., family, school, peer group, welfare office) with which they interact.
- The focus on the here-and-now situation and possibilities for intervention contributes to a neglect of history.
- There is no recognition or analysis of oppressive social structures that produce inequality.

NEED FOR A PROGRESSIVE SOCIAL WORK VISION

We have witnessed in the past decade an increasing body of social science writings criticizing our present social order because of its failure to provide satisfying levels of living for large numbers of citizens. These criticisms are important for social work because they identify and illuminate the sources and reasons for many of our social problems and show us what we are struggling against. However, although critical analysis may show us what we are fighting against, by itself it does not show us what we are fighting for. As Galper (1975: 140) states, 'We need more.' We need a picture or a vision of alternative social arrangements that we can work towards. We need a goal—a conceptualization of 'a society in which every person is afforded maximum opportunity to enrich his or her spiritual, psychological, physical, and intellectual well-being' (Galper, 1975: 147). As Nevitte and Gibbons (1990: 140) note in their discussion of social change, 'A preference for social change in the abstract is meaningless.' Also, McNally (2002), in discussing anti-capitalist movements, argues that radical movements cannot change societies without a vision. It may be possible to resist dominant forces by engaging in the powerfully negative act of saying 'no'. But without a clear vision or alternative, that accomplishment of saying 'no', while immensely important in terms of building confidence and capacities for struggle, only postpones the battle. To shift from the defensive to the offensive requires a vision of a different kind of future.

We are passing through a period of history when societal visions or Utopian models of society have not been widely discussed. With the post-war welfare state in place and financed by an ever-growing economy, many believed that society by a process of evolution had reached its pinnacle (Galper, 1975). However, the fiscal crisis of the state and the calling into question of the welfare state have cast shadows of doubt on this notion. Presently, many of our comfortable and cherished assumptions about the nature of our society and its ability to respond genuinely to human needs are in doubt. We seem now to need visions of alternative societies. 'Given the dire [social] condition of the planet, it is . . . urgent that we formulate alternatives which are at once radical, comprehensive, and practical' (Wineman, 1984: 159). Without such alternatives or visions there is a danger that we will become victims of distorted notions of justice, well-being, and solidarity, thus denying many people their rightful place in society. Fortunately, given the apparent collapse of (or at least reconstituted) globalism, there is a beginning return to discussions of visions or ideas of a different type of world—one based on social justice—as evidenced by such works as Ferguson, Lavalette, and Whitmore's book, *Globalisation, Global Justice and Social Work* (2005) and Finn and Jacobson's article, 'Just Practice: Steps Toward a New Social Work Paradigm' (2003).

Because social work often deals with the casualties and victims of society, it, too, must become involved in questioning our present social arrangement. Given social work's belief in the inherent dignity and worth of the person, it must ask itself what type of society best promotes this ideal. Given social work's belief that people have a right to develop fully and freely their inherent human potential and to live productive and satisfying lives free from domination and exploitation by others, those in social work must ask what social arrangements best accommodate these values. In other words, what type of society best promotes the values, ideals, principles, and beliefs espoused by the social work profession? What is the vision that social work should pursue?

Unfortunately, it would be impossible to reach consensus among social workers on such a vision of society. A major obstacle to developing and articulating a universally accepted social work vision is the existence of the two incompatible views of current society, social welfare, and social work. Not even a common value base or a professional code of ethics is enough to unify the profession with respect to the coexisting conventional and progressive views. The Canadian Association of Social Workers' (CASW) *Code of Ethics*, as noted by Woodsworth (1984), consists of 'competing, even conflicting philosophies', and has been described by Lundy and Gauthier (1989: 192) as 'an amalgam of competing ideologies that are at times contradictory and even antagonistic to one another'. The contradictory nature of the welfare state (i.e., its social care and social control functions) is expressed within the *Code of Ethics* in that ideas of conservatism, liberalism, and collectivism are all represented. As indicated previously, the viewpoint taken here is progressive.

FORWARD TO THE PAST: THE 2005 CASW CODE OF ETHICS

If the espoused values of social work were to be used to formulate a social work vision, the nature and form of that vision would differ depending on whether a conventional or progressive view was used. For the past decade, I have used the 1994 CASW *Code of Ethics* as a point of departure for writing about progressive social work theory and practice and for contributing to progressive social work ideas, views, and visions. In spite of competing and conflicting ideas and ideologies within the 1994 *Code*, it contained sufficient progressive content to carry out these tasks. Thus, it was with considerable anticipation that I recently reviewed a copy of the new 2005 CASW *Code of Ethics*. I thought that it would be even more progressive than its 11-year-old predecessor. It is not. It reflects a 'liberal-humanist' approach to social work that seeks to comfort victims of social problems, rather than a critical approach that seeks fundamental social change (i.e., transformation).

Although in some regards there are a few improvements over the 1994 *Code*, such as the delineation of ethical responsibilities in its accompanying *Guidelines* (absent in the 1994 *Code*), the new *Code* has retreated to an era when there was no vision or articulation of what social work wanted, when no statement of social philosophy existed, and when the primary task of social work was to help people cope with, adjust to, and/or fit back into the very society that caused them problems in the first place. In other words, the new *Code* emphasizes residual ideas and regressive practices while it de-emphasizes or omits progressive elements from the 1994 version. Although space does not permit an exhaustive critique, a number of major limitations are presented here.

1. *No philosophical statement or vision.* The 1994 *Code* (p. 7) contained the following philosophical statement: 'The profession of social work is founded on humanitarian and egalitarian ideals.' These two social ideals provide a vision of a society (one characterized by humanitarianism and egalitarianism) for social work to pursue. Without such a vision, what type of society should social work have as its goal? What is it that gives social work a sense of direction? The new *Code* is silent on this issue. It does state in its preamble (p. 3) that '[t]he social work profession is dedicated to the welfare and self-realization of all people', but it does not offer an opinion on what type or kind of society would best promote this principle. Is it our current North American society with its value base of individualism and cutthroat competition? Or is it a society based on a different set of values that are more consistent with social work values? Humanitarianism and egalitarianism denote a society characterized by social, economic, political, and cultural equality where every person is of equal intrinsic worth. Without such social ideals, what is it that

inspires social work? What is its social raison d'être'? Why doesn't the *Code* have a vision statement along the following lines?

> The vision of the profession of Social Work is to help create and contribute to a world where there are no great inequalities of wealth or income, where economic and political power is more evenly distributed, where human need is the central value of distribution of society's resources, where diversity of culture is celebrated, where people have greater control over their own lives, and where all persons are afforded maximum opportunity to enrich their physical, spiritual, psychological, and intellectual well-being.
>
> (taken from the *Vision Statement* of the
> Faculty of Social Work, University of Manitoba)

2. *The client is no longer the primary professional obligation*. Whereas the 1994 *Code of Ethics* was unequivocal in stating that a 'social worker shall maintain the best interest of the client as *the primary* (emphasis added) professional obligation' (p. 9), the new *Code* states, 'Social workers maintain the best interests of clients as *a priority* (emphasis added) with due regard to the respective interests of others' (p. 3). In other words, no longer is the client the primary obligation of the social worker, but just one 'other' priority. Given that the best interests of the client often conflict with the interests of the agency (or of more powerful others), whose interests are likely to win out in such conflicts—the client's or one's employer? The 2005 *Code* has taken away a powerful tool for resisting policies and directives of workplaces that mitigate against the best interests of clients.

3. *A limited view of social justice*. Although the new *Code* identifies the pursuit of social justice as a value, it presents a limited and limiting view of social justice. That is, social justice is defined only in terms of distributing or redistributing society's resources (i.e., distributive or redistributive justice), which excludes doing anything about the social institutions, policies, processes, and practices responsible for the inequitable distribution in the first place. A (re)distributive view of social justice simply compensates victims of social injustice and does nothing to change a society characterized by inequality along lines of race, class, gender, age, sexuality, and so on.

4. *The fallacy of equal opportunity or universal impartiality*. A regressive stance in the new *Code* is found in 'Value 4: Integrity in Practice', where it is stated that 'Social Workers strive for *impartiality* in their professional practice' (p. 6; emphasis added). Impartiality is a liberal-humanist notion that was adopted as a professional norm by mainstream social work dating back to at least 1958, when Wilensky and Lebeaux called for it to become part of the social work 'professional self'. The notion of professional impartiality specifies the desirability of providing social work services to people without regard to gender, class, race, sexuality, age, and so on. In other words, all people should be treated equally. However, as Galper pointed out in 1975, and as feminists and anti-racist writers argued in the 1980s and 1990s, although perhaps well-intentioned, this mandate carries with it a limited notion of fairness. By treating people equally, we are assuming that the standard

of equality is 'equality of opportunity', thus ignoring important social differences. Equality of opportunity assumes that people start from the same place and compete equally for resources, including social welfare benefits and social work services. Persons and/or groups may be equal before the law, but not all people or groups start out at the same position, which means that not all people or groups are able to exercise their rights or access resources or use their opportunities to the same extent as more privileged groups. If some groups are in a better position to use opportunities because of their social position and the resources available to them, then notions of impartiality and equal opportunity discriminate against other groups (e.g., Aboriginal groups, poor people, people of colour, refugees, disabled persons) who have been historically marginalized in our society. The whole fallacy of the impartiality position is that social groups differ with respect to their ability or capacity to use opportunities and to access services. To treat all social groups as if they were all the same is to maintain the inequalities that exist among them. Social work cannot be colour-blind or gender-blind.

5. *Acknowledgement of diversity*. Ethical Guideline 1.2 in the new *Code*, titled 'Demonstrate Cultural Awareness and Sensitivity', contains a subclause 1.2.2: 'Social Workers *acknowledge* the diversity within and among individuals, communities and cultures' (CASW, 2005: 4; emphasis added). Given our so-called pluralistic or multicultural Canadian society and the fact that the present white majority is predicted to become a minority within 20 years, why does the *Code* not make a stronger and more positive statement about culture, such as 'Social Workers celebrate and promote the diversity of culture'? Use of the word 'acknowledge' could be interpreted to mean 'recognize' only or 'tolerate', rather than appreciate. Recognition or acknowledgement of diversity is part of the multicultural model of social work that now has over 10 years of critique from the feminist, anti-racist, post-colonial, postmodern, Aboriginal, and other progressive social work perspectives, and this model has been rejected in favour of an anti-oppressive or 'politics of difference' approach to diversity (see Mullaly, 2002). Why are we going back a decade in our *Code of Ethics* with respect to issues of difference and diversity?

6. *Limited self-determination*. The *Code* states under Ethical Guideline 1.3, 'Promote Client Self–Determination and Informed Consent', that with respect to agency records, 'Social Workers . . . provide them [clients] with honest and accurate information regarding . . . the client's right to view professional records and to seek avenues of complaint' (p. 5), but this does not go far enough. If we are talking about promoting or maximizing 'client self-determination', the *Code* should stipulate that service users have the right to write their own recordings or tell their stories and to have them placed in the file along with any other document they may wish to have placed there. By not clearly stating so, we continue to privilege professional knowledge over personal experience—something for which the profession has been criticized by various service user groups and contemporary social theorists.

Given this critique of the 2005 CASW *Code of Ethics*, what kind of Code of Ethics would suit social workers who are interested in fundamental social change (i.e., social transformation)? Jeffry Galper developed such a code back in 1975. More recently, two Australian progressive social workers, Heather Fraser and Linda Briskman (2004), developed a Code that would be more relevant to progressive social work practice in the new millennium (Box 2.3). They point out that this Code is not a definitive or final declaration, but a way to open discussion with progressive social workers around the world. This Code is presented here so that a comparison might be made with the CASW 2005 *Code of Ethics*.

BOX 2.3   CODE OF ETHICS FOR PROGRESSIVE SOCIAL WORKERS

1. We regard as our primary obligation to be the welfare of all humankind, across the globe, not just those in our immediate vicinity.
2. We understand the contradictions inherent in delivering social work services in a capitalist society. We know that the state can be both oppressive and supportive.
3. We never claim to be 'apolitical' or 'neutral' and we define social justice in political, material and global terms, not just psychological terms.
4. We respect the need for resources and decision-making processes to be fairly shared, and we realize that this will be hard to achieve given the current political order.
5. We recognize the importance of language and try to show sensitivity through the words that we use. However, we realize that we might 'get it wrong'.
6. We value processes as much as 'products' or 'outcomes', and we are—at the very least—skeptical of using violence to deal with conflict.
7. We define power in possessive and relational ways. This means that while we are wary of calling anyone 'powerless', we are also aware of the way dominant groups can exercise power over people who are oppressed on the basis of race, gender, class, ability, age, sexual orientation and geographical location.
8. Because we strive to live in a society where people are able to exercise their human rights, we try to democratize our professional relationships as well as our personal ones.
9. We do not see financial profit as the primary motive in life. Thus, we do not uphold the tenets of global capitalism nor do we value paid work over that which is unpaid.
10. While we appreciate the importance of group bonds, we are wary of the way nationalism can be used to deride and exclude others. In so doing, we seek to work with people from diverse backgrounds in equitable-and culturally sensitive-ways.
11. We value education for the ways it can be used to develop critical consciousness.

12. We respect the need for oppressed groups to sometimes 'go it alone'. Yet, we do not presume this will always be their preference. Instead, we are open to providing support/resources to oppressed groups in a manner that they suggest will be useful.
13. While developing knowledge that will be useful to social transformation, we speak up whenever we can about acts of unfairness that we see, using all sorts of media to broadcast our observations and ideas.
14. We recognize the potentially conservative nature of all methods of social work and strive to radicalize all forms of social work that we undertake. As we do this, we avoid individual acts of heroism or martyrdom, preferring instead to work in collaboration with others.
15. We do not see ourselves sitting outside society, or as liberators of the 'needy' or the 'downtrodden'. Rather, we try to use the benefits derived from our professional status to work against the exploitation of individuals and groups.
16. We try to do all this in everday, reflexive ways, without posturing as self-appointed experts.
17. Given the obstacles that confront us, we realize that fatalism, cynicism and despair may set in. To prevent this we try to keep a sense of humour, have fun with others and incorporate self-care activities into our lives.

Source: Fraser and Briskman (2004).

Given the absence of an articulated social philosophy in the CASW 2005 *Code of Ethics* and its regressive elements, I will continue to use the much more progressive 1994 *Code* to develop a progressive vision for social work. I encourage all Canadian social workers who are concerned with progressive and emancipatory forms of practice to do the same and to protest the new *Code* for its inadequate, incomplete, and regressive response to social problems and social injustice. As we move further into the new millennium the profession of social work needs a more forward-looking rather backward-looking *Code of Ethics*. Specifically, we must look back to the 1994 *Code* in order to move forward. The following statement of philosophy from that earlier *Code* is central to a progressive approach.:

The profession of social work is founded on *humanitarian* and *egalitarian* ideals. Social workers believe in the intrinsic worth and dignity of every human being and are committed to the values of *acceptance, self-determination* and *respect* of individuality. They believe in the obligation of all people, individually and collectively, to provide resources, services and opportunities for the overall benefit of humanity. The culture of individuals, families, groups, communities and nations has to be respected without prejudice. (CASW, 1994: 7; emphases added)

THE FUNDAMENTAL VALUES OF SOCIAL WORK

The following discussion of the values identified in the above statement of philosophy embodies that part of social work that challenges rather than supports our present social order. Values consist of beliefs, preferences, or assumptions about what is good or desirable for people. They are not assertions or descriptions of the way the world is, but rather how the world ought to be. Values do not stand alone but exist in systems of thought and are organized in such a way that they have a relative importance to other values. Fundamental or primary values represent ideals or goals that a profession attempts to achieve, that is, the end product. Secondary or instrumental values specify the means to achieve these goals or desired ends.

Because 'the profession of social work is founded on humanitarian and egalitarian ideals' (CASW, 1994: 7), these ideals must form the cornerstone of social work's ideal society. Fundamental values cannot be compromised by such notions as economic individualism and/or competitive capitalism. If we do not have a society based on humanitarian principles then we have a society based, in whole or in part, on principles of inhumanity. If we do not have a society based on egalitarianism then we have a society based, in whole or in part, on principles of inequality. If we have a society based, in whole or in part, on principles of inhumanity and inequality, then our secondary or instrumental values of social work—acceptance, self-determination, and respect (CASW, 1994)—are meaningless, since there must be consistency between our primary values and our secondary values.

Humanism

'Humanitarianism' tends to be used interchangeably in the social work literature with the term 'humanism'. While some writers contend that there are some differences in meanings between the two terms, other sources contend that the popular use of the term 'humanitarianism' means the practice of the doctrine of 'humanism' (*Webster's New Collegiate Dictionary*, 1980). The latter usage will be adopted here, and henceforth the term 'humanism' will be used more generally since most of the reference material for this chapter employs this term.[3]

A definition supplied by the *Dictionary of Philosophy* (Saiflin and Dixon, 1984) describes humanism as 'a system of views based on the respect for the dignity and rights of man [*sic*], his value as a personality, concern for his welfare, his all-round development, and the creation of favourable conditions for social life'. This view of the person recognizes that the individual should be the focus of all societal decisions. A society based on humanism would not only recognize the universal nature of human need but would actively attempt to provide to everyone conditions conducive to physical survival, mental health, self-respect, dignity, love, a sense of identity, the opportunity to use one's intellect, and happiness (Hardy, 1981a). Such a commitment must be based on social equality, co-operation, and collective orientation (Gil, 1976a), and consideration of all economic decisions ought to be based on their implications for human welfare (Galper, 1975).

Goroff (1981) has articulated his view of a society based on humanism as one in which: (1) each individual is seen as a person with inherent dignity and worth and not as an object with utility; (2) relationships among human beings are non-exploitative, co-operative, and egalitarian; (3) resources created by human beings through their labour are distributed so as to provide each person with the goods and services to meet his or her needs without denying others theirs; and (4) each individual has equal opportunities to develop his or her fullest human potential. There is consensus in the social welfare and social work literatures that our present North American society does not contain these humanistic characteristics.[4]

Because it has been suggested by some writers on the subject of the philosophy of social work that the values of social work are firmly rooted in humanism (e.g., Payne, 1997; Ife, 1997), we should be aware of the limitations of humanism. A common criticism of humanism is that it is ahistorical and does not consider the social context of people's lives—that is, it overlooks the implications of inequalities (Clark and Asquith, 1985; Rojek et al., 1988) and does not contain a structural analysis of oppression (Ife, 1997). Certainly, notions of 'acceptance' in social work have been influenced by humanism in that social work practice has often excluded concern for the material hardships of service users (Biehal and Sainsbury, 1991). Psychoanalytic, client-centred, and family therapies, for the most part, have focused on introspection, self-realization, and interpersonal dynamics rather than on the social context of people's lives. An example of overlooking material impoverishment and social context is the fact that poverty was rediscovered in the 1960s by people other than social workers.[5]

Another criticism of humanism comes from post-colonial writers (see Gandhi, 1998, for a discussion of this point), who point out that humanism is a Western concept that assumes a Western superiority over all other cultures and societies. As well, postmod-ernists criticize humanism (particularly radical humanism) for overlooking discourse, subjectivity, and subject position (Pease, 2003). However, the position adopted here is that there are different versions of humanism and that such forms as a critical humanism (Ife, 1997), or a radical humanism (Howe, 1987; Mullaly and Keating, 1991), which emphasize dominant ideology and consciousness, are essential for developing progressive forms of social work. I agree with Bob Pease (2003), who argues that radical forms of humanism can contribute to progressive forms of social work practice if they are supplemented by critical theory traditions of materialist perspectives emphasizing material conditions and lived experiences; Marxist and feminist Freudian views emphasizing the unconscious and repression; and postmodern perspectives emphasizing discourse, subjectivity, and subject position. Also, as I will be argue in Chapter 9, radical humanism must be accom-panied by another perspective on social interpretation and social change, that is, radical structuralism. An elaboration of these ideas is presented in Chapter 9.

Egalitarianism

Although more than one meaning can be ascribed to the term 'egalitarianism',[6] the one that forms part of a progressive social work ideology is that of 'social equality'. David

Gil (1976a, 1998) has written eloquently and extensively on the notion of social equality from a social work perspective. He argues that if we wish to establish a society based on social equality we need to explicate the meaning of this overused, yet elusive, concept. The central value premise of social equality is that every person is of equal intrinsic worth and should therefore be entitled to equal civil, political, social, and economic rights, responsibilities, and treatment.

Implicit is the belief 'that every individual should have the right and the resources to develop freely and fully, to actualize his [or her] inherent human potential, and to lead as fulfilling a life [as possible] free of domination, control and exploitation by others' (Gil, 1976a: 4). Social equality is a correlate of humanism, as the dignity of the person cannot be achieved if some people have control over others, have preferred access to life chances, or have more power concerning public affairs: 'Genuine democracy, liberty and individuality for all are simply not feasible without social equality' (Gil, 1976a: 4). A society based on social inequality is based on the value premise that people differ in intrinsic worth and therefore are entitled to different rights and to as much power, control, and material goods as they can gain in competition with others. Humanistic ideals cannot be reached in such a society.

Social equality does not mean monotonous uniformity; rather, it aims at the realization of individual differences in innate potentialities, not at the division of available resources into identical parts for every member of society. The key element in arriving at a humanistic and egalitarian society is the development of a true collectivist spirit. This means taking seriously the fact that people form a social entity called a society when they live together. This does not mean uniform blandness or submission to the group, but it recognizes that decisions made in those areas affecting the whole must be subjected to collective thought and to collective action in the light of collective needs and resources.[7] Collectivism implies participatory decision-making, not hierarchical decisions made at the top and passed down. People should have a say in the decisions that affect any area of their lives—social, economic, political, work, the distribution of society's resources, and so on. This type of decision-making cannot occur in a society based on social inequality.

In sum, humanism (humanitarianism) and social equality must form the twin pillars of an ideal social work society. These fundamental values, and not inequality, rugged individualism, and cutthroat competition, support the dignity and intrinsic worth of people. To realize these fundamental values society must be arranged according to the principles of collectivism, participatory decision-making, and co-operation and not according to the practices of exploitation, distribution of resources according to economic profit rather than social need, and hierarchical, elitist decision-making. A social work vision of society is based on the premise that the present set of social arrangements is not a natural phenomenon but is, instead, the result of person-made decisions. 'People can be self-determining about social forms and can shape and reshape them to meet their current needs' (Galper, 1975: 151). In other words, given the political will, a society can develop a social order that promotes human welfare. In addition to meeting people's individual needs, it is part of the progressive social work mission to promote this political will. Gil (1990: 20–1) reminds us that social work practice cannot be politically neutral: 'it either confronts and challenges established societal institutions or it conforms to them openly or tacitly. [Social work] practitioners should avoid the illusion of neutrality and should consciously choose and acknowledge their political philosophy.'

THE SECONDARY (INSTRUMENTAL) VALUES OF SOCIAL WORK

Social work's secondary or instrumental values stem from its fundamental values and contribute to the goals of humanitarianism and egalitarianism. 'They dictate the ways the [social] worker should interact with others in carrying out his [or her] professional activities so as to actualize the primary values, that is to achieve the desired ends or goals' (Pincus and Minahan, 1973: 39). Three secondary values highlighted in the preamble of the 1994 Canadian Association of Social Workers' *Code of Ethics* are respect, self-determination, and acceptance. The operationalization of these three values is assumed to contribute to the situation where the worth and dignity of people are realized. We affirm people's worth and dignity by showing respect for them, by allowing them maximum feasible self-determination, and by accepting their individualities.

Statham (1978: 34) argues that these instrumental values are meaningless in societies based on economic individualism rather than on social equality:

> Social workers affirm their belief in the worth of each person by virtue of their humanity and see them as having needs in common, but the society in which they operate distributes rewards unequally, not because of faulty mechanisms which can be remedied by social work or reform, but because the allocation of rewards is intended to operate in this way.

Do we not negate the respect we extend to clients in our interpersonal relationships with them if we accept a social order based on economic individualism with its inevitable consequences of poverty, homelessness, deprivation, and unemployment? By accepting a person's individuality are we also accepting her or his social and economic conditions? And how can we practice self-determination with people who do not possess the economic and social resources necessary for choices to be realized? Self-determination often has meaning only for those possessing the economic resources and social status necessary to implement choice. In a society based on inequality, self-determination is not possible for persons who are powerless 'to resolve, by their individual efforts, the problems created, for instance, by inadequate income, housing, or by unemployment' (Statham, 1978: 27).

It would seem, then, that social work's instrumental values are illusory if, as Biehal and Sainsbury (1991: 249) suggest, 'They are not seen in the context of people's lives—notably the context of differences in power.' It is not enough to show respect and acceptance for people and offer them choices restricted by their social position in society.

Cries for acceptance of rights for people are empty slogans if the reality of power (to exercise rights) is ignored. Social work must also be concerned with realizing a society that promotes social work values rather than one that negates or compromises them. It would seem that only a society founded on humanitarian and egalitarian ideals could accommodate these secondary values. Surely, an imperative for social work is to work towards the establishment of a social vision based on its own value position.

A PROGRESSIVE PERSPECTIVE OF SOCIAL WORK IDEOLOGY

An ideology is a consistent set of social, economic, and political beliefs. It serves as the foundation and determines the nature and world view of particular social paradigms. Social work has historically been practised in an arena of conflicting beliefs. There has always been some degree of conflict between the social, economic, and political beliefs of the larger society and those espoused by the social work profession in general and by the progressive sector of the profession in particular. Social workers presently operate at the meeting place of the conflict between the dominant values of liberal capitalism and the dominant social work values of humanitarianism and egalitarianism.[8]

Many social workers also experience conflict within their own social, economic, and political beliefs. For example, social workers may subscribe to humanitarian social beliefs about the dignity and worth of people but also subscribe to our present capitalist economic system based on competition and exploitation, without realizing the inherent conflict between their humanitarian social beliefs and their capitalist economic beliefs. As well, many social workers may believe that self-determination is a laudable goal but will not question our present system of representative democracy where self-determination and meaningful participation are not options for large numbers of people.

Although social workers espouse many humanitarian and egalitarian beliefs, insufficient attention has been paid to integrate these beliefs in any consistent fashion. Thus, an articulation of social work ideology must entail a delineation of specific social beliefs, economic beliefs, and political beliefs that are consistent with one another. Otherwise, the present hodge-podge of beliefs will continue to present conflict, inconsistency, and uncertainty to social workers in their everyday practice, and will do nothing in terms of informing social workers of the nature and form that society would assume if it were to be congruent with social work ideology.

Social Beliefs

David Gil (1976a: 242) has described in humanistic and egalitarian terms the nature of the relationship between people and the society in which they live:

> All humans, everywhere, despite their manifest differences and their uniqueness as individuals, should be considered of equal intrinsic worth. Hence, they should be deemed entitled to equal social, economic, civil, and political rights, liberties and

obligations. Societal institutions . . . should assure and facilitate the exercise of these equal rights, and the free, autonomous, and authentic development of all humans.

This view of people is one in which persons are considered to be social beings. John Friedmann (1973) contrasts this view of social beings with economic individualism, which perceives people as independent, gratification-maximizing individuals with no social responsibility for others. What distinguishes people as social beings from people as economic individualists is that the former view is based on the notion of community and the latter on the notion of the 'rugged individual'. Whereas the economic individualist equates public well-being with the mere aggregation of individual interests, the social view of persons recognizes public well-being as a more complex construct made up of not only the aggregate of its members but also the relationships among them.

Friedmann argues that the view of people as social beings is essentially moral whereas the view of people as economic individualists is essentially amoral. As a social being a person is a thinking and feeling animal who stands in relation to others as a person. His or her recognition of the other person as one like him or herself establishes the manner in which their relationship will be fulfilled. People will treat others as they themselves would want to be treated. A society built on the image of economic individualism would be simply 'a bundle of functional roles . . . superordinated, subordinated, or equal and either useful to you or not', a relationship based on a 'suspicion of mutual exploitation' (Friedmann, 1973: 6, 5). In the economic individualist view the notion of the public well-being is arrived at by summing the individual utilities in the marketplace. The worth of a person is judged mainly by what he or she earns and/or owns. Community, which is the cornerstone of civilized life, is not possible with such an amoral foundation. 'Without community, there can be no justice, and without justice, life becomes brutish and destructive of both the self and others' (Friedmann, 1973: 4).

In addition to its moral weaknesses, an economic individualist view ignores the realities of our modern industrial society (Mullaly, 1980). For example, specialization and division of labour require people to depend on one another for provision of those goods and services they cannot provide for themselves; some contingencies, such as accident, illness, inflation, and recession, are beyond the control of the individual; and if left on one's own, the individual tends to be overwhelmed by forces of which he or she is only dimly aware, which subjugate him or her to a role of decreasing importance and present problems with which the person has no means to cope (Ross, 1967).

Economic Beliefs

In *The Politics of Social Services* (1975), Jeffry Galper outlines a set of economic beliefs consistent with social work values. He contrasts these beliefs with the practices of competitive and capitalist economy, which is based on the criterion of profitability. Galper contends that if we are to be successful in creating a world conducive to human well-being, then we must find a way to dominate, rather than be dominated by, economics.

Neither the invisible hand of the marketplace nor the present partnership of government and big business ensure that social priorities will dominate economic decision-making.

Galper (1975: 142–3) argues that in our present economic system goods are produced, decisions made, and the number and nature of jobs available for people are determined on the basis of profitability. The consequences of this system are:

> an overabundance of goods that do not add up to a fundamental sense of well-being for most people, an absence of goods that we need but that are not profitable to produce, jobs that are destructive to people who hold them, a national psychology organized around competition and consumption, ecological destruction, and exploitation of large parts of the rest of the world to enable us to maintain our standards of material achievement. Human well-being is not, as it should be, the rationale for our actions.

Galper contrasts our present economic system with one where all decisions of production are based on the criterion of human need. In other words, decisions about what should be produced and in what quantities, as well as when, where, and how, should be made according to their impact on our overall well-being. Galper uses two examples: (1) the decision to produce cars would not be made exclusively on the basis of their saleability but on the basis of such social criteria as the relative emphasis to be given to private versus public transportation, pollution, use of raw materials, safety, and the nature of the work experience for people; and (2) a new factory would be located not just according to the availability of raw materials, labour, and transportation, or for political gain, but according to the development needs of the various regions of the country. An economic system consistent with social work ideals would assure each person full economic rights, and the distribution of wealth, goods, and resources would be much more equitable than presently exists.

In sum, to be consistent with social work ideals, the economic system must be rationalized from a social perspective. It must be viewed as the means to achieve those social goals to which social work aspires, not as an end in itself. Goods must be produced for their utility rather than their profitability, and consideration should be given to all the costs (social, economic, ecological, and so on) of production. Finally, the distribution of wealth, rather than following social Darwinian notions, must be made according to social determinations—those factors that contribute to the well-being of all citizens, not just to those who own the means of production. These principles are, of course, contradictory to and inconsistent with the laissez-faire principles of our present liberal-capitalist economic system.

Political Beliefs

Social work subscribes to the democratic ideals of self-determination, participation, and an equal distribution of political power. In fact, much of social work practice is directed towards individuals and groups, helping them gain or regain autonomy and control over their lives. However, there are basically two methods by which democracy can be practised: representative democracy and participatory democracy.

We all are used to the representative form of government. Pateman (1970, cited in Hardy, 1981b: 17) describes and analyzes this system of democracy:

> The characteristically democratic element . . . is the competition of leaders for the votes of the people at periodic, free elections. Elections are crucial to the democratic method for it is primarily through elections that the majority can exercise control over their leaders through loss of office. . . . The decisions of leaders can also be influenced by active groups bringing pressure to bear during inter-election periods. 'Political equality' in the theory [of representative democracy] refers to universal suffrage and to the existence of equality of opportunity of access to channels of influence over leaders. . . . The level of participation by the majority should not rise much above the minimum level necessary to keep the democratic method working; that is, it should remain at about the level that exists in Anglo-American democracies.

Although this model of democracy is relatively efficient in terms of the time it takes to make decisions, its weaknesses have been well documented in the literature (Galper, 1975; Hardy, 1981b; Naiman, 1997; Wharf and Cossom, 1987). (1) Political elites at times make decisions that are not responsive to the wishes of the electorate. (2) Interest pressure groups may gain some sectional advantage at the expense of more general welfare. (3) Unorganized sections of society may be ignored or exploited by powerful, organized sections. (4) The right to vote every few years is inconsistent with the notion of democracy. (5) Such a system promotes and relies on a considerable degree of passivity in the majority of people. (6) In the absence of participatory principles, those who make decisions will be those who have benefited most from the system and, therefore, have the least commitment to changing it. 'Though democratic in the way it is chosen, representative government has been shown to be elitist in the way that it operates' (Lees, 1972: 39).

By way of contrast, participatory democracy would produce a very different world (Hardy, 1981b). It would permit and encourage greater popular participation in non-governmental bodies like industry, trade unions, political parties, corporations, schools, universities, and the like (Lees, 1972; Naiman, 1997). In addition, it would delegate a larger share of public power to local communities small enough to permit effective and meaningful general participation in decision-making:

> Participation in politics would provide individuals with opportunities to take part in making significant decisions about their everyday lives. It would build and consolidate a sense of genuine community that would serve as a solid foundation for government. The first and most important step is to recognize that personal self-development is the moral goal of democracy and that direct popular participation is the chief means of achieving it. When this is generally accepted, then society can get

on with the largely technical job of thinking up new and better means for increasing popular participation. (Lees, 1972: 41)

Surely, given social work's values and ideals with respect to egalitarianism, self-determination, and so on, participatory democracy rather than representative democracy is the preferred form of democracy.

Summary of Social Work Ideology

The amalgam of the above social, economic, and political beliefs comprises social work's ideology. Social beliefs are based on the person as a social being. Economic beliefs are based on the notion that human well-being is the major criterion for economic decision-making. And political beliefs are based on people having the right and the responsibility to participate in those decisions that affect their lives. Taken together, these beliefs constitute social work's ideology for progressive social workers (see Table 2.2). This ideology comprises an interdependent, consistent, and mutually reinforcing set of ideas and ideals that should underpin the type of society that best promotes social work's fundamental values of humanism and egalitarianism.

SOCIAL WORK AND SOCIAL PROBLEMS

All social work activity is concerned with social problems, that is, with alleviating, eliminating, or preventing social problems and the deleterious effects they have on people. However, although poverty, mental illness, and deprivation may constitute objective phenomena, the analyses, interpretations, and explanations of these phenomena are subjective. In other words, a social problem may be seen as a set of objective circumstances but it includes a subjective interpretation. Such interpretations are defined largely in terms of ideology and group interests. For example, the existence of poverty will be explained differently by a conservative than by a Marxist, the former attributing poverty to a defective individual and the latter attributing it to a defective social arrangement (i.e., capitalism). The implication for social work is that the individual living in poverty would be treated in a punitive or remedial manner by a conservative social worker but would be treated as a victim of an oppressive social order by a progressive or critical social worker.

Although the values of social work are generally considered progressive and humanistic, its definitions or explanations of social problems have not always been progressive or humanistic. Because social work has been reluctant to elevate the discussion of its values to a societal level, there has been no agreed-upon goal or product with respect to the type and form of society social work is seeking. In the absence of a publicly articulated social vision, social work falls victim to the prevailing paradigm. That is, without a clear vision of itself and of the society within which it exists, social work has tended to accept as a given the current social order or paradigm. This means that social work 'theory and practice become accommodated only to that which is possible within existing

TABLE 2.2   OVERVIEW OF PROGRESSIVE SOCIAL WORK IDEALS AND BELIEFS

Social Beliefs	Humanitarianism (humanism)
	Community
	Equality
Economic Beliefs	Government intervention
	Social priorities dominate economic decisions
	Equitable distribution of society's resources
Political Beliefs	Participatory democracy (self-determination) in both governmental and non-governmental areas
View of Social Welfare	An instrument to promote equality, solidarity, and community
	Ideal = social welfare state or structural model
Principles of Social Work Practice (taken from the 1994 CASW *Code of Ethics*)	Treat people with respect
	Enhance dignity and integrity
	Facilitate self-determination and self-realization
	Accept differences
	Advocate and promote social justice

organizational constraints' (Moreau and Leonard, 1989: 235). With no alternative social order defined or articulated, social work becomes part of the existing social order, helping people to adjust to it or cope with it or attempting to make small changes within the system rather than attempting to make fundamental changes that transform the system.

Social work, by being part of the present paradigm and in the absence of an alternative, tends to take on the prevailing definitions or explanations of social problems. In Canada and the United States, social problems have been defined mainly within conservative-liberal perspectives. Most internally derived social work theory-building has been in the methods or means of social work practice rather than in the goals or desired ends of social work practice. As long as social work avoids the task of articulating its desired ends or vision it will continue to treat objective social problems with the subjective prescriptions of the prevailing paradigm. To date in North America, most social work explanations of social problems and most social work interventions have been based either on 'individual pathology' (conservative ideology) or 'general systems/ecological' explanations (liberal ideology) of social problems. Such approaches, of course, do not guarantee that social problems experienced by large numbers of people will be dealt with adequately or effectively. Radical or critical explanations of social problems have only recently become part of the social work theory landscape, but these still occupy a minority position. This is because, to date, socialist/Marxist, feminist, anti-racist, anti-oppressive, anti-homo-phobic ideas and analyses have not been major parts of the prevailing paradigms in North America.

In sum, although social work espouses a set of values considered progressive, its approach to resolve social problems has not been progressive. In the absence of an articulated social vision or goal consistent with its value base, social work has accepted by default the mainstream definitions and explanations of social problems, which have come from the prevailing North American ideologies of conservatism and liberalism. The critical question arising from this situation is whether or not social work ideology is consistent with either conservatism or liberalism. Or is it more consistent with an ideology that does not prevail in North America? A related question is whether or not social work's progressive and humanistic ideology is consistent with or in conflict with its current theory base and practice.

THE IDEAL SOCIAL WELFARE SYSTEM: A PROGRESSIVE VIEW

Every industrial democracy in the Western world has developed a social welfare system to deal with the vagaries of the market economy. Although all states have policies of intervention, the forms of these interventions often differ, as do their purposes. Furniss and Tilton (1977) have aggregated the different forms of intervention into three models of social welfare states: the positive state, the social security state, and the social welfare state. These models are described below in terms of the type of intervention employed, the groups in society benefiting from the intervention, and the vision of society that inspires each model. The first two models correspond to Wilensky and Lebeaux's (1965) typology of the residual model (the positive state) and the institutional model (the social security state). The third model corresponds to Mishra's (1981) description of the struc-tural model of welfare.

The Positive State or Residual Model of Welfare

The main goal of the positive state is to protect the interests of business from the diffi-culties of unprotected markets and from potential redistributive demands. The policy emphasis is on government–business collaboration for economic growth. Business yields much of its market decisions to government in return for financial assistance at home and political support abroad. The positive state aims at minimal full employment to keep consumption up, labour costs down, and labour unions weak. The current process of globalization is being driven, in large part, by values and principles of the positive state.

The preferred social welfare instrument is social insurance, which is consistent with economic efficiency and encourages 'proper' work habits. As well, it functions as social control by tying people's eligibility for social insurance benefits to their participation in the labour market. The beneficiaries of the positive state tend to be those who, under conditions of laissez-faire individualism, prosper most readily. The vision of the positive state is not at all similar to that of social work. Rather, it is one of rugged individualism within the context of balanced economic growth and protection of business interests (Mishra, 1981). It is the model of welfare favoured by neo-conservatives. The United States best typifies this model.

The Social Security State or Institutional Model of Welfare

The key concept of the social security state is that everyone who is a casualty of the industrial order has a right to a guaranteed minimum of social security. This collective responsibility for individual maintenance recognizes that a society based on competitive capitalism cannot provide universal security and that the state has a duty to fill this void. Theoretically, it is possible to eliminate poverty by establishing the national minimum income at an adequate level. The vision of a social security state is based on government–business co-operation where the guaranteed national minimum is financed by pursuing an economic policy of maximal full employment and public employment as a last resort. These economic and social policies are intended to be of direct benefit to every citizen and to overcome the limitations of social insurance provisions.

The social security state does not contain egalitarian social and economic ideals. The governing principle is 'equality of opportunity' where all are equal in status before the law but unequal in material resources, life chances, and political power. It represents what Furniss and Tilton (1977) call 'a modern and noble version of the Liberal ideal'. Great Britain (before Thatcherism) and Canada and Australia (before Howard), to a lesser extent, typify the social security state, although there has been a drift towards the positive state in all three jurisdictions

The Social Welfare State or Structural Model of Welfare

Unlike the goal of minimalist-full employment of the positive state or of maximalist-full employment of the social security state, the social welfare state has as its goal full employment. This requires government–union co-operation in the labour market. Equally important to the social welfare state are two other policies: environmental planning (in its most comprehensive form) and solidaristic wages. Environmental planning encompasses regulation of property to preserve amenities, prohibition of activities resulting in pollution, urban planning, and development of new communities. In short, this policy represents an effort to inject collective and social values into a society founded on the good life of the individual. The solidaristic wage policy counteracts the tendency towards concentration of assets and income, narrows differentials among groups of wage-earners, and extracts for labour a larger piece of the national income.

The social welfare state aims to promote equality and solidarity. It seeks more than a national minimum for citizens in attempting to achieve a general equality of living conditions. It substitutes public services, such as the public provision of health care, child care, and legal services, for social insurance programs. These services are available to all, not just to the under-privileged. The social welfare state envisions extending the locus of political and economic power and increasing citizen participation in all areas of living. It is similar to what Mishra (1981) calls the structural model of welfare. Although no country at present typifies the social welfare state, Sweden best approximates it among Western industrial democracies.

Social work must reject the positive state as a welfare system because it violates its fundamental values of humanism and egalitarianism and its corresponding set of social, economic, and political beliefs. The social security state contains some humanistic elements but lacks egalitarian ideals. The social welfare state, on the other hand, is most congruent with social work values, beliefs, and principles. Thus, progressive social workers must work towards and attempt to achieve this form of society if they are to remain true to their own ideals. However, the social welfare state or the structural model of welfare is not possible to achieve in our present society because it rests on a set of values contradictory to those of neo-conservative or liberal capitalism.

CONCLUSION

In this chapter the two major approaches to social work, the mainstream and progressive views, were presented. Using the progressive perspective as a point of departure, the argument here is that social work needs a progressive vision of society and social work practice if it is to be true to its primary values of humanitarianism and egalitarianism. The new 2005 CASW *Code of Ethics* contains little potential to develop such a view; indeed, the 1994 *Code* is a much more progressive document. Using the 1994 *Code*, elements of a progressive alternative vision of society were presented (see Table 2.2). The question for social work is, which of the major societal paradigms is most congruent with this alternative vision? In other words, is there a paradigm that approximates or is consistent with social work's primary values of humanitarianism and egalitarianism, as well as its secondary or instrumental values? These instrumental values include respect for the individual as a social being, the domination of economic decisions by societal decisions, participatory democracy, and a social welfare system that contributes to equality, solidarity, and community. The next four chapters will examine various social paradigms in an attempt to answer this question.

CRITICAL QUESTIONS

1. What does a 'progressive view' mean and why is it important to social work?
2. Why does social work need a code of ethics?
3. Why does social work need a professional association? Why doesn't social work organize itself into a union instead of a professional association?

4. How do you respond to the charge that social workers advocate for more spending on social programs only to guarantee themselves jobs?
5. Why has social work not been able to exert a significant influence on social policy decisions?
6. How and in what direction do the media influence people's opinions about social work and social programs?

The Neo-Conservative Paradigm

The modern conservative is engaged in one of man's oldest exercises in moral philosophy, that is, the search for a superior moral justification for selfishness.
—*John Kenneth Galbraith (1908–2006)*

Conservatives are not necessarily stupid, but most stupid people are conservatives.
—*John Stuart Mill (1806–73)*

INTRODUCTION

This chapter presents an overview of the traditional concept of 'conservatism' as was originally conceived in the late eighteenth and early nineteenth centuries and compares it to its modern form or what has come to be known as 'neo-conservatism'. Also presented is a summary of what conservatives believe about the inherent nature of human beings, the nature of society, the role of the nation-state, the substance of social justice, and social change. Neo-conservative ideology is deconstructed into its constituent parts or sets of social, economic, and political beliefs and an attempt is made to show how these beliefs underpin and shape the explanations neo-conservatives hold about social problems and the role and nature of the welfare state. A picture of what social work practice would look like within a neo-conservative/liberal context is outlined, as is a critique of neo-conservative beliefs. Finally, neo-conservative ideals are compared to those of progressive forms of social work.

CONSERVATISM

Conservatism is a set of beliefs that 'springs from a desire to conserve existing things, held to be either good in themselves, or better than the likely alternatives, or at least safe, familiar, and the objects of trust and affection' (Scruton, 1982: 90). This view implies a distrust of sudden or radical change. Conservatives prefer to maintain traditional institutions and processes, which should only be modified with extreme caution. The political consequences of these beliefs are a suspicion of state interference, a sympathy towards property rights, and an acceptance of inequalities with respect to class, education, status, and wealth (Roberts, 1971).

The purest source of conservative principles is found in Edmund Burke's *Reflections on the Revolution in France*, published in 1790 (Rossiter, 1968). Burke (1729–97) wrote during a time of turmoil (the 1780s) in France—a parliamentary system had been created, the Declaration of the Rights of Man was adopted, the last remnants of feudalism were abolished, the property of the Catholic Church had been nationalized, and the rationalism of the Enlightenment had replaced tradition as the surest guide to human conduct. These changes occurred with lightning rapidity and caused Burke to predict correctly that turmoil and despotism would follow such a radical break from the past (Dickerson and Flanagan, 1986). 'The result was the emergence of a political faith that celebrated the beauties of stability and tradition' (Rossiter, 1968: 294).

Burke's conservatism, an amalgam of economic liberalism (free-market economy) and social conservatism (respect for the past and a hierarchical view of society), has been adopted by most Anglo-American conservatives (Dickerson and Flanagan, 1986). Benjamin Disraeli, a late nineteenth-century Prime Minister of Britain, John Adams, second President of the United States, and John A. Macdonald and George-Étienne Cartier, two of the chief founders of Canada, are examples of political leaders who subscribed to the Burkean world of order, tradition, hierarchy, private property, laws, and customs. Conservatism in these terms is often found to be the ideological foundation of conservative political parties such as the Conservative Party of Britain, the Republican Party of the United States, the Liberal Party of Australia, and the Conservative Party of Canada.

Conservatism was the dominant ideology in nineteenth-century Britain and North America, and although it started to wane in the latter part of the nineteenth century it remained dominant until the Great Depression of the 1930s. Then, many conservative notions fell into disrepute and were replaced by liberal ideals and beliefs, including a new economic theory developed by John Maynard Keynes and a new social policy direction contained in the Beveridge Report of 1942. Following World War II the state was seen as a force for implementing a more just and equitable society, and a growing welfare state represented the means of implementation (Dickerson and Flanagan, 1986). The absence of serious recession, steady economic growth, and full employment (with some national fluctuations) made it seem that 'the old order of capitalism with its crude dogma of laissez-faire, endemic business cycles of boom and bust and chronic unemployment had . . . been left behind in a major evolutionary advance' and that acceptance of '[t]he mix of values and institutions represented by the welfare state . . . symbolized the new social order' (Mishra, 1989: 172).

In light of such beliefs the events of the 1970s, such as the oil crisis, a worldwide recession, stagflation, and the fiscal crisis of the state, came as a real shock and were not resolved by reformist liberal mechanisms and policies. Although never dead, conservative ideas and rhetoric have been revived as a way of explaining what went wrong with the mixed economy of the welfare state and as a guide to economic recovery and prosperity (Mishra, 1989). Political parties advocating conservative ideas and solutions have been elected in Britain (1979, 1983, 1987, and 1991), the United States (1980, 1984, 1988, 2000, and 2004), Australia (1996, 1998, 2001, and 2004), and Canada (1984, 1988, and 2006). Within the past two decades even those political parties traditionally advocating more progressive forms of welfare capitalism have pursued neo-conservative policies when elected: the federal Democratic Party elected in the US in 1992 and 1996; the federal Liberal Party elected in Canada in 1993, 1997, 2000, and 2004; the Australian Labour Party elected in 1983, 1984, 1987, 1990, and 1993; the British Labour Party elected in 1997, 2001, and 2005.

NEO-CONSERVATISM

The resurgence of conservative ideas, policies, and rhetoric, along with an attack on the welfare state, has been variously referred to as anti-collectivism (George and Wilding, 1976, 1985), rugged individualism (Djao, 1983), and the New Right (Mishra, 1984), but will be referred to here as neo-conservatism, which is more consistent with popular usage. Basing their economic and social views on the classical doctrines of laissez-faire and individualism, neo-conservatives have called for a return to the economic values of the private marketplace. Their solutions to the current crises are to attack government deficits by cutting profligate social spending, to rely on the private sector to restore economic growth, to eliminate or reduce the power of unions, to deregulate industry, and to limit the controls on multinational corporations (Riches, 1986).

Resnick (1984) describes three different but complementary elements running through neo-conservative thought. (1) People's excessive expectations are seen as a threat to representative government. Hence, government's role should be reduced, individual rights diminished, and more traditional values, such as authority and obedience, reinstated. (2) The state should follow laissez-faire policies and reject government interventions; demand management of the economy should be replaced by supply-side economics; deregulation, privatization, and severe limits on government spending should be imposed; and balanced budgets should be the central goal. (3) Traditional concepts of morality and religion should be asserted to control the permissiveness of modern society, and school prayers, the sacredness of pregnancy, law and order, and anti-communism should be the four foundations of the good society. Rossiter (1968) has identified some of the persistent philosophical themes of modern conservatism:

- the imperfect nature of people, where unreason and sin lie under the mask of civilized behaviour;
- the natural inequality of people in mind, body, and character;
- the necessity for social classes;
- the need for a ruling and serving elite;
- the existence of a universal moral order supported by organized religion;
- the primacy of private property;
- the limitations of human reason, and the consequent need for traditions, institutions, symbols, and prejudices.

What, then, is new about neo-conservatism? That is, what are the differences between the conservatism of the last century and the first half of this century and the neo-conservatism of the 1980s, 1990s, and 2000s? Most writers suggest that there is little difference. Dickerson and Flanagan (1986: 105), for example, state, 'We continue to use the traditional term conservatism because we see no fundamental change in ideology, even though popular support for conservative views has increased.' Mishra (1984: 173) contends that the only difference is the context (i.e., welfare capitalism) and that the doctrine is the same: 'Remove the context and the associated rhetoric and there is little that is new—that cannot, for example, be traced back to the classical doctrines of Adam Smith (individualism and free market) and Herbert Spencer (social Darwinism).' Most writers suggest that neo-conservatism represents a more sophisticated presentation of conservative doctrine rather than a different doctrine (Mishra, 1989).

Neo-conservatives have blamed much of the economic crisis on the welfare state. Mishra (1989: 171) says, 'It is one thing when economic growth stops . . . and governments find that they have to economize on social [expenditure]. . . . It is quite another thing when economic recession . . . become[s] the occasion for a general attack on the basic principles and practices of the postwar welfare state.' Neo-conservatives have argued that the welfare state has created both economic and social problems. The American neo-conservative writer, Charles Murray (1984, cited in Rice and Prince, 2000), argued that the welfare system ignored three (conservative) premises: that people respond to sticks (disincentives) and carrots (incentives); that people are inherently amoral and would rather not work; and that people must be held accountable for their actions. Economically, neo-conservatives argue that the welfare state is too big and too expensive, and also inefficient because it allows (or encourages) workers to drop out of the labour market, thus depriving the economy of needed labour and increasing welfare costs at the same time. Socially, neo-conservatives contend that the welfare state has fractured traditional family life, eroded the work ethic, legitimated unearned leisure time without shame or penalty, and encouraged undesirable behaviour (Stoesz and Karger, 1990). For example, the US Attorney General in the administration of George H.W. Bush blamed the 1992 Los Angeles race riots, which followed the 'not guilty' verdict in the trial of the policemen who beat Rodney King, on the liberal social programs of the Kennedy and Johnson administrations. Social expenditures were cited as encouraging too many inner-city black females to have children out of wedlock, and these children, the products of sexual abandonment without proper families, it was claimed, were responsible for the looting and rioting. To the neo-conservative, then, social welfare programs represent the cause rather than the cure for many social problems.[1]

A difference between traditional conservatives and neo-conservatives is that the latter group is much more sophisticated in its criticisms and attacks on the welfare state. Traditional conservatives were content to snipe at social programs from the sidelines using clichés about welfare cheats, bleeding-heart social workers, and self-interested bureaucrats (Stoesz and Karger, 1990). Right-wing think-tanks that attempt to give neo-conservative ideas intellectual legitimacy have emerged in all Anglo democracies. There are the London Institute of Economic Affairs and the Centre for Policy Studies in Britain, the Hoover Institute, the Cato Institute, and the Heritage Foundation in the United States; the Australian Institute for Public Policy, the Centre for Independent Studies (CIS), and the Institute of Public Affairs (IPA) in Australia (Mendes, 2003); and there are the moderately conservative C.D. Howe Institute and the more right-wing Fraser Institute in Canada, both of which are funded mainly by 'big business' (Naiman,1997; Rice and Prince, 2000). All have made serious proposals to restructure the welfare state (consistent with market solutions for social problems) rather than to eliminate it. Examples of such proposals are: to transfer as much welfare responsibility as possible from the federal government to lower levels of government and to the private sector; to transfer money from welfare to workfare programs; to encourage the involvement and participation of private citizens in the provision of many welfare services (i.e., set up food banks, soup kitchens, emergency shelters, and so on). Mullaly (1994) has argued that the current restructuring of the welfare state is occurring along class lines, with money being taken out of general welfare programs for the working class and redirected into fiscal welfare, i.e., grants, tax breaks, and the like for corporations and wealthy individuals, and into occupational welfare, i.e., perks and fringe benefits for the managerial and professional sectors of the working class, which are subsidized through the tax system. The result of this restructuring is that social benefits are redistributed away from those most in need (the poor) to those least in need (the wealthy). The class nature of this restructured welfare state is, of course, consistent with the neo-conservative belief in hierarchy and/or aristocracy (Sigurdson, 2002).

Given the confusion over use of the terms 'neo-conservatism' and 'neo-liberalism', what is the difference between them? It was pointed out in Chapter 1 that some writers maintain that there is no difference and show that the two terms are often used interchangeably. However, there is, in fact, a crucial difference. Although both perspectives subscribe to similar economic ideas and principles, that is, to fiscal conservatism in conservative terms and classical free-market doctrine in liberal terms, they differ with respect to social doctrine (see Table 3.1). Whereas neo-liberalism is mainly an economic ideology (shared with neo-conservatives, but not as extreme or as absolute) that advocates an economic arena free from government control or restriction, neo-conservativism is just as much a social ideology (Green, 2000). The latter calls for a return to the value norms of the traditional two-parent family and to traditional male and female roles and decries the progressive changes that have come about from such social movements as feminism, gay and lesbian rights, and multiculturalism (Sigurdson, 2002). This social ideology also is hostile towards easier divorce laws and same-sex relationships—especially same-sex marriage (Lavelette and Pratt, 1997). These ideas have found their way into the Conservative Party of Canada via its previous Reform Party/Canadian Alliance base, as well as in the Republican Party in the United States. With respect to the latter, in early 2005 the Republican branches (federal and state) of government sought to interfere with the judicial system in a case where a husband in Florida gave permission to turn off the life

**TABLE 3.1   NEO-CONSERVATISM: FISCAL CONSERVATISM PLUS
SOCIAL CONSERVATISM**

Conservative Focus	*Values*
Fiscal conservatism	Espouses classical liberal economic doctrine, but in more extreme/absolute form.
	Views a free market as the means of distribution of income, resources, and life chances.
	Sees government 'intervention' as government 'interference'.
	Believes in restricted public spending and monetarist economic policy.
	Champions global free trade.
	Wants only minimal taxation and a minimal (residual) welfare state.
	Expresses hostility towards labour unions.
	Insists on private ownership of the means of production.
	Believes that profit is the purpose of production.
	Upholds private property and inheritance rights.
Social conservatism	Believes that the traditional, heterosexual, married couple with children is the cornerstone of society.
	Claims that the ideal society is hierarchical, patriarchal, authoritarian, and inequitable.
	Is skeptical about immigration, especially when it involves people of colour.
	Expresses hostility towards same-sex relationships, divorce laws, and multiculturalism.
	Accommodates the religious right with its literal interpretations of the Bible, strong views on sin, and rejection of non-Christian religions.
	Sees human life as sacred from conception to death; thus, abortion and euthanasia are wrong/sinful.
	Abhors the changes that have occurred because of such social movements as the women's movement, gay and lesbian rights, and the human rights movement.
	Views poverty not as an economic problem but as culturally determined through values, behaviours, attitudes, and a lack of ambition transmitted across generations.

support system attached to his wife (Terri Schiavo), who had been in a vegetative state for over a decade. President George W. Bush and his brother, Jeb Bush, the Governor of Florida, were part of this intervention, with the President claiming that he was upholding a sacred Republican belief in 'a culture of life' (i.e., anti-abortion and anti-euthanasia). This claim is truly ironic when one considers that President Bush ordered the invasion of Iraq, that the United States is one of the very few Western democracies that employs capital punishment, and that the state of Texas, where he was Governor, executes more people than any other state. This social ideology of neo-conservatism is also the bedrock of the so-called 'Moral Majority'—the religious, fundamentalist right wing of the American population—one leader of which, the televangelist Pat Robertson, in 2005 called for the assassination of Venezuela's democratically elected leftist president, Hugo Chavez. Neo-liberals, for the most part, do not subscribe to this fundamentalist religious belief system or to this extreme ideology. They still prefer a reform brand of liberalism (albeit a watered-down version) that seeks to keep the free market but to purge it from some of its worst abuses (to be discussed in the next chapter).

Before we consider the specific ideological (social, economic, and political) beliefs of neo-conservatives, a brief overview of the views that neo-conservatives hold with respect to human nature, the nature of society and the state, social justice, and social change will be presented. The relationship between these neo-conservative views and the neo-conservative social, economic, and political ideals that constitute neo-conservative ideology is symbiotic. In other words, these views and ideals are mutually supportive of each other and inter-related, with each contributing to the overall neo-conservative world view or paradigm.

VIEWS OF THE NATURE OF HUMANS, SOCIETY, THE STATE, SOCIAL JUSTICE, AND SOCIAL CHANGE

As mentioned in Chapter 1, what we believe about *human nature* will largely determine how we think we should be governed (Sigurdson, 2002). It will also determine our explanations for social problems, our social welfare solutions for dealing with those problems, and the nature and forms of our social work practices. What, then, do neo-conservatives believe about what it means to be human, in other words, what is our human essence? Thomas Hobbes (1588–1679) gave the classic conservative (and neo-conservative) view of human nature. He wrote that humans are isolated and selfish creatures, driven by the twin forces of appetites (pleasures or desires) and aversions (pains). Individuals are motivated by gain (profit) and power (control of others), and if left to their own devices, life would be 'solitary, poor, nasty, brutish, and short' (Hobbes, 1981 [1651]: 185–6). Thus, Hobbes concludes that to avoid the violence and anxiety and constant war 'of every man [person] against every man [person]' (p. 185) that comes from this natural condition, the only rational course of action is to give up or trade some individual freedom and live in a formally organized state to gain the security needed to satisfy individual needs. In other words, civil society is only an expedient or necessary evil and not a conservative value or ideal. Jeremy Bentham (1748–1832) further developed this notion of human nature by arguing that all human behaviour can be explained by the two primary motives of pleasure and pain (theory of psychological hedonism). He argued that it was only 'rational' (natural) for the individual to pursue self-interest over the interests of all others and that one must use his or her 'reason' in this pursuit. Bentham believed that community or society interests were a fiction, for by nature there only existed the sum of the individual interests of its members.

The *nature of society*, as suggested by Bentham, is only equal to the sum of individual interests. It has no rights or values or collective interests in and of itself. Bentham and David Ricardo (1772–1823), an early political economist who developed the classical school of economic theory further than anyone before him, argued that society is simply a convenient way of referring to the sum of the contracts that free individuals entered into with one another. Milton Friedman, the twentieth-century neo-conservative economist and adviser to Reagan in the US and Thatcher in Britain, held that there are no social goals other than the aggregate of individual goals. In this way, society is reduced to so many contracts and agreements between the individuals who, in total, comprise the society. It does not stand above or apart from individuals. There is no idea that the whole is greater than the sum of its parts. There is no 'sociological imagination' (Mills, 1959). Margaret Thatcher once remarked, when asked a question about society, that 'there is no such thing as society; there are only individuals' who live within a particular state or nation. Although conservatives grudgingly accept the existence of classes, they have tended to de-emphasize the class concept by downplaying the importance of the concept of society; that is, society is comprised mostly of individuals, not classes. Ironically, conservatives subscribe to notions of hierarchy and aristocracy and the maintenance of such. Rather than social classes, however, conservatives have tended to see individuals who are either morally superior or inferior. Burke, who had an aristocratic belief in a natural hierarchy of persons, characterized the morally superior as 'the wiser, the more expert, and the more opulent', and the morally inferior as 'the weaker, the less knowing, and the less provided with the goods of fortune'. Of course, with this distinction, those who had wealth were regarded as morally superior and those without 'opulence' were regarded as morally inferior. Thus, a conservative imperative was to maintain the position of each group. In other words, the status quo was to be 'conserved' because it would not be good for the morally inferior to obtain positions of power.

If, as neo-conservatives claim, society only represents the sum of individual contracts, then what is *the role of the nation-state* (government)? Hobbes partially answered this when he stated that in exchange for some security, which was necessary for them to meet their individual needs, individuals must give up some freedoms to the state. Thus, to the neo-conservative the primary role of the state is maintain law and order for the orderly management of trade and commerce. It is to act as impartial arbiter in trade and contract disputes. But anything beyond protecting people's lives and property by maintaining law and order becomes, in the eyes of neo-conservatives, a threat to liberty (Sigurdson, 2002). And, of course, part of the task of maintaining law and order was and is to assure the compliance of subordinate groups (individuals) with the goals, needs, and interests of the ruling class (i.e., the morally superior, the aristocracy, the bourgeoisie, and other elites).

Social justice, to neo-conservatives, is based on the belief in individual responsibility. That is, every individual has a responsibility to look after him or herself. Only when people do not carry out this responsibility do problems such as unemployment, lack of resources, and inadequate housing occur. Neo-conservatives would guarantee a formal equality of right to participate in the free market and then rely on the free market to provide an equilibrium of societal benefits (Sigurdson, 2002). That is, there should be no legal discrimination banning groups such as people of colour or women from applying to educational programs or running for office. Further, a fair system of competition will produce fair results and, therefore, the state should not be used to provide specific advantages for historically disadvantaged groups (Sigurdson, 2002). Affirmative action programs are viewed as socially unjust by neo-conservatives because they are seen to be programs of reverse discrimination. Social equality is not a value choice of neo-conservatives. They believe that material inequality can be a good thing. In 1786, for instance, Joseph Townsend, an influential clergyman in England, published anonymously a little book called *A Dissertation on the Poor Laws by a Well-Wisher to Mankind*, in which he argued that 'poverty was a necessary spur [incentive] to human activity' (cited in de Schweinitz, 1943: 115).

Neo-conservatives are relatively content with the way things are (i.e., with the status quo) and would defend institutions from reformers. The status quo—traditional social values and accepted ways of doing things—best serves the interests of the market, and any attempt to change the fundamental institutions is regarded as a threat to existing social relations (i.e., to the existence of a morally superior dominant group and a morally inferior subordinate group). Neo-conservatives are highly skeptical of attempts to improve life through social policy and social intervention, which they call 'social engineering'. They prefer the tried and true to the new and experimental. Neo-conservatives realize that some change is inevitable, but insist that *social change* should be gradual and evolutionary rather than rapid and revolutionary. Neo-conservatives point out that biological evolution has occurred over millions of years (since creation for many religious conservatives, especially in the US) and, therefore, contend that social change should follow the same course of normal, natural, divine, and evolutionary change.

Table 3.2 summarizes neo-conservative beliefs with respect to human nature, the nature of society, the state, social justice, and social change.

The next three sections look at specific ideological beliefs of neo-conservatism along social, economic, and political lines. Some of these beliefs overlap with the views outlined above. These views and the subsequent ideological beliefs are mutually reinforcing. Taken together, they represent the neo-conservative position today. When compared to the progressive perspective of social work presented in the previous chapter, it is obvious that there is little, if any, agreement or common ground between neo-conservatism and progressive social work.

TABLE 3.2   A SUMMARY OF NEO-CONSERVATIVE VIEWS

Concept	Views
Human nature	Isolated and selfish individuals.
	Behaviours determined by pleasure and pain.
	Motivated by gain (profit) and power (control over others).
	Not natural (but necessary) for humans to live in society.
	Individuals are either morally superior or inferior.
Society	No such thing as society, only individuals.
	Equal to the sum of individual interests (no collective interests).
	Series of individual contracts that free individuals enter into with one another.
Nation-state	Necessary evil that maintains law and order.
	Referee role in trade and contract disputes.
	Assures conformity of subordinate groups to interests of dominant groups.
Social justice	Individuals have responsibility to look after themselves.
	There are no social problems, only personal problems that occur when individuals do not look after themselves.
	Every individual should have the right (and responsibility) to participate in the free market.
	Affirmative action is reverse discrimination; socially unjust.
	Poverty is a good thing as it teaches discipline and provides incentive.
Social change	Content with existing social institutions and social relations.
	Skeptical of social engineering (i.e., social intervention).
	Any social change should be slow and evolutionary.

SOCIAL BELIEFS

The central social values of neo-conservatism are freedom or liberty, individualism, and inequality (George and Wilding, 1976, 1985). Liberty is seen primarily as the absence of coercion. People must be as free as possible to exert themselves to the utmost limit of their abilities to the advantage of the individual person, which in turn will have a beneficial effect for society (in economic terms, a trickle-down effect). Any government promotion of social values that interfere with one's freedom is counterproductive. Yet, if coercion is to be avoided, there must be sanctions against those who would use it. The state, therefore, uses the threat of coercion to avoid coercion by any individual. This institutionalization of coercion is perceived by neo-conservatives as benefiting everyone equally in spite of the stratified nature of society and the concentration of power within certain groups. Thus, one of the inherent contradictions of a neo-conservative society is that coercion by the state is the instrument of liberty.

Individualism is a necessary correlate of liberty. The dominant theme of individualism is that the individual must have as much liberty as possible to pursue his or her own interests and to bear the consequences of his or her actions. If everyone in society adheres to the principle of the pursuit of self-interest without harming others, then society will run smoothly. Only when people fail to carry out their obligations or when government interferes with one's liberty do problems occur for the individual and for society. Individualism perceives people as imperfect beings who, therefore, must be controlled by sanctions and rules enforced by the state. Individualism also attributes a large role in the socialization of people to voluntary organizations and to institutions such as the family, the school, and the church. When these voluntary institutions fail in their socialization function, the coercive role of the state is invoked.

Social equality and liberty are seen by neo-conservatives as contradictory. They fear that equality of incomes from work will destroy people's work incentives, including the social esteem that accompanies certain occupations. Politically, social equality implies that powerful groups would have to share their political power, which could only occur through government coercion. Thus, to achieve social equality necessitates interference with the equality of freedom (including the freedom to be poor rather than being coerced into affluence by the state). Equality of freedom is the only equality accepted by neo-conservatives and, in fact, is their supreme value. But this equality of freedom is bound to produce material and political inequality. Thus, neo-conservatives support equality of freedom and social inequality. Obviously, these values foster a social Darwinian 'survival of the fittest' view that any form of state intervention into people's freedoms is contrary to the laws of nature, leading potentially to a restriction on the power and authority of the fittest members of society and an enhancement of the weak and unfit.

ECONOMIC BELIEFS

The fundamental economic values of neo-conservatism are laissez-faire economics, competitive capitalism, and private property accumulation. Descriptively, the term 'laissez-faire' (leave alone) refers to minimal government interference (as opposed to intervention) with the lives and activities of private citizens, especially in regard to their economic activities. The role of the state is to ensure the provision of the basic conditions for free competitive capitalism by maintaining law and order, enforcing contracts, protecting property rights, and defending the nation against attacks by other nations. It does not interfere in the economy by either holding back the successful or helping the unsuccessful.

Laissez-faire is a prerequisite for competitive capitalism. Reference is often made by neo-conservatives to the 'natural laws' of the competitive marketplace (laws of supply, demand, and price determination). A society that ignores or interferes with these natural laws, it is assumed, will run into trouble as surely as a person who ignores the law of gravity. Neo-conservatives believe that competitive capitalism, based on voluntary exchange rather than on coercion, is the best model for an economic system (Friedman, 1962, cited in Djao, 1983). The free market protects everyone's interests: the consumer, the seller, the employee, and the employer. The consumer is protected because he or she can buy from other sellers. The seller is protected because there are other potential consumers. The employee is protected because there are other employers he or she can work for, and so on. This whole economic process is carried out unfettered by any authority. If government were to interfere by attempting to regulate and restrict competition, or to hamper the efficient and successful, or to help the inefficient and unsuccessful, the results would be to upset the delicate but perfectly balanced natural economic system. All society would suffer and be poorer for it. The best economic policy of government is to leave the economy alone.

One of the freedoms cherished by neo-conservatives is the right to acquire, accumulate, and own property (land, material and natural resources, means of production, and so on) and to use one's property as one sees fit. Private ownership is not only consistent with neo-conservative social beliefs of liberty, individualism, and inequality, it also is the driving force behind the economic system. Private ownership provides the means for making profits and thus is the incentive in a competitive free market for persons to work hard to maximize their material and spiritual well-being. If people were not allowed to keep the fruits of their labour and to dispose of them in any fashion they wish, there would be reduced incentive to work hard and the economy, as a whole, would suffer. Individuals are responsible for providing for themselves out of resources they manage to control. This notion forces people to attempt to increase their share of available resources, as any increase in property is perceived as an increase in material security and social status. To the neo-conservatives the appropriation of material resources is the fundamental principle around which a society's system of provision and the entire social order should be constructed.

POLITICAL BELIEFS

The major political beliefs of neo-conservatism are: rule by a governing elite; subjugation of the political system to the economic system; law, order, and stability; and paternalism. Conservatives have always found the concept of democracy to be problematic, and it is important to remember that when modern democracy as we know it, that is, representative democracy, first appeared on the world stage only property-owning males were allowed the vote. Politics is restricted in meaning to the 'art of governing', which is too important to be left to anyone but the most able and best prepared, who, of course, are inevitably members of the elite ruling class. To extend political rights to the masses is to run the risk of decisions being made by the wrong people, that is, by non-members of the established elite who, therefore, cannot be legitimate rulers. The Family Compact of Upper Canada (Ontario) in the nineteenth century and the hierarchy of the Roman Catholic Church of Lower Canada, which dominated Quebec life well into the twentieth century, are examples of conservative ruling elites in Canada.

The belief in ruling elites is no mere relic of political history but is used today by neo-conservatives as a political explanation for the economic and social crises confronting Western industrial societies. 'A ruling class, unlike a democratically elected government, is expected to serve the interests of those who control the economy' (Marchak, 1981: 71). In a democracy political parties must compete with one another for votes. In this electoral competition excessive expectations are made on governments, pushing them further and further into responsiblity for everything. The result, according to neo-conservative thought, is government overload: demands on government far exceed its capacity to meet them effectively. This situation is characterized by public expenditure out of control or by government itself expanded out of control, and has been brought about by increasing democratization (Mishra, 1984). The neo-conservatives would like to see this process reversed or, at least, curtailed.

Neo-conservatives blame much of the recent fiscal crisis discussed in Chapter 1 on excessive government intervention and regulation. They would resolve this crisis by curtailing democratization of the political process and by depoliticizing the economy. If society is to benefit from economic activity, then, it is claimed, we must put up with the costs (e.g., unemployment, inadequate wages, questionable labour practices) of a free market. The role of government should be to protect, to support, to assure, and to enhance the workings of a free market. It should not be the role of government to regulate, interfere with, or explicitly allow unions, professional associations, or other interest groups to modify the spontaneous workings of the market. Thus, although neo-conservatives believe in a strong central state, its sphere of activities must be restricted to such things as national defence and protecting individual rights and freedoms.

Neo-conservatives place a premium on the maintenance of a social hierarchy, and much of past conservative effort has been to *conserve* rather than reform the legal, political, social, and economic status quo. Originally such a perspective was justified on religious grounds, but today there is a strong psychological attraction for conserving rather than reforming (Pritchard and Taylor, 1978). In other words, much of neo-conservative rhetoric is based on the assumption that people have a basic psychological need for security and will opt for a social system they are familiar with, even though it may contain many flaws, rather than take a chance on one they have not experienced and are unfamiliar with. Thus, much of neo-conservative political rhetoric is focused on law and order and on preserving the 'old' ways and values. Any change or reform is perceived as a threat to social stability and social continuity.

Another political belief of neo-conservatives is 'paternalism for those whom society designates as not responsible' (George and Wilding, 1976: 32) or, in Poor Law terminology, 'the deserving poor'. This form of government activity is seen as a necessary evil (the alternative is to let people die) rather than as a means of reducing inequalities. Although the risk of abuse is great (in terms of expanding the categories of people considered as not capable of taking responsibility for themselves), there is no avoiding the need for some degree of paternalism. The amount of assistance must be the lowest acceptable to society. In return for this *noblesse oblige* the neo-conservative ruling elite would expect conformity and loyalty from its citizenry.

VIEW OF SOCIAL PROBLEMS

In accordance with its views of human nature and society, and its social, economic, and political beliefs, neo-conservatism holds that people should provide for themselves by exercising their individual freedoms and choices in the competitive marketplace. In other words, everyone should provide for his or her own needs through work, savings, and the acquisition of property. Only those persons who do not carry out these obligations (the unfit, the lazy, and the inferior) encounter problems. Even if people become ill and cannot look after themselves, the judgement is often that they should have made arrangements to cover such contingencies and it is up the family to look after them in the first instance. And because these problems are of their own making, they do not deserve help from government or from hard-working, responsible, and honest taxpayers. In fact, neo-conservatives believe that helping those who fail to provide for themselves reinforces idleness and dependence on government and encourages others to avoid efforts to support themselves. An exception to this rule is that if people are judged to be in difficulty through no fault of their own (i.e., disabled persons, dependent children, older persons), they may be eligible for some help through a residual welfare system (discussed in the previous chapter). History has shown, however, that this group of 'deserving poor' has always been numerically under-represented.

The neo-conservative view of social problems seldom considers structural or environmental sources of social and economic problems, but attributes such problems to individual weakness, deviance, or heredity. Social problems are viewed as personal problems and the focus is on the troublesome person or family. The problem is supposed to be caused by defects of the mentally ill person or the drug addict or the poor person or the criminal. The family also is seen as the source of personal problems because, consistent with social Darwinian thought, unfit parents will produce unfit children. In other words, parents who are lazy, dishonest, and inferior will produce children with similar characteristics. Neo-conservative writer George Gilder (1981) contends that welfare programs and the decline of traditional family values and traditional family patterns (not sexism, racism, or unemployment) cause poverty and that any cause-effect relationship between racism or sexism and poverty is a myth perpetrated by social workers and feminists. In all cases, the analysis of social problems is the same. The individual is separated from society and a biographical portrait of deficiencies is constructed as the source of the person's troubles.

The neo-conservative view of social problems is consistent with the 'social pathology' perspective that was central to the thinking of early American sociologists. Their work was infused with moral indignation formulated in terms of a medical model wherein many social problems were the work of sick or pathological individuals, that is, people who are defective, delinquent, dependent, and deficient. The solution to social problems according to these early sociologists was to educate the pathological troublemakers in middle-class morality (Rubington and Weinberg, 1995). This perspective on social problems, which is often referred to as the 'personal deficiency approach', has informed the diagnostic, functional, and psychosocial traditions in social work (Coates, 1991). The impact that the larger social environment has on personal problems is not considered.

BOX 3.1   THE DOUBLE STANDARD OF NEO-CONSERVATIVES

From approximately 1985 to 1995 I was Chair of the Social Work Department at St Thomas University in Fredericton, New Brunswick. During that time I was a frequent media commentator on various social policy issues. I often found myself on panels discussing the impacts of provincial or federal budgets or new legislation or particular social policies. Along with myself, the panels usually consisted of a businessman (never a businesswoman), an accountant or economist, a right-wing academic (usually a political scientist or management professor), and someone from the Chamber of Commerce or the Real Estate Board. Given this makeup of panel members, it is obvious that I was the 'token' left-winger whose views would be out of step with the others, who were usually conservative in their positions. Inevitably, I found myself being written off and/or patronized by the other panel members, including the media person who chaired the panel. I like to think that I held my own in these panel discussions not only because I knew my stuff and was relatively articulate in expressing my views, but also because the (neo-conservative) positions of the others were usually indefensible.

I remember one particular radio panel where we were discussing a recent provincial budget in which there were several cutbacks (again) to social programs. I took my usual position that these cuts were morally bankrupt, short-sighted in terms of social arithmetic as they would lead to higher social and economic costs over time, discriminatory as they picked on vulnerable groups, and so on. The business leader on the panel said to me in a patronizing way, 'Well now Bob, you have to understand that when you give someone something for nothing, you don't do them any favours. You just make them lazy, irresponsible parasites. Why would you want to reward them for doing nothing?' Because of his patronizing attitude, *I decided to go for his jugular!*

I said to Mr Big Business Leader, 'Could I ask you a somewhat personal question that relates to what you just said?' Looking a little bewildered, he replied, 'Yes, I guess so.' I asked him, 'When you die, I assume that you will not leave your children anything which you own. Is this right?' He stated in a rather annoyed manner, 'Of course I will. Why would you even ask that?' To which I replied, 'Well, you just made the argument that giving someone something for nothing will damage their character by making them lazy, dependent, and irresponsible. And, since I am sure you love your children, I assumed that you wouldn't want to do that to them or reward them for doing nothing. You know that it would be better if they worked for whatever they got rather than you giving it to them on a silver platter.'

There was a long silence on the part of everyone on the panel while Mr Big Business Leader, who now realized that he was hoisted on his own petard, was looking very uncomfortable and at a loss as to what to say. The moderator intervened and said, 'We should perhaps move on.' But, having been patronized, I didn't want to move on, so I said, 'No, I asked this guy a question and I want to hear his answer. He just condemned everyone who has had to suffer the indignity of seeking some kind of help from society, and I want to know how he justifies this *double standard* where it is okay to help his children even when they are not in need, but it is a big social sin to help others out who are in need.' Another long silence. Finally, the moderator said that we *really* had to move on. I don't recall Mr Big Business Leader saying too much for the rest of the panel discussion.

VIEW OF SOCIAL WELFARE

George and Wilding (1985, 1994) explain how neo-conservatives are fundamentally hostile to a developed social welfare state. Any provision of more than basic government services is believed to have unnecessary and undesirable social, economic, and political consequences. Socially, the more services the state provides, the more it weakens the traditional sources of welfare: the family and local voluntary organizations such as the churches. These sources will not only disappear over time, but so, too, will the individual's ability and willingness to provide for his or her own needs. Economically, government assistance, above a basic subsistence level, diverts human and capital resources from the productive sector, undermines work incentives, is provided inefficiently, and encourages consumption of unneeded services. Politically, social welfare undermines individual freedom, weakens public respect for government and the political process, and may lead to dictatorial regimes. In essence, the neo-conservatives see the 'welfare state' as a misnomer because government intervention actually leads to a state of 'diswelfare'.

The free-market system, according to the neo-conservatives, is the main source and origin of welfare. Even social services should be delivered through the market by private commercial practitioners/entrepreneurs. The model of social welfare most consistent with neo-conservative thought, and that has the free market as its central concept, is 'residual' (Wilensky and Lebeaux, 1958). This is based on the neo-conservative belief that social welfare programs (both private and public) should only come into play when the normal channels for meeting needs—the family and the market economy—break down.

When these preferred structures of supply are not functioning properly or when an individual cannot make use of them because of illness or old age, a third mechanism for fulfilling need—the social welfare system—is brought into play. This residual structure attends to emergency functions only, and it is expected to withdraw when the two normal or regular structures, the family and the economic system, are again working properly. All social welfare assistance should be minimal and must not threaten or undermine the operations of the marketplace, nor must it erode wage earners' sense of responsibility for themselves and their families.

Because of its temporary, residual, and substitute nature, social welfare often carries a stigma of charity and abnormality. This concept of social welfare formed the basis of the Elizabethan Poor Laws, which divided the poor into two groups: the deserving (dependent children, the elderly, the disabled) and the non-deserving (employable adults). The former group might have been eligible for residual welfare; the second group was not. That this model of social welfare is consistent with such neo-conservative values as individual responsibility, the free market, and minimal government intervention is readily apparent. The residual model of welfare is similar to Furniss and Tilton's (1977) 'positive state' model of social welfare described in the previous chapter, where it was argued that it should be rejected by the social work profession because it is based on value premises diametrically opposed to those of social work.

Mishra (1989: 174) contends that neo-conservatism challenges all persons who believe in an adequate and fair welfare state:

> neo-conservatism is openly and unashamedly partisan and one-sided. It has forced upon the world of social welfare the realization that what we are involved in is essentially a contest over values, beliefs and interests rather than some objective necessity dictated by the economy. In breaking the consensus of ideas and practices over the welfare state it has thrown an open challenge to those on the side of social welfare to make an adequate ideological response.

SOCIAL WORK PRACTICE WITHIN THE NEO-CONSERVATIVE PARADIGM

Given: (1) the neo-conservative views on the nature of human beings, society, the state, social justice, and social change; (2) such neo-conservative values as individual responsibility, inequality, survival of the fittest, and laissez-faire; (3) a neo-conservative view of social problems as originating from individual weakness and deviance; and (4) a neo-conservative conception of social welfare as temporary, abnormal, and residual, therefore the nature of social work practice within neo-conservatism would be one of control and coercion of people. Emphasis would be placed on getting people to accept their personal, family, and social obligations and not on social or environmental reform.

Because the nature of human beings is viewed as contentious, competitive, and self-absorbed, social work must use coercive measures to make sure that people look after themselves. All other sources of assistance must be explored before a person would be considered eligible for any kind of financial help. A means test is an integral part of the residual model of welfare. Separation of the deserving poor from the non-deserving poor would be a primary function of social workers in a neo-conservative society. Investigation and monitoring of people's living, work, and financial situations would occur regularly to control abuse of social welfare systems and programs. Because of the belief that social problems are mainly due to individual fault and deviance, then suspicion, moralism, and punitive attitudes would be qualities held by social workers. The primary task of social work under neo-conservatism would be to teach people how to do without the welfare state.

Individual behaviour within the neo-conservative paradigm is seen within a limited social context that hardly extends beyond an individual's family. In other words, neo-conservatives attribute problems to an individual's dysfunctional family, and it is not likely that the source of personal/social problems will be considered to extend beyond the boundary of the family. A dysfunctional family is not viewed as a victim of the social order, but as a pathological social unit. Social work with pathological families would consist of coercing, cajoling, and convincing individual family members to adjust their behaviours and to carry out their individual responsibilities to themselves, to one another, and to society. Threats of removing children and other intimidation tactics would be major tools used in working with families.

Rather than focus on helping, social work would emphasize control of people's behaviour by way of such methods as 'case management' in order to remove any threat to the established social order. This is so because, according to the neo-conservatives, society can only function effectively and efficiently as long as everyone carries his or her own weight. Once the principle of individual responsibility starts to break down, then the whole society is in danger of collapsing. If individual pathology cannot be controlled by social work, then it must be neutralized by other state mechanisms such as asylums and prisons.

One possible exception to the controlling and coercive nature of social work within the neo-conservative paradigm would be its treatment of the so-called 'deserving poor'. Because a judgement has been made that the deserving poor are in need through no fault of their own, likely they would not be treated as punitively as their 'non-deserving' counterparts. However, there is always the problem of determining who is deserving and who is not. As well, the history of the Poor Laws tells us that those judged deserving have always been numerically under-represented. Even in working with the deserving poor, social workers would be expected to exhort and cajole as much money and help as possible from the poor person's family for the maintenance of its unfortunate member.

Iatridis (1983: 101) sums up the effects of neo-conservatism on social work:

> neo-conservatism creates a special crisis for social workers because this ideology is the antithesis of social work theory, practice, philosophy, values, objectives, and commitments—of everything, in fact, for which the profession stands.

CRITIQUE OF THE NEO-CONSERVATIVE PARADIGM

Neo-conservative thought forms much of the intellectual support for recent social policy in Canada, the United States, and Britain. An excellent overview of the criticisms of neo-conservative doctrine has been presented by Mishra (1984) and is summarized here.

(1) Although there may be a grain of truth in many neo-conservative arguments, there is a tendency to exaggerate this grain of truth and to generalize on the basis of insufficient evidence. For example, neo-conservatives often convey the impression that budget deficits have been occurring regularly since World War II because of Keynesian economic practices, when, in fact, it has only been since the recession of the 1970s that sizable deficits began to emerge.

(2) Neo-conservative thought and argument vary in terms of theoretical sophistication but, on the whole, tend to be one-sided and based on highly selective evidence. For example, neo-conservatives often blame Britain's economic ills on its welfare state, but no mention is made of other European countries such as Germany and Austria with well-developed welfare states that also enjoy excellent economic growth, low inflation, and low unemployment. They are simply ignored.

(3) Neo-conservatives offer a biased view of how government functions. They criticize governments for not being decisive enough and for not taking quick action. They fail to see that government is not the same kind of undertaking as a business seeking profit. Hence, what is presented as government failure—for example, 'weakened' authority because of greater democracy and more participation—may in fact be government's strength.

(4) Neo-conservatives possess an inadequate conception of the role of democracy and politics in modern societies. It was mentioned earlier that neo-conservatives would like to see the capitalist market economy depoliticized as much as possible, that is, that elected governments should not be allowed to interfere in the market. This would be a reversal to the growth of the modern state and of citizenship that has been occurring over the past 100 years. It would negate the responsibility a democratically elected government has for the nation's well-being by not allowing it to exercise control and regulation over the economy.

(5) Based on the values of individualism, liberty, private property, and inequality, neo-conservatism has little appreciation of the concepts of social justice and social integration as vital elements of modern, industrial democracies.

CONCLUSION

This chapter presented an overview of conservative ideology and showed how it shaped neo-conservative beliefs about the reasons why we have social problems and what to do about them. It also provided an overview of neo-conservative beliefs about the nature of people and society, the role of state, the meaning of social justice, and social change. The social, economic, and political beliefs of neo-conservatives were outlined, as were the neo-conservative views of the welfare state and the proper role of social work. Table

TABLE 3.3   OVERVIEW OF NEO-CONSERVATIVE AND SOCIAL WORK IDEALS

	Neo-Conservatism	*Social Work*
Social Beliefs	Freedom (from government coercion) Individualism Inequality	Humanitarianism (humanism) Community Equality
Economic Beliefs	Free market Competitive capitalism Private ownership	Government intervention Social priorities dominate economic decisions Equitable distribution of society's resources
Political Beliefs	Elite rule Depoliticization of economic system Law, order, and stability Paternalism	Participatory democracy in both governmental and non-governmental areas
View of Social Welfare	Fundamentally hostile Ideal = residual model	An instrument to promote equality, solidarity, and community Ideal = structural model
Nature of Social Work Practice	Use of coercive measures to make people look after themselves Control people's behaviour Poor Law treatment of separating deserving from non-deserving Emphasize investigation and monitoring to prevent cheating the system	Treat people with respect Enhance dignity and integrity Facilitate self-determination and self-realization Accept differences Advocate and promote social justice

3.3 outlines the principal beliefs of neo-conservatism and contrasts them with the fundamental beliefs of progressive social work. After examining the major beliefs and ideals of each, one can conclude only that neo-conservatism and progressive social work are incompatible. The social, economic, and political beliefs of each contradict one another, as do their respective views of the welfare state. Although social work practice does contain coercive and controlling elements, they tend to be imposed by outside bodies such as the state and the authorizing agency. They are not self-directed functions of progressive social work. Neo-conservatism's eighteenth-century assumptions about economic, human, and social behaviour conflict with those of social welfare and are the antithesis of progressive social work.

CRITICAL QUESTIONS

1. How closely do you think the following political parties adhere to conservative ideology?
   - federal Conservative Party in Canada
   - Republican Party in the US
   - federal Liberal Party in Australia
   - Conservative Party in the UK
2. The term 'human nature' suggests that certain innate characteristics or traits are common to all people. For example, conservatives claim that humans are *by nature* greedy individuals and competitive. However, socialists claim that humans are *by nature* social beings and co-operative. Is there any such thing as a human nature and, if so, what is it? Or are human traits and characteristics socially determined?
3. How would neo-conservatives explain street crime in low-income areas? How would they explain white-collar crime such as cheating on your income tax? How would they explain corporate crime such as manipulating markets or dipping into shareholders' money? Are any of these crimes more respectable in a neo-conservative's eyes than others? Why?
4. Why has neo-conservatism been so successful in influencing social policy over the past three decades?
5. Which groups in society are most supportive of neo-conservative ideas?
6. How would you respond to the following neo-conservative claims?
   - If we abolished the minimum wage, we would increase youth employment.
   - Too many teenaged girls are having babies so they can get welfare.
   - Aboriginal people will never get ahead as long as government gives them welfare, free housing, and free education and doesn't collect any taxes from them.

The Liberal and Neo-Liberal Paradigms

The state has no place in the nation's bedrooms.

— Pierre Elliott Trudeau (1919–2000)

INTRODUCTION

This chapter presents a brief historical overview of liberalism and attempts to clarify and differentiate among several forms of liberalism such as classical or market liberalism, contemporary or reform liberalism, welfare liberalism, and neo-liberalism. It also provides an overview of liberal views or beliefs about human nature, the nature of society, the role of the nation-state, the meaning of social justice, and social change. The social, economic, and political beliefs that constitute liberal ideology are examined and we explore how these beliefs shape the explanations of liberals with respect to the causes of social problems and the nature and role of the welfare state. A picture of social work practice within the liberal paradigm is presented along with a discussion of how mainstream social work thought and practice developed within a liberal discourse. Even today, the bulk of social work education, literature, and practice is shaped by and reflects liberal ideology. A critique of liberalism is provided and a comparison and contrast of liberal ideals is made with those of progressive social work.

LIBERALISM(S)

Liberalism comes from the Latin word 'liber', meaning free. It comprises a set of beliefs based on the assumption that there should be as much individual freedom as possible in any civilized society while allowing for essential constraints (Roberts, 1971). Although liberalism developed as a coherent system of ideals and practical goals mainly in the eighteenth and nineteenth centuries, it has a long and rich tradition (Smith, 1968). It has roots in Greek philosophy and literature, in Roman law, and in several religious traditions, including Christianity, and was fostered by the Renaissance and the Reformation. It is the result of the convergence of a number of broad social and political trends and forces. Today, the term 'liberalism' is confusing, made only more confusing when the word is preceded by the prefix 'neo'. John Gray (1989, cited in O'Brien and Penna, 1998) claims that it is more realistic to think in terms of 'liberalisms' in the plural. To some it means individualism in the extreme, where the only goal of social organization is to maximize individual autonomy and freedom; to others it means the promotion of collective strategies for social development while maintaining a commitment to individual freedom (O'Brien and Penna, 1998). In this chapter we distinguish among the terms 'liberalism', 'neo-liberalism', 'classical liberalism', and 'reform liberalism', but the major emphasis will be on 'reform liberalism' since this form guided the development of the twentieth-century welfare state, at least in North America, and reform liberalism is what separates the neo-conservative from the neo-liberal.

When discussing liberalism it is important to distinguish the older classical liberalism from contemporary or reform liberalism. As mentioned in the previous chapter, classical liberal economic doctrine is today referred to as neo-liberalism. Classical liberalism, sometimes called 'market' liberalism, is similar to conservatism as both developed in the eighteenth and nineteenth centuries, mainly in Britain and Western Europe, and both used the same writers and thinkers as the source for many of their ideas and theories.[1] Reform liberalism, which developed in the twentieth century, acknowledged the role of the state in allowing the capitalist free market to function (Naiman, 1997). Whereas classical liberals saw the state in negative terms as a threat to individual freedom, reform liberals view the state in positive terms as promoting freedom for those who otherwise might not achieve it. Great inequalities in market power make one person's freedom another person's oppression. Also, reform liberals view the state as a means to remedy some of the abuses of the free market, such as child labour, slum housing, tainted food, and so on (Smith, 1968). Thus, economic freedom and the free market are not accorded the same primacy in reform liberalism as in classical liberalism (Dickerson and Flanagan, 1986). Another major difference between classical and reform liberalism lies in the concept of equality that each holds. Equality to the classical liberal means only that everyone abides by the same rules (laws) and does not extend to a desire or responsibility to ameliorate inequality of wealth, status, or power. This is similar to the neo-conservative belief that there should be an equality of right (and responsibility) to participate (i.e., work) in the market. Equality to the reform liberal means equal opportunity, that is, the everyone should have the same opportunity to compete in the market place for wealth, power, and prestige (Naiman, 1997). Such competition will lead to a status hierarchy where one's location is determined by a system of meritocracy. Thus, liberals accept inequality. The reform liberal does not wish to eliminate inequality but seeks to reduce its excesses by using the power of the state to provide opportunities, such as public education or public health care, that would not be available to some people without government intervention. In short, reform liberalism tries to modify the free market without abolishing it. Table 4.1 outlines some of the major 'liberalisms'.

From their inception in Canada, Britain, and the United States, conservative thought and ideology helped to shape the welfare states and continue to exert a great deal of

TABLE 4.1   *LIBERALISM(S)*

Classical liberalism (developed alongside the growth of early capitalism)	Shared origins with conservatism (history, place, intellectual foundations). Economic doctrine (i.e., free market) is similar to fiscal conservatism, but not as extreme or absolute. Government spending distorts market forces and causes budget deficits. Unemployment is caused by government interference (giving workers an alternative to employment) and by behaviour of unemployed people (voluntary withdrawal from job market). Business should be privately owned and be free from government interference in order to make a profit and create jobs Corporate taxes, minimum wages, and workplace legislation squeeze out jobs. Unfettered laissez-faire capitalism is the ideal economic system. Social doctrine espouses individualism, inequality, and guaranteed freedoms. Poverty is desirable because it provides a labouring class.
Reform liberalism	Recognizes that the state can play a positive role in helping to reduce the worst excesses of a competitive market system by employing Keynesian economic policy, i.e., by planning and regulating capital, but keeping private ownership and profits. Recognizes that capitalism produces winners and losers and believes that the state should be used to provide fair chances (i.e., equal opportunity) to compete by ensuring that no individual be discriminated against on the basis of gender, race, class, etc. Thus, human rights legislation is a liberal goal. Believes that capitalism causes social problems for many and that the state should provide a minimum living standard (i.e., a welfare state) for those hurt by capitalism. Believes in the social doctrine of liberty, individualism, and inequality, but that they should be modified on humanitarian (concern for the individual) and pragmatic (concern for society as a whole) grounds. The state can be used to mediate the struggle between capital and labour and bring about an accord between the two.

(continued)

TABLE 4.1   (CONTINUED)

Neo-liberalism	This is a modified amalgam of the doctrines of classical liberalism and reform liberalism.
	Fiscal crisis led to a repudiation of Keynesian economic policy and a return to the belief that a free market economy is necessary to provide the resources for social programs and government services.
	The goals of reform liberalism are still laudable, but many are impractical and some can only be achieved (afforded) if we return to classical liberal economic principles and practices and reduce the scope and level of assistance of social programs.

influence today. However, the dominant paradigm that accompanied the emergence of the post-war welfare state in Canada and the United States, and to a lesser extent in Britain,[2] is reform liberalism. Although challenged by neo-conservatism today, reform liberalism is still the dominant social ideology in Canada. In other words, Canadians live in a liberal society where both the existing social welfare states and social work practices have been influenced mainly by reform liberal ideology since World War II. Therefore, it is crucial for the social work profession to be informed of, and to understand, the social, economic, and political beliefs that in large part shape our welfare state and determine the nature of our practice.

George and Wilding (1985) believe that the term 'liberalism' today stands for such a wide spectrum of political ideology that it has lost all meaning. Instead, they use the term 'reluctant collectivism'. Djao (1983) follows the lead of George and Wilding and refers to liberalism as 'modified individualism'. The term 'liberalism' will be used in this book, however, because, as with 'conservatism', it is more consistent with popular usage and is more widely used in Canadian social, economic, and political literature. Nevertheless, the terms 'reluctant collectivism' and 'modified individualism' are useful in distinguishing liberalism from conservatism and at the same time suggest what they have in common. Whereas conservatives subscribe to an absolute form of individualism, liberals, particularly reform liberals, subscribe to a modified version of individualism and/or to a reluctant form of collectivism.

As noted above, reform liberals share many of the same values with neo-conservatives: beliefs in freedom, in individualism, and in competitive private enterprise. However, they hold fewer absolute values in that they accept intervention into the economy on the basis of pragmatism and humanism. Their pragmatism is based on a conviction that although capitalism may be the best economic system, it is not self-regulating. It requires regulation and control to function efficiently and fairly. Their humanism is based on a recognition that capitalism is hurtful to many people. Concern for the human implications of capitalism led John Maynard Keynes and William Henry Beveridge in Britain,

John Kenneth Galbraith in the US, and Leonard Marsh and Harry Cassidy in Canada to lead British and North American societies to reject conservative thought and to adopt the reform liberal paradigm (George and Wilding, 1985).

The views of liberals with respect to the nature of human beings, society, the state, social justice, and social change are presented below. Again, these views are common to both reform liberalism and neo-liberalism, although they are less strictly applicable to neo-liberal thought.

VIEWS OF THE NATURE OF HUMANS, SOCIETY, THE STATE, SOCIAL JUSTICE, AND SOCIAL CHANGE

Whereas neo-conservatives share a belief in the imperfection of *human nature*, seeing in the individual varying degrees of weakness, immorality, and irrationality (Sigurdson, 2002), liberals hold a more favourable view of human beings. They assume that people are naturally moral and rational (Bastow and Martin, 2003) and that, given certain social conditions (e.g., equal opportunity and freedom from societal interference), the individual can improve him or herself. In this way, liberals implicitly connect the well-being of society to the well-being of the individual. L.T. Hobhouse (1864–1929), one of the great historians of British political thought and a founding father of British sociology, and the English philosopher Jeremy Bentham (1748–1832) argued that the liberal notion of 'individuality'could not be realized without the state taking action 'to secure the conditions of self-maintenance for the normal healthy citizen' (Hobhouse, 1994: 174). Individualism and social needs were thus conceived as mutually self-sustaining (Bastow and Martin, 2003). Human nature is dual in that it is both egoistic (self-interest) and altruistic (concern for others). In other words, decisions made by an individual go beyond a simple notion of economic greed to include a moral concern for others. Although inequality of life circumstances is a normal outcome of fair competition in the market, persons should not become so destitute that they are unable look after themselves.

Similar to neo-conservatism, liberalism holds an atomistic view of *the nature of society* whereby individuals interact with each other to satisfy their individual interests, but liberals differ from neo-conservatives with respect to their view that there is also a collective interest. Unlike conservatives, who developed a social doctrine of social Darwinism based on Darwin's notion of 'survival of the fittest', reform liberals were influenced by Charles Darwin's work that stressed co-operation and evolution, and developed a theory of society in which collectivism represented a higher stage of human evolution. This theory allowed liberals to justify state welfare and social reform as part of the progressive logic of social development and to ground their normative theory in the 'objective' terms of scientific theory. Twentieth-century liberalism also drew from the science of biology the notion of society as an 'organism' or entity of mutually interdependent parts. This notion reinforced the view of liberal reformers (mentioned above) that the well-being of the individual cannot be considered apart from the health of the entire organism (Freeden, 1978, cited in Bastow and Martin, 2003). It is important to note that twentieth-century reform liberalism was challenged by socialist ideas and movements, which undoubtedly made it more receptive to notions of collectivism and social reform.Unlike classical liberals, reform liberals recognize the existence of classes, but they rationalize this by claiming that equality of opprotunity means that people can climb the social ladder if they really try.

Given the reform liberal's belief in social development, collective interests, and a mutual relationship between the well-being of the individual and that of society, then *the role of the state* goes beyond that of an umpire or arbiter of disputes among individuals with respect to contracts made between them. It includes a role of intervening into and regulating (to a degree) the social, economic, and political life. The major role of the state would be to operationalize the concept of 'equal opportunity' and make the race of life fairer by implementing human rights legislation, placing legal restraints on corporate and professional conduct, providing public programs for all citizens such as public education and health care, and helping those disadvantaged by capitalism (Bastow and Martin, 2003; Naiman, 1997).

Social justice to the reform liberal is based on a distribution or redistribution of resources, which, of course, is consistent with a belief in equal opportunity. Liberals, by way of state intervention, would redistribute income and some goods and services through the tax system and/or social welfare system. No attention is given to the source or cause of the maldistribution in the first place, only to its consequences. Part of a just society is that individual rights are protected in legislation such as Canada's Charter of Rights and Freedoms and provincial human rights statutes, and a major human right is the right to participate/compete in society without being discriminated against on the basis of race, class, gender, and so on. Inequalities of circumstances are acceptable as long as they are based on merit or effort (i.e., competing successfully on a fair playing field) and not on heredity or some other social characteristic. That is, unequal rewards go to those with unequal skills and effort.

Whereas neo-conservatives would defend society and institutions from any attempts by reformers to bring about *social change*, preferring instead slow, evolutionary change, reform liberals would use the instrument of government to modify society in order to make it fairer for individuals to compete in the market. However, only modest alterations to society would be made. In the end, both conservatives and liberals accept current social arrangements and would not attempt to make fundamental social change. In other words, liberals would make changes *within* the system rather than changes *of* the system—it would remain the same system. After any liberal social change we would still have a capitalist society where structured inequality is acceptable (Naiman, 1997). Reform liberals would make changes in order to help society function better, that is, they would fine-tune society but not change its fundamental nature. Liberal social intervention would be designed to help the individual cope with, adjust to, or fit into the existing society. Galper argued in 1975 that liberal social reform is an illusion as the present society is not reformed by liberal social change; rather, it is consolidated and/or reinforced.

The next three sections look at the specific ideological beliefs of reform liberalism along social, economic, and political dimensions. These reform liberal values are

TABLE 4.2   A SUMMARY OF LIBERAL VIEWS

Concept	Views
Human nature	Moral and rational.
	Egoistic and altruistic.
	Competitive and co-operative.
	Motivated by self-development and progress.
	Requires a healthy social environment to flourish.
	A complex organism with interdependent parts.
	Can be modified by government intervention.
	Classes are recognized, but can be transcended by effort.
Nation-state	Promotes fair competition among members via state intervention.
	Protects and enhances our natural rights.
	Acts in best interests of all society.
	Reduces the worst excesses of capitalism by (limited) regulation of the economy and by developing a welfare state.
	Promotes consensus and harmony among interdependent parts of society.
Social justice	(Re)distributive model of social justice.
	Individual rights are protected by legislation.
	A modern welfare state compensates victims of capitalism.
	Equal opportunity provides everyone the means to succeed.
	Individual success and upward mobility occur on basis of individual effort and merit.
Social change	Social reform is valued as long as it improves society for individuals, but does not fundamentally change its nature; i.e., social change must be ameliorative, not transformative.
	Social reform is needed to attend to the socially defined needs of the population—public health care, pensions, unemployment assistance, student aid, etc.

tempered today by classical liberal economic principles. In other words, the drive for social reform and a well-developed welfare state is not as great today as during the three decades following World War II. With its emphasis on individualism (albeit in a modified form from that of conservatism), on inequality of circumstances, and on maintaining an economic system that victimizes some groups of people, there is an obvious disjuncture between liberalism and progressive social work, as outlined in Chapter 2.

SOCIAL BELIEFS

The central social values of liberalism are essentially the same as those of neo-conservatism, but they differ in degree. Both groups believe in freedom and individualism and both are non-egalitarian. As mentioned above, however, liberals modify or qualify these values somewhat by pragmatic and humanistic concerns. For example, while neo-conservatives and liberals regard freedom as an essential value, neo-conservatives view freedom simply as freedom from the arbitrary power of governments, whereas liberals include in their value the freedom from such social evils as unemployment, disease, and squalor. To protect this latter freedom would obviously necessitate some form of state intervention that would be unacceptable to neo-conservatives.

Individualism is a key value of liberals. All government action should have as its goal the maximization of an individual's pursuit of self-interest. The purpose of government intervention is to maximize individual welfare. It attempts to remove obstacles to self-sufficiency. Whereas neo-conservatives measure the total well-being of society by simply summing up the well-being of all individuals in that society, reform liberalism also has a collective interest. There is recognition that a healthy social environment is related to individual well-being. Classical liberals do not speak of classes because society is viewed as a collection of individuals rather than as a class or stratified society. This view helps to absolve people from responsibility for the well-being of others in society. There is no obligation or responsibility for others. Anything done for others is carried out either on pragmatic grounds (i.e., it is more efficient or it will dispel social unrest) or on humanitarian grounds, which often leaves deprived or disadvantaged persons to the vagaries of charitable and paternalistic whims of others. People as social beings may be recognized as such, but because of the equal opportunity thesis they are left to their to their own devices

Those liberals who do recognize that classes exist and that some classes fare much better than others in a capitalist society would contend that social and economic mobility is possible because of equal opportunity. In other words, some people in society may be suffering, but if they work hard and take advantage of the opportunities available to them they can get out of their present situation and move to a higher class ('socio-economic position' in liberal terms). Liberals accept inequality of circumstances because of their profound belief in equal opportunity, which means that we are all equal before the law. No one has any more freedoms or liberties than anyone else. Everyone has access to education, the job market, health care, social services, and so on. If a person fails in society it is because he or she did not take advantage of available opportunities. Liberals do not consider the possibility that some people in society, because of their social position and resources, may be in a better position to exploit these so-called available opportunities than others. To use an analogy, if one person has a 50-metre headstart in a 100-metre race, it is not likely that the other person will ever catch up. A small number of individuals, because of their great wealth, control the race and set it up in such a way to prevent most people from winning. Furthermore, the children of the wealthiest people start the race so close to the finish line that they can be the slowest runners and still win (Naiman, 1997). The Achilles heel of the equal opportunity concept is that not everyone starts out at the same place in life. Therefore, some people have an unfair advantage and preferred access to these 'equal' opportunities. Karger (1987: 8) states, 'The fallacy of the entire argument is that true equality of opportunity is unattainable in an unequal society.'

Although liberals are not egalitarians, they do think that inequalities should and could be reduced based on humanistic and/or pragmatic grounds. Humanistically, liberals are aware of the ugliness of poverty and would seek to eliminate it, which is a different concern from the search for equality. Pragmatically, a wider distribution of income will: (a) increase aggregate demand, thus lessening unemployment, and (b) reduce social tension. From this point of view, however, egalitarianism destroys incentives, weakens social cohesion, and threatens the freedom of the individual (George and Wilding, 1985).

ECONOMIC BELIEFS

The fundamental economic value of liberalism is competitive capitalism based on free enterprise, but with some government regulation. This type of economic system is often called a mixed economy as opposed to the neo-conservative's laissez-faire economy. Although both neo-conservatives and liberals subscribe to a capitalist economy, liberals do not share the neo-conservative belief that an unregulated free enterprise system works well.

Liberals have four major criticisms of capitalism (George and Wilding, 1985). (1) Capitalism is not self-regulating. Without state intervention it cannot solve the economic problems it has created for itself, such as cyclical recession, structural unemployment and underemployment, inflation, large discrepancies in wealth and income, and regional disparity. (2) Capitalism is wasteful and inefficient, and misallocates resources. With each recession the productive capacity of nations is wasted as factories and people lie idle. If left by itself capitalism will result in private affluence and public squalor, which are morally unacceptable to humanistic liberals and politically dangerous, as public squalor can lead to crime, violence, and social unrest. (3) Capitalism will not by itself eliminate poverty and injustice. By its very nature (material acquisition, competition, survival of the fittest), capitalism produces and perpetuates poverty and inequality. (4) Capitalism leads to the interests of the economically dominant groups being identified as the national interest. These groups have, for example, convinced government and the people that industrial development, which is of interest to the capitalists, is really in the national interest. Consequently, giant corporations have little difficulty getting government to spend money on roads, technological development, research, and so on, while the care of the old, the ill, the poor, and others is neglected because no economically powerful group has spoken in their interests.

In spite of these significant criticisms of capitalism, liberals do not believe that it should be abolished. Rather, they believe it should be regulated because the faults of capitalism, in their view, are technical in nature rather than fundamental and can be made good by government action. However, liberals would still place limitations on this government action because they believe that: (1) once the technical problems of capitalism are solved the system will regulate itself; (2) capitalism is naturally superior as a source of initiative and liberty; and (3) government action, while necessary for freedom, is always a potential threat to freedom (George and Wilding, 1985).

Because liberals do not seek to change the given economic system, most of their interventions into the economy will be symptom-focused and ameliorative rather than structural. Fiscal and monetary actions will be designed to compensate for such instabilities inherent in capitalism as recessions, unemployment, and inflation, and will not be designed to overcome the systemic roots of these problems (Gil, 1976). In other words, government intervention into the economy is intended to fine-tune it rather than to change its basic nature.

POLITICAL BELIEFS

The fundamental political beliefs of liberalism lie in representative democracy (Marchak, 1981) and pluralism (Sills, 1968). Liberals argue that direct participation in the day-to-day business of government by the electorate is impossible. Rather, the essence of modern-day democracy rests in the popular control of elected representatives. Control is exercised through the competition of people running for office, selection by the people of representatives in periodic elections, limitations on the power elected representatives can exercise while in office, and removal of the incumbent representatives if they fail to perform to the people's satisfaction. In sum, the ultimate control within a representative democracy rests with the people who elect and hold accountable a representative government.

Representative democracy is based on the principles of free and regular elections, a broad suffrage, and the existence of a party capable of forming an alternative government (Lees, 1972). A fuller discussion and analysis of representative democracy was presented in Chapter 2, where it was contrasted with the concept of participatory democracy. In addition, it was argued that social work ideology is more consistent with participatory democracy as a model than with the liberal choice of representative democracy.

According to the liberals universal suffrage has led to a transformation of political systems in Western democracies from institutionalized ruling-class governments of the eighteenth and nineteenth centuries to open and democratic structures, where the ordinary citizen now has direct and immediate access to his or her elected representative. However, 'modern society has become considerably more complex during the twentieth century and "political power" has become more "diffused" and more "corporate"' (Pritchard and Taylor, 1978: 93). In other words, governments are more involved in a whole range of issues and areas, and a host of competing interests and pressure groups have emerged with the aim to influence the decisions of elected representatives.

The above brings us to the second fundamental political belief of liberals—that in a representative (liberal) democracy political power is divided among competing interest groups so that no one group dominates another, let alone dominates the government.

This view of political power is called pluralism. The government acts as an independent arbitrator (umpire) of these competing interest groups, controlling their activities by a set of rules called the law through which it acts as the guardian of the public interest and of individual rights. Thus, it is claimed, no government can fail to respond to the wishes of its citizens because the individual is heard through his or her membership in particular interest groups and at election time.

Few serious commentators believe that liberal democracies are totally accessible. Some of the limitations of the pluralist view are: (1) as with any type of competition there will be winners and losers, so that the strongest and best-organized interest groups will have their interests prevail over their counterparts; (2) not everyone belongs to an organized interest group; (3) some powerful interest groups may gain sectional advantage at the expense of the general welfare; and (4) the elites within the various interest groups may make decisions that are not responsive to the needs or wishes of the memberships.

VIEW OF SOCIAL PROBLEMS

Unlike neo-conservatives, liberals do not place the blame for social problems squarely on the shoulders of the individual or his/her family. 'They accept the failure of the market to meet basic needs, the inability of the contemporary family to meet needs it supposedly met in the past and that economic growth will not, on its own, abolish poverty' (George and Wilding, 1976: 62–3). The imperfections of capitalism cause problems for some people, and this perception is different from the neo-conservative belief that it is the individual who causes problems for him or herself. In other words, whereas neo-conservatives attribute social problems to weakness, deviance, or heredity of the individual, liberals attribute such problems to social disorganization inherent in an urbanized and industrialized capitalist society and a globalized economy.

Although liberals focus more on society as the source of social problems, the personal deficiency view is not dropped completely. Society is viewed as a complex whole or organism consisting of individuals interacting within numerous interdependent social systems such as the family, the workplace, and the school. Liberals believe that these systems are based on consensus and have legitimate functions that contribute to the healthy functioning of society because they are expected to integrate individuals into the larger society (Carniol, 1984). They recognize, however, that the numerous interdependent social systems that comprise society are not perfect and may not adequately provide the resources needed for healthy functioning. The various systems may get out of tune with one another in a society that experiences urbanization, industrialization, technological change, migration, globalization, and so on. These movements or forces upset the equilibrium among systems and between people and social systems, thus precipitating social disorganization. In turn, this social disorganization produces stress and personal disorganization: mental illness, alcoholism, family breakdown, crime, spousal and child abuse, even community disintegration (Rubington and Weinberg, 1995). Because social problems are caused by some systems out of tune with one another, the solution to the problem is to fine-tune these systems and restore equilibrium. This may involve personal change and/or system change, but in all cases 'such changes are accommodative to the status quo' (Carniol, 1984: 188).

From the disciplinary vantage point of social work, the social disorganization view of social problems is an improvement over the personal deficiency view held by neo-conservatives because it recognizes the role that society plays in creating social problems. The systems perspective of liberalism is found in most major introductory social work texts and in the curriculum of most schools of social work. An outgrowth of this perspective is the ecological view of social problems, which assumes an 'optimal goodness of fit' between the individual and society (Germain, 1979). Thus, if personal disorganization occurs the social worker would try to change either the individual or a particular subsystem or both. This approach has contributed to a plethora of generalist and/or eclectic social work approaches. However, because liberals believe that our present liberal democratic social order, although flawed, is superior to all others, then any social change proposed by the liberal worker will be limited to fine-tuning the system rather than overhauling it. Any change will occur within the system and will not involve a fundamental change of the system. That is, after the change, liberal capitalism will still be intact.

In short, liberals believe that social problems occur mainly because of instrumental or technical flaws in the capitalist system that cause personal disorganization for some people. They also believe that the capitalist system is the most efficient form of economic organization and must be preserved. Therefore, the response to social problems is not to alter the system dramatically but to: (1) purge it of as many inefficiencies as possible by way of minor social reform (i.e., system-tinkering); and (2) purge it of injustices by tending to those persons who are hurt by the system.

This view of social problems is much more humane and benign than that held by neo-conservatives. Liberals believe that even when people conform to their roles in society and attempt to carry out their social responsibilities, they will sometimes experience problems because of events (technological change, cultural changes, etc.) beyond their control. Thus, weaker members of society may succumb to the stresses they experience and will require care, cure, and protection. This approach to social problems has been termed 'humanist liberal' (Lee, 1986) and 'liberal humanist' (Coates, 1991). In spite of this humanistic aspect, liberals share two views with neo-conservatives with respect to social problems. First, liberals see individuals rather than social classes or social groupings as casualties of capitalism. Individuals remain the central unit of analysis rather than sexism, racism, and so on. Second, neither liberals nor neo-conservatives give serious consideration to the possibility that the unequal distribution of resources in society may have a connection to social problems (George and Wilding, 1985).

VIEW OF SOCIAL WELFARE

Liberals accept the social welfare state as an instrument for correcting and modifying the negative aspects of capitalism. They do not see the welfare state as a means for pursuing social equality or for promoting social or economic change (George and Wilding, 1985). Its role is to be reactive (i.e., to deal with existing social problems) rather than to be proactive (i.e., to use the welfare state to achieve greater equality or to extend democracy into areas outside of the political sphere).

A primary goal of a liberal social welfare state is to achieve for all citizens the 'social minimum'. This concept has been described by Leonard Marsh (1950: 35), architect of Canada's social security system, as 'the realization that in a civilized society, there is a certain minimum of conditions without which health, decency, happiness and a "chance in life" are impossible.'[3] In other words, society should use the welfare state to guarantee a minimum income to purchase the basic necessities of life and to ensure that everyone has access to basic (minimum) levels or standards of health care, housing, and education. However, liberals do not believe that governments are responsible for providing more than a minimum. A social welfare system that has as its primary goal a social minimum was described in Chapter 2. It was argued that such a welfare system, termed the 'social security state' or 'institutional model', although containing some humanistic elements, must be rejected by progressive social workers because of its lack of egalitarian ideals. It does not seek to reduce inequalities above the social minimum, nor does it promote solidarity or attempt to extend social, economic, or political democracy.

The 'institutional conception' of welfare is based on the assumption that industrialization and urbanization are natural processes of human progress (Wilensky and Lebeaux, 1965), and while they have brought higher standards of living to many people they have also brought disruption to some people who have had to bear most of the social costs of industrial progress. These people, it is argued by liberals, should be protected and compensated by state welfare programs. Unlike the neo-conservative residual conception of welfare, people in need are not considered to be lax, immoral, or irresponsible but are considered genuinely in need. Therefore, there is a reduced use of the humiliating means test, little suggestion of abnormalcy, and decreased stigma attached to social welfare programs. The institutional conception does not do away with family responsibility, but it recognizes that in a modern, complex, industrial society families may need help in carrying out their obligations. Social welfare programs represent a first line of defence against the exigencies of a capitalist society, not a residual function. That is, the institution of welfare should take its place alongside all other social institutions in society rather than coming into play only after all other social institutions have failed. This view dispenses with moralizing about the shortcomings of people in need. In short, industrialization, urbanization, and the development of the welfare state are viewed as normal, logical, evolutionary, and inevitable processes in human progress. The purpose of the welfare state, according to this view, is not to change society but to make good for its defects.

SOCIAL WORK PRACTICE WITHIN THE LIBERAL PARADIGM

Because we in Canada live in a liberal democratic state most of our social work practice is determined by the values, beliefs, and tenets of liberalism. Galper (1975) argues that the greatest determinant of the kind of practice that social workers will engage in is the social-economic-political culture in which social work operates. In other words, not only is the social welfare system a reflection of the larger society, so, too, is social work practice. Taken together they form a paradigm, and in the case of Canada it is a liberal paradigm.

The above is not to suggest that social work practice in Canada is based purely on liberalism. Social work ideology is another major determinant of the nature of social work practice. For example, social work subscribes to egalitarianism and some of our social work practice in Canada lies outside the liberal paradigm, especially that which seeks to transform our capitalist system. (Certainly, however, this is not yet an integral part of many social workers' practice.) Two other determinants of the nature of social work practice are historical continuity and competing paradigms. Canada was a conservative society before World War II; thus, our social welfare system and our social work practice have retained some features of control and coercion. The paradigms competing with liberalism in Canada are neo-conservatism, which supports the retention of coercive social work practices, and social democracy, which supports transforming Canada from a capitalist to a social democratic state. In spite of these other influences, however, social work practice today in Canada is based primarily on liberal values.

Social workers carry out basically three activities within the liberal paradigm: (1) personal reform based mainly on general systems theory; (2) limited social reform based mainly on the ecological model of practice; and (3) advocacy based on a pluralist view of society. The nature of these activities is determined by the liberal's belief that social problems are caused by social disorganization, an undesirable but unavoidable outcome of capitalism. And because they can do nothing about the occurrence of social disorganization, social workers must focus their attention on its negative consequences.

One way of dealing with the effects of social disorganization is to take those people who have fallen out of the game and direct them back to the starting point. They must be counselled and helped to learn more effective methods and patterns of communication so that they can enter into and maintain healthy relationships in all areas of their life. Or, they must be rehabilitated or resocialized so that their attitudes and behaviour are more congruent with the expectations that society places on them. Or, they must undergo psychotherapy and have their ego defence mechanisms strengthened so that they can better cope with competing and conflicting demands imposed on them. General systems theory is widely used by social workers in this area because of its assumption that the system (society) is basically okay but that some people need help getting back into it or coping with it.

Another possible way of helping those people who are negatively affected by social disorganization is to try and make some changes in the person's immediate environment. Given that the capitalist system has some flaws, it may be possible to make minor reforms without affecting the working of the overall system. This could mean the removal of a family member, for example, in the case of family tension and dysfunction. Or, it might mean a change in a public school's policy or program to better accommodate children from a disadvantaged group. Or, it could mean some labour legislation to make work conditions less stressful. These changes are reactive, as they focus on the effects of social disorganization and not on its causes. Many would argue that the root cause is the capitalist system itself. The ecological approach is often used with this activity as the ecological model assumes that a 'goodness of fit' or natural harmony exists between the person and society. What is not considered is that the system itself could be bad and that we are looking for a goodness of fit between a person and a bad system.

A third area within the liberal paradigm where social workers often find themselves working is that of advocacy. Much time and effort is expended by social workers in attempting to obtain programs, services, compensation, and/or recognition for various individuals and groups in society who are injured by the capitalist system. Promoting the well-being of the homeless by advocating for housing programs and lobbying government for job protection legislation for minorities are examples of advocacy work, which again focuses on the consequences and not the causes of social disorganization. It is based on the pluralist view that society consists of competing interest groups, with some winning and others losing. It is often the job of social workers to help the losers get back into the competition.

These three areas of social work are based on the belief that the liberal-capitalist system is superior although it causes problems for some people. The job of social work is to work with capitalism's casualties for mainly humanitarian reasons. By doing so, social workers working within the liberal paradigm do not connect these people with economic structure, class, race, or gender. To make these connections we must look to paradigms other than neo-conservatism and liberalism.

CANADA AS A LIBERAL STATE

The political science literature reveals that there are three major political ideologies in Canada: conservatism, liberalism, and socialism (Horowitz, 1968, cited in Campbell and Christian, 1999; McCready, 1980). There has been influence from other ideological perspectives, such as populism, progressivism, social credit, and nationalism, but these have not been as influential, as distinct, or as long lasting as the three major political ideologies. And, although Canada has three major political ideologies, they have not been and are not now of equal strength. There is agreement in the literature that the dominant and pervasive political ideology in Canada since World War II has been liberalism (see Campbell and Christian, 1999; Horowitz, 1996; Marchak, 1981). As Bell and Tepperman (1979: 232) emphasize, 'liberalism is not just numerically dominant [in Canada]. It dominates because it is the ideology of the dominant class: it has the full force of the state, church, media, and educational system behind it: it has been trained into all of us.'

For the most part all three major political parties in Canada are steeped in liberal ideology.[4] The federal Liberal Party adheres to the beliefs, principles, and values discussed in this chapter. It has been the dominating and ruling party of the federal government of Canada for most of this century. The Progressive Conservative Party of Canada, although a conservative ideological party at one time, was essentially a liberal party before the amalgamation of the Progressive Conservative Party with the Canadian Alliance to constitute the Conservative Party of Canada (which is currently a blend of conservatism coming from the Canadian Alliance/Reform Party members and liberalism coming from the Progressive Conservatives). Even the national New Democratic Party, which claims to be a social democratic political party, 'has survived as a liberal reform movement, rather than as a fundamentally different ideological position' (Marchack, 1981: 14).

The fact that liberalism has been and is the dominant and pervasive political ideology in Canada is of considerable importance in understanding the development of the Canadian social welfare state. As liberalism replaced conservatism as the dominant ideology of Canada beginning in the 1940s, Canada's social welfare state gradually shifted away from a residual form towards an institutional form of welfare[5] (notwithstanding some of the regressive policies of federal and provincial governments in Canada in the past 25 years). Social policy or social welfare choices are limited or bound by the social, economic, and political beliefs of liberalism. Obviously, those who subscribe to an established dominant ideology will not purposely seek its transformation or undoing. In fact, the elite or dominant class will attempt to protect and strengthen their ideology because, in so doing, they protect and strengthen their own positions in society. Thus, social policy in Canada does not threaten individualism, capitalism, inequality, or any other pre-eminent value of liberalism. In sum, even though there has been a shift to the right on the part of all major political parties, Canada remains a liberal society and its social welfare system not only reflects liberalism and its attendant values, it reinforces them as well.

CRITIQUE OF THE LIBERAL PARADIGM

A few words must be said about the theoretical incapacity of the liberal paradigm to explain certain social, economic, and political phenomena in a liberal society. Marchak (1981) provides an impressive amount of data that reveal some of the realities of Canadian society that liberalism does not explain: there is poverty in the midst of affluence; there is evidence of interference in the political process by privately owned corporations; there is a persistent division of the population along economic lines that liberals refuse to recognize as a class division but that is inexplicable otherwise; and the decisions of large corporations more profoundly affect the lives of people than do the actions of politicians. These empirical facts of a liberal society are not accounted for by liberal ideology.

Liberalism accounts for differences among individuals in terms of quality of life as due to individual differences in talent or effort or due to imperfections in the system. According to liberals, the consequences of the former can be alleviated and of the latter can be corrected or reformed. However, the evidence does not substantiate these beliefs but suggests, rather, that there are consistent and persistent differences among identifiable groups in Canada with respect to wealth, power, and access to goods, services, and social institutions. The evidence also shows that these differences are attributable not to individual characteristics but to social characteristics such as ethnicity, gender, age, place of residence, and family of origin (Curtis et al., 1988; Marchak, 1981). The foremost criticism of liberalism is that it has failed to reform the system to correct the causes of these differences. Writing on the Canadian situation, Marchak (1981: 42–3) articulates this criticism:

> Regional inequalities persist in spite of equalization payments; poverty persists in spite of a welfare system; the taxation system is finally unable to redress the considerable imbalances between the rich and the poor. These are puzzles that the liberal ideology, with its emphasis on individual achievement, equality of opportunity, a market-place for competing talents, and an openness to reform, cannot explain.

Naiman (1997: 193) argues that liberalism is similar to capitalism in that both are 'rife with contradictions'. On the one hand, it draws us towards seemingly admirable social goals such as equal opportunity, democracy, and individual human rights and freedoms, but on the other hand, it does so in a way that masks structural inequality, which 'sets limits on these very aspirations'.

A major criticism of welfare capitalism (i.e., the welfare state in a liberal-capitalist society) is that, although it was set up to modify (i.e., humanize) the negative impact of capitalism on people, it actually reinforces capitalism and thus, indirectly, contributes to many of the problems it seeks to eliminate. The reason for this is hardly surprising. The social welfare state is like any other social institution. It has been established within the social, economic, and political context of liberalism and is bound to reflect and support the context from which it comes and within which it operates. In addition to attending to the immediate needs of some people who are hurt by capitalism, it also carries out socialization, social control, and stabilization functions for the prevailing social order by reinforcing the norms, behaviours, institutions, and values of liberalism.[6]

> Paradoxically, then, implicit in the social services is the affirmation of oppression and exploitation of humans by humans, and the negation of equality of rights, responsibilities, and dignity and of genuine liberty and self-actualization for all. The social services [welfare state] are thus revealed not as part of the solution of issues of provision in our society, but as a factor in the maintenance of the human problems they pretend to treat and prevent. (Gil, 1976: 60)

Table 4.3 compares and contrasts the ideals of social work with those of liberalism. The differences between the two sets of ideals are not as great as those between neo-conservatism and social work. However, the differences and contradictions between liberalism and social work ideals are too great to be reconciled. With respect to social beliefs, although liberalism believes in a certain amount of humanism, it also subscribes to individualism and inequality, which contradict social work's beliefs in community and equality. And although liberalism subscribes to a limited amount of government intervention, it does not believe that society's resources should be distributed equitably among all citizens. Liberalism's belief in representative democracy and pluralism contrasts with

TABLE 4.3   OVERVIEW OF LIBERALISM AND SOCIAL WORK IDEAL

	Liberalism	Social Work
Social Beliefs	Freedom Individualism Inequality (all the above modified by humanitarianism and pragmatism)	Humanitarianism (humanism) Community Equality
Economic Beliefs	Competitive capitalism with some government intervention (i.e., mixed economy)	Government intervention Social priorities dominate economic decisions Equitable distribution of society's resources
Political Beliefs	Representative democracy Pluralism	Participatory democracy in both governmental and non-governmental areas
View of Social Welfare	An instrument to modify negative aspects of capitalism Ideal = institutional model Provides a social minimum	An instrument to promote equality, solidarity, and community Ideal = structural model
Nature of Social Work Practice	Personal reform Limited social reform Advocacy	Treat people with respect Enhance dignity and integrity Facilitate self-determination and self-realization Accept differences Advocate and promote social justice

social work's belief in participatory democracy. As a consequence of the above differences in ideals and values, liberalism holds a different view of the nature and purpose of the welfare state than does social work. Whereas liberalism perceives the social welfare state as a means of providing people with the social minimum, progressive social work believes the purpose of the social welfare state is to go beyond providing a bare minimum by promoting equality of living conditions, solidarity among citizens, and a sense of community.

With respect to social work practice it has been suggested here that: (1) a liberal society actually causes many of the problems that social work seeks to resolve; and (2) social work practice within liberal boundaries actually reinforces and perpetuates many of the inequities social work claims to be against. Thus, it seems that the social work profession should reject the liberal paradigm if it is to remain true to its own values, beliefs, and principles. This does not mean that social work should abandon the three basic social work activities practised within the liberal paradigm—personal reform, social reform, and advocacy. It does mean, however, that the limitations of these activities must be recognized and that another dimension of social work practice must accompany them. This other dimension, referred to in this book as structural (or transformational) practice, is the subject of later chapters.

LIBERAL HEGEMONY IN SOCIAL WORK

One of the characteristics of a dominant paradigm is that it is able to reproduce itself by socializing members of society into accepting the structures and social relationships it espouses. Literature and the media, for example, shape the thoughts and understandings of members of society. This socialization or reproduction is not necessarily a conspiratorial activity on the part of the ruling elite. However, it is only logical to expect that the people who run the media and people who write books and articles will reflect their world views and understandings of subjects in their work. Social workers are no different. Most social work educators and writers in North America have been socialized not only into liberal societies but into a liberal view of social welfare and social work as well. Given this socialization, it is not surprising that most of the social work literature in North America accepts the liberal paradigm. A few Canadian examples are presented below to illustrate this point.

BOX 4.1 AN EXAMPLE OF LIBERAL HEGEMONY IN SOCIAL WORK

One day while working on this chapter I decided to share my critique of systems theory and the ecological approach with my colleagues by way of an e-mail in order to stimulate thinking and discussion about the nature of social work practice. One colleague replied by e-mail, expressing her disagreement that systems/ecological approaches essentially humanized the system rather than changed it fundamentally. A slightly modified version of her argument follows.

Bob—Systems/ecological theory has as one of its tasks to examine ways to effect change *in the system* (emphasis added) so it can better meet the needs of clients. For example, the social worker can do this through advocacy with another agency in regard to how its policies are being interpreted for a client; the clients can also be encouraged or coached to work *to make changes in one of their systems (family, school, friendship network, etc.)* [emphasis added]. In some approaches to family therapy, parents are coached to advocate on behalf of a child with the school system, the justice system, etc.

In my view, my colleague has given the classic description of liberal social work. Although the work she speaks about is important, by itself it does not fundamentally challenge or change the larger social system in any way. The changes that my collegue seeks are all changes *within the system* and not changes *of the system*—a critical distinction. No thought is given to the possibility that the source of problems lies not within the system but is the system itself, because of its various forms and sources of oppression (the subject of Chapter 10). My colleague, in my view, equates any kind of change brought about by a social worker as structural change, when in fact *it is the nature of the change* that differentiates mainstream (liberal) social work from progressive/structural social work. The former attempts to make life a little better for people by tinkering with or fine-tuning or adjusting the system. The latter attempts to make a contribution to fundamental change of the system itself, that is, to make a dent in the situations or processes of social inequality that fall along lines of class, gender, age, race, and so on.

Three widely used introductory textbooks in schools of social work on the Canadian welfare state are Andrew Armitage's *Social Welfare in Canada* (1975, 1988, 1996, 2003), Dennis Guest's *The Emergence of Social Security in Canada* (1980, 1985, 1997), and Frank McGilly's *An Introduction to Canada's Public Social Services* (1990, 1998). Most social work students in the last three decades have been exposed to one or more of these texts during the course of their studies. Two recent Canadian social welfare textbooks, Ernie Lightman's *Social Policy in Canada* (2003) and Steven Hick's *Social Welfare in Canada: Understanding Income Security* (2004), add to the pool of liberal thought applied to Canadian social welfare. What do students learn about society, social welfare, and the relationship between the two by reading these books? In a word, students learn 'liberalism'. To date, there is no progressive or critical Canadian social welfare textbook along the lines of the 1990 American book by George Martin, *Social Policy in the Welfare State*, and the British book by Fiona Williams, *Social Policy: A Critical Introduction—Issues of Race, Gender and Class* (1989). Though not strictly Canadian nor introductory, Peter Leonard's *Postmodern Welfare: Reconstructing an Emancipatory Project* (1997) would fall into the critical (postmodern) school of social welfare thought.

Although societal flaws are pointed out in each book, neither Armitage, nor Guest, nor McGilly calls for a different social order. Carniol (1984) points out that Armitage analyzes industrialization to show how it causes the disorganization that brings about social welfare provisions—a liberal view of social problems and social welfare. In the most recent edition of his book (2003), Armitage states that the philosophical position is that of liberalism. Four of the themes in Guest's historical overview of the development of the Canadian welfare state are liberal notions and/or goals:

1. The shift from a residual model of welfare to an institutional model is seen as laudable.
2. A goal of the Canadian welfare state is described as being to provide a basic minimum to all Canadians.
3. Dependency is redefined as being the result of industrialization and urbanization rather than being the consequence of individual fault.
4. The growth of the welfare state is understood as being instrumental in leading to a growth of citizenship status.

McGilly (1990: 39, 12) writes unabashedly from a liberal perspective: 'the assumptions and predilections underlying this text may be characterized as liberal, pluralist, and interventionist.' His stated definition of social welfare (policy) is 'society's struggle to keep up with the consequences of advancing industrialization'. As Carniol (1984: 192) notes, such logic implies that social welfare services exist only 'because of their humanitarian values, which are consistent with our society's desire to implement minimal standards of social responsibility'.

Although Ernie Lightman (2003) challenges many of the economic assumptions associated with liberalism, he states that it is not about revolution and that he seeks a better deal for people within a market society. Steven Hick (2004) presents an overview of the major ideologies with respect to some social welfare issues, but states that he does not argue a position, leaving it to the reader to decide his or her own course of action. My view is that by not taking a position, the current dominant liberal perspective will remain relatively unchallenged.

There are no Canadian introductory social work textbooks of the same stature as the social welfare texts discussed above. This means that Canadian social work students tend to be exposed to one or more of the standard American introductory social work textbooks that make prominent use of liberal approaches to social work systems theory, ecological models, eclectic methods, and so on. A content analysis of American introductory social work textbooks published between 1985 and 1995 found: minimal coverage of progressive or feminist social work scholarship; some coverage of these two sets of scholarship presented in a way that reduced their political charge and transformative potential; a narrow theoretical base—the main theories presented were general systems theory and the ecological approach; for the most part, only liberal feminism; and no critical analysis of capitalism (Wachholz and Mullaly, 2000). The few Canadian textbooks on social work are similar in orientation (i.e., liberal humanism) to most of the American texts. Shankar Yelaja's *An Introduction to Social Work Practice in Canada* (1985) is framed in the ecological perspective, as is Lawrence Shulman's *The Skills of Helping Individuals and Groups* (1979),[7] where the focus is on mediation (striving for a successful fit) between the individual and society. Steven Hick's *Social Work in Canada: An Introduction* (2002) is the first legitimate Canadian 'introductory' social work textbook of which I am aware. Maybe because of its introductory nature there is a lack of critical analysis on the nature of social work, only description. As in his book on social welfare, Hick does not take a position and does not critically analyze either mainstream or progressive approaches to social work. Thus, the book, by default, reinforces social work as a liberal practice. There is no questioning in any of these books of the fundamental nature of our present liberal-capitalist society or any suggestion that social work should consider a different paradigm.

CONCLUSION

In conclusion, social workers, like all Canadian citizens, are socialized into a liberal paradigm (although the nature of this paradigm has shifted to the right in the past decade or so). Because they work within a liberal social welfare institution their practice will reflect, protect, and promote the liberal view of how society should operate. Rather than challenging inequality or the capitalist system, which is based on inequality, social work in Canada has favoured large-scale government programs to compensate for the chronic and acute ills of an industrial liberal society and to ameliorate the resultant suffering. In identifying with liberalism the social work profession has accepted, almost uncritically, the notion that more and larger social service programs can overcome society's multiple social problems. Viewing social problems as technical matters rather than as political or moral problems, Canadian social workers have become planners, researchers, administrators, and front-line workers of ever-increasing social service bureaucracies. This approach to social problems, where more services and programs are seen as the solution to social problems, contrasts with the neo-conservative belief that fewer services and programs are needed. It also contrasts with the social democratic and Marxist belief that the issue is not one of more or fewer social services but one of a different social order.

CRITICAL QUESTIONS

1. What is the difference between 'Liberal' and 'liberal'?
2. In order to promote a certain concept of equality, Western democracies have developed a number of codes or categories of rights such as civil rights, political rights, human rights, social rights, the Canadian Charter of Rights and Freedoms, and so on. What makes these different sets of rights a liberal idea? From a social justice and/or progressive social work point of view, what is their major limitation?

3. The federal Liberal Party in Canada has been referred to as 'the governing party' because it has been in power for most of the time since World War II. Many political commentators attribute this electoral success to the location that the Liberals occupy on the political spectrum—that is, in the centre. Why would this location help the Liberal Party win elections?

4. Should men and women always and in all ways be treated equally?

5. List the major textbooks used in your social work courses. Can you identify a dominant ideological perspective of each book? How many books tend to be liberal; how many are progressive? If a book does not state or infer a political position, do you think it supports a status quo or a social change position?

The Social
Democratic Paradigm

Let us always remember the founding principle of our [social democratic] party,
which is how we look after each other, not how we look after ourselves. This is the
principle of how I have tried to live my life personally and politically.

—*Tommy Douglas (1904–86) in one of his last speeches,*
at an NDP function in 1983

INTRODUCTION

Because social democracy and the next paradigm to be examined, Marxism, are associated with socialist ideology, a section on socialism precedes the discussion of social
democracy. The major reason for including an overview of socialism is to dispel the
following myths sometimes associated with socialism—that it represents a single unified
social doctrine; that it is anti-democratic and totalitarian; and that the recent events in
Eastern Europe prove that socialism is unworkable and all but dead. Like the previous
two chapters, a summary is presented of what social democrats believe about human
nature, the nature of society, the role of the state, the meaning of social justice, and social
change. As well, social democratic ideology is examined along the lines of its social,
economic, and political beliefs and how these beliefs affect their particular views on the
causes and remedies of social problems, the nature and role of the welfare state, and the
nature of social work practice that is in accordance with the social democratic paradigm.
A comparison is made between social democratic ideals and those of progressive social
work, and finally, a critique of social democracy is presented.

SOCIALISM

Socialism to North Americans is probably the least understood and most misunderstood
of all schools of political thought. The terms associated with the range of political and
theoretical positions within socialism, such as anarchism, communism, Marxism, social
democracy, and syndicalism, cause confusion. As well, through our North American
liberal/conservative socialization, socialism has been presented to us by the media,
by our educational system, by our politicians, and by our other social institutions as

totalitarian and atheistic. This is especially so in the United States, where a psychology of Cold War paranoia existed for so many years. The United States is probably the only Western democracy without a socialist political party at the national level. Canada does have a national socialist party, the New Democratic Party, but it has never placed higher than third in any national election. There have, however, been socialist governments in some of the provinces.[1]

In spite of the vagueness and the negative picture painted of it in North America, socialism has strong appeal to many people all over the world, with national socialist governments having been democratically elected in all continents except North America. Even in North America, socialist values such as community and social justice have been popular with many groups, including progressive social workers. As a political theory socialism is a relative newcomer, but it has emerged in the twentieth century as a set of ambitious philosophical and political doctrines with a vision of human nature that connects the two (Scruton, 1982). One noted writer (Nove, 1989: 170) has defined socialism as:

> an alternative to a society still based largely on private ownership and private profit. Generations of reformers and revolutionaries envisaged a world in which there would be no great inequalities of income and wealth, where common ownership would prevail, where economic (and political) power would be more evenly distributed, where ordinary people would have greater control over their lives and over the conditions of their work, in which deliberate planning for the common good of society would replace (at least in part) the elemental forces of the marketplace.

There are certain characteristics that all schools of socialist thought accept, although in varying degrees. Four of particular importance are: (1) a planned economy geared towards the fulfillment of human need of all rather than a free market geared to profits for a few; (2) public ownership of productive property for the benefit of all rather than private ownership for the benefit of a restricted circle of private owners; (3) equality of condition, or at least the serious effort to reduce, as much as possible, major inequalities of wealth, income, social status, and political influence; and (4) a belief that selfishness is the result of living in our present flawed social institutions and that social change can produce less selfish people who are concerned with the welfare of others (Dickerson and Flanagan, 1986). These four characteristics or objectives will result from and, at the same time, support each other. Flowing from these four characteristics are certain socialist policy objectives, such as an elimination of privilege in all its forms, an opposition to inheritance, a defence of the welfare state, and a strong affiliation with the labour movement (Scruton, 1982).

While these characteristics represent the major areas of consensus among all schools of socialism, there is a fundamental source of disagreement among socialists: how to obtain and maintain the political power necessary to realize their common objectives. Disagreement among socialists tends to occur mainly over the means to achieve certain ends and not on the ends or goals themselves. A few historical events of modern socialism are highlighted below to distinguish for the reader some of the differences among the major socialist camps.[2]

Although socialism has a long history dating back to an early association with Christianity, it was given its classic formulation by Karl Marx and Friedrich Engels in their *Communist Manifesto* (1848). They departed from their Utopian socialist predecessors by rejecting the belief that social change for the betterment of humanity could occur by appealing to reason. Marx and Engels believed that socialism could only come about by the political victory of the working class (i.e., the proletariat). Marx's attitude towards capitalism was one of total rejection rather than reform and he devoted most of his intellectual efforts to proving how it was both inhuman and unworkable.

Marx believed that the contradictions of capitalism—its association with imperialism and wars, overproduction, cyclical and deepening recessions, worsening conditions of workers—and the alienation of the working class would eventually become so intolerable that the working class, led by socialist intellectuals such as Marx himself, would eventually take over the state and use it to abolish capitalism. A system of social and economic collectivism termed communism would then be instituted by the proletariat. This system would involve communal ownership of all property and a classless social structure, and work would be directed by and performed willingly in the interests of the community as a whole—'from each according to his/her ability, to each according to his/her needs' (Roberts, 1971: 38). At this advanced stage of development, the state would wither away as 'people would learn to conduct their affairs without a centralized apparatus of coercion' (Dickerson and Flanagan, 1986: 116). According to Marx, all forms of domination and hierarchy would disappear.

Marx did not believe that the transformation from capitalism to socialism could be automatic; rather, it would require a deliberate political struggle on the part of the proletariat. Marx's view of the nature of this political struggle has been a source of major disagreement among Marxist scholars. One group makes the case that, based on the number of times Marx (and Engels) advocated forcible measures (i.e., violent revolution) as the means for workers to assume political power and based on the number of times that Marx denounced reform as the means to transcend capitalism, there can be little doubt that his real convictions lay in revolutionary socialism (Becker and Barnes, 1978). Other Marxist scholars point out the occasions when Marx and Engels suggest or admit that a peaceful overturn of the social order might be possible and conclude that Marx actually had a dual approach to the gaining of power: (1) *revolutionary socialism* (use of forcible measures) in those countries where constitutionalism and rule of law did not exist; and (2) *evolutionary socialism* (election of an organized workers' political party) in constitutional countries with a parliamentary system (Dickerson and Flanagan, 1986). The revolutionary socialist writers explain Marx's comments on peaceful means as tactical concessions he made to the reformist wing of the socialist party so that it would not split from the major party.

Whether or not Marx's revolutionary theory excluded peaceful means, his emphasis on forcible revolution caused a group of English socialists to repudiate revolutionary socialism and to advocate evolutionary socialism instead. This group formed the Fabian Society in England (1884), which developed social democracy in Britain and eventually created the country's official social democratic political party—the Labour Party (1906). The Fabian Society represents one of the earliest divisions among socialists and was based on disagreement, not with the goals of socialism, but with the means of achieving them. Evolutionary socialism in the form of social democracy spread to Germany in the latter part of the nineteenth century and soon after became the dominant form of socialism in Europe. Only in Russia did the revolutionary socialists remain in the majority (Becker and Barnes, 1978).

Social democratic parties have been elected in most Western European countries and have actually governed for most of the post-war era in the Scandinavian countries. In 1999, nine of the 11 European Union governments were dominated by social democratic parties and they have not hesitated to use their new-found powers to assert changes in the political order that the neo-conservative regimes of the early 1990s had attempted to establish (Rundle, 1999). Socialism, in the form of social democracy, is a familiar part of contemporary politics, but it has been considerably diluted from its original Marxian version. The modern-day social democratic paradigm is presented in the next section of this chapter.

Although social democracy has become the major school of socialist thought in Western Europe, revolutionary socialism held sway in Russia. The absence of a parliament and a constitution in Russia during the early years of the twentieth century made evolutionary socialism irrelevant in that country. There were no democratic institutions or legal working-class organizations that could be used as the base of operations to transform Russian society from within. In February 1917 Czar Nicholas II was dethroned and a constitutional democracy established, and in October of the same year Vladimir Lenin led the Bolshevik Revolution and seized control of the state. Lenin deviated from Marx's theory of revolutionary socialism, because the conditions in Russia were so different from those of Western Europe. Faced with an economically and industrially backward country with a small working class and with a large peasant class, Lenin believed the socialist party had to be controlled from the top and that revolutionary consciousness had to be transmitted by intellectuals to the working class (Dickerson and Flanagan, 1986). This, of course, was inconsistent with Marx's belief that the revolution was to grow from the spontaneous class consciousness of the proletariat or working class.

To solidify his control over the country and the socialist party Lenin centralized political power, calling it 'democratic centralism'. Lenin rationalized this action as being consistent with Marx's revolutionary theory. Marx believed that there had to be a transition period between the end of capitalism and the beginning of advanced communism. Marx did not believe that people could throw off the yoke of capitalism one day and live as adjusted, productive communists the next day. A period of adjustment and transition was needed for the technological and social foundations to be put in place that would be necessary for the achievement of an advanced communist state. The old state machinery must be destroyed and a new state constructed to serve as the means to attain the final communist commonwealth where there is neither oppressor nor oppressed (Becker and Barnes, 1978). Marx's strategy for this transition period was for a government comprising workers to be set up that would actually function as a 'dictatorship of the proletariat'. This government/dictatorship would ignore the rules of law until the revolutionary fervour and violence subsided, and would gradually phase itself out as the transition to communism was made (i.e., the state would wither away).[3] Marx called this transition period socialism. During this transitional stage between capitalism and advanced communism the means of production would be taken into public ownership and the provisional government would oversee a new order of legality and a new system of rights that would allow the emergence of true common ownership and the eventual abolition of the state (Scruton, 1982).

Lenin exercised Marx's notion of dictatorship of the proletariat and outlawed all political opposition, even socialist opposition. His extensive use of dictatorship and his constant postponement of the withering away of the state appalled socialists of Western Europe. As a result, the world socialist movement split irreparably. Those who approved of Lenin and his methods organized themselves in communist parties in every country and adopted Marxism modified by Leninism as the official party ideology. Those who opposed Lenin regrouped under the social democratic banner and became the most prominent school of socialism in the Western world. Russian communism, with an extended dictatorship of the proletariat, was implemented by Lenin, developed by Stalin, and imposed by force on the less advanced nations of Eastern Europe using a distorted version of Marx's theory of revolutionary socialism as a rationale. Fourteen semi-autonomous regions and countries in Eastern Europe and Western Asia were eventually annexed by Russia under the title of the Union of Soviet Socialist Republics.

Communist parties still exist in most Western European countries. The label applied to them today is 'Eurocommunism' and they differ from Russian communism in the very important area of political freedom. Although Soviet leaders did bring many reforms to the economic system in line with Marxist egalitarian ideology, they did not do the same in the political arena. Public ownership replaced private ownership and inequalities in wealth, income, and life chances were greatly reduced in the Soviet Union. However, the egalitarian and democratic elements of Marxism did not spread to the political life of the Soviet Union. Its political system may be described as totalitarian and monistic. No political parties except for the Communist Party were legally allowed, no other ideologies were permitted expression, and civil and political rights were denied. In effect, the Soviet Union had a socialist economy and a totalitarian political system, so that any social security experienced by citizens was overshadowed by the existence of political insecurity (Mishra, 1981). This totalitarian nature of Soviet society violated Marxist socialism, and Eurocommunist parties took exception to it. Eurocommunism, unlike Soviet communism, subscribes to a pluralistic and parliamentary democracy where more than one ideology and one political party are allowed.

The fall of the Russian-led Soviet empire is now history. However, as this brief description of socialism suggests, the fall of Russian communism does not represent the fall of socialism or of its ideas. Russian communism represented one school of socialist thought, albeit a prominent school. Many would argue that it represented a distorted view of socialism because all that was achieved politically was the transfer of control from an old ruling class of aristocrats to a new elite of bureaucrats. Socialism originated as a doctrine concerned about the oppression of the working class. It would be difficult to find a true socialist today who would argue that the Russian experience contributed to the political emancipation of the proletariat in the former Soviet Union. However, the Communist (or socialist) governments did reduce inequalities in Russia and guaranteed the general population a modicum of universal health care, pensions, jobs, and education. Socialist ideology did influence all spheres of life except for the political life of the Russian population.

In sum, socialism does not represent a single unified ideology and it is not anti-democratic. Although the goals of socialism are essentially common to all schools, the major area of disagreement is the appropriate means to transcend capitalism. The fall of the Soviet bloc does not represent a failure of socialism (Mishra, 1999). Its economic failures are due more to its centralized 'command-administrative' socialism, which failed to generate stable growth and development, stifled workers' initiative, lagged behind in technological innovation, and misdirected new investment (van Houton, 1992). Its political failures were due more to its totalitarian practices. With the Soviet type of socialism gone, most socialists today hope that socialism will be able to learn from the mistakes of the Soviet experience, to reaffirm its claim to democracy, and to re-establish itself as the logical 'political expression for collectivist and egalitarian impulses' (Jacques, 1990: 16).

Although there are several schools of socialist thought, the two major schools appear to be social democracy and Marxism (Mishra, 1999). Many social welfare and social work writers divide socialists ideologically into these two groups: (1) social democrats, who believe that social transformation of capitalism can occur by using the working-class institutions within capitalism such as the welfare state, trade unions, and the election of social democratic political parties; and (2) Marxists, who believe that social transformation can occur only by using alternative organizations to state bureaucracies (George and Wilding, 1985; Mullaly and Keating, 1991; Pritchard and Taylor, 1978). This division of socialists is adopted in this book.

SOCIAL DEMOCRACY

Just as socialism consists of a range of theoretical and political divisions, social democracy occupies a wide area on the political spectrum, bordering on liberalism at one end and Marxism at the other end. The divisions between social democracy and these other ideologies are not always clear (George and Wilding, 1994). For many people, social democracy is only a well-developed form of liberalism and they question whether or not social democracy is even a form of socialism. For others, social democracy is only a few steps away from Marxism. This chapter and the next will clarify these issues by presenting the similarities and the differences between social democracy and liberalism, and between social democracy and Marxism.

Most Canadian, Australian, and British social policy writers, when writing about social democracy, use British Fabian social democracy as their reference point. This may be reasonable in terms of gaining an understanding of British social democratic values, beliefs, and principles. The danger, however, is that the British experience with a social democratic government may become the expectation for social democratic governments in all countries. Because the Labour government (Britain's social democratic party) did not fulfill the expectations that many socialists anticipated, the Marxists (and many social democrats) now believe that capitalism cannot be transformed into socialism with a social democratic government. However, if one looks beyond Britain to Sweden, which has had a social democratic government for almost all the years since 1932, one might draw a different conclusion. This issue will be taken up later in this chapter.

It should be noted here that although there is not a 'neo-social democracy' as such, there is another variant of social democracy that emerged in the 1990s, which is commonly known as 'the Third Way'. Anthony Giddens is the intellectual architect of the Third Way, and Tony Blair, the Labour Prime Minister of England, is the social democratic political leader who has developed and implemented Third Way policies more than any other national leader. Third Way thinking and policies have impacted on social democratic parties in Canada and Australia and also influenced Bill Clinton's social policies when he was the President of the United States. Basically, Third Way supporters claim that it is a new left-of-centre political ideology that incorporates the best aspects of social democracy and neo-conservatism or neo-liberalism. The Third Way is discussed more fully in Chapter 8.

The following section provides an overview of social democratic views on the nature of human beings, society, the state, social justice, and social change. Since social democracy and Marxism are both socialist paradigms, there is an overlap between them with respect to their views, beliefs, and fundamental values. This will become more evident in the next chapter.

VIEWS OF THE NATURE OF HUMANS, SOCIETY, THE STATE, SOCIAL JUSTICE, AND SOCIAL CHANGE

What is our basic *human nature*? Are we independent individuals or social animals? Contrary to the neo-conservative belief that humans are by nature independent individuals for whom group membership is voluntary or to the liberal belief that humans are by nature independent individuals who require a healthy community to develop their individuality, social democrats (and all socialists) believe that humans are by nature social animals. The former position was championed by those early writers who were instrumental in formulating both conservativism and classical liberalism as ideologies, such as Thomas Hobbes, John Locke (1632–1704), and Edmund Burke. The latter position (called communitarianism) can be traced to Aristotle (384–322 BC), Jean-Jacques Rousseau (1712–78), and Karl Marx (1818–83) among others. Aristotle argued that only a beast or a god (the subhuman or the superhuman) could live without being a member of a community, for it is only in commune with our fellow citizens that we attain our full human potential (Sigurdson, 2002). In short, 'all humans need other humans to achieve their humanity' (Berry, 1986: 6). Socialists believe that human nature is good and inherently perfectible, and that humans may realize their inherent potential if the right environment is created by using their capacities for responsible and rational action (Sigurdson, 2002). A question that arises here is that if humans are essentially good, then why is it so difficult for us to get along? Whereas neo-conservatives adhere to Hobbes's argument that it is because we are by nature selfish and avaricious, socialists would subscribe to Rousseau's argument that it is because humans have introduced private property into their lives, which has led to inequality, selfishness, and the concentration of power in the hands of a few. In other words, Rousseau's thesis is that humans are basically good, but have been corrupted by the socio-economic-political environment, which today is characterized by capitalism, patriarchy, racism, ageism, and so on. Socialists believe that this goodness can be recaptured if social conditions are put right by humans using their inherent human capacity for co-operation and consensus (Sigurdson, 2002). However, as indicated above and as will be discussed below, socialists disagree on the means (evolution vs revolution) of putting social conditions right.

Socialists, including social democrats, subscribe to Marx's argument that the *nature of society* or community is not some optional extra; rather, it is definitive, and outside this arena the individual is an unreal abstraction. The collective good is considered primary because it determines, in large part, the well-being of individuals. Society is not owned or controlled by a powerful few because such a system would violate the collective human nature of people. Given this collective nature, all persons would participate in its governance. Like Aristotle, socialists believe that because humans are by nature social beings then society is natural. Without society individuals would not be what they are, because any individual talent or ability still requires the co-operation of others for it to be effectively exercised (Berry, 1986). As well, we can only develop a sense of self or identity by associating or interacting with others because our sense of self is largely determined by feedback from others and comparisons to others.

Unlike neo-conservatives and liberals, social democrats believe that the *role of the state* is to promote the collective good and play a positive role in the economy. Social Democrats believe that the state should carry out public control (not necessarily public ownership) of the major means of production to meet social needs rather individual profit, regulate the market and bring about greater equality in the distribution of society's resources, increase democracy in both the political and economic spheres, and protect the environment through centralized planning. Underpinning this role of the state is an emphasis on co-operation and a corresponding de-emphasis on competition. Social democrats do not see this role of the state being carried out satisfactorily in a capitalist society, but believe that by electing social democratic governments and building the welfare state that the preconditions for a socialist society can be put in place as part of the transformation from capitalism to socialism.

Michael Meacher (1977: 36, cited in Berry, 1986: 8) articulates the *nature of a just society* from a socialist or communitarian perspective as one where the members of that society govern their interrelationships by the ideals of 'sharing, co-operation, altruism' and where the values are 'more equal sharing of the material benefits of society, greater sharing in the key decisions rather than subjection to artificial hierarchies of command, and greater sharing of opportunities to develop one's full potentials'. Such a society, Meacher claims, 'abhors class domination and individualist aggrandizement at the expense of others.' Sigurdson (2002: 102) states that 'while liberals are content with an equality of opportunity, socialist justice requires an actual equality of condition', although he points out that for social democrats this 'is more of an ideal than a practical goal.' Although class inequality is a major source of injustice, social democrats recognize and seek to eliminate other sources of injustice and oppression, such as patriarchy, racism, sexism, ageism, ableism, and xenophobia.

Although socialists agree that capitalism must be transformed to a socialist society, they disagree on the *nature of social change* to carry out this transformation. Whereas communists, some Marxists, and other radical socialist camps believe in the necessity for total, revolutionary change, sometimes through violent means, social democrats insist on working within the parliamentary system and achieving socialism through democratic and evolutionary change. Social democrats would promote a variety of redistributive measures such as graduated or progressive tax systems, full employment policies, and well-developed social welfare programs. Social democrats would progressively develop the welfare state and use it as a stepping stone towards a socialist society. Social democratic social change would gradually transform existing social institutions and practices from those that serve individual interests to those that serve collective needs and ends.

As with the chapters on neo-conservatism and liberalism, the next three sections here look at the specific ideological beliefs of social democracy along social, economic, and political lines. Unlike neo-conservatism and liberalism, both of which accept competitive capitalism and its associated inequality, social democracy, like Marxism, seeks to transform the current set of unequal social relations to a socialist society. This is not to say that social democrats or Marxists believe that socialism represents a Utopian society where everyone is happy and makes the same wages and where there are no social problems or bad behaviours. In fact, as mentioned above, there will be considerable variability among socialist societies depending on the unique set of cultural and historical characteristics of each (Naiman, 1997). Just as each capitalist society is unique, so each socialist society will be unique. However, all social democratic societies will have, to some degree, the views outlined in the section above and the beliefs outlined below.

SOCIAL BELIEFS

Social democrats stress three central values—equality, freedom, and fellowship—and two derivative values—democratic participation (the derivative of equality and freedom) and humanitarianism (the derivative of equality and fellowship) (George and Wilding, 1985).

Arguably, the primary social democratic value is equality, which rests on four inter-related grounds—social integration, economic efficiency, natural rights, and individual

TABLE 5.1   SUMMARY OF SOCIAL DEMOCRATIC VIEWS

Concept	Views
Human nature	Humans are social animals. Rational, free-willed, and responsible. Co-operative and consensual. Inherently good. Humans will tend to actualize potentials in a supportive environment.
(Socialist) Society	Communal in nature. Characterized by equality, solidarity, and co-operation. Competitive capitalism and inequality are antithetical to a healthy society. The common or collective good is primary. Widespread participation in decision-making.
Nation-state	Role is to regulate the economy, level out society's social and economic inequalities, and protect the environment. Used to promote participation of citizenry in economic and non-economic decision-making Resources of the state are used to pursue goals of equality, social justice, democracy Balances the interests of different groups in society, ensuring that no group becomes dominant.
Social justice	Equality of condition as a social goal. Absence of a ruling class or group. Entitlement (to society's resources) tied to individual need and not to the nature or worth of work. All forms and sources of oppression must be challenged.
Social change	Society is a human rather than a transcendental construct. Capitalism must be transformed to a socialist society using peaceful means. Mode of social transformation should be evolutionary.

self-realization. With respect to social integration, social democrats believe that a reduction in inequalities reduces feelings of isolation or alienation and creates a greater sense of belonging or social cohesion (George and Wilding, 1985). With respect to economic efficiency, a society characterized by gross inequalities experiences little social mobility, which means that many talented people will not rise to a position where they can use their talents and abilities. With respect to natural rights, inequality means that some people have greater opportunity and/or greater power than others, not because of merit but because of the luck of the genetic lottery in that some are born into families of wealth and influence. Finally, inequality often denies the individual the opportunity to realize his or her full potential, which in effect diminishes people's basic humanity. In spite of a consensus that there must be greater equality in all areas of life, social democrats do not agree on a definition of equality or on how much equality is desirable (George and Wilding, 1985). Where liberals are content with an equality of opportunity, social democrats talk about equality of condition, but more as an ideal than a practical goal. The social democratic objective is to narrow the gap as much as possible between rich and poor (Sigurdson, 2002).

Among the key social values social democrats hold, freedom ranks with equality. David Gil (1976b) argues convincingly that freedom for all is the central socialist value but can only be achieved if greater social equality is attained first. If some people have greater resources than others, they have greater freedom to control their conditions of life, which conversely means that some people have less control or freedom to make choices with respect to their life conditions. Social democrats believe that genuine freedom for all can come about only through government action rather than, as neo-conservatives believe, through government inaction. Only government, according to the social democrats, can create the conditions of social equality vital for the attainment of freedom for all.

The third central social value of social democrats is fellowship or collectivism, which means 'cooperation rather than competition, an emphasis on duties rather than rights, on the good of the community rather than on the rights of the individual, on altruism rather than selfishness' (George and Wilding, 1985: 74). A capitalist society does not subscribe to the value of solidarity. Rather, it encourages people to use their power and abilities for self-interest and to treat others not as people but as commodities to be bought, sold, or used to further one's own end. Social democrats reject such attitudes and behaviour.

Two other social values strongly held by social democrats—democratic participation and humanitarianism—were noted earlier. Democratic participation should extend to all areas of life, not just to the political and economic areas. For example, in the workplace employees should have a voice in the conditions of their work and employers should not be able to exercise arbitrary power or control over workers. In the areas of health and social services, lay people should have a say in formulating policies about the delivery of these services since they are the actual and potential beneficiaries. Social democrats believe also that people should be able to enjoy certain minimum standards of living and that social distress should be eliminated. Therefore, they would like to see a higher proportion of the nation's wealth spent on these goals, with proportionately more spent on deprived groups (George and Wilding, 1985).

ECONOMIC BELIEFS

The central economic beliefs of social democrats are government intervention, public control of the means of production and distribution, and a more equitable distribution of income and opportunities. Just as social democrats do not agree on how much equality is desirable, neither do they agree on how much government intervention should occur, or on the extent of public control of the means of production and distribution, or on how equitable the distribution of income should be. Opinions vary from the Marxist belief that total public ownership is necessary to achieve socialist goals to the liberal belief that regulated capitalism is all that is necessary to achieve socialist goals.

George and Wilding (1985) present five criticisms that social democrats have of a free-market economy. (1) There is no social purpose or collective goal as individuals pursue their own interests, which results in social misery for many. (2) The free market is fundamentally unjust as it has no clear principles for distributing rewards other than a moral right to extract what one can without breaking the law. (3) The free market is undemocratic as decisions important to many, if made at all, are made by an elite few in privacy. (4) The free market is inefficient because without government regulation it leads to environmental devastation, regional economic disparities, periodic economic recessions, an oversupply of fundamentally useless products, and an undersupply of socially necessary goods and services. (5) The distribution of goods and services in a free-market economy does not include goods and services needed by those experiencing illness, old age, or life circumstances such as widowhood.

To overcome these inherent deficiencies of a free-market economy the social democrats would attempt to replace the anarchy of capitalism and the motives of private gain with rational economic and social planning for the common good. In other words, economic mechanisms would be put in place to control the means of production and distribution. These mechanisms could include the Marxist notion of state ownership (i.e., nationalization of private ownership) as well as government regulation of private ownership, and the development of workers' co-operatives, consumers' associations, and credit unions. The question of nationalization has caused a division in the social democratic camps, fundamentalists believing that nationalization is the only way to achieve socialist goals and reformists claiming that separation between ownership and control can achieve the same goals.

Both fundamentalist and reformist social democrats condemn gross inequalities of income, opportunities, and living conditions. Pay equity, progressive taxation policies, the elimination of inheritance of large fortunes, an emphasis on human rights, and affirmative action programs are mechanisms favoured by social democrats to reduce inequality. Again, the questions of how much redistribution of resources is equitable and how far the wealth of the rich should be reduced are not answered unanimously by the social democrats.

POLITICAL BELIEFS

The fundamental political beliefs of social democrats are: (1) the state has a positive role to play in society; (2) capitalism can be transformed into socialism by a social democratic government; and (3) the state should encourage broad participatory decision-making in all areas of life.

Social democrats view the state as an agent for redistributing benefits and resources. It is seen as acting independent of, and often in opposition to, market mechanisms (Djao, 1983). Only the state, through legislation and government action, can protect the freedoms of the less powerful citizen from the ravages of the more powerful, and only the state can bring about certain changes and promote an ethic of collective preference over that of individual interest (Mendes, 2003). Through the state the political process governs the economic process rather than the reverse, that of economics determining politics. The rationality of planning, under a social democratic regime, guides society, not the magical forces of laissez-faire.

Social democrats believe that government planning can transform capitalism into socialism without endangering individual freedom, contrary to the belief of neo-conservatives (George and Wilding, 1985). Social democrats believe that it is just as possible to plan for freedom as it is for tyranny. Many social democrats claim that a social democratic government could use the state machinery (the government, the civil service, and the judiciary) to implement radical changes in capitalist society,[4] and that over time, with proper public education about the benefits of its radical program, the citizenry would accept these changes and true democracy would flourish more than it does under capitalism. Social democrats, on the whole, believe that these changes must come through peaceful means and that violence would only contaminate socialism. Social democrats also believe that one of the major ways of transforming capitalism into socialism is to develop the social welfare state, which emphasizes distribution according to need and not according to one's social position.

Social democrats subscribe to the principle and practice of participatory decision-making in both the economic and political spheres (Naiman, 1997). It is believed that this form of decision-making would spread responsibility, reduce power concentration, and increase productivity (George and Wilding, 1985). Social democrats would promote more worker control in industry and work organizations, more service user involvement in the delivery of public services, such as health or social services, and more community development directed at boosting the power of people with respect to local, regional, and national governments. Of course, these involvements would essentially be of a decision-making nature and not merely of a cosmetic consultative nature.

VIEW OF SOCIAL PROBLEMS

Basically, two competing sets of theories in the sociological literature attempt to explain the nature of society and the nature and cause of social problems. 'Ultimately, all social theories, whether they acknowledge it or not, either support the present social arrangements or advocate changing them' (Naiman, 1997: 18). These two competing sets of theories are the *order* and *conflict* (or change) perspectives of society, which are rooted in nineteenth-century history and social thought. Essentially, order theories are of a social system characterized by equilibrium, stability, continuity, consensus, integration, and social control. Order theories perceive social problems to be caused when members of a society do not learn to revere its institutions or respect its rules (Reasons and Perdue, 1981). Functionalism or structural functionalism, with its roots in the sociology of August Comte, Herbert Spencer, Max Weber, Émile Durkheim, and Talcott Parsons, is probably the best known of the order theories (Naiman, 1997). As will be discussed in Chapter 9, neo-conservatism and (neo-)liberalism adhere to order interpretations of society and social problems, whereas social democracy and Marxism adhere to conflict interpretations.

Conflict or change theories view the nature of society as a contested struggle among groups with opposed aims and perspectives (Horton, 1966). In pursuing their own interests they are often in conflict with one another. Reasons and Perdue (1981) set out some of the major tenets of conflict theory. In the contested struggle among groups the state is an important agent because it is used as an instrument of oppression by the dominant class for its own benefit. Social inequality is a consequence of coercive institutions that favour the dominant groups, and this social inequality is a primary source of conflict. In sum, conflict theorists see society as conflict-ridden rather than as stable, orderly, and integrated, and they question a social order marked by differences of race, class, gender, age, and so on. All conflict or change theories are informed by the ideas of Karl Marx (Naiman, 1997).

Although there are several schools of conflict/change thought the two main theories, according to George and Wilding (1985), are the social conflict and the class conflict schools. The social conflict school believes that the sources of conflict are diverse and numerous and include such elements as race, religion, profession, region, gender, and economic status. Social democrats subscribe to the social conflict school. The class conflict school sees the conflict between the two major economic classes—the owners of production and those who must work for them—as the most important conflict in society. And because class conflict originates from the production system of capitalism, the only way it can be resolved is to abolish the capitalist system itself. Class conflict theory is, of course, synonymous with Marxist theory.

Racism, poverty, pollution, and other social problems, from the social conflict view, are actually contests among various groups over the acquisition or control of desirable resources such as wealth, privilege, and political power. Because these issues are actually clashes of interest they represent political conflicts. Conflict theorists would prefer to call these conflicts 'political conflicts' or 'social conflicts' because the term 'social problems' implies some kind of social sickness that can be treated more successfully by the 'dispassionate intervention of experts' than by political action (Rule, 1971).

In short, social problems, according to social democrats, are not the result of deviance, as the neo-conservatives believe, or of industrialization, as the liberals believe, but are normal consequences of the way society is organized. Thus, they cannot be dealt with by technical means or administrative reforms. They can only be resolved by a reorganization of the society that caused the problems (conflicts) in the first place.

VIEW OF SOCIAL WELFARE

When talking about socialist views of the welfare state a distinction must be made between a welfare state within a socialist society and a welfare state within a capitalist society. For all socialists (Marxists and social democrats) the ideal welfare system, which would be consistent with socialist values and an integral part of a socialist society, is what Mishra (1981) calls a 'structural model' of welfare. Although both social democrats and Marxists subscribe to this ideal socialist model of welfare, they differ in their views on the nature and functions of our present capitalist welfare state. Mishra (1981: 133) outlines the socialist conception of a welfare state:

> Central to the socialist view of welfare is the notion that 'to each according to his [*sic*] needs' should be the guiding principle of distribution. In other words collective consumption—that is, typically universal, comprehensive and free social services such as health and education—constitutes the basic model of distribution under socialism.

Social democrats believe that the above form of equal distribution of societal resources is possible only after the production and distribution of all resources has come under state control (either by nationalization or by regulation). Only then will the market, the family, and private property cease to be the basic means of distribution of income and opportunities. The main feature of the structural model of welfare is that it considers welfare (distribution according to need) to be a central social value. The users of social services are not merely citizens entitled to a basic minimum of civilized life (as liberals believe), but are members of a socialist community whose needs are to be met to the fullest extent possible (Mishra, 1981).

Consistent with the socialist principle of participation of people in all areas of life, the structural model of welfare includes citizen participation in social services decision-making rather than strict control by administrators and experts. This emphasis on lay power or deprofessionalization of the social services would necessitate a demystification of professional knowledge (e.g., medical knowledge) and a decrease in the power, status, and authority of professionals in the social welfare field. This does not mean that lay people would be delivering health, education, and other social services, but that they would have a much greater say in how they are to be delivered and how they are to be administered.

Another vital principle of the structural welfare state is prevention. Many socialists (particularly Marxists) do not believe that preventive services can be established in a capitalist system because: (1) social services are viewed by socialists as institutions that tend to problems created by a system that neglects human needs; and (2) where the social welfare state is controlled by professionals primary consideration is given to professional interests rather than to service-user interests. For example, Mishra (1981) contends that the Soviet Union placed much greater emphasis on preventive medicine because lay people had more say than professionals concerning health policies.

Although it is instructive to become informed about the social democratic ideal or preferred model of welfare, progressive social workers need to know the social democratic view of welfare capitalism. How does the welfare state in capitalist societies relate to the structural welfare model and to social democratic beliefs, principles, and values? If a social democratic party were elected to national office in Canada, for example, what would have to be done to its present welfare state to achieve social democratic goals?

Social democrats consider the welfare state to have followed a course of historical pragmatism (Mishra, 1981). In other words, social problems have accompanied industrialization, urbanization, and technological change and have had to be attended to by the state. In the course of dealing with these problems the state has had to reconcile various group conflicts by compromise or by siding with one group and ultimately instituting a social policy to deal with the problem. Over time, this method of piecemeal social engineering has produced an accumulation of social policies that constitutes the welfare state.[5]

Social democrats value the welfare state for what it can and does achieve within a capitalist state. However, they want the welfare state to do more. Social welfare should further justice and prevent problems rather than deal only with situations of injustice and the treatment of problems; social welfare should promote equality of opportunity; social welfare should reduce all inequalities, not just eliminate poverty; and social welfare should promote greater control of social services by lay people rather than by administrators and experts (George and Wilding, 1985).

Perhaps the major belief of social democrats with respect to the social welfare state in a capitalist society is that it can be used as a stepping stone towards a socialist society. Because social welfare programs and services represent a break with the free-market doctrine of distribution, social democrats think that the advantages of such a system would be seen by the general public as preferable to that of the free market, thus aiding in the transformation from a capitalist to a socialist society. Social democrats are aware that a welfare state, by itself, will not provide a just society. This can occur only if the means of production and distribution come under public control, either by ownership or by regulation. However, the failure of the Labour government in Britain to live up to the expectations placed on it by social democrats has been interpreted by some to indicate that the welfare state only supports and strengthens capitalism, while others now see the road from capitalism to socialism as longer and more perilous than originally perceived.

It should be noted here that although the welfare state was widely assumed by social democrats to be an emancipatory project in that the state would provide a wide range of public services to even up the life chances of individuals and groups, it has been criticized by feminists, people of colour, postmodernists, and others as being another institution of domination. Beneath the socialist rhetoric of liberation and equality and universalistic ideas underpinning the modern welfare state, postmodernists along with feminists, people of colour, and other oppressed groups have criticized the welfare state for not acknowledging and/or for suppressing and discriminating against 'diversity in cultures, sexualities, abilities, ages and other human characteristics' (Leonard, 1997: xiii). Any attempt by social democrats to reconstruct the welfare state as an emancipatory project must take into consideration these criticisms. More will be said about postmodern deconstruction and reconstruction of the welfare state in Chapter 7.

SOCIAL WORK PRACTICE WITHIN THE SOCIAL DEMOCRATIC PARADIGM

The nature of social work practice within our present capitalist society will be determined by the view of social democracy that one holds. If one views social democracy as a well-developed extension of liberalism (as many writers contend was the view of British Fabians), then that person's practice of social work will be quite different from one who believes that capitalism must be transformed into socialism in order to deal effectively with our modern social problems. The former would concentrate on a social work practice of individual and humanitarian care while the latter, in addition to performing tasks of individual and humanitarian care, would seek to create forces that would contribute to the transformation of capitalism to socialism.

Fabian social democracy, as will be argued below, violates too many principles of socialism even to be considered as socialism. Therefore, social work practice according to this view will not be discussed here, for it would not differ significantly from liberal social work practice. An overview of social work practice based on the social democratic belief that the welfare state can be used as a stepping stone towards socialism is presented here.

Social democratic social work practice has a dual function: (1) to tend to the immediate and legitimate needs of people or groups of people who lose out in the ongoing group conflicts that occur in capitalist society over the acquisition of material resources and power; and (2) to work towards the transformation of capitalist society to one that adheres to those social, economic, and political beliefs and values of social democracy. That is, social work must aim towards the creation of a socialist state. Underpinning this view of social work practice is the belief that our present set of social arrangements can be transformed by working through the existing political and social institutions, which, according to the social democrats, 'are relatively accessible, are democratic, and are therefore capable of radical reform' (Pritchard and Taylor, 1978: 96–7).

The above belief is different from that of Marxists, who believe that alternative organizations and institutions must be established outside the existing system to challenge the power of the capitalist state. In other words, social democrats believe that social work can contribute to radical changes in society by working within the existing system, but Marxists tend to believe that social work must operate outside the existing system or else it will become incorporated into the present social order and end up protecting it rather than changing it.

The dual function of social democratic social work—to provide practical, humanitarian care and to further the democratization and restructuring of society along socialist lines— means a politicized and radical social work profession. This does not mean, however, that the two functions are mutually exclusive, that you cannot carry out both at the same time. Indeed, as a reforming profession, social work must help simultaneously both the individual and society to evolve along more socially concerned lines. For example, a social democratic social worker may work with someone who is considered deviant or disruptive. The task would be to help this non-conformist to cope with his or her non-conforming but not necessarily to abandon it—an important qualification, as Pritchard and Taylor (1978) point out. The non-conforming behaviour may not be at fault, but rather society's rules, norms, or expectations. More will be said about this in Chapter 9.

Much of social democratic social work practice at the micro level would be to normalize and depersonalize the problematic situations in which many people find themselves. In other words, the social worker would explore the social context of the situation with the service user and analyze it along social democratic lines to see if a relationship exists between the problem and capitalism. For example, if the problem is unemployment and over one million Canadians are unemployed, this does not mean that we have over one million unique personal problems. Rather, we have one social problem affecting over one million workers and their families. In other words, 'the personal is political.' As well as the incidence of unemployment, the reasons why capitalism needs and produces unemployment would be discussed with the service user. Subsequently, a plan of action would be jointly determined and would include helping the person deal with his or her individual situation of unemployment, at the same time exploring ways that can contribute to a transformation of the existing capitalist system. At the macro level, social democratic social workers, through their professional organization or association, would act:

> as a legitimate pressure-group operating within the present socio-political structure and campaigning for both specific policies and a general reorientation of strategy and/or philosophy (i.e., for policies based upon a more egalitarian, redistributive system which would also be far more concerned than at present with the achievements of social justice, the extension of welfare services and the protection of the rights of the underprivileged in society generally). (Pritchard and Taylor, 1978: 4)

The macro or political task, then, is to mobilize as much support as possible for social democracy, in general, and for social progress among social services users, in particular. Social democrats believe it is important to educate 'both the "advantaged" and the "disadvantaged" in an acceptance of the interdependency of different sections of society' (Pritchard and Taylor, 1978: 95). The social work profession, therefore, must join forces with other socialistic organizations and institutions, such as the labour movement and social democratic political parties, to gain an ever-increasing control of the various institutions of the state and move eventually to a position where the attainment of a fully socialist system becomes possible. Such a project, however, must be informed by the post-modern deconstruction/critique of social democacy in general and the modern welfare state in particular so that it does not continue to be an institution of social exclusion and domination (see Chapter 7). If the welfare state is to become a radical force for progressive social and political change (i.e., a stepping stone to socialism), it is absolutely imperative that social work become politicized and radicalized. This is so because social work is a key sector within the welfare state structure and has an important influence on welfare state ideology.

BOX 5.1   SOCIALISM AND ATHEISM

Since teaching social work from an explicitly political position (i.e., socialist), I have experienced a number of hostile reactions from a few students (and from a few parents) over the years, especially on those occasions when I would claim that, given the collectivist principles and lifestyle of Jesus Christ, he would be called a socialist today. I remember one occasion in the mid-1980s when I was teaching in the social work program at St Thomas University, which is a small Catholic, liberal arts university located in Fredericton, New Brunswick. The president of the university at that time was a Roman Catholic priest. There were a few first- and second-year students in my Introduction to Social Welfare class who were offended by my socialist approach to social welfare and social work. They were also under the belief that all socialists were atheists, as this was part of the myth and stereotype attached to socialism at the time by many uninformed North Americans. They decided among them that they would go to the president and complain that there was a socialist and atheist who was teaching in his Catholic university and that they did not think they should have to be subjected to heretical and sinful views in the classroom. At the time I was a practising Roman Catholic who attended Mass in the university chapel every Sunday morning. The president's response to the student complaint was that he did not care about Dr Mullaly's political views but, for their information, he did see him at Mass every Sunday, but could not remember seeing any of them. (God bless this president!).

CRITIQUE OF THE SOCIAL DEMOCRATIC PARADIGM

Some of the major criticisms levelled at social democracy are: it does not move capitalist society closer to a socialist society but only changes the face of capitalism; its anti-nationalization stance is inconsistent with one of the basic tenets of socialism; it leads to a centralized and elitist control of planning and decision-making; and the welfare state has not produced the desired reduction in inequalities. An overview of these criticisms and a response to each of them follows.

A common criticism of British social democracy is that although the social democratic Labour Party was the dominant political force in Britain for most of the sixties and seventies, it did not use this power to create an alternative to capitalism but adapted the labour movement to an acceptance of the existing system. Legitimation and public acceptance of social democracy in Britain seem to have been gained at the expense of socialism (Pritchard and Taylor, 1978). However, as mentioned previously, it does not logically follow that the course of social democracy in Britain must be the course of social democracy everywhere.[6] Writing from Sweden on that country's experience with a social democratic government for all the years between 1932 and the present (except for 1976–82 and a brief period in the nineties), Himmelstrand et al. (1981: 26–7) state that there are good theoretical and empirical reasons for 'rejecting the simplistic notion of social democracy simply as a tool of capitalist development'. The authors present some recent Swedish social democratic reforms concerning the work environment and the relative power of labour and capital that would seem to change significantly the relations of production in a socialistic direction. Based on the Swedish experience, it would seem that social democracy may be used as a path to a socialist state, though this path is longer and more complex than originally conceived by social democrats.

A second criticism of social democracy, that its anti-nationalization stance is antithetical to socialism, also is rebutted by the Swedish example. Swedish social democratic policy has been to separate ownership of the means of production from its control. Rather than risking a huge backlash as a result of nationalizing industry, the Swedish social democratic government has gained control of industry through legislation and regulation. In other words, by regulating industry the Swedes can practically achieve the same economic and social goals as if they owned industry. In fact, the Swedes would point to the British experience of nationalization as contributing to capitalist development in that the compensation paid to the capitalists for nationalizing their firms was profitably reinvested elsewhere. One of the effects, then, was to see public industry subsidize private capitalism (Hughes, 1973). All this is not to say that Swedish social democrats are not interested in the labour force gaining capital ownership. Some of the recent Swedish workplace reforms move in this direction but without use of the draconian action of nationalization.[7]

The criticism that social democracy leads to a centralized and elitist control of planning and decision-making is also based on the British experience with social democracy. The trade union section of the Labour Party emphasized the democratic role of the working class within the transition to socialism, but the Fabians, who gained political control, actually opposed the idea of working-class control and mass participatory democracy. The Fabians believed that the working class was an alien mass incapable of understanding the complexities of modern society. British social democracy thus consisted of substituting for the capitalist class an elite of disinterested experts to control the new socialist society subject to control by the people through the parliamentary system (Pritchard and Taylor, 1978). Again, this elitist form of social democracy can be contrasted with the massive participation that goes into the decision-making process in Sweden. At any one time 200 to 300 parliamentary-sanctioned commissions of study[8] are looking at various public policy issues. All relevant individuals, organizations, and interest groups are consulted before a preliminary report is drafted. They are consulted again on the contents of the preliminary report, after which a final report is drafted and presented to parliament for debate and policy formulation. The point to be made is that one of the fundamental social-political values of social democracy is participation in decision-making. It seems illogical to dismiss social democracy as elitist and undemocratic on the basis of what happened with one country's experience.

Another criticism is that it has not produced a significant reduction of inequalities. It was originally thought by social democrats that many socialist objectives, including greater equality, could be achieved through the welfare state. But as Mishra (1981) points out, the British welfare state has failed to achieve a significant redistribution of income and opportunity. Market forces have counteracted the effects of egalitarian policies (for example, fringe benefits or occupational welfare has reduced the levelling effects of a progressive income tax system). Inequalities of income and wealth stubbornly persist in Britain and other social democratic countries. The universality of social services has meant that both the rich and poor have benefited from them. And, social welfare has not resulted in an inter-class transfer of resources. 'Those who use the social services by and large pay for them' (Pritchard and Taylor, 1978: 65). The response of the social democrats to this criticism is to acknowledge that there are deficiencies in the present welfare state. But they would argue that the welfare state is the creation of the Labour Party; without it many people would be much worse off than they are today; and with more time and the proper political will the welfare state can be further developed to the point where its socialistic aims can be achieved. Other social democratic writers, such as Furniss and Tilton (1977) and Esping-Andersen (1990), argue that social democracy can achieve socialistic goals and point to the social democratic Scandinavian countries and their respective social welfare states because they have achieved much greater equality of income and opportunity than most other Western democracies.

A final criticism of the social democratic paradigm to be looked at here is part of the critique that postmodernism has of all paradigms or ideological thought structures or 'grand narratives'. Although more will be said about this critique in subsequent chapters, its basic criticism of left (socialist) politics and social democratic welfare states is presented here. An essential idea of nineteenth- and twentieth-century socialism was that it was a unifying concept that could mobilize mass populations for the historic task of transforming capitalism. The socialist/social democratic political party was considered to be the vehicle for this transformative process. However, socialist parties also reflected in their organization and culture the forms of domination and exclusion that existed in the larger society. In particular, white males provided the leadership of such parties (Leonard, 1995), with *others* being excluded on the basis of culture, race, gender, sexuality, and so on—resulting in a situation, as Peter Leonard (1997: 18) states, where 'their voices [were] silenced, their very existence as active subjects erased from "history"'. The social democratic view of the welfare state was that of an ever-expanding universalism that would improve the life chances of the entire population, but especially the working

TABLE 5.2   OVERVIEW OF SOCIAL DEMOCRATIC AND SOCIAL WORK PARADIGMS

	Social Democracy	*Social Work*
Social Beliefs	Humanitarianism Collectivism Equality Freedom Democratic participation	Humanitarianism (humanism) Community Equality

Economic Beliefs	Government intervention
	Public control of the means
	  of production and distribution
	Equitable distribution of
	  income and opportunities
		Government intervention
		Social priorities dominate
		  economic decisions
		Equitable distribution of
		  society's resources

Political Beliefs	Participatory decision-
	  making in all areas of life
	Capitalism can be
	  transformed by a social
	  democracy
	The state has a positive
	  role to play in society
		Participatory democracy in
		  both governmental and
		  non-governmental areas

View of Social Welfare	Welfare capitalism can be
	  used as a stepping stone
	  to a socialist state
	Ideal = social welfare state
	  or structural model
		An instrument to promote
		  equality, solidarity, and
		  community
		Ideal = structural model

Nature of Social Work Practice	Provide practical
	  humanitarian care to
	  casualties of capitalism
	Further the democratization
	  and restructuring of
	  society along socialist lines
		Treat people with respect
		Enhance dignity and
		  integrity
		Facilitate self-determination
		  and self-realization
		Accept differences
		Advocate and promote
		  social justice

class. It became, as Giddens (1994) points out, a welfare state based on a model of traditional family and gender patterns with programs aimed primarily at supporting male participation in the paid labour force with a secondary set of programs oriented towards families without a male breadwinner.In other words, the welfare state was essentially an institution used by social democrats in their 'class struggle'. Any reconstruction or reconceptualization of the welfare state as a project of emancipation must be informed by this postmodern critique. It must avoid the modernist illusion of essentialism, the practice of social exclusion, the tendency to privilege Eurocentric views of the world, and it must involve all oppressed groups in a dialogue of liberation.

Table 5.2 shows that, unlike neo-conservatism and liberalism, there is a high degree of compatibility between the social democratic and social work paradigms. They share many of the same social, economic, and political beliefs and there are no contradictions between the two sets of ideologies. Both have the same attitude towards the nature and some of the functions of the social welfare state. It would appear that social democracy (and eventually socialism) is one possibility as the kind of society that best meets and actualizes social work's values, principles, and ideals. If this is so, then a heavy emphasis would be placed on the structural components (restructuring society along socialist lines) of social work practice. In other words, social work practice would become much more like that described in this chapter.

CONCLUSION

This chapter presented an overview of social democracy as a prominent school of socialism. An attempt was made to dispel some of the negative myths held about socialism, especially in North America. It examined social democratic beliefs about human nature, the nature of society, the role of the state, the meaning of social justice, and social democratic attitudes towards social change. It also looked at social democratic ideology and how social democrats would view and treat social problems, and it described the nature and role of social work from the social democratic paradigm. As well, it compared social democratic ideals with those of progressive social work and concluded that there was much more convergence between the two than exists between progressive social work and either neo-conservative or liberal ideals. A critique of the social democratic paradigm was also outlined.

CRITICAL QUESTIONS

1. Socialism is all about equality, but no socialist would call for total and complete equality in all aspects of life. How much equality do you think is desirable or acceptable?

2. Jesus Christ has been described as a radical and a socialist because he lived according to collectivist principles, wanted more sharing of society's resources, challenged (and was crucified by) the status quo. However, it is often the most conservative groups in society such as the religious right or the Moral Majority who most decry socialism and support conservative causes. How do you account for this apparent contradiction?

3. The NDP in Canada and the Labour parties in Britain and Australia call themselves social democratic parties. How close do you think the particular social democratic party in your country comes to the social democratic ideals, beliefs, values, and social policies described in this chapter? Has there been a shift (right or left) in their positions over time? If so, why?

4. Early socialists based their analysis on the premise of a 'class struggle'—that there were irreconcilable differences between the two classes in society—i.e., the capitalist class (bourgeoisie) and the working class. What are the major limitations of this analysis today?

5. What do your family (nuclear and extended) and your friends think or believe about socialism? Is there any difference in the opinions of the two groups? If so, what are they and why do you think they exist?

The Marxist Paradigm

. . . the philosophers have only interpreted the world, in various ways; the point is to change it.

—*Karl Marx (1975 [1845]: 423)*

INTRODUCTION

This chapter presents a brief introduction to Karl Marx, the times in which he lived, and how the man and his era contributed to the school of social and socialist thought called Marxism. It also provides an overview of Marxist beliefs with respect to human nature, the nature of society, the role of the state, the meaning of social justice, and the Marxist attitude towards social change. An examination is made of the Marxist view of welfare, both in capitalist and socialist societies, and of the explanation for social problems held by Marxists. A picture of social work practice in accordance with Marxism is painted and a contemporary critique of Marxism is outlined. Finally, a comparison of Marxist ideals with those of progressive social work is made.

MARXISM

As mentioned in the previous chapter, the two most important schools of socialist thought are social democracy and Marxism. Marxism includes Karl Marx's own writings as well as the writings of others whose ideas and analyses are close to those of Marx. Marx's basic philosophy was humanistic, as he was deeply concerned about the well-being and life chances of the working class in Victorian England. With the rise of capitalism he saw the increasing degradation of industrial workers who had no control over their work process or product and who had to live in squalor, insecurity, and poverty (see Box 6.1). At the same time as workers' lives were reduced to a subsistence level, the industrial land-owners (i.e., the capitalists) became enormously wealthy and their lives greatly enriched materially and politically (Djao, 1983). Marx's attitude towards this system was one of total rejection rather than of reform and he devoted most of his working life seeking to prove that capitalism was both unworkable and inhuman (Mishra, 1981).

BOX 6.1   THE COMMUNIST MANIFESTO

The year is 1848. In Ireland, thousands of people are starving to death. Thousands more are migrating to swell the slums and warrens of English cities. Manchester, Liverpool, and all of the other rapidly expanding urban centres of English capitalist production are paradoxical places. They have pleasant shopping centres, leafy suburbs, and grand architectural monuments to the rich and powerful. They also seethe with poverty and pollution, disease and dissent. In France, King Louis Philippe has abdicated the throne and Paris is burning behind barricades erected by the people against government forces. In Germany there is rebellion, counter-rebellion, and slaughter. All over Europe dissatisfaction with political and economic oppression erupts here and there into insurrection and war. In the English Parliament sits a Whig (classical Liberal) government, glowing with ideological fervour over its free-market theories and policies, determined to keep control over economic life and expand the riches flowing into the coffers of the bourgeois class. Its Poor Law system of welfare relief maintains the shackles of stigma and penury around those unable to find, or unable to carry out, paid labour. In London, a young philosopher, Karl Marx, and his colleague and patron, Friedrich Engels, present to the Communist League, a small group of left-wing radicals, a manifesto for transforming the world: the Manifesto of the Communist Party. It is a document filled with ominous warnings for the complacent bourgeoisie, rich in the rhetoric of revolution. From its opening portent—'There is a spectre haunting Europe—the spectre of Communism'—to its closing call to arms, it is both a brilliant piece of political propaganda and the key that unlocks the whole of Marxist theory.

Source: From O'Brien and Penna (1998: 46).

Marx's view of welfare or well-being is that it is a social norm based on the values of solidarity and co-operation. 'In concrete terms, welfare manifests itself in the social recognition of human need and in the organization of production and distribution in accordance with the criterion of need' (Mishra, 1981: 69). In a Marxist society production would be governed by social criteria and the fruits of labour, produced through co-operation, would be distributed according to the needs of people. Thus, a welfare society in the Marxist sense is one where the well-being of people is of primary consideration and where the mode of production is set up to meet human need rather than to make profits. To Marx, capitalism represented the very antithesis of a welfare society (Mishra, 1981).

For Marx, the central feature of any society is its mode of production—the way its system of productivity is organized. The mode of production determines the structure of society and its processes. In other words, the way society earns its living accounts for its political system, its educational system, the nature of its art and music, its ideology, its riches, its poverty, and how people relate to each other. The capitalist mode of production consists of the following structural (inherent) elements through which wealth, poverty, and inequality are generated and reproduced: private ownership of the means of production; production for profit; private property and inheritance; and the distribution of income and resources through the market mechanism (Mishra, 1981).

Marx did not believe that a welfare society could exist under capitalism. The dominance of the market as a distributive mechanism of income and life chances denies human need and social solidarity altogether. Coercion and competition rather than co-operation and solidarity are the bases of capitalist social organization. Welfare, as a central value, cannot make much headway in such a society. If welfare were to be institutionalized as a central value (i.e., production governed by social criteria and distribution determined by human need), private ownership of the means of production would have to transfer to public ownership. There are different interpretations of how Marx saw this transformation occurring: by reform or by revolution. This has been the source of much debate by contemporary Marxists.

In sum, Marxism is relevant to social welfare and social work on two counts. First, it provides a comprehensive theory of society that explains directly the nature and development of the welfare state and, indirectly, the nature and functions of social work practice in capitalist society. Second, it offers a normative theory about the transcendence of capitalism and the establishment of a welfare society whose central feature is to meet human need (Mishra, 1981).

The following section provides an overview of Marxist views on the nature of human beings, society, the state, social justice, and social change. As mentioned in the previous chapter, because social democracy and Marxism are both socialist paradigms, there is an overlap between them with respect to their views, beliefs, and fundamental values. As will become evident, however, there are also differences.

VIEWS OF THE NATURE OF HUMANS, SOCIETY, THE STATE, SOCIAL JUSTICE, AND SOCIAL CHANGE

For Marx the essence of *human nature* is that people are creative producers. This is not an individual attribute of people but a communitarian trait—by activating this essence people create a true community of human beings. 'To produce as an authentic human being is to express this deep communality' (Berry, 1986: 4). Not only is production an expression of an individual's own activity, but this individual satisfies the needs of another human being through this productive activity. And, Marx argued, by satisfying the needs of another, the producer is acknowledged as a complement to (even a necessity of) his/her own self. This process is mutual, and by attaining such complementarity between and among people, they are realizing their 'human communal nature'. 'Accordingly all humans need other humans to achieve their humanity. Their interrelationship is thus one of basic complementarity' (Berry, 1986: 6).This communal production is what makes humans distinct. Although animals and insects may produce under the compulsion of physical need, they lack the self-consciousness, autonomy, and free will of human beings. Humans, then, are active creators of self and their social environment. Marx recognized that human nature is not static, however, as it changes with different social contexts, becoming competitive under capitalism and co-operative under socialism. It is when humans lose control over the production process and from the product of their labour (through a forced division of labour and exploitation perpetrated by capitalism) that the person becomes alienated from his or her true essence and from society. De-alienation requires the radical transformation of society and its fundamental institutions.

For Marx and Engels, production is not only the basis of individual human nature but of the *nature of society* or collective life as well. 'Every society has to produce food, goods, shelter, and so on, in order to reproduce both its individual members and its social system' (O'Brien and Penna, 1998: 50).The way in which a society organizes its production proccesses is called the *mode of production*. A mode of production consists of a combination of the means of production and the relations of production. The means of production include labour, land, tools, machines, factories, and so on that are organized in particular ways. For example, in a capitalist society the mode of production is privately owned, with the class structure, in its most simple form, consisting of owners and those who must work for them. Thus the relations of production are characterized by a confrontation between the two camps because they have competing interests (i.e., profits vs wages). The relations of production in a capitalist society are unequal and take the form of a class struggle between the owners of production (the bourgeoisie or ruling class) and the workers who produce (the proletariat). In a socialist society the means of production would be publicly owned and because there would be no owners and everyone would contribute according to their ability and receive according to their needs, the relations of production would be characterized by social equality where there would be no economic class structure. The nature of a socialist society from a Marxist perspective is the same as that described in the previous chapter in regard to social democratic views and beliefs.

The Marxist perspective of *the nature or role of the state* in a socialist society is similar to that of social democrats. The Marxist view of the role of the state in a capitalist society, however, differs from that of social democrats in that they are much more skeptical about the state having any transformative potential. The state and other social institutions are seen 'to act in opposition to the real interests of all members of society by constituting an "illusory community", which then serves to disguise the real struggles that classes wage against each other' (O'Brien and Penna, 1998: 55–6). Over the course of history each particular method of production gave rise to a political situation that furthered the interests of the economically dominant group. During feudalism, the interests of the aristocracy or landowners were protected by the law, the monarchy, the army, the suppression of the serfs, and so on. During the period of capitalism, the interests of the capitalists are protected by the law, the churches, the family, the education system, the political system, the media, a false sense of social consciousness perpetrated on workers, and so on. Marx and Engels referred to the 'executive (leadership) of the modern state' as nothing 'but a committee for managing the affairs of the whole bourgeoisie' (i.e., capitalists or ruling class) (O'Brien and Penna, 1998: 56). In sum, the role of the state in a capitalist society is viewed by the Marxists to be a tool and servant of the ruling class used to control the working class in that all laws, political decisions, policies, and actions of government are in the interest of the capitalists, that is, the ruling class.

The concept of *social justice*, from a Marxist perspective, is similar to that from a social democratic point of view, and is best captured in Marx's statement about how goods in society ought to be distributed: 'From each according to his [one's] ability, to each according to his [one's] needs' (Marx, 1970 [1875]). Marx did not believe that it was fair when workers, who worked to produce the goods, received so little for their labour and the capitalists, who did not work to produce the goods, received a disproportionate share of the product's value. Marx believed that entitlement should not be tied to the nature of work or the worth of work, but to individual need itself. In this way, individual contribution to social wealth was separate from social consumption. These assumptions are based on a different model of human nature from those held by conservatives and liberals. Marx believed that individuals had a claim on society's resources, not on the basis of unequal individual endowment, but on the basis that everyone is equal by virtue of being a human being. Thus, the ultimate or ideal form of a just society to Marx was a classless society.

Social change, according to the Marxist perspective, is constantly occurring and is brought about directly through class struggle. In their earlier writings, Marx and Engels claimed that capitalism was doomed because the internal and inherent contradictions of capitalism (emphasis on accumulation, exploitation of workers, imperative of growth leading to overproduction) would eventually lead to its self-destruction. The leading force for this destruction would be a self-conscious, organized, and majority-size working class who would seize the means of production and turn these means to the service of its own needs. In their more analytical works, however, Marx and Engels acknowledged that the logic of capitalism was much more complex and adaptive. Both struggle and counter-struggle existed, with the classes mobilizing forces and developing strategies to further their own interests. In other words, much of the working class bought into capitalism and attempted to get as much out of it as they could. This co-optation, of course, fragmented the working class, reduced its class consciousness, and made the idea of social transformation seem unrealistic. This topic has been the subject of a number of distinct philosophical schools of Marxism or neo-Marxism (e.g., the Frankfurt School of critical theory, the existentialism of Jean-Paul Sartre, structuralism, the cultural Marxism of Antonio Gramsci and the Birmingham Centre for Contemporary Cultural Studies, political economy perspectives, feminist and anti-racist perspectives, and so on). These schools and perspectives have moved Marxism well beyond a simple class analysis by encouraging a series of reconstructions and reformulations of Marxist theory. Unfortunately, too many social workers and social work writers have not informed themselves of these developments and have dismissed Marxism as an interesting but outdated theory of society and social change. *Nothing could be further from the truth.*

TABLE 6.1   A SUMMARY OF MARXIST VIEWS

Concept	Views
Human nature	Humans are communal beings. Creative producers (production is the basis of human nature). Active creators of self and their social environment. Conscious, autonomous, and free-willed. Human nature changes with different social contexts.
Society	Production is the basis of the nature of society. Mode/organization of production (i.e., the means and the relations of production) determines the nature of society.
Role of the state	Same as social democratic view regarding a socialist state. State in a capitalist society furthers the interests of the economically dominant group. Social institutions used to control and co-opt working class and other subordinate groups in capitalist society.
Social justice	From each according to one's ability, to each according to one's needs. Entitlement not tied to worth of work but to human need. People are valued on the basis of being human, not on the basis of some notion of superiority/inferiority. Ideal form of social justice is a classless society.
Social change	Social change is constantly occurring and is brought about by class struggle. Inherent contradictions of capitalism are the leading force for its destruction. Capitalism has, so far, been able to mutate and adapt, and thus co-opt many of its opponents. There are several neo-Marxist schools of social change.

SOCIAL BELIEFS

Marxists adhere to the three central values of socialism: liberty, equality, and fraternity. Liberty, to the Marxists, can only exist if certain other conditions are present in society (George and Wilding, 1985). Without a substantial degree of economic security and equality, freedom is an illusory concept. Without these conditions some people will have more resources than others and, therefore, will have more privileges, more influence, and more liberties. Whereas neo-conservatives and liberals believe that civil rights are synonymous with liberty or freedom, Marxists believe that these rights or liberties can only be exercised fairly if they are complemented by social freedom—freedom from want, freedom from unemployment, and so on—and by opportunities to work, to earn, to develop oneself, to enjoy life. The Marxists do not believe that true liberty for all can occur in a capitalist society based on inequality. Thus, while neo-conservatives equate liberty with inequality and liberals equate liberty with equal opportunity, Marxists equate liberty with equality of economic circumstances or human emancipation that can only be achieved under socialism. George and Wilding present the Marxist concept of equality based on the writings of two Marxist writers, Harold Laski (1925) and John Strachey (1936). Equality does not mean sameness to Marxists; rather, it means the absence of special privilege and the availability of opportunities to all. Differences in wealth or status are consistent with Marxism as long as they can be reasonably explained, all can attain to them, and they are necessary for the common good. Economic equality does not mean equal incomes, for it would not be fair to reward unequal efforts exactly the same and it would not be fair to reward unequal needs with the same amount of social benefit. Also, a strict interpretation of 'distribution according to individual need' is recognized as problematic because individual need is difficult to define. Rather than 'absolute equality', some Marxists view equality as 'relative equality' with every need related to the social or civic minimum that, when not met, prevents one from attaining effective citizenship. These needs must be satisfied before dealing with needs above the social minimum and, after the satisfaction of basic needs, differences in reward must be built into the system to acknowledge varying contributions of individuals in different occupations.

The third central social value, solidarity or collectivism, reflects the communitarian nature of people and is antithetical to individualism. It views the individual as a social being in the sense that his or her thoughts and actions are influenced by those of others and vice versa. Collectivism recognizes people's need for each other and suggests that a good society is one without barriers to people living harmoniously and co-operatively with one another. According to this view of people, government intervention is legitimate, necessary, and beneficial.

ECONOMIC BELIEFS

The major economic beliefs of Marxists are public ownership of the means of production (brought about by nationalization of private enterprises), distribution of resources according to need, industrial democracy, and a planned economy.

Unlike the social democrats, the Marxists do not believe that the means of production can be controlled by regulation in a capitalist society. Private ownership creates two main classes—the capitalist class and the working class—locked in a structurally antagonistic relationship because their basic interests (profits versus wages) conflict with each other. Class conflict, then, is an inherent part of capitalism and can only be abolished by the abolition of the private ownership of the means of production.

The means of attaining public ownership advocated by the Marxists is nationalization, which they justify on both political and economic grounds (George and Wilding, 1985). The private ownership of the means of production has resulted in a concentration of economic power in the hands of the capitalist class in Britain, the United States, Australia, and Canada, and this inevitably has meant a concentration of political power in the same hands. Also, it is considered immoral by Marxists that profits are produced through the labour of the workers, but are reaped by shareholders who do not have to work. In this way, workers feel alienated from the work process and suffer psychologically, which in turn reduces economic production. To deal effectively with these political and economic problems the Marxists would nationalize private enterprise.

The second Marxist economic belief flows from the Marxist notion of social justice outlined above: 'each person should contribute to society according to his or her abilities and be rewarded by society according to his or her needs.' Although this principle is problematic in its implementation, most Marxists would adhere to it in some form. For example, some Marxists would establish minimal standards of living necessary to retain full citizenship in society and would ensure that everyone in society was living up to these standards before dealing with needs above the social or civic minimum (Laski, 1925, cited in George and Wilding, 1985). Other Marxists would follow Marx's theory of revolutionary socialism by distinguishing between distribution according to the quality of work done under socialism (i.e., the transformation stage of socialism) and distribution according to individual need under communism (i.e., the final stage of socialism when capitalism has been abolished) (Strachey, 1936, cited in George and Wilding, 1985). These Marxists point out, however, that distribution according to need requires both economic affluence on the part of the state and a different value system than that which underpins capitalism.

Industrial democracy, that is, a democratic workplace, is a third Marxist economic belief. Marxists generally accept that nationalized industries in a socialist society must be democratically run with maximum participation on the part of workers. As George and Wilding point out, the benefits of industrial democracy are many and varied—it extends and gives real meaning to political democracy; it reduces industrial conflict and promotes industrial co-operation; it enhances individual work satisfaction; and it increases work productivity, which in turn increases the overall standard of living of society.

The final Marxist economic belief is that government planning with the widest form of participation must be a central feature of a socialist society (George and Wilding, 1985). Rather than laissez-faire or free enterprise, the Marxists aspire to a planned economy (as part of a planned society) where the market is subordinated to purposes upon which members of society have agreed. The Marxists believe that, contrary to the neo-conservative argument, planning enhances democracy and efficiency and is less susceptible to government corruption (George and Wilding, 1985). Obviously, the combination of nationalization and industrial democracy would make it easier for governments to formulate and integrate economic and social policies.

POLITICAL BELIEFS

The central political beliefs of the Marxists are government planning, a participatory democracy, a parliamentary system of government, and the view that capitalism can be transformed only by class conflict. The Marxist belief in government planning has been discussed above and the Marxist attitude towards participatory democracy is similar to that of the social democrats.

The suppression of parliamentary democracy during the Soviet era in Eastern European countries, which were referred to as socialist by much of the media and by many commentators in capitalist countries (understandably, since the leader of the Eastern bloc was the Union of Soviet *Socialist* Republics), caused many people to believe that Marxism is anti-democratic (George and Wilding, 1985). However, a belief in parliamentary democracy by most contemporary Marxists is unmistakable, as evidenced by its acceptance in Western Europe's Communist parties. The idea of a one-party socialist state is inconsistent with the concept of democratic socialism.

The Marxists believe that any significant social change can come about only through class conflict. This belief is different from that of the social democrats, who believe that capitalism can be transformed by social conflict between racial, religious, and other interest groups (including classes) aided by a progressive social democratic government. Although early Marxists recognized other conflicts in society in addition to that which exists between exploited wage earners and the owners of the means of production, they believed these other conflicts could be resolved within the legal conditions of capitalism. Early Marxists were united in their belief that class conflict would sooner or later lead to the downfall of capitalism. Neo-Marxists are not as absolute in this regard. For example, Marxist feminists view patriarchy and classism as twin evils and do not think that the elimination of one would necessarily mean the end of the other. Similarly, anti-racist theorists do not think that the abolition of class exploitation will end racism. They point to the example of Jewish people who, as a group, have achieved middle-class status, which means that they receive higher than average incomes (Blalock, 1967) that tend to tie them in more with capitalism. However, anti-Semitism remains a primary hate crime in Canada. Jews and other middle-class visible minorities in various times and in various places have been accused of being clannish, aloof, and disloyal to their country, and of being parasites who drain the economy (Sanderson, 1995). Given modern developments of Marxist theory and analysis, the road to social transformation is not as clear as it was 100 years or even 50 years ago. This change may come peacefully or violently, although most contemporary Marxist writers advocate peaceful means. Unlike social democrats, who believe that the welfare state can be used as a vehicle for socialist change, most Marxists view the welfare state as a social institution supporting capitalism (see below). They would, instead, focus their efforts on labour as the primary vehicle for socialist change, but would not rule out other social movements contributing to this goal.

VIEW OF SOCIAL PROBLEMS

Unlike neo-conservatives, Marxists do not see so-called social problems as the result of individual fault. Nor do they view social problems as the result of industrialization, as the liberals do, or as the result of social conflict among various groups, as the social democrats do. Rather, social problems are 'the result of the capitalist form of production and its accompanying forms of social relationships' (George and Wilding, 1985: 109–10). Marxists believe that the term 'social problem' mystifies structural issues of inequality, oppression, and alienation by turning them into individualistic issues of deviance, inadequacy, or pathology.

For example, a Marxist analysis of poverty shows that it will never be resolved or eliminated in a capitalist society because capitalism needs poverty. Poverty carries out the following functions for capitalism:

- Poverty helps to keep wages down and profits up. When people are poor, they will accept low wages to purchase basic necessities, and when there are many poor people, one of the ways they will compete for jobs is by working for lower wages than the other person.
- Capitalism needs a workforce that will perform its dangerous work and carry out its menial tasks. People living in poverty often have to perform these tasks just to survive. For example, a disproportionate number of African Americans, Hispanic Americans, and poor white people are on the front lines in fighting America's wars (with affluent white men occupying positions as generals, Pentagon officials, and White House politicians). Similarly, those who work in coal mines are decidedly not the sons of the well-to-do, and while right-wing American politicians rail against illegal Mexican migrants and propose a border barrier fence costing billions of dollars for 'security', these same migrants do the dirty or dangerous jobs that others refuse. It is often poor (and illegal) immigrants and people of colour who are forced to clean public washrooms and pick up cigarette butts and styrofoam coffee cups around campuses and other public areas.
- Poverty enhances feelings of superiority (i.e., self-righteousness) of the non-poor.
- Poor people are often used as scapegoats for societal ills. For example, government deficits of the 1970s and 1980s were often blamed on generous social welfare programs that were needed because poor people were considered to be too lazy to work.
- Programs developed to deal with poverty employ large numbers of people, thus contributing to a lower unemployment level.
- Many private organizations make profits via government contracts in delivering services to poor people. (There is a good deal of money in poverty, only poor people are not getting much of it.)

- Poor people are often pointed out as examples of what will happen to a person if he or she does not conform to the (capitalist) society's expectations, such as becoming a productive member of the workforce (see Box 6.2 below).

BOX 6.2   'SHAPE UP OR YOU WILL END UP IN THE POOR HOUSE!'

I grew up in Saint John, New Brunswick, during the 1950s. Near the house in which I lived was a body of water called Courtney Bay. Right across the Bay from our house was an old 'Municipal Home' operated by the county. It was, in fact, a poor house since the Poor Laws in New Brunswick were not repealed until 1960. Living in the 'Home' were older people who had been there for years. They had originally been committed or forced to enter the poor house because they had no other means of support. On sunny days they would sit outside in front of the Home where they would be on display for people going by. They were decrepit, forlorn, and very old looking, especially to a young boy driving by on his bicycle. My father, as one of his forms of discipline, would take me outside our house, point across the Bay to the poor house, and say 'If you don't behave yourself better, you will end up in that poor house.' Of course, this terrified me and I would be on my best behaivour—for a day or two.

Marxists believe that by focusing on the victims of inequality, oppression, and alienation and calling them criminals, drug addicts, or poor people, we are actually labelling them as troublemakers. Consequently, we neglect the social conditions of inequality, powerlessness, and institutional violence that form the basis of our troubled society. Instead, the Marxists would trace these problems back to the social relationships determined by capitalism, not to the individual. Personal problems are rooted in capitalist politics. For some problems, such as poverty, the explanation is direct and simple; for others, such as crime, it is less direct and more complex. In sum, Marxists believe that social problems are caused by the capitalist system. Therefore, they cannot be abolished by social policy in a capitalist society but only by the abolition of capitalism.

Marx is arguably the founder of a body of social theory called 'critical social theory'. His ideas and emancipatory intentions have been extended by many notable theorists. As its name suggests, critical theory is critical of existing social institutions and practices and locates the sources of social problems (i.e., domination) within them. Critical social theory seeks to change a society whose institutions, practices, and processes are exploitative and discriminatory to one that is emancipatory and free from domination. Marxism is perhaps the earliest form of critical social theory and was based on an analysis of capitalism and its exploitation of workers. More recent forms of critical theory are emancipatory forms of feminism, anti-racism, anti-oppression, liberation theology, post-colonialism, and structural social work (Mullaly, 2002). Some of these theories will accord primacy to one particular form and source of oppression (e.g., anti-racist perspectives); others will attempt to accommodate multiple forms of oppression in their analyses and theories (e.g., anti-oppression and structural social work). More will be said about critical social theory in Chapter 9.

VIEW OF SOCIAL WELFARE

The ideal social welfare system in the Marxist view is the same as that espoused by social democrats or by any socialist group—the structural model of welfare. Its major attributes are that social services should be distributed according to need; they should be universal, comprehensive, adequate, and free; prevention is a primary social welfare principle; and there should be participation on the part of lay people in determining policy.

Marxists, however, as noted previously, do not agree with the social democrats that the welfare state under capitalism provides a stepping stone to a socialist society. Instead, Marxists believe that although the welfare state does provide minimal help to some people, its main function is to support and strengthen the liberal-capitalist system. The welfare state represents one of the contradictions of capitalism. On the one hand, it works towards greater degrees of human well-being by tending to the immediate needs of some people. On the other hand, it denies and frustrates the pursuit of a just society as it supports and reinforces conformity to the very institutions and values that generate the problems the welfare state was established to deal with in the first place.

Two obvious questions arise from the Marxist contention that the welfare state does not move capitalist society any closer to a socialist society but, instead, supports and strengthens capitalism. Why does the welfare state prop up capitalism? How does it do this? The simple explanation of why the welfare state supports capitalism is that this is its principal raison d'être in a capitalist society—to protect capitalism. The welfare state is established within a certain political and economic context. Because of that liberal-capitalist context, the welfare state is part of a symbiotic relationship with all other major (liberal-capitalist) institutions in society. All activities and reform efforts of the welfare state are governed by the logic and requirements of capitalism. Marxists perceive all capitalist social institutions as functioning to promote conformity to capitalism. This perception is part of the fundamental Marxist belief that the government in a capitalist state represents the interests of the capitalist class. How the welfare state promotes conformity is described below.

According to Marxists the welfare state in a capitalist society operates (1) to reduce working-class antagonism to the existing social order, (2) to increase efficiency of the economic system, and (3) to underwrite many of the costs that the owners of capital incur. Marxists believe that many of our social welfare measures are actually tactical concessions made to labour to avert social disruption or other threats to the social order. The classical example is the social insurance reforms introduced by Bismarck in Germany in the late nineteenth century. These reforms were initiated to crush revolutionary socialism—a growing political force in Germany—and to win over German workers. Some Marxists view social welfare reforms as ransom for social harmony that the working class has squeezed out of the government, while other Marxists believe they are given freely by government but with an ulterior motive—co-optation of the working class. In either case, the effect is to cool out any drastic social reform efforts that would challenge capitalism.

Marxist analysis argues that the capitalist welfare state acts as a corrective for the inherent inefficiency of capitalism. Left on its own the capitalist system of production tends towards regular cycles of depressions and recessions, overproduction, underconsumption, falling profits, and stagflation. The state has been forced to intervene to enable the capitalist system to overcome these recurrent tendencies towards economic crisis. The more advanced the economy, the more government intervention seems to be needed. Thus, the welfare state, in this analysis, is largely the result of the functional needs of capitalism.

The welfare state also enhances the profitability of capitalist businesses by underwriting many of the costs associated with the capitalist system of production. Through public spending in the areas of education and health, the private sector has available to it an educated and healthy workforce without any direct costs to it. As well, our social insurance and other public financial assistance programs put money directly into the hands of consumers of the goods and services produced by the private sector, which keeps consumption at a higher level than it would be without social welfare programs. The welfare state also reduces costs to the private sector associated with accidents on the job (workers' compensation) and unsafe working conditions. A Canadian Labour Congress study found that between 20 and 30 per cent of fatalities from cancer can be traced to the effects of chemicals and other products used on the job. Of course, publicly financed health care picks up the tab for the medical costs associated with these fatalities (Finn, 1979, cited in Buchbinder, 1981).

Many social programs certainly subsidize private enterprise indirectly. James O'Connor (1973: 6) offers a more complete explanation of how the welfare state props up capitalism. He argues that the capitalist state must try to carry out two basic but apparently contradictory functions—accumulation and legitimation:

> The state must try to maintain or create the conditions in which profitable capital accumulation is possible. However, the state also must try to maintain or create the conditions for social harmony. A capitalist state that openly uses its coercive forces to help one class accumulate capital at the expense of other classes loses its legitimacy and hence undermines the basis of loyalty and support. But a state that ignores the necessity of assisting the process of capital accumulation risks drying up the source of its own power, the economy's surplus production capacity and the taxes drawn from this surplus. . . . the state must involve itself in the accumulation process, *but it must either mystify its policies by calling them something that they are not, or it must try to conceal them* (emphasis added).

O'Connor separates the economic (capital accumulation) functions of the state from the social welfare functions. The former aim at serving the needs of capital by helping to increase profit, by offering tax incentives, by encouraging labour mobility, and the like. However, a government seen to attend only to the interests of the minority but powerful capitalist class will not be accepted by the working class. To legitimize itself to the working class, therefore, the government must also appear to represent their interests. It does this, in part, by developing a welfare state that the government claims strives towards fairness, equity, and justice. Marxists believe, however, that the welfare state does not live up to these claims because, in fact, much of the government's social welfare activities actually enhance capital accumulation. Thus, the functions of capital accumulation and legitimation may appear to be contradictory, but Marxists would argue that experience has shown they are mutually reinforcing and favour the capitalists.

Marxist critics have no difficulty citing evidence to substantiate their claim that the welfare state is the same as any other liberal capitalist social institution in that it functions in such a manner to protect dominant class interests. Galper (1975) provides an insightful analysis of how social welfare programs support and nurture liberal capitalism. Most public financial assistance programs support the labour market by making people's eligibility for assistance dependent on their past experience and present relationship to the job market. Even programs such as daycare depend on the needs of the dominant class for labour, as daycare spaces tend to increase during periods of low unemployment and are cut back during recessions. Eligibility for many social welfare programs also depends on conforming to society's prevailing values. For example, public assistance regulations are often used to control the behaviour of recipients in such areas as parenting, sexual conduct, and market purchases. The fact that social welfare programs are often under-funded and provide minimal assistance gives the message to those who depend on such programs that people who cannot make it in the private market cannot really count on a public support system for much help. Also, they had better behave in a socially acceptable manner or they could easily lose the minimal benefits they do receive.

Even those government actions that have no obvious effect on increasing profits or ensuring a ready workforce for private enterprise are viewed skeptically by Marxists. For example, the factory legislation enacted during Karl Marx's time in England was often not enforced. A contemporary example of governments appearing to act in the best interests of all citizens but not interfering with capital accumulation of private enterprise is found in the fact that some very good anti-pollution legislation exists, but it is often not enforced when it is violated by large industries.

Mishra sums up the main features of the Marxist view of welfare:

1. True welfare (i.e., a social norm based on solidarity, co-operation, and human need) involves the regulation of working and living conditions and the distribution of society's resources based on human need.
2. As a socio-economic-political system, capitalism is the antithesis of true welfare.

3. True welfare can begin to be partially established in a capitalist society through the collective efforts of workers. Given the nature of capitalism, however, the chances for meaningful and lasting reform are slight.

4. In a class-divided society, the government and society largely attend to the interests of the dominant class. However, the universality of the state requires it to act (or appear to act) on behalf of all classes. Thus, the capitalist state is two-faced with respect to welfare. Social programs may be accepted in form but not realized in substance.

5. True welfare can be established fully as a social norm only after the means of production have been nationalized and the free-market/private property system abolished.

6. Social welfare in a capitalist society contributes to the efficiency and smooth working of the capitalist economy.

7. Social welfare in a capitalist society has an important social control function—to moderate class conflict and stabilize the social order.

8. Not surprisingly, the initiative for social welfare programs often comes from sectors of the dominant class.

9. Attempts to reform the capitalist system only lead to new economic and social contradictions. The welfare state has stabilizing as well as destabilizing effects on the capitalist social structure.

10. To avoid wrongful ideological conclusions, welfare activities in a capitalist society must be seen in conjunction with its other interventions and activities.

In light of these beliefs about welfare, orthodox Marxists reject the notion that the welfare state in a capitalist society holds any potential for socialism. They differ, therefore, from social democrats, who believe that the welfare state, the trade union movement, and social democratic parties all have potential for socialist transformation and should be used in this fashion. However, not all Marxists reject the welfare state out of hand as a vehicle for socialism. It depends on whether one has adopted a revolutionary or an evolutionary Marxist perspective.

SOCIAL WORK PRACTICE WITHIN THE MARXIST PARADIGM

The crucial question for the Marxist social worker is whether or not radical social and political change can come about through the social welfare institution in a capitalist society. The answer depends on whether one is a 'revolutionary' or an 'evolutionary' Marxist.[1] Although both types of Marxists favour the attainment of a socialist state, they differ on the means of such attainment. The evolutionary Marxist believes that a socialist state can be created by working within existing social institutions and organizations that have potential for socialism, such as the trade union movement and the welfare state. The revolutionary Marxist does not believe that any socialist potential is inherent in any capitalist social institution (except the trade unions, which comprise a working-class movement) and, therefore, seeks to create and develop counter-institutions and organizations to challenge the power of the state.

It is difficult to see how a revolutionary Marxist could even practise social work in a capitalist society. Since social work occurs within the welfare state, which is rejected as a base of operations by revolutionary Marxists, what or where would be the basis of attempts to stimulate, create, and develop socialist institutions and organizations? Revolutionary Marxists maintain that social work has political potential for socialism only if it would dispose of its social reform illusions and join in the 'revolutionary movement'. However, they do not say how this could be done or who would employ revolutionary social workers. Unless one is self-supporting or employed by a radical union, there do not appear to be many opportunities for revolutionary Marxists to practise social work in a capitalist state. Social work practice within the social welfare institution is seen by orthodox (revolutionary) Marxists as perpetuating an unworkable and undesirable system of capitalism because it is used as 'a mechanism for identifying and absorbing potential social revolt against the status quo' (Pritchard and Taylor, 1978: 5).

Evolutionary Marxists do not reject the capitalist state as a vehicle for socialist change:

> There is, indeed, a significant number of evolutionary Marxian socialists arguing
> . . . for the creation of a socialist system . . . through the relatively untainted and
> indigenous institutions of the working class; most notably the trade unions and the
> welfare state. (Pritchard and Taylor, 1978: 89–90)

In other words, evolutionary Marxists believe that the welfare state can be used as a stepping stone towards socialism. In this regard they appear to have much in common with those social democratic social workers who attempt to create forces in their social work practices that would contribute to the transformation of capitalism.

The differences between social democratic social work practice and evolutionary Marxist social work practice would be more of degree and emphasis than of kind. Both would attend to the needs of people who have been hurt by capitalism and both would attempt to restructure society along socialist lines. However, the evolutionary Marxist social workers would undoubtedly emphasize the latter task more than would their social democratic counterparts.

> The ultimate function of [Marxist] social work must be to raise community, and thus
> ultimately political, consciousness by exposing the assumed class nature of existing
> society . . . the greater the 'awareness' the greater the potential for conflict between
> working-class activists and 'authority'. (Pritchard and Taylor, 1978: 85)

To reiterate the Marxist position on social work practice, both revolutionary and evolutionary Marxists would attempt to raise socialist political consciousness. However, the revolutionary Marxist social worker, as part of this process, would attempt to undermine the acceptance of, and support for, the very institution of which his or her profession is a part—as Pritchard and Taylor (1978: 109) point out, 'a dangerous but not altogether ignoble role!' Evolutionary Marxist social workers, on the other hand, would join their radical social democratic counterparts and attempt to radicalize the power structure within the welfare state by means of increased participation, decentralization, and democratization and 'to extend and fortify the working-class and socialist incursions into capitalism' (Pritchard and Taylor, 1978: 107). Eventually, it is believed, such actions would lead to a position where the attainment of a fully socialist state becomes possible. Most of the recent Marxist or neo-Marxist social welfare and social work literature falls within the 'evolutionary' school, but does not ignore the revolutionary Marxist skepticism when analyzing the welfare state and social work as instruments for emancipation of oppressed groups.

CRITIQUE OF THE MARXIST PARADIGM

As a social theory Marxism is 'probably the best single theory available for a critical understanding of capitalist society. That is its major strength' (Mishra, 1984: 97). Part of this critical understanding is the way in which the Marxist view locates the welfare state within capitalism rather than seeing it in isolation. The view of the welfare state as a necessity for capitalism because it makes capitalism more efficient and productive while controlling the workforce and legitimizing capitalism is a major contribution of Marxism. However, as a theory of building a socialist state it 'remains sadly inadequate' (Mishra, 1984: 97). It has not come to terms with the entire historical experience of existing socialism. In fact, as Mishra points out, the actually existing socialism (i.e., Soviet Socialism) was for many years an embarrassment to Western Marxists. There is no working model of advanced socialism that Marxists can point to. There are, however, many social democratic countries that have been influenced by Marxist ideas. In fact, most Western European states are social democratic, but as mentioned above, Marxists do not consider social democracy to be a fully developed form of socialism. With respect to Marxist-governed nations, a number of interesting developments have occurred recently in Latin America, especially in Chile, Bolivia, Brazil, and Venezuela where left-leaning governments now hold political power. Each of these countries had been hurt by neo-conservative economic politicies associated with globalization and carried out by the World Bank, the International Monetary Fund, and the World Trade Organization. As a result, socialist governments have been elected in these countries and have implemented economic reforms contrary to those advocated and imposed by global economic leaders.

The classical Marxist view that capitalist societies comprise two monolithic classes and that all conflict in society runs along class lines has been criticized on the basis of being incompatible with the realities of contemporary societies (George and Wilding, 1994; Mishra, 1984; O'Connor, 1973). The working class is divided along white collar and blue collar, private and public sector, rural and urban workers, skilled and unskilled workers, managerial and professional status, and so on. And it is very questionable whether all conflicts in society are based on class or capitalist oppression. For example, is the enemy of oppressed women capitalism or patriarchy? Are all racial conflicts or religious conflicts actually class conflicts? It should be noted here, however, that since at least the late 1970s neo-Marxist analyses of society and social welfare have incorporated gender and race dimensions. Both Ferguson et al. (2002) and O'Brien and Penna (1998), for example, consider how other world views, such as feminism, anti-racism, and post-modernism, have supplemented Marxism and reduced the charge against it of being a totalizing and Eurocentric grand narrative. There have also been recent attempts (e.g., Ferguson et al., 2002; Mullaly, 2002) to use Marxist theory to analyze and explain oppression. And there has long been an alternative Marxist tradition to that of early Marxism, which emphasized structural determinism to the exclusion of the role of human agency in the 'making of history'.

The traditional Marxist claim—that the state is the representative of the capitalist class and that all issues dealt with by the state are directly or indirectly relevant to the stability and reproduction of the capitalist system—is doubtful. As George and Wilding (1985) point out, a group of policy issues, including abortion, adoption, divorce, capital punishment, and drug addiction, are mainly moral in nature and have nothing to do with the survival of capitalism. These authors present other considerations that have to be accounted for when assessing the autonomy of the state to act against the interests of the capitalist class:

- the political ideology of the government (a social democratic government is more likely to pursue anti-capitalist policies than a conservative government);
- the nature of public opinion (public opinion, such as the public's wish for anti-pollution legislation, will often set limits on pro-capitalist policies);
- the power of the working class (when the working class is well organized, governments have to take notice of the demands of trade unions).

With respect to its view of the welfare state, Marxism is in the unenviable position of trying to balance both sides of a contradiction. 'Social welfare may help shore up capitalism, materially and ideologically, but it also represents a gain for the working class in its struggle against exploitation' (Mishra, 1984: 81). This is the classical dilemma for Marxists. During good times Marxists have tended to focus on the broader political implications of the welfare state, often neglecting or denigrating its benefits to individuals and families. However, during periods of attack on the welfare state from the right, Marxists become its staunchest champions. 'In this sense, Marxism represents a paradoxical theory of emancipation' (O'Brien and Penna, 1998: 74).

Table 6.2 shows that Marxism and social work ideology share many of the same values and ideals. It will be recalled from the previous chapter that there was also a high degree of compatibility between social democratic and social work ideologies. Because the social democrats and the Marxists both want the same thing—a socialist state—they naturally share many of the same primary values. There is much consistency among social democracy, Marxism, and social work in terms of their primary values. Each has egalitarianism as a central value and both social democracy and social work have humanitarianism as an explicit central value while Marxism has it as an implicit central value (i.e., Marxism seeks to abolish capitalism for humanitarian reasons). The major difference among the three sets of belief systems is that whereas social democracy and social work perceive the welfare state to be a stepping stone towards a better society, Marxists tend to perceive it as a mechanism that props up capitalism, although they concede that it has, in part, come about through the efforts of the working class.

Before dismissing Marxism as a possible course of action for social work, we should be cognizant of the contributions it has already made through such earlier writings as Ian Gough's *The Political Economy of the Welfare State* (1979), the Macmillan series of *Critical Texts in Social Work and the Welfare State* edited by Peter Leonard in the late 1970s and early 1980s, Peter Leonard and Paul Corrigan's *Social Work Practice under Capitalism* (1978), Bailey and Brake's *Radical Social Work* (1975), two American books—Piven and Cloward's *Regulating the Poor: The Public Functions of Welfare* (1972) and Jeffrey Galper's *The Politics of Social Services* (1975), a Canadian book by Steven Wineman, *The Politics of Social Services* (1984), and, from Australia, Harold Throssel's *Radical Essays in Social Work* (1975). As Ferguson et al. (2002) point out, these books represented an important break from the tradition of social administration (as an approach to social policy) and its essential empirical assumption that all we needed to do to combat social problems was to obtain more and better services. In short, they broke with the liberal or psychosocial approaches of social work. George and Wilding (1994) contend that Marxism remains the most insightful and satisfactory model in explaining the development of the welfare state. In assessing the potential of Marxism for social work today, we should also be cognizant that many contemporary writers (I include myself along with Jim Ife, 1997; Peter Leonard, 1997; Ferguson et al., 2002) are attempting to reconstruct, reformulate, and revitalize Marxist theory informed by feminist, anti-racist, postmodern, and other critiques. We and many, many others believe that a Marxist view of the dynamics of advanced capitalism, class, the state, culture, alienation, and oppression can help us make sense out of a range of current social welfare and social work issues and debates. But unlike two or three decades ago, we do not believe that Marxism by itself holds the key to social transformation and emancipatory forms of social work practice.

CONCLUSION

This chapter presented an overview of Marxism as one of two prominent schools of socialism (the other being social democracy). An attempt was made to establish the historical and social context within which Marx lived and wrote and to extend some of his ideas and analyses about such things as social welfare, capitalism, oppression, and social problems to today's realities. An attempt was made to dispel some of the negative myths and stereotypes held by many in North America about Karl Marx and Marxism thought. The chapter examined Marxist beliefs about human nature, the nature of society, the role

TABLE 6.2 OVERVIEW OF MARXIST AND SOCIAL WORK IDEALS

	Marxism	*Social Work*
Social Beliefs	Liberty Collectivism Equality	Humanitarianism (humanism) Community Equality

Economic Beliefs	Public ownership of
	   means of production
	Industrial democracy
	Distribution of resources
	   according to need
	Planned economy
		Government intervention
		Social priorities dominate
		   economic decisions
		Equitable distribution of
		   society's resources

Political Beliefs	Government planning
	Participatory democracy
	Parliamentary system of
	   government
	Transformation of capitalism
	   by class conflict
		Participatory democracy in
		   both governmental and
		   non-governmental areas

View of Social Welfare	Welfare capitalism props
	   up capitalism but also
	   represents the fruits of
	   working-class efforts
	Ideal = social welfare
	   state or structural model
		An instrument to promote
		   equality, solidarity, and
		   community
		Ideal = structural model

Nature of Social Work Practice	Revolutionary Marxists see
	   no social change role for
	   social workers in capitalist
	   society
	Evolutionary Marxists'
	   practice of social work is
	   similar to that of Social
	   Democrats, but emphasizes
	   'class conflict' more
		Treat people with respect
		Enhance dignity and integrity
		Facilitate self-determination
		   and self-realization
		Accept differences
		Advocate and promote social
		   justice

of the state, the meaning of social justice, and social change. It also looked at Marxist ideology and how Marxists would view and treat social problems, and it described the nature and role of social work in accordance with the Marxist paradigm. As well, it compared Marxist ideals with those of progressive social work and concluded that there was much more convergence between the two than exists between progressive social work and either neo-conservative or liberal ideals. It also concluded that, since both are socialist paradigms, there is much in common between social democracy and Marxism. One of the major areas in which they differ is the means to transform capitalism to a socialist society. A critique of the Marxist paradigm was also outlined.

CRITICAL QUESTIONS

1. Which approach do you believe that socialism, in general, and social work, in particular, should adopt in pursuing the transformation of capitalist society to one of socialism—evolution or revolution? Why?
2. Marx believed that capitalism contained internal contradictions that would eventually lead to its demise. Can you think what some of these contradictions might be?
3. The United States is probably the only Western democracy without a socialist political party. Why do you think this is?
4. An idea inspired by Marxism to help eliminate or reduce intergenerational inequality and families building up huge fortunes is to do away with inheritance. What do you think of this idea?
5. A few key Marxist concepts or ideas are 'alienation', 'internalization of a socially constructed identity', 'social production and reproduction', and 'the control of society not by an army or police, but by the ideas of the ruling class'. What do these ideas mean and how are they related to social problems?

Feminist, Anti-Racist, and Postmodern Critiques

How wrong it is for a woman to expect the man to build the world she wants, rather than to create it herself.

—Anaïs Nin (1903–77)

The overall impact of postmodernism is that many other groups now share with black folks a sense of deep alienation, despair, uncertainty, loss of sense of grounding even if it is not informed by shared circumstance.

—bell hooks

INTRODUCTION

In the previous four chapters, four paradigms were presented—two that support capitalism and two that seek its transformation to some form of socialist or collectivist society. Although these paradigms were presented as different from one another, some similarities and overlaps were also indicated. These four paradigms and their respective ideological bases were the major world views for much of the nineteenth and twentieth centuries, and they have formed the basis for most social theory and social work theory and practice. There have been other perspectives, such as ultra-right-wing ideologies of fascism and Nazism and ultra-left-wing ideologies of anarchism and communism. However, these latter perspectives and/or movements have not been as long-standing or as popular in Western democracies and, therefore, are not discussed here.

Over the past two decades or so, two significant developments have brought the relevance of paradigms or political ideologies as world views into question. First, as noted in Chapter 1, capitalism has been transformed from its rigid and centralized post-war form to a flexible (for the capitalists at least) and global form, thus making much of the earlier analysis of capitalism irrelevant. We have witnessed the declining power of nation-states to intervene in their own economies; the spread of terrorism; increasing disparities between rich and poor; the fall of many state socialist regimes; national trade union movements in disarray; the virtual collapse of leftist politics in the developed nations; and continuing oppression on the basis of class, gender, culture, sexuality, age, race, and so on. Given these and other events, many people today are skeptical about the relevance of the dominant paradigms in the face of the rapid social, economic, political, and cultural changes that have occurred since the early 1970s.

The second development that has questioned the legitimacy of paradigms and ideological foundations has been the emergence of postmodern and post-structural thought. They have challenged many of the theories, universalistic ideals, and discourses that underpin the traditional paradigms. For example, discourse theorists reject any claim that ideologies or paradigms have core characteristics that give them a 'true' and independent meaning 'outside' of the interpretation given by their specific discourses (Rorty, 1999; Bastow and Martin, 2003). It has been suggested that the era of grand theoretical perspectives (such as social paradigms) is over. Rodger (2000: 16) argues that 'the key nineteenth- and twentieth-century political ideologies such as Marxism, Socialism, Communism, Liberalism, and even Feminism, are no longer regarded as offering convincing understandings of social and political life in the twenty-first century.' Some of the reasons for the current skepticism with respect to traditional ideological analysis are explored below. As well, a summary of some postmodern and post-structural critiques of paradigms, political ideologies, and the modern welfare state are presented.

Certainly, legitimate and substantive criticisms were made of the dominant paradigms and ideological frameworks from other perspectives prior to the more recent postmodern critiques. These criticisms have come from a number of sources, but the major critiques have emanated from various forms of feminism and from anti-racist writers. Feminists have criticized the paradigms for not addressing women's issues, thus rendering women invisible, while those writing from a critical race perspective have faulted them for being colour-blind. An overview of the feminist and anti-racist critiques of the dominant paradigms is presented in this chapter, followed by the postmodern/ post-structural critique. The examination here is not exhaustive. For example, a couple of emerging critiques are the political ecology or 'green' critique (e.g., Coates, 2003) and the Aboriginal critique (e.g., Hart, 2002).

The purpose of this chapter is not to discard ideological analysis as a tool for understanding social phenomena or to reject the analytical value of the paradigms outlined in the previous chapters, in particular social democracy and Marxism. Rather, feminism, anti-racism, postmodernism, and other critiques can help to correct, inform, and revitalize the paradigms and political ideologies, which in turn will contribute to our understandings of social theory, social welfare formations, and social work practice.

FEMINIST CRITIQUE

Although postmodernism provides a powerful critique of the traditional paradigms, many contemporary scholars concur with Knuttila (2002: 224), who says that:

> The most important and systematic critique of the analytical and explanatory capacities of the older theoretical approaches has come from scholars and activists

associated with various schools of feminist thought. As new questions were posed concerning the nature and role of the state, especially as it relates to sex and gender relations, the existing approaches were found wanting in two related, but different aspects.

These two aspects are: (1) that there is overwhelming evidence that the state plays a central role in the domination of men and the subordination of women; and (2) this evidence has led to demands that the existing ideological and theoretical frameworks be revised to account for the role of the state in maintaining dominant patriarchal and heterosexual relations that characterize Western society. This section looks at the analysis of gender inequality and the critiques that have been made of the traditional paradigms for being gender-blind.

Although there are different forms or groupings of feminism, the common thesis is that the relationship between the sexes is one of inequality or oppression. All schools of feminism attempt to identify the causes of gender inequality and to remedy it, but they differ in terms of their beliefs as to which agency produces and reproduces inequality (Macey, 2000). Feminist critiques are primarily concerned with two themes: (1) the ways in which the gendered nature of social institutions and practices have been ignored and gender neutrality has been assumed in traditional social science literature; and (2) the ways in which issues of particular importance to women have been marginalized or excluded from the social welfare agenda (Woodward, 1997).

Feminists draw attention to the fact that women experience a different social world—including the welfare state—than men. Rice and Prince (2000: 182–3) present some of these differences in the Canadian context, which are very similar to those of other Anglo democracies.

- Women have the greatest responsibility for the family, including child care and elder care (i.e., women are 'cradle-to-the-grave' caregivers).
- Women are disproportionately the victims of male violence.
- Women are among the poorest groups in Canadian society.
- Women head over 80 per cent of single-parent families.
- Over half of Canadian women will be widows, whereas only 20 per cent of men will be widowers.
- Women constitute almost 60 per cent of the seniors population and 70 per cent of all persons aged 85 and over.
- Women still experience occupational segregation in many sectors of the labour force and receive lower earnings, benefits, and pensions.
- Women remain significantly under-represented in legislatures, cabinets, the courts, and in senior levels of public services and business corporations.
- There are gender inequalities with respect to access to social programs, benefit levels, rights, and redistributive outcomes.
- Women experience more adversely the results of cutbacks to social services.

The paradigms and political ideologies presented in Chapters 3–6 were, of course, all constructed by men and reflect the world as seen and experienced by men. This male construction includes the four welfare models as well. For example, although the four welfare models fall along the traditional left-to-right political ideological spectrum, they all feature a male breadwinner, a female bread-maker, and a dependent family. Giddens (1997: 75) states that 'welfare programmes have been aimed mainly at supporting male participation in the paid labour force, with a "second tier" of household programmes oriented towards families without a male breadwinner.' All four paradigms also assume that a clear separation exists between the private sphere of home, family, and the unpaid domestic work of women and the public sphere of paid work, the market, and the state (Boyd, 1997, cited in Rice and Prince, 2000). One of the key contributions of the feminist movement has been its recognition that 'the personal is political' (and vice versa), which has helped to break down the traditional treatment of separating the private individual or family from political influences. Another common assumption underpinning all four paradigms was the belief in the maintenance of the family as integral to society's stability. This belief formed part of what feminists call the ideology of 'familism' (Neysmith, 1991; Williams, 1989), which comprises a set of ideas that characterizes the '"normal" or "ideal" family form as one where the man was the main breadwinner and his wife's main contribution to the family was through her role as mother, carer and housewife, rather than as a wage-earner and who was therefore, along with her children, financially dependent upon her husband' (Williams, 1989: 6). Those families not conforming to this normal family model were thus viewed as somewhat deviant and potentially problematic.

Although all feminists may agree on the existence of gender inequalities, they are fundamentally divided on the causes of these inequalities and on the strategies for effecting social change. They also differ on the nature and extent of women's subordination. It is possible to subdivide feminism into a large number of categories or schools. Williams (1989), for example, uses six categories. Here, three schools of feminism are outlined: liberal feminism, socialist feminism, and radical feminism. These groupings are consistent with the categorization that many other writers use (e.g., Armitage, 2003; George and Wilding, 1994; Knuttila and Kubik, 2000; Woodward, 1997).

It should be noted here that there is no school of 'conservative feminism' since the essence of feminism is to do something to rectify women's inequality. There are, of course, conservative women who advocate for a return to the days when women remained in the home as homemakers, abortion was illegal, and feminism did not exist (e.g., a Canadian group that calls itself 'REAL Women').

Liberal Feminism

'First-wave' feminism of the nineteenth and early twentieth centuries used the language of liberalism to demand formal equality (equal opportunities and equal civil rights) with men. This first wave focused on social issues, such as temperance, and on gaining the vote for women. Since the 1960s, 'second-wave' feminism has sought equality and civil rights, with the emphasis on reforming existing institutions. Williams (1989: 44–5) summarizes the essence of liberal feminism:

> The belief that society's treatment of women violates their rights to liberty, equality and justice, and in addition creates a waste of women's skills and abilities, is the basis of liberal feminism . . . . Consistent with liberal thought, the focus of liberal feminist activity is the state, which is seen as a neutral, disinterested arbiter or referee open to the influence of reason and political pressure. Inequality is the result of gender discrimination and gender-biased laws and social practices.

The liberal feminist remedy for gender inequality is to reform (not transform) social and political institutions. Biological differences between men and women are not seen by liberal feminists as a significant barrier to gender equality. 'Claims about women's biology determining their inequality have no place in liberal feminism, which rejects any influence of biology in favour of a view that women are conditioned and socialized into the roles they play' (Williams, 1989: 49). Liberal feminism denies the relevance of any differences between women and men and, with respect to women as the ones who bear children, then laws, policies, attitudes, and behaviours must be changed to accommodate this. Liberal feminists argue that the state can minimize any role that biology may play in interfering with women's freedom to compete and use their skills and abilities by guaranteeing rights to contraception and abortion, maternity leave, and publicly funded daycare (Williams, 1989).

Other feminists have levelled a number of criticisms against liberal feminism (see George and Wilding, 1994; Williams, 1989). (1) Liberal feminism is said to be naive and simplistic because it overlooks the capitalist and patriarchal nature of the state. (2) Liberal feminism fails to see that the status quo, which disadvantages women, actually benefits men, who are unlikely to surrender their privileged position without resistance. (3) Historically, liberal feminists have restricted their analysis of gender inequality to the public sphere, and by simply pursuing the extension of opportunities in the public sphere they overlook a crucial part of women's lives and ignore the truism that the personal is political. Williams (1989) points out that contemporary liberal feminism has drawn on work (social learning theories) done on the socialization of girls within the private sphere of the home. (4) Liberal feminists seek equality of opportunity in male terms, which fails to account for current gender differences and other structural forces. Women are simply not in a position to compete equally with men because of the still prevailing domestic division of labour and patriarchal assumptions about their caring role. (5) Liberal feminist strategies are criticized as primarily benefiting white, highly educated middle-class women and having little relevance to poor women and/or women of colour. (6) Both socialist and radical feminist groups point out that although women for the past 200 years have been proving the irrationality of women's inequalities in the face of liberal ideas of justice, equality, and liberty, very little has been achieved by the law or state reforms only.

Although liberal feminism is criticized by other feminist schools, its strongest point might be its commitment to action for social justice now. It has brought about some reforms in the public sphere such as the workplace, education, wages, pensions, civil and social rights, and so on. It has developed various strategies for social change that have been adopted by other feminist groups (although for different reasons). However, while such reforms are absolutely necessary to improve women's lives in the here and now, they are not sufficient in themselves. They have helped ameliorate the position of (some) women in society, but as with liberalism, in general, liberal feminism has done very little to address such structural forces as classism, patriarchy, and racism in society—forces that relegate many women to a second-class citizenship. 'Reforms and laws cannot undermine the institutionalization of women's oppression within the very structures of the labour market, the family, education system and the welfare state' (Williams, 1989: 47). These shortcomings have resulted in many feminists looking elsewhere for analyses, theories, and strategies that address structural causes of gender inequality.

Socialist Feminism

Socialist feminism covers a range of political strategies and actions and interpretations, but in general it is influenced by social democratic and Marxist thought, as well as by liberal feminist ideas. Socialist feminism attempts to locate an analysis of women in society within a socialist or Marxist analysis of capitalism. However, it does not consider women's oppression to be a simple subset of the overall oppression of the working class. Socialist feminism accepts Marxism for its powerful tools of historical and materialist analysis of the relationship of the working class to the capitalist mode of production, and for its view of the role of the working class in transforming society (Hartmann, 1986; Williams, 1989). However, Williams (1989: 57) articulates the caution socialist feminists have about classical Marxism:

> socialist feminists have also been critical of classical Marxism for ignoring the signifi-
> cance of the specific oppression of women, and of the practices of socialist groups
> and organizations representing the working class, especially the trade unions, for
> seeing the struggles by women against aspects of oppression as irrelevant or 'dividing
> the working class.'

Heidi Hartmann (1986: 2–3) argues that socialism and feminism need each other in the struggle to overcome both class and gender oppression in capitalist society. She says of Marxism, 'While Marxist analysis provides essential insight into the laws of historical development, and those of capital, in particular, the categories of Marxism are sex blind.' Of feminism, she says, 'Feminist analysis by itself is inadequate because it has been blind to history and insufficiently materialist.' Her proposed solution is a 'more progressive union of Marxism and feminism' that would simultaneously analyze the structures and dynamics of both capitalism and patriarchy. Williams (1989: 57) summarizes this socialist feminist position:

> The concern of contemporary socialist feminists then, has been, at a theoretical level, to present a materialist analysis of women's oppression under capitalism which does not reduce all forms of women's oppression to the requirements of capitalism but does attempt to take account of the concept of patriarchy, and at a practical level, to demonstrate the importance, indeed the centrality of women's issues and struggles to the struggle for socialism: *there can be no socialism without women's liberation, and no women's liberation without socialism* (emphasis added).

There is much contentious debate within socialist feminism about the forms of practice it ought to take. However, with respect to theoretical development, Williams (1989) summarizes a few areas of general agreement: the importance of understanding that the differences between men and women's behaviour are socially constructed and not biologically caused; the necessity of recognizing the personal as political; and the significance, for solidarity, in recognizing the different as well as shared experiences of oppression of women of different classes, races, ages, sexual orientation, and so on. With respect to forms of practice, she notes the following types of advances made by socialist feminists:

- In relation to welfare strategies, many socialist feminists have put their energies into women's groups and organizations fighting for improved health, housing, income security, child and elder care, education, and employment services.
- Many socialist feminists have joined social democratic political parties and have campaigned for women's issues to become part of their socialist party's platform.
- Many socialist feminists have been elected to work within trade unions, especially within the public sector. For example, in Canada, Shirley Carr, who became the first female president of the Canadian Labour Congress (and the first woman in the world to head a national labour organization), championed legislation to address women's equality, maternity leave, child care, sexual harassment, and concerns about health and safety in the workplace.

A major focus of socialist feminism is the interrelationship between capitalism and patriarchy. This has involved an analysis of women's 'dual role'—(1) their *productive* activities in the public sphere as a reserve army of labour, drawn into the labour market when the labour supply is short and eased out of the labour market when there is an oversupply of workers; (2) their involvement in the *reproduction* not only of the labour force, but also of social relations through their role in the private sphere (i.e., in the home) as they produce the next generation of workers and care for the current generation (Rowbotham, 1989, cited in Woodward, 1997). Williams (1989: 68) argues that socialist feminism is the most fruitful of the feminist approaches because it draws attention to women's dual role and demands 'the reorganization of the sexual division of labour and an end to the divisions between paid and unpaid work'. In terms of the welfare state, this means changing the concept of welfare so that it no longer underpins female dependency or the sexual division of labour, where caring is seen as women's natural work, and it no longer privileges the male breadwinner/head of household model of the family. Socialist feminists do disagree as to the greatest source of women's oppression—capitalism or patriarchy or the interface of the two—and they also differ in their analyses as to the root of patriarchy (see Williams, 1989: 57–69, for a discussion of these important questions).

Radical Feminism

One group—radical feminists—believes that neither the liberal feminist nor the socialist feminist approach is radical enough. Liberals focus on reforming social institutions and practices by changing sexist values, norms, and ideas; socialists argue for a fusion of class analysis with an understanding of female oppression in a patriarchal social system. Radicals, however, believe that they both miss the fundamental form of oppression experienced by women—that women as a class or group are oppressed by men as a class or group (Robbins et al., 1998). The term 'sexual politics' (Millett, 1970) has been used to describe unequal power relations between men and women, and patriarchy is seen as the primary source of women's oppression both personally and institutionally.

Patriarchy has been defined in two ways by radical feminists—male power and control over women's sexuality and male power and control over women's biology in terms of their reproductive capacity (Williams, 1989). In regard to sexuality, radical feminism holds that throughout history men have constructed and controlled women's bodies to serve their own needs and interests. The possibility of male violence serves as the perpetuation of male domination over women by force. This analysis has been behind feminist campaigns against male violence (e.g., take back the night marches), war, nuclear proliferation, pornography, and incest (Williams, 1989). The second radical definition of patriarchy, which sees it as the fundamental class oppression giving rise to other forms of oppression, was first discussed in Shulamith Firestone's powerful treatise, *The Dialectic of Sex: The Case for Feminist Revolution* (1970). For Firestone the basis of class is biological, and one class (males) has dominated the other class (females) throughout history largely because of women's biological role in species reproduction. Because of the biological processes of childbirth, women are forced to depend on men for long periods of time, which has resulted in the emergence of larger patterns of male domination and female subordination. Thus the abolition of patriarchy can only be possible by relieving women of their biological reproductive role by every means possible—family planning, abortion, 24-hour child-care centres, artificial reproduction (Firestone, 1984).

Radical feminism has made important contributions to feminist theory and political action. It has drawn attention to problems that other feminist perspectives do not emphasize, for example, rape, domestic violence, sexuality, and reproductive technologies. It emphasizes 'the personal is political' analysis as a guiding principle more so than other feminisms. Some radical feminist positions developed out of what is called the 'woman-centred' stage of second-wave feminism (Lerner, 1979, cited in Woodward, 1997). This position gave priority to women's experience as the focus of all study and the source of social and cultural values. For example, a critique of motherhood was a major concern of some radical feminists in the 1970s (e.g., Rich, 1977) who, on the one hand, celebrated motherhood as an essentially female experience, but, on the other hand, critiqued it as a social institution under patriarchy that distorted women's experiences. In the 1980s and 1990s radical feminists extended Millet's concept of patriarchy as sexual politics to include heterosexism as a source of female oppression (Rich, 1980; Jeffreys, 1986, cited in Woodward, 1997). The women-centred approaches of radical feminists have been instrumental in establishing separate social services provided by women for women, such as women's refuges, and in challenging the sexism of the medical profession by establishing 'well-women' clinics and health centres where women can be treated by a female doctor and where the emphasis is on the provision of information to women about their own bodies. Radical feminism has also been important in terms of establishing women-only counselling services for victims of male violence, and these services, in turn, have been important for exposing the patriarchal assumptions held by the police and the courts about female sexuality (Williams, 1989).

Radical feminists (along with socialist feminists) have also critiqued the internal culture of social welfare organizations for its patriarchal nature. Wendy Weeks (1992), a leading feminist social welfare writer in Australia, points out that most public and private welfare organizations have been structured by men and, therefore, tend to be characterized by such male characteristics as: male dominance rather than gender equality; competition and independence rather than co-operation and interdependence; hierarchical rather than flat structures; rational control with an emphasis on technology; and a devaluing of subjective experience (cited in Armitage, 2003). Alternative social services organizations established by feminist social service workers are characterized in varying degrees by a democratic organizational culture:

- participation of workers and service users in decision-making;
- a shared or agreed-upon model of leadership;
- the accommodation of caring responsibilities within the organization's operations and employment policies;
- consensus and discussion as the basis of decision-making rather than decisions being made by those in senior positions within the organization or by majority vote;
- a respectful workplace free from harassment.

The incorporation of these feminist concepts and values has not been easy since they fly in the face of the patriarchal nature and structure of social services organizations in Western society. However, as Armitage (2003: 183) states, 'the goal of a more equal and democratic workplace for workers and service users represents an important challenge. If human service organizations cannot produce a more equal and equitable environment in their own sphere of activity, how can they expect to introduce these values to the wider community?'

In spite of its contributions to social theory, political action, and to the social welfare state and social work practice, radical feminism has been the subject of wide-ranging criticism. A major criticism is that by defining patriarchy in terms of biological differences, radical feminism may have distanced itself from the economic reductionism of Marxism (i.e., explaining women's oppression in terms of the needs and operation of capitalism). Rather, it has fallen victim to biological reductionism, which traps women back into their biology. In other words, radical feminism tends to reduce the complex issue of women's inequality to a simple single explanation—biology. Radical feminism has been accused of creating a 'false universalism' by assuming a commonality of interests and positions among women that is at odds regarding differences of interest among them with respect to race, culture, class, and so on. The other 'false universalism' is derived from the radical feminist definition of patriarchy whereby all men are considered to be oppressors. Finally, radical feminism has been criticized for being naive or idealist in the extreme because it rests on the hope of social change through the encouragement of woman-centred values and practices to counter and overcome society's dominant male values and practices.

Conclusion

Feminism exposes the glaring omission inherent in all four dominant paradigms—that of a gender analysis of women's inequality in society and of how the state contributes to women's oppression. Included in this analysis is the role that the welfare state has played in this oppression. Feminism challenges the assumed gender neutrality of the paradigms and of the post-war welfare state. 'There can be no doubt, then, that the state in capitalist society is vitally important to the construction, production, and reproduction of sex and gender relations' (Knuttila and Kubick, 2000: 193). The three feminist perspectives presented above all focus on this common concern, but offer different analyses and explanations of women's subordination in society and different strategies for correcting it. In addition to its gender analysis, feminism has developed social theory that includes social and political practice. 'It is through campaigns that feminists have put women and women's concerns on the public agenda, and the explanations which feminists offer for what their research and struggles reveal derive from listening to women's voices' (Woodward, 1997: 92).

In recent years, feminist theory, along with other modernist social theories, has been criticized on a number of fronts. People of colour, in particular black feminists, have referred to the above feminist perspectives as 'white feminism' because of their omission of race and racism in their analyses of women's oppression. Postmodernism, in general, and postmodern feminists, in particular, have criticized feminism as being a historically and theoretically modernist movement based on such universalisms as a unitary image of woman and for espousing grand narratives in their theory-building. The next section looks at the anti-racist critique of the dominant paradigms, which includes a critique of 'white feminism' and the modernist welfare state.

ANTI-RACIST CRITIQUE

Just as white feminists critiqued the traditional paradigms and older social theory for being male-dominated, people of colour have criticized the paradigms and theories for their failure to account for racism. Because the ideologies of conservatism, liberalism, socialism, and Marxism were developed largely in Europe during a period of history when the population of Europe was mainly white and the dominant group (including those who developed these ideologies) consisted mainly of white males, it is little wonder that the ideologies reflect gender and race biases. And, just as white feminists criticized these ideologies and their derived social theories for being gender-exclusive, so did women of colour criticize both the ideologies and white feminism for being colour-blind. Although questions about race had bothered feminists through the 1970s, it was not until the 1980s that women of colour became an organized force and introduced a new 'radical women of colour' perspective into the feminist public culture (Seidman, 1998). They criticized the dominant political paradigms for reflecting the interest of white, bourgeois males and they (particularly black women, Latina women, and Aboriginal women) criticized the women's movement for focusing on the experiences, values, and interests of white, middle-class women (e.g., Lorde, 1984; Davis, 1981; Moraga and Anzaldua 1983).

Defining Race and Racism

From the time of Enlightenment and with the popularization of Darwinian theories of evolution, race became associated with visible biological differences. Physiological characteristics, such as skin colour, facial features, and brain size, were used to identify and/or categorize different 'races', and with the development of social Darwinian ideas these characteristics were often used to rank the peoples of the world in an assumed order of superiority and inferiority (Penkith and Ali, 1997). This kind of thinking led to the implementation of eugenicist immigration policies in such countries as the United States and Sweden, which discriminated against certain social groupings such as Jews and people of colour. Today, we know from the science of genetics that comparative studies of various population groups have shown that there is much more statistically significant genetic diversity within these groups than among them. 'To geneticists, the physiological differences associated with "race" have no more significance than hair or eye colour' (Penketh and Ali, 1997: 103).

Because the use of race as a way of categorizing people lacks scientific validity and any evidence from biology, then it is a social construction, a way of making sense of the world by dividing people into assumed biological categories (Thompson, 1998). If there is no scientific basis for the concept of race, why does the term continue to be used? Husband (1987: iii) answers this by writing that 'one reason for its continuing vitality is that, beneath its apparent simple reduction of complex individuals and societies to self-evidently basic units there lies a highly complex body of emotive ideas.' These ideas constitute 'racism'.

Elsewhere (Mullaly, 2002), I have described racism as the belief that human abilities are determined by race, that one race is superior to all others and, therefore, has the right to dominate all other races. The assumption that racial classifications can be made on the basis of biological differences underpins racism. Skin colour, for example, may be considered to be associated with other biological differences such as intelligence. 'Essentialism is part of racism in that there is a belief that everyone belonging to a particular racial group possesses the same characteristics' (Thompson, 1997). A partial answer to the question posed above—that if there is no scientific validation of racial categorization, why do we still have such categorizations?—is that such classifications carry out certain ideological political functions for the racially dominant group (i.e., white people). Racial categories are not value-neutral, but constitute a hierarchy of racial groups in which white people as a group are dominant because of their socially constructed superiority (Ahmad, 1990).

Effects of Racism

The assumption of racial superiority has had substantial negative effects on people of colour within most European societies and the countries they colonized. People of colour are subject to disparaging stereotypes and are oppressed at the personal, cultural, and structural or institutional levels of society (Mullaly, 2002). The effects of racism at the personal level include the imposition of an identity by the racially dominant group that is often stereotyped, essentialist, and inferior. On the surface, there appears to be no escape from this negative identity, as people of colour are reminded of it every day in their interactions with the dominant white group. There is also a tendency on the part of non-white groups to accept and internalize this socially constructed and imposed identity and to act in ways that reinforce the stereotypical identity in the eyes of white people.

In today's society there are many cultures but one dominant culture, which reflects the norms, values, shared patterns of thinking, and world views of the dominant group (i.e., a white, male, bourgeois group). All other cultures are viewed as inferior and, therefore, the solution to the problems members of these groups experience could be resolved if they would assimilate into the dominant culture. And, of course, it is rather difficult for a person of colour to assimilate into the racially dominant white group (see Mullaly, 2002, for more discussion on oppression and anti-oppressive social work practice at the cultural level). At the institutional or structural level, Sidanius and Pratto (1999) present an impressive amount of empirical data and powerful evidence showing that racism can be found in all the major areas of an individual's life in European, Australasian, and North American societies. The major areas where racial discrimination occurs on a daily basis include employment, financial opportunities, housing and retail markets, education, health care, and the criminal justice system. Elsewhere (Mullaly, 2002), I summarize the effects of racism experienced by Aboriginal people in Canada and make the argument that racism in particular and oppression in general at the structural level constitutes a form of *socially sanctioned violence*. This 'structural violence' leads to a slow, agonizing, unpunished, and premature death for countless numbers of subordinate people all over the world on a daily basis. In the next chapter I elaborate on this concept of 'structural violence'.

There are three major responses to race and racism in the literature: assimilation, multiculturalism, and anti-racism (or the politics of difference). The first two are based on an assumed notion that the dominant white culture is superior to all others. Assimilationism would have all other cultures and races reject their own cultures and accept and integrate, as much as possible, into the dominant culture. Multiculturalism accepts and may even celebrate the idea of a plurality of cultures in today's society, but there is still a superior culture to which all others must defer. This is reflected, for example, in the Canadian Constitution, where the languages of the two 'founding' peoples—French and English—are specifically recognized as 'official' while 'the preservation and enhancement of the multicultural heritage of Canadians' is also claimed as a societal value (Constitution Act, 1982, sections 16, 27). Similarly, the anti-racist approach accepts that there are many different cultures in society, but it differs from multiculturalism in that the fundamental belief is that there are no superior and inferior cultures. Cultural differences should be celebrated and cultural equality must be pursued. These approaches are discussed in more detail and in the context of structural social work practice in Chapter 11.

Black Feminist Critique

The criticisms of white-dominated feminism from black feminists in the 1980s were important for the development of feminist theory, feminist strategy, and therefore, for the feminist critique of the welfare state. Williams (1989: 69) notes that '[a] significant amount has been written articulating the experiences of Black women, how their relationship to work, the family, men, sexuality, reproduction, the state, including the welfare state, is structured by "*race*" as well as by gender, and how this renders their experiences different from those of white women.' Women of colour argued that they not only suffered from oppression as women, but also as people of colour, and often as poor persons as well. The simultaneous experiences of black women with respect to sexism, racism, and classism not only compounded these oppressions but reconstituted them in specific ways. For example, white feminists who enjoy the privileges of 'whiteness' and bourgeois social standing could afford, economically and politically, to pursue a separatist agenda. Black women, however, cannot pursue a separatist agenda since they must forge bonds of solidarity with black men to fight racism and classism (Seidman, 1998).

Black feminists have criticized how the concept of patriarchy has been used in a number of ways.

- It emphasizes women being oppressed as women, which overlooks the differences of power between women, particularly the racism of some white women and the racism of the state along with its sexism.

- White women have greater access to society's power structure (e.g., to the courts) than do women of colour.
- The patriarchy of black men cannot be equated with that of white men. There is more solidarity between white men and white women than there is between white males and black males.
- The white feminist criticism of the family as a site of oppression is not as appropriate to the experience of blacks, where the black family has been the site of resistance in struggles against slavery and current struggles such as against police brutality, discrimination in housing and employment, and so on (Williams, 1989).

Black feminists did not wish to subvert the core status of the category of women, but sought to make it more inclusive by expanding the range of legitimate identities that women could claim (Seidman, 1998). Instead of a unitary female identity, black feminism led to a diversity of feminist standpoints—each reflecting a particular class and racial positioning of women. Feminist women of colour sought to expand the category of 'women' to include them by viewing gender, class, and race as interconnected.

Conclusion

Just as feminism exposed the glaring omission in the dominant paradigms of a gender analysis of women's inequality and the ways that the state contributed to women's oppression, so, too, did people of colour (particularly black feminists) expose the omission of a race analysis of inequality along lines of race and how the state contributed to the oppression of people of colour. Furthermore, while black feminism criticized mainstream feminism for being colour-blind, the 1980s lesbian feminism also criticized mainstream feminism for its heterosexual leanings and argued against the dichotomous nature of female and male sexual values and for expanded sexual expression and choice for women. By the mid-1980s a multitude of voices spoke about women's social differences. 'New feminist identities surfaced: women of colour, working class women, sadomasochistic lesbians, and postcolonial women' (Seidman, 1998: 263). They all criticized mainstream feminism for repressing women's differences and for imposing controls on women's bodies and behaviours.

> Mainstream feminism was criticized for functioning as a disciplining, normalizing force that reinforced dominant Eurocentric, middle class, White social norms. Drawing on the poststructural critique of essentialism and foundationalism, a new social and cultural force in feminist cultural politics was born: postmodern feminism. (Seidman, 1998: 264)

Postmodern feminism is, of course, part of the larger postmodern and post-structural critique of modernist thought, which includes the dominant paradigms, ideologies, and models of welfare. It is to this critique that we now turn.

POSTMODERN CRITIQUE

Postmodernism, Social Welfare, and Social Work

The application of postmodern ideas to institutions such as the welfare state, which define modernism, can cause confusion. The position taken here is similar to that of other writers, including Ben Agger (1992, 1998), Peter Leonard (1997), and John Rodger (2000). In this view, postmodernism is not a fully developed or coherent or singular theoretical perspective but a critique of modernity and modernist thought. This does not mean a total condemnation and rejection of modernism. Rather, postmodernism provides an essential ingredient to inform and revitalize progressive social thought such as social democracy, Marxism, feminism, and anti-racism. The modernist project of emancipation (i.e., to resist and overcome domination) is not over. It continues, as Leonard (1997: xiii) states, 'under changed historical conditions—economic, cultural, social—and with a newly reflective ability . . . to understand the contradictions of emancipatory projects of the past as well as that of the present.' A major purpose here, then, is to show how postmodernism can contribute to a reconstructed project of emancipation as it is still expressed within socialist, feminist, anti-racist, anti-oppressive, and other struggles against domination. In other words, although postmodernism does not replace modernist progressive thought, it supplements, corrects, informs, and revitalizes modernism.

Unfortunately, there has been a general reluctance among social work and social policy writers to engage with postmodernism. Carter (1998) has suggested that social policy is just about the last social science to take up the postmodern challenge. Commenting on the lack of postmodern material in social policy studies, John Rodger (2000:15) writes:

> Ideological concepts common in the lexicon of social policy analysis such as neo-liberalism, democratic socialism, welfare pluralism and collectivism all lack a referent to the wider social and cultural influences which are at work in determining the shape of a future welfare society. While students of social policy have become accustomed to making sense of the welfare state debate through the clash of neo-liberal and socialist politics, they have been slow to recognise that the debate has moved on from a polarised choice between state or market . . . .

Both Carter and Rodger call for social policy students to engage with the substantial postmodern literature that describes contemporary social change and sensitizes us to the social, economic, political, and, especially, cultural context within which social policies are being formulated for the new century. The nature of society and politics is changing and we need to engage with ideas that until recently have been unfamiliar to students of social policy and social work. Writers in Britain (e.g., Howe, 1994; Parton, 1994) and Australia (e.g., Pease and Fook, 1999) have taken up the postmodern challenge sooner than their North American counterparts. Notable exceptions in Canada are Adrienne

Chambon and Allan Irving (1994), Chambon, Irving, and Epstein (1999), and Peter Leonard (1994, 1995, 1997).

Surprisingly, many contemporary social welfare and social work writers openly reject postmodernism as having any potential for understanding social welfare formations or contributing to social work knowledge. Writing from Australia, Fitzpatrick (2002: 14) and Mendes (2003: 5) argue that postmodernism is relegated 'to sit on the sidelines of social conflicts, rather than promoting collective campaigns for social and economic justice'. Similarly, some British writers (e.g., Ferguson and Lavalette, 1999; Philo and Miller, 2000) have accused postmodernism of being in vogue, but 'increasingly [it is] recognized as contributing to a moral relativism and a stance of "ironic detachment" which is untenable in the face of the economic and ecological crisis facing humanity' (Ferguson et al., 2002: 15). The noted Canadian social welfare writer, Andrew Armitage (2003), claims that post-modernism is a recent form of socialism, which I am sure horrifies postmodernists, as one of their fundamental beliefs is the rejection of all grand narratives or totalizing ideo-logical schemes such as capitalism and socialism. Armitage says of postmodernism, 'The critique of welfare institutions by the postmodernists is searching but the conclusions tend to endorse an anarchy that would be a complete contradiction to the concept of a just and peaceful society' (p. 180). Colleen Lundy (2004: 43), in her book on structural social work practice, states that it 'remains to be seen the degree to which postmodernism can contribute to the emancipatory project and offer a "solution" to social work practice and social problems in our society. In my view, broad-based social change and social justice are more likely to occur through a collective struggle . . . . A focus on subjectivities while retreating from the broader structures will neither serve our profession nor the people we serve.'

Although each of the above writers acknowledges some of the legitimate criticisms that postmodernism has made of the traditional social policy and social work approaches to social change, they all dismiss postmodernism without showing how they would address these criticisms. At the very least, the positions of these writers appear to be based on a lack of awareness that there is more than one form of postmodernism, including a critical postmodernism where the intention is not to reject all modernist thought or abandon the modernist project of emancipation, but to forge links between critical theory (Marxism, feminism, anti-racism, etc.) and postmodernism. It is this critical postmodern perspective that is adopted here. Some of the major criticisms that postmodernism and post-structuralism make of modernist concepts such as paradigms and ideological forma-tions are identified below. Rather than rejecting these criticisms and insights, it is my intention to use them in an attempt to inform and help revitalize modernist progressive social welfare and social work thought.

Postmodern Critique of Modernism

Although a full discussion of modernism and postmodernism is well beyond the purview of this book, a brief outline of some of the major postmodern criticisms of the concept of paradigms is presented here. More discussion of postmodernism will follow in Chapter 9, where postmodernism is brought into a theory of structural social work. The project of modernity, which came into focus towards the end of the eighteenth century, promised that the domination of nature by science and the accumulation of objective, pure knowledge acquired by a rationale subject using impartial scientific means would yield freedom from want, scarcity, and so on (Harvey, 1989). Doctrines of equality, liberty, and faith in human intelligence (once educated) abounded. '[T]he intellectual foundation of modernity was a belief in the power of reason over ignorance, order over disorder, and science over superstition that would allow humanity to achieve progress and emancipation' (Mullaly, 2001: 307). A selected list of postmodern and post-structural criticisms of modernist thought (including paradigms and ideologies) are contained in Box 7.1 and discussed below.

BOX 7.1   POSTMODERN/POST-STRUCTURAL CRITIQUE OF MODERNIST IDEAS

Postmodernism:

- Rejects the idea that there is objective social knowledge containing an absolute truth.
- Rejects the idea of an objective, value-free scientific method that makes reality accessible.
- Rejects the notion of universalism, such as a universal human subject or a universal set of human needs.
- Rejects a belief in 'essentialism', such as an essential human nature.
- Rejects the myth that modern history reflects a progressive road towards humanist goals.
- Rejects attempts to develop overarching frameworks (paradigms, ideologies) or all-encompassing theories (e.g., Marxism) that attempt to establish an underlying reality.
- Rejects the notion that there exists a fixed human identity characterized by coherence and unity rather than by fragmentation.
- Rejects the binary or oppositional structure of modernist thought.
- Criticizes modernist use of language and dominant discourses that reflect dominant-subordinate relationships.
- Rejects the notion that power is concentrated (rather than dispersed) and rests within certain areas of the social structure (e.g., the ruling class).

The rejection of modernist beliefs by postmodern writers, perhaps most notably Michel Foucault, is by now well known. Social theories and philosophical traditions that envisage a universal subject (e.g., the working class, the rational individual), an essential human nature (e.g., self-interested, altruistic), and a global human destiny in which human history is claimed to represent a unilinear and progressive development are rejected by postmodernists (Lemert, 1994, cited in O'Brien and Penna, 1998). Claims to universality, reason, and order often mask the interests of those making them. 'Imperialist nations, ruling classes, males, whites, heterosexuals, doctors, psychiatrists [social workers] and criminologists have all claimed that their perspective defines a universal and rational outlook. By doing so they have effectively silenced other nations, other classes, other genders, other races, those of other sexual orientation, patients, the mad and prisoners' (Smith, 1993: 31). Because the pursuit of scientific truths in human affairs has at times led to repression and control, postmodernists reject all totalizing belief systems or grand narratives that seek to impose some kind of ideal order on society in the interests of society.

Postmodernism joins with critical social theorists and feminists in criticizing the assumptions that underpin positivism, and thus rejects positivism—the collection and analysis of observable 'objective' data—as the pre-eminent method for carrying out research. The claim that the only valid research occurs from objective, impartial, unbiased, neutral, rational observation of social phenomena that reveals or creates innocent knowledge, verifiable thanks to rigorous scientific tests, has been rejected by critical theorists of the Frankfurt School in the 1950s, by second-wave feminists, by postmodernists, by critical race theorists, by indigenous scholars, and by researchers from other marginalized groups. These groups have all argued that traditional research draws from a narrow foundation of knowledge based on the social, historical, and cultural experiences of bourgeois white males who have been in charge of the research enterprise since the beginning of the Enlightenment. The researcher's social location and political commitments are obscured by methodological claims to objectivity and neutrality. Brown and Strega, 2005: 11) address this point:

> The histories, experiences, cultures, and languages (the 'ways of knowing') of those on the margins have been devalued, misinterpreted, and omitted in the academy, where . . . only certain conceptualizations of information are counted as 'valid' (objective and therefore authoritative) knowledge. In this process, many ways of knowing, which Foucault (1980) referred to as 'subjugated knowledges', have been excluded or trivialized.

Although critical social theory, which is associated with progressive forms of socialism and underpins progressive forms of social work, shares with postmodernism many of the same criticisms of positivism, Strega (2005) criticizes it for its continuing commitment to the idea that reality can be uncovered (e.g., socialism is superior to capitalism; people are social animals rather than desert islands). Thus, it implicitly continues to support hierarchical dualisms and the inequities engendered in these dualisms.

Bastow and Martin (2003) point out that global warming along with environmental disasters such as Chernobyl undermined the belief in the mastery and control of nature by science and led many to believe that unfettered economic production and consumption were leading to ecological devastation. Furthermore, the whole premise of uninterrupted economic growth, which all traditional paradigms require in order to fund either the expansion of business (neo-conservatism) or the expansion of the welfare state (liberalism and social democracy), has been called into question by postmodernists and others.

The notion of an essential 'human nature' is rejected by postmodernists and post-structuralists. The dominant modernist paradigms, adherents claim, have positive essences or core characteristics that give them a true and independent meaning and/or identity outside the interpretation of a specific discourse (Rorty, 1999, cited in Bastow and Martin, 2003). Postmodernists argue that an essential human nature exists only within the discourse of each paradigm and that this essential human nature varies from paradigm to paradigm. Such essentialist thought makes all human beings the same and, therefore, they should all be treated the same, no matter what differences may exist with respect to time, social context, culture, or other social characteristics. Postmodernists argue that ways of thinking and acting are produced by a network of social forces within which we are immersed rather than by some innate characteristic of the individual. The individual or subject is not an autonomous self-producing agent, but a product of changing culture and discursive fields (Ashe, 1999). Post-structuralism starts from the assumption that no fully formed or complete identities pre-exist social interactions. Rather, individuals occupy a plurality of shifting and overlapping identities (the workplace, the home, political struggle, the legal system, gender, class, age, sexuality, race, and so on) that construct them in relation to others through different discourses and changing conditions. Workers, for example, have modified the meaning of what it is to be an employee through struggles that have changed social relations in the workplace (Bastow and Martin, 2003). Similarly, various social service user movements have changed the meaning of what it is to be a 'client' of certain social services organizations.

The modernist notion that a (different) set of rational assumptions underpins each paradigm is also rejected by postmodernists. For example, each paradigm assumes in a different manner that the totality of society can be objectively understood and that social division or conflict exists because of a failure to recognize the rational order beneath the surface of the conflict. Postmodernists reject such assumptions because they contain oppressive political implications. The idea that there is some 'true' understanding of society 'legitimises the coercion of those unwilling to recognise the validity of such claims' (Bastow and Martin, 2003: 148). This can lead to the logic that people must be forced to be free (e.g., the Marxist concept of 'dictatorship of the proletariat' or the neo-conservative goal of freeing people from government providing health and education services to them).

Post-structural critics of modernist epistemology have highlighted and critiqued the 'binary' or 'oppositional' structure of Western thought, arguing that it is based on a series of prejudicial dualisms, such as mind/body, public/private, reason/emotion, culture/nature, human/animal, white/non-white, man/woman, rich/poor, straight/gay, and so on. The terms contained in these dualisms are held to be opposites, mutually exclusive, and logically contradictory since one cannot be both at once. Dualisms thus exclude all kinds of other possibilities that do not fall neatly into one of the two fixed meanings of the dualism. And, as Lloyd (1999) points out, they also contain an implicit value judgement, where the first term is more highly valued than the second. Thus, binary oppositionals not only restrict our thinking and our identities, they do so by establishing hierarchies. Post-structuralists call for more fluid understandings of these concepts. For example, the post-structural feminist, Judith Butler (1990), suggests that, instead of the binary structure of gender (male/female), we work with the notion of a multiplicity of genders, which introduces these concepts as social constructions rather than as natural constructions. Deconstructionism would be the tool used to expose the hierarchical, binary oppositions and rhetorical devices that produce claims to truth and reality. Some examples of binary oppositions that form part of the dominant paradigms are: capitalism/socialism, competition/co-operation, statutory welfare/voluntary welfare, individualism/community, and free market/government intervention.

For example, the dominant discourse in many schools of social work in Canada, the US, and Australia, and among many social work educators, includes 'general systems theory' and/or 'ecological models' as core social work knowledge in spite of 30 years of damning critique (more about this in Chapter 9). Use of these borrowed concepts represents an appropriation of material from biology that appeals to the authority of 'science' (i.e., an incontestable, authoritative truth) to create the appearance that social work is based on hard science. In this way, the possibility of developing alternative theories and practices (such as structural social work or feminist social work) is reduced because they are not scientific enough.

Traditional social science tended to believe that language simply reflected reality and that knowledge was obtained and/or given through language. However, postmodernism and post-structuralism have helped to show us that there are many realities, not one universal reality, and that language does not have the properties of absolute truth but is historically, culturally, socially, and politically contextualized. Language is not politically neutral, as evidenced by Howe's (1994: 522) summary of the relationship between power and language. Whereas modernist beliefs contended that increasing knowledge of the essential and true nature of things produced power, postmodernism reversed the process: 'Those with power can control the language of the discourse and can therefore influence how the world is to be seen and what it will mean. Language promotes some possibilities and excludes others; it constrains what we see and what we do not see.'

A related concept to language is that of 'discourse'. Discourse is a term widely used and variously interpreted. In modernist usage, it usually refers to talking or to a way of talking within a circumscribed area of discussion, as in a 'discourse about the economy', or is used to delineate how a topic is discussed, as in 'social work or other professional discourse' (Strega, 2005). Discourse, in this way, is considered to be a way for people to discuss a particular topic, with its role in producing, reproducing, or transforming social structures, relations, and identities being overlooked (Fairclough, 1992, cited in Strega, 2005). Discourse, however, includes not only language, but the rules governing the choice and use of language and how the ideas and language will be framed (Mullaly, 2002). A discourse is a framework of thought, meaning, and action (Thompson, 1998), which does not reflect knowledge, reality, or truth but creates and maintains them. 'Knowledge', according to Foucault, is produced by discourse—it is 'the way in which power, language, and institutional practices combine at historically specific points to produce particular ways of thinking' (Featherstone and Fawsett, 1994, cited in Stainton and Swift, 1996: 77). With respect to ideology, each ideology or paradigm has its own discourse that consists of a set of assumptions about the social world. And, although there is always more than one discourse at any particular time, one discourse usually dominates. The dominant discourse(s) today largely reflects the interests of global capitalism, patriarchy, and people of European descent. And, as Agger (1989) points out, even our textbooks are largely written within this dominant discourse. The knowledge presented in the social science literature assists in the reproduction of the existing social order through: (1) the incorporation of ideas that support the current socio-economic-political-cultural order; and (2) the suppression and/or marginalization of scholarship that seeks to challenge or transform it (Wachholz and Mullaly, 2000).

> By virtue of being developments of modernist thought, the welfare state and social work have also been subject to postmodern critique. Because the world is characterized by diversity, multiplicity, pluralism, and conflict rather than by sameness, unity, monism, and consensus, postmodernists believe that no group should try to define the reality, needs, interests, or experiences of another group. The welfare state and social work have tended to overlook differences and diversity and have, instead, carried out policies and practices of homogenization, exclusion, bureaucratic control and surveillance, hierarchical decision-making and professional expertise. A cornerstone of postmodernism is its concern for language and discourse. It criticizes modernism for its use of dominant discourses that reflect class, gender, race, and other forms of dominant-subordinate relationships and it criticizes professions, such as social work, for controlling the discourse of their practices by using pathological, diagnostic, and professional vocabularies that exclude and disempower service users. (Mullaly, 2001: 307)

Limitations of Postmodernism and Post-Structuralism

Although postmodernism would seem to offer valuable critical insights of many modernist foundational concepts and ways of gathering knowledge, it is not without its limitations—especially with respect to social justice issues. A fuller critique of postmodernism is presented in Chapter 9, but some of its limitations with respect to concerns of progressive social work include the following:

- A number of writers (e.g., Agger, 1998; Ife, 1997; Thompson, 1998) argue that although postmodernism rejects all meta-narratives, it, too, is a meta-narrative.

- With its emphasis on difference, relativism, and cultural diversity, postmodernism lacks any potential for solidarity among groups (a prerequisite for social movements) experiencing oppressive conditions (Leonard, 1990).
- By its rejection of all meta-narratives, hooks (1991) points out, subordinate groups are left disempowered at the very point at which they need to demand emancipation in the name of universal notions of justice and equality.
- Harvey (1989) asks that if, as the postmodernists insist, we cannot aspire to any unified representation of the world, or see it as a whole with connections and differentiations rather than as constantly shifting fragments, how can we ever act coherently to change it?
- By rejecting possibilities of emancipation and social progress, postmodernism is nihilistic (Thompson, 1998). 'The nihilism of postmodernism shows itself in two symptoms: an inability to specify possible mechanisms of change, and an inability to state why change is better than no change' (Crook, 1990: 59).
- It does not account for structural oppressions along the lines of class, race, gender, and so on, as its pluralist perspective views power as being dispersed throughout society and not concentrated in the hands of a few (Ife, 1997).
- Ife (1999) indicts the postmodern view that human rights are somehow relative, which, although it has appeal to those who wish to be culturally sensitive, is also used to justify the oppression of minorities in places like East Timor, the maintenance of low wages and abhorrent working conditions, ethnic cleansing, and other human rights violations.
- Postmodern analysis, which is often used to deconstruct mainstream assumptions, can result in supporting mainstream assumptions because of its lack of a political agenda (Moosa-Mitha, 2005).
- Much postmodernist writing can be accused of 'obscurantism'—a form of arcane language that distances and alienates many readers through its unnecessarily obscure references and constructions (Thompson, 1998). There is a quality of 'linguistic elitism of postmodern discourse' (Leonard, 1997), which is ironic for a body of thought that emphasizes the significance of language in relation to power.

Other limitations and weaknesses of postmodernism with respect to progressive notions of social welfare and/or social work have been noted by several authors (e.g., Eagleton, 1996; Leonard, 1994, 1995; Rossiter, 1996; Smith, 1993; Smith and White, 1997; Taylor-Gooby, 1994).

In view of the legitimate critiques that postmodernism has of many (modernist) values, ideals, and goals associated with progressive social welfare and social work, on the one hand, and in view of the limitations and weaknesses of postmodernism in relation to these progressive values, ideals, and goals, on the other hand, what is one to do? As will be argued further in Chapter 9, there is a need to forge links between modernist critical theory and postmodernism (see, e.g., Agger, 1991, 1998; Leonard, 1990, 1994, 1997; Pease and Fook, 1999; Thompson, 1998; Mullaly, 2001). Outlined below are some areas where the postmodern critique can inform and assist in revitalizing some of our progressive and emancipatory notions with respect to paradigms and ideological formations

Postmodernism, Paradigms, and Ideology

In the past two decades a revival of interest in ideologies has occurred, which reflects the fact that ideology has not come to an end, as Daniel Bell (1965) had argued in the 1960s. Nor have we reached the 'end point of mankind's [*sic*] ideological evolution' (i.e., that capitalist or liberal democracy has won the competition for ideological pre-eminence for all times), as Fukuyama (1992: xi) argued in the 1990s. 'Instead, the ideological frames through which people interpret and experience their world are recognised increasingly as an ever-present feature of modern life. . . . As such, ideologies are rooted in social relations of power, and seek either to legitimise existing social orders or to delegitimise them' (Bastow and Martin, 2003: 15).

Part of the revival of interest in ideologies, however, has been the emergence of *discourse theory*, which offers a different way of studying ideologies from the traditional analysis of major political concepts. Instead of analyzing ideological formations as to how they look at such notions as 'human nature' (e.g., individual vs social), universal values (e.g., co-operation vs competition), and 'great books' (e.g., *Das Kapital* vs *The Wealth of Nations*), discourse theory does not limit itself to dominant political traditions and the theoretical arguments over preferred social and political arrangements derived from these traditions. Discourse theory recognizes 'that the world is made meaningful not simply by political concepts and ideals but also by popular notions, common sense values, and often quite irrational prejudices about peoples and their innate characteristics that are rarely formulated as ideologies' (Bastow and Martin, 2003: 4). Proponents of discourse theory such as Bastow and Martin (2003: 16–17) argue that the focus of analysis is 'more on the contingent, open-ended and contestable features of discourse than on stable, relatively closed and incontestable features of ideologies'.

It would seem, then, that discourse analysis enables us to rethink the nature of political ideologies and paradigms. Rather than being guided by fixed and immutable symbolic frameworks, discourse analysis opens up further possibilities for defining the world and seeing how to change it. In brief, discourse analysis requires us to 'think outside the box' to discover new connections and relationships between ideas. Discourse theory allows us to deconstruct ideologies to see how their assumed essentialisms are in fact contingent and relational. This helps us to consider possibilities that fall outside traditional ideological frameworks. It also helps to examine the relationships (i.e., shared ideas and patterns of understanding) among them. For example, an assumption of economic progress and rationality underpins both socialist and liberal ideologies (Bastow and Martin, 2003). Discourse theory is useful, as well, in exposing any discriminatory or oppressive ideas and beliefs that may underpin a dominant discourse. And we can develop 'counter-discourses' based on the ideals of equality, fairness, and social justice.

Other postmodern correctives to our progressive (socialist and Marxist) paradigms include using postmodern thought to inform and revitalize the modernist ideal of emancipation. Peter Leonard (1997: 28) argues that, consistent with postmodernism, the narrative or discourse of emancipation must be one of uncertainty—'a story without guarantees as to the outcome'. However, a universal discourse of justice and equality has always been central to the historic emancipatory struggles against domination. Leonard counters the postmodern rejection of these universalisms by pointing out that they are socially constructed and culturally produced within a specific historical period of short duration. 'They are, therefore, culturally relative and are not necessarily shared, even as ideals, by other cultures.' Postmodernism fosters the idea that other culturally produced conceptions of human well-being, such as African, Aboriginal, Asian, and so on, can take their place alongside those of the Euro-centred West. Of this Leonard says:

> we slowly start to learn that it is possible to think differently than we have previously thought, perceive the world differently, even feel differently. But the fact that the narrative of emancipation is a ship which sails in a sea of different cultures and diverse social conditions enables us, at least, to envisage a process of arriving at some agreed values, which we can call *universal by consent*, and which are established as a result of political struggle which resolves itself in a consensus amongst those striving for emancipation. (Leonard, 1997: 28)

What might be agreed? Leonard uses the example of the 'value of diversity', which immediately provides a critique of social forces in any particular paradigm or otherwise whose objective or function is to attain homogenization or Oneness by disregarding the fact of difference.

Thompson (1998) points out that the postmodern concept of difference has two meanings. First, it is often used to refer to change, development, or movement, or what Thompson calls difference as flux. In this respect, difference is in opposition to essentialism. Second, it also refers to the multiplicity of social divisions that characterize present-day society. Difference here is seen to be in opposition to normalization—the tendency to impose restrictive social norms at the expense of diversity. 'In both these senses, difference is an important concept that can be used to challenge oppression—in the first case, the oppressive nature and consequences of essentialism and, in the second, the range of oppressions that includes sexism, racism, ageism and disablism' (Thompson, 1998: 61). Incorporating the value of difference or diversity into progressive paradigms/ideologies should help to prevent the social welfare policies and social work practices of 'homogenization, exclusion, bureaucratic control and surveillance, hierarchical decision-making and professional expertise' that have occurred within the dominant paradigms and that were discussed above.

The postmodern emphasis on difference includes 'cultural diversity' as a value, not just as a concept. Although culture (values, norms, and shared patterns of thought) is discussed in more detail in Chapter 9, it is important to note here that progressive social workers, along with feminists and social activists, have tended to lump culture in with other structural forces as part of the 'personal is political' model of social analysis. However, thanks to postmodernism and cultural studies, we now have a better understanding of how culture mediates the effects of the person on the political and the effects of the political on the person. Without a solid understanding of culture and how it mediates these relationships, there is a danger of endorsing an assumed superior culture, thus elevating William Ryan's concept of 'blaming the victim' for social problems from the individual level to the cultural level. The 'personal is political' model of analysis is extended to include culture as a working model of anti-oppressive and structural social work in Chapter 9.

BOX 7.2   THE PERSONAL IS POLITICAL: AN INSURMOUNTABLE LEAP OF FAITH?

If there is a social work 'mantra' at all, it has to be that 'the personal is political.' This slogan was popularized by the women's movement in the 1970s, although it was first used by African Americans in the 1960s in their struggle for civil, political, and social rights. The profession of social work during the late 1960s and early 1970s was characterized by a tension-filled, often acrimonious split between the clinical stream and the policy stream, the micro and the macro, direct practice and indirect practice, counselling and community development, and so on. Desperate for unification and a common identity, the profession made several attempts at unification: development of a unitary framework or theory base; imposition of a concept borrowed from biology (general systems theory) as core or fundamental knowledge for *all* social work; and implementation of a generalist model of social work education at the BSW level. All attempts failed to unite the profession, which has at one of its continuum the individual as the unit of analysis and intervention and at the other end all of society (national or global). It is no wonder that social work in the late 1970s and early 1980s latched onto the phrase 'the personal is political' like a hungry dog to a bone. Borrowing (a favourite social work pastime) the analysis from the women's movement, social work thought that it had finally secured the unifying mechanism.

'The personal is political' analysis exposed (if not clarified) the link between the individual and society. The individual impacted on society and, in turn, was impacted on by society. The individual and society were not isolated entities; there was a clear relationship of interdependence. You could not understand one without understanding the other. The slogan became a social work homily that permeated (with varied intensity) the social work curriculum. Its recitation could be heard in the classroom, at faculty meetings, at student events, at demonstrations, in general conversation, in arguments, at thesis defences, and so on. Because feminists took the leadership in developing the analysis and putting it into practice, those social work courses that focused on gender issues tended to be more advanced in terms of incorporating the analysis into everyday social work practice.

In spite of all this, many social workers, once in the field, still do not put 'the personal is political' into practice. To expect social workers to do so is an insurmountable leap of faith—this leap from analysis to practice is too great. By extending 'the personal is political' analysis to include the cultural level, the insurmountable leap of faith between the personal and the political perhaps can be reduced. The cultural level is located between the personal and the political and is the cement that reinforces oppression at the personal and structural levels (Dominelli, 1997).

Moosa-Mitha (2005) identifies an important post-structural contribution to the theory supporting the traditional socialist paradigms and earlier progressive social work. The binary thinking that is part of the dominant paradigms can be *deconstructed* to move beyond simple dichotomous relationships. For example, binary thinking about oppression assumes the existence of an oppressed and an oppressor. However, a more complex notion of oppression recognizes and acknowledges that a person can be both an oppressor and oppressed at the same time (Mullaly, 2002; Razack, 1998, cited in Moosa-Mitha, 2005). This recognition of multiple relationships is associated with the fact that persons occupy more than one social identity and challenges the tendency to essentialize people on the basis of a singular social location or identity, such as class or gender or race. And, as discussed above, essentializing has been part of the dominant paradigms and has been manifest in social policies and social work practices.

As the title of his 1997 book, *Postmodern Welfare: Reconstructing an Emancipatory Project*, suggests, Peter Leonard argues that postmodernism can contribute to a reconstruction of the welfare state as an emancipatory project:

> An emancipatory project of welfare under the conditions of late capitalism must turn its face against the kind of totalizing programme which was the ideal of many of the protagonists who established the old welfare state. It cannot be based upon some overall grand *plan*, some new, complete *reorganization* of welfare, because the over-ambitious planning, programming and organization of welfare institutions, its professionals and subjects, produced the paradox that a commitment to welfare resulted, to a large degree, in a system of domination in the interests of exclusion, homogenization and the defence of expert power. (p. 163)

Leonard deconstructs the modernist welfare state (a precondition for reconstruction) to reveal our knowledge and beliefs as historically and culturally specific products, which can no longer be legitimated by reference to the universal authority of *reason*. Then, in a most 'unpostmodern' way (by his own admission), he suggests some elements of reconstruction:

- 'The obligation to acknowledge and, whenever possible, to celebrate difference is a fundamental ethical assumption of a reconstructed welfare project.' (p. 164)
- The experiences of clients, patients, and welfare recipients being subjected to the professional gaze of experts with assumed superior knowledge must be de-pathologized and renamed as the effects of racism, classism, sexism, and other discourses and practices of domination.
- To counteract the homogenizing tendency of the welfare state, co-authorship of joint narratives about problems, needs, and claims must be emphasized. Because every narrative is open to interpretation, a dialogue of the interpretations gives priority to the recognition of a diversity of subjects.
- The dominant discourse of welfare is laden with binary classifications such as good mothers and bad mothers, workers and shirkers, deserving and non-deserving, independent and dependent. Discourses on these binaries must be deconstructed to show their exclusionary and oppressive consequences and reconstructed within welfare discourses of emancipation. For example, interdependence is a common experience in all human societies. 'A politics of welfare, . . . if it is to be emancipatory, demands a rejection of discourses on dependence and independence and in their place argues for a discourse on *interdependence*.' (p. 158)

In sum, postmodernism has much to contribute to our understandings of paradigms or ideological formations, to the idea of welfare as an emancipatory project, and to social work as vital part of that project. Postmodern contributions to structural social work are the subject of subsequent chapters.

CONCLUSION

In this chapter three different critiques of the dominant paradigms and/or ideological formations were presented. Different schools of feminism have criticized all four paradigms for being gender-exclusive. As well, feminism has contributed to the development of critical or progressive social theory in general and to social welfare and social work theory in particular. Similarly, anti-racist or critical race theorists have criticized the paradigms for being colour-blind and not including the lived experiences of people of colour. They, too, have contributed to progressive social theory and social work thought and practice. However, earlier forms of feminist and anti-racist analysis have, in turn, been criticized for their modernist ideas. A brief overview of the postmodern critique of modernism was presented in this chapter as well. Feminist and critical race theories and analyses have benefited from postmodern insights and ideas with respect to informing, complementing, and supplementing many of their earlier modernist ideas and concepts.

Hopefully, progressive social work and social welfare theorists will also benefit from postmodern insights and ideas.

Some writers and scholars argue that a new brand of politics based on a reformulation of social democratic thought now exists. This is an alternative view to the old politics of class and social division found in the traditional paradigms. Proponents claim that this alternative addresses many of the postmodern criticisms of the traditional paradigms in that it moves beyond such ideological oppositionals as market versus state and individual versus community, which are integral parts of the dominant paradigms. This so-called new brand of social thought and politics is known as 'the Third Way' because, as is claimed by proponents, it represents a partnership between many of the oppositional or conflicting values, ideas, and policies that are inherent in the old paradigms. In other words, the claim is that it represents an alternative or compromise to the sets of ideas and values that underpin both capitalism and socialism. The next chapter examines the Third Way in an attempt to evaluate this claim.

CRITICAL QUESTIONS

1. Can a man be a feminist? Why or why not?
2. Over the past 15 years or so, I have heard many young female social work students say that feminism today doesn't mean anything to them, that they have not experienced any gender discrimination in their lives, and that they wish their older feminist peers would just get over it. Is feminism relevant to today's social and political life?
3. Which school of feminism—liberal, socialist, or radical—do you think that progressive social work should adopt?
4. An argument sometimes heard is that only members of a particular oppressed group can really understand the hardships and problems experienced by that group. Therefore, only members of any particular oppressed group should practise social work with that group. In other words, only female social workers should work with women, only Aboriginal social workers should work Aboriginal persons, only visible minority social workers should work with visible minorities, and so on. What do you think of this position?
5. Conversely, can social workers from subordinate groups work with members of dominant groups, such as female social workers working with men, Aboriginal workers with white people, and so on?
6. I once received a term paper (from a female social work student) that argued that 'males' constituted an oppressed group. Do you think that men can ever be oppressed solely on the basis of being a male?
7. Can there be a pure form of postmodern social work practice? Why or why not? If so, what would it look like?

The Third Way

The Third Way represents a transformation of social democratic ideology in the face of the challenging conditions of globalization, whilst retaining the essential guiding thread of achieving social equality.

—Anthony Giddens (1998)

The Third Way is but an ideological façade behind which capitalism continues on its brutal and destructive way.

—Callinicos (2001: 120)

INTRODUCTION

Social democracy, as outlined in Chapter 5, has a major competitor in some jurisdictions today. It is commonly called the Third Way and is associated with the New Left (also called New Labour in the UK and Australia) as opposed to the Old Left (or Old Labour). Some proponents claim that it is a genuinely new 'left-of-centre' political ideology that incorporates the best of social democracy and neo-conservatism (or neo-liberalism) at a time of global social and economic change (Mendes, 2003). However, the intellectual champion of the Third Way in the United Kingdom, Anthony Giddens (1998), claims that the Third Way is not new, but represents a reformulation of social democratic thought, without which the survival of social democracy is in danger.

This chapter presents the major ideas and values of the Third Way; some of its policies and programs that have been proposed and/or implemented; the limitations and critique of the Third Way; and the role that social work plays in Third Way jurisdictions, such as the UK. This chapter assesses whether or not the Third Way adequately addresses the criticisms of the dominant ideological formations that have come from feminism, critical race theory, and postmodernism, as described in the previous chapter.[1]

The concept of a 'third way' has actually been appropriated from the Swedish social democrats, who in the 1980s characterized the Scandinavian approach to welfare as the 'third way' between the free market and state socialism. Since the demise of East European communism, the Third Way has been redefined and now appears to be centred on the concept of 'communitarianism' and the strengthening of civil society without abandoning a role for the state, nevertheless emphasizing individual responsibility and de-emphasizing collective rights (Rodger, 2000). Tony Blair, the three-term Labour (social democratic) Prime Minister of Great Britain, is the political leader most associated with

Third Way philosophy and policy (see Blair, 1998). Other prominent political advocates of Third Way thinking and policies are former US President Bill Clinton (under the term 'New Progressivism'), the former German Prime Minister, Gerhard Schroeder (see Blair and Schroeder, 1999, who argue for a distinctly European Third Way), and the former leader of the Australian Labour Party, Mark Latham. Although the New Democratic Party in Canada (federally and provincially) has not articulated a Third Way philosophy or ideology, various Third Way social and economic policies have been adopted by provincial NDP governments in Manitoba and Saskatchewan.

Third Way proponents claim that it represents a brand of politics based on principle rather than on dogma, presents a rational answer to the challenges of globalization, and is an alternative to the politics of class and social division often associated with supposedly confrontational leftist political parties. It has been adopted by some political parties and advocates of the left who still claim to be working in that tradition (Bastow and Martin, 2003), such as those identified above. Third Way opponents argue, on the other hand, that it is a dilute imitation of neo-conservative politics in that it accepts the predominant role of the market in addressing social problems. Bastow and Martin (2003) assert that the Third Way is difficult to classify because it deliberately evades the traditional categories of left and right politics. It is positioned at the centre or middle of the ideological or political spectrum, but purports to be 'radical'. Bastow and Martin (2003) argue that the Third Way represents the 'radical centre'.

Third Way social democrats consistently argue that they are not part of the traditional oppositional 'right-left' confrontation between particular values and policy choices. They claim that they have moved beyond ideological oppositionals by using both the 'market' and the 'state' in a governing partnership, by emphasizing both 'rights' and 'responsibilities' in their concept of citizenship, and by focusing on both the 'individual' and 'community' as the basis of social order (Bastow and Martin, 2003). The question for many, however, is where has the Third Way moved to? This chapter examines the Third Way and attempts to answer this question. More specifically, it explores the Third Way to see if it addresses the critiques of the traditional paradigms made by feminists, anti-racists, and postmodernists. In other words, does the Third Way accommodate such issues as gender, race, diversity, difference, essentialism, and a universal human subject that were omitted from the dominant modernist paradigms?

THIRD WAY ARGUMENTS AND DISCOURSE

The philosophy and principles of the Third Way have been articulated by Tony Blair (1988) and his intellectual guru, Professor Anthony Giddens (1998), in their respective books, each titled *The Third Way*. They claim that the Third Way is an alternative to the free-market model of the neo-conservative or neo-liberal state, and to old-style socialism of both the undemocratic Soviet, command-economy type and the old social democratic model with a mixed economy and universal, collectivist welfare state (Jordan, 2000). Giddens does not accept the thesis that the Third Way is a bridge between the right and

the left. Rather, he argues that new ideas and policies are needed to renew social democratic values under new, globalizing conditions (Giddens, 1998). These conditions, which
include the development of the knowledge economy, telecommunications technology,
and the decline in traditional social identities and moral obligations, make the traditional
values of social democracy, such as equality of outcome and social solidarity based on
collective needs, hopelessly outdated as policy options (Bastow and Martin, 2003). In
their place, the Third Way has adopted the following values:[2]

- equality (of opportunity, not outcome);
- protection of the vulnerable;
- freedom as autonomy (personal freedom; choice);
- no rights without responsibilities (individual responsibility; obligations
  corresponding to social rights);
- no authority without democracy (empowerment; devolution of power);
- cosmopolitan pluralism (social inclusion as the basis of social justice);
- philosophic conservatism (but not politically conservative; a modernizing
  perspective that accepts the logic of globalization as an opportunity).

As Carling (1999) points out, the Third Way largely accepts capitalism as a means of
delivering these values and aims to modify (or complement) the effects of capitalism by
way of the following policy goals: lifelong learning; a balance of rights and responsibilities; promoting independence through work; and provision for genuine need. Giddens
(1998) claims that social democracy's belief in the nation-state as the administrator of a
type of social justice is no longer feasible because the state no longer has the capacity to
control a national economy in the face of global capitalism.

Similarly, Giddens argues that the right-wing neo-conservative movement has also
proved unsuccessful in regenerating national economies. Commenting on Giddens's
ideas, Bastow and Martin (2003: 4) state that:

> market-led strategies destroy the social basis of stable growth by abandoning the
> individual to the vagaries of profit maximisation. Whilst it has contributed to the
> expansion of global markets, neo-liberalism's [neo-conservatism's] tolerance of vast
> social inequalities and, in some instances, its conservative defence of traditional
> forms of social organisation such as the Church and marriage place it outside of any
> reasonable discussion of social change.

In sum, Giddens believes that neither traditional social democracy nor neo-conservatism, because of their rigid adherence to particular forms of economic and social development, can respond with any flexibility to the challenging conditions of a globalizing
environment. These changes, according to Blair (1998) and summarized by Bastow and
Martin (2003: 50), are: 'the internationalization of trade conditions under processes of
globalization; the rapid development of new technologies and their effects on jobs, skills

and education (the 'knowledge economy'); the transformation of women's social and economic roles; dissatisfaction . . . with unresponsive and often ineffective political institutions'. For Giddens and others, these changes and challenges have exhausted any solution to deal with them from the Old Left or the Old Right, which dogmatically emphasized the role of either the state (Old Left) or the market (Old Right) in delivering economic growth. The Third Way, Blair argues, pragmatically balances the responsibilities of state and market in meeting these challenges. He outlines four broad policy objectives in which the government assumes a new role (Blair, 1998, cited in Bastow and Martin, 2003: 51):

1. a government that enables (rather than commands) in a dynamic, knowledge-based economy where the power of the market is harnessed to serve the public interest;
2. a government in partnership with a civil society of strong communities empowered by rights *and* responsibilities;
3. decentralization and partnership;
4. a foreign policy based on co-operation with international partners.

Other tenets of the Third Way include the following:

- Class and structural inequalities no longer form the basis of social or political action. Instead, local communities are likely to be the major source of social and economic empowerment.
- Taxes should be reduced in line with international competition. High rates of taxation are no longer considered to be effective in reducing poverty.
- Poverty is redefined as a form of *social exclusion*, emphasizing the social as well as financial exclusion of people from the mainstream institutions and opportunities.
- Structural inequalities do not cause poverty, but the absence of attachment to work, family, and other community resources that ensure individual responsibility.
- The free market and successful entrepreneurs should be left relatively unhindered by government regulations.
- Governments should encourage the emergence of social entrepreneurs who use market principles to create wealth and growth at the local level.
- Significant power and resources should be transferred from the public sector to local (voluntary) community organizations and leaders. (Bastow and Martin, 2003; Blair, 1998; Giddens, 1998, 2000; Mendes, 2003)

Clearly, the Third Way represents an attempt to modernize or change the role of government away from both ends of the political spectrum (i.e., focused on the state or the market as a solution to social ills) to confront the challenges of a global economy. In place of a laissez-faire (neo-conservative) state and/or a state whose role is that of a large-scale provider, the Third Way state is to be harnessed and steered from the centre in the drive for global competitiveness (Ferguson et al., 2002). Third Way proponents call this process 'modernization', which is a code word for reforming social institutions to meet the demands of globalization. Whereas neo-conservatism would also attempt to change social institutions and would not bother with the negative consequences of globalization (i.e., the people hurt by globalization processes), the Third Way's modernization program would attend to the victims of classism, racism, sexism, and other forms of social exclusion, but would not deal with the structural causes of these forms and sources of oppression. A crucial element in this process of modernization is the reform of the welfare state.

THIRD WAY WELFARE REFORM

A major reason why Third Way welfare reform has been so popular is the political skill that governments (especially the Blair Labour government) have used in promising main-stream voters that welfare spending will be used to build a new system that promotes employment and independence. A central premise is the idea that the welfare system should demand more from those who receive assistance (no rights without responsi-bility) and that recipients should make themselves more employable through available programs of education, training, and work experience.

Third Way rhetoric is, in many regards, quite similar to that of neo-conservatism with respect to ideas about social welfare. It includes bestowing the importance of the work ethic, the negatives of welfare dependency, the responsibility of recipients to accept opportunities offered, and the struggle against welfare fraud. However, as Mendes (2003) points out, there are differences among the ways that these policy objectives might be carried out. For example, President Clinton's Personal Responsibility and Work Oppor-tunity Reconciliation Act was punitive in that it imposed time-limited welfare payments, compulsory workfare programs, and the denial of benefits to unmarried teenage mothers along with the assignment of them to the care of government-appointed guardians or trustees. The sole purpose of this scheme seemed to be to push recipients off the welfare rolls (O'Connor, 1999, cited in Mendes, 2003). In contrast, Blair's Third Way appears to use the carrot rather than the stick approach. Sole parents are not obliged to participate in welfare-to-work programs, and there is a stronger emphasis on job creation, wage subsidies, and the provision of education and training programs for welfare recipients (Mendes, 2003).

Social policies that enhance economic competitiveness such as welfare-to-work (workfare) programs are part of Third Way welfare reform. Also, the Third Way ques-tions the degree to which social services should be provided by the state and empha-sizes instead the role of private agencies—in partnership with the state (Ferguson et al., 2002). The role of the state becomes that of enabler rather than provider of social welfare programs. In Giddens's own words, the aim is '[i]nvestment in human capital wherever possible, rather than direct provision of economic maintenance. In place of the welfare state we should put the *social investment state* (emphasis added), operating in the context of a positive welfare society' (1998: 117). An important concept in Third Way ideology is that of social exclusion, which Giddens uses to replace the concepts of poverty and inequality. He argues that social exclusion is not about gradations of inequality but about mechanisms (i.e., personal and structural characteristics) that detach or remove groups from the social mainstream. Thus, a Third Way social policy goal becomes 'social inclusion' or bringing people back into the social mainstream. To do this the welfare system must focus on making socially excluded groups more employable through education and training. In Giddens's 'social investment state', equality is achieved by equipping citizens better for participation in a competitive economic environment (Jordan, 2000). Difficulties with this view and other Third Way notions are presented below.

In addition to the above Third Way reforms of the welfare state, Ferguson et al. (2002) identify the following reforms that have been carried out by the Blair government and have also been pursued or discussed in the other Anglo democracies. While Third Way thinking and action has been to reduce the role of the state in certain economic and social areas, the power of the state has been enhanced in other ways. Law-and-order issues have been a prominent area where interventions in the form of 'tough love' measures have been implemented. For example, the processes of criminalization have been extended through curfews, parenting orders, and the removal of homeless people from the streets of some towns and cities. The Blair government has continually linked social exclusion to issues of crime, truancy, and other forms of anti-social behaviour. The Third Way response has involved a greater disciplinary role on the part of the state. The family is expected to operate as a moralizing and socializing influence on family members, whose breakdown is considered to be the cause of many, if not all, of society's social problems. In other words, dysfunctional families are the cause of educational failure, crime, violence, economic dependence, and so on. Therefore, parenting classes for parents of delinquent and anti-social children have become a central part of Third Way politics, a politics that is consistent with neo-conservative notions that reinforce family hierarchies and women's oppression (Lavalette and Mooney, 1999).

The Third Way's preference for market solutions can be seen in the British experience with respect to the Blair government's record in the areas of health, housing, and education (see Ferguson et al., 2002). Traditionally opposed to privatization, the Labour Party under Tony Blair, once in power, became not only supporters but champions of privatization legislation. Once referring to itself as the party of the National Health Service (NHS), it has increasingly turned over to the private sector not only the building of hospitals but the running of them as well. In the area of housing, the Blair government has overseen the transfer of much of the public housing stock to an assortment of partnerships, co-operatives, and housing associations. It has rationalized this action by using neo-conservative rhetoric and ideology along the lines that the privatization of housing promotes choice, self-reliance, and responsibility (Ferguson et al., 2002). The Blair government has placed much emphasis on modernizing the education sector as it links education and employability in its eagerness to increase Britain's capacity to compete in the global economy. A major policy employed by the Third Way to modernize the education sector is to adopt business practices in the provision of education and the management of schools, including their privatization (and commoditization and marketization).

As with their tough love policies towards law-and-order issues, Third Way proponents display a moral authoritarianism in almost every aspect of government's political strategy, as evidenced by the language used by Home Secretary Jack Shaw in attacking 'squeegee merchants, asylum seekers, and social security fraudsters' (Blunkett, 2001, cited in Ferguson et al., 2002). Another example is the statement by the Secretary of State for Social Security, Alastair Darling, who threatened people in receipt of welfare: 'We're toughening up the penalties for those who persistently steal from the taxpayer. So from now on, if people commit fraud more than once, there will be no second chances. Two strikes and they're out' (*Herald*, 28 Nov. 2000, cited in Ferguson et al., 2002: 173). In addition to attacking welfare recipients, Blair has attacked Britain's public-sector workers for resisting the changes sought by his Third Way policies. In particular, teachers and social workers have been accused of failing to embrace reform. It seems that whereas the key objective of Old Labour was 'to control the market and free the people', under New Labour (Third Way) it is a story of 'controlling and regulating the working class—and freeing the market'. An outline of Third Way welfare reforms is presented in Box 8.1.

BOX 8.1 THIRD WAY WELFARE REFORM GOALS

- Make work pay by decreasing social insurance programs, increasing means-tested benefits for those outside the labour market, and giving support to low-wage workers through the income tax system.
- Change the role of government from provider of welfare services to enabler by contracting with private-sector agencies to deliver services.
- Insist that those in receipt of benefits must avail themselves of opportunities (training programs) to become financially independent.
- Coerce change in those welfare recipients who are unwilling to change their behaviour and attitudes regarding work and self-responsibility.
- Impose programs of 'tough love' on individuals and families exhibiting or responsible for delinquent and other forms of anti-social behaviour.
- Treat welfare recipients, asylum seekers, unemployed people, beggars, and poor people in general with suspicion and moral disapproval.

Although much of the writing about the Third Way comes from and focuses on the British/Tony Blair experience, Third Way ideas have also influenced social welfare thinking and policies in all other Anglo democracies. As mentioned above, the Bill Clinton administration implemented many Third Way policies, although in a more draconian manner than in Britain. The British and Australian Labour (social democratic) parties have a long history of exchanging ideas, agendas, and policies for government. Between 1983 and 1996 the British Labour Party used its Australian counterpart as a model in view of the electoral success Labour enjoyed in Australia under the leadership of Bob Hawke and Paul Keating. Since the election of Tony Blair (and of John Howard and the right-leaning Liberal Party in Australia) this process has been reversed, with many in the Australian Labour Party (ALP) looking to Blair's Third Way as a model to emulate (Mendes, 2003).

The New Democratic Party in Canada does not have the same relationship or exchange of ideas with Britain's Labour Party as does the Australian Labour Party. Nevertheless, many Third Way ideas have been adopted by the NDP without all the Third Way rhetoric. The federal NDP has been the most reluctant to adopt Third Way ideas. Likely, not expecting to become the governing party allows it to retain many of its traditional social democratic values and principles. Rejection of Third Way ideas by the federal party, in fact, led Bob Rae, the former NDP Premier of Ontario and a strong supporter of Third Way policies, to leave the NDP in protest. However, like their provincial counterparts, the federal party is not remotely interested in challenging capitalism nor has it been since the dismantling of its internal Waffle Movement in 1972.[3] Campbell and Christian (1999) contend that the federal NDP is now preoccupied with creating new alliances with progressive groups in Canadian society—the trade-union movement, environmentalists, feminists, gay rights activists, and farm and community groups—around specific policy issues, which may be at the expense of their prior commitment to developing a structural model of the welfare state.

At the provincial level, one of the most successful New Democratic Parties, led by Premier Gary Doer, is now in its second term as the governing party in Manitoba. In spite of a weak opposition, however, the Doer government has not responded with any consistency to issues along social democratic lines. An editorial in *Canadian Dimension* (March/April 2003), 'Manitoba: What the NDP Does When It Governs', acknowledged some good things that the Doer government did (increased availability of daycare, reduced university and community college tuition fees, and election finance reform), but then focused on the government's record as a supposedly social democratic government:

> For a party that claims to represent the interests of the poor and powerless, it is also notable that the Doer government has refused to raise Manitoba's welfare rates over its term in office. [The government raised the rates in its second term by $20 a month, which meant that rates are still lower than they were in 1995 when the Conservative government cut the basic living allowance to $175 per month.] . . . Is it a wonder Manitoba has the second-highest child-poverty rate in Canada? . . . Even measured against its own social-democratic standards, this government must be a disappointment to its followers. The federal party calls for electoral-reform measures like proportional representation, a move this government has not considered. Municipal governments across the continent are registering their opposition to a war in Iraq, a gesture this government could easily make, but has not, despite the stand of the federal party. Nor has it shown any interest in combating new moves within the WTO to open up health care, education and other social services to transnational capital—rules that will clearly impact on provincial policy.

Although some Third Way elements may be attached to the Manitoba NDP and its current government—an acceptance of capitalism, inadequate focus on poverty, some talk about tough love measures with respect to law-and-order issues—there has not been an outright acceptance of the Third Way. The rhetoric of the Doer government is more pragmatic than ideological, which is undoubtedly intentional.

Ralph Klein, the Conservative Premier of Alberta, used the term 'Third Way' to describe his notion and desire to privatize health care in the province. However, what he was talking about is a Fraser Institute-inspired neo-conservative concept of a private 'for-profit', two-tiered system rather than a partnership between government and privately operated heath-care units.

In sum, Third Way welfare reform resembles somewhat that of neo-conservatism but with a slightly different rhetoric attached to it. Whereas continental European and Scandinavian countries chose to increase social insurance contributions as a response to the rising unemployment that accompanied globalization, the Anglo democracies imposed reductions in spending on their public services and economic competition on their least well-endowed citizens (Jordan, 2000). They also shifted towards means-tested benefits, made these conditional on work effort, and allowed wages at the lower end of the labour market to fall. And as Ferguson et al. (2002) argue, the Labour government of Tony Blair has continued the neo-conservative policies of welfare reform via the Third Way.

SOCIAL WORK PRACTICE UNDER THE THIRD WAY

Obviously, a social worker working under a Third Way regime would be expected (by the government) to carry out its policies, administer its programs, and deliver its services in accordance with Third Way philosophy and objectives. For social workers in Australia and New Zealand this has meant much the same as for social workers in Canada and the US, that is, working within a neo-conservative paradigm. Britain is a special case in that Blair had such antipathy for the public service, in particular teachers and social workers, that he seldom used public social work agencies as vehicles for social welfare reform. Rather, he preferred to create new agencies and roles, often with a specific enforcement emphasis using face-to-face interventions by officials—frequently called counsellors or advisers, but not social workers (Jordan, 2000).

The vilification and de-professionalization of social workers that occurred under the Conservative governments of Margaret Thatcher and John Major in Britain has continued under Blair (Ferguson et al., 2003; Jordan, 2000). In fact, many social workers are now reluctant to refer to themselves as social workers in the present political climate. The title of social care worker is replacing that of social worker, as evidenced by the name of the accrediting body for social work educational programs—General Social Care Council rather than the General Social Work Council. A top-down implementation of social policy continues, and the suspicion of the public sector, including social work, which originated during the Thatcher era, has not changed. This has marginalized social work with respect to some of the progressive initiatives of the Blair government, such as those focusing on the social and economic regeneration of deprived districts via employment zones, single regeneration grants, and a social exclusion unit (Jordan, 2000).

Part of the de-professionalization of social work has come about by the emphasis the British government has placed on competency-based education, risk assessments, and evidence-based approaches to practice. The scientism and positivism of these latter two concepts have been discredited in the social sciences for many years as methodologically unsound and yielding misleading conclusions. Emphasis on the former concept has resulted in many graduates (who are not social workers) of competency-based programs taking over social work jobs. They may have a set of skills that can be applied in a work setting, but they are not educated to be critical thinkers or reflective practitioners. They are, however, easier to control by their political masters. Even within social work education, community work and community development, which had been part of mainstream social work in the 1970s, have now fallen right out of the curriculum in social work programs (Jordan, 2000). In Canada, the movement towards competency-based social work education is presently being advocated by some elements within the federal government (e.g., those working on free-trade agreements) and by some provincial governments (e.g., Alberta and Manitoba). And risk assessments are employed in several provinces, most notably in child protection and probation services.

Looking at the British experience of social work practice within a Third Way regime, Jordan (2000: 15) sums up the position and role of social work:

> What is distinctive about the Blair agenda is its strongly moral rhetoric and its reliance on 'people changers'—agents to transform attitudes, cultures, practices and decisions both among service providers and service users. But not only are social workers not to be such agents themselves; they in turn are to be changed—controlled, regulated and quality-assessed [i.e., tested in applications of risk assessments and competencies], in ways that will tie them more closely to their statutory tasks and to ministerial guidance.

Jordan (2000: 220) says of the overall program of the Third Way: 'Successful implementation of a programme for equal worth, opportunity, responsibility, community and justice [espoused Third Way values] cannot take the forms that the [Blair] government prescribes.' He then summarizes his view of what social workers ought to do when working within a Third Way context:

> There is nothing esoteric or mystical about these methods [of practice within the Third Way]—they stem from the ordinary rules of communication and co-operation between members of a community, respecting each others' identities and values and trying to make sense of their shared social world. Social work has no need to be ashamed of the fact that its expertise consists in the systematic and disciplined application of principles of decency and respect to all its interactions with service users who are also fellow citizens.

Thus, social work must remain a human and creative activity that uses imagination, empathy, and commitment as well as reason and evidence, and engages with people's emotions and vulnerabilities as well as their rights and obligations. In a culture of rapid change and uncertainty, what social work would have to be ashamed of is if it came to represent rigidity, resistance, and stagnation, or stigma, blame, and exclusion. It should also be ashamed if it is boring and oppressive, rather than energizing and liberating.

POTENTIAL FOR A PROGRESSIVE POLITICS

The Third Way's pragmatism is often read as neo-conservatism by its critics on the left. However, there are writers who believe that the combination rather than the transcendence of left and right stands for a new ideological framework. Driver and Martell (2000) argue that this novel mixture offers opportunities for new ways of formulating policy that would not have been possible in the Old Left view of social democracy, for example, combining social justice measures with economic efficiency. They also point out inherent pitfalls in this approach—the Third Way may find compromises between once opposed options, but it cannot resolve their tensions, which are always present and that remain permanent features of the political and policy-making landscape. For example, the egalitarian outcomes of social justice cannot be reconciled with the inegalitarian dynamics of the market (Driver and Martell, 2000, cited in Bastow and Martin, 2003: 63).

Assuming the validity of even this critique of the Third Way, it is difficult to see how it could be considered to be a progressive force offering radical opportunities for those committed to a democratic and pluralistic politics. Bastow and Martin (2003: 142) argue, however, that the discourse(s) of the Third Way has the potential for a renewed radical politics. They encapsulate the modernist beliefs of those on the left as follows:

> For much of the twentieth century, being on the left meant a number of related things: an attachment to social and political change as a form of progressive improvement of individual and social life; the formal and substantial achievement of equality amongst individuals in industrial societies; the reorganisation of wealth and power in favour of the poor; and the democratisation of state and society. . . . Socialists, social democrats, communists, syndicalists, anarchists, radical liberals, feminists: all saw in the advances of the previous one hundred years the as yet unfulfilled opportunity to surpass various forms of oppression and inequalities. To be on the left signalled an awareness that social improvements were still unfinished, that modern society could bring emancipation . . ..

Following the identification of these modernist beliefs of the left, Bastow and Martin (2003) present a number of dislocations that have undermined or diminished these traditional assumptions and beliefs. These dislocations are essentially some of the same criticisms that postmodernism has made of modernist thought, namely, that neither Eastern nor Western versions of socialism proved to be radically emancipatory;

the emergent distrust of grand narratives along with a 'rejection of the feasibility of the modernist project to bring about the emancipation of humanity from poverty, ignorance, and the absence of enjoyment' (Lyotard, 1984, cited in Bastow and Martin, 2003: 144); the reduced power and authority of the nation-state with respect to the welfare state and economic independence in the face of globalization and regionalization (e.g., European Union, NAFTA); global warming and events such as Chernobyl undermined the belief in the mastery and control of science over nature; and new social movements, such as the struggles over race, sexuality, and the environment, have disrupted class (i.e., the trade union movement) as the primary social movement and have made it more difficult for people to feel like members of a homogeneous political community. These changes, Bastow and Martin argue, have brought into question the traditional beliefs and assumptions of social democracy, and it is this questioning that the Third Way seeks to address by its 'modernization' program. And, as suggested above, this modernization is considered by Third Way advocates as the cure to the problems accompanying globalization. Flexible labour markets, education, retraining/re-skilling, and partnerships with the private sector all are part of the modernization program.

Having presented a postmodern critique of traditional (i.e., modernist) social democracy; and having identified its modernization program as the Third Way's reformulation of social democracy, Bastow and Martin then pose a critical question with respect to the Third Way—'can we square this social democratic Third Way with a radical democratic politics?' (p. 146). In addressing this question the authors draw on the work of Chantal Mouffe (2000), who explicitly rejected New Labour's Third Way for reducing complex relations of power in society to a simple competition of interests that can be harmonized through dialogue: 'This is the typical liberal perspective that envisages democracy as a competition among elites, making adversary forces invisible and reducing politics to an exchange of arguments and the negotiation of compromises' (Mouffe, 200: 110–11, cited in Bastow and Martin, 2003: 147). Within this perspective, consensus is the goal of democratic politics, which leads to an emphasis on shared identity rather than difference and to agreement rather than conflict. Mouffe argues that this perspective would proclaim 'flexibility' to be a modern social democratic aim, and that 'to believe that one can accommodate the aims of the big corporations with those of the weaker sectors is already to have capitulated to their power' (Mouffe, 2000: 120, cited in Bastow and Martin, 2003: 147). Although Bastow and Martin agree that the emphasis on consensus evades antagonisms such as free markets versus social equality, or reduces them to mere debating points, they curiously ask whether this holds for all forms of the Third Way. They then outline the celebrated work of Laclau and Mouffe, *Hegemony and Socialist Strategy: Toward a Radical Democratic Politics* (2001). Laclau and Mouffe argue for a renewed socialism (what they call 'the radical democratic imaginary') informed by postmodern ideas. These ideas include abandoning rationalist and essentialist assumptions, accepting that a vision of a social order can never be fully reconciled, ensuring that there are no universally privileged sites of conflict, and developing space in which a number of social antagonisms irreducible to economic issues can be regarded as equal and where a plurality of social and political identities can be formed around agendas of anti-racism, anti-sexism, and other forms of anti-oppression.

Having outlined some of the arguments of Laclau and Mouffe, Bastow and Martin (2003) then claim that this 'radical democratic imaginary' represents a form of the Third Way because each shares many of the same concerns—anti-essentialism, social identities viewed as contingent social constructions, the rejection of totalizing logic, a skeptical view of universalisms, transcendence of ideology, and so on. The problem with this position is that although Laclau and Mouffe's socialist strategy and the Third Way may share many of the same concerns, this does not mean that they will share the same explanations, solutions, approaches, or strategies for dealing with these concerns. Furthermore, to say that the Third Way has the potential to become the radical political expression of the left flies in the face of the substantial criticisms of Third Way policy and practice outlined in this chapter. Bastow and Martin, it seems, are arguing that the Third Way could become a form of radical left politics if it is informed by postmodern thought. However, Tony Blair's Third Way does not fulfill this condition. Maybe Laclau and Mouffe's 'radical democratic imaginary' has the potential to become a radical Third Way, but given that one of the characteristics of the Third Way is its position near the centre of the political spectrum and that Laclau and Mouffe are attempting a revitalization of the socialist left, this is highly doubtful. Ramesh Mishra (1999: 71) summarizes the issue of identifying the Third Way:

> Although a good deal is heard nowadays about the 'third way'—between traditional social democracy and neoliberalism—the ideas and policies of its practitioners, such as Bill Clinton or Tony Blair, amount to a gentler and kinder version of neoliberalism rather than a different approach to the economy and social protection.

In other words, if it walks like a duck and talks like a duck, there's a pretty good chance it is a duck!

CRITIQUE OF THE THIRD WAY

Although some criticisms of the Third Way were alluded to in the preceding sections, a summary of the major criticisms are presented here. Important questions are raised by the attempts of the Third Way to bridge such traditionally oppositional policy choices and values as the market vs the state, responsibilities vs rights, and the individual vs community. Bastow and Martin (2003: 3) ask these critical questions:

> In abandoning a principled defence of one side over the other, the Third Way exhibits its central claim to have moved beyond ideological antagonism. But moved where? What are the limits to the reliance on the market or the state? When do rights have precedence over responsibilities and vice versa? How can the needs of the individual be reconciled with those of the community?

There does not appear to be a new principle beyond the traditional antagonisms that would allow the Third Way to answer these questions. In the absence of such a principle, many have accused the Third Way of being vague, elusive, opportunistic, or simply facile (Bastow and Martin, 2003; White, 2001).

Mendes (2003) outlines several other criticisms from the left, which have been noted by Giddens himself (2000) in his attempt to answer them. Critics argue that the Third Way:

- Contains policies that victimize already vulnerable people.
- Emphasizes participation in the labour force at the expense of other forms of contributions to the community.
- Ignores the concentration of private wealth and power and its exercise in the interests of the powerful.
- Has no effective way of dealing with ecological issues other than endorsing technological change.
- Does nothing for losers in the globalization process, which produces winners and losers, since it accepts the world view of the winners.
- Redirects obligations of the collective community to the individual.

Bill Jordan, the noted progressive British social work writer, identifies some additional limitations of the Third Way in *Social Work and the Third Way* (2000). Third Way attempts to counter the selfishness and greed associated with economic individualism are applied only to those people who must rely on welfare benefits and not to those in mainstream society. Jordan also finds fault with the notion of 'social exclusion' replacing poverty and inequality as the focus of the Third Way's social programs. 'Social exclusion' refers to the mechanisms, such as education and the work ethic, that exclude people from the mainstream. Therefore, Third Way social policy is more about making people employable (thus equipping them better for participation in a competitive economic environment) through education and training and less about redistribution of resources after people are excluded from the mainstream. The problem with this view is that the solution (education/training) is inconsistent with progressive views of social justice—it does nothing about the conditions that caused the person to be in a deficit situation in the first place. In other words, it is a reactive policy that may help a particular individual, but it does nothing about the structural causes of social exclusion or poverty. To use an old metaphor, it is the same as treating a malaria victim, but doing nothing about the malaria-carrying mosquitoes.

Bastow and Martin (2003) summarize some of the literature that criticizes the Third Way for lacking continuity and coherence with respect to any social doctrine. Although Blair and Giddens claim that the Third Way represents a renewal of social democracy, not its abandonment, the view exists that the Third Way has simply adopted neo-conservative policies and principles (Hay, 1999; Hattersley, 2001; Marquand, 1999; Vincent, 1998, cited in Bastow and Martin, 2003). The evidence for this view rests on the Blair government having adopted the policies of the Thatcher neo-conservative government on crime, education, and public-service funding and on its refusal to renationalize the public services she privatized. 'Underlying these questions of policy, critics argue, is the acceptance of inequalities brought about by a market economy and the necessity for the individual[s] to rely on their own efforts to ensure their well-being, not on "handouts" from the state' (Bastow and Martin, 2003: 58). Critics use these actions to defend their claim that the Third Way has abandoned socialism in general and social democracy in particular. Bastow and Martin (2003), however, cite Bevir (2000), who argues that ideologies are not totally closed or fixed systems, but contingent and changing as new problems are faced. In other words, identifying similarities between different ideological traditions (such as conservatism and socialism) does not mean a wholesale transformation from one ideology (e.g., social democracy) to another (e.g., neo-conservatism). Bastow and Martin (2003) argue that it is incorrect to classify the Third Way in terms of the traditions from which it draws because this overstates the unity of these traditions. They point out that while New Labour (i.e., the Blair government) draws on various strands of neo-conservatism, neo-liberalism, and social democracy, both in principle and practice, many critics have labelled it neo-conservative, which they argue is an oversimplification because it misses many of its nuances, however contradictory.

In addition to its apparent lack of continuity with previous notions of social democracy doctrine, Bastow and Martin (2003) also outline another charge made against the Third Way—that it is incoherent as a political ideology. In the absence of any stable principle against which to judge various aspects of its policies, it is criticized for being opportunistic and intellectually eclectic. Powell contends that the Third Way does not seem to be based on any clear ideology or 'big idea' that unites its various claims and policies, and consequently it appears to formulate policy on the fly (Powell, 2000: 53, cited in Bastow and Martin, 2003: 61). Thus, rather than having developed a new synthesis of left and right into a new ideology, critics claim that the Third Way has simply combined or mixed principles traditionally associated with the closed ideological systems of the left and right, which has resulted in a pragmatically broad approach to policy-making. This has allowed New Labour, critics argue, to appeal to popular attitudes and sentiments, usually those that grab headlines. More often than not, these involve an appeal to the reactionary common sense of the so-called 'ordinary person on the street'. Policies claiming to be 'tough on crime', that tackle welfare 'scroungers', and appeal to the values of 'hard-working people' reveal an effort to speak to the public in the language of tabloid papers (Powell, 2000: 54, cited in Bastow and Martin, 2003: 62).

CONCLUSION

An overview of the Third Way was presented in this chapter with an examination of some of Tony Blair's (Third Way) policies, reforms, and their outcomes. Social work practice under a Third Way government was also examined, and it was concluded that, in the UK at least, Third Way social work is closer to neo-conservative social work than it is to progressive forms of social work. The argument that the Third Way has potential for a progressive politics was reviewed and rejected. It was concluded that Third Way policies are not progressive even though they are cloaked in such terms of progressive rhetoric as 'citizenship' and 'social inclusion'. Any paradigm or approach that provides social services in partnership with business, and that does not seek greater substantive equality, cannot be considered to be progressive. Not only must structural social work reject the Third Way on ideological grounds, it must also do so because Third Way politics does not deal with such issues as race, gender, and long-term structural inequalities that were identified in the previous chapter as omissions in the traditional paradigms. In sum, the Third Way is not progressive nor is it sensitive to feminist, anti-racist, and postmodernist concerns.

CRITICAL QUESTIONS

1. Do you think the Third Way is a viable form of social democracy? Why or why not?
2. Ralph Klein, the Premier of Alberta, presented in 2005 a plan for Alberta's health-care system that he called the 'Third Way' because it has a public component if people cannot afford private health care and a private component for those who can afford private health care. What do you think about this two-tier system? Does it address the principle of equity?
3. A Third Way movement in Canada, supported by some governments, claims that the market is incapable of providing social services and that the state model of social welfare can no longer be the provider of social services in an age of globalization. Therefore, what is needed is a 'social sector' or 'social economy' where voluntary organizations at the local level provide needed social services. What do you think of such a model?
4. Competency-based social work education consists of teaching basic sets of skills that a social worker will use in practice. They are observable and measurable. What is wrong with a social work program based solely on a competency-based model?
5. What is a 'tough-love' approach to social policy and social work? Can you think of some examples? What do you think of such an approach?

PART 2

Structural Social Work Theory and Oppression

A Reconstructed Theory of Structural Social Work

We can be for theory or we can be against theory, but we can never be without theory.

INTRODUCTION

Following an argument that theory is an imperative for any type of social work practice, a number of elements are presented in this chapter, which, taken together, constitute the theoretical basis and framework for the new structural social work: its socialist ideology; its radical social work heritage; its critical social theory base; its social change perspective; its dialectical analysis; its inclusion of all forms of oppression; and its conceptual framework that incorporates and integrates these components into a transformative and emancipatory form of social work practice. In the present edition these elements are reconceived in light of the postmodern, feminist, and anti-racist ideas discussed in Chapter 7.

THE IMPERATIVE OF THEORY FOR SOCIAL WORK

Many social workers either turn cold or rebel at the mere mention of theory. Theory is often viewed as esoteric, abstract, and something people discuss in universities. Practice, on the other hand, is seen as common sense, concrete, and occurring in the real world. Social work is viewed by many as essentially a pragmatic profession that carries out practical tasks. Theory has little direct relevance and actually obscures the true (i.e., practical) nature of social work. Spontaneity and personal qualities of the social worker are more important than theory (Barbour, 1984).

Reinforcing this anti-theoretical orientation of many social workers is the way the social work curriculum is ordered and presented in social work educational programs. Students leave the university and their theory-based classroom courses to go out into community agencies to learn field practice. This theory/practice dilemma is a constant problem for social work educators concerned with the integration of theory and practice (Barbour, 1984; Pilalis, 1986; Reay, 1986). Exacerbating the tension between classroom and field settings is the fact that social work students in their field placements come into contact with practising social workers who are skeptical of the theory being taught in social work courses and who emphasize instead the value of experience (Barbour, 1984). Students are often described as (or accused of) being naive, idealistic, and in need of 'seasoning' (i.e., practical experience).

This tendency on the part of many social workers to elevate theoretical ignorance to a level of professional virtue is wrong for two main reasons: (1) theory is part of everyday life—we all use theory; and (2) theoretical ignorance is not a professional virtue but an excuse for sloppy and dishonest practice (Howe, 1987). We often use theories in our everyday lives without even being aware that we are doing so. When we see dark clouds in the sky and tell ourselves it is going to rain, we have expressed a theory about the relationship between dark clouds and water falling from the sky. Imagine if we could not make generalizations about things and every time we saw a dark cloud we had to get wet in order to conclude that it was going to rain (Williams and McShane, 1988).

Just as we use theories in our everyday life, often without realizing it, social workers, too, often use theories in their everyday professional lives without realizing it. David Howe (1987) takes to task those 'practical-folk' social workers who declare that their practice is not related to theory by showing that all practice is theory-based. Social workers who appeal to common sense or declare themselves to be pragmatists or announce they are eclectics see people and their situations in one way or another. Perceptions are never theory-free because they are based on certain fundamental assumptions about the nature of people, society, and the relationship between the two. These assumptions enable social workers to make sense of any situation, and making sense is what Howe (1987) calls a 'theory-saturated activity'. And just because a social worker cannot imagine how else to view a particular situation does not mean that it is not related to theory. It just means that this one taken-for-granted reality (theory) is the social worker's entire world of sense. In other words, those persons who call themselves common sense, pragmatic, or eclectic social workers base their practice on personally constructed theory rather than scientifically constructed theory.

A review of the literature by Howe (1987) on what service users want in social workers and a review of the professional literature by Fischer (1978) on what makes social workers effective converge on two aspects of practice: (1) social workers must create the conditions conducive to a trusting, caring, and accepting relationship; and (2) social workers must make deliberate use of well-articulated theories and methods that organize and direct practice in a way that is systematic and recognized by both worker and service user.

Without going into a discussion of them, theory carries out four basic functions: description; explanation; prediction; and control and management of events or changes. Social work is a practice-based profession that pursues all four of these functions: it describes phenomena; it attempts to explain what causes them; it predicts future events, including what will happen if certain interventions occur; and it attempts to control and manage events or changes at all levels of human and social activity (Reynolds, 1971). 'If drift and purposelessness are to be avoided, practice needs to be set within a clear framework of explanation, the nature of which leads to a well-articulated practice' (Howe, 1987: 17).

SOCIALIST IDEOLOGY

Returning to the four societal paradigms discussed in Chapters 3–6, we will now try to answer the question posed at the end of Chapter 2, 'Which of the societal paradigms is most congruent with a progressive view of social work?' That is, which paradigm is most congruent with the fundamental values of humanitarianism and egalitarianism; with the instrumental values of respect, self-determination, and acceptance; with a social belief in the individual as a social being; with an economic belief whereby societal decisions dominate economic decisions; with a political belief in participatory democracy; and with a social welfare system that emphasizes equality, solidarity, and community?

To help answer the above question a schematic outline of the four paradigms is presented in Table 9.1. Both neo-conservatism and liberalism adhere to the basic values of capitalism, with the former advocating a purer form (less government intervention) than the latter. Conversely, both social democracy and Marxism adhere to the basic values of socialism, although they differ on the means to achieve a socialist state. While a major goal of the capitalist paradigms is to maintain basic capitalist structures in North America, the socialists would have as their major goal the transformation of these capitalist structures to socialist structures. The implication for the social work profession is that by deciding which societal paradigm is most congruent with its ideology, social work is also deciding its position with respect to preserving or changing the society within which it is located.

As we have already seen, and as is clear from Table 9.1, social work ideology has much more in common with the socialist paradigms than it does with the capitalist paradigms.[1] If social workers truly believe in the values and ideals they espouse, then they cannot subscribe to and try to maintain a social order that contradicts and violates many of these same values and ideals. If the social work profession is to be true to itself it must, first of all, realize that in North America, at least, it embodies one of the contradictions of capitalism. The profession is based on humanitarian and egalitarian ideals but operates within a social order based on an inequality whereby a minority dominates (controls and exploits) the majority. Second, in light of this awareness, social workers must do something about it. They must try to change the present social order to one that is more compatible with their own world view. To bring about this transformation they must go beyond critical analysis of our capitalist social system and develop transformational theory or what is termed here structural social work theory.

Although structural social work may align itself with socialism, it must be a *revitalized socialism* and not the 'old' socialism of the twentieth century, which reflected a project of emancipation rooted in domination. This revitalized, socialism must engage with post-

TABLE 9.1   OVERVIEW OF FOUR PARADIGMS

	Neo-Conservatism	Liberalism
Social Beliefs	Freedom (or liberty) Individualism Inequality	Freedom Individualism Inequality (all of the above modified by humanitarianism and pragmatism)
Economic Beliefs	Laissez-faire Competitive capitalism Private ownership	Mixed economy or welfare capitalism
Political Beliefs	Élite rule Dominance of economic system Law, order, and stability Paternalism	Representative democracy Pluralism
View of Social Problems	Caused by individual weakness, deviance, or heredity	Caused by social disorganization, which is inherent in a capitalist system
View of Social Welfare	Hostile toward a well-developed welfare state Goal is to relieve destitution Ideal welfare model = residual system	Used to modify negative effects of capitalism Goal is to provide a social minimum Ideal welfare model = institutional system
Nature of Social Work Practice	Coerce people to look after themselves Social control Poor Law treatment Emphasize investigations to prevent abuse	Personal reform Limited social reform Advocacy

(continued)

TABLE 9.1 (CONTINUED)

	Social Democracy	Marxism
Social Beliefs	*Primary Values* Freedom Collectivism Equality *Derivative Values* Humanitarianism Democratic participation	Freedom Collectivism Equality
Economic Beliefs	Government intervention Public control of economy Equitable distribution of income and opportunities	Public ownership of economy Industrial democracy Distribution according to need Planned economy
Political Beliefs	Participatory democracy Capitalism can be transformed by a social democracy The state has a positive role to play in society	Participatory democracy Government planning enhances democracy Transformation of capitalism by class conflict
View of Social Problems	Caused by various social conflicts inherent in a capitalist society	Caused by social relationships (owners vs. workers) inherent in capitalism
View of Social Welfare	Welfare capitalism can be used as a stepping stone toward socialism Ideal welfare system = structural model (goal is to promote egalitarianism)	Welfare capitalism props up capitalism but also represents efforts of the working class Ideal welfare system = structural model
Nature of Social Work Practice	Provide practical, humanitarian care to casualties of capitalism Restructure society along socialist lines	Revolutionary: no social change role possible in a capitalist society Evolutionary: essentially the same as social democracy

modernism, as well as with feminist, anti-racist, and other struggles against domination, and demand the acknowledgement and celebration of diversity in cultures, sexualities, races, ages, abilities, and other human characteristics that were excluded, suppressed, or discriminated against within an unreconstructed modernist version of socialism (Leonard, 1997). In other words, structural social work must align itself with a form of socialism that is informed and reconstituted by the feminist, anti-racist, postmodern, and other anti-oppressive critiques outlined in Box 9.1.

BOX 9.1 TOWARDS A RECONSTRUCTED SOCIALISM

- Move beyond the preoccupation of the old socialism with class as the primary source of oppression and include the voices and experiences of all oppressed groups.
- Deconstruct the gender neutrality of old socialism and its oppressive assumptions about women's responsibilities in society to eliminate its gender exclusion and its patriarchal base.
- Deconstruct the colour-blindness of old socialism and its oppressive assumptions about white superiority to eliminate its preoccupation with pursuing mainly the interests of white persons in general and white, bourgeois males in particular.
- Deconstruct the role of the state in maintaining dominant patriarchal and heterosexual relations and replace this narrow politics with a politics of difference that seeks true social equality.
- Reorganize the sexual division of labour by breaking down the separation between the private sphere of home, family, and unpaid work and the public sphere of paid work, the market, and state.
- Deconstruct the assumptions about traditional family forms and gender systems that underpin much public policy and most welfare models and reconstitute socialism so that it reflects the multiple forms of families that are present today.
- Be cognizant of the claim of many socialist feminists that there is a relationship between capitalism and patriarchy and that socialism and feminism complement and need each other.
- Deconstruct the (Eurocentric) dominant culture and reconstruct the concept of culture so that cultural differences are celebrated and cultural equality is a value of a reconstituted socialism.
- Bridge positive and liberating aspects of socialism's modernist critical theory tradition with those of postmodernism by:
    - retaining ideals of social justice, emancipation, and equality in a way that respects difference, diversity, and inclusion;

- working on the interstices of materialist philosophies and critical postmodernism;
- avoiding totalizing belief systems and essentialisms, on the one hand, and politically disabling fragmentation along with witless relativism, on the other.
• Challenge fatalistic ideas, such as the belief that today's situation is evolutionary and inevitable—what was made by a small elite can be unmade and/or remade.
• Expose 'Third Way' politics as an excuse for individualism and blaming victims, and develop the socialist counter-discourse of why we need government intervention today.

It must be acknowledged that many persons today, both inside and outside social work, are skeptical of socialism as a working model for society. Given the fall of the Berlin Wall, the dictatorial nature and subsequent failure of Soviet socialism, and the rise of neo-conservatism, many people have given up on any notion of a socialist alternative. This skepticism has been reinforced by a nihilistic school of postmodern thinking that dismisses meta-narratives or broad interpretive schemas like those employed by Marx or Freud, and thus rejects socialism and most other forms of Enlightenment reason. However, it must also be acknowledged that many persons today, inside and outside social work, including many (critical) postmodernists, still subscribe to such socialist values as social justice, equity, collective care, and structured opportunities so that all classes, races, genders, cultures, sexualities, ages, and abilities may attain personal and social fulfillment. Although socialism as an ideology, or as a meta-narrative, may have fallen out of favour with many progressive thinkers, its ideals and values have not. Structural social work, like any other radical social work approach, has always been underpinned by socialist ideology, but today it must be a reconstructed or reconstituted socialism.

THE HERITAGE OF STRUCTURAL SOCIAL WORK THEORY

Historical Overview

Structural social work is part of the larger radical social work movement and, therefore, adheres to certain themes common to all schools of radical social work. These themes are outlined in the 'radical social work' section below. Structural social work theory is the term adopted here for a number of reasons. First, the term 'structural' is descriptive of the problems that confront social work in that they are an inherent, built-in part of our present social order. Our social institutions function in such a way that they discriminate against people along lines of class, gender, race, sexual orientation, disability, and so on. Second, the term 'structural' is prescriptive for social work practice as it indicates that the focus for change is mainly on the structures of society and not solely on the individual. Third, structural social work theory appears to be more flexible and inclusive, and, in many cases, more realistic, than most other radical theories. For example, it is not only concerned with one group of oppressed people, such as the poor, but with all groups who are victims of the present social order. Also, it does not restrict social work practice to either inside or outside the existing social welfare system. And, finally, much of the developmental work of structural social work theory has been carried out in Canada, where it has assumed the status of a major social work perspective.

'Structural social work' is a term first used by Middleman and Goldberg in 1974. However, although these authors identified the social environment as the source of social problems, they attributed them to the liberal notion of social disorganization. Nowhere do they call for wholesale social change, nor do they present a social or ideological analysis of capitalism. Instead, their prescription for social problems falls within the ecological approach. Middleman and Goldberg (1974: 26) state that 'the assumption that inadequate social arrangements are predominantly responsible for the plight of many clients of social agencies suggests the need for social workers who can *help people to modify the social situations that limit their functioning*' (emphasis added). Although Middleman and Goldberg point out much that is wrong with capitalism (without mentioning capitalism, using instead the term 'social environment'), nowhere do they call for its overthrow. There are many radical social work writers in the United States, but none, other than Middleman and Goldberg (see also Goldberg-Ward and Middleman, 1974), have used the term 'structural social work' to describe their particular radical approach.

Arguably, most radical social work literature has originated in Britain. As with the American literature, however, very few radical writers use the term 'structural social work'. Ann Davis (1991: 71) is one exception. In 'A Structural Approach to Social Work' she presents two contrasting approaches of structural social work that are offered in the literature:

> These two broad approaches which offer a contrasting analysis of, and ways of working with structural issues, provide different starting points for social workers in training and practice. The first, in arguing for maintenance within given conditions, promotes a consensual view of practice in which recognition of the discrimination suffered by vulnerable groups is dealt with through advocacy within organizational and political givens. The second, in arguing for change of existing structures which perpetuate inequality, promotes an adversarial view of practice which simultaneously seeks to alleviate and transform the conditions in which oppressed clients find themselves.

The latter approach corresponds to the view of structural social work presented in this book.

Most of the developmental work on the structural approach to social work has been carried out in Canada. It was pioneered by Maurice Moreau (1979, 1990; Moreau and Leonard, 1989) at the School of Social Work at Carleton University in the mid-1970s with the help of many of his colleagues at Carleton,[2] the University of Montreal,[3] and the Université du Québec à Montréal.[4] This approach was presented by Moreau as an umbrella for the major radical themes of Marxism, feminism, radical humanism, and radical structuralism (Carniol, 1992; LeComte, 1990). One of the unique features of this structural approach was that it did not attempt to prioritize different forms of oppression—classism, racism, patriarchy, heterosexism, and so on—into some kind of hierarchical listing of most to least fundamental or most to least debilitating (Moreau and Leonard, 1989). Rather, the structural approach views various forms of oppression as intersecting with each other at numerous points, creating a total system of oppression (see Sklar et al., 1986; Wineman, 1984). Another notable feature of the structural approach is that it does not restrict itself to working only with social institutions. Instead, it is a generalist model of practice requiring knowledge and skills for working with individuals, families, groups, and communities, always making the connection between the personal and the political (Carniol, 1992; LeComte, 1990).

The structural social work approach has continued to develop in Canada since the mid-seventies. Moreau continued researching and writing on the subject until his death in 1990. The structural approach continues to be an integral part of the Carleton School of Social Work program, although it does not appear to be the rallying framework it was in the late seventies and during most of the eighties (LeComte, 1990). At least four other Canadian schools of social work publicize their programs as being structural or structural/feminist in orientation.[5] In addition to its analytical and theoretical appeal, the experience of many graduates from structural schools with respect to the practical relevance of structural social work is very promising (LeComte, 1990; Moreau and Leonard, 1989). Although there was a lull in structural and radical social work publications during most of the eighties, there has been a significant resurgence since 1989.[6] The radical/structural social work literature of the nineties, for the most part, has attempted to deal with one of the major criticisms of the previous radical social work—that it was long on analysis but short on practice. Fook's (1993) book on radical casework, Ife's (1995) book on community development, and Martin's (1990) and Williams's (1989) books on social policy are examples of applying structural concepts and analyses to particular areas of practice. As well, much of anti-oppressive social work has developed from structural social work (see Mullaly, 2002).

Radical Social Work

Clark and Asquith (1985) have noted that social workers who are committed to some type of socialist vision, ranging from 'mild social reformism to revolutionary Marxism', are attracted to the radical social work perspective. Langan and Lee (1989a) contend that many social workers (socialist and non-socialist) are attracted to this perspective as well because they have found that conventional theory is inappropriate for dealing with the social reality of so many people. This perspective chastises conventional social work for failing to develop a critical self-awareness and for often pathologizing oppressed people by offering individualistic explanations of social problems. The radical perspective also 'urges social workers to get involved in socialist political action as much in their own interests as in the interests of those who depend upon their services' (Langan and Lee, 1989a: 4). The progressive view of social work discussed in Chapter 2 corresponds to the radical perspective. Davis (1991: 70) summarizes the radical argument:

> social workers need to understand the nature of state power and the role of social work as an element of state control and oppression, and to construct an approach to practice which is underpinned by this understanding. Such practice must be directed at challenging and changing structures which oppress.

Beginning with the Settlement House movement, social work has always had a radical element. Bertha Reynolds, an American Marxist social work academic and activist during the 1930s and 1940s, argued that to be a good social worker, one had to be a radical (Withorn, 1984). 'Like many other radical social workers, Bertha Reynolds . . . viewed the rise of radical social work as consistent with the ethics and values of the profession' (Wagner, 1990: 6). In spite of its long history, however, radical social work has only developed a substantial literature and following since 1975 with the publications of Bailey and Brake's *Radical Social Work* in Britain, Jeffry Galper's *Politics of Social Services* in the United States, and Harold Throssell's *Social Work: Radical Essays* in Australia. That these three publications were written independent of one another, in three different English-speaking continents, but at the same time and with similar alternative approaches to conventional social work practice, and that they corresponded with the emergence of the world economic crisis and the fiscal crisis of the state should not be surprising. It is completely consistent with one of the features of the concept of a paradigm that when the dominant paradigm is no longer able to evade anomalies or to explain crises, competing paradigms will begin to emerge or re-emerge.

Because of radical social work's association with socialism, which is an extremely broad tendency, there is a wide range of opinion among radical social workers (Clark and Asquith, 1985). Different shades of socialism coexist under the radical social work label.[7] Evidence of these differences is found in the following list of names that have been applied to radical social work: critical social work (Allan et al., 2003; Carniol, 1979; Hick et al., 2005); Marxist social work (Corrigan and Leonard, 1978; Longres, 1986; Wineman, 1984); political social work (Withorn, 1984); progressive social work (Jones, 1983; Smid and van Krieken, 1984); radical social work (Bailey and Brake, 1975; Galper, 1975; Langan and Lee, 1989b; Pritchard and Taylor, 1978; Simpkin, 1979; Statham, 1978); socialist social work (Galper, 1980); socialist welfare work (Bolger et al., 1981); and structural social work (Davis, 1991; Middleman and Goldberg, 1974; Moreau, 1979; Moreau and Leonard, 1989). These nominal differences suggest that there is less homogeneity among radical social workers than is often believed by both enthusiasts and critics. Mullaly and Keating (1991) contend that the above schools of radical thought tend to fall into one of three traditional schools of socialist thought—social democracy, revolutionary Marxism, and evolutionary Marxism—and that these three perspectives differ on: (1) the place of radical social workers in the capitalist welfare system and whether they work within or outside it; (2) the fundamental source of oppression in a capitalist society; and (3) the priority given to the personal versus the political in a strategy of social transformation. These differences reflect disagreement on the means for transcending capitalism rather than any disagreement on the goal of social transformation itself.

There are also several areas of agreement. Mullaly and Keating (1991) have identified nine common themes found in the radical social work literature, with expected differences in emphasis:

1. Capitalism is rejected in favour of socialism.
2. Liberal reformism is rejected as a way of dealing with social problems.
3. The capitalist welfare system carries out interrelated political and economic functions that prop up capitalism.
4. Social welfare as a societal norm is antithetical to capitalism.
5. Conventional social work perpetuates social problems.
6. The 'individual vs society' is a false dichotomy as private troubles cannot be understood or treated apart from their social or political causes.
7. The feminist perspective is an epistemological imperative for radical social work; it not only decodes sexism and patriarchy but links the personal and the political better than any other theory and emphasizes transformational politics.
8. Classism and patriarchy are not the only oppressions concerning radical social workers; racism, ageism, heterosexism, imperialism, and ableism are increasingly viewed as structurally oppressive forces.
9. Professionalism distances professionals from service users and serves the former at the expense of the latter; unionization is the preferred mode of organization for radical social workers.

These major areas of agreement among radical social workers are not static. As radical social work theory continues to develop, other areas of agreement will emerge.

STRUCTURAL SOCIAL WORK AS A CRITICAL SOCIAL THEORY

Structural social work is part of a school of social theory known as critical theory. Critical theory provides criticisms and alternatives to traditional, mainstream social theory, philosophy, and science. It is motivated by an interest in the emancipation of those who are oppressed, is informed by a critique of domination, and is driven by an goal of liberation (Kellner, 1989). Critical theory concerns itself with moving from a society characterized by exploitation, inequality, and oppression to one that is emancipatory and free from domination.

Karl Marx is arguably the founder of critical theory. His ideas and emancipatory intentions have been extended and developed by the Frankfurt School (most notably Theodore Adorno, Max Horkheimer, and Herbert Marcuse) and by its heir apparent, Jürgen Habermas (see Jay, 1973). 'The basic idea of their "critical theory" is that since persons cannot be free from that about which they are ignorant, liberation depends in the first instance on recognition of that which imprisons the human mind or dominates the human person' (Sabia and Wallulis, 1983: 4).

In *Critical Theory in Political Practice* (1990: 3) Stephen Leonard defines critical theory:

> A critical theory of society is defined as a theory having practical intent. As its name suggests, it is critical of existing social and political institutions and practices, but the criticisms it levels are not intended simply to show how present society is unjust, only to leave everything as it is. A critical theory of society is understood by its advocates as playing a crucial role in changing society. In this, the link between social theory and political practice is perhaps the defining characteristic of critical theory, for a critical theory without a practical dimension would be bankrupt on its own terms.

Critical theory, then, is different from most social science theory constructed according to the canons of scientific inquiry. Traditional social theory may describe and explain social processes, but it is quite independent of political practice. Its commitment is to the advancement of objective knowledge by attempting to understand the world as it really is. Conversely, critical theory is committed to change the world 'in ways that can help "emancipate" those on the margins of society by providing them with insights and intellectual tools they can use to empower themselves' (S. Leonard, 1990: xiii).

Leonard (1990) contends that there are three requirements or undertakings of a critical theory: (1) it must locate the sources of domination in actual social practices; (2) it must present an alternative vision (or at least an outline) of a life free from such domination; and (3) it must translate these tasks in a form that is intelligible to those who are oppressed in society. Current examples of theory that satisfy these requirements and, therefore, are critical theories (by definition) in practice are Paulo Freire's 'pedagogy of the oppressed', 'liberation theology', and some forms (i.e., transformative forms) of feminist theory (S. Leonard, 1990).

In accordance with the above requirements of a critical theory, structural social work theory is a critical theory. It is critical of existing social, economic, and political institutions and practices and seeks to change them. It has articulated an alternative social vision (or at least an outline) consistent with progressive social work values in which life is free from domination. And, as will be seen in the following chapters, its major thrust is to involve people in its social analysis and in its political practice. Other forms of social work theory are also critical theories according to the above criteria—transformative forms of feminist social work, anti-racist social work, anti-oppressive social work, and Aboriginal anti-colonial social work.

Ben Agger (1998: 4), one of the leading critical social theory writers in North America, points out that there is not one critical theory but a 'theory cluster', that is, a number of different theories can be considered to be critical theories. He argues that for a theory to be considered as a critical social theory (CST), it must have the following features:

- CST opposes positivism (i.e., belief in an objective, value-free scientific method) because knowledge is not simply a reflection of an inert world, but is an active construction by theorists who necessarily make certain assumptions about the world they study, which is not a value-free activity.
- CST distinguishes between the past and the present, largely characterized by domination and exploitation, and a possible future free from these phenomena. This future can be realized through concerted political and social action.
- CST argues that domination is structural, i.e., people's everyday lives are affected by such social institutions as politics, the economy, and culture.
- CST argues that structures of domination are reproduced through people's internalized oppression or false consciousness.
- CST argues that social change begins in people's everyday lives—sexuality, family, workplace. Thus, CST rejects determinism in favour of the power of agency (personal and collective).
- CST conceptualizes the bridge between agency and structure as dialectical, i.e., structure conditions everyday experience, but knowledge of structure can help people change social conditions.
- CST holds people responsible for their own liberation and cautions them not to oppress others as part of the liberation process. (Agger, 1998: 4–5)

As with Stephen Leonard's three undertakings of critical theory, structural social work also adheres to Agger's criteria of critical social theory. By any account, structural social work theory is a critical theory.

There are actually two competing perspectives of critical theory—modernist and postmodernist version—and there are a number of versions of postmodernism, with the critical postmodern school containing emancipatory purpose. Both the modernist and postmodernist views are committed to a conception of social theory that is emancipatory in intent and politically engaged, but neither has been able to make good this commitment (S. Leonard, 1990). The major difference between the two is that whereas modernism believes it has the potential for overcoming domination and oppression in all its forms, postmodernism indicts this belief and views modernism as another form of enslavement. In Chapter 7 a brief overview of the postmodern critique of modernism was presented, along with the some of the limitations of postmodernism and its utility for reformulating the old socialist paradigm. Here I will present a brief summary of modernism and post-modernism before arguing that it is a false dichotomy or binary opposite to choose one or the other as a basis for structural social work theory and practice; both are necessary.

It should be noted at the outset that a substantial literature on postmodernism has developed over the past two decades in both the humanities and the social sciences. However, some still tend to impose a clear, complete, and time-defined break—what could be called a 'great divide'—between anything written in the period now known as modernity (from the Age of Enlightenment around the end of the eighteenth century up to the present or recent past, which includes most critical social theory writings) and writings in the era of postmodernity (from around 1970 to the present, according to David Harvey [1989]). Such a position is uninformed, uncritical, and non-scholarly. Although there are major differences between the two, often overlooked or not known in the first place is the fact that postmodernism and critical social theory share a common intellectual heritage. The postmodern writers Baudrillard, Derrida, Foucault, and Lyotard all wrote within the period of modernity, did not reject progressive causes, and based their critiques of the Enlightenment on the thinking of Nietzsche and Heidegger. The latter is seen by many to be the archetype and trend-setter of postmodernism. Both Heidegger and Nietzsche influenced the Frankfurt School's critique of civilization. Both sets of critiques reject the Cartesian philosophy of identity (with its omission of the Other), the emancipatory myth of teleology, and positivism (Nietzsche declared not only God dead, but all imposter gods such as philosophy and science).

Modernism

Habermas (1983) contends that the project of modernity came into focus in the eighteenth century even though the preconditions of modernity were put in place much earlier, during the Renaissance transition from the Middle Ages to the modern world. Enlightenment thinkers of the eighteenth century sought 'to use the accumulation of knowledge generated by many individuals working freely and creatively for the pursuit of human emancipation and the enrichment of daily life' (Harvey, 1989: 12). The increased domination of nature by the scientific revolution promised freedom from scarcity and want and reduced the risks of natural calamities. The project of modernity was to develop rational forms of social organization and to use rational thought to liberate people from the irrationalities of myth, religion, and superstition and to release them from the arbitrary use of power that characterized European life prior to that time (Harvey, 1989; S. Leonard, 1990). Doctrines of equality, liberty, faith in human educated intelligence, and universal reason abounded, and it was expected that 'the arts and sciences would promote not only the control of natural forces but also understanding of the world and of the self, moral progress, the justice of institutions and even the happiness of human beings' (Harvey, 1989: 13).

In this modernist project human beings were freed from the beliefs that everyone and everything belonged to a preordained place in the grand scheme of things and that all they could do was contemplate the wonder of it all. Prior to modernism no one should question, let alone attempt to change, the world as it was given to us by Divine Providence

(Howe, 1994). Modernist thinkers detached themselves from the universe 'in order to examine it, probe it, penetrate it, fathom it, see of what it is made, understand how it works, explain it, control it, use it, and exploit it [for the betterment of all people]' (Howe, 1994: 514–15).

On the surface, it would seem that the project of modernity would be a worthwhile endeavour. However, its commitment to reason as the sole determinant of knowledge has proved problematic because scientific reasoning became the model. Given the success of science in understanding and dominating the natural world in the interests of human welfare, modernists adopted scientific rationality, objective knowledge, and the development of grand theories (including socialism and capitalism) as the way of understanding the social world and as the means of attaining human emancipation. By the nineteenth century the newly established social sciences (the inheritors of the Enlightenment project) had adopted positivism as the dominant and legitimate means of pursuing knowledge. Thus, the demand for objective, empirically verifiable knowledge led to the dismissal of normative concerns and, more importantly, to a dogma that knowledge for its own sake ought to be pursued. Legitimate knowledge was restricted to that most closely resembling natural and universal laws, which guided the physical sciences (S. Leonard, 1990). The twentieth-century experience, with its holocausts, two world wars, militarism, devastation of the environment, threat of nuclear annihilation, and the nuclear bombing of Nagasaki and Hiroshima, shattered the emancipatory ideal of modernism.

Modernist thought contained a host of difficult problems and contradictions. For example, who could claim to possess superior reason and knowledge and under what conditions would this reason and knowledge be exercised as power? Whose Utopian plan should be adopted and what guarantees existed that it would not become oppressive? What should be the relationship between the means of obtaining knowledge and the ends to which it would be put? (Harvey, 1989). Questions like these are ignored in traditional social science with its focus on developing knowledge for the sake of knowledge and with no attempt to connect theory to any political practice.

Modernist critical theory departs from traditional social theory in a number of areas and, in so doing, has attempted to address (but not necessarily resolve) a number of the above criticisms of modernism. It is normative in nature and practical in intent; it rejects such scientist elements of positivism as 'science is the only means of obtaining knowledge' and that objectively verifiable facts constitute the only legitimate form of knowledge; it does not believe that the subjects who create the knowledge can be distinguished from the objects of that knowledge; and it subscribes to the belief that knowledge and a commitment to human emancipation (i.e., theory and practice) cannot be separated. The best-known critical theorists—Marx,[8] members of the Frankfurt School, and Jürgen Habermas—all have addressed these issues in varying degrees.[9] In spite of the problems associated with the project of modernity—its crimes against humanity in the name of progress and order, its grand theories of individual and social development that are Eurocentric and androcentric, and its professional discourses and practices that actually homogenize, monitor, and control subordinate populations (supposedly in their own interests) (Leonard, 1995)—its emancipatory intent would still appear to be a laudable goal for those concerned with human well-being and social justice. There is consensus that Marx, the Frankfurt thinkers, and Habermas were unable to conceptualize the practical intent of their critical theories. However, rather than abandoning modernist critical theory altogether, maybe the means of achieving the Enlightenment ideal of human emancipation has to be rethought. To assist in this task, the ideas, ideals, and practices of postmodernism are examined below to see what, if any, insights it might hold for critical theory.

Postmodernism

Although Marx, the Frankfurt School, and Habermas have had a tremendous influence on critical social theory scholars, a rival perspective to modernist thought has assumed major attention in the past two decades. This rival perspective belongs to a tradition of rejectionist criticism of modernity that calls for a 'total break with the Enlightenment' (Fraser, 1985: 165–6). This tradition, as noted above, goes back to Nietzsche and Heidegger, and more recently it includes the French post-structuralists (e.g., Lyotard) and arguably its most influential proponent, Michel Foucault. Foucault presents a compelling critique of many modernist ideas and concepts, even though he describes his work as having emancipatory intent (Leonard, 1990).

It is important to understand that postmodernism is not restricted to postmodern social theory (Agger, 1998). It includes postmodern architecture, art, and design as well as postmodern literary and cultural theory. With respect to postmodern social theory, a range of perspectives will deeply affect the kind of politics that might emerge from them. At one end of the continuum, postmodernism is a conservative, individualistic, and nihilistic doctrine that believes there is no potential for solidarity among oppressed persons or for social change efforts because every person is his or her own moral agent—a position that Ife (1997) calls an ' anything goes brand of politics' and what Geertz (1986) calls 'witless relativism'. At the other end of the postmodern social theory spectrum are those writers who have taken postmodern analyses and criticisms of modernity as essential ingredients in an attempt to revitalize critical social theory. Examples of some of these latter theorists include Ben Agger, Stanley Arnowitz, Terry Eagleton, Nancy Fraser, David Harvey, Frederic Jameson, Douglas Kellner, and Timothy Luke. Examples of such theorists within social work and social welfare include Jim Ife (1997, 1999), Peter Leonard (1997), Bob Mullaly (2002), and Bob Pease and Jan Fook (1999). This book and its development of the new structural social work follow this 'critical postmodernist' approach.

Although there is no agreement about when the world entered its postmodern phase, David Harvey, in his celebrated book, *The Condition of Postmodernity: An Enquiry into the Origins of Cultural Change* (1989), contends that it emerged as a full-blown though still incoherent movement somewhere between 1968 and 1972. He documents how this cultural transformation from modernism to postmodernism occurred in such areas as architecture, art, literature, urban planning, philosophy, theology, and all other arenas of intellectual activity. Although the nature and depth of this transformation is debatable, there is no doubt that, in the words of Huyssens (1984), 'in an important sector of our culture there is a noticeable shift in sensibility, practices and discourse formations, which distinguishes a post-modern set of assumptions, experiences and propositions from that of a preceding period' (cited in Harvey, 1989: 39).

The postmodernists[10] reject the modernist's claim that modernism has brought about material and social progress for some populations because, at the same time, it has also meant exploitation, impoverishment, cultural destruction, and death for others through its association with modern imperialism, colonialism, economic development, and warfare (Leonard, 1994). Postmodernists observe that universal truths arrived at by rational thought are often used to transform both the natural and social worlds according to those universal principles. In doing so, differences are often abolished, sometimes through force in the name of collectivism and historical inevitability (Howe, 1994). Modernist claims to universal truths omit the experiences and forms of knowledge generated by women, non-Europeans, and the most subordinated classes (Leonard, 1994). The pursuit of scientific truths in human affairs has at times led to totalitarianism and Utopian visions that, in turn, have repeatedly led to repression and control. Therefore, post-modernists reject all totalizing belief systems or meta-narratives, such as Marxism and socialism, which seek to impose an ideal order on society (Howe, 1994).

Instead of believing in a single reality derived from a single rationality, discourse, or meta-narrative, postmodernists claim that different realities exist at any one time and that these are constantly being defined and redefined by different actors in different contexts (Ife, 1996). Thus, any attempt to develop a universal explanation of history, politics, or society simply imposes one particular definition of reality on all situations at all times and in all places. Such an imposition has no validity because no centres of authority and truth, and no meta-narratives of progress, emancipation, and perfection, compel universal consensus (Lyotard, 1984).

To the postmodernist, truth is not centred in a particular form of human reasoning. It is decentralized and localized in different places at different times. In fact, many truths are dispersed across time and place (Howe, 1994). Postmodernists reject the idea of one correct answer or one best way of doing or understanding things. 'There is a refusal to accept that some cultural groups and their ways of thinking have a monopoly on the truth' (Howe, 1994: 520–1). Postmodernism also does not accept traditional disciplinary boundaries, as these represent parochial attempts to define and impose particular views on society (Howe, 1994; Ife, 1996).

Because postmodernists believe that phenomena such as truth, power, and repression are localized and contextualized rather than universalized, they believe that difference and pluralism ought to be celebrated rather than subsumed inappropriately under some universal banner. The world is characterized by diversity, multiplicity, pluralism, and conflict rather than sameness, unity, monism, and consensus. No group should try to define the reality or experience of another group. 'The relativist, in contrast to the universalist, believes that all forms of behaviour are local; there can be no such thing as human nature, for what is "natural" in one part of the world will be regarded as "unnatural" in another' (Howe, 1994: 524). This relativism has been the basis for attacks against sexism and patriarchy by feminists, against ethnocentrism by visible minorities, and against inherently oppressive social structures by disabled persons and many other marginalized groups. The world is a plurality of different cultural groups, each with its own systems of meaning and understanding and its own perceived needs and purposes (Howe, 1994).

Unlike many modernists, postmodernists do not believe that power is ultimately located within the state. Rather, power is to be found in different localities, contexts, and social situations. The prison, the school, the asylum, the hospital, and the social worker's office are all examples of places where power is dispersed and built up independently of any systematic strategy of class or gender or ethnicity. What happens at each locality cannot be explained by some overarching theory (Harvey, 1989). Foucault believed that only through a multi-faceted and pluralistic attack on localized practices of repression can any global challenge to capitalism be mounted without reproducing all the multiple repressions of capitalism in a new form (Harvey, 1989).

As pointed out in Chapter 7, a cornerstone of postmodernism is its concern for language and discourse. It severely criticizes modernism for the totalistic nature of its use of dominant discourses because these reflect class, gender, race, and other forms of dominant relationships (Leonard, 1994). Howe (1994: 522) summarizes the relationship between language and power:

> Whereas modernity believes that increasing knowledge of the essential and true nature of things produces power, postmodernity reverses the formula, recognizing that the formation of a particular discourse creates contingent centres of power which define areas of knowledge, passing truths and frameworks of explanation and understanding. Those with power can control the language of the discourse and can therefore influence how the world is to be seen and what it will mean. Language promotes some possibilities and excludes others; it constrains what we see and what we do not see.

Another core concern of postmodernism is otherness—that 'all groups have a right to speak for themselves, in their own voice, and have that voice accepted as authentic and legitimate' (Harvey, 1989: 48). Postmodernists criticize the imperialism of an enlightened modernity that presumes to speak for others with a unified voice. This belief in otherness offers the potential for liberation to a whole host of groups (e.g., visible minorities, colonized people, poor persons) and to a whole host of social movements (e.g., women's movement, environmental movement, gay and lesbian liberation movement).

In its concern for difference, for the difficulties of communication, for the complexity and diversity of cultures, interests, and the like, postmodernism exercises a positive influence. The theories and language of modernism tended to gloss over important differences and failed to pay attention to important details and disjunctures. Postmodernism has been especially important in acknowledging the multiple forms of otherness as they emerge from differences in subjectivity, gender, class, race, and so on. It is this aspect of postmodernism that Leonard (1990) says gives it a radical edge.

Although postmodernism offers a useful critique of the oppressive aspects of modernism, it also contains contradictions and limitations with respect to realizing its emancipatory intent. Some of the limitations of postmodernism were outlined in Chapter 7. Some others are presented here. Postmodernists seem to overlook the fact that much of the world is still modernist and that ideology is still a driving force for many people and groups. Much of the postmodern rhetoric appears to avoid confronting the realities of political economy and global power. While postmodernists have argued for otherness, difference, localism, and fragmentation, capitalism has taken another course—globalization of capital accumulation that is being used to subjugate the very groups and localities for which postmodernism expresses its concern. By denying the existence of universal phenomena and by fragmenting people under the banner of localism, is postmodernism not aiding and abetting this subjugation?

Harvey (1989) asks that if, as the postmodernists insist, we cannot aspire to any unified representation of the world, or see it as a whole with connections and differentiations rather than as constantly shifting fragments, how can we ever act coherently with respect to changing it? The simple postmodernist answer is that we should not even try to engage in a global project because any coherent representation or action is either illusory or repressive. This leaves the question open as to what path localized struggles should take to add up to a progressive, rather than regressive, attack on the central forms of capitalist and other structural sources of oppression.

Postmodernism does not accept the notion of historical progress, as the very idea of progress implies an acceptance of a meta-narrative. History and experience are reduced to a series of pure, fragmented, and unrelated presents. Such a breakdown of the temporal order abandons all sense of historical continuity and memory, which means that a pursuit of better futures cannot take place (Harvey, 1989). To the extent that our identities are the creation of our histories, and to the extent that our historically constituted identities are a matter of power/knowledge constraints, postmodernism 'eludes the difficult task of articulating the kind of collective action required to transform our relationships with others in emancipatory ways' (Leonard, 1990: 79). Although postmodernism allows for the development of alternative realities, it does not suggest what these might be and its absence of normative elements precludes any direction to take (Ife, 1996).

Ife (1997) points out a few other contradictions and limitations of postmodernism. It does not account for structural oppressions such as race, class, and gender, as its pluralist perspective sees power as being dispersed throughout society and not concentrated in the hands of a few. By emphasizing difference and localism it reduces any potential for solidarity among groups experiencing the commonality of oppression (whatever its source). A related criticism made by Ife is that, by its rejection of universal meta-narratives, postmodernism is also rejecting the importance of universal discourses that are at the foundation of most social justice movements, such as the peace movement, the environmental movement, the women's movement, and the human rights movement.

By drawing attention away from structural issues and universal notions of social justice, postmodernism appears to have an essential conservative element that can be used as a convenient legitimization for an 'anything goes' brand of politics; it allows for a multiplicity of visions and not just those concerned with social justice. And its emphasis on relativism could be used to justify many human rights violations (e.g., those in China). A final limitation noted here, again taken from Ife, is that by advocating universal skepticism and a universal discourse of difference while indicting all universal truths, postmodernism is self-contradictory.

Implications of Modernism and Postmodernism for Structural Social Work Theory

Modernist and postmodernist critical theory obviously differ in many respects. In fact, each almost represents the very antithesis of the other. However, there are also commonalities between the two. Both stand against domination and oppression and both have failed to reach their emancipatory intent. As well, both fulfill the three criteria of critical theories outlined by S. Leonard (1990). (1) They are both critical of our present social order and locate the sources of domination in actual social practices (although each may identify different practices). (2) They both have, or in the case of postmodernism allow for, many different, alternative visions of society. Modernist critical theory seeks a society based on socialist or collectivist principles, and although critical postmodernism allows for many alternative visions only those concerned with human liberation are legitimate, given its emancipatory intent. (3) Both perspectives have a practical intent, as both see the involvement of marginalized populations as a necessary part of this praxis, albeit in different ways. Critical social theory (both modernist and postmodernist) is a partisan enterprise, because it involves standing alongside oppressed and marginalized populations against exploitation and domination, and both perspectives claim to do this.

Structural social work does not perceive these two perspectives on critical theory to be completely dichotomous or polarized. Instead, it views each as having strengths and limitations that the other does not and seeks to use the strengths of each as a corrective for some of the limitations and contradictions of the other. The following are some examples that reflect this attempt.

One of the major strengths of modernist critical theory is that it attends to pervasive structural issues of oppression and domination, particularly in the areas of class, gender, and race. It recognizes commonalities among all forms of oppression, such as the nature of dominant/subordinate relations, the dynamics and consequences of oppression, and the hegemony of the view of the dominant group and how it is reinforced by social institutions. For example, the deficit situation and sufferings of people may result from social forces of which they are unaware or about which they have little knowledge or understanding. Such is the global nature of capitalism, patriarchy, racism, and the like. A structural analysis helps them to understand and normalize their position in a capitalist, patriarchal, racist society. In turn, understanding and normalization help to free them from feelings of guilt and blame for a situation that they did not cause and open possibilities for solidarity and collective action with other oppressed persons and groups. In other words, a structural analysis links the personal with the political by enabling people to relate their personal experience with oppression to a broader political understanding.

The contribution of critical postmodernism to a structural analysis is to help us recognize that although oppression and exploitation may be universal phenomena, they will be experienced differently by different people living in different places in different contexts. For example, a poor person living on the streets of Toronto would experience poverty differently from a poor person living in rural Newfoundland. An understanding of these differences, along with their meanings for people, would be obtained by the structural social worker through dialogue with those experiencing oppression and then used to inform the larger structural analysis to determine what action should be taken to combat this oppression. Consistent with Foucault's belief, by fighting in a multi-faceted way local practices of oppression, while recognizing that they are attached to broader practices, global oppressions are challenged.

Modernist critical theory emphasizes solidarity among oppressed people, but does so through various meta-narratives. For example, Marxism calls for solidarity of the working class against capitalism and feminism calls for solidarity among women against patriarchy. Solidarity among those who have had common experiences of oppression has been the essence of modernist critical theory's political practice. Solidarity underpins all significant social movements. It is the glue that holds coalitions and alliances together and provides them with their strength, as measured by the numbers of people acting for change. Without solidarity among oppressed people, resistances to the dominant social order are dispersed and weakened. However, the politics of solidarity have often neglected the politics of difference and have reflected in their own organization and culture the very forms of domination and exclusion that existed in the wider societies (Leonard, 1995). Marxism, for example, has often overlooked other forms of oppression, such as patriarchy and racism, and has often viewed the working class as a homogeneous group whose members are equally exploited, not recognizing stratification, ethnicity, gender, and other types of differences within it. Early second-wave feminism also called for solidarity and unity among oppressed 'sisters' without regard to race, social position, and the like, thus failing to acknowledge other forms of oppression experienced by many women. Postmodernism helps the structural social worker develop a new politics of solidarity—one that pursues the idea of fractured identities where differences within particular oppressed groups 'are always given attention, contextualized with reference to their specific geographical location in the world, their class position, and their place within the structures of race and ethnicity . . . age, sexuality, and differences of ability' (Leonard, 1995: 7). In sum, solidarity within and among oppressed groups is crucial in the quest for emancipation, but to avoid various forms of oppressive inclusions and exclusions that have occurred in the past it must incorporate a progressive politics of difference.

Another important area for the structural social worker is that of language and discourse. Most social work activity is carried out through language and discourse, whether counselling, writing reports, reading research and journal articles, or articulating analyses of personal and social problems. Like everyone, social workers are immersed in language (Howe, 1994). The modernists believed that language simply reflected reality and that knowledge (obtained or given through language) was empowering. The task of progressive social workers, then, was to increase their own knowledge of oppression and use their knowledge and analyses when working with marginalized groups. However, the postmodernists have shown us that there is no one universal reality, but many realities, and that language does not have the properties of absolute truth but is historically, culturally, and socially contextualized and largely reflects the interests and world views of dominant groups. Thus, any discourse will include some pieces of information and exclude others.

As well, the messages received may be different from what was intended by the sender. The knowledge historically used by social workers has been that of 'expert' knowledge derived from objective, scientific, and professional sources and has reflected a Eurocentric, patriarchal, and bourgeois bias rather than the lived reality of oppressed persons (Leonard, 1994). This expert knowledge has been disempowering for marginalized populations because it reproduces relationships of hierarchy and subordination and excludes the voices of the very people with whom social work claims to be concerned. Structural social workers would facilitate the authentic voices of marginalized groups to be heard (Ife, 1996) and use this communication to inform and modify their professional knowledge and analyses. This process (called dialogical communication) would be used by both the social workers and the oppressed persons to gain a fuller and more accurate understanding of the particular historical, cultural, and social situation they are confronting. It not only is empowering for oppressed persons to be heard, but it provides social workers with fuller, more accurate information than the traditional privileged, and assumed objective, universal knowledge. This approach recognizes the centrality of language and communication in developing emancipatory theories and practices. Structural social work is committed to respecting the plurality of ways in which human beings find their own voices, while also being committed to solidarity with those who are struggling, against the imposition of others, to find those voices.

In sum, the structural social worker does not perceive modernist and postmodernist critical theory to be totally dichotomous. This approach is similar to that of some other writers (Ife, 1997; Leonard, 1994, 1995) in that it seeks to use the strengths of each to correct the limitations and contradictions of the other. Allan (2003a: 50) argues that critical social work must find a way of keeping the two approaches together, but 'maintain the tension between the two and work with the contradictions, debates and uncertainties that emerge from taking this position.' This view of two opposing sets of forces or theoretical positions acting upon each other constitutes what is called a dialectical relationship (to be discussed in a subsequent section of this chapter). Structural social work as a critical theory is best summarized by Stephen Leonard (1990: 269):

> Domination and oppression take a variety of forms, and because of this, enlightenment and emancipation will also take a variety of forms. From this it should be

clear that any adequate account of critical theory must be cognizant of the need to be sensitive to the plurality and difference that defines our identities and characterizes our lives, and it must also be attentive to the need to open a philosophical and political space in which individuals can find their own voices, however plural and different they may be. At the same time, a critical theory cannot ignore the harsh reality of those who are victims of history; it must be in solidarity with those victims, or it risks seeing its aims and conclusions transformed into idle posturing and hopeless despair. Plurality and solidarity: these must be the watchwords of critical theory.

CLASSIFICATION OF THEORY

There is no shortage of social work knowledge. Many students, in fact, often believe there is an overabundance of knowledge. Social work textbooks and professional journals contain a plethora of theories and theoretical positions. As if the problem of reading and understanding the various theories were not difficult enough, many writers have attempted to group or classify them according to some simple differences. But because any classification scheme is to a degree arbitrary, social work theories are classified in different ways. This has tended to muddy the theoretical waters for social workers. Since these classifications do exist, however, they must be mentioned. Some of the more common classification schemes in social work are outlined here.

1. *Objective vs subjective theories.* Theories either seek to discover the real objective nature of things (e.g., behavioural theories) or they reflect the subjectively generated explanations of what things mean for people (e.g., client-centred theories).
2. *Individual change vs social change theories.* This classification is based on the notion that social work has a dual function. Theories seek to explain how personal change can be brought about or they seek to explain how social change can be realized.
3. *Macro (policy and planning), mezzo (community and organizations), and micro (individual, family, and small group) theories.* These are based on the level of social unit on which social workers focus.
4. *Grand, mid-range, and practice theories.* These theories are based on different levels of abstraction. Grand theories are highly abstract and provide comprehensive conceptual schemes (e.g., Marxism). Mid-range theories offer an explanation for a particular phenomenon or group of phenomena (e.g., labelling theory) or model of intervention (e.g., family therapy). Practice theories are located at a more specific level of action and comprise practice principles (e.g., establishing a trusting relationship with service users).

Other common classification schemes of theory include: 'normative vs non-normative' and 'theory of practice vs theory for practice'.

Most of us have come to believe that the world is comprised of 'facts' that can be put together into a coherent package known as 'the truth'. However, as suggested in the first section of this chapter, there is usually more than one explanation or theory for the same set of phenomena. Theories are not laws—they are explanations for certain phenomena, and there can be more than one explanation for the same phenomena. Put differently, there are a number of competing broad theoretical frameworks (sometimes called paradigms) that explain the same facts in different ways (Naiman, 1997: 13). This does not mean that an objective reality cannot exist outside our own individual perceptions of it. For example, there may be agreement that poverty exists among certain groups, but the explanation of why it exists will differ. Given the fact that theoretical explanations will differ, the scheme used here to classify theories consists of two competing perspectives of the social world—the 'order' perspective and the 'conflict' or 'change' perspective.[11] These two perspectives are both all-inclusive and mutually exclusive: all social theories fall within one perspective or the other, but not in both. Order theories are sometimes called mainstream, conservative, or traditional, while change theories are sometimes called radical, critical, progressive, or conflict. Order theories focus on and support the current social order while change theories focus on the lack of social justice in the current social arrangements and lead us to change them. Other reasons for selecting this classification scheme are: (1) it is used by many social science writers when discussing social theory; (2) it not only accommodates the notion of paradigm as used in this book but recognizes that it is the core of social science (i.e., research is carried out within a paradigm once its boundaries have been established); and (3) it makes the connections among ideological preferences, mid-range social work theories, and actual social work practice.

ORDER AND CONFLICT/CHANGE PERSPECTIVES

Order and change perspectives represent two competing views on the nature of people, society, and social problems. The former views society as orderly, stable, and persistent, unified by shared culture and values, and a consensus on the desired form of society and its institutions. The latter views society as a continually contested struggle among groups with opposing views and interests. From a change perspective, society is held together not by consensus but by differential control of resources and political power. The neo-conservative and liberal paradigms, as well as conventional social work, are based on the order view (i.e., maintenance of the capitalist system). The social democratic and Marxist paradigms, as well as structural social work, are based on the change view (i.e., transformation of the capitalist system). 'As a generalization, groups or individuals committed to the maintenance of the status quo employ order models of society. . . . Dissident groups, striving to institutionalize new claims, favour a conflict (change) analysis of society' (Horton, 1966: 703).

Reasons and Perdue (1981) proposed two sets of logically interrelated and essential assumptions, one underpinning the order view of society and one underpinning the change view (They use the term 'conflict' rather than 'change'). Table 9.2 contains a modified version of these assumptions, which concern: (1) the nature of human existence; (2) the nature of society; (3) the nature of the relationship between the two; and (4) the nature of social problems.

Order Perspective

The order perspective, which presently dominates North American social thought, is associated with Durkheim and Weber and more recently with Talcott Parsons. Parsons is usually regarded as the founder of an explicitly functionalist theory of society (McDaniel and Agger, 1984), which is synonymous with a systems analysis (i.e., structural-functional analysis) of society and social problems (Horton, 1966).

Society. Any society is comprised of people who are by nature competitive, acquisitive, self-absorbed, individualistic, and therefore predisposed towards disorder. To establish and maintain order, enduring social institutions are created and rules (laws) established so that human interaction can be regulated. In this way all parts of society can be co-ordinated so that members of society and society's organizations and institutions all contribute to the support, maintenance, and stability of the social system. The basic assumption is that there is agreement on the values and rules of society so that they, along with the social institutions regulating the system, must be learned, respected, and revered by everyone. 'We learn what is expected of us in the family, at school, in the workplace and through the media' (Howe, 1987: 35).

Social problems. If a person does not behave in ways expected of, say, a parent, a wage earner, or a law-abiding citizen, it is assumed that something went wrong in that person's socialization process. To ensure itself against disequilibrium, society will attempt to return the person to normal functioning through its social institutions. If society's official agents, such as teachers, social workers, or police, fail to correct or control the malfunctioning or out-of-step person, then he or she may have to be removed from society and the individual's behaviour neutralized by institutionalization. This removes a threat to social stability and also serves as an example to other would-be non-conformists and deviants.

Because it is assumed that there is essential agreement among members of society on the nature of the prevailing institutions and supporting ideology, their existence is taken for granted and the existing order legitimated (Reasons and Perdue, 1981). And because these institutions and their supporting ideology fend off disequilibrium, discontinuity, and disorder of the system, their preservation becomes a social imperative. These assumptions about social institutions being good, necessary, and agreed to, as well as the belief that people are contentious and must be controlled, lead order theorists to conclude that social problems are best described and understood by focusing on lower levels or plateaus of society than on the societal or structural level. In other words, order theorists look at three levels of society for describing, analyzing, and explaining social problems:

(1) the individual level, (2) the family level, and (3) the subcultural level (Reasons and Perdue, 1981).

At the individual level the source of social problems is found within the person him or herself: a person is not conforming to the rules, norms, and expectations of society because of some individual trait. Poverty, mental illness, drug addiction, and criminal activity are blamed on supposed personal defects. As Reasons and Perdue point out, at the individual level social problems are personalized. Poverty and crime, for example, are blamed on some defect of the person and what emerges is 'a biographical portrait that separates the individual from society' (Reasons and Perdue, 1981: 8). Individuals are carefully scrutinized (diagnosed, assessed) to discover the explanation for the problem. One of the most clear-cut examples of an order theory at the individual level is 'biological determinism', which locates the explanation for human behaviour in some aspect of human biology (i.e., genes, chromosomes, anatomy, etc.). If social behaviour is biologically based rather than socially based, then the focus is on changing the person rather than changing society.

Examples of the above type of explanation would include Cesare Lombroso's explanation of criminal activity being caused by persons who are physically distinct from non-criminals. Freud's psychoanalytic theory where intra-psychic phenomena were hypothesized as the determinants of maladjusted behaviour is another example. Much of social work's earlier casework and psychodynamic practices were based on individual explanations of social problems. Sociobiology is a contemporary development of a theory that holds that genetic information explains social behaviour. As recently as 1988 a psychology professor from the University of Western Ontario created international controversy when he published an article alleging that race was connected to intelligence, sexual restraint, and personality, among other personal characteristics (Rushton, 1988).

Most order theorists and most social workers, because they operate from a systems perspective or employ an ecological model when dealing with social problems, are not satisfied with individual levels of explanations of social problems. From this comes the liberal concept of social disorganization. As detailed in Chapter 4, this concept is based on the notion that the present liberal-capitalist social order contains some defects that create disorganization and bring harm to some people, and the job of social work (and other occupations) is to rectify these defects (i.e., to fix the parts of society not working properly so that society works better and is able to persist). Systems theory and an ecological approach to social work, however, do not try to change the essential nature of the system but deal with individuals and/or environmental influences within the system. The types of environmental influences most frequently dealt with by social workers practising from an order perspective are the family and the subculture.

The family as an important social unit has received enormous attention from social workers and others since the early sixties. Family disorganization has been cited as an explanation for most social problems that social workers deal with. The family is routinely analyzed in an attempt to find its contribution to situations of poverty, juvenile delinquency, mental illness, alcoholism, family violence, poor school performance,

TABLE 9.2   ASSUMPTIONS OF ORDER AND CONFLICT/CHANGE PERSPECTIVES

	Order	*Conflict/Change*
Nature of Human Existence	competitive, contentious, individualistic, and acquisitive	co-operative, collective, and social
Nature of Social Institutions	must endure and regulate human interactions (political, economic, educational, religious, family) to avoid disorder	dynamic with no sacred standing; facilitate co-operation, sharing, and common interests
Nature of Society	consists of interdependent and integrated institutions and a supportive ideological base; viewed as an organism or system with each part contributing to the maintenance of the whole	in a society of structural inequality the social nature of human existence is denied with social institutions serving private rather than public interests
Continuity of Social Institutions	prevail because of agreement (consensus) among society's members	prevail in a class-divided society because of control and coercion
Nature of Relationship between People and Society	members are expected to conform and adapt to consensus-based social arrangements	acceptance, conformity, and adaptation to a coercive social order is questioned
Nature of Social Problems	socialization will occasionally fail whereby reverence for institutions and respect for rules will not be learned; such occurrence on a large scale is a social problem	faulty socialization is more a matter of defective rules than defective control; rules are problematic

(continued)

TABLE 9.2   (CONTINUED)

	Order	*Conflict/Change*
Approach to Social Problems	a) behaviour must be changed through resocialization (rehabilitation, counselling, etc.) or neutralized through formal systems of state control (criminal law, prisons, asylums, etc.)	institutions and ideology must be changed to protect social nature of human existence
	b) social change can only involve minor adjustments that are consistent with the nature of the existing system	behavioural change can only involve minor adjustments consistent with co-operative and collective nature of society; massive commitment to behavioural change is a form of blaming the victim
Paradigms	neo-conservatism liberalism	social democracy Marxism

and so on. Family therapy was viewed as almost a panacea to society's problems and 'family dysfunction' replaced 'individual pathology' as the popular explanation for social problems (but did not eliminate individualistic explanations). Rather than blaming social problems on some defect of the person, problems are attributed at the family level to poor parenting, undeveloped communication skills, and the like. Rather than a 'sick' individual being blamed for social problems, as neo-conservatives contend, problems are blamed on 'maladaptive' or 'dysfunctional' families. Social problems become family problems.

Explanations of social problems at the subcultural level of society focus on various categories of people who are distinct from the larger majority population by reason of such features as race, ethnicity, and class. Subculture theorists believe these distinctive groups have distinctive subcultural values that put them at a disadvantage or in conflict with the larger or dominant culture (Reasons and Perdue, 1981). Social problems are not blamed on the individual or the family at the subcultural level, but are attributed to one's culture.

An example of a subcultural theory is the 'culture of poverty' or what is often termed 'the cycle of poverty theory', which attempts to explain poverty. The culture of poverty theory assumes there are common traits among poor people (feelings of inferiority, apathy, dependence, fatalism, no sense of deferred gratification). These traits are passed on to subsequent generations through the process of socialization so that by the time poor children are of school age they have internalized the basic traits of poverty and are not psychologically prepared to take advantage of the opportunities available to them. No thought is given to the possibility that many of these so-called traits of poor people are actually adaptations and adjustments on the part of the poor to cope with poverty rather than actual causes of poverty.

Another subcultural theory is the 'cultural deprivation theory', which attempts to explain the situation of North American Aboriginal peoples and other minority groups. This theory attributes the second-class status of Aboriginals and other minorities to an inferior culture. In other words, Aboriginal culture is inadequate to prepare persons to function properly (successfully) in the larger society. Examples include: Aboriginal parents do not read to their children; they do not take vacations abroad to expand their children's horizons; there is low motivation for school achievement or for work; there is no concept of the importance of time; welfare and alcoholism are part of this inferior culture. The end result is that children of Aboriginal ancestry are culturally deprived. Once so labelled, of course, they are expected to fail in school and often do so.

Both of the above subcultural explanations of social problems are part of a larger process of 'blaming the victim'. William Ryan (1976) outlines this process:

1. Identify the problem.
2. Study those affected by the problem and discover how they are different from the rest of society.
3. Define the differences, which are in fact the effects of injustice and discrimination, as the causes of the social problem.
4. Assign a government bureaucrat to invent a humanitarian action program to correct the differences by changing the people affected by the problem.

Thus, the solution to social problems originating at the subcultural level is to try to untangle, correct, and make up for the deficiencies of these inferior cultures by changing the people from them. This strategy involves counselling, resocialization, cultural enhancement services, upgrading, rehabilitation, and community education programs. In effect, people are worked on so they can better fit into the mainstream, into the culture of the majority. This process of acculturation leaves society's social institutions unchanged. It is better to change a minority culture than to change social institutions so that they can accommodate the minority culture.

Social work and the order perspective. Within the order perspective social work would operate at the three levels where social problems are seen to occur—the individual, family, and subcultural levels. Because the social order is assumed to be accepted by members of society, then the primary function of the social worker is to preserve it. Both the neo-conservative and the liberal paradigms subscribe to the goal of preserving the capitalist system. In the case of neo-conservatism, social work preserves the capitalist society by coercing and controlling persons who stray from the capitalist way of life. From a liberal perspective, social work preserves the capitalist system by helping people to adjust and cope, or by modifying the immediate environments of persons, or by advocating on behalf of certain groups that have been disadvantaged by capitalism.

Most current social work theories and practices today are based on the order perspective. Major activities are personal reform, limited social reform, and advocacy, all of which are carried out in an effort to humanize capitalism, not to change it. The major theories—psychoanalytic, family therapies, general systems theory, and the ecological approach—all emanate from the order perspective. In the case of psychoanalytic theory the major task is clearly personal reform. In the case of family therapy and general systems theory the major task is to repair the harm or disruption that has upset the healthy functioning of the family or the equilibrium of the system. The ecological approach aims to find the best fit between the person and the system. In none of these theories or approaches is any thought given to the possibility that the source of the problem lies not within the system but is the system itself. This critical omission is the Achilles heel of conventional, mainstream social work carried out in the order tradition.

This is not to say that structural social workers would never use general systems theory or the ecological approach. These perspectives are useful in that they provide the social worker with a snapshot of the current situation with which they are dealing. They identify the relevant actors and organizations in an individual's life and help clarify the relationships among them. However, by themselves, they only describe situations and do not provide any causal explanations for a problem or situation. Unlike critical social theories such as structural social work that contain analyses and explanations for social problems, they offer no theoretical explanation whatsoever for any social phenomena such as poverty, social inequality, or differential levels of power, prestige, and influence in society. Although systems and ecological approaches may include a person's immediate environment (i.e., one's family, school, workplace, community), they do not deal with larger-order structural phenomena. By emphasizing only those aspects of the social environment considered amenable to social work practice, systems theory and the ecological approach ignore broader structural social forces, which in effect reinforces social inequality (Gould, 1987, cited in Pease, 1991).

Pease (1991) has summarized some of the major criticisms and the structural variables that are unaccounted for in systems and ecological models of social work practice:

- They are focused more on stability and preserving the status quo than on social change (Moreau, 1989).
- They assume no conflict among the goals of different groups and no clash of interests between marginalized and dominant groups (Gould, 1987).
- They consider existing power inequalities in society to be the norm (Marchant, 1986).
- They ignore the roles of power and wealth in maintaining inequality and exploitation (Gould, 1987).
- They fail to challenge class, gender, race, and other forms of oppression based on social, economic, and political arrangements (Moreau, 1989).

For the structural social worker these variables are critical for understanding social problems and developing emancipatory forms of social work practice. To this list of criticisms of systems and ecological approaches to social work practice, Finn and Jacobson (2003) add the following: they are so vague and general that they give little specific guidance for practice; the approach's focus on the 'here-and-now' situation and intervention contributes to a neglect of history; while the language offers a metaphor for conceptualizing the person-environment relationship, the translation into practice is not so clear (Rossiter, 1996); feminist scholars such as Walters, Carter, Papp, and Silverstein (1988, cited in Finn and Jacobson, 2003) have noted that systems certainties such as boundaries, roles, and balance actually encode and reinforce the gender stratification of the larger society rather than challenge it; the emphasis on the 'fit' of persons within a social context tends to support rather than question the dominant order and accentuates strategies for adaptation to rather than transformation of existing structural arrangements (Coates, 1992); the approach is reliant on an uncomplicated view of both the person and the environment as it assumes that both are stable, knowable, and non-problematic (Rossiter, 1996); and finally, the approach adheres to liberal notions of the person as an autonomous individual and assumes a basic distinction between the individual and society rather than acknowledging the dialectical relationship between them.

> In short, systems and ecosystems perspectives offer little basis for critical engagement with questions of power. They tend to naturalize arbitrary power differences, and they assume rather than question the dominant social, political, and economic order. These approaches are premised on the positivist view of the social world as a single, objective, and ultimately knowable reality. They offer no epistemological base through which to consider multiple constructions of social reality and the power of thought, language, and structured social interactions that shape these constructions. Systems and ecosystems perspectives focus on extant, 'observed' relations and practices rather than on a critical analysis of how these relations and practices have come to be constructed in a particular manner and at a particular historic moment. (Finn and Jacobson, 2003: 60–1)

Change Perspective

The harmony and consensus extolled in the order perspective as characterizing society are not recognized in the change perspective. Or, if they are, it is because of an illusion created by the dominant group in society to lead the less powerful into accepting an unequal social order in which the dominant group is the main beneficiary (Howe, 1987). The change perspective is strongly identified with Karl Marx (and therefore with socialism) and a variety of later writers loosely associated under the umbrella labels of 'critical', 'political economy', 'progressive', and 'radical'.

Society. Change theorists accept the view of society as a system of interrelated parts but do not believe the parts are held together by consensus and shared interests and values. Rather, they see society comprising inherently opposing groups with respect to interests, values, and expectations. These groups compete for resources and power and those who win exercise their control and power by imposing an ideological world view that holds capitalism as the best of all economic systems (McDaniel and Agger, 1984). Part of the ideological climate or hegemony established by the dominant group is the formulation of laws, the creation of social institutions, and the distribution of ideas that favour the dominant group. This results in structured inequality marked by vast differences in wealth, status, and power, and the social nature of human existence is denied (Reasons and Perdue, 1981).

Change theorists do not accept the present social order. They want radical change. A truly just order can come about only through the radical reorganization of society, not through the extension of social control (Horton, 1966). Change theorists' vision of society is one where a new economic order of production is realized that would bring with it new social relations, with no one group dominating another (Howe, 1987).

Social problems. Horton (1966) tells us that conflict analysis is synonymous with historical analysis, an interpretation of intersystem processes that brings about the transformation of social relations. A key concept in this analysis is alienation (Naiman, 1997), which means a separation from the social system and a separation of people from each other in a society that reduces them to commodities (i.e., the only value they have is what they can obtain in the labour market). To the order theorist this situation is known as 'anomie', which occurs when people lose their sense of collective consciousness. The role of the state, from the order perspective, is to promote this collective consciousness in order to protect and preserve the status quo. To the change theorist this situation is known as 'alienation' and the progressive response would be change. In sum, the order theorist perceives anomie as synonymous with deviance and disorganization and the task is to bring people who have been separated from society and from each other back into society. The change theorist views the same situation as alienation and the task is to change the society that creates and perpetuates inequality and alienation.

Change theorists do not believe that social problems normally originate within the individual, the family, or the subculture, as do order theorists, but 'arise from the exploitive and alienating practices of dominant groups' (Horton, 1966: 704). Given the nature of a society marked by inequality and structured along lines of class, gender, race, age, and so on, the explanation for social problems must lie at a higher societal plane than those perceived by order theorists. For change theorists the societal plane where social problems are more realistically described, analyzed, and explained is at the structural level (Reasons and Perdue, 1981). This level includes society's institutions and its supportive ideology. At this level a social problem is defined as:

> a condition that involves the social injury of people on a broad scale. The injury may be physical in manifestation (as with disease stemming from a health service geared to income), social-psychological (as with alienation), economic (as with poverty), political (as with the oppression of dissident groups), or intellectual (as

with nonexistent or inadequate education). Social problems ensue from institutional defects and are not to be best interpreted or understood through individuals, families, or subcultures. Thus, the social problem as such is not an aberration but rather a normal consequence of the way in which a society is organized. (Reasons and Perdue, 1981: 12)

Reasons and Perdue (1981) point out that the above definition of social problems does not mean that change theorists ignore individuals, families, and subcultures as areas for study. The difference is that change theorists will always connect these societal planes with the broader structural order of society. In other words, the change theorist will always look to public issues (i.e., social institutions and their supportive ideology) as the source of private troubles. And because social problems are rooted in the social order they cannot be resolved by technical or administrative reforms. They can only be resolved by a massive reorganization or transformation of the social system. In sum, the major postulates of the social change or conflict perspective are:

1.   Society is the setting within which various struggles occur among different groups whose interests, values, and behaviours conflict with one another.
2.   The state is an important agent participating in the struggle on the side of the powerful groups.
3.   Social inequality is a result of coercive institutions that legitimate force, fraud, and inheritance as the major means of obtaining rights and privileges.
4.   Social inequality is a chief source of conflict.
5.   The state and the law are instruments of oppression controlled and used by the dominant groups for their own benefit.
6.   Classes are social groups with distinctive interests that inevitably bring them into conflict with other groups with opposed interests. (Reasons and Perdue, 1981: 13–14)

Social work and the change perspective. The change or conflict social worker must fight for change at all social, economic, and political levels. A conflict analysis of society reveals who is benefiting from established social arrangements; it shows how domination is maintained; and it suggests what must be done to bring about changes in power and resources. To assist the victims of an oppressive social order the social worker needs to know who holds the power, whose interests are being served by maintaining the status quo, and what devices are being used to keep things as they are (Howe, 1987).

Because social democracy and socialism are based on social change thought, then social work from a change perspective would be very similar to the nature and type of social work practice outlined in Chapter 5 (social democratic social work) and in Chapter 6 (evolutionary Marxist social work). Social work would have a dual function: (1) to provide practical humanitarian care to the casualties of a capitalist social order; and (2) at the same time, to further the democratization and restructuring of society along socialist lines.

The change-based dual function of social work does not preclude intervention at the individual, family, and subcultural levels. The difference is that instead of dealing with each of these levels by itself, the connection between people's private troubles and the structural source of these troubles would be made in every case. Rather than looking within the individual or within one's family or within one's subculture for the source of distress, the way in which the larger social order perpetrates and perpetuates people's problems would be identified and discussed with the person or group experiencing the distress. Although change social workers would do many of the same things that order social workers would do, many differences emanate from the different explanations each holds about the nature of society and of social problems. These differences will be discussed in the next three chapters.

THE DIALECTIC IN STRUCTURAL SOCIAL WORK

One of the most prominent aspects of structural social work is its dialectical analysis and approach to practice. The concept of dialectic is an essential component of structural social work theory. It sensitizes practice to the opposing and contradictory forces within capitalism,[12] the welfare state, and social work, and it helps social work avoid the construction of false dichotomies or dualisms that have been part of the social work tradition. This tradition is actually two traditions—an idealist tradition that persuades individuals they can effect great changes through self-determination, and a structural determinist tradition that sees individuals as the victims of a deterministic social environment that cannot be changed. Neither tradition comprehends the dialectic between the individual and the social world—the individual is both the creator of the social world and is created by the social world.

Naiman (1997: 13–14) summarizes the main principles of 'dialectics':

- *Everything is related*. Nothing in the universe is isolated, but, rather, all things are dependent on each other. This relationship may be direct or indirect, and therefore, nothing can be understood in isolation.
- *Change is constant*. Nothing in the universe is final, absolute, or immutable. Everything is in a continual process of change with the replacement of old forms by new forms preserving the viable elements of the earlier form. Change is neither linear nor circular, but more like a spiral.
- *Change proceeds from the quantitative to the qualitative*. Change usually occurs gradually and cumulatively over time. At some point, however, the cumulative or quantitative changes result in a qualitatively (i.e., radically) different nature or form. In other words, small changes eventually add up to something quite different from what existed in the first place.

- *Change is the result of the unity and struggle of opposites.* We tend to think in terms of binary opposites—good or bad, right or wrong, beautiful or ugly, true or false, capitalist or socialist, and so on. Dialectics emphasizes the unity of these binary opposites—things can contain within them two opposing forces at the same time. The tensions or contradictions between these opposing tendencies eventually become the basis for social change.

Dialectical analysis is based on a view of society and social processes as containing contradictory opposites that must be unravelled and understood. A dialectical social work theory recognizes the false dualisms of orthodox social work theory and attempts to replace them by recognizing the symbiotic relationship between contradictory elements with all their attendant mutuality. For example, the welfare state has both social care and social control functions, it contains both liberating and oppressive features, and it represents both the fruits of the struggles of oppressed people and a mechanism used by the dominant group to 'cool out' the powerless.[13] Without a dialectical understanding of social process, false dichotomies or dualisms are constructed and incorporated into social work theory and practice. The social welfare state and social work may be viewed by one group as solely part of the state apparatus that controls and oppresses people (e.g., orthodox Marxists), while another group may view them as instruments of human liberation representing only humanitarian concerns (e.g., conventional social workers). A dialectical perspective recognizes that social welfare and social work contain both of these contradictory forces. Given this dialectical perspective the strategy for structural social work is to maximize the emancipatory potential of social welfare and social work and to neutralize or minimize their repressive elements.

The modernist versus postmodernist debate discussed above is another example of a duality or false dichotomy that a dialectical analysis can help to clarify. Modernism, with its emphasis on universalisms, historical continuity, and solidarity, is often contrasted with postmodernism's emphasis on difference, present realities, and fragmentation. A dialectical analysis helps one to see the world as possessing some universal truths (e.g., capitalism, oppression of subordinate groups) but with different people in different localities with different ethnicities, social positions, and so on experiencing universal phenomena differently. Dialectical analysis helps one to connect the personal with the political. The aim here is to make an attempt to integrate parts of modernism (the *thesis*) with parts of postmodernism (the *antithesis*) and arrive at a *synthesis* of the two, although it will be an incomplete synthesis. Without a dialectical analysis, the temptation would be to opt for either modernism or postmodernism as a perspective on which to base one's critical theory (as too many have). This would, of course, result in the potential contributions of one or the other being omitted, which in turn would render a disservice to those suffering exploitation and subordination.

A question addressed by a dialectical perspective is whether or not individuals are subjects (creators of their social structures) or objects (created by their social structures). Wardell and Benson (1978, cited in Rachlin, 1991: 267) argue that they are both:

Fundamental to the dialectical view is the conception that human beings actively produce their social and material world. In doing so they objectify themselves in the form of social relations and material objects. This productive dimension of social life exists because human beings are able to imagine future social arrangements and then engage in purposeful activity to create those arrangements. . . . The instability of societies stems from this reflexive process since human beings may set out to intentionally reconstruct their world. This production process undermines established arrangements, edging them toward fundamental change. And, at critical junctures, people may act jointly to construct alternatives. . . . But because of the form of the present social structure, human beings may be only partly conscious of themselves, others, and the alternative possibilities when producing their social world . . . the production of social life is [not] random or extremely relative. The social structure of any society sets limitations upon what can be produced and by whom. . . . Any social structure will limit and restrain the production of future alternatives, but the same structure contains openings through which human beings can construct innovative alternatives to the present limitations.

Mullaly and Keating (1991) contend that many of the philosophical, theoretical, and practical disagreements that exist among radical or progressive social workers are actually due to the inadvertent acceptance on the part of many of certain false dichotomies. They further argue that a dialectical approach would lead to greater integration of theory and better informed radical practice. In the chapters on social democracy and Marxism three schools of socialist thought were identified—social democracy, evolutionary Marxism, and revolutionary Marxism. These three schools differ with respect to their individual prescriptions for social transformation. Two questions fundamental to structural social work and that would elicit disagreement among the socialist schools are:

1. Should structural social workers work inside or outside the social welfare system?
2. Do structural social workers concentrate on changing people's consciousness as a prerequisite to social change (i.e., radical humanism) or do they concentrate on changing material conditions and structural patterns as a prerequisite to changing people's consciousness (i.e., radical structuralism)?

The following responses to these questions should help to explain and clarify the dialectical nature of structural social work.

1. *Where should structural social workers work—inside or outside of the social welfare system?* Social democrats appreciate the welfare state within a capitalist society for providing people with a minimum standard of living, but they believe it should also promote greater equality and social justice. They view the capitalist welfare state as a stepping stone towards a socialist society and, therefore, advocate working within the system. Revolutionary Marxists believe that the capitalist welfare state promotes the

survival, not the transformation, of capitalism. Therefore, they maintain that structural social workers should work outside the welfare system and support welfare rights groups, co-operatives, self-help groups, and other alternative services and organizations that challenge capitalism. The evolutionary Marxists join with the social democrats in their belief that the welfare state can be used to transform capitalism, but agree with the revolutionary Marxists that many welfare state activities support and preserve capitalism. Thus, they would work within the system but would separate the forces for socialist change from the forces that preserve capitalism.

A dialectical analysis recognizes the place of human consciousness in the creation and recreation of human circumstances, but also recognizes that circumstances affect people and shape their consciousness. The state is shaped both by the logic of capitalism, patriarchy, and racism and by the conscious struggles of people along lines of class, gender, and race. Modern states contain both emancipatory and repressive forces (Frankel, 1979). This requires structural social workers to work both inside and outside the welfare state.

2. *Radical humanism vs radical structuralism: which comes first, the personal or the political?* Although radical social workers recognize the connection between private troubles and public issues, there is disagreement on which should come first in a strategy of political transformation, the personal or the political. Should changing people (by consciousness-raising) be a prerequisite to changing society or is the redistribution of wealth and power necessary to change people's consciousness? The former approach is known as 'radical humanism' and the latter as 'radical structuralism' (Burrell and Morgan, 1979). Each reflects a different set of ontological (the nature of being) and epistemological (the nature of knowledge) assumptions.[14]

Radical humanism is a subjectivist orientation to social change and radical structuralism is an objectivist orientation. Each provides a different answer to the question, 'Are we creators of or created by our social reality?' Subjectivist radical humanism holds that knowledge and social reality are created in people's minds through personal experience (Howe, 1987), and that no social facts exist because we create our own social reality. Conversely, objectivist radical structuralism holds that knowledge and social reality are external to the individual, that social reality is composed of concrete structures, and that this external social reality has a deterministic impact on an individual's development and circumstances (Burrell and Morgan, 1979; Howe, 1987).

Obviously, radical humanists and radical structuralists favour different means (i.e., social work practices) to achieve a society free from inequality. The former, who believe that personal consciousness-raising precedes political change, focus their efforts on raising people's consciousness about how inequalities shape, limit, oppress, and dominate their experiences (Howe, 1987). By understanding how capitalist hegemony operates to make people accept their subjugation they can free themselves to regain control over their present experiences and their destiny (Carniol, 1984; Howe, 1987). Paulo Freire's work in consciousness-raising among oppressed persons is relevant to the subjectivist approach of radical humanists. Radical structuralists, who believe that reality resides in the social world rather than in the person, focus their efforts on changing material conditions and structural patterns along socialist lines. With enough changes a socialist society would become the new reality. Radical structuralists would organize and mobilize social service users, trade unions, and other social activist groups to achieve this transformation. This approach involves consciousness-raising focused on the reality of unfair social structures and how they are perpetuated rather than on constrained individual reality. Each of these approaches to social transformation contains limitations.

> Radical humanism naively and optimistically assumes that raising people's consciousness will effectively address social problems and expose an exploitative social system. It ignores the fact that power and privilege, whether rooted in class, gender, or race, is [*sic*] not likely to be relinquished without a struggle and that part of this struggle would involve supporting the ideological hegemony required to continue to control people's consciousness. Radical structuralism is overly simplistic and deterministic in its understanding of the complexity of human need and the depth of oppression. It is difficult to understand how describing external power empowers people to change it. (Mullaly and Keating, 1991: 67)

A dialectical analysis would view these two different approaches to radical practice as a false dichotomy. Although both link private troubles and public issues, they dichotomize praxis (political practice) along personal–political lines. Subjective reality and objective reality are irrevocably locked into a dialectical relationship. We are conscious creators of our surroundings, using thought, information, and emotion to act and to choose. At the same time, we are created by our surroundings. A dialectical approach to structural social work avoids the simplistic linear cause-effect notion of historical materialism and the naive romanticism associated with the notion of totally free human will (Mullaly and Keating, 1991). Dialectical analysis helps to illuminate the complex interplay between people and the world around them and to indicate the role of social work within society. 'We are not only objects of the prevailing social order, we must also be subjects who are able to move beyond it' (Mullaly and Keating, 1991: 72). In short, structural social work incorporates both these radical traditions into its theory base, recognizing that they constitute a dialectical whole rather than distinct and contradictory approaches. It is not a question of which comes first, the personal or the political. Neither is a prerequisite to the other; both must occur conjointly (Allan, 2003b).

INCLUSION OF ALL FORMS OF OPPRESSION

As mentioned in Chapter 7, radical social work initially focused only on the oppression of white, male members of the working class (Langan and Lee, 1989a). Feminism challenged this narrow focus to include the role and function of patriarchy in its analyses. Feminist theory and analysis have been enormous sources of information, inspiration, and instruction for radical social work, in general, and structural social work, in particular.[15] Feminist insights on the way patriarchy structures virtually all social institutions, such as families, the market, and the welfare state, have been incorporated into structural social work analyses (Dominelli and McLeod, 1989; Langan and Lee, 1989b; Leonard, 1990; Rojek et al., 1988; Williams, 1989). Given its increasing importance as a major social work perspective (Baines et al., 1991; Collins, 1986; Eichler, 1988; Van Den Bergh and Cooper, 1986), along with the predominance of women among the users and providers of social work services, the feminist perspective is imperative for structural social work.

Feminist analysis not only decodes patriarchy and stresses the links between the personal and political better than any other theory, it, like structural social work, emphasizes transformational politics (Van Den Bergh and Cooper, 1986; Withorn, 1984). Some feminist theorists do not limit this transformation to a constituency of women but seek the end of domination and oppression of all people.

> It [feminism] is a vision born of women, but it addresses the future of the planet with implications accruing for males as well as females, for all ethnic groups, for the impoverished, for the disadvantaged, the handicapped, the aged and so on. (Van Den Bergh and Cooper, 1986: x)

Although feminists share the basic view that patriarchal society is oppressive, different feminist analyses exist with respect to the fundamental source of oppression in society and, therefore, how to deal with gender inequality. In their frequently cited *Feminist Frameworks*, Jagger and Struhl-Rothenberg (1978, 1984) identify four feminist approaches, which were discussed in Chapter 7 (although Marxist feminism was encapsulated within socialist feminism). Liberal feminism accepts liberal capitalism and seeks to reform it by removing gender-based discrimination from all social institutions. As such, because it accepts liberal capitalism, it is largely incompatible with structural social work. Socialist feminists believe capitalism and patriarchy are co-determinants of oppression. Marxist feminists believe that capitalism is the fundamental form of oppression, but that patriarchy is the fundamental source of oppression. Both socialist and Marxist feminists see the solution to ending sexism as transforming capitalism into socialism. Radical feminism places gender ahead of class, asserting that patriarchy is responsible for women's oppression. Control over women's reproductive capacity is often favoured as a social change strategy. Socialist, Marxist, and radical feminists have much to offer structural social work theory and practice in their understanding of the nature and dynamics of patriarchy (Mullaly and Keating, 1991).

Just as early radical social work ignored patriarchy as a source of oppression, so, too, did it largely ignore racism as a source of oppression (Dominelli, 1997; Langan and Lee, 1989b). And just as black women criticized the early feminist movement for overlooking the special and more complex situation of women of colour, so, too, have black social workers criticized the early radical social work movement for largely overlooking anti-racist social work practice (Freeman, 1990; Hutchison-Reis, 1989; Shah, 1989; Small, 1989).

Racism institutionalizes the myth of white superiority by creating social structure and processes that support this pattern of domination. The political, social, and economic marginalization experienced by people of colour reinforces racist beliefs within white society and helps to maintain the oppression of non-whites. It [racism] legitimizes inequality on the basis of personal-cultural characteristics while obscuring its structural roots. (Mullaly and Keating, 1991: 57)

Feminist writers have shown that a radical social work practice that ignores gender reproduces sexist practices; in the same fashion, black activists have shown that a 'colour-blind' social work practice reproduces racist practices. An anti-racist structural social work practice would raise the consciousness of practitioners and service users about the oppressive effects of racism and its interplay with capitalism and patriarchy.

Just as feminism and anti-racism now occupy prominent positions in the structural social work literature, other non-classist forms of oppression are also being incorporated into this literature. The emphasis given by postmodernism to issues of difference should facilitate and accelerate this process of inclusion. Today, structural social work includes in its analysis the roles and functions of colonialism of North American Aboriginal people, imperialism of Third World countries by developed nations, and heterosexism as well as ageism and ableism and other forms and sources of oppression. Oppression will be the subject of the next chapter.

BOX 9.2 DEVELOPMENT OF A THEORETICAL ORIENTATION

Early in my academic career if someone had asked me what my theoretical orientation was, I would have answered unhesitatingly—'Marxist'. However, with the critique of Marxism that accompanied the emergence and development of feminist scholarship and that included a progressive feminist analysis of social welfare and social work, I adjusted my theoretical orientation and became a 'pro-feminist Marxist'. Subsequently, as people of colour criticized Marxism and feminism for being colour-blind and omitting race as a source and form of oppression, I became an 'anti-racist, pro-feminist, Marxist social worker'.

The problem for me was obvious. As more groups would develop and articulate an analysis of their respective sources and forms of oppression, my theoretical label would continue to expand. Thus, I was relieved when Maurice Moreau began to develop his idea of structural social work. This view concerned all forms and sources of oppression and did not regard any particular oppression as primary or more important than others. That is not to say that all oppressions are equally severe; rather, it recognizes that many groups in society find themselves in a position of second-class citizenship, not because of anything they did, but because of some group characteristic or trait that they possess and over which they have no control. When people ask me today what my theoretical orientation is, I answer by

> saying that I am a 'critical' social worker. 'Critical', today, of course, has a meaning quite different from what it did 25 years ago. It has moved from a narrow Marxist view to an all-inclusive view of oppression—as have I.

As the above marginalized groups make their voices heard, hopefully with some help from structural social work, their experiences with and analyses of their subordinate positions in society, including their exploitation and oppression, will be incorporated into structural social work theory, as were the feminist and anti-racist experiences and analyses. Obviously, the theory base of structural social work is not static. It will continue to grow and develop as more information on the experiences of all oppressed groups is received from the oppressed themselves. This will assist in the development of a dialectical politics of difference and solidarity within structural social work theory and practice.

STRUCTURAL SOCIAL WORK: A CONCEPTUAL FRAMEWORK

Based on a reconstituted socialist ideology, located within the radical social work camp, grounded in critical theory, and operating from a social change view of society, structural social work views social problems as arising from a specific societal context—liberal/neo-conservative capitalism—rather than from the failings of individuals. The essence of socialist ideology, radical social work, critical theory, and the change perspective is that inequality: (1) is a natural, inherent (i.e., structural) part of capitalism; (2) falls along such lines as class, gender, race, sexual orientation, age, ability, and geographical region; (3) excludes groups from opportunities, meaningful participation in society, and a satisfactory quality of life; and (4) is self-perpetuating. Writing from Britain, Pond (1989, cited in Davis, 1991: 65) presents some reasons why social workers should attend to inequality as a major part of the structural context in which they practice:

> The distribution of economic rewards between different groups in the population and different parts of the country is an important determinant of the nation's economic and social structure. Economic and social inequality are inextricably intertwined, and the distribution of income and wealth, the extent of poverty and privilege, have their effects on living standards, life chances and opportunities. Individuals' health and well-being are influenced by their position in the labour market, income and access to economic resources. Thus, class differences in health (for example) have persisted, despite an overall improvement in national standards.
>
> Moreover, inequalities in wealth have political implications, providing the wealthiest individuals with access to economic, social, and sometimes political

power. For this reason, inequalities can become self-perpetuating, having an influence on the institutions that reinforce the class structure.

Given this view of social problems, structural social workers seek to change the social system and not the individuals who receive, through no fault of their own, the results of defective social arrangements.[16] Thus, the goal of structural social work is twofold: (1) to alleviate the negative effects on people of an exploitative and alienating social order; and (2) to transform the conditions and social structures that cause these negative effects. This goal involves a two-tiered process: immediate relief or tension-reduction on one level accompanied by longer-term institutional and structural change.

As mentioned previously, the term 'structural' in structural social work is both descriptive and prescriptive. It is descriptive in the sense that the major source of social problems is identified as being the way our society is structured. It is prescriptive in the sense that because social problems are rooted in our social structures, then the structures must be changed, not the individual, the family, or the subculture adversely affected by social problems. Even if it were possible to change everyone presently harmed by our social structures, the source of these problems—our social structures—would still be there to harm, oppress, and alienate more people along lines of class, gender, race, and so on. Figure 9.1 illustrates the general structural arrangement of any society. Figure 9.1 could just as well represent a bridge constructed by engineers. There is a foundation or base (i.e., substructure) of the bridge upon which the rest of the bridge stands. The substructure of a bridge is usually situated underground or underwater, which is why it is called the *sub*structure, as the prefix 'sub' means 'under' and is usually hidden from view. It is the 'invisible' structure of the bridge. Sitting on the bridge's foundation are the pillars or the columns of the bridge, which carry or support the deck of the bridge (i.e., its superstructure).

Translating the example of a bridge into a societal structure, the substructure or foundation of society consists of a dominant ideology, which is transmitted to all members of society through the process of socialization and determines the nature of a society's institutions and the relations among its people. The dominant ideology or belief system of a society constitutes the 'hidden' or 'invisible structures' that are part of the larger concept of social structures. The social institutions (pillars or columns) of a society rest on the foundation or ideology of that particular society, and the social relations (i.e., deck or superstructure) of society, in turn, rest on and are supported by the social institutions. Because each of the three levels of the social structure is an integral part of the total structure, they must all be changed in the work of social transformation. If the foundation of society is comprised of liberalism, for example, the social institutions of that society and its social relations will rest on, reflect, and carry out liberal beliefs, values, and ideals. In turn, the social relations will also reflect liberal beliefs, values, and ideals so that they (the social relations) will be characterized by inequality, individualism, capitalism, and so on. In other words, the social institutions and social relations of a particular society will be determined by the dominant ideology and, in turn, will operate in a manner consistent with and supportive of the dominant ideology.

FIGURE 9.1 STRUCTURAL VIEW OF SOCIETY

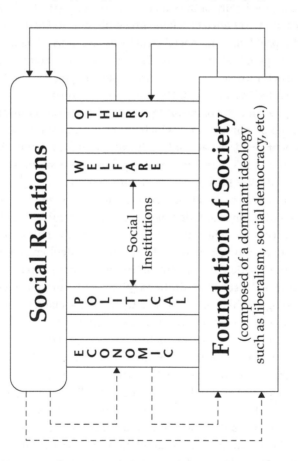

Superstructure

Consisting of:

i) social institutions that carry out society's functions; and

ii) social relations among all social groups

Substructure

an ideology that underpins all social institutions and determines the nature of social relations

Social Relations

ECONOMIC   POLITICAL   WELFARE   OTHERS

Social Institutions

Foundation of Society

(composed of a dominant ideology such as liberalism, social democracy, etc.)

→ determine

- - -▸ reinforce

Fundamental social change presents a difficult challenge. Each level of the social structure is interdependent and mutually reinforcing of the other levels, which suggests that a serious approach to social change must occur at all three levels. At the substructural level, the dominant ideology must be challenged by engaging in consciousness-raising by exploring with people the alienating and oppressive features of our present liberal-capitalist system, which is characterized by oppression falling along lines of race, class, gender, culture, age, and so on.[17] At the level of social institutions not only must the social welfare institution be changed so that its control functions are minimized and its liberating features maximized, but all social institutions must change in a similar manner.[18] At the level of social relations we must not only attempt to break down the superordinate–subordinate relations around us, we must also attend to the way we live our own personal lives so that we do not contribute to the reproduction of our present social relations, which are often based on classism, sexism, racism, and so on.[19]

The ultimate goal of structural social work is to contribute to the transformation of our current society to one that is more congruent with our reconstituted socialist principles. Carniol (1990: 22) says of this transformation:

> A new form of intervention would call for a restructuring of our major institutions, so that they become answerable to the public rather than being strictly controlled by a relatively small class of people composed primarily of white wealthy males. Without such transformation those social problems now experienced will be perpetuated endlessly into the future, with bandaids being busily applied by a profession that should know better.

This goal of social transformation is illustrated in Figure 9.2.

Langan and Lee (1989a: 13) articulate the challenge for radical social work:

> It is possible to be simultaneously committed to a set of socialist principles and to helping people as a social worker. What is much less clear is how it is possible to connect the two in a manner that allows them to merge into forms of feasible practice in the here and now.

We now turn to this dual task of helping people while simultaneously working towards the transformation of the liberal and/or neo-conservative paradigm. Given the inroads that neo-conservatism has made in the past three or so decades with respect to replacing liberalism as the dominant paradigm, it is imperative that structural social work develop theory and praxis for its commitment to socialist principles.

CONCLUSION

Box 9.3 summarizes some of the major theoretical assumptions and ingredients of the new structural social work that were presented and discussed in this chapter.[20]

FIGURE 9.2 TRANSFORMATIONAL GOAL OF STRUCTURAL SOCIAL WORK

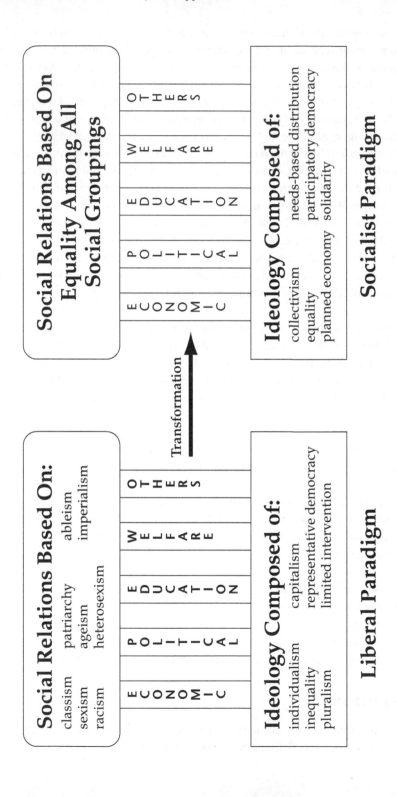

BOX 9.3   MAJOR ELEMENTS OF THE NEW STRUCTURAL SOCIAL WORK

- Social problems are built into the structures (social institutions, social processes, social practices, and social relationships) of society.
- Focusing on the individual as the cause of social problems is blaming the victim. For social problems to be resolved, social structures must change.
- Social inequalities are mainly structural in nature and not the result of innate differences.
- Society functions in ways that discriminate against people along lines of class, gender, race, and so on.
- The state's institutions, such as the law and educational system, function as instruments of oppression and benefit the privileged groups.
- The traditional dichotomy between the individual and society needs to be challenged; individual problems cannot be understood separate from the social context.
- Social structures, ideology, and personal consciousness are interrelated—each element or component of society impacts on the others.
- Knowledge is not objective, and the knowledge of the dominant group forms the ruling ideas in society and reflects the interests of the dominant group, often at the expense of subordinate groups.
- A social change perspective must be adopted as a response to social problems and oppression.
- Conventional social work perpetuates social problems by focusing on personal change and/or limited social reform rather than fundamental social change.
- Capitalism should be rejected in favour of some kind of reconstituted democratic socialism.
- No single source or form of oppression can claim primacy. All sources and forms of oppression are to be rejected, and no hierarchy of oppression is developed.
- The welfare state in a capitalist society props up capitalism and operates in a way to reproduce all oppressive social relations.
- The positive and liberating aspects of modernist critical social theory and of critical postmodern theory are both of central importance.
- Emphasizing either 'individual agency' or 'structural forces' as the focus for social change is overly reductionist. To understand social problems and develop structural approaches, both are necessary.
- The dominant order must be challenged and resisted by developing counter-discourses to victim-blaming, free-market glorification, welfare dependency, etc.
- An anti-oppressive approach to social work should be adopted (see next chapter).

To conclude, all societies establish organizations to carry out certain functions that are essential for their maintenance. Examples include an economic system to ensure the production, distribution, and consumption of needed and desired goods and services; an education system to provide persons with the knowledge and skills needed to participate in the workforce; and a welfare system to attend to the needs of economically deprived persons. These organizations are called social institutions. These institutions, along with their procedural rules of operating, the policies governing their operations, and their social practices, are known as 'social structures'. These structures affect everyone in society.

Traditional critical social theory has always emphasized social structures as the major source of social problems. Because these social structures were initially established by and continue to be dominated by a particular social group—bourgeois, white, Christian, heterosexual males of European descent—they primarily reflect and reinforce the assumptions, views, ideals, culture, social position, and interests of this group. Furthermore, this group enjoys its privileges and power at the expense of subordinate groups such as the working class; people of colour; non-Christians; gay, lesbian, bisexual, and transsexual persons; women; and so on (Mullaly, 2002). Our social structures are imbued with sexism, racism, patriarchy, and classism in that there is a privileged or dominant group within each of these social divisions that has more social, political, and usually economic power than the subordinate groups. The domination of men over women, affluent persons over poor people, white people over persons of colour, physically able people over physically and mentally challenged people, and so on has 'been so internalized into the structures of society that [it has] also become intrinsic to the roles, rules, policies and practices of [social] institutions' (Haney, 1989: 37).

This domination is not usually a conscious or intentional choice on the part of the dominant group, as few people would consider themselves to be oppressors. Paulo Freire (1994) argues that it is more a case that the dominant group is not aware of any viable alternative social, economic, or political structure. Members of the dominant group perceive their situation of having more not as a privilege that may dehumanize others, but as their God-given right for having taken advantage of the opportunities that are available to everyone (in their view). Little thought is given to the possibility that access to opportunities and resources is largely based on one's social position or location (i.e., one's class, gender, race, etc.) rather than strictly on merit or effort. Awareness of the oppressive nature and functions of our present social structures is an essential element of structural social work theory and practice. To that end, the next chapter focuses on the nature, dynamics, causes, and consequences of oppression.

CRITICAL QUESTIONS

1. When you hear that someone is a 'radical', what is the image that first comes to your mind? Where does this image come from? Can you think of any political purpose that such an image might serve?

2. A tenet of structural social work is that oppression often originates from within or is caused by social structures because they treat people differently (favourably or unfavourably) according to their race, gender, class, age, sexuality, and so on. Furthermore, some of these structures are invisible. What are some examples of invisible structures and how do they contribute to oppression?

3. One group of young people lives in comfortable homes in a crime-free and mostly white neighbourhood. These young people all attend the finest schools, have extra money from their parents when they want it, wear the latest teen fashions, and will make use of family connections to get good jobs when they are finished school. Another group of young people lives in a neighbourhood with slum housing, heavy traffic, and a high level of street crime. The schools they attend lack resources and have a high annual rate of teacher turnover, and their parents cannot afford extra help for them. They wear 'Sally Ann' clothes and spend most of their time on the streets because there is always tension at home and a steady stream of bill collectors, social workers, and the police at their doors. Which group do you think tends to see society as stable, orderly, and full of opportunities, and which group do you think sees society as chaotic and crisis-ridden with no legitimate opportunities?

4. Why are there only theories and no laws in social work and in the social sciences like there are in the physical and natural sciences?

5. Give some examples of where or how our social structures or institutions are racist, sexist, ageist, classist, and so on.

Oppression: The Focus of Structural Social Work

The oppressed are allowed once every few years to decide which particular repre-
sentatives of the oppressing class are to represent and repress them.

—*Karl Marx*

INTRODUCTION

Much mention was made in the previous chapter of oppression and subordinated populations. Indeed, the primary focus of structural social work is oppression. Its socialist ideology, its social change perspective, its critical theory base, its dialectical analysis, and its inclusion of multiple forms of oppression all point to oppression as the major source of social problems and not to individual deficiency or to social disorganization. Most structural social work practice is carried out with, or on behalf of, oppressed people. Therefore, it is crucial to have an understanding of the nature of oppression, its causes and sources, its production and reproduction, its dynamics, its effects on the oppressed, including its internalization, and the social functions it carries out in the interests of the dominant groups (i.e., the oppressors) in society. These are some of the topics discussed in this chapter. As with the preceding and following chapters this chapter is informed by critical social theory, particularly that of Marx, the Frankfurt School, Habermas, critical postmodernism, feminism, and critical race theory.[1]

THE NATURE OF OPPRESSION

To understand what oppression is, it is necessary to know what oppression is not. Since people are social beings and live in societies, no one is free from social structures. Such structures consist of boundaries, barriers, expectations, regulations, and so on. One could make a loose argument that everyone in society is oppressed because one's choices or freedoms are restricted by the simple existence of social structures. For example, when a person drives an automobile she/he is obliged to buckle up the seat belt, to drive (in North America) on the right-hand side of the road, and to obey all traffic laws and regulations.

These restrictions on our freedom cannot be regarded as oppressive. Not everything that frustrates or limits or hurts a person is oppressive. So, if one wishes to distinguish between what oppression is and is not, one has to look at the social context of a particular restriction, limit, or injury (Frye, 1983).

Everyone suffers frustrations, restrictions, and hurt. What determines oppression is when these happen to a person not because of individual talent, merit, or failure, but because of his or her membership in a particular group or category of people, for example, black people, women, poor people, and gay and lesbian persons. 'If an individual is oppressed, it is by virtue of being a member of a group or category of people that is systematically reduced, molded, immobilized. Thus, to recognize a person as oppressed, one has to see that individual as belonging to a group of a certain sort' (Frye, 1983: 8). Of course, not all groups in society are oppressed. Nor are all oppressed groups equally oppressed. Those in the dominant mainstream of our society are less likely to be oppressed and more likely to be among the oppressors. Women are oppressed (by men) as women. Men are not oppressed as men. Non-whites are oppressed (by whites) as non-whites. Whites are not oppressed as whites. Gay and lesbian persons are oppressed (by heterosexuals) as gay and lesbian persons. Heterosexuals are not oppressed as heterosexuals. This is not to say that oppression is a simple matter of dividing society into two groups: bad people (i.e., the oppressors) and victimized people (i.e., the oppressed). It is much more complex, as most people are oppressed in some aspects of their lives and oppress others in other aspects of their lives.

In addition to being group-based, oppression is described by almost all writers on the subject to be relational. There must be a dominant group who oppresses and a subordinate group who is oppressed. The former occupies positions of power, influence, and privilege that are used to maintain their position, often at the expense of the subordinate group(s). Gil (1998: 11), for example, argues that once oppression is 'integrated into a society's institutional order and culture, and into the individual consciousness of its people through socialization, oppressive tendencies come to permeate almost all relations.' Gil points out, however, that the intensity of oppression is not constant, but will vary over time. In other words, oppression occurs among (groups of) people in their everyday relations with each other.

BOX 10.1 MISUSE OF THE CONCEPT OF OPPRESSION

Unfortunately, some writers will feel pressure to seek the approval of their peers and will attempt to 'jump on the bandwagon' of certain frameworks that may be popular at certain times and in certain places (Naiman, 1997). Because 'anti-oppressive social work' currently enjoys theoretical popularity, as evidenced by its inclusion in the Standards of Accreditation of social work programs in Canada by the Canadian Association of Schools of Social Work (CASSW), some writers have made claims about oppression that violate its relational nature. For example, a 2003 Canadian social work textbook on working with people experiencing addictions was entitled by its authors (Rick Csiernik and William Rowe), *Responding to the Oppression of Addiction: Canadian Social Work Perspectives.* My question is, who is the dominant group that is oppressing another group and who is the subordinate group that is being oppressed by a dominant group? Which groups are involved in an oppressive relationship? People experiencing problems with addictions may be oppressed along lines of class, race, gender, and so on, but they cannot be oppressed by addictions. No group is enjoying a position of power, privilege, influence, and opportunity because it is oppressing those people who are addicted. Although addiction to alcohol or drugs or gambling involves hardship and misfortune, it does not determine oppression. Oppressed groups will disproportionately experience certain problems because of their second-class or inferior position in society, but the problem itself is not oppressive. Subordinate group members may be more susceptible to health and social problems than members of the dominant group, but the health or social problem is not the cause of oppression. Health and social problems may be symptoms or outcomes of oppression, but they are not causes of oppression. Only people oppress people.

Besides being group-based and relational, another feature of oppression is that it is not accidental (nor is it usually intentional).

> The experience of oppressed people is that the living of one's life is confined and shaped by forces and barriers which are not accidental or occasional and hence avoidable, but are systematically related to each other in such a way as to catch one between and among them and restrict or penalize motion in any direction. (Albert et al., 1986: 19)

Since oppression is perpetrated and perpetuated by dominant groups and is systematic and continuous in its application, a logical question is: why does it occur? The simple and correct answer is that oppression occurs because it benefits the dominant group. Oppression protects a kind of citizenship that is superior to that of the oppressed. It protects the oppressors' access to a wider range of better-paying and higher-status work. It protects the oppressors' preferential access to and preferential treatment from our social institutions. The oppressed serve as a ready supply of labour to carry out the menial and dangerous jobs in society, and they also serve as scapegoats during difficult times for the dominant group, often being blamed for inflation, government deficits, recessions, social disruptions, and the like. In short, oppression carries out certain social functions for the dominant group by ensuring that society reproduces itself and maintains the same dominant-subordinate relationships.

The dominant group in society may not really subscribe to oppressive behaviour as a means of protecting its favourable position. Most people do not consider themselves to be oppressors. In fact, most people probably believe that oppressive behaviour should not be a part of a democratic society. Why, then, do they engage in oppressive practices? Paulo Freire (1970: 45) eloquently answers this question:

> The oppressors do not perceive their monopoly on having more as a privilege which dehumanizes others and themselves. . . . For them, having more is an inalienable right, a right they acquired through their own 'effort', with their 'courage to take risks'. If others do not have more, it is because they are incompetent and lazy, and worst of all is their unjustifiable ingratitude towards the 'generous gestures' of the dominant class. Precisely because they are 'ungrateful' and 'envious', the oppressed are regarded as potential enemies who must be watched.

Thus, the view the oppressors hold of the oppressed is that they constitute a dangerous class that must be controlled for the good of the whole society. The ways this social control is carried out are discussed below.

BOX 10.2 MYTHS THAT PERPETRATE AND PERPETUATE OPPRESSION

- *Myth of scarcity.* There is not enough to go around, which deflects attention away from the fact that a small minority owns most of the world's resources.
- *Myth of might makes right.* The majority rules even if it means tyranny of the minority.
- *Myth of objective information.* It is possible for one group (mainly white, bourgeois males) objectively to observe humanity, thus becoming the authoritative knowers.
- *Stereotyping.* All members of a group are the same.
- *Blaming the victim.* People are the architects of their own misfortune and oppression.
- *Competition and hierarchy.* Human beings are competitive by nature and aspire to be ahead/above others (from Anne Bishop, 2002).
- *Myth of supremacy.* The dominant educational system, with its emphasis on Western civilization, leads to a belief in the supremacy of a white, Western, male culture.
- *Myth of class.* Most people believe they belong to the middle class, which lives in harmony with a 'higher' (superior) class. This belief mandates and then sanctions a dominant and a subordinate class (from Haney, 1989).

OPPRESSION AS A SOCIAL JUSTICE ISSUE

In defining social justice as 'the elimination of institutionalized domination and oppression', Young (1990: 15) contends that contemporary philosophical theories of justice do not conceive justice so broadly. Instead, they restrict themselves to an interpretation of social justice as the morally proper distribution of benefits and burdens among all society's members. The benefits to be distributed would include both material resources, such as wealth and income, and non-material social goods, such as rights, opportunities, and power. Issues of distributive justice are analogous to persons dividing a stock of goods and comparing the amount or size of the portions. Injustice, according to this distributive notion of social justice, would be defined as a situation where one group has a monopoly over a particular good. Even explicitly socialist discussions of social justice fall within the distributional theory, as the principles of distribution (need vs market) are paramount to social justice. What distinguishes the distributive perspective of social justice, then, is the tendency to see social justice and distribution as co-extensive concepts (Young, 1990).

Welfare capitalism and conventional social work have also adopted the distributional concept of social justice in that their focus has been on the distribution and redistribution of income and other resources (often defined in terms of some kind of social minimum). Discussion has tended to centre on inequalities of wealth and income and the extent to which the state can or should alleviate the suffering of the poor and disadvantaged. Indeed, the immediate provision of basic goods and services for people suffering severe deprivation must be a first priority for any group or program seeking social justice. Any conception of justice must take into account the vast differences in the amount of material goods that exist in our society, where thousands starve and live on the streets while others can have anything they want (Young, 1990).

From a structural perspective a major limitation of the distributional theory of social justice is identified by Iris Marion Young in *Justice and the Politics of Difference* (1990). Equating the scope of social justice only with distribution is misleading in two ways: (1) the social processes and practices that caused the maldistribution in the first place are ignored; and (2) the limits of the logic of extending the notion of distribution to such non-material goods and resources as rights and opportunities are not recognized.

Ignoring Social Processes and Practices

Young notes that the distributional view of justice assumes a social atomist or individualist perspective of people in that they are externally related to the goods they possess and only related to one another in terms of a comparison of the amounts of goods they possess. The institutional contexts within which distribution occurs are ignored. These institutional contexts go beyond a narrow Marxist account of the mode of production and include all social structures and practices, the rules and norms that guide them, and the language and symbols that mediate social interactions within them. This context affects distribution—what is distributed, how it is distributed, who distributes it, who receives it, and what the outcome is. An example presented by Young (1990: 23) is economic inequality. Discussions of distribution often omit the decision-making structures that determine economic relations in society.

> Economic domination in our society occurs not simply because persons have more wealth and income than others, as important as this is. Economic domination derives at least as much from the corporate and legal structures and procedures that give some persons the power to make decisions about investment, production, marketing, employment, interest rates, and wages that affect millions of other people. Not all who make these decisions are wealthy or even privileged, but the decision-making structure operates to reproduce distributive inequality and the unjust constraints on people's lives.

Limits of Extending Distribution to the Non-material

Advocates of the distributive theory of justice claim that any issue of justice, including such non-material things as rights and opportunities, may be treated as 'goods' or some aggregate of things to be possessed and/or distributed and redistributed. Young argues that such treatment produces a misleading conception of the issues of justice involved, as it reifies aspects of social life that are better understood as functions of rules, relations, and processes than as things.

Distributing or redistributing rights and opportunities is not the same as distributing or redistributing income, as rights and opportunities are not possessions. Some groups may have rights and opportunities that other groups do not have, but extending them to the groups that do not have them does not entail that the formerly privileged group must surrender some of its rights and/or opportunities as it does in the case of a redistribution of income. Rights are not things but relationships; rights are institutionally defined rules specifying what people can do in relation to others. 'Rights refer to doing more than having, to social relationships that enable or constrain action' (Young, 1990: 25). In other words, people may have certain rights but be unable to exercise them because of particular constraints based on class, gender, race, and so on. For example, a poor person may have a right to a fair trial but be unable financially to hire proper legal counsel.

Similarly, opportunity refers to doing rather than to having. It is a condition of enablement rather than of possession and usually involves a system of social rules and social relations, as well as an individual's skills and abilities. Having opportunities may lead to securing material goods such as food, shelter, and a job, but it is no guarantee that these goods and services will be secured. Just as people may have certain rights but are unable to exercise them, so, too, might people have certain opportunities but be constrained from using them because of particular social relations and practices. For example, in Canada we may say that Aboriginal persons have the opportunity to obtain an education, but education occurs in a complex context of social relations. Aboriginal people tend to have inferior schools, fewer material resources, and less access to tutors and computers, as well as the experience of culture shock in off-reserve schools. This is not to say that distribution is irrelevant to educational opportunities, but that opportunity has a wider scope than distribution (Young, 1990).

Certainly, then, the distributive theory of social justice contains a major limitation. By focusing on something that must be identifiable and assignable it reifies social relations and processes and institutional rules. It gives primacy to substance over relations, rules, and processes by conceiving of people as social atoms, thus failing to appreciate that individual identity and capacities are themselves the products of social relations and processes (Taylor, 1985, cited in Young, 1990). Such an atomistic social ontology ignores or obscures the importance of institutional contexts and rules and social relations and processes for understanding issues of social justice. An adequate conception of social justice must understand and evaluate these social phenomena as well as the substance of distribution (Young, 1990).

Heller (1987) suggests a conception of justice that includes social phenomena. She views justice as primarily the virtue of citizenship wherein persons collectively consider problems and issues facing them within their institutions and actions, under conditions free from oppression and domination, with reciprocity and mutual tolerance of differences. Young argues that this conception of justice shifts the focus from distribution issues to procedural issues of participation in deliberation and decision-making. A norm would be just only if people who follow it have an effective voice in its consideration and acceptance. A social condition would be just only if it enabled all people to meet their needs and exercise their freedoms. A social process would be just only if it were an inclusive process with respect to different social groupings. A social practice would be just only if it is in accordance with how people carrying it out would like to be treated themselves. Social injustice from this perspective entails not only an unfair distribution of goods and resources, but includes any norm, social condition, social process, or social practice that interferes with or constrains one from fully participating in society, that is, from becoming a full citizen.

This concept of social justice is empowering because it goes beyond a concern with distribution to include the institutional conditions necessary for the development and exercise of individual capacities and collective communication and co-operation (Young, 1990). Oppression consists of institutional conditions that inhibit or prevent one from becoming a full participant in society. A society may be evaluated as just to the degree that it contains and supports the institutional conditions necessary for the promotion of the universal value that everyone is of equal intrinsic worth. For all those concerned with developing an adequate conception of social justice and for those committed to social justice in practice, oppression must be a central concern.

THE ORIGINS OF MODERN-DAY OPPRESSION AND THE POLITICS OF IDENTITY

Modern-day classism, sexism, racism, homophobia, ageism, and other forms of oppression are not superstitious carry-overs from the Dark Ages. On the contrary, Young (1990) states that nineteenth- and early twentieth-century scientific and philosophical discourse explicitly proposed and legitimated formal theories of race, sex, age, and national superiority. Also, she contends that the methods of science and the attributes of the scientist have, in part, contributed to the formulation of these theories of superiority/inferiority. The social construction of these theories that present a white, bourgeois male as the perfection of human form and equate the virtues of manliness with the virtues of respectability is discussed below.

There has been much criticism of modern scientific reason by critical theorists, feminists, and postmodernists. These criticisms, which were summarized in the previous chapter, have, in part, punctured the authority of modern scientific reason. A major part of this criticism has been directed at the construction of the scientist and philosopher as knowers or subjects standing outside the objects of knowledge—autonomous, objective, and neutral. The subject is a socially detached observer, standing in the immediate presence of reality but without any involvement in it. Moreover, as Foucault (1977) notes, these observations are not mere passing looks but normalizing gazes that assess their object according to some hierarchical standard. Some of the particulars or attributes of the object are then defined as deviant or are devalued in comparison to the norm.

Young (1990) cites recent scholarship that has revealed the white, bourgeois, male, European biases attached to the notion of a rational subject or knower. That is, the virtues of the scientist have also become the virtues of masculinity—detachment, careful measurement and the manipulation of instruments, comprehensive generalizing and reasoning, and authoritative speech supported by evidence (Keller, 1985; Merchant, 1978, cited in Young, 1990). Those articulating and carrying out the code of modern scientific reason were white, bourgeois males speaking for themselves and unmindful that there might be other positions. In other words, they became not only the knowers or truth-seeking subjects, they also created or embodied the standards against which all other groups (objects) were measured. This already privileged group assumed the privilege of the authoritative subject of knowledge, and groups that they defined as differing became the objects of their distancing and mastering observations.

> The imposition of scientific reason's dichotomy between subject and object on hierarchical relations of race, gender, class, and nationality . . . has deep and abiding consequences for the structuring of privilege and oppression. The privileged groups lose their particularity; in assuming the position of the scientific subject they become . . . agents of a universal view from nowhere. The oppressed groups, on the other hand, are locked in their objectified bodies, blind, dumb, and passive. The normalizing gaze of science focused on the objectified bodies of women, Blacks, Jews, homosexuals, old people, the mad and feeble-minded. From its observations emerged theories of sexual, racial, age, and mental or moral superiority. (Young, 1990: 127)

Nineteenth-century theories of race that explicitly assumed white, male, bourgeois, European body types and facial features as the norm were given legitimation and naturalized by scientific discourse (Young, 1990). Using this norm as the measuring stick, these theories posited that all other bodies were considered either degenerate or less developed. This superior body type by nature also determined directly the intellectual, aesthetic, and moral superiority of persons in this group over all other types (West, 1982).

In addition to a superior body type, the nineteenth-century ideal of beauty was primarily an ideal of manly virtue—a strong, self-controlled, rational man distanced from sexuality, emotion, and everything disorderly or disturbing (Mosse, 1985; Young, 1990). 'In much nineteenth-century scientific discourse . . . whole groups of people are essentially and irrevocably degenerate: Blacks, Jews, homosexuals, poor and working people, and women' (Young, 1990: 128–9). Women were considered to be physically delicate and weak, childlike mentally, and prone to irrationality and madness. The notion of whiteness was identified with reason, while blackness was associated with body (Kovel, 1970). This allowed people who were white to identify themselves as possessing reason and, therefore, to be the subject of knowledge, and to identify people of colour as the objects of knowledge (Said, 1978). Nineteenth-century discourse often extended the concept of 'black' to depict Jews and gays and lesbians. A new discourse on old age occurred in this time period, too, shifting it from an association with wisdom and endurance to an identification with frailty, incontinence, and senility (Cole, 1986, cited in Young, 1990). All groups that did not meet the norm of the young, white, bourgeois man were objectified in varying degrees as degenerate others.

This normal/abnormal or good/bad distinction did not guarantee respectability and superiority for all white bourgeois men, however, as even they were subject to disease and deviance, especially if they succumbed to sexual impulse. The nineteenth-century medical and moral literature is replete with male fears of becoming effeminate. Therefore, manly men must protect their health and beauty by exercising control over sexual urges. Bishop (1994) contends that during this period every oppressed group was assigned at least one negative sexual myth, usually that the oppressed group is sexually out of control, immoral, or perverted. Thus all women secretly want to be raped; gays and lesbians are perverts who engage in unnatural sex acts and want to seduce children; poor people breed like rabbits; black men want to rape white women; black women are more highly sexed than white women; Aboriginal women cannot say 'no'; disabled and old persons have no sexuality. These stereotypic attributes reinforced the socially constructed and 'scientifically' legitimated belief that groups other than young, white, bourgeois males were inferior and degenerate.

THE DYNAMICS OF OPPRESSION

It could be argued that the racial, gender, class, mental, and other theories of superiority generated by nineteenth-century scientific reason have been discredited by twentieth-century research and social movements. Numerous pieces of social legislation and social rules in the form of proclaimed civil, political, and human rights are now available to the oppressed, as are affirmative action and employment equity programs that express a commitment to equality among social groups. Ideologies of natural superiority and group domination no longer seem to hold the influence they once did in our society. However, the position taken here is that various forms of oppression still are rooted in contemporary society, but they appear in different manifestations having both continuities and discontinuities with past structures.

Oppression does not occur today through some coercive rule of law or because of the evil intentions of a dominant group. It occurs through the systemic constraints on subordinate groups that take the form of unquestioned norms, behaviours, and symbols and in the underlying assumptions of institutional rules. In other words, modern-day oppression is structural.

> In this extended structural sense oppression refers to the vast and deep injustices some groups suffer as a consequence of often unconscious assumptions and reactions of well-meaning people in ordinary interactions, media and cultural stereotypes, and structural features of bureaucratic hierarchies and market mechanisms—in short, the normal processes of everyday life. We cannot eliminate this structural oppression by getting rid of the rulers or making new laws, because oppressions are systematically reproduced in major economic, political, and cultural institutions. (Young, 1990: 41)

To understand the meaning and practice of oppression Foucault (1977) suggests that we go beyond viewing oppression as the conscious and intentional acts of one group against another. Instead, oppression is often found in such areas as education, the production and distribution of goods and services, public administration, the delivery of health and social services, and the like. In other words, many people contribute to maintaining and reproducing oppression in carrying out many of their day-to-day activities, yet they do not understand themselves to be agents of oppression (Young, 1990). This is not to say that members of oppressed groups are never intentionally harmed, as evidenced by rapes of women, physical attacks on gay men, lockouts of workers, and harassment of people of colour. Nor does it mean that members of oppressed groups never oppress others, as evidenced by verbal attacks of the working poor on the non-working poor, physical attacks by youth gang members belonging to one oppressed group against youth belonging to another oppressed group, racial biases held by people in some ethnic or religious communities, or attacks by members on others belonging to the same oppressed group. In spite of these acts of intentional oppression, the contention here is that most oppression today is systemic and unintentional, built into our social institutions, and carried out unconsciously in our day-to-day activities.

LEVELS OF OPPRESSION

Oppression occurs at three levels: the personal or individual level, the cultural level, and the structural or institutional level (Dominelli, 1997; Mullaly, 2002; Thompson, 1997). Each of these three levels or locations is interdependent, interactive, and mutually reinforcing with respect to the other levels, and, in turn, is supported, reinforced, and influenced by the other two levels. In other words, each level of oppression influences and reinforces oppression on the other two levels. Thompson (1997) has named this multi-dimensional perspective the 'PCS' (personal, cultural, structural) model of analysis.

The personal or individual level is located within the cultural and structural contexts of society, and the cultural level is located within the structural context (see Figure 10.1). Although we may examine oppression at only the personal level or at one of the other two levels, it will be an incomplete examination because one's thoughts, attitudes, and actions can only be understood in the larger context(s) with an awareness that the three levels continuously interact with one another. In some respects, the PCS model of analysis is an elaboration of the 'personal is political' analysis of feminists, social activists, and progressive social workers (Mullaly, 2002). It retains the 'personal' and the 'political' by recognizing that social problems are political or structural by nature and that they cause personal difficulties for many people. Furthermore, just as structural forces affect people, so, too, do people affect structures. This insight has been behind all social change movements, from small acts of individual resistance to large social movements. The PCS model adds to this perspective an intermediate level, which is the cultural level. Culture (values, norms, and shared patterns of thinking) tended to be lumped in as part of the structural level in the 'personal is political' model. However, today, thanks to the development of contemporary cultural studies, we have a greater understanding of how the dominant culture of a society reflects and reinforces the oppression of subordinate cultures on the other two levels. Culture, as a level or location of oppression, helps to address the concern expressed in Chapter 7 (see Box 7.2) about the utility of 'the personal is political' as a useful tool in everyday social work practice.

Oppression at the personal level comprises those thoughts, attitudes, and behaviours that depict a negative pre-judgement of a particular subordinate group. It is usually based on stereotypes and may be overt or covert. Oppression at the cultural level consists of those values, norms, and shared patterns of thinking and acting, along with an assumed consensus about what is right and normal, that, taken together, endorse the belief in a superior culture. It acts as a vehicle for transmitting and presenting the dominant culture (i.e., the culture of the dominant group) as the norm, the message being that everyone should conform to it. Oppression at the structural level refers to the means by which oppression is institutionalized in society. It consists of the ways that social institutions, laws, policies, and social processes and practices all work together primarily in favour of the dominant group at the expense of subordinate groups. At this level oppression is given its formal legitimation.

THE MULTIPLICITY AND PERSISTENCE OF OPPRESSION

A person's identity is associated with physical, psychological, social, and cultural variables such as appearance, personality, social status or class, social roles, and race

FIGURE 10.1 PCS MODEL OF OPPRESSION

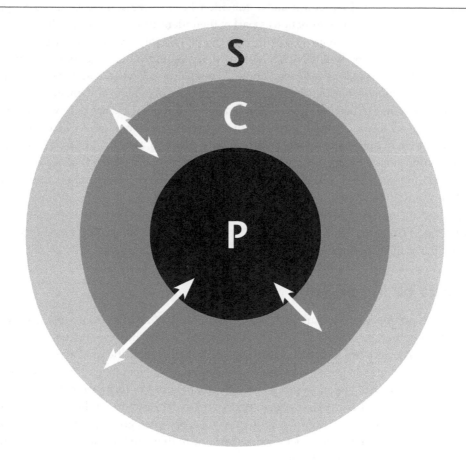

or ethnicity (Mullaly, 2002). One's identity is seldom, if ever, determined solely by one characteristic although one characteristic may be a major marker in most situations (e.g., one's gender or skin colour). The individual does not possess a single social identity, but multiple identities that shift and change over time or in different contexts. Persons may be identified in various ways as they tend to be members of many affinity groups. Black persons, for example, may be rich, poor, old, or gay. These differences produce different identities as well as potential conflicts with other black people and affinities with some white people. Oppressed people are seldom oppressed along one dimension only, but tend to be multiply oppressed.

Given the fact of multiple identities and the wide array of forms and sources of oppression, most oppressed people belong to more than one category of oppression. Anne Bishop (1994: 61) states, 'we are oppressors in some parts of our identity, and oppressed in others.' She suggests that it would be easier to fight oppression if a line could be drawn between oppressors and oppressed. This means that most oppressed people also have access to some form of superiority and domination. Because many disadvantaged people have at least one form of domination as part of their identity, it is very difficult to wage a campaign to eliminate oppression. Although the individual may want to see the end of oppression in those parts of his or her identity that are subordinate (e.g., poverty, homosexuality), he or she may be very reluctant to surrender the power and privilege that come with that part of personal identity that is dominant (e.g., maleness, affluence).

The net effect of defending those parts of our identity that give us relatively favourable treatment in society while contributing to the oppression of others is to keep the whole system of oppression in place. As long as separation, competition, and hierarchy among subordinate groups exist, there is no potential for solidarity and collective action on the part of oppressed groups, which leaves the status quo protected. Only a complete and complex understanding of our own contradictory roles as oppressors and oppressed will allow us to recognize our shared interests and to resist rather than co-operate with oppression (Bishop, 1994). Mullaly (2002) presents an overview of a few models that attempt to depict the intersecting and multiple nature of oppression.

FORMS OF OPPRESSION

Although all oppressed groups, such as the poor and working-class people, women, people of colour, gay men and lesbians, disabled persons, elderly citizens, Jews, and Aboriginals, experience some obstacles to developing their capacities and to participating fully in society, it is impossible to give one essential or universal definition of oppression. Iris Young (1990) has developed a set of five categories or forms of oppression that encompass both distributive issues of injustice and social structures, relations, and practices that go beyond distribution. Although not all oppressed groups experience all five forms of oppression they do experience at least one of them and usually more than one. A summary of each is presented below.

Exploitation

Exploitation refers to those social processes whereby the dominant group is able to accumulate and maintain status, power, and assets from the energy and labour expended by subordinate groups. Exploitation is primarily experienced by working-class persons, women, and people of colour.

With respect to workers, capitalism systematically transfers powers from workers through the private ownership of the means of production and through markets that allocate labour and the ability to buy goods. As well, the powers of workers are diminished by more than the amount transferred, because workers also suffer material deprivation and a loss of control over their work, which results in a loss of self-respect.

The injustice of class division goes beyond the fact that a few people have enormous wealth while many people have little. Exploitation is realized through a structural relationship between the have and have-not groups. Social rules about what work is, who works for whom, how work is to be compensated, and how the results of work are to be distributed and used all operate through a systematic process to produce and reproduce relations of power and inequality.

Women are exploited not only in the Marxist sense that they are wage workers or that their domestic labour is simply subsumed in the wages a family receives, but also in terms of their nurturing, caring, and smoothing over of workplace tensions (Alexander, 1987; Young, 1990). Women expend energy and expertise that are most often unnoticed and unacknowledged (while they simultaneously perform their work in their paying jobs) in ways that enhance the wealth, status, or comfort of others, usually of men who thereby are released to carry out work considered more important and creative, both aspects of which are more highly rewarded than the work of the subordinate women. In other words, the power, freedom, and status enjoyed by men are attributable significantly to women who work for them and in a way that constitutes a systematic and unreciprocated transfer of power and energy from women to men (Young, 1990).

Along with class and gender, Young (1990) argues that there is also a race-specific form of exploitation. It is carried out by members of non-white groups performing menial tasks for white people. Wherever racism exists in a predominantly white society there is an expectation that members of non-white groups will carry out servant roles for the dominant white group—domestics, bellhops, maids, non-professional nannies, porters, busboys, janitors, dishwashers, and the like. In addition to servile, unskilled, minimum wage, and low-status work with little autonomy, these jobs involve a transfer of energy whereby the servers enhance the status of the served.

To Young's contention that menial labour constitutes a form of exploitation, another form of work—dangerous work—can also be considered exploitative. During times of war, poor working men, both white and black, are usually on the front lines of the battlefield while white bourgeois males—high-ranking officers and officials in departments of defence—direct operations far from the front lines and take credit for victory. The coal-mining industry and the fisheries have historically employed (in the former case) or relied on (in the latter case) resource-poor people to go into the mines to dig and extract the coal or to go on the waters to catch the fish, while the owners of the mines or the fish-processing plants, who determine wages or the price of the fish catch, seldom leave their safe and comfortable corporate headquarters. Female workers are subject to sexual harassment on the job, a type of corporate violence to which men typically are not exposed. Many female workers who make their living by making repetitive wrist, arm, and back movements, such as secretaries and other keyboard operators, are subject to repetitive strain injuries such as tendonitis and carpal tunnel syndrome (DeKeseredy and Hinch, 1991).

The above forms of exploitation cannot be eliminated by a redistribution of material resources. As long as current structural relations and institutionalized practices remain unaltered, the process of transferring energy and labour from the exploited to the dominant group will reproduce an unequal distribution of goods and benefits. 'Bringing about justice where there is exploitation requires reorganization of institutions and practices of decision-making, alteration of the division of labor, and similar measures of institutional, structural, and cultural change' (Young, 1990: 53).

Marginalization

Marginalization affects primarily people of colour, old and young persons, many single mothers and their children, physically and mentally disabled people, unskilled workers, and North American Aboriginals. These groups constitute a growing underclass permanently confined to the margins of society because the labour market cannot or will not accommodate them.

Young (1990) suggests that marginalization is perhaps the most dangerous form of oppression because it excludes whole groups of people from useful and meaningful participation in society, which, in turn, may lead to severe material deprivation. Even though advanced capitalist societies have put in place modern welfare systems to deal with material deprivation, in North America, at least, welfare redistribution has not eliminated large-scale suffering, and in the present political climate there is no assurance that the welfare state will continue. As well, the welfare state in liberal democracies has been criticized for denying those who become dependent on it of certain rights and freedoms that others take for granted (Galper, 1975, 1980). Welfare bureaucracies have often treated poor people, old persons, and disabled individuals who rely on them for support and services with punitive, demeaning, patronizing, and arbitrary policies and regulations that interfere with their basic rights to privacy, respect, and autonomy.

Even when material deprivation is not present, marginalization may still occur. Many old people, for example, have the material means to live comfortable lives, but they are excluded from meaningful social participation and cannot exercise their capacities in socially defined and recognized ways. Most of society's productive and recognized activities are related to age and work. Thus, in their marginality, older people are often subject to feelings of uselessness, boredom, and a lack of self-respect.

Marginalization constitutes a basic feature of injustice and oppression. To overcome it requires both a restructuring of productive activity to address a right of participation within the wage system and establishing some socially productive activity outside the wage system.

Powerlessness

Powerlessness consists of inhibitions in the development of one's capacities, a lack of decision-making power in one's working life, and exposure to disrespectful treatment because of the status one occupies. It affects primarily non-professional workers, but also people of colour and women to a lesser extent. It is based on the social division of labour but is more complex than the traditional Marxist model of class exploitation in that it recognizes the distinction between the 'middle class' and the 'working class' to be a social division of labour between professionals and non-professionals.

Most workplaces in advanced capitalist societies are organized hierarchically, with direct participation of workers being rare and decisions (in both the private and public sectors) being imposed on workers and citizens. However, this decision-making power is often mediated by agents who may have no say in the decision, but do exercise power and authority over others in carrying out decisions and policies. The powerless are those who do not have power or authority even in this mediated sense; they 'exercise little creativity or judgement in their work, have no technical expertise or authority, . . . and do not command respect' (Young, 1990: 58–9). Non-professionals suffer this type of oppression; professionals (white males at least) do not.

The status privilege of professionals has three aspects (Sennett and Cobb, 1972, cited in Young, 1990). First, a professional develops her or his capacities and gains recognition by obtaining a university education and through subsequent professional advancement with an accompanying rise in status. Second, professionals have considerable work autonomy relative to non-professionals and usually have some authority over others, whether subordinate workers or clients. Third, the privileges of the professional extend beyond the workplace to a whole way of life or culture that has respectability associated with it. The norms of respectability in our society—in terms of dress, speech, tastes, and demeanour—are those of a professional culture. If one wishes to make a good impression, whether in seeking a bank loan or applying for a job, one likely will try to look 'professional' or 'respectable' as part of his or her efforts. Typically, professionals receive more respectful treatment in our society than non-professionals.

The power and respectability that accompany the privileged status of being a professional also involve racist and sexist dynamics. People of colour and women who are professionals must prove their respectability again and again. When it is not known that they are professional persons they are often not treated with respect or deference, but when others become aware that the individual is, for example, a university teacher or a business executive, the person will often receive respect. Conversely, working-class white men are often accorded respect until their working-class status is discovered.

Although the injustices of powerlessness have distributional consequences they are more fundamentally issues of the division of labour and bring into question the social division of those who make decisions and those who carry out these decisions. This social division of labour provides a plausible explanation for so many social workers being co-opted by our present social system that oppresses so many people. As professionals, social workers are able to exercise their capacities through their university training and through the professional development that occurs throughout their careers. In addition, they are able to exercise considerable power over others and receive the respect that goes with the privilege of professionalism. It requires considerable commitment as well as energy to work at transforming the society that has given the social worker some degree of power and privilege.

Cultural Imperialism

Exploitation, marginalization, and powerlessness all refer to relations of oppression that occur through the social division of work. Feminists and black liberation theorists, among others, have identified a further form of oppression—cultural imperialism. This form of oppression comes about when the dominant group universalizes its experience and culture and uses them as the norm. Through a process of ethnocentrism the dominant group, most often without realizing it, projects its experience and culture as representative of all humanity. Our social institutions are based on the culture and experiences of the dominant group, and our educational system, the media, the entertainment industry, literature, and the marketing of products reinforce this notion of a universal culture. We are socialized into this ethnocentric view of the world. Cultural imperialism is experienced in varying degrees by all oppressed groups.

The dominant group reinforces its position by measuring other groups according to the dominant norms. Thus, the differences of women from men, black people or Aboriginal people from white people, Jews from Christians, gay men and lesbians from heterosexuals, and workers from professionals become largely constructed as deviance and inferiority. These 'other' groups experience a double and paradoxical oppression. Stereotypes are used to mark them at the same time their own experiences and perspectives are rendered invisible.

The stereotypes applied to the culturally imperialized brand them as deviant and inferior, and are so pervasive in society that they are seldom questioned. Examples are that Aboriginal persons are alcoholic and lazy, gay men are promiscuous and perverted, women are good with children, black people are drug addicts and criminals. The fact that culturally dominated groups tend to be defined from the outside not only renders their own experiences and perspectives invisible to the dominant group, but forces oppressed groups to look at themselves through the eyes of a dominant group that views them with contempt or amusement (Du Bois, 1969, cited in Young, 1990). 'This, then, is the injustice of cultural imperialism: that the oppressed group's own experience and interpretation of social life finds little expression that touches the dominant culture, while the same culture imposes on the oppressed group its experience and interpretation of social life' (Young, 1990: 60). To overcome cultural imperialism it would seem that a necessary step would be for culturally oppressed groups to take over the definition of themselves and assert a positive sense of group difference.

Violence

Almost all oppressed groups suffer systematic violence simply because they are members of a subordinate group. Violence includes not only physical attack, but harassment, ridicule, or intimidation, which serves the purpose of stigmatizing group members. The oppression of violence lies not only in direct victimization, but in the constant fear that violence may occur, solely on the basis of one's group identity.

Women have reason to fear rape; people of colour have reason to fear harassment; gay men and lesbians have reason to fear unprovoked assaults; striking workers have reason to fear attacks by police or strikebreakers. Violence is structural when it is tolerated, accepted, or found unsurprising by the dominant group, or when perpetrators receive light or no punishment. Violence is a social practice when people from the dominant group seek out people from oppressed groups to beat up, rape, or harass. To reform institutions and social practices that encourage, tolerate, or enable violence against members of specific groups will require a change in cultural images, stereotypes, and the day-to-day reproduction of dominance and aversion.

The above summary of Young's (1990) five faces of oppression avoids the problems associated with both the unified and the pluralistic accounts of oppression. The former tends either to leave out groups that even the theorist thinks oppressed or to ignore important ways in which groups are oppressed. The latter fails to accommodate the similarities and overlaps in the oppression of different groups, on the one hand, and, on the other hand, falsely represents the situation of all group members as the same.

Young's framework avoids the above reductions and exclusions. Rather than a full theory of oppression, the five forms of oppression function as objective criteria for determining whether or not individuals and groups are oppressed. Each criterion can be operationalized and applied through the assessment of observable behaviour, status relationships, distributions, texts, and culture. Although the presence of any one of these five conditions is sufficient for calling a group oppressed, different oppressed groups exhibit different combinations of them, as do different individuals within these groups. Comparisons can be made of the ways a particular form of oppression occurs in different groups, or of the combinations of oppression that groups experience. Obviously, this framework has significant potential for helping social workers understand better the oppression of people with whom they work in their professional practice.

OPPRESSION AS STRUCTURAL VIOLENCE

The term 'social or structural inequality' is part of an academic and professional discourse that reduces its political charge and impact by 'covering over' the structural violence experienced by members of subordinate groups all over the world. Furthermore, by not including the violent consequences and correlates of social inequality in its discourse and practice, the profession of social work is, in effect, an agent (perhaps unwitting) in limiting healthy and productive living and in contributing to premature rates of death. Structural social workers and anti-oppressive social workers view social inequality as more than notions of deprivation, disadvantage, and redistribution. It is part of a socially sanctioned process whereby people are hurt, maimed, and killed in ways that are unseen and unpunished.

As mentioned above, the recent literature on anti-oppressive social work presents oppression as occurring at three levels—personal, cultural, and institutional or structural (Mullaly, 2002; Thompson, 1998, 2001). Oppression at the structural level refers to the means by which oppression is institutionalized in society. It consists of the ways that our social structures (i.e., social institutions, laws, public policies, social processes and practices) all work together primarily in favour of the dominant group at the expense of subordinate groups. Structural oppression may be overt and visible, such as when the state does not recognize gay and lesbian marriages or does not allow these persons to have other family rights (e.g., inheritance, pension benefits, right to visit a partner in a hospital when only family members are allowed). However, most oppression at the structural level today is covert or hidden. Covert structural oppression occurs when our social institutions, laws, policies, and practices disproportionately allocate goods, services, and opportunities with a positive social value (e.g., good health care, decent housing, a good job) to dominant group members and disproportionately allocate goods, services, and limited opportunities with negative social value (e.g., inadequate housing, incarceration, poor health care) to members of subordinate groups. Some of the ways that this inequitable distribution occurs will be looked at below.

Covert oppression at the structural level is a powerful force in maintaining group-based hierarchies. First, it appears to contradict the spirit and intention of the civil and human rights legislation and the principles of liberty and equality that have been developed over the past hundred years to prohibit institutional discrimination and to extend citizenship status to previously excluded groups. Second, its hidden nature results in many dominant and subordinate group members not recognizing it, which may result in subordinate group members blaming themselves for their own oppression (i.e., internalizing their oppression). Even if recognized, its hidden and subtle nature makes it very difficult for subordinate groups to employ collective action to bring it to an end. The belief that modern Western democracies are largely free from discrimination and oppression at the structural level is not only held by the lay public, but is widespread among political commentators, public intellectuals, and a number of scholars (Sidanius and Pratto, 1999). However, the evidence overwhelmingly contradicts this belief. Rather than social equality and equal opportunity, widespread institutional or structural oppression affects all the major areas of an individual's life—employment, housing, health, education, financial opportunities, and treatment by the criminal justice system. Structural oppression constitutes a total environment or what Sidanius and Pratto (1999: 129) call a 'circle of oppression'.

The term 'social inequality' is widely used by social work and social policy personnel to refer to a differential or inequitable distribution of goods, services, and opportunities whereby members of dominant groups enjoy satisfactory levels of living while members of subordinate groups live in states of deprivation. As mentioned above, one of the traditional tasks of the social welfare state and social work has been to attempt to reallocate or redistribute goods and services to members of subordinate groups so as to reduce deprivation and disadvantage. This activity, sometimes referred to as distributive or redistributive justice, does nothing about the social, economic, and political processes and practices that disproportionately allocate goods, services, and opportunities in the first place. Furthermore, by focusing on the reduction of deprivation and disadvantage as the goal, we tend to overlook or not even recognize the fact that the deprivation and disadvantage, which are associated with social inequality, lead to higher rates of morbidity and to premature death for countless numbers of subordinated people all over the world.

The social inequalities that occur because of oppression at the structural level go beyond an inequitable distribution of society's resources. The African-American psychiatrist and scholar, Hussein Bulhan (1985), argues, for example, that structural oppression is a form of violence because it negatively affects human growth and development; it interferes with the inherent potential of individuals; it limits productive and healthy living; and it brings about premature death. Bulhan's (p. 135) definition of violence links it with structural oppression: 'Violence is any relation, process, or condition by which an individual or a group violates the physical, social, and/or psychological integrity of another person or group.'

Violence at the personal level is relatively easy to detect and control as it usually involves direct action in which the act of violence and its consequences are observable. The perpetrator and the victim are normally distinguishable, and the purpose of the violence can be verified and its effects can be assessed. Structural violence is a much more complex and higher-order phenomenon. It is a feature of social structures and social institutions. The social processes, relations, and practices associated with social inequities often span generations. They are deeply ingrained in people and dominate everyday living. 'Structural violence involves more than the violation of fairness and justice. . . . [it] leads to hidden but lethal inequities, which can lead to the death of those who lack power or influence in the society' (Bulhan, 1985: 136).

Thus, rather than a quick death by state execution or a personal act of lethal violence, structural oppression in the form of such inequities as inadequate income, substandard or no housing, unemployment, and lack of health care leads to a slow, agonizing, unpunished, and premature death for countless numbers of subordinated people all over the country, not to say world, on a daily basis. To understand this better we can look at how resources and opportunities are distributed inequitably in six areas of everyday living, along with the resultant violent consequences of these social inequities.[2]

Discrimination in the Housing Market

- Although most Western nations have housing legislation and programs, broad-based covert and systematic discrimination still relegates many subordinate group members to areas that are impoverished, under-serviced, and dangerous.
- Housing discrimination is found at each stage of the housing search, from initial information concerning availability, to efforts made to conclude transactions, to the availability of financing, and to the final location of housing.
- People of colour were given much less information from agents on available units for sale.
- People of colour did not receive the same level of positive comments on prospective homes from agents or were not offered the same special incentives to take a rented apartment as were given to white persons.

- People of colour were more likely to be asked to call the agent back than have the transaction pursued immediately.
- People of colour were more likely to be directed to an area (low income, greater minority populations, substandard schools, higher crime rates) other than the one originally requested.
- The same treatment as above has been experienced by single mothers and young people looking for housing.

Discrimination in the Retail Market

- Retail outlets located in neighbourhoods occupied by subordinate groups charged higher prices for the same goods as stores located in neighbourhoods occupied by dominant groups.
- For goods that have negotiations attached to them in terms of prices (e.g., cars), people of colour pay more than white people and women pay more than men for the same goods even when the location of the retail outlet is controlled.
- People of colour regularly experience targeted surveillance in retail outlets (e.g., being followed by security persons).
- Subordinate group members receive more instances of rude and disrespectful treatment from retail outlet personnel.

Discrimination in the Labour Market

- Work is a major determinant of one's perceived worth, social position, and general well-being. By allocating various kinds of jobs to different social groups, societies produce and maintain group-based social dominance and privilege.
- There is widespread discrimination against women, people of colour, non-European ethnicities, non-Christian religions, poor persons, and other subordinate groups in all Western countries.
- Subordinate group members are last hired and first fired, receive less pay, have fewer opportunities for on-the-job training, and have less chance for promotion.
- The level of market discrimination is greater:
  - for jobs requiring more rather than less contact with people;
  - in the private sector over the public sector;
  - for jobs requiring fewer qualifications;
  - when for-profit employment agencies are used;
  - in jobs that are narrowly rather than widely advertised;
  - during times of economic recessions.
- Although most job discrimination is covert, a significant number of businesses discriminate overtly.
- Social policies that address problems of discrimination in the labour market, such as affirmative action and employment equity, are the very policies that are most

unpopular with the dominant group, and, therefore, may not be sustainable in the long run.

Discrimination in the Education System

- Both the quantity and quality of education is lower for subordinate groups than for dominant groups. Four mechanisms of institutional discrimination help to produce these differential outcomes.
  1. *Differential funding.* Children in dominant groups receive a larger proportion of public education resources for their education.
  2. *Differential referral.* Children who are poor, non-white, and from particular neighbourhoods are more likely to be regarded as emotionally disturbed or mentally challenged and referred to special education or remedial classes.
  3. *Differential tracking.* Students from subordinate groups are more likely to be channelled into non-academic or vocational programs and students from dominant groups are more likely to be channelled into academically enriched classes regardless of academic abilities.
  4. *Differential teacher expectations.* Students regarded and treated by teachers as dull fall below the performances of those regarded and treated as bright, and subordinate group children usually are placed in the first category and dominant group children in the second category.

Discrimination in the Health-Care System

- All national and international studies looking at health status found that subordinate groups experience higher morbidity and premature mortality rates, while those at the top of the social hierarchy are generally in better physical and psychological health (Aboriginal people in all countries with an Aboriginal population rank far at the bottom).
- Subordinate group members are less likely to have access to the economic and social resources that promote health (i.e., plentiful and high-quality food, living and work environments that are not dangerous or stressful, and access to immediate and high-quality medical care).
- In addition to lack of resources or ready access to medical care, subordinate populations experience considerable discrimination within health-care systems that take three forms according to Sidanius and Pratto (1999):
  1. *Differential treatment by health-care professionals.* Studies found that white persons received higher levels of care than black people for coronary problems, extreme kidney failure, and cancer. Poor people have lower immunization rates than affluent persons and black persons have lower immunization rates than white people. Similarly, mammography rates were lower for black women than for white women and lower for poor persons than for affluent persons.

Disfiguring medical procedures (castrations, amputations) were higher among black people than white people.

2. *Differential dissemination of health-care information.* Controlling for all other factors, it was found that black women were given less prenatal information than white women on smoking cessation and alcohol use.

3. *Discriminatory physiological effects.* Studies show that the psychological experiences of racial discrimination contribute to the negative health status of subordinate groups (i.e., high blood pressure and other stress-related illnesses).

Interestingly, one study (Krieger and Sidney, 1996) reported lower blood pressure among black persons who would challenge racial discrimination than among those who accepted what they regarded as unfair discrimination. This finding supports Frantz Fanon's (1963) thesis that resistance to oppression has positive physical and psychological effects on oppressed persons. This is an important piece of information for developing an anti-oppressive social work practice.

Discrimination in the Criminal Justice System

- There is a substantial over-representation of subordinate group members within the criminal justice system (e.g., indigenous Australians are imprisoned at a rate of more than 15 times that of non-indigenous Australians, African Americans are incarcerated at a rate of 6.8 times that of white Americans, and Aboriginal people in Canada experience an incarceration rate three times higher than that for non-Aboriginal Canadians, though these rates are considerably higher in the western provinces) (Dickason, 2006: 271).

- Controlling for all legally relevant variables (e.g., type and seriousness of crime, criminal record), subordinate groups have a higher likelihood of: being arrested, having more serious charges laid against them, having higher amounts of bail, being more likely to be convicted, having a more severe sentence imposed, and having less likelihood of probation or early parole.

- A Canadian study found that prison guards are more likely to subject black prisoners to harsh treatment, especially when a considerable degree of interpretational discretion is allowed (Cole and Gittens, 1995).

- One American study looked at police violence across the Americas and found that police brutality against subordinate group members often results in institutional rewards rather than in punishment (Chevigny, 1995, cited in Sidanius and Pratto, 1999).

- Crimes committed by subordinate group members against dominant group members were more severely punished than those committed by the latter against the former.

In Canada, as with all countries with an Aboriginal population, Aboriginal people, by all indicators, experience the highest levels of social inequality and, therefore, suffer most from structural violence, as shown below:

- Nearly half (47.2 per cent) of First Nations families live below the poverty line (Oberle, 1993).
- The average life expectancy of Aboriginal people is 10 years less than that for Euro-Canadians (Health and Welfare Canada, 1991a).
- Twenty per cent of First Nations children are removed from their families by child welfare authorities (Clarke, 1991).
- The infant mortality rate is double the national average (Health Canada, 1994).
- Suicide rates for adolescent girls is seven times the national rate and four times higher for male adolescents (ibid.).
- Incarceration rates and alcohol and drug abuse are much higher than in the general population (Health and Welfare Canada, 1992).
- Family violence is disproportionately high among Aboriginal families (Chappell, 1997).

Among other subordinate groups experiencing oppression and structural violence are older Canadians. For these people, poverty, loneliness, and a sense of uselessness contribute to Alzheimer's and related dementias (Health and Welfare Canada, 1991b), very high suicide rates (Health Canada, 1994), and abuse of prescription drugs (Health Canada, 1989). Canadian women experience violence (Statistics Canada, 1993), poverty (National Council of Welfare, 1996), and workplace discrimination with respect to wages, occupational segregation, training, and pensions (Canadian Advisory Council on the Status of Women, 1990).

An examination of the living situation of almost any subordinate group anywhere in the world is likely to show it experiencing oppression in all or most of the above areas. That is, subordinate groups will, for the most part, suffer directly from lack of adequate employment, low income and poverty, inadequate housing, discrimination in the retail market, lack of educational opportunities, inferior health care, and over-representation within the criminal justice system. These inequities constitute structural violence in that people who experience them consequently suffer from disproportionate levels and incidences of stress, anguish, frustration, alienation, and exclusion, and these factors result in differential rates of mortality (i.e., lowered life expectancies), morbidity, incarceration, homicide, suicide, and infant mortality. There can be no doubt, as Bulhan (1985) argues, and as did Fanon (1968) before him, that oppression at the structural level leads to violence at the intrapersonal level (e.g., suicide and self-mutilation), at the interpersonal level (e.g., homicide and domestic violence), and at the institutional level (premature death because of social inequalities). What makes this type of violence so insidious is the fact that no recognized perpetrator or intention is normally identified as responsible for the violence. Commenting on structural violence elsewhere (Mullaly, 2002: 121), I concluded that:

> structural inequalities often have violent effects or outcomes. Terms such as 'social inequality' and 'structural inequality' tend to cover up the violent outcomes that many

people from subordinate groups experience. Structural inequalities are much more than one person or one group having a greater quantity of or more access to social goods, rights, and opportunities. They are more than violations of philosophical notions of fairness, equity, and justice. Structural inequalities are socially sanctioned forms of physical and psychological violence, which over time will lead to hurtful discrimination and slow, agonizing, premature, and unpunished death. The term 'structural violence', I contend, more accurately reflects the realities of oppressed persons. 'Structural inequality' is a somewhat abstract, technical, bourgeois, and polite term that covers up its violent outcomes. We should call it what it is—*socially sanctioned structural violence.*

RESPONSES OF OPPRESSED PEOPLE TO THEIR OPPRESSION

There are two major sets of responses that oppressed people may make with respect to the oppression they experience: (1) accommodation and compliance through a process of inferiorization; or (2) rejection through a process of collective resistance and a politics of difference (Adam, 1978; Young, 1990). Both sets of responses are discussed below.

Inferiorization

Members of oppressed groups are defined in ways by the dominant group that often devalue, objectify, and stereotype them as different, deviant, or inferior. Their own experiences and interpretation of social life find little expression that touches the dominant culture (Young, 1990). Because they find themselves reflected in literature, the media, formalized education, and so forth either not at all or in a highly distorted fashion, they suffer an impoverished identity (Adam, 1978). The paradox of this situation for oppressed populations is that at the same time they are rendered invisible by the dominant group they are also marked as different.

This lack of a strong self-identity will, in many cases, lead to an internalization of the dominant group's stereotyped and inferiorized images of subordinate populations (Young, 1990). This internalized oppression, in turn, will cause some oppressed people to act in ways that affirm the dominant group's view of them as inferior and, consequently, will lead to a process of inferiorized persons reproducing their own oppression. Through a process of cultural and ideological hegemony many oppressed people believe that if they cannot make it in our society, if they are experiencing problems, then it is their own fault because they are unable to take advantage of the opportunities the dominant group says are available to everyone. It is, as Paulo Freire (1970) said, as if the oppressor gets into the head of the oppressed. People understand their own interests in ways that reflect the interests of the dominant group.

When people internalize their oppression, blaming themselves for their troubled circumstances, they will often contribute to their own oppression by considering it as unique, unchangeable, deserved, or temporary (Adam, 1978), or else blame other significant people in their lives such as parents or family. Oppressed persons often contribute to their own oppression, also, by psychologically or socially withdrawing or engaging in other self-destructive behaviours, which causes them to be rejected by others. This, in turn, confirms the low image they may have of themselves (Moreau and Leonard, 1989). The radical psychiatric movement considers all alienation to be the result of oppression about which the oppressed have been mystified or deceived. That is, the oppressed person is led to believe that he or she is not oppressed or that there are good reasons for his or her oppression (Agel, 1971).

Paulo Freire (1970) discusses several stances oppressed people may adopt that either reinforce or contribute to their own oppression. Fatalism may be expressed by the oppressed about their situation—'There is nothing I can do about it' or 'It is God's will' are common expressions of fatalism. However, this fatalistic attitude is often interpreted as docility or apathy by the oppressor, which reinforces the view of the oppressed as lazy, inferior, and getting all that they deserve. Horizontal violence often occurs among oppressed people whereby an Aboriginal, for example, may strike out at another Native person for petty reasons (which again reinforces the negative images held by the dominant class of subordinate groups). Self-deprecation also occurs when a group hears so often that they are good for nothing that in the end they become convinced of their own unfitness. Moreau and Leonard (1989) and Adam (1978) call this process inferiorization. Another characteristic of some oppressed persons is that they feel an irresistible attraction towards the oppressor and his or her way of life. This affirms, of course, the belief that oppression is legitimate and that it is more desirable to oppress than to be oppressed.

It must be noted that such responses are not irrational on the part of those oppressed persons who use them. Although they may appear to be peculiar, unnatural, or neurotic, they are actually rational coping mechanisms employed in everyday life to lessen the suffering of oppression—despite the fact that they are ineffective because they function to sustain domination. Adam (1978) identified seven such responses.

1. *Mimesis*. One response to oppression is for a member of a particular oppressed group to mimic or imitate the behaviours and attitudes the dominant group displays towards that group in an attempt to gain a slightly more privileged status. Some examples are: often the harshest critics of the non-working poor are the working poor (who repeat all the punitive and moralistic accusations held by the dominant group), even though both groups suffer the oppression associated with poverty; an organized women's group called REAL Women of Canada has been unrelenting in its attack on what it sees as the efforts of the feminist movement to diminish the importance of the family as the bedrock of society; 'Uncle Tom' black persons historically have been given positions of authority over other black persons and then treat their subordinates as inferiors rather than as compatriots.

Each oppressed group has a small class of converts and apologists who assist the dominant group in the preservation of the status quo by conforming to the values of their 'masters'. Impressed with the small privileges that go with their 'borrowed status', they savour them and will often defend them with fear and harshness. Often the converts will, over time, identify more with the dominant group than with their own community, thus presenting the community with a chronic threat.

2. *Escape from identity*. To avoid or ease the burdens of oppression some inferiorized persons will attempt to escape from the 'composite portrait' (with its accompanying range of social penalties) used by the dominant group to define their particular place in society. Although it may be regarded as neurotic behaviour in that one cannot escape from what one is, to the person attempting to flee from his or her identity, this escape is an attempt to move into another social category—one with fewer social penalties attached to it. However, escaping one's identity personalizes failures on the part of the person who rejects by recognizing or denying that one is a member of a subordinate group. Examples are: Jews who converted to Christianity solely to escape their primary identity (e.g., in Nazi Germany and during the times when immigration policies of some countries such as Canada during and after World War II discriminated against Jews); gay and lesbian persons who enter into heterosexual marriages to be socially accepted; people of one colour or ethnicity who 'pass' as being members of the dominant group or of the subgroup to which they belong socially/occupationally.

Escape from identity, like other inferiorized responses to oppression, functions as a false consciousness that subordinates the person to the rationality of oppression. As well, it successfully isolates the person from others who share the same form of oppression. This false consciousness and the atomization of oppressed people serve to maintain the status quo with respect to dominant–subordinate relations in society.

3. *Psychological withdrawal*. Oppressed persons may adopt a cautious, low-profile conservatism as a way of decreasing their visibility (and social penalties) and compensating for a disfavoured identity. Overly visible behaviour by fellow members is strongly condemned as it gives the rest a bad name (e.g., the 'loudmouthed' black, the 'pushy' Jew, or the 'swish' homosexual). An effort to reduce the hazards of a high-risk environment outweighs active resistance. This coping effort is often manifest in psychological responses such as passivity, lethargy, and submission. Afro-Americans during the period of slavery and Jews in Nazi concentration camps often exhibited these psychological characteristics. Obviously, psychological withdrawal fails to confront the oppressive order.

4. *Guilt-expiation rituals*. Sacrifice is classically conceived as the destruction of a victim for purposes of maintaining or correcting a relationship with the 'sacred' order. Some oppressed persons will see the dominant order as sacred and immutable, and to atone for the guilt of not being able to become full-fledged members they will engage in certain conscious or unwitting guilt-expiation rituals. These rituals become manifest in certain self-mutilating alterations, such as black people straightening their hair and lightening their skin; gay men acquiescing to aversive therapy such as extended electro-shock treatment to atone for their imputed transgressions; and the ultimate self-sacrifice by suicide of Aboriginal persons and others as a guilt-ridden response to oppression.

5. *Magical ideologies*. Some oppressed people will see their situation with respect to the dominant group as so immutable that they will appeal to 'divine' ways out of their

oppressed condition, such as fantasies that may lead to neuroses, astrology, superstition, messianism, and even gambling. The appeal is made to someone or something else full of power and authority to fix what is wrong. Internal blinders shield the person from confronting the real menace causing his or her inferiorized situation and lead the person on a search for a magical solution.

6. *In-group hostility.* Hierarchies provide a self-perpetuating dynamic that allows the dominated to console themselves through a comparison with yet more degraded people. It constructs what Adam (1978) calls a 'poor person's snobbery' that sets up a superior–inferior relationship among persons in oppressed groups similar to that between dominant and subordinate groups. It can occur on an intergroup basis, as in the case of white, working-class members oppressing black people, or within an oppressed group, such as closet gay people ridiculing homosexuals or light-skinned black people treating their darker-skinned compatriots with disdain. In this way the dynamics of oppression are reproduced by dominated groups themselves.

7. *Social withdrawal.* Social withdrawal is a coping strategy in which the oppressed person externalizes identity conflict into the immediate social environment. The oppressed person will develop repertoires of behaviours for different audiences. That is, he or she will behave in one way when in contact with the dominant group (usually assuming a low profile to escape attention) and in another way when in contact with the subordinated community (in a way that affirms with others his/her true identity). Social withdrawal does not challenge or negate the dominant view of the oppressed group, as it is a means to placate the powerful other. For example, black parents will often advise their children to avoid (withdraw from) confrontation with the dominant white society as a means of coping with harassment. In effect, this behaviour contributes to a strategy of invisibility, but also supports the dominant view that black people are by nature servile and passive.

The other side of social withdrawal is that it permits the first move towards reconciliation with identical others. As oppressed individuals withdraw from the dominant group by acts of compliance and communicate with other members of their subordinated community, they may discover their identity with them. That is, they become acquainted with their identity as defined by their own group, as opposed to the identity that has been defined and imposed on them by the dominant group. A dialectical movement towards integration occurs as community members discover each other and, in the process, discover themselves. Although the discovery of self and community requires some degree of social withdrawal from an inhospitable social environment controlled by the dominant group, the danger is that it may lead to a ghettoization, which, though seeming safe from the dominant group, probably is also stifling and confining for the oppressed. The ghetto or haven is a response to oppression and potentially a first assertion of community. It has the potential for developing true identity, a sense of community and solidarity. Confidence within oppressed groups can grow so that members are able to 'come out' and assert their authentic identity and differences in ways that contravene the prevailing rationality of the dominant group.

EMANCIPATION OF OPPRESSED GROUPS: ASSIMILATION, MULTICULTURALISM, AND A POLITICS OF DIFFERENCE

In contrast to the above inferiorized coping mechanisms that comply with or accommodate oppression, three emancipatory sets of politics attempt to overcome oppression: assimilation through a politics of integration; multiculturalism through a politics of cultural pluralism; and collective resistance through a politics of difference. Assimilationism would render equal social status to everyone according to the same principles, rules, and standards, while a politics of difference would sometimes require different treatment for oppressed groups (Young, 1990). The former has been the traditional approach of social work, as evidenced by its emphasis on 'impartiality', whereas the latter is more consistent with structural social work's emphasis on democratic cultural pluralism.

Assimilation

Wasserton (1980, cited in Young, 1990) outlines three reasons for choosing the assimilationist ideal of liberation. First, by imagining a society in which class, race, gender, and so forth have no special social significance, one sees more clearly how these categories unnecessarily limit possibilities in our existing society for some people. Second, a clear and unambiguous standard of equality and justice for all is promised, and any group-related differentiation or discrimination would be suspect. That is, any social benefits distributed differently according to group membership would be viewed as unjust. Third, the assimilationist ideal eliminates the situation of group differences resulting in social differences. Thus, people would be free to develop themselves as individuals. In sum, assimilationism promises a 'deal'. The identities, cultures, and values of oppressed groups are to be surrendered for the promise or opportunity of improved life chances. Submission to the social rules of the superordinate group supposedly mitigates the barriers confining subordinate groups (Adam, 1978).

Some writers, such as Young (1990) and Adam (1978), have criticized assimilation as a goal of liberation politics. Today in North American society, and in many other societies, there is widespread agreement that no person should be excluded from political, economic, or social activities because of ascribed characteristics. However, group differences continue to exist, and certain groups continue to be advantaged. Although some persons from disadvantaged groups have succeeded in improving their overall life chances, the general scheme of allocating privilege and resources has remained unchanged (Adam, 1978).

Young (1990) outlines three ways that assimilationism, by ignoring group differences, has oppressive consequences. First, assimilationism entails bringing formerly excluded groups into the mainstream, but this means coming into the game after the rules and standards have already been set and having to prove oneself according to these rules and standards. The privileged group, of course, defines the standards against which all will be measured, and because their privilege involves not recognizing these standards as culturally and experientially specific, they are perceived to be the ideal of a common, universal, and neutral humanity in which all can participate regardless of race, class, gender, and so on. Because the standards are in fact group-specific to the dominant class, they put subordinate groups at a disadvantage in trying to measure up to them, and for that reason assimilationist policies perpetuate their disadvantage.

Second, the notion of a universal humanity devoid of group differences allows dominant groups to overlook or not recognize their own group specificity. The assimilationist's blindness to difference perpetuates cultural imperialism because the subordinate groups are the ones that must drop their culture and adopt the dominant culture, which is assumed as a common, universal humanity.

Third, assimilationism often produces an internalized devaluation by members of subordinate groups. Assimilationist participation means to accept an identity other than one's perceived own and to be reminded by others and by oneself of one's other identity. As a result, children of non-English speaking groups may become ashamed of the accents of their parents, women control their tendency to cry, and gay and lesbian couples avoid displaying affection to each other in public.

Multiculturalism

Multiculturalism as a concept and as a public policy issue dates back to the 1970s in most Western industrialized countries. Although there have been many progressive activists and supporters of multiculturalism, Agger (1998) contends that the concept of multiculturalism has been appropriated to some extent by some schools of postmodernism and that, consequently, a change in meaning has occurred. Basically, Agger argues that multiculturalism is a recognition and acceptance of cultural pluralism, but it does nothing to change the situation of there being one dominant culture with all others subordinate to it. This situation violates the position of earlier multicultural activists that there not be a hierarchy of cultures (this position has now been adopted in the 'politics of difference' approach as outlined below). Multiculturalists today will acknowledge and accept cultural pluralism and will often equate multiculturalism with annual ethnic celebrations. Although many self-proclaimed advocates of multiculturalism may enjoy these annual exotic fesitivities, some of these same people will show little interest in or knowledge of the struggles, blocked opportunities, and second-class citizenship that members of these subordinated cultures experience on a daily basis (Mullaly, 2002).

The dominant theory of multicultural social work in Canada, the US, and Australia is that of cultural sensitivity. The aim of this theory is to increase worker and agency awareness of and sensitivity to different cultural norms and to reduce (but not eliminate) institutional racism. Cultural sensitivity enables white social workers to better establish a 'helping relationship' with members of other races and cultures to make services more accessible and to advocate for the enactment of equal rights legislation. Although the cultural sensitivity model represents an advance over the colour-blind and assimilationist (melting-pot) approach to issues of race and culture, it can actually, without intending it, allow racism to persist, but in a more 'respectable' form (Ahmad, 1991; Thompson, 1997). The cultural sensitivity model ignores the fact that cultures and races are ranked in order of perceived merit and it ignores the power relations in Western society between people of colour and white people, both historically and in the present (Ahmad, 1991; Williams, 1989).

The Politics of Difference

As an alternative to assimilation and multiculturalism, Adam (1978) argues for collective resistance to assimilation and/or to an acceptance of a dominant culture on the part of subordinated groups. He emphasizes the importance of community for developing self-identity, solidarity, and resistance to domination. Communication among members of a subordinate group over time engenders social networks and language that nurture collectivization and a new understanding of their life situation—one defined by the group itself.

> Shared experiences identify effective strategies for coping with social limitations, methods of survival and self-betterment, sources of freedom and joy. Brotherhood or sisterhood is not the simple correlate of, for example, physical resemblances; it is the mutual creation . . . of each member by the other. (Adam, 1978: 122)

Young (1990) elaborates on this notion of community by calling for a 'politics of difference' as the means of overcoming oppression. Rather than attempting to transcend group differences as the assimilationist approach would do or simply to accept them as the multicultural approach would do, the politics of difference seeks equality among all socially and culturally differentiated groups, where mutual respect and affirmation of one another in their differences would occur. Group differences are considered positive and desirable rather than a liability or disadvantage or simply a fact. The positivity of group difference is liberating and empowering in that the identity the dominant group has taught them to despise would be reclaimed, affirmed, and celebrated. This positive view of one's specific culture and experience makes it increasingly difficult for the dominant group to parade its values and norms as universal and neutral.

The politics of group difference also promotes a notion of group solidarity against the individualism of liberal humanism. It is recognized that a positive view of one's specific group requires separate organizations that exclude others. This does not eliminate the need for coalitions among groups or the need for oppressed groups to combat other types of oppression (e.g., white people against racism or men against sexism), but it is a recognition that group autonomy is an important vehicle for empowerment and the development of a group-specific voice and perspective (Young, 1990).

Young notes that many fear that asserting group differences will lead to a justification of subordination. However, she contends that a politics of difference confronts this fear because it presents group difference not as essential, other, or exclusively opposed, but as ambiguous, relational, and shifting, marked by specificity and variation. In this way group differences are conceived as relational rather than defined by substantive categories and attributes (Minow, 1985, 1987, 1990, cited in Young, 1990). A relational view of difference does not focus on the attributes of groups as the measure of difference, but on the interaction of groups with institutions (Littleton, 1987, cited in Young, 1990).

In this relational view, the meaning of difference becomes contextualized (Scott, 1988, cited in Young, 1990). Group differences are conspicuous, depending on the groups compared, the purposes of the comparison, and the point of view of those making the comparison. Such contextualized understandings of difference undermine essentialist assumptions. Young (1990) provides the following example to underscore this point. Wheelchair-bound persons are different from other people in terms of athletics, health care, and social service support, but they are not different in many other respects. At one time disabled persons were excluded and segregated from society because the differences between able-bodied and disabled were conceptualized as extending to all or most capacities.

A relational understanding of group difference rejects exclusion. Differences among groups do not mean they are different in all respects. They have overlapping experiences, common goals, and shared attributes. The assumption that oppositional categorization is inherent in group differences must always be challenged. A relational and contextualized understanding of difference also undermines the notion of an essential individual identity. Persons have many different identities as they tend to be members of many affinity groups, not just one. Black persons, for example, may be poor, rich, old, or gay. These differences produce different identities as well as potential conflicts among other blacks and affinities with some whites. Thus, contextualizing the meanings of difference and identity helps us to see the differences that may exist within affinity groups. Oppressed persons are seldom oppressed along one dimension only. As we have seen, they tend to be multiply oppressed. 'In our complex, plural society, every social group has group differences cutting across it, which are potential sources of wisdom, excitement, conflict, and oppression' (Young, 1990: 172–3).

A politics of difference, of course, has serious implications for policy-making. A goal of social justice (and structural social work) is social equality. As discussed previously, social equality not only refers to an equitable distribution of social goods but to full participation of everyone in society's major institutions and to the socially supported opportunity for all to develop and exercise their inherent capacities. Although in Canada, and in many other Western societies, formal legal equality exists for most groups, these societies still are marked by extreme social inequality. Instead of policies that are universally formulated and thus blind to differences of class, race, gender, age, and so forth, a politics of difference would require policies that reflect the specific situations of oppressed groups. 'Groups cannot be socially equal unless their specific experience, culture, and social contributions are publicly affirmed and recognized' (Young, 1990: 174).

A politics of difference would require a dual system of rights: a general system of rights for all, and a more specific system of group-conscious rights and policies (Young, 1990). We already have a precedent for such a system in the form of civil, political, and human rights for all citizens, along with some affirmative action and employment equity programs for some groups who have historically been disadvantaged in our society. To extend this dual system of rights to the point that there would be effective recognition and representation of the voices and perspectives of oppressed groups (as opposed to interest groups), Young proposes the implementation of institutional mechanisms and public resources supporting: (1) the self-organization of subordinate groups whereby group members could achieve collective empowerment and a reflective understanding of their collective experiences and interests in the context of society; (2) group analysis and generation of policy proposals in institutionalized settings where decision-makers are obliged to demonstrate that their deliberations have taken relevant group perspectives into consideration; and (3) group veto power regarding specific policies and decisions that affect a group directly, such as land use for Aboriginal communities or reproductive rights for women.

STRUCTURAL SOCIAL WORK WITH OPPRESSED GROUPS

An understanding of oppression has several major implications for structural social workers. First, recognizing the limitations of a distributional model of justice is important because this helps in avoiding the pursuit of a more equitable distribution of goods and services without attending to (and thereby reifying) the institutional rules and the social processes and practices that caused the maldistribution in the first place. The goal of structural social work is not simply to compensate and care for victims of oppression. It is to transform the entire constellation of oppressive rules, processes, and practices. Only a theory of social justice that has oppression as its central concern can accommodate this goal.

Second, an understanding of how oppression and its dominant–subordinate relations have been socially constructed is important if social work is to avoid notions and practices of 'blaming the victims'. Only by knowing that oppression is a social construction can social work embark on a deconstruction of oppressive practices and a reconstruction of society characterized by true social equality.

Third, only an understanding of oppression as a systemic situation that is produced and reproduced in everyday social processes and practices—and an awareness that oppression carries out several important social functions for the dominant group—will lead to structural solutions. Otherwise, social work will continue to treat oppression as a technical problem (e.g., as a lack of 'goodness of fit' between the individual and society) amenable to technical solutions rather than as the moral and political (i.e., structural) problem that it is.

Fourth, an understanding of the various forms of oppression allows structural social workers to make more sense of the situation of oppression of those they serve. All forms of oppression are not the same and will, therefore, require atuned responses and actions. This knowledge will also enable the social worker to engage in a more meaningful way in consciousness-raising and normalization activities with oppressed persons.

Fifth, at a micro level of social work practice, an understanding of personal or individual oppression and the various types of internalized oppression will enable the structural social worker to better understand how oppressed persons may be experiencing and coping with their situation of oppression. Through dialogue, this knowledge will assist the worker in sorting out with members of subordinate groups helpful and counterproductive responses to their oppression.

Sixth, at the macro level of social work practice, an understanding of the politics of difference will help the structural social worker to encourage and support group-specific organizations and groups or the establishment of new ones. These are important mechanisms for oppressed people discovering themselves, reclaiming their identity, creating community and solidarity, and developing a group-specific voice and perspective. The politics of difference will also encourage structural social workers to advocate for policies and decision-making mechanisms that give full recognition and representation to the voices of oppressed groups.

These, then, are some implications that a theory of justice, based on a politics of difference and having oppression as its central concern, would hold for structural social work. They may be viewed as the 'what is to be done' aspect of combatting oppression. The elements of 'how to do it' are the subjects of the following two chapters.

CONCLUSION

This chapter looked at the concept of oppression along a number of dimensions. Oppression was described as a type of second-class citizenship that is assigned to people, not on the basis of lack of merit or failure, but because of their membership in a particular group or category of people. Oppression exists and persists because of the number of positive functions it carries out for the dominant group at the expense of subordinate groups. A number of myths that help to rationalize and perpetuate oppression were presented. It was argued that the (re)distributional model of justice that has historically underpinned the modern social welfare state and social work practice only compensates victims of oppression and does nothing to alter the causes of inequality. Furthermore, it was argued that structural inequality goes beyond a simple notion of an inequitable distribution of society's resources because social inequalities lead to higher rates of morbidity and to slow, agonizing, premature, and unpunished death for countless numbers of subordinate persons all over the world on a daily basis.

Although there are different forms, sources, levels of severity, and experiences associated with oppression, a common set of dynamics is engaged between dominant and subordinate groups. Iris Marion Young's five categories of oppression, of which all oppressed groups experience at least one, were presented. This categorization is adopted here because it includes both distributive issues of social justice and social practices that go beyond distribution. A model of oppression that located oppression at three levels—personal, cultural, and structural or institutional—was outlined. The multiple nature and persistence of oppression were discussed and two sets of responses (acceptance and resistance) to oppression by subordinate groups were outlined. Finally, some implications of adopting oppression as the major explanation for social problems for structural social workers were presented.

CRITICAL QUESTIONS

1. Studies have shown that members of dominant groups are often unaware of their many privileges and take them for granted. Furthermore, the studies show that members of subordinate groups tend to be more aware of the privileges that members of dominant groups enjoy. Why is this? What are the implications of this for social workers, who are usually members of dominant groups working with members of subordinate groups?

2. Identify those characteristics of yourself that make you a member of dominant groups (e.g., class, gender, race, age, religion, sexuality, ableness, etc.). Make a list of privileges that you have in society that are associated with each of your dominant group characteristics.

3. Compare your lists of privileges with the lists compiled by those in your class who are not part of the dominant groups of which you are a member. In other words, if you are a male, how does your list of privileges compare to the lists that were compiled by the female members of your class? Similarly, if you are white, how does your list of privileges compare to the lists compiled by the non-white members of your class?

4. Take any source or form of oppression, such as poverty, racism, sexism, homophobia, or ageism, and identify some of the ways it is carried out at the personal, cultural, and structural levels. What would a structural social worker do with this information in his or her social work practice?

5. A single, poor, black mother of three small children is experiencing problems in several areas of her life. She is often turned down by employers for jobs in which she is qualified. She has difficulty finding (being accepted by landlords) decent housing for her family. She often receives derogatory treatment from store clerks, her children's teachers, hospital/medical personnel, employees delivering public services, and others with whom she interacts as a consumer or customer. Is there one subordinate characteristic (single parent, race, class, gender) that is most responsible for the degrading and insulting treatment that she receives on a daily basis?

6. Does the composition of the profession of social work in Canada reflect the diversity of the country's population? Should it? Why or why not?

PART 3

Structural Social Work: Practice Elements

Working Within (and Against) the System: Radical Humanism

They sentenced me to twenty years of boredom, for trying to change the system from within.

— from 'First We Take Manhattan' by Leonard Cohen, 1986

INTRODUCTION

The ultimate goal of structural social work is to contribute to the transformation of society. To accomplish this goal social work must operationalize an ideology within a society where another ideology dominates. To carry out this task the social worker should possess the following attributes:

- an awareness of the limitations of our present society as a satisfactory social system;
- a vision of society where the satisfaction of human need is the central value;
- an awareness that social work is a political activity that either reinforces or opposes the status quo;
- an awareness that social problems are not amenable to individual, family, or subcultural solutions;
- an awareness that critical social analysis is itself an important social work skill;
- an awareness that structural social work is much more than an approach to practice—it is a way of life.

The guiding principle for structural social work practice is that everything we do in some way contributes to the goal of social transformation. This does not mean that the legitimate, here-and-now needs of people are ignored. Rather, structural social work practice comprises a simultaneous two-pronged approach: (1) to provide practical, humanitarian care to the victims and casualties of our patriarchal, liberal-capitalist society; and (2) to restructure society along socialist lines. This two-pronged approach to practice is consistent with the concept of dialectic discussed in Chapter 9.

The purpose of this chapter is to present certain practice elements that characterize structural social work practice and that therefore distinguish it from mainstream, conventional social work practice. Although these practice elements are presented and analyzed separately here, in reality they cannot be separated so easily, for they are all interrelated, functionally intertwined, and mutually reinforcing. These elements of practice operationalize structural social work theory. Through the practice of this structural social work theory, social workers will contribute to the long-term transformation of our present society by tending to the short-term needs of people within the social welfare institution—the very system that oppresses both those who depend on it and those who work within it.

The theory of structural social work does not consider any level of social work practice as inherently conservative or oppressive. Nor does it consider that one level of practice is inherently more progressive and liberating than another. For example, Galper (1975) has shown how community organization, as it has traditionally been practised, is just as conservative as traditional casework. A substantial literature (see Agel, 1971; Allan et al., 2003; Caspary, 1980; Fook, 1993; Forbes, 1986; Longres and McLeod, 1980; Lundy, 2004; Vazala-Martinez, 1985) shows how casework or clinical work can be emancipatory as opposed to oppressive for the service user. The major distinction between liberal mainstream social work practice and structural social work practice is that the former reflects and perpetuates the present social order whereas the latter attempts to transform it.

The approach to structural practice within the social welfare system emanates from the *radical humanist* school of thought. As presented in Chapter 9 this approach is based on the belief that changing people by personal consciousness-raising on a massive scale is a prerequisite for changing society. This consciousness-raising, which is carried out by structural social workers with service users and with co-workers, focuses on raising people's awareness of how a society characterized by dominant–subordinate relations shapes, limits, and dominates the experiences of members of subordinate groups, thus alienating them from social structures, from each other, and from their true selves. Only by becoming aware of how others define us to suit their own interests and by understanding how ideological hegemony makes our subjugation appear acceptable can we become free to begin to regain control over our lives and our destiny (Carniol, 1984; Howe, 1987; Mullaly and Keating, 1991). In sum, radical humanism is predicated on the belief that before social transformation can occur, personal transformation must take place. This assumption is rejected by structural social workers, who believe that it is not a case of personal change coming first or of social change coming first (the latter comes from the *radical structural* school of social change—discussed in Chapter 9 and further discussed in the next chapter). Rather, both approaches carried out simultaneously (in a dialectic) are necessary. The women's movement is one of the clearest examples where both approaches were carried out simultaneously. In combating sexism and patriarchy, much use was made of women's consciousness-raising groups that helped large numbers of women become aware of the pervasiveness, oppressive effects, and dynamics of gender discrimination in society. With this awareness, women put pressure on the system to change its gender biases. At the same time, leaders in the women's movement put pressure on the political structures to enact legislation and policies that addressed gender inequality. Many people (mainly men) then adjusted to the new social reality (i.e., legislation and policies promoting gender equality) before they had a real understanding or awareness of gender oppression in society.

The remainder of this chapter is divided into two major sections. The first section discusses certain elements of structural social work practice that help to operationalize radical humanist thought when working with users of various social agencies, services, and programs. The second section focuses on ways that help social workers not only survive working in mainstream social work bureaucracies but to change them from within as well. The material in this chapter also addresses a number of myths (see Box 11.1 below) often associated with progressive social work approaches in general, but structural social work in particular.

BOX 11.1 COMMON MYTHS HELD ABOUT STRUCTURAL SOCIAL WORK

- It is a militant, unreasonable, and irresponsible approach to practice—a relic of the 1960s and 1970s.
- One must work at the macro level and carry out large-scale social changes; otherwise one is not working structurally.
- There is nothing that an individual social worker can do to change the system.
- It denies all conventional social work practice such as counselling, micro skills, direct practice, family therapy, etc.
- Social work should be about people and not about politics.
- Structural social work is strong on critique, but short on practice.
- By focusing on social structures and forces, structural social work absolves people of all personal responsibility for their actions.
- You will lose your job if you practice structural social work in an agency.
- Structural social work is just too hard for the average person. It alienates one from other workers and leads to burnout and self-destruction.

WORKING WITH SERVICE USERS

Intrapsychic and Interpersonal Work

As noted in Box 11.1, one of the myths held by many about structural social work is that such work ignores all conventional social work activities such as working with people who are in crisis or who are hurting in the 'here and now'. Nothing could be further from the truth! Structural social workers are keenly aware that: (1) over time oppression results in damaging psychological effects in a person's intrapsychic and interpersonal areas; and (2) before one can take action against social structures that are negatively affecting his or her social position and functioning, work has to be carried out with individuals that encompasses intrapsychic and interpersonal processes. As well, crisis situations, including a lack of material necessities such as food, shelter, and clothing, and safety issues must be alleviated before political action can be contemplated.

Intrapyschic work. Geraldine Moane (1999), a critical psychologist, reviewed a series of studies and summarized the effects of oppression on psychological functioning: a sense of inferiority or low self-esteem, loss of personal identity, fear, powerlessness, suppression of anger, alienation and isolation, and guilt or ambivalence (see Mullaly, 2002, for a

---

BOX 11.2 A PSYCHOLOGY OF LIBERATION

Psychological approaches to social problems have been criticized as, at best, unrealistic and, at worst, as contributing to the maintenance of social problems. Earlier versions of progressive social work have accused clinical or counselling social workers, psychologists, psychiatrists, and other helping professionals of supporting the status quo by: controlling or managing the dangerous (i.e., oppressed) classes; cajoling or coercing victims of social problems to accept and adjust to the very systems that victimized them in the first place; diverting attention away from the real source of social problems—an oppressive society; attempting to humanize an inhumane society; and promoting personal development through 12-step and other programs. Too often, critics have charged, people experiencing social problems have entered therapy or counselling because of problems associated with their oppression only to focus on their childhood, family, and endless analysis of their feelings. Psychotherapy and personal development become substitutes for political action.

The above 'anti-psychological' position not only overlooks the obvious psychological consequences of oppression, but also the psychology of both dominant group and subordinate group members. As well, it homogenizes all perspectives in psychology and overlooks the critical and liberation schools of psychological thought that also criticize mainstream psychology for its inattention to social variables. The critical and liberation schools of psychology start with the premise that psychological patterns can only be understood by analyzing the social context in which individuals live their lives. Members of this school, such as Moane (1999) and Fox and Prilleltensky (1997), seek 'to develop a political explanation of psychological phenomena, and to harness psychological insights for the purposes of political activism' (Moane, 1999: 182). 'Internalized oppression' is a focus of liberation psychologists in that they analyze psychological patterns associated with internalized oppression and develop psychological processes for breaking out of internalized oppression and bringing about social change. Moane calls this a *psychology of liberation*.

In sum, structural social work is not anti-psychological. It is 'anti-mainstream psychological', and 'pro-liberation psychology'. The latter recognizes that breaking out of the oppression associated with social problems, whether at the psychological or at the political level, requires changes in both psychological and social patterns. Not attending to the need for social change means that social conditions continue to affect individuals and shape psychological functioning in oppressive ways, and not attending to psychological change means that any desired social change will be undermined by negative psychological patterns. Both are necessary.

discussion of these factors). The main aim of structural social work in the intrapsychic area is to: (1) counteract these damaging effects of oppression; and (2) build strengths in the individual for developing a community of solidarity with others and for taking individual and/or collective action against oppression. Individual work, group work, or community work may be used separately or in some combination to pursue these goals.

Often an individual will require counselling to deal with the psychological effects of oppression and to become emotionally ready to participate in a group. This can take the form of introspective counselling or behavioural therapy or any other type of individual work that helps to stabilize a victim of oppression, relieve some hurt, change some symptoms and behaviours, and build some strengths. The important point for structural social work is that, regardless of the individual approach used, it must not de-contextualize human activity or treat it in a de-socialized or ahistorical way (Bulhan, 1985). Otherwise, personal changes may become concessions to the current social order whereby the person has been helped to adjust to it rather than to change it. 'As well, individual work is not an end in itself, but the means to connecting or reconnecting with other persons similarly oppressed so that they might together reflect on their situation and engage in collective actions to change it' (Mullaly, 2002: 172). The need for both collectivization and conscious-ness-raising as crucial structural social work activities are discussed below.

One of the criticisms made of any kind of social work (including structural social work) is that it is potentially oppressive, especially at the one-to-one intrapsychic level. This type of criticism was articulated best by Bulhan (1985: 271), who, with respect to any kind of therapeutic intervention or helper–helpee relationship, asked, '[F]or how can an intervention liberate the patient from the social oppression when the "therapist–patient" relationship itself is suffused with the inequities, nonreciprocity, elitism, and sado-masochism of the oppressive social order?'. Bulhan is referring to inequities such as the power of the professional (therapist, social worker) and the powerlessness of the service user, the comfort of the professional's office (often alien to the service user), the professional's values (often foreign to the service user), and the professional's discourse that differentiates expert from layperson or professional from client. Given this power imbalance, Bulhan asks: 'Is it therefore surprising that the oppressed have not come in droves to seek help from mental health professionals, and, if a few of them turn to "therapy" as a last resort, that they soon drop out and return to their own travails?'

To avoid reproducing oppressive patterns and relationships while working with oppressed persons two essential themes of structural social work must be kept in mind at all times. First, people experiencing social problems or oppression must be the agents of their own change, whether it is personal, cultural, or social. Of this Moane (1999: 183) says, 'Change is a process which individuals undergo in their social context and through their own processes. It is fundamental that this process of change is experienced by individuals as one in which they are in control, rather than as a re-enactment of patterns of domination. . . . Developing agency is itself a central part of the liberation process.' The second theme to help avoid the reproduction of oppression is to ensure that one's structural social work practice is *critically reflective*. This takes the form of the social worker engaging in a reflective conversation with the situation, which as Thompson (1998: 204) argues, 'can be used to promote an ethos in which equality issues [including the relationship between the social worker and the service user] are openly and explicitly on the agenda.' He further argues that the reflection must be critical with respect to not taking any existing social arrangement or structure for granted. Otherwise, the reflection becomes another routine, uncritical form of practice that legitimates existing relations of social inequality. Critical reflection is discussed more in a subsequent section of this chapter.

Interpersonal work. There is widespread agreement in the literature that to become part of a group process with other persons who are experiencing similar problems or are in similar situations is the most effective way for them to: (1) develop political awareness; (2) self-define a more genuine identity than the one imposed on them by the dominant group (e.g., 'welfare bum', 'lazy Aboriginal', 'inferior black culture'); (3) develop the confidence to assert their more authentic identity (e.g., Aboriginal persons as a resilient group of people who have survived hundreds of years of colonization and policies of assimilation); and (4) establish solidarity with similar others to take action against their oppressors (Bishop, 2002; Freire, 1994; hooks, 1993; Leonard, 1997; Mullaly, 2002; Pharr, 1988). Consciousness-raising is a critical element in the process of liberation, and the most effective way for engaging in consciousness-raising is in groups. These two elements of structural social work (i.e., consciousness-raising and collectivization) are discussed below, along with a number of factors that assist in the process of consciousness-raising. Taken together, they provide the framework and guidelines of a structural approach to interpersonal work.

BOX 11.3 WHERE DO I START AS A STRUCTURAL SOCIAL WORKER?

As an exercise for a class of students in Australia, I asked them where they would begin with service users—given a structural explanation for social problems. One student wrote the following passage that I think helps to answer this question that so many students new to structural social work have.

Because the explanation for social problems goes far beyond the individual, structural social work becomes much more than just dealing with the problems of individuals. It is about challenging the dominant order, and doing what we can on the personal, cultural, and structural levels to work towards a society that is free of oppression. So then, given our understanding that oppression (domination, subordination, and privilege) is the root cause of social problems, what will our practice look like?

Whichever way we look at society, it is made up of individuals. Much of social work practice involves dealing with individual people, and taking a wider view of society does not exclude working with people on the personal level. I believe one of the most important things we can do for people at the personal level is simply to listen to them. Everyone has his or her story, and everyone's story deserves to be heard. Everyone's story will be different, as we all experience our lives in our own unique way.

We need to explore the oppression in people's lives and allow them to verbalize how they are feeling. We mustn't assume that we understand what someone has experienced because we have heard similar stories before, or have had similar experiences ourselves. Nor should we assume that because we can identify one form of oppression in someone's life, that it is the main reason for concern. We need to respect the people we are dealing with, and their views of what is happening in their lives.

The act of listening in itself can be part of the healing process. It indicates that you consider the person worth listening to, and that she or he has value. By listening carefully to the service user, a dialogue can develop, where ideas and knowledge can be shared and assumptions challenged. Listening to someone's story also gives the opportunity of naming the oppression or oppressions, and placing them in a political framework. Making these connections and normalizing the experiences can all be part of a powerful process. It may not solve someone's structural problems, but it can give a greater understanding of what is happening to her/him, and why.

The fact that persons have survived the various forms of oppression in their lives indicated that they have strengths, and that they have used these strengths to develop strategies. By identifying what strategies have worked for them in the past, an indication may be given as to what direction they may move to in the future. If strategies haven't been successful, it may be possible to relate this to structural objects, and a political dialogue can follow.

An important aspect of structural social work is to respond to the psychological damage that oppression causes. This will involve building up self-esteem and confidence. The act of listening and of identifying strengths that people possess is the beginning of this. People also need to express their feelings of shame, guilt, and repressed anger. It may be possible to redirect this anger and for it to be used in a constructive way, just as our own anger can be used constructively.

—Reproduced with thanks to Liz Deutscher

The Personal Is Political

One of the myths held about structural social work is that such work is carried out only at the macro level. Most progressive social writers today (e.g., Gil, 1998; Leonard, 1997; Mullaly, 2002; Thompson, 1998) agree that social work interventions are limited if they focus on only the individual level or the structural level. Bulhan (1985) points out that the former, which focuses only on the here and now and individual problems of people, tends to lose sight of people's shared victimization and the need for social transformation and often results in a minimalist view of change or a conservative outlook that blames the victim. The latter, which works towards social transformation, tends to become a paternalistic imposition of change from the top and disengages the person on whose behalf the changes are sought. Both approaches fail to adopt a dialectical perspective whereby interventions at both the individual/personal level and the societal/political level are carried out simultaneously, with each informing and influencing the other.

Although social work has always espoused an awareness of the connection between the personal and the political,[1] the emphasis for the most part has been on personal change, adjustment, and/or coping. This emphasis, of course, is consistent with the order view of society discussed earlier. In fact, a dichotomy emerged in social work practice in that most social workers chose and worked within the areas of casework, group work, and family therapy (i.e., intervention on a personal level), leaving the larger socio-political issues to a minority of community organization and social policy social workers. Social workers who subscribe to a change or conflict analysis of society view this split as a false dichotomy (Mullaly and Keating, 1991) and would point to what C. Wright Mills (1959: 3) said about the relationship between the individual and society: 'Neither the life of an individual nor the history of a society can be understood without understanding both.'

The traditional split between micro and macro social work practice has served to weaken the link between the personal and the political, which is at the heart of social work. This split is often reinforced by the ways the curriculum is organized in schools of social work and by the structures within which social workers are employed. Curriculum tends to be divided along micro-macro lines; most social agencies are mandated to provide personal services without engaging in political or macro-level practice; and those agencies that focus on social policy, social action, or larger social change tend not to see the provision of personal services as part of their mandate. The artificiality of such organizational constraints needs to be challenged. Although they may reflect the current political reality of separating the personal from the political, they do not reflect the social reality of people's lives or the reality of good social work practice. How can a direct practitioner be effective if she or he omits the cultural or community or societal context of the people with whom she or he works? Similarly, how can a social policy or community practitioner be effective if he or she lacks interpersonal, listening, and communication skills? In terms of skills, the differences between micro and macro social workers are much less than might appear on the surface (Ife, 1997).

'The personal is political' stands for a method of analysis developed and refined by feminists for 'gleaning political insights from an analysis of personal experience—in particular, female experience' (Collins, 1986: 215). Most writers today use the statement when analyzing or discussing how the socio-economic political context of a society is critical in shaping who we are in terms of our personality formation and what we are in terms of our personal situation (Mullaly and Keating, 1991). Social work deals with many personal issues, troubles, and situations. If the personal is political, then social work is political, also.

The premise that the personal is political has two major implications for social work practice. First, it signals that a social worker's individual practice has certain political ends. This applies to all social workers. Personal practices inevitably contain political ends. For conventional social work the political end is to maintain the status quo. This is done by personalizing social problems. For structural social work the political end is to change the status quo and leave oppression behind. This does not preclude intervention at the individual or family level, but instead of dealing with each of these levels by itself the connection between private troubles and the structural source of these troubles is made in every case. Each structural social worker must see her or his individual work as an integral element of the larger movement of social transformation.

The second major implication that 'the personal is political' has for social work practice is that it forces the worker beyond carrying out mere psychosocial manipulations, which in effect pathologize those people who are forced to use social work services. Understanding that private troubles are often linked to political (structural) forces enables the worker to begin a discussion of the relationship between the personal and the political (i.e., consciousness-raising) with the persons experiencing difficulties and to explore the personal situation of the person within its larger social context to see if there are connections between the two (i.e., normalization). This activity often has the effect of reducing some of the internalized guilt and blame (i.e., internal oppression) that many people experience as part of their troubled situations. This has to be carried out with a high degree of both personal and social empathy on the part of the structural social worker. These processes, along with some of the techniques that facilitate them, are considered below.

As discussed in Chapter 7, structural social work owes a great deal to feminist analysis. It has shown us the nature and extent of patriarchy in our society and it has given us ways of dealing with women's oppression that do not further contribute to it. Too much of conventional social work practice locates the source of many problems women face within the person herself. This psychologizing of what are essentially problems of the larger society contributes to women's oppression by failing to see a woman in the context of a patriarchal society and by placing the blame for all her troubles squarely on the shoulders of the woman experiencing them. Because of the many social workers who have been actively involved in and/or influenced by the feminist movement, there is now a major social work perspective and practice based on feminist theory and analysis.[2] In addition, feminist social work writers have shown us that sexism exists within the welfare state and within our own profession (Walker, 1977; Weeks, 2003; Williams, 1989). And, of course, becoming aware of, identifying, and analyzing sexism in social work are prerequisites to purging us of it.

Given the global and normalized nature of the forces of capitalism, patriarchy, and racism and the limited analyses of them by the mainstream media, the felt needs and sufferings of many people often are consequences of forces of which they have little knowledge or understanding. However, a 'personal is political' (i.e., structural) analysis holds the potential for a powerful force for change. If people are helped to relate their disempowerment and experiences of oppression at a personal level to a broader political understanding, there is a basis for moving beyond 'coping and adjustment social work practice' to a practice that attacks the alienating and oppressive institutional and thought structures of our current society.

'The personal is political' as a method of analysis has relevance and utility for dealing with all sources of oppression in our society. It can be used to understand better the nature and extent of racism in our society and how it contributes to the oppression of visible minority groups. It can be used to understand better the nature of colonialism and how it contributes to the oppression of Aboriginal persons in our society and to the oppression of developing countries by the industrial and post-industrial societies. It can be used, as well, to better understand oppression based on classism, ageism, physical disability, mental disability, heterosexism, and so on. What conventional social workers treat as private problems belonging to isolated individuals, structural social workers would treat as public problems belonging to a society characterized by oppression along these various lines. However, the concern expressed in Chapters 7 (see Box 7.2) and 10 about the difficulty in translating 'the personal is political' analysis into social work practice should be kept in mind. The practice problem is that it seems to be a giant leap between the personal and the political, so much so that many practitioners retreat to working at the personal level only (and some at the political level only) so that the dialectic between personal problems and their structural causes is lost. This is not to suggest that the structural social worker excuses irresponsible behaviour or bad choices by adopting a simplistic 'it's all society's fault' approach when dealing with situations of service users. However, a distinction must be made between 'excusing' and 'explaining' irresponsible behaviour. Personal responsibility is discussed in more detail in a subsequent section of this chapter. The PCS model of oppression presented in Chapter 10 helps us out of this dilemma as it separates culture from social structure and reminds us that oppression also occurs at the cultural level situated between the personal and structural levels. 'The personal is political' is still a powerful analytical tool, but an awareness that a dominant culture helps to legitimize and institutionalize oppression provides the structural social worker with specific targets to change—oppressive stereotypes, dominant discourses, norms, values, and shared patterns of thinking (see Mullaly, 2002, for an overview of anti-oppressive social work at the cultural level).

Empowerment

From the discussion in Chapter 10, it is obvious that oppression leads to the alienation and powerlessness of the subordinate classes. Most definitions of power or powerlessness refer to the control or lack of control persons have over their environment and their destiny. Oppressed people, as individuals, have limited choices over most aspects of their lives and are often ruled by forces of which they are not even aware. A tenet of mental health is that, 'Throughout life, the feeling of controlling one's destiny to some reasonable extent is the essential psychological component of all aspects of life' (Basch, 1975, cited in Pinderhughes, 1983).

One of the insights of postmodernism is that everyone has some measure of power and that it was a limitation of earlier modernist forms of progressive social work to assume that members of subordinate groups had no power. Yet, although no one is without power, it is equally wrong to assume that power differentials do not exist—including the power difference between social workers and their service users. At a societal level, dominant groups not only have more power than subordinate groups, they also frequently use it to maintain this power differential and the privileges that come with it. Gil (1976b) argues that the lack of control that oppressed people experience over their life situation and their destiny robs them of their essential human dignity, for without any real control life becomes meaningless. We drift through it, controlled by others, used by others, and devalued by others for the interests of others. Oppression, then, violates or contradicts such important social work values and beliefs as self-determination, personal growth and development, the inherent dignity and worth of persons, social equality, and democracy.

A key concept of structural social work is 'empowerment'. However, empowerment is a contested concept and one that has been appropriated by neo-conservatives. With respect to its contested nature, Allan (2003b) points out that earlier forms of mainstream social work and some progressive perspectives regarded it as a process whereby social workers would give power to the people with whom they worked. And, with respect to its appropriation, empowerment takes on another meaning for neo-conservatives. For example, many neo-conservative politicians have promised to empower oppressed persons to look after themselves by reducing the scope of and/or taking away the benefits of the welfare state. These two meanings of empowerment are quite different from that of structural social workers, who view it as a process through which members of subordinate groups reduce their alienation and sense of powerlessness and gain greater control over all aspects of their lives and their social environments. The definition and concept of empowerment that are most consistent with structural social work were developed by Gilles Rondeau (2000: 218):

> I define empowerment as a process that enables the transition from a state of passivity to one of activity and control over one's life. . . . [I]t essentially means a process of change where people stop being passive and become active, that is, they take charge and become active players in their own lives. By becoming active, they attempt to take, or take back, control of themselves and their environments.

Empowerment, as a goal and a process, has been a recurrent theme in social work (Freedberg, 1989). However, since the 1980s it has been receiving increasing attention in social work theory and practice (Simon, 1990). Some writers view empowerment as the major goal of social work intervention (e.g., Gutierrez et al., 1998; Pinderhughes, 1983; Rondeau, 2000), while another 'calls for a revision of social work practice theory in a way that defines the major function of social work as empowering people to be able to make choices and gain control over their environment' (Hasenfeld, 1987: 487). Empowerment is typically understood as a process through which people reduce their powerlessness and alienation and gain greater control over all aspects of their lives and their social environment. Simon (1990) points out that (1) empowerment has its basis in the self-help or mutual aid traditions and in the civil and human rights activities of the 1960s; and (2) because of the many groups, organizations, and professions involved with empowerment in all its dimensions, it should be considered as a social movement. 'Empowerment, in short, is a series of attacks on subordination of every description—psychic, physical, cultural, sexual, legal, political, economic, and technological' (Simon, 1990: 28).

As a dialectical process empowerment occurs in two ways. Consistent with radical structuralism, empowerment for some disciplines and groups is essentially a political and economic process whereby these structurally oriented groups will actively attempt to gain more power and influence over those organizations and institutions, such as schools, hospitals, and the workplace, that impact their lives. This area of empowerment will be examined in more detail in the next chapter. Consistent with radical humanism, the empowerment process involves the psychological, educational, cultural, and spiritual dimensions involved when individuals are helped to understand their oppression and to take steps to overcome it.

Simon (1990) points out that empowerment is a compelling topic for social work for three major reasons. First, the people that social workers work with tend to be in marginal and disadvantaged positions and are among the most oppressed, alienated, and powerless. Second, social work is a profession disproportionately staffed by women, who themselves comprise a group that historically has been oppressed and powerless, even within the profession of social work (Cummings, 1980). And third, 'Social workers of both genders are no strangers to the experiences of being discounted, scapegoated, dislodged, underpaid, and overlooked by legislatures, public administrators, executive directors of agencies, colleagues in other professions, academics, clients, and the public' (Simon, 1990: 34). We know first-hand the meaning of occupational subordination.

This trinity of interests in empowerment should serve as a catalyst for social work to continue to devise theory and strategies for working with oppressed and disempowered groups, including the profession itself. Hasenfeld (1987) contends that empowerment must occur on at least three levels in social work: (1) at the worker/service-user level, where activities are carried out to increase the service user's power resources; (2) at the agency level, where organizational policies should be aimed at increasing people's power resources rather than conformity to prescribed behaviours; and (3) at the social policy level, where the formulation and enactment of policy decisions are influenced by those directly affected by them. Consistent with the PCS model of anti-oppressive social work, Mullaly (2002) and Thompson (1998) contend that empowerment as a practice must occur at three levels—the personal, cultural, and structural levels. At the personal level, which is the major focus in this chapter, the emphasis is on helping individuals to gain greater control over their own lives through intrapsychic and interpersonal work by, for example, alleviating the psychological damages caused by oppression and enhancing confidence. At the cultural level, assumptions, stereotypes, and discourses of the dominant groups that perpetuate dominant–subordinate relations are deconstructed and challenged. And, at the structural level, power relations rooted in the institutions of society are resisted and challenged. Empowerment at the cultural and structural levels is discussed in the next chapter.

Should empowerment take place at the personal level before structural empowerment can occur? Dalrymple and Burke (1995) believe that this should be the case. Although, as suggested earlier, crisis situations might have to be resolved or some intrapsychic damage might need to be repaired before proceeding to structural analyses or social action, I concur with June Allan (2003b) when she argues that in order to avoid the traps of creating dualisms, structural social workers need to work with persons at all levels of empowerment, and that this may be done simultaneously (but not always). Many inherent difficulties are involved in empowerment work, but if three considerations are kept in mind at all times the process of empowerment will be greatly facilitated. First, social workers cannot empower others but can only aid and abet in the empowerment process. Service users 'who are empowered by their social workers have, de facto, lost ground . . . in their battle for autonomy and control over their own environment and existence'. The role of social work is to provide 'a climate, a relationship, resources and procedural means through which people can enhance their own lives' (Simon, 1990: 37). The relationship between social worker and user is one of collaboration, with the latter retaining control of the purpose, pace, and direction of the collaborative effort.

A second important aspect of the empowerment process is that instead of being an expert problem-solver the social worker becomes engaged in a mutual learning situation with the service user (Moreau and Leonard, 1989). The worker should not assume that a compatibility of interests exists between service user and worker (Hasenfeld, 1987). What could be more presumptuous and more disrespectful on the part of a social worker than to think that she or he knows exactly what the problem is and what the solutions are? To avoid this elitist, expert, disempowering practice, social workers should: (1) continually update their knowledge of the history of race, gender, class, and other relations of subordinate groups (i.e., know as much as possible about the groups one is working with) (Simon, 1990); and (2) help the service user define and contextualize his or her situation and problems while always encouraging him or her to question and to express disagreement or reservations about particular interventions that the social worker might suggest (Moreau and Leonard, 1989).

A third aspect of empowerment for social workers is to avoid exploiting the helping encounter for our own benefit (Pinderhughes, 1983). It was mentioned that social work experiences subordination as an occupation. Also, we are often stigmatized because of our association with marginalized groups. Thus, we may be vulnerable in terms of compensating for the powerlessness we experience at work and may use our professional role to gain a sense of power. Rather than empowering the people with whom we work we may actually reinforce their victim status by playing the role of benefactor and exploiting the power differential between ourselves and service users.

Consistent with the principle of linking the personal with the political, empowerment-based social work transcends the micro and macro levels of practice and today includes work at the cultural level as well. At the micro level the social worker helps the individual not only to take more control of his or her life, to set goals, to access resources, and to articulate needs and ambitions, but also to create or join associations or organizations of members of similar social groupings. These organizations (e.g., anti-poverty groups, women's organizations, Aboriginal groups) constitute the focus of macro social work discussed in the previous chapter and further discussed in the next chapter. The fact that there were (and still are in many workers' minds) two major levels of social work practice has historically created tension between micro and macro practitioners (Ife, 1997). Social workers at the micro level have often believed that the larger aims of social change pursued by macro workers are unattainable, and thereby have devalued the importance of social change. Conversely, social workers at the macro level have often believed that individual approaches to helping are simply affirmations of the status quo, thus devaluing the skilled work of many social workers.

The 'old' structural social work model incorporated both approaches to empowerment within the day-to-day work of each social worker and within the social work profession as a collective (Ife, 1997). Individual empowerment is not possible unless the individual understands the connection between individual powerlessness and its structural/political sources through a reflection on her or his own experience not only as an individual but as a member of one or more oppressed groups. Similarly, at the macro level, empowerment work must incorporate the lived experiences, the personal stories, and the impact of oppression on the individual lives of the people who constitute the membership of the various groups or organizations of oppressed persons. The link between the personal and the political is made not just at the analytical or theoretical levels, but at the practice level of empowerment-based structural social work. And, of course, empowerment work today must include an awareness of how the dominant culture both oppresses subordinate groups and supports and reinforces social institutions that serve the dominant group through dominant discourses, stereotypes, and popular or mass culture (see Mullaly, 2002). The medium in which these links are made is through a consciousness-raising dialogical relationship.

Ife (1997) makes an important point about empowerment when he calls on social workers not to speak on behalf of oppressed groups, but to facilitate the voices of the marginalized themselves to be heard. In the current socio-economic-political climate, marginalized persons do not have a legitimate voice, and what voice they do have tends to be devalued by politicians, who are themselves also overwhelmed by the corporate sector. Well-intentioned advocacy by social workers who speak on behalf of marginalized groups is actually disempowering. It only reinforces marginalization in that oppressed people still do not speak for themselves and, thus, are further excluded from political discourse. As well, the perception may be that social workers are using marginalized people to represent their own views and interests rather than those they claim to represent. Structural social workers must work alongside oppressed groups to help them find and make their own voices heard. This involves helping them to define their own needs, to develop the skills and vocabulary required to articulate these needs, to gain access to public forums to address the structures of power and domination, and to help legitimize these authentic voices by supporting them in every way possible. The role of the social worker in empowerment-based social work is one of facilitator and supporter. The ideal of empowerment connects the personal with the political. It requires both good interpersonal skills and political and organizational awareness and understanding.

Empowerment is not a technique but a goal and a process. As a goal, it will not be reached overnight, just as the oppressive conditions within our current social order will not suddenly disappear. As a process it is ongoing. Components of empowerment work are feelings and beliefs about self-efficacy; ideas and knowledge and skills for critical thinking and action; knowledge and skills (including the process of reflection, learning, and relearning) to influence invisible and external structures (Dalrymple and Burke, 1995; Gutierrez et al., 1998, cited in Allan, 2003b). This process of empowerment is not linear, and no one area is considered more important than another (Gutierrez et al., 1998). It applies just as much to community development projects, policy formulation and implementation, and social action campaigns as it does to work with individuals and groups. 'Hence there is a broad range of strategies that could be drawn on to facilitate empowerment' (Allan, 2003b). Some of the elements of empowerment work are presented below.

The major premise underpinning empowerment is that people are not objects to be exploited, to be controlled, or to be oppressed. People are subjects, human beings with inherent dignity and worth that should not be conditional on race, gender, class, or any other inherent characteristic. All people should have reasonable opportunities and choices over their life situation and their social environments. Empowerment is a goal and a process for overcoming oppression.

CONSCIOUSNESS-RAISING

Although the idea of revolutionary praxis involving both subjective and objective elements was formulated by Marx, the more recent versions have come from Paulo Freire, the contemporary women's movement, and a host of recent writers concerned with social justice and anti-oppression (Gil, 1998; Dominelli, 1997; Freire, 1994; Leonard, 1997; Moane, 1999, Mullaly, 2002; Thompson, 1997, 1998; Young, 1990). Consistent with the precept that the personal is political, consciousness-raising is legitimized on the basis of the relationship between the social order and human misery. 'Thus, consciousness-raising involves the politicization of people' (Longres and McLeod, 1980: 268). As awareness of social injustice and oppression grows, oppressed people are more able to identify the causes of their oppression and are less likely to blame themselves (Longres, 1986; Midgely, 1982). Freire developed a total pedagogy based on the 'conscientization' of the peasant population living in Latin America. With a similar set of ideas and purposes the women's movement has used consciousness-raising as a powerful tool for combatting gender oppression and empowering women.

There are two elements to consciousness-raising:

> First, consciousness-raising is reflection in search of understanding dehumanizing social structures. Second, consciousness-raising is action aimed at altering societal conditions. The two must go hand in hand; action without reflection is as unjustifiable as reflection without action. (Longres and McLeod, 1980: 268)

The techniques used in consciousness-raising are similar to those used in conventional social work, with one significant difference. Conventional social work is introspective, often motivating people to change their behaviour and adjust to their circumstances. Consciousness-raising, on the other hand, encourages people to gain insights into their circumstances with a view to changing them (Midgely, 1982).

Consciousness-raising is obviously an important part of intrapsychic and interpersonal work in that with increased awareness of injustice and oppression, oppressed people are better able to identify the structural causes of their negative emotions and interpersonal difficulties. Part of the intrapsychic and interpersonal work may involve personal development through individual counselling or by taking a course such as assertiveness training or leadership development, which have been found to increase self-confidence and assertiveness (Mulvey, 1994, cited in Moane, 1999), two characteristics needed for social change activities. However, without a social analysis, such courses may reinforce and perpetuate a 'blaming the victim' ideology by overemphasizing human agency and cultivating the belief that problems in living can only be solved through personal change (Kitzinger and Perkins, 1993; Mulvey, 1994). Thus, although personal development may be a first step for many in an ongoing process of empowerment and change, it should be framed within a structural analysis of oppression and social injustice.

Obviously, consciousness-raising is part of the radical humanist school, as it is predicated on the belief that reflection must precede action. Although it sees practical action as an outcome, consciousness-raising places its initial emphasis on the understanding of oneself in the context of the social order. As Leonard (1984: 210–11) points out, 'The hegemony of the ruling class involves the domination of its world view, a view which drenches individual consciousness and which must therefore be actively struggled against at the level of consciousness.' Thus, changes of consciousness regarding social relations are a precondition of the transformation of those relations.

Although a certain amount of consciousness-raising may occur in individual counselling sessions (e.g., providing statistics to the oppressed individual with whom one is working, providing some factual information about some aspect of his or her oppression, exploring some of the functions that a particular form of oppression carries out for the dominant group), most effective consciousness-raising occurs in groups of persons who share the same form of oppression (Longres and McLeod, 1980; Young, 1990). Elsewhere (Mullaly, 2002), I pointed out that there is widespread agreement among many anti-oppressive writers and progressive social work writers that to become a member of a group process with other persons who are similarly oppressed is the most effective way for oppressed persons to develop political awareness of their situation. In such a group context, the members can self-define a more authentic identity than the one imposed on them by the dominant group, develop the self-confidence to 'come out' and assert their more authentic identity, and establish solidarity in order to take action against their oppression (Adam, 1978; Bishop, 2002; Dominelli, 1997; Freire, 1994; Herman, 1992; hooks, 1993; Ife, 2001; Leonard, 1984; Pharr, 1988; Withorn, 1984).

Much of consciousness-raising occurs in the form of political education whereby structural social workers, in the course of their daily service efforts, explore with service users their experiences with oppression and how to challenge and resist it. Consciousness-raising can occur by linking people's personal problematic situations with their political causes so that oppressed people 'become more aware of the structures and the discourses that define and perpetuate their situations of oppression' (Ife, 2001: 151).This type of education is not a process of depositing knowledge (i.e., the banking concept of education) into the head of a service user (Bock, 1980), nor is it a process of haranguing people about social injustice (Longres, 1986). Allan (2003b: 65) cautions us that although consciousness-raising may open up possibilities for action, it can also be 'oppressive and patronizing if it is based on the assumption that the practitioner's consciousness is superior and is to be imposed on the people with whom s/he is working.' First and foremost, consciousness-raising must involve reflection based on the service user's experience and individual consciousness, and not solely the worker's. This does not mean that the structural social worker will not introduce new ideas or challenge beliefs held by the service user, however. Rather, the political education process takes the form of a dialogue where both the social worker and the service user assume roles of mutual sharing and learning.

The service user will present his or her world view and where he or she sees him/herself fitting into this view. The social worker, in turn, will ask questions that might expose any of the service user's stereotypical or socially conditioned assumptions. This type of questioning is called '*critical questioning*', which is different from 'normal questioning' (Fook, 1993) because it focuses on any socially conditioned answer. An example is a response a social worker might give to a woman who says, 'If I just tried harder to be a good wife and mother, I might still have my family.' The worker could say, 'And why do you think that?' Such a response, however, might imply that there is one correct answer and the woman could respond, 'because it is the woman's job to look after her family'. Alternatively, a structural social worker would respond by asking a critical question such as, 'Is that what you think or what you think is expected of you?' This use of critical questioning has the potential for persons to explore their expectations and how they feel they have to act. It may also provide the opportunity for the woman to understand the extent to which her life may represent her own personal choices on the one hand or social conditioning on the other (Fook, 1993).

To facilitate this process of dialogue, mutual learning, and critical questioning, the social worker must express empathy to signal to the service user that his or her world view and explanation of any difficulty is understood by the social worker. Empathy 'is a large part of the substance of critical consciousness for a social worker' (Keefe, 1980: 389). In her seminal book, *Radical Casework*, my friend and former colleague, Jan Fook (1993), extends the concept of empathy beyond 'personal empathy' to include 'social empathy'. The former refers to a social worker's ability to understand by experiencing or merging with the experience of another with respect to his or her perceptions, feelings, and ideas of his or her own personal world. Social empathy refers to the worker's ability to empathize with the service user's perceptions, feelings, and ideas about the social world. This is a valuable tool to link the personal and the political in the service user's situation. What Fook has called 'social empathy', Jessup and Rogerson (1999) call 'structural empathy'. Examples of translating these concepts into practice are contained in Box 11.4 below.

BOX 11.4 SOCIAL OR STRUCTURAL EMPATHY

Social Empathy
'Take the following exclamation by a bored and frustrated housewife: "Men always get what they want!" This can be empathically reflected [back to the woman] in at least two ways. The first picks up the personal experience: "You feel you never get what you want?" The second highlights her perceptions of the social condition: "You think men get a better deal than women?" A socially empathic response would ideally combine the two and draw attention to the links about them: "You don't think you ever get what you want because men always get a better deal than women?"'

—(Fook, 1993: 112)

Structural Empathy
Working with a woman who has abused drugs and alcohol and who is now separated from her children and her partner, who was physically abusive, a social worker might ask, 'Can you tell me what rights you believe you have as a mother, wife and individual?' and 'What resources do you need to get your children back?' (Jessup and Rogerson, 1999: 173, cited in Allan, 2003b: 66). Other structural empathic questions in this situation are: 'Tell me, what do you think the role of mother and partner should be?' 'Where do these expectations come from?' 'How do you differ from these?'

—(Jessup and Rogerson, 1999: 174, cited in Allan, 2003b: 66)

A major topic of dialogue between social worker and service user is how our present society works, including the social functions carried out by poverty, sexism, racism, heterosexism, and so on. If members of various subordinate groups realize that their personal difficulties are related to their membership within a particular oppressed group and that their oppression is socially useful to the dominant groups, then this awareness should alleviate much of the internalized guilt and blame that exist. In turn, awareness of their oppression, coupled with the energy unleashed from not feeling guilty or responsible for their subordinate status any more, should lead to some kind of social action against that oppression. For this consciousness-raising to be successful, however, it must be based on people's experiences and not on some foreign, academic critical analysis imposed on people in sophisticated quasi-Marxist jargon. 'Consciousness-raising methods require the same sensitivities to self-determination and relationship-building that traditional . . . [social work] requires' (Longres, 1986: 31).

Often, service users will demonstrate what Marxists call 'false consciousness' or what anti-oppressive writers call 'internalized oppression' (Ruth, 1988) in that they understand their troubles and behave in ways that promote the interests of the dominant groups in society (Longres, 1986). At the same time, a part of all of us tells us that society is not working in a way that supports a satisfying and enriching life for large numbers of people. From a structural social work perspective we should look for and reinforce that part of the service user's perspective that is aware of social oppression (Galper, 1980). In this way we are not imposing a brand of politics unrelated to the normal events of service users. Instead, we are focusing on their experiences in an empathic, respectful, and relevant manner.

Some examples may help clarify the discussion so far. People who are forced to apply for welfare benefits will often express humiliation, guilt, and shame because they have been socialized into believing that everyone in society should be able to make it on their own. One of the ideological myths of capitalism is that equal opportunity exists and that only the lazy, the inferior, and the weak do not take advantage of opportunities available to everyone. To be on social welfare is a sign of weakness, inferiority, and laziness. When people seek social welfare benefits or any other kind of social service, we must help them deal with their pressing immediate problems. Most people cannot develop a larger critical perspective of their distress until they experience some symptomatic relief.

However, we have an obligation as structural social workers to move beyond symptomatic relief, since we know the symptoms will likely reappear (Galper, 1980). We must participate in the consciousness-raising experience of the welfare recipient by discussing why poverty exists in a capitalist society (i.e., the social functions it carries out); why the receipt of social welfare is seen as a failure in our society; the social control functions of social welfare; and how it operates in the best interests of capitalism and the dominant groups in society. In other words, a structural analysis of the welfare recipient's situation and experiences is discussed in an empathic manner at a level and in a language that the recipient understands. As mentioned previously, although most people are victims of false consciousness or internalized oppression, everyone knows to some extent that society is not working in the interests of large numbers of people. Similarly, many social welfare recipients have some awareness that their situation is not necessarily or completely of their own doing. It is these thoughts that the structural social worker uses to begin the consciousness-raising process.

Consciousness-raising should always be based on the service user's situation and experiences. Oppression is group-based, so consciousness-raising should focus on a structural analysis of the position the service user's group occupies in society. If we are working with senior citizens, then the structural social worker must know all about ageism. If this analysis is discussed in a meaningful way with senior citizens, then part of that discussion will include how many of the problems experienced by senior citizens—limited housing options, inadequate or non-existent home care, high cost of drugs, meagre pensions, transportation difficulties—are not caused by senior citizens, but stem from a society that treats people as commodities where, if you are a non-producer and have no market value as a worker, then you have no social value.

Longres and McLeod (1980) make two additional points about consciousness-raising as social work practice. First, because consciousness-raising focuses on the negative features of society and politicizes people around these features, then structural social workers who engage in this practice will not be favoured by politicians, by administrators, and by many conventional social workers. Consciousness-raising will not make life easier for the social worker. Second, although consciousness-raising should be a cornerstone of social work practice, it does not represent the totality of practice; giving support, dealing with crises, providing hard services, advocacy, making referrals, and helping to make people's immediate lives more bearable are also important activities. It should also be noted here that consciousness-raising is greatly enhanced when it occurs on a group basis. More will be said about this later. Four activities that are part of the consciousness-raising process: normalization, collectivization, dialogical relationships, and reframing or redefining situations are presented below.

Normalization

Normalization assists in the consciousness-raising process. Its purpose is to dispel any notion that any particular difficulty experienced by an oppressed individual is unique and idiosyncratic only to that individual, when in fact the difficulty is a logical outcome of oppression and is being experienced by many members of a particular subordinate group. It is a way of learning that many others of the same social grouping, whatever it might be, also experience the same problems and that in their situation it is not unusual to have such problems. Many oppressed persons will internalize feelings of guilt, shame, and self-blame for their oppressive living conditions because they have been socialized into accepting the dominant culture's messages that they are the architects of their own misfortune. In other words, they believe that they are responsible for causing the social problems they are experiencing. Normalization breaks with that part of conventional social work that does not look at an individual as part of a social group subject to all the vagaries involved in a dominant–subordinate relationship. Normalization is an activity consistent with Cloward and Piven's (1975: xiii–xiv) contention that:

> we have to break with the professional doctrine that ascribes virtually all of the problems that clients experience to defects in personality development and family relationships. It must be understood that this doctrine is as much a political ideology as an explanation of human behaviour. It is an ideology that directs clients to blame themselves for their travails rather than the economic and social institutions that produce many of them. . . . This psychological reductionism—this pathologizing of poverty and inequality—is, in other words, an ideology of oppression for it systematically conceals from people the ways in which their lives are distorted by the realities of class structure.

The point has already been made that structural social work is not anti-psychological. However, it does not automatically assume pathology or deviance on the part of someone who is experiencing problems. It understands that the political, cultural, and economic context of our present society, which is characterized by dominant–subordinate relationships, favours the dominant group at the expense of the subordinate groups. Unlike conventional social workers, structural social workers never overlook class, gender, race, and the like as possible sources of personal problems.

One of the first normalization activities is to deal with the service user's notion that the problem or situation being experienced is something unique to that service user. This may be done in two ways: individually and collectively. First, giving some factual information to the service user may help him or her to see that other people are in the same situation. For example, people are socialized into believing that those who are not working in the labour market are in some way defective and, therefore, are responsible for their unemployed status. However, if the unemployment rate for a community is

10 per cent, there obviously are more workers than there are jobs, so that some people, through no fault of their own, will not be able to find work. And if there are one million unemployed people within a labour force of 11–12 million (as there were in Canada during the recession of the early 1980s), this does not mean that there are one million unique problematic situations caused by one million individual workers. Rather, there is one social problem affecting one million workers and their families, and a problem of this magnitude is well beyond the control of any individual negatively affected by it. If persons experiencing unemployment are able to place their situation in the wider political and economic context and understand that there are many other people like themselves, much of the guilt and blame that have been internalized should be allevi-ated. Unemployment is a structural problem that negatively affects lower socio-economic groups but is encouraged by the dominant group so that the latter will benefit by having an available workforce to compete with each other for carrying out dangerous and menial jobs at subsistence wages, which of course contributes to larger profits for the dominant group.

Feminist social workers are able to provide female service users with all kinds of infor-mation on how our patriarchal society oppresses women, how it causes problems for them, and how it then convinces them that they, themselves, are responsible for the emotional, financial, marital, and family problems they might encounter. Normalizing information helps to combat internalized oppression and to reject blaming-the-victim explanations. An example is that of an abused woman who believes that she is one of a very tiny minority of women, and because this happens to so few, there must be something she is doing to cause her partner to abuse her. Providing some basic statistical information, such as abuse rates of women, should help normalize this woman's situation and dampen her internalized belief that, somehow, she has brought this abuse on herself. Once the internalized guilt, shame, and blame are eliminated or alleviated, a certain amount of energy is freed up that can be used to take a deeper and broader look at the situation and deal with it in a more fundamental way (Galper, 1980).

A second and more effective normalization activity is to link the service user with others experiencing similar situations and problems. One of the difficulties of trying to normalize a service user's situation on an individual basis is that 'the weight is too strongly distributed in favor of individual uniqueness and private troubles' (Longres and McLeod, 1980: 273). The collective sharing and consciousness-raising that occur within these types of self-help groups show people that their situations and problems are not idiosyncratic but are part of a larger social dynamic.

In sum, normalization puts situations and problems in their proper political, economic, cultural, and social context. The emphasis is not on the uniqueness or indi-viduality of a service user's situation but on the sameness and common ground of the service users. It is a way of reducing guilt and raising self-esteem and opens the possi-bility of analyzing the structural causes, dynamics, and consequences of social problems and oppression. A precondition for carrying out normalization activities is that the social worker is able to move beyond the traditional diagnostic mindset that ascribes all social problems to personality defects and family dysfunction. If this diagnostic mentality remains in place, chances are greatly reduced that the service user will be able to move beyond the traditional 'personal inadequacy' perception of social problems.

Collectivism

Collectivism is a primary social value of both of the socialist paradigms. Collectivism recognizes that people are social beings who depend on one another for the satisfaction of most of their primary and social needs. It is the antithesis of individualism and, therefore, should be reflected in structural social work practice. Galper (1975: 213) points out that because we live and experience problems within a social context, the analysis of the causes of problems, the development of awareness of the extent to which problems are widely shared, and the mobilizing of activity towards the solutions of these problems must take place in conjunction with others. '[I]t is important for all of us to experience the power of a mutual, collective exploration of the dilemmas we face . . . the group context of practice goes further than the individual context in pointing toward solutions.' Thompson (1998: 147) supports Galper's position when he says, 'because inequality is a political issue, responses to it are often of a collective nature. That is, people band together to tackle the problem by challenging the ideologies and social practices that sustain it.' Leonard (1984: 208) makes a similar point when he says, 'through the practice of *collective consciousness-raising*, the individual's experience is contextualized by an understanding of the social order which stands against the dominant messages contained in the ideological inculcation of subordinate people' (emphasis added). In other words, problems and solutions often are defined differently in consciousness-raising groups of service users than they are in the traditional 'individual pathology' approach.

Longres and McLeod (1980: 273) conclude that 'The first step to consciousness-raising is forming groups based on common social statuses' and that 'consciousness-raising in a holistic way is only possible within groups' because such a medium is free of what Corrigan and Leonard (1978) call the 'cult of individualism'. This does not deny the necessity for individual work with service users, for it is recognized that many people will feel overwhelmed in a group or that a group focus overshadows their immediate personal needs. Some individualizing is necessary to show care, respect, support, and encouragement to participate in a group process. As mentioned above, initially the situation may call for the relief of any pressing and immediate stress as well as a demonstration of personal and social empathy for the service user. Once the initial crisis is dealt with and a trusting relationship is established, the service user will be in a better position to look at his or her situation in a broader but more fundamental way with others.

Groups of service users may serve a number of different purposes: therapy, consciousness-raising, political action, or a combination of these. If such groups already exist, the structural social worker should refer all service users he or she comes into contact with to these groups. For example, a structural social worker should refer anyone in receipt of, or applying for, social welfare to any welfare rights or anti-poverty organizations that might exist in the community. As well, structural social workers should support such groups however they can, including alerting such groups to policy developments that have the probability of negatively affecting them (Galper, 1980). Although structural social workers should support mutual aid groups of service users, they should not violate the social work value of self-determination by attempting to lead them. Withorn (1984: 110) underscores this point when she discusses the functions of mutual aid groups:

> Political practice means establishing groups of clients, not staff-led therapy groups, but 'mutual aid' groups, in the best sense. Such groups can discuss common concerns and organize joint demands on workers. They can also provide support and assistance to each other. We do not live in a socialist society: we cannot organize real 'mass organizations'. Any efforts will be compromised and feel contrived. But the presence of such groups could help articulate client demands: They may be a safe place for sharing 'bootleg' information about the agency, and they may give clients a place to do their own 'power analysis'.

To these functions of the collective process Leonard (1984: 210–11) would add two psychological benefits: (1) positive changes in the conception of the self occur; and (2) people are able 'to move away from the cult of individualism which dominates people's lives within capitalist societies'. These can also be consciousness-raising groups in which members are involved in social analysis of their oppressive conditions and dynamics. They can also be social or political action groups in which members strategize, plan, and carry out campaigns to challenge and change oppressive social conditions, policies, and practices. Groups are usually dynamic, change over time, and may shift from one focus or purpose to another, as illustrated in Box 11.5.

In working with groups organized on the basis of a common status, the social worker ideally is assigned to groups that share his or her gender, race, class of origin, and so on. Maurice Moreau (n.d.) cites research showing that if the social worker is of the same social group as that with which he or she is working, (1) the worker is better able to empathize with the group members; and (2) the group members tend to explore themselves much more than when the social worker has a different background. The caution for the worker, however, is not to project his or her own life experience onto the service users.

Eight practices that Moreau and Leonard (1989: 124) use for the operational definition of collectivization are useful here:

1. Drawing a service user's attention to the links between her/his personal difficulties and the similar problem situations of other service users.
2. Putting service users of the same agency who are living in similar problem situations in touch with each other.

3. Grouping service users for the purpose of mutual aid.
4. Grouping service users for the purpose of creating necessary resources the agency itself should provide.
5. Grouping service users for the purpose of creating necessary resources other agencies should provide.
6. Grouping service users for the purpose of changing problematical aspects of the agency.
7. Grouping service users for the purpose of changing aspects of other agencies and organizations that are problematic to service users.
8. Referring service users to larger social movements directly related to their situations.

Adam (1978) makes an important point with respect to the collective process by showing that it is not always (if ever) a linear process. He acknowledges that when individuals who are similarly oppressed come together, a dialectical movement towards integration of the group occurs whereby group members discover each other, and, in the process discover themselves. However, for this discovery to occur, a certain withdrawal from the inhospitable environment controlled by the dominant group may be necessary. Thompson (1998) argues that greater progress can often be made by the subordinate group if members of the dominant group (including the social worker) are not present or involved with meetings, planning, etc. of the subordinate group. He gives the examples of some women's groups and some groups of black people who deliberately exclude men and white persons, respectively, from meetings. Leonard (1997) also notes that some degree of segregation is a necessary element for emancipation and symbolic community identity. He points out that some groups have developed their own social services, which are more relevant to their needs than are many mainstream agencies, but they still participate in the larger social services network. Adam (1978) issues a caution with respect to segregation. He points out that it could lead to a ghetto-type situation, which, although it may offer some degree of comfort and safety from the dominant group, could also be stifling and confining to oppressed individuals.

The segregation process does not mean that the social worker has no involvement with the group. Mullaly (2002: 177) makes two points in this regard:

First, social workers who have had some prior involvement with some group members should not feel rejected if they are not invited to or are excluded from such groups. Letting group members know that you are available to them on an individual or group basis may be all that you can do at this time. Second, knowing the importance of the liberating functions carried out by segregated groups, the anti-oppressive social worker should encourage the formation of such groups and support them in every way possible. There will still be plenty of opportunities to work with oppressed persons on a group basis . . . .

BOX 11.5 THE BRISBANE WOMEN'S READING GROUP

Several years ago I was invited to speak to a class of social work students at the University of Queensland in Brisbane, Australia. The students in this class were taking a specialization in radical/structural social work co-ordinated and taught by Dr Bill DeMaria. On this day, a few graduates of this program were also in attendance to speak to the students about some of their experiences as structural social workers. One of the graduates related a work experience that I think illustrates several essentials of collectivist structural social work.

She had recently graduated and obtained a job with the Commonwealth (i.e., federal government, which is responsible for social security in Australia) in the Department of Income Assistance (Centrecare). She was given the task of working with a group of single-parent mothers who were regarded by the department as potential 'child protection' cases (simply because they were lone parents and in receipt of welfare). The young structural social worker managed to obtain some funds from the department for child care and transportation so that the women could attend a weekly group meeting. The social worker set the meeting up as a reading club whereby the women would read a book selected from a number of books suggested and then purchased by the worker. The group would then discuss the book at their weekly meeting. This program was sold to Centrecare as a way for the women to get out of the house once a week for a needed break.

Initially, the books were of general interest, but over time, as the group bonds became established and the worker gained the trust of the women, feminist books were introduced. The women would read these books, some of which critically analyzed the place of women in a patriarchal society such as Australia and others that looked critically at such topics as discriminatory (to women) spousal and child support legislation; gender-discriminatory welfare legislation and policies, and so on. The women were encouraged by the worker to talk about their own lived experiences with respect to the texts that they read.

The worker described the process of consciousness-raising and normalization that occurred with the women in the group. Initially, the group operated along the lines of a therapy group, but over a short period of time anger set in, which was directed towards adding a political dimension to the group's activities. The group developed and carried out strategies to change some of the moralistic and punitive legislation and regulations that negatively affected them as a group of oppressed persons (i.e., as women with children who were dependent on welfare).

Redefining

Redefining is a consciousness-raising activity in which personal troubles are redefined in political terms, exposing the relationship between objective material conditions and subjective personal experiences. Society, as discussed earlier, is characterized either by order or by change, and each view defines social problems differently. According to the order view, social problems emanate from individual defects, family dysfunction, or subcultures outside the mainstream. The social change view ascribes most social problems to the present set of social relations where the dominant group controls the subordinate groups. Because social agencies are established within the present liberal-patriarchal-capitalist system they tend to embody the ideology and thought structure of the larger system, that is, an order perspective. This includes the problem definition that underlies all services and social work–service user interactions. Rose and Black (1985) argue that the thought structure of operating assumptions that typically characterizes social agencies validates the North American political economy and invalidates users of social services. They contend that the validation of North American social reality and invalidation of service users are hidden (not stated or publicized or even recognized by many) and pervasive. Rose and Black (1985: 26) cite a study by Warren et al. (1974) of 54 agencies in nine cities:

> people either needing service or failing to fit into already established service delivery patterns were defined as defective; their difficulties in living, rather than resulting from poverty, underemployment, discrimination or inadequate care were seen as results of their individual behaviors or values . . . whether the defect was located in individuals' intellect, personality, discipline or values or in family structure or neighborhood, one or more of these factors were taken to be the determinants of the client's social position in society. Agency responses, in the form of programs and service designs, for example, were incapable of recognizing poverty as an inherent structural characteristic of our society; incapable of recognizing race, sex, age or handicap as structurally and historically determined aspects or characteristics of American society.

Contributing to the entrenchment of this personalist definition of social problems within social agencies is the fact that this thought structure benefits these agencies in two ways. First, it allows them to attribute program failure either to service-user defects (i.e., they are not capable of utilizing help) or to a form of quantitative management rationality. This latter factor permits the agency to make continuous demands for more funds and resources, which is the second way the agency benefits from adopting the prevailing problem definition (Rose and Black, 1985). According to Rose and Black there are several effects on service users of such a problem definition. (1) It invalidates the service user by validating the larger system. (2) It decontextualizes the service user because it severs his or her subjectivity from the objective and materialist context that frames and shapes all social life. (3) It shapes people's behaviour to correspond to the given social reality and the more one deviates from this 'proper and appropriate' behaviour, the more severe is society's treatment. (4) It saturates service users with pejorative vocabulary, a language of pathology and deviance that contains such concepts as diagnosis, treatment, symptoms, acting-out behaviour, resistance, and so on. (5) It forces service users to accept the problem definition imposed on them, in other words, to accept a false reality. If one were seeking an operational definition of oppression these five effects on service users of the prevailing definition of problems would be a good starting point.

Redefining represents an alternative social reality, an alternative definition of problems. 'It [redefining] asserts the primacy of reconnection to objective circumstances as the central problem to be addressed, and an ever-present theme to be interwoven in every aspect of practice' (Rose and Black, 1985: 36). Validation is derived from reconnecting people to their objective social and historical context. The task, rather than working on personal change and accommodation to society, is to engage people as producers and participants in comprehending and acting on their contextual environment. Redefining involves the social worker and service user in a process of deconstruction and reconstruction. In every instance explanations of problems that are self-blaming are challenged, deconstructed and examined in terms of the service user's specific situation, and reconstructed or redefined in terms of their connection with the larger socio-economic-political system. As with consciousness-raising and normalization, priority is given to group rather than individual work because the former is consistent with collectivization and mutual sharing among persons with similar social statuses, which produces more meaningful consciousness-raising.

Moreau (n.d.) outlines a number of redefining or 'reframing' techniques. These include the following: critical questioning (discussed above); dialectical humour (Frayne, 1987, cited in Moreau, n.d.); metaphors and storytelling (Gordon, 1978); cognitive dissonance (Festinger, 1975); the checking of inferences (Middleman and Goldberg, 1974); mental imagery (Rosen, 1982); persuasion (Simons, 1982); and the use of silence (Bourgon, 1988). Such techniques help to contextualize not only the service user's problem situation but often the service user's behaviour. Behaviour that may be labelled as inappropriate and self-destructive according to the personalist problem definition may be relabelled as perfectly appropriate and normal with an alternative problem definition. Lundy (2004: 139) offers the following simple ways of operationalizing the concept of 'redefining' or 'reframing'. She says that service users are often hard on themselves and may accept responsibility for a situation that is structurally caused. The structural social worker will, in such instances, engage the service user in a process of reflection and, in a tentative fashion, offer another way of looking at the situation by saying something like, 'Do you think another explanation might be . . .', or 'Another way of looking at it could be . . .', or 'I see it another way.' Narrative therapists use a number of techniques to help people see situations in ways that are not self-blaming. Externalizing the problem in conversation helps to remove the problem from the identity of the service user and to see it differently (Lundy, 2004).

An example may help to make this discussion more concrete. Many graduates from the social work program at St Thomas University (a structural program) in New Brunswick, where I had been a faculty member, are employed in departments of social services where one of the services is 'child protection'. They report that the problem definition of child abuse and neglect is that these occur because of inappropriate behaviours and attitudes on the part of parents. Case recordings of non-structural social workers highlight personal inadequacies, emotional immaturity, poor coping skills, and family dysfunction as the areas to focus on in working with child abuse and/or neglect situations. Large amounts of money are spent each year in providing family therapy training to the social workers so that they might work more effectively with child protection families. If there is any mention that maybe the service users' problems are largely material and structural or institutional, it is dismissed as either incorrect or by stating that 'There is nothing we can do about that. Our job is to work with these families.'

The problem definition of the social agency is that child abuse and neglect are problems of personal inadequacy, when, in fact, child abuse and neglect are in large part a class problem. Contrary to the myth of classlessness, which is part of the current system's thought structure, both evidence and reason lead to the unmistakable conclusion that 'child abuse and neglect are strongly related to poverty, in terms of prevalence and of severity of consequences . . . . adherence to the myth [of classlessness] diverts attention from the nature of the problems and diverts resources from their solution' (Pelton, 1978: 617). This is not to say that child abuse and neglect do not occur among other socio-economic classes; the evidence does indicate, however, that the great preponderance of abuse and neglect and the greatest severity of abuse and neglect occur among those who have the fewest resources to work with, who are struggling the most to secure the basic necessities of life, and who have the greatest number and most sustained pressures on them—that is, the poor—especially poor women (see Karen Swift's *Manufacturing 'Bad Mothers': A Critical Perspective on Child Neglect* [1995]). This is not an excuse for child abuse or neglect but it is an explanation. The job of the structural social worker, then, is to redefine the problem from one of personal pathology to one of class. This should be done not only with the service user but should be stated at case conferences, and the case recordings should be redressed to reflect the service users' problems as largely material and institutional.

This is not to imply that child abuse and neglect are only matters of class. Physical abuse, emotional abuse, and sexual abuse each have their own distinct set of dynamics. The argument here is that class impacts on these dynamics and that adequate material conditions are often a more realistic solution than sending people to parenting courses when they may not know where their next meal will come from or if they will have a roof over their heads, or even if they will still have children to parent.

One of the myths about structural social work (see Box 11.1) is that it does not allow for personal responsibility. That is, in linking all personal situations to larger social or political structures and forces, it removes all blame from the person for any seemingly irresponsible or bad behaviour. When people make bad choices, the criticism of structural social work is that it takes on a 'society made me do it' response, which is similar to the 'it's all a capitalist plot' critique of critical social theory explanations for social problems. Structural social work does not overlook or accept irresponsible or bad behaviours on the part of individuals. However, it does not blame or pathologize people for such social phenomena as poverty, racism, sexism, and so on.

Unlike mainstream 'blame the victim' types of explanations for social problems, structural social work recognizes that the reasons for people's behaviours are much more complex than a simple dichotomy of the person being good or evil. When people suffer from all the injustices and indignities of oppression over a long period of time and must struggle to obtain the basic necessities of life, they will often develop coping behaviours that help them to survive day to day that, on the surface, might seem to be morally wrong or self-destructive. As well, when individuals lack the resources or opportunities to live their lives in productive and socially acceptable ways, they will often use ways and means to get by that are not socially acceptable. And, as in the case of child abuse or neglect, these are not excuses for seemingly bad or irresponsible behaviours; they are explanations. Thus, structural social workers would not accept or overlook personal irresponsibility, but neither would they condemn the person as bad or evil because of it. They would work with the individual to extinguish or neutralize such behaviour, but in their work they would recognize that such behaviour is linked to larger oppressive forces in society and, therefore, would take a broader approach than simply 'fixing up' the person.

Dialogical Relationships

Normalization, collectivization, and redefinition are the means of carrying out consciousness-raising. The medium within which these activities are carried out is dialogue, between the social worker and the service user and among service users. Dialogue is the vehicle for uncovering people's subjective reality and opening it to critical reflection.

> Dialogue cannot be professional interviewing, application of therapeutic technology, instructions for improved functioning, or casual conversation. It is purposive in both process and focus. It directs itself to validation of the oppressed as persons, attempting to demonstrate their capacity to inform you, and it struggles to direct the content towards depiction and analysis of the objective situation. . . . To unveil oppressive reality is to be willing to enter it more fully, to encourage the elaboration of expression, to support the expression of experiences, to initiate the early steps in critical reflection. (Rose and Black, 1985: 45)

To be able to engage in meaningful dialogue the structural social worker must develop a dialogical relationship with service users—a relationship based on horizontal exchange rather than vertical imposition (Freire, 1970). A dialogical relationship is one wherein *all participants in the dialogue are equals*, wherein each learns from the other and teaches the other. Power is shared as much as possible between worker and service user and each is considered to have different but equivalent wisdom and experience so that they mutually engage in theory-building and action (Allan, 2003b). Professional knowledge is not privileged over knowledge gained from lived experiences (Ife, 2001).Of course, the social worker will have some skills and insights that the service user does not have, but the service user has experiences and insights that the worker lacks. The structural social worker must make conscious efforts to dispel any myths of expert technical solutions to fundamental political problems. Wisdom, experience, and expertise are accepted and validated 'from below' as well as 'from above' (Ife, 1997). The worker may pose problems but not solve problems, as this latter activity must be shared between worker and service user(s). Both work together so that they can ask the questions as well as think about the answers. As a result, both will come to a better understanding of the issue, both will learn, and both will act (Ife, 1997). Consciousness-raising can only occur within the context of a non-authoritarian relationship. Criticism of conventional social work practice has often centred on its elitist, impersonal, and overly technical approach. 'In essence, a dialogical relationship is exchanging, comparing and communicating, rather than indoctrinating, proselytizing and generally issuing a "communiqué"' (Moreau, 1979: 89).

As structural social workers we do not want to reproduce with service users the kinds of social relations that have oppressed them in the first place. One of the contradictions of social work practice is that it attempts to provide practical humanitarian care for people in distress, yet it often provides this care in a superordinate (helper-helpee), authoritarian (worker has the answers), and mystical (helping process is not explained) way. A dialogical relationship minimizes these aspects. Burghardt (1982: 215) points out that 'one of our pivotal, potentially "insurrectionary" roles can be to produce relationships between client and worker that run counter to the dominant social relationships produced elsewhere.' Such relationships are not only conducive to structural social work practice but they challenge the ideological hegemony of the larger society.

To demystify social work activities, techniques, and practices, social workers must not be possessive of them, but must make them broadly available to people at large as part of their job. For instance, the use of any technique, skill, or process is an opportunity to demystify it by discussing its origins, purpose, and other situations where it might prove useful and by encouraging the service user to ask questions. The content of service users' files should be made available to them, and they should have the right to be present at all conferences that affect them. Hidden strategies and manipulative approaches are not used and the rationale behind all questions asked by the worker is explained (Moreau, n.d.).

In discussing empowerment Moreau and Leonard (1989: 82–7) present the following dialogical practices:

- sharing with the service user the content of case recordings;
- directly involving service users in the decisions that affect them;
- directly involving the service user in providing feedback on the kinds and quality of services provided;
- reducing the social distance between worker and service user by use of self-

disclosure, casual dress, giving the rationale for techniques and questions, personal empathy, home visits, first names, direct clear speech, and use of body language;

- sharing with the service user one's personal biases and limits as part of the 'helping' contract;
- providing information on the role of the agency, the rights of the service user, and letting her/him know the worker is there to serve the service user.

In conclusion, consciousness-raising is the approach used for working with service users, just as empowerment is the goal and process of structural social work for challenging oppression, and 'the personal is political' provides the critical analysis at this level. Normalization, collectivization, and redefining are the techniques used in consciousness-raising. All structural social work at the personal level is carried out through the medium of dialogical communication and relationships. Two Australian structural social work educators (Fraser and Strong, 2000) developed a set of interviewing skills that provided the focus of a course they taught on structural social work skills. These skills, which capture much of the discussion above, are presented in Box 11.6. Those skills that the authors identified as traditional are listed from 1 to 3 and the remaining 6 skills (with an asterisk) are broadly identified as structural interviewing skills. All students were assessed on how well they were able to demonstrate competence on these skills in role-playing situations.

BOX 11.6 INTERVIEWING SKILLS FOR STRUCTURAL SOCIAL WORKERS

1. Capacity to *engage* clients at the beginning.
2. Demonstration of *warmth, empathy, sensitivity,* and *respect* to all clients in the group.
3. Management of *shared* air time.
4. Ability to facilitate a broad *definition* of the problem.*
5. Attention to the *different perspectives* held by various members in the client group.*
6. Appropriateness of probes and questions to facilitate a consideration/ reflection that the impact of *class/gender/race/sexuality/ability/age* might have on the problem.*
7. Interviewer's use of non-judgemental and *non-pathologizing* language.*
8. Overall ability to elicit discussion that explores problems from a *critical perspective.**
9. Ability to demonstrate confident handling of proceedings without becoming *dogmatic* or *authoritarian.**

IN THE BELLY OF THE BEAST: SURVIVING AND CHANGING THE WORKPLACE

Most social workers work in agencies, whether they are public or private. The question most often asked of me by social work students and practitioners is, *'How can I practice structural social work and not get in trouble with my agency or even lose my job?'* Although the short and glib answer is 'by being smart (i.e., strategic) about what you do', there is of course much more to it than that. There are a number of ways a structural social worker can survive within and challenge or change social agencies that hold the same oppressive thought and ideological structures as the larger society. Although social work by itself cannot eliminate oppression and injustice, it can help to erode oppressive structures and practices starting within its own arena for struggle—the social agency.

Contradictions of Agencies as a Basis for Radicalization

The basic contradiction of most mainstream or conventional social agencies and services is well known: they 'deny, frustrate and undermine the possibilities of human liberation and a just society, at the same time that they work toward and, in part, achieve greater degrees of human well-being' (Galper, 1975: 45). Social agencies and services provide social care and social control at the same time. This is their basic contradiction, and within this contradiction we can carry out structural social work practice.

Agencies and services are organized so that 'they support and reinforce conformity, among both clients and workers, to the very institutions and values that generate the problems to which the services were addressed in the first place' (Galper, 1975: 46). To receive services, people are often forced to accept roles and behaviours for themselves that reinforce and support the status quo.[3] And social workers are constrained in a variety of ways by various means, such as being subject to traditional individual supervision, a reward structure based on conformity to agency need rather than on service user need, heavy caseloads that yield little opportunity to step back and consider the larger picture, requirement to use 'risk assessments' that focus on individual traits as an explanation for social problems rather than on structural factors, and computerization with programmed problem definitions and solutions.

While structural social workers recognize that conventional social agencies do not offer sufficient solutions to social problems, are too often inadequate within their own terms, frequently constrain workers to behave in ways that are deleterious to service users, and offer limited opportunities for a rewarding social work career, the vast majority of social workers find themselves working somewhere in 'the system'. Structural social workers need to support one another and, because there are limited opportunities for employment with alternative social agencies (to be discussed in the next chapter), with radical unions, or in other positions geared to undermine the system, most social workers will continue to be employed by mainstream agencies. Thus, the challenge to the structural social worker is to remain true to one's structural mission while not alienating oneself from management and from other workers in the agency.

Most social workers enter their work because of a concern for people and an interest in responding to social problems. However, studies show that 'it is adjustment to the bureaucratic reality of the job that causes the most discomfort among new workers and is the most responsible for the loss of "idealism"' (Withorn, 1984: 160). Understanding the contradictory functions of social agencies helps one to make sense out of the frustrations, limitations, and obstacles experienced by the worker. Many progressive social workers believe their only option for structural social work practice is that of 'protecting the poor, the sick, the criminal, and the deviant against the agencies' (Cloward and Piven, 1975: xii). Their belief is that they must become 'guerrillas in the bureaucracy' and undermine the agency at every turn from their political underground position (Withorn, 1984). But not all agencies are alike and, as Withorn notes, not all the negative aspects of social service work can be attributed to the social control functions of mainstream social agencies. Some of the features of mainstream agencies that tend to control and/or pacify its social workers are presented in Box 11.7.

BOX 11.7 CONTROL AND PACIFICATION FEATURES OF MAIN-STREAM SOCIAL AGENCIES

- The dominant assumption of mainstream social work is that agencies carry out no political functions.
- All oppressive features of the larger society are reproduced in social agencies (i.e., classism, racism, sexism, ageism, heterosexism, etc.).
- Agency-based definitions of social problems and solutions tend to personalize social problems and pathologize service users.
- Success orientation encourages workers to toe the line and not rock the boat.
- Most social agencies are organized hierarchically, with top-down management, and provide little opportunity for input by front-line workers.
- Day-to-day demands on workers detract from looking at the larger picture of how the agency functions to support dominant–subordinate relations of the larger society.
- Traditional supervision is carried over from student field instruction days where supervisors review all cases with the worker to ensure she/he is practising within agency expectations.
- The service orientation of agencies has been replaced by 'rule orientation' in many cases.
- Radicalism, radicals, and progressive forms of social work are discounted as unrealistic and naive.
- There is always the implicit threat of unemployment if one steps outside the agency rules.

Given a structural understanding of the nature, operations, and political functions of social agencies, social workers should be able to operate above the political underground in combining social care with our structural social work goals. (Guidelines for carrying out a structural analysis of one's field placement or workplace may be found in the Appendix.)

> The overriding goal must always be to politicize the workplace so that activists, clients, and fellow workers understand the political dimensions of the work and take the greatest advantage of the contradictions of the system. This can only be done by a self-conscious strategy that is sensitive to specific workplaces with their particular personalities, structures, and political imperatives and is aware of broader bureaucratic, economic, and social realities. (Withorn, 1984: 200)

The contradictions present in most social agencies and the fact that social workers always have some measure of autonomy permit us to undertake more intra-organizational change than is often believed possible. And, as Scurfield (1980) and Patti and Resnick (1972) point out, and as discussed in Chapter 2, according to our own *Code of Ethics* our primary obligation is to the people we serve and not to the agency that employs us. The legitimation for radicalizing the agency is derived from our ethical obligation to place professional values above organizational allegiance. The challenge for structural social workers is to work within the 'social care–social control' contradiction and maximize the agency's emancipatory potential while neutralizing its control function. Some of the ways to do this are presented below.

Radicalizing and Democratizing the Agency

The purpose of politically radicalizing the agency is to emphasize its service function and to de-emphasize its control function. In order to carry out this purpose it is necessary to engage in 'anti-capitalist practice' within the agency (Burghardt, 1982: 191). This opposes those assumptions of professional social organizations that flow from the prevailing thought and ideological structures of our liberal-capitalist society. If one of the goals of structural social work is to transform society from capitalism to socialism, then a logical place to begin is with the social welfare institution of which we are a part and, more specifically, with the social agency within which we work. Thus, as we practise anti-capitalist social work we are also practising socialist or structural social work. We de-emphasize capitalist values and practices while emphasizing socialist values and practices. This means we must challenge the agency's traditional definitions of problems and their resultant oppressive policies, attempt to democratize the agency, strive for more egalitarian relationships within the agency, and defend the service user from the agency. Of course, as structural social workers concerned with all forms and sources of oppression, we would extend the concept of 'anti-capitalist practice' to 'anti-oppressive practice'. We would challenge all sexist, racist, ageist, etc., definitions of problems and policies and practices that occur within the agency. Box 11.8 presents some 'overt' activities that structural social workers can carry out to protect service users from regressive agency policies and practices and that contribute to changing the workplace.

BOX 11.8 OVERT STRUCTURAL SOCIAL WORK ACTIVITIES TO CHALLENGE OPPRESSION IN THE AGENCY

- Push for definitions of problems and solutions that are grounded in people's lived realities and do not blame victims.
- Ensure that case recordings reflect these realities.
- Every staff meeting or supervisory session is an opportunity to raise questions about traditional assumptions and conventional approaches.
- Circulate articles that contain structural analyses of problems dealt with by your agency.
- Bring in structural speakers who will have analyses different from the agency.
- Work through your union and/or professional association to raise concerns about work requirements that force workers to harm service users.
- Develop brochures outlining the rights and entitlements of service users and distribute them routinely.
- As a regular and routine part of your practice refer all service users to existing alternative groups and organizations (to be discussed in next chapter).
- Push for more peer and group supervision and decision-making.
- Seek out and network with sympathetic co-workers. Develop collective approaches and support others.
- Confront any behaviour or comments that defame/demean service users or reflect negative stereotypes.
- Have realistic expectations; accept that change takes time but is nonetheless worth pursuing.

In calling for social workers to become 'organizational operators' (i.e., those who seek to have a positive influence on the organization), Thompson (1998) would add the following to the above list:

- Promote practice that is critically reflective.
- Make the value base equality and the affirmation of difference open and explicit.

When agency policies and definitions of people's problems are based on assumptions of individual deficiencies, family dysfunction, or cultural inferiority, the structural social worker has an obligation to confront these oppressive assumptions. Workers can press for definitions of these problems that are grounded in people's social, economic, and political circumstances. When to press and how to press are two considerations when challenging personalist interpretations of structural problems. With respect to the first consideration Galper (1980: 198) says, 'Every staff meeting offers an opportunity to raise questions, to challenge conservative assumptions, and to encourage coworkers to do the same. Every supervisory session provides an opportunity for political encounter.' The most effective strategy for presenting these challenges is not based on confrontation, but focuses on asking questions about current practices while presenting information that leads to a different definition of the problem. For example, at a staff meeting of a child protection unit of a provincial Department of Social Services that views child abuse/neglect problems as essentially family problems to be solved by family therapy, one could ask, 'Why are we doing all this family therapy work when we know from our own experience that if most of the families we work with had a decent job with a decent income they wouldn't be having so many problems? Also, these articles that I have here [and which are then distributed] clearly show that most child abuse and neglect situations are problems related to poverty and not to bad parents.'

Most social agencies are managed from top to bottom. The social work literature is replete with accounts of how this hierarchical management model works against the front-line worker's attempts to deliver an adequate and quality service to people (see, e.g., Withorn, 1984; Simpkin, 1979; Carniol, 2005). Policies are formulated at the top of the organization with little or no input from workers, let alone service users, and are passed down the line for implementation. This type of management is anti-democratic, as it excludes worker or service-user participation. It promotes inequality in that a small elite makes the decisions and imposes them on workers, and results in oppressive policies because the decision-making is based on the myths, assumptions, and stereotypes inherent to capitalism, patriarchy, etc. Thus, part of the struggle for structural social workers is to democratize the workplace. This may take various forms, such as union activity to build and increase service-user participation in the decision-making process, more peer supervision, development of a consultative relationship with supervisors rather than that of a boss–subordinate relationship, and a struggle to implement more democratic means of sharing decisions, responsibilities, and information. Much more research and many more written accounts of democratic collective experiences of administering and delivering services are needed.[4]

In addition to challenging personal pathology definitions of social problems and attempting to democratize social agencies, structural social workers must also confront all agency policies and practices that oppress or negatively affect service users in other ways. Major areas of concern are to maximize the service user's access to resources, benefits, or services provided by the agency, to link service users together and support service-user advocacy groups, and to combat any behaviour that demeans or defames service users. It is preferable, of course, for the structural social worker to use overt means in performing these tasks, but in many situations workers are forced to use covert strategies. This presents a dilemma for social workers, but social work's *Code of Ethics* is clear in this regard. The social worker's primary responsibility is to the service user, and when the needs of the service user conflict with the needs of the agency the social worker has an ethical and professional responsibility, first and foremost, to the service user.

Moreau and Leonard (1989) call the maximizing of client use of an agency's services or benefits 'defence of the client'. The aim of this defence is to maximize the client's use of resources while minimizing their negative effect. Moreau and Leonard outline five (covert) practices that defend the service user within the worker's own agency and two practices that defend the service user in relation to outside agencies. The five practices within the worker's agency are:

1. Provide service users with confidential inside information on how best to present a request for service from the agency.
2. Alter or falsify statistics to satisfy organizational requirements, all the while giving more time to needy service users. (For example, an agency may require that each service user receive a monthly home visit, which is virtually impossible because of the heavy caseloads. A worker may report that he or she has fulfilled this requirement, but in fact has not because he or she has chosen to give more attention to those service users who are most in need. At the same time the worker has the obligation to protest the heavy caseload to the agency, to his or her union, and so on.)
3. Deliberately avoid recording certain facts, for example, a welfare recipient received some money from an outside source that, if reported, would be deducted from his or her welfare.
4. Turn a blind eye to a service user's violation of policies, rules, or procedures of the agency, for example, residency requirements for eligibility of a service.
5. Become involved in making efforts to change organizational rules, regulations, or practices that work against the needs or interests of service users.

The two practices of defending the service user in relation to outside agencies are:

1. Provide service users with confidential 'inside' information on how to present a request for service from another agency.
2. Turn a blind eye to a service user's violation of rules, policies, or procedures of an outside organization, for example, violation of a probation order or illegally receiving a financial benefit.

[NOTE: At no time should a social worker become involved in breaking rules or altering or falsifying agency-required statistics unless the well-being of the service user is compromised by not doing so. It is only when the well-being of a service user is threatened by some penalty or sanction by the agency that these practices should be considered. A structural social worker always weighs the risks associated with any action that may be outside the normal way of operating. As the Australian social work writer B. Lane (1997: 39) says, using an Aussie metaphor, 'perhaps as social workers, we need to become skilled at swimming with the crocodiles while accomplishing our tasks. Being an advocate for social justice requires the talent to know when to risk and when to wait.' When engaging in such action, it must be done in a thoughtful and considered manner. Otherwise, there is a danger of getting caught or having your action backfire, and you could be responsible for all kinds of negative results—including giving the rest of us structural social workers a 'bad name'. On the other hand, it should be remembered that many social workers, without telling anyone, break rules on a daily basis mainly because of bureaucratic priorities that interfere with the social worker performing his or her job.]

Another way of enhancing the service user's power and influence within the agency is to link service users with one another and to outside advocacy groups. Just as groups enhance consciousness-raising, so, too, they enhance the ability of service users to challenge destructive agency policies. Groups of service users should be supported in every way the social worker is able to do so, such as providing information (including so-called confidential information), referring other service users to the group, forewarning the group of destructive policy discussions being held within the bureaucracy so that they might prepare to counter them, and identifying workers within the agency the group can trust and those who should be avoided.

Finally, in carrying out anti-oppressive or structural work within the agency, social workers must confront any behaviour that demeans or defames service users. Derogatory remarks about service users by workers are far more common than they should be. Blair's classic study of welfare workers (1973, cited in Withorn, 1984: 202) found that anti-client statements served as a way of affirming social solidarity among workers and were part of the normative culture of the workplace in that these derogatory remarks were often used by workers to show others that they were not 'naive or sentimental about clients'. Just as racist or sexist remarks or jokes are unacceptable, so, too, are anti-client statements because all such statements perpetuate stereotypes and devalue people. Such behaviour can be initially dealt with in subtle ways, such as not laughing or responding to it, or by silence, or by disapproving looks, or by a general discussion at a staff meaning about such behaviour and what it represents. If, as Withorn (1984) notes, subtle tactics do not work, then structural workers may have to resort to overt disapproval such as taking the offending person aside and telling him or her that you are offended by this person's derogatory humour, that you have given all the non-verbal and indirect cues you could to get that message across, but to no avail, and if it continues you will have no choice but to report or complain to management about the behaviour.

Protecting Ourselves

Social agencies are often repressive because they enforce service-user conformity to capitalist values and relations. Also, they 'enforce worker conformity through direct coercion, subtle pressures and ideological indoctrination' (Galper, 1975: 196). Therefore, any attempts at democratizing or radicalizing the agency put the worker at risk. However, the risks to the worker are probably not as great as is often assumed. It was pointed out earlier in this chapter that the inherent contradictions of agencies give the worker some latitude for structural work. Although most agencies contain repressive elements, usually their goals are couched in terms of equality, democracy, social justice, human need, and optimal service. These stated goals, along with a certain degree of autonomy that the worker enjoys, give the worker a foothold for structural practice within the agency. Furthermore, by keeping certain guidelines in mind, structural social workers can minimize the likelihood of any kind of serious reprisal from the agency. Some of these guidelines are found in Box 11.9.

BOX 11.9 PROTECTING OURSELVES FROM REPRISALS

- Form a caucus of 'like-minded' people and use it for peer support and collective action.
- Know your agency—legislation impacting on it, agency policies, formal and informal power relations, points of vulnerability, who can and cannot be trusted—and use this knowledge strategically to promote anti-oppression.
- Become valuable to the agency by doing your work in a competent manner.
- Avoid adventurism and martyrdom.
- Work through your union and /or professional association to promote anti-oppression.
- Avoid militant confrontations. Searching questions are usually more effective than accusations or attacks.

Thompson (1998) presents a number of guidelines for 'elegant challenging' by social workers. If challenging the actions or attitudes of others that are punitive, moralistic, and/or oppressive in the workplace is to be effective, it needs to:

- Be tactful and constructive rather than a personal attack.
- Avoid 'cornering people' and allow them to save face.
- Pay attention to an appropriate time and place to challenge rather than immediately challenge at all times.
- Not be punitive—the aim is to promote equality and anti-oppression and not to create unnecessary tensions and hostilities.
- Acknowledge explicitly or implicitly the vulnerability of all of us with respect to oppressive practices.
- Be undertaken in a spirit of compassion and social justice rather than taking the high moral ground.

Galper (1980) originally presented some of the above guidelines for radical or structural practice in social agencies and argued that, if followed, they would minimize the risks of reprisal by the agency against the worker. He says that the first step is to be competent in carrying out the agency's assigned tasks. If a worker is competent, he or she will be of value to the agency. In turn, the agency will be more tolerant of efforts at democratization and radicalization than it would be if the worker was not competent. If a structural worker is incompetent, then the agency has an easy reason for getting rid of her or him. Galper also cautions us to avoid 'adventurism or isolation'. The structural activities we carry out within the agency should not be overly militant, irrational, or destructive. What is the sense of making a public scene over a principle if your action gets you fired (unless this is your strategy)? People cannot continue to carry out structural practice in the agency after they are fired. For example, what is the sense of jumping on top of the coffee table and yelling Marxist slogans such as, 'Social Workers of the world unite! Capitalism sucks!' We know that. What good comes about by making the 'big splash', if it means you are gone tomorrow? More realistically, challenging the entire belief system of a supervisor in a strident, face-to-face confrontation can only alienate. Martyrs are of limited practical use for ongoing structural work within agencies. Another important guideline is to know your agency—its history, policies, points of vulnerability, and the people in it—who is likely to be supportive, who is not to be trusted.

There is consensus in the literature that the most important way of protecting ourselves, not just from agency reprisal but also from burnout, is to have peer support. Withorn (1984) contends that a 'workplace caucus' of 'politically compatible people' is essential to combat the bureaucracy's inherent tendency to divide workers through hierarchy and specialization. Such caucuses provide support to members, facilitate consciousness-raising of the workers' situation, enable planning to radicalize the agency, and give members a sense of collective and individual efficacy to change their agency. Galper (1980) echoes the need for a caucus of radical/structural workers and says that the process of establishing such a caucus does not have to start in a grandiose way but may begin with two or three like-minded workers meeting informally. Sherman and Wenocur (1983: 377) believe that a mutual support group of workers 'weakens the impact of the disempowering socialization process in an organization by creating an alternative subculture governed by workers' values'. And, finally, a study of graduates from a structural social work program in Canada found that peer support either from within or from outside the agency was the most important factor in carrying out structural social work practice (Moreau and Leonard, 1989). Donna Baines (1997: 314–15), a progressive social work writer, provides the clearest example of the functions that can be carried out by a caucus (see Box 11.10). This example is taken from her practice as a social worker in a culturally diverse, impoverished inner-city community in the United States where she was part of a caucus of progressive social workers.

BOX 11.10   THE CONSPIRACY

'Jokingly referring to ourselves as "the conspiracy", we shared stories and our outrage over lunch. Without the support of these colleagues, I would have found it difficult to resist the dominant discourse that blames individuals for all their problems. Instead, we continually reframed our problems and our clients' problems to be the result of structural and systemic forces and sought solutions that went beyond those just for individual cases.' Baines goes on to talk about the importance to the group of the practice principle, 'Build ties to oppositional groups outside the workplace'. 'This principle is especially important for maintaining a sense of social solidarity. It concretizes certain aspects of the personal-is-political equation and provides alternatives for clients and practitioners, as well as resources and important information on specific and broader struggles for social justice. It is seen as essential for social workers to remain grounded in a social-movement sense of services, rather than an individualized view of clients' problems. For time to time, members of "the conspiracy" at the hospital fed information to community groups, spoke at public meetings, and tried to connect clients to activist organizations. These tiny efforts helped us tie our everyday concerns and struggles to larger strategies and visions for social justice and social change.'

CONCLUSION

This chapter presented an overview of structural social work practice that emanates from the radical humanist school of thought. The focus is on working directly with individuals, families, groups, and communities as well as working within conventional or mainstream social agencies. Several practice elements were presented that should facilitate the ultimate goal of structural social work—to contribute to the social transformation of society while carrying out practical, day-to-day, humanitarian care to victims and casualties of social problems and oppression. These practice elements, which emerge from the critical or social change explanation for social problems, help to differentiate conventional practice from structural social work practice. Structural social work does not consider any level of social work practice to be inherently conservative or oppressive, nor does it consider any level to be inherently progressive or emancipatory. A number of myths regarding structural social work were examined and debunked.

The second part of the chapter addressed the most contentious aspect of structural social work—how can it be carried out in a mainstream agency without the social worker receiving some kind of reprisal, including the loss of one's job? A number of guidelines and strategies were presented for democratizing and changing the culture and practices of those workplaces that define social problems in individual terms and that hold the same oppressive thought and ideological structures as the larger society. Issues and strategies for protecting oneself from reprisal were discussed. There are risks involved in attempting to change the social agency from within, yet a number of ways exist for protecting ourselves and our jobs. We can do our work well, we can plan strategies that take into account the tolerance of the agency, and we can work collectively. The alternative to working within and against the agency is to work within and *for* the agency. The former entails risks of retaliation by the agency. The latter entails risks of cynicism, despair, and burnout because we deny much of the social, economic, and political reality around us (Galper, 1980). Put in these terms, it would seem that working within and against the system/agency is the better choice.

CRITICAL QUESTIONS

1. Identify as many stereotypes as you can with respect to the following oppressed groups: poor people, Aboriginal persons, women, immigrants, gay and lesbian people, black persons, older people. Where do these stereotyped views come from? What functions do you think they carry out for the dominant group?

2. Why did you originally choose social work as an occupation? What were your initial beliefs about the place of social work in society? Have they changed at all? If so, in what way? What has been your biggest surprise about social work?

3. Most people recognize the relevance that sociology and psychology hold for social work practice, but why should social work students have to study economics, politics, culture, women's studies, and Native studies?

4. What is your idea about 'good communication' between a social worker and a service user? Can you identify any class or cultural assumptions in your answer?

5. How do you usually deal with conflict? Is there anything in particular that makes it easier or more difficult for you to deal with or manage conflict?

6. Structural social workers do not blame people for the social problems that they may experience. However, structural social workers do not adopt an 'anything goes' approach to people's behaviour or attitudes and they do hold people accountable for their actions. What kinds of responses would you make to service users who are abusing or neglecting their children or who lie to you or who are breaking the law for personal gain?

Working Outside (and Against) the System: Radical Structuralism and Working within Ourselves

The question is not 'is there life after death?', but 'is there life after birth?'
—*Saul Alinsky (1909–72)*

INTRODUCTION

The previous chapter presented and discussed a number of structural social work practice elements that may be carried out in the course of one's work within the traditonal social welfare system. This chapter considers a number of modes and forms of structural practice outside the social welfare system and outside the formal practice of social work. The reason for carrying out structural practice outside the system is that the system places institutional limits on much of our social work practice. Although much good work may be carried out within the system, it 'must be linked to struggles for structural change outside agency walls. In practice, this means the worker should keep in touch with and support parallel social change movements going on outside of social agencies' (Moreau, 1979: 89). As well as structural social work practice outside the system, this chapter presents several strategies and guidelines that should help us on a personal level as we encounter the myriad obstacles and issues associated with structural social work.

Structural social work practice within the system is based mainly on the radical humanist school of changing people's consciousness on a massive scale as a prerequisite to changing society. Structural practice outside the system is based mainly on the radical structural school of changing material conditions and oppressive structural patterns such as patriarchy, racism, and ageism. These would be replaced by a socialist society that, once in place, would become the new social reality for people. By itself, each approach has limitations, which were discussed in Chapter 9. Both are necessary.

This chapter discusses each of the following as arenas for carrying out structural social work practice outside the social welfare system: alternative services and organizations; coalitions, social movements, and new social movement theory; unions;

professional associations; electoral politics; a revitalized public sector; challenging and resisting the dominant order; and the moral premise of social welfare—universal human needs. It also looks at the following personal aspects of the worker in carrying out structural social work practice and in living our lives as structural social workers: critical self-reflection; self-care; having realistic expectations; using anger in a constructive way; and making the political personal in our own lives.

WORKING OUTSIDE AND AGAINST THE SYSTEM

Alternative Services and Organizations

If we are to contribute to social transformation, then a logical starting point is the workplace. However, structural social workers should not focus on the workplace to the exclusion of overall social change efforts outside their agency walls. Changing the social relations within agencies does not, by itself, change the basic elements of our dominant–subordinate social order with its severe discrepancies of wealth and power, domination by giant corporations, a dependence on industrial production that pollutes our environment, and patriarchy, sexism, racism, ageism, etc. And, as Carniol (1987: 109–10) points out, we may help someone obtain better housing or the full entitlement of a welfare benefit or cut through red tape or overlook a few rules or regulations so that the individual does not lose a needed benefit or service, but we know: (1) that most of the benefits or services we deliver are inadequate; and (2) that we have done nothing to change those structural causes of the person being oppressed and in need in the first place.

One of the ways for structural social workers to contribute to social transformation is to create, develop, and/or support alternative social service organizations.

> If a cohesive radical movement is to emerge, focus on an alternative human services policy and program could serve an important integrating function. Because the recipients of human services are overwhelmingly poor and/or female and/or people of colour and/or young or old, it is an issue which creates bridges between the 'narrow' interests of pivotal oppressed groups. Because human services implicate economic and political and social issues, radical alternatives could create a 'cutting edge' in efforts to achieve comprehensive change. (Wineman, 1984: 20)

Alternative services and programs are counter-systems to mainstream social agencies and can be used ultimately to develop 'a base from which larger social changes can be eventually effected' (Moreau, 1979: 87). These kinds of organizations usually come about because traditional, mainstream social services have been set up by the dominant group and tend to operate in accordance with dominant norms, values, and expectations. In other words, mainstream agencies and organizations are culturally specific (i.e., to the dominant culture) and sometimes will unintentionally contribute to the oppression of subordinate populations.

Alternative services and organizations are founded on different principles, values, and ideals from our traditional liberal services and organizations. They provide opportunities for subordinate groups to come together and engage in collective action. 'Joining a group can help shift people from individual views toward the development of collective views' (Allan, 2003b: 70), that is, personal issues are discussed in their political context. Alternative services and organizations facilitate consciousness-raising, solidarity and alliances, and lobbying to change oppressive rules, practices, conditions, and institutions (Allan, 2003b). They attempt to institutionalize new forms of social relationships by incorporating community control, mutual social support, and shared decision-making. These function to meet the needs of people in the community and are growth-producing for those working within them. 'Alternative services usually spring from the work of a specific oppressed community or movement' (Carniol, 2005: 110). Examples of alternative services are welfare rights groups, tenant associations, rape crisis centres, transition homes for battered women and their children, off-reserve Native friendship centres, gay and lesbian associations, ex-psychiatric groups, Alcoholics Anonymous, and prisoners' societies.

Structural social workers do not see alternative services and organizations as competitive or disruptive to the operations of mainstream services and organizations. They understand that alternative services represent attempts by people associated with them to connect the personal with the political and to gain control over their own destiny. Structural social workers would support alternative services in a variety of ways:

- by becoming involved with them to the extent that they can without endangering their employment in mainstream agencies;
- by providing material resources, since alternative organizations are usually strapped for funds (e.g., money, stationery, photocopying);
- by providing inside information from one's own organization (e.g., notice of a pending policy that will negatively affect the alternative organization so that it can prepare to rebut or fight it);
- by referring users of a mainstream service to an alternative service (e.g., most persons applying for public assistance would benefit from membership within a welfare rights group);
- by encouraging the formation of such services or organizations where none exist.

Structural social workers must be careful not to romanticize alternative organizations. Anyone who has ever been associated with such an organization will know how difficult it is to work collectively and co-operatively and to share all decision-making when we, as North Americans, have been socialized into working and living in social institutions where hierarchy, specialization, and an overreliance on rules prevail. Withorn (1984) cautions us that old habits die hard, our expectations for alternative services are often too grand, and we may not always be clear on what an anti-capitalist, anti-racist, feminist practice is. In addition, Carniol (1987) warns those workers who have developed a critical awareness and are involved with alternative services against becoming arrogant and self-righteous and forgetting the importance of listening to and learning from the very groups we see as most oppressed. Most writers on the subject of alternative services point out the problem of funding these services because of a strong push towards co-optation by establishment funding agencies such as United Way and government departments.

Alternative services and organizations, then, clearly have some limitations. By themselves they will not bring about the transformation of the welfare state (contrary to revolutionary Marxist thought), but they do make an essential contribution to this goal. They embody the values, beliefs, principles, and practices of structural social work. They provide building blocks by which we learn workplace democracy. And they become prototypes of social service organizations of the future, providing us with positive and hopeful glimpses of what might be (Carniol, 1987: 130).

Social Movements, New Social Movement Theory, and Coalition-Building

As has been emphasized, one of the major goals of structural social work is to transform our present patriarchal, liberal-capitalist society to one based on a different set of values and social arrangements. However, by itself, social work cannot transform society; it can only contribute to its transformation. The previous chapter focused on ways and means that structural change can be carried out on a daily basis within the social welfare system generally and within our agencies particularly. On a more macro scale, social work can contribute to social transformation by forming coalitions and alliances with other groups and organizations also committed to changing the destructive social relationships and operating principles of our present society. Social work must become part of a social movement. Galper (1980: 114) warns us as structural social workers that if we do not strive 'to build a revolutionary social movement, we can rightly be accused of failing to take seriously our own analysis of the need for fundamental change.'

The concept of social movements has been variously defined as 'a wide variety of collective attempts to bring about change in certain social institutions or to create an entirely new order', as 'socially shared demands for change in some aspect of the social order' (Sills, 1968: 438, 445–6), and as 'an organized effort, usually involving many people representing a wide spectrum of the population, to change a law, public policy or social norm' (Barker, 1987: 153). From these definitions it is obvious that the goal of a social movement is to bring about some kind of social change. It is important, however, to distinguish between two different types of social change: social reform and structural change. The former refers to improving or altering existing laws, policies, and social conditions without changing the fundamental nature of society. The latter refers to fundamental changes in the very nature of the social, economic, and/or political order of society. The former is concerned with changes within the present social order and is usually associated with liberal social work based on the order view of society. The latter is concerned with changes of the present social order and is usually associated with social democratic or Marxist social work based on the conflict or change view of society. Obviously, given its goal of social transformation, structural social work is more concerned with movements of structural change than with social reform movements (though it does not ignore or necessarily refuse to work with reform groups). Many individuals and groups of individuals in society have gone through consciousness-raising processes similar to that of structural social workers and have concluded that social transformation of our present society is necessary.

An integral part of social movement work is to build coalitions (see Dluhy, 1990) with such groups and, together, to seek structural social change. The biggest obstacle to building coalitions is that many groups with potentially shared political interests will focus solely on their respective single issues. This tendency has some obvious problems, which Biklen (1983: 210–11) delineates in his discussion of self-help groups: (1) social issues are defined in a narrow parochial fashion; (2) single-issue groups often fail to make alliances with other groups whose interests they share because there is no awareness of the common causes of the oppression that each group experiences; (3) when single-issue groups focus on single issues they may even compete with each other for resources, attention, acceptance, and political dominance; and (4) even when a single-issue group effects change in a particular area it is not likely to bring about broad social change.

Wineman (1984: 159) contends that the biggest obstacle to coalition-building is the ability of the 'big business-government' alliance 'to create and sustain deep divisions among oppressed people'.This segmentation of oppression has historically been manifest in perceived conflicts of interest running along lines of class, gender, race, age, disability, sexual orientation, and so on. With this segmentation each group is prone to analyzing society along parochial lines wherein a single but different basic source of oppression is identified by each group. For example, conventional Marxist analysis places economic organization and class oppression as the fundamental societal problem; Black persons, Aboriginal people, and other people of colour may identify racism as the fundamental source of oppression; women's organizations may identify patriarchy as the fundamental source of oppression.

A major inherent weakness in traditional coalition-building and social movements was that they were organized mainly around class issues to challenge the excesses of capitalism. Thus, while the old social movements may have achieved power as the voice for disadvantaged workers, they also silenced the voices women, people of colour, minorities, and young people entering the workforce (Fisher and Kling, 1994). The global economy without national regulation and control has undermined the old-style social movements. New social movement theory has developed around five characteristics that differentiate new from old social movements (Fisher and Karger, 1997). First, they are organized around geography or communities of interest and much less often at the workplace. Second, they are organized around cultural identities, such as people of colour, gay, lesbian, and bisexual persons, students, peace activists, anti-globalists, and ecologists where labour becomes one constituency among many. Third, the predominant ideology is that of a neo-populist view of democracy that rejects hierarchy, communism, or nationalism. Fourth, the struggle over culture and social identity plays a greater role in community movements than it did in the work-based movements of the past. Fifth, new social movement strategies focus on empowerment and community autonomy, thus seeking independence from the state rather than state power.

Although new social movement theory gives social work more diversity by expanding the number of participants and the number of struggles being fought, it presents a significant challenge as well. How, in a postmodern context, do we continue to promote diversity and polyvocal discourse and, at the same time, find the commonalities needed to challenge global capitalist politics and culture? In other words, how do we combine a politics of difference with a politics of solidarity in practice? As Wineman (1984: 163) points out, the problem with each oppressed group identifying a single source of oppression is 'that it at once fails to create a basis for unity which respects the dignity and felt experience of all the oppressed . . . who are supposed to become unified, and it fails to generate a practical strategy . . . [to] challenge all forms of oppression.' Without unity a competition emerges among oppressed groups for resources and attention. And, as with any competition, there are winners and losers. Thus, social Darwinian principles of survival of the fittest dominate social change efforts, with a few oppressed groups making some gains while others fail to. In fact, the gains some oppressed groups may make are often at the expense of other oppressed groups. Meaningful social change is denied because nothing was done to change the basic nature and structures of society that caused the oppression in the first place.

The dominant group in society has become very proficient at using this situation to its advantage by playing one oppressed group against another and exacerbating tensions among them. For example, the dominant group will often categorize oppressed people in ways that cause tension and hostility among them: working vs non-working poor, the troubled single-parent family, the Aboriginal problem, the black ghetto, and so on. This 'divide and conquer' behaviour on the part of the dominant group effectively obscures the commonalities that underpin the situation of these and other oppressed groups.

Overcoming the imposed divisiveness among oppressed groups and other barriers to coalition-building requires several actions and strategies. One essential element of successful coalition-building is to create a 'mutual expression of solidarity' (Wineman, 1984: 182). This does not mean that one oppressed group must submerge its perceived interests in the name of unity. Rather, members of groups oppressed in one way will identify with members of groups who are oppressed in other ways, regardless of the severity (but not pretending that all oppressions are equally severe). This kind of mutual identification is necessary to overcome competing claims of who is more oppressed and to bring about the unity required for successful movement-building.

Mutual identification of one another's oppression, by itself, is insufficient to generate a strategy and process that effectively challenge all forms of oppression. Mutual identification may lead to various oppressed groups supporting each other in the struggles of each against the immediate source of their respective oppressions. For example, groups oppressed by classism may identify with the oppression experienced by groups oppressed by racism or sexism. But this identification with other oppressed groups may not go any further than sympathetic understanding unless it is recognized that all forms of oppression are related. 'Different oppressions intersect at innumerable points in everyday life and are mutually reinforcing, creating a total system of oppression in which one [category of oppression] . . . cannot be addressed in isolation from all the others' (Wineman, 1984: 169). It may be true that sexism is at the base of gender inequality and that racism is at the base of racial inequality and that classism is at the base of economic inequality, but it is also true that inequality is a value and an established practice in our present patriarchal, liberal-capitalist society. It makes no political sense for workers to demand economic equality but to ignore gender inequality as someone else's problem or for women to demand gender equality but ignore racial inequality. Although each oppressed group may fight oppression on its own front, the recognition that we live in a society that requires inequality for its very survival will cultivate coalitions among groups by providing them with a common goal—the transformation of our present society based on inequality to one based on true equality, not just equal opportunity.

A goal of social transformation necessitates a shared ideological position among various oppressed groups. This common base provides the cement for building and maintaining coalition structures. Without a common ideology there is no common cause, issues are viewed in a parochial fashion, and single-issue reform becomes the goal of each group. The net result is that if any change occurs it is only a minor change within the system and not a fundamental change of the system itself. System-tinkering is liberal-style social change.

Not unrelated to a goal of social transformation is a shared political analysis as a prerequisite for coalition-building. Whatever the original causes of various forms of oppression, the fact is that they have become culturally ingrained into our present society and have themselves become mutually reinforcing. Coalition-building for purposes of broad structural change becomes more crucial but more realistic when oppressed people understand that the same political and economic elite that pursues globalization as an economic goal and allows the devastation of our environment for profit is also responsible for the immoral and gross inequalities of living conditions between rich and poor; that the same political and economic elite that promotes imperialist policies abroad for economic gain is also responsible for policies at home that discriminate against the poor, women, people of colour, gay, lesbian, and bisexual persons, and so on; and that the same political and economic elite that promotes militarism for political and economic domination is also responsible for consumerism whereby people measure their own and others' worth and social standing in terms of what they own. This kind of awareness makes it imperative for structural social workers to join with the women's movement, the peace movement, the environmental movement, the human rights movement, and any other movement seeking a transformation of society in order to end oppression of any kind.

An important dynamic of oppression that should facilitate coalition-building is that 'no category of oppression, however distinct, creates an irreducible group which is only oppressed in one way' (Wineman, 1984: 167). Racism does affect people of colour, but people of colour include the working class, women, gays and lesbians, the young and old, and the disabled. In turn, classism affects the working class, but the working class consists of women, people of colour, gays and lesbians, the young and old, and the disabled. Most oppressed people are multiply oppressed both individually and in groups. This dynamic should help oppressed groups overcome any tendency towards single-constituency movements if there occurs within oppressed groups what Wineman (1984: 220) calls 'a flowering of internal caucuses based on sex, race, class, sexual orientation, age, disability, and various combinations of these characteristics'. An internal caucus is a recognition of the fact that people bring their particular identities of oppression with them into various struggles. A caucus of women within an anti-poverty group's struggle against economic exploitation becomes a link between women's organizations and poor people's organizations. An Aboriginal women's caucus within an anti-poverty group becomes a link between Aboriginal, women's, and anti-poverty organizations. These internal caucuses not only manifest overlapping oppressions among single-constituency organizations but become the points of contact between various oppressed organizations and spearhead common goals and joint actions (Wineman, 1984: 221). This notion of 'internal caucuses' is discussed further within the 'professional associations' section below.

Progressive Unionism

An effective practice of structural social work must include the trade union movement as a major vehicle for carrying out its social transformation mandate. Most people are aware that unions have struggled historically to improve working conditions and pay for union members. What is less well known is the fact that the trade union movement has been at the forefront in urging governments to introduce and improve social programs such as old age pensions, employment insurance, public health care, and daycare. During periods of cutbacks the trade union movement has led the resistance and opposition to the attacks on the welfare state (Carniol, 2005: 103; Corrigan and Leonard, 1978: 144). Unions provide social workers with opportunities for worker empowerment in the workplace, for better understanding of class issues, for contributing to the development of economic and social alternatives, and for participating in coalitions with other workers, consumer groups, and progressive social movements. To realize these potentialities, however, social workers must be familiar with the two opposing views of the nature and purpose of unionism that exist within and outside the trade union movement.

Jeffry Galper (1980: 157) uses the concepts 'class-conflict' and 'class-collaborationist' to differentiate radical and non-radical unionism. The former, based on workers' awareness that they constitute a distinct class in society, views the role of unions as protecting and advancing the interests of the 'total' working class, and to do so necessitates the eventual abolition of capitalism. The latter, based on a lack of workers' awareness that they constitute a distinct class in society, views the role of unions as protecting and advancing the interests of the union membership only by fighting for a larger share of the wealth that workers produce within the context of capitalism. The trade union movement in Sweden typifies (although not exactly) the class-conflict view of unions, and unions in the United States represent the closest case of a pure class-collaborationist viewpoint. Great Britain and Canada fall in between these two types, with Britain closer to the class-conflict view. Canada, because of its proximity to the United States and because many unions in Canada were once (and some still are) controlled by American unions, is closer to the class-collaborationist view than most trade union movements in other countries (Heron, 1996).

Obviously, if unions are to become an effective vehicle for promoting the welfare state and for socialist transformation, they must adopt a class-conflict view. A class-collaborationist view is based on the conservative-liberal belief that there is a harmony of interests between capital and labour. American unions often opposed social welfare schemes such as social insurance because they were seen as a rival to the protection unions had secured for their members through bargaining (Fraser, 1979). As a result, they obtained an extensive but inequitable occupational welfare system instead of an adequate public welfare system that would cover more people (Mishra, 1981). Piven and Cloward (1977) argue that the American trade union movement has not been a force for social welfare concessions in the post-war era. And, in view of the fact that the proportion of the US labour force that is unionized has been declining for the past several decades, it is unlikely that the trade union movement in that country will be a significant political force in the near future.

A class-conflict view is based on the belief that there is an inherent conflict of interests between capital and labour. Whatever one group gets is at the expense of the other group (i.e., profits vs wages). This view also recognizes that the welfare state in capitalist societies has benefited the working class, but it has benefited the capitalists even more by subsidizing certain costs of production, such as maintaining an educated and healthy workforce and guaranteeing a certain level of consumption of goods and services purchased with social welfare benefits. As long as capitalism exists there will never be a true welfare state based on the principle of distribution according to need.

The progressive class-conflict concept of unionism has much in common with structural social work. Both reject capitalism as a social and economic system and seek to replace it with a social order where human need is the central organizing principle. Both reject narrow, self-interested individualism in favour of collective association, rights, and responsibilities. Both reject elitist, hierarchical decision-making and advocate active participation in and control over all aspects of one's living and working conditions. And both reject exploitation and oppression based on such grounds as class, gender, and race, with the progressive union movement focusing on its elimination specifically in the workplace.

Another major reason for structural social workers to become involved with the trade union movement is, as noted above, that the growth of the welfare state is, in part, a product of the union movement (Carniol, 2005; Flora and Heidenheimer, 1981; Fraser, 1979; Furniss and Tilton, 1977; Mishra, 1981; Wilensky, 1975). International comparisons show that those countries with extensive and well-organized labour movements, such as Austria, Germany, and the Scandinavian countries, tend to have extensive and well-developed welfare states. And, conversely, those countries without a high percentage of the workforce unionized tend to have primitive welfare states. For example, the United States, which has the lowest rate of organized workers in the Western industrialized world (less than 20 per cent), also has the least developed welfare state.

Mishra (1981: 113) outlines four ways in which organized labour has contributed to the development of the welfare state. First, the growth of labour movements is often perceived by the ruling classes as a threat to capitalism, and to reduce this threat the ruling classes have often conceded social programs to the working class. Bismarck's social legislation in Germany in the latter part of the nineteenth century is a good example. Second, ruling classes and liberal and conservative governments have often implemented social welfare programs being promoted by socialist parties and that were very popular with the working class. An example would be Canada's public health-care program, which was originally a socialist party idea but was legislated by bourgeois governments to dampen the rising popularity of the socialist (CCF/NDP) party. Third, labour movements have themselves demanded social legislation as a means of improving the life situation of working-class people. And fourth, social democratic governments, as in Sweden and Great Britain, have aligned themselves with labour movements as a means of transforming capitalist societies to socialism.

In addition to its contributions to the development of the welfare state, unionism holds many benefits for social workers. Several writers have commented on these benefits (see Carniol, 2005, for some examples). Galper (1980) views unions as fertile ground for radical social work. Besides being necessary for the protection of workers' jobs, wages, and benefits, unions are an important source of political education and growth because they help us understand that conflict is real in our society despite our having been socialized into an anti-conflict ethic. Unions can provide the experience of collective work, organizing, and engaging in political analysis. Union negotiating allows workers to have a say about service provisions and delivery, such as caseload sizes, and to have input into policy formulation and decisions. Galper also believes that unionism provides a counterbalance to the elitist, exclusionary, and self-serving tendencies that characterize the 'ideology of professionalism'. Withorn (1984) shares this belief.

Carniol (2005) suggests that active union membership has potential for social workers to empower themselves in the workplace by working towards greater industrial democracy, by linking broader issues such as employment equity, better pension legislation, and daycare to the more traditional 'bread and butter' issues, and by forming important links with other workers and other social movements. Corrigan and Leonard (1978) believe that the union movement is the only powerful force defending the welfare state against cuts and that social workers must use the union to defend both themselves and the interests of service users. Wineman (1984) thinks that unions enhance worker control, sensitize social workers to issues of class, contribute to the growth of economic and social alternatives, and facilitate social worker participation in coalitions.

Wagner and Cohen (1978) believe that unionization symbolically draws a line between social workers and their employing agency, and helps to crystallize the fact that the workplace is an arena of conflict, with administrators and workers often having different interests. They argue that social service settings raise political questions more readily than industrial settings in that social workers daily observe the lives of victims of capitalism and the failure of reformist solutions. To challenge the system, social workers can provide important leadership to the rest of the working class, as they have done in Latin America and in parts of Europe.

Although it is imperative that structural social workers recognize the strength of the union movement as the most economically well-organized working-class organization with potential for taking on capitalism, the weaknesses and limitations of the current union movement must also be understood. Corrigan and Leonard (1978) note that the major limitation of the union movement is its apparent lack of political consciousness and activity. They point out that, historically, trade unions were created to advance and defend the interests of the working class within capitalism and that we should not be surprised to find that many workers do not have an inherent belief in revolutionary change. Panitch and Swartz argue that the trade union movement in Canada has been co-opted—unions have become large bureaucracies preoccupied with technocratic proce-dures at the expense of mass mobilization, and consequently fail to see the state as a constituent part of capitalist domination (Carniol, 2005; Panitch and Swartz, 1988). Nor are workers free from the racism, sexism, and conservatism that are part of the larger societal consciousness. Feminists have criticized unions for being dominated by white males who are often homophobic, for being focused on product rather than process, and for ignoring the needs of women, people of colour, and other sexual/cultural/ethnic iden-tities (Carniol, 2005). To realize the revolutionary potential of the union movement, union members must understand how social transformation is in their best interests and how it has a direct material importance. Galper (1980) also addresses this issue by suggesting that the union movement has to move away from a class-collaborationist mentality to one of class conflict if its revolutionary potential is to be tapped. Without a class-conflict mentality, unions simply become one more socially reproducing bureaucracy with which to contend.

Professional Associations

Unlike unions, professional associations, as a form of organization, are not the products of an inherent conflict among particular groups in society. They are, in fact, created by society to carry out particular functions for society and not to oppose society. Given the fact that professional associations are part of the current social structure, the critical ques-tion for structural social workers is: Can professional associations of social workers be used as another means of social transformation?

Mullaly and Keating (1991) have summarized the main radical social work criticisms of professionalism. First, professionalism emphasizes technical aspects of helping, such as impartiality, emotional neutrality, and apolitical service. Thus, it masks the political component of social work practice and perpetuates the notion that capitalist social relations are natural and normal functions of an industrialized society. As well, professionalism promotes technical solutions to problems, implying that these problems are individual rather than larger social and political problems.

Second, by organizing into an exclusive group based on academic credentials, professionalism divides social workers from other workers and from persons who use social work services. By requesting certification from the state, professional social workers implicitly align themselves with the state. In exchange for state recognition, social workers are required to deliver services that contain elements of oppression and control. In effect, professionalism blinds social workers to issues of class, particularly their own class position and class function.

Third, by organizing themselves into social and occupational hierarchies professional social workers are practising inequality. By treating social problems as individual misfortunes, they promote individualism. And by accepting an ethic of 'service to others' they disempower those they would serve. The messages conveyed are that intervention should focus on people and not on social structures, and that the best source of helping rests with the 'expert' social worker and not within the service user.

Finally, the history of professionalism, such as in law and medicine, indicates that such hierarchical organizations benefit the professionals, not the service users. Despite its 'service to others' ethic, professionalism becomes self-serving as professionals tend to seek personal, social, economic, and political power for themselves.

The above criticisms of professionalism have led many radical social work writers (Carniol, 2005; Galper, 1980; Hardy, 1981; Laursen, 1975; Wagner and Cohen, 1978; Wilding, 1982; Withorn, 1984) to reject professionalism and/or to opt for unions as the most appropriate form and means for social workers to organize to pursue social transformation. However, not all radical writers and certainly not all social workers believe that there is necessarily an incompatibility between unionism and professionalism as means of engaging in collective forms of organization. Three separate studies, one Canadian (Lightman, 1982) and two American (Alexander et al., 1980; Shaffer, 1979), found that the majority of social workers do not believe that unionism and professionalism are incompatible. A more recent study (Reeser and Epstein, 1990) looked at the correlations between professionalization and activism among rank-and-file social workers in 1968 and 1984. It found, contrary to the speculation of radical critics of professionalism, that professionalization is not associated with a neutralist political ideology and that participation in political activities was associated with greater institutionalized activism. The study also suggested that differences in activism among social workers is likely to be a product of factors independent of professionalization, such as different recruitment patterns, different background characteristics, and so on.

The position taken here is that structural social workers should join professional associations for the same reason they should join unions—to engage in collective action with the purpose of social transformation. Given the present class-collaborationist nature of most unions in North America and the evidence cited above, which suggests that professionalism by itself does not deter social activism, it is a false dichotomy to present unionism as the radical form of social work organization and professionalism as the conservative form. Most social workers will belong to both a union and a professional association. Just as structural social workers work within the social welfare institution to radicalize it and to use it as a means of social transformation, so, too, should they join professional associations for the very same purposes. To argue that 'working within' only applies to one institution in our society and not to others is contradictory and illogical. Moreau and Leonard (1989) argue that to refuse to join professional associations means to abandon its membership to the right wing.

One of the criticisms of professionalism is that it tends to be self-serving in that narrow interests to increase the well-being of its members are pursued. Leslie Bella (1989) has outlined some actions of the Canadian Association of Social Workers (CASW) that did not seek direct benefits to its members but instead were carried out for the broader purposes of public welfare. The CASW has fought for progressive tax reform to bring more equity and justice to the present system in Canada. It has also defended social programs and it sought changes to such legislation as the (now defunct) Canada Assistance Plan[1] that would bring more fairness and integrity to Canada's welfare state. The CASW also campaigned against free trade with the United States and has become an active member of the peace movement. It opposed Reagan's 'Star Wars' defence plan, advocated compensation for victims of the internment of Japanese Canadians during World War II, lobbied for sanctions against South Africa during its apartheid era, and has made presentations to several commissions, committees, and task forces. More recently the CASW has frequently spoken out on social and political issues. It distributed a 'political kit' to inform its members of the positions of the various political parties running for office in the January 2006 election with respect to social work and social welfare matters. One may quarrel with the success or effectiveness of these actions and whether or not they are radical or only reformist, but the CASW cannot be accused of being purely elitist and self-serving.

To prevent professional associations from falling victim to the conservative forces of professionalization and becoming supporters of the status quo, some guidelines should be considered. Wilding (1982), for example, has expressed concern about the lack of mechanisms for consumer groups to comment on those aspects of professionalism that ultimately impact on the users of social work services. Just as front-line social workers should be able to participate in formulating social policy, so should service users have some input into professional associations. Lay representation on the boards of professional associations and the establishment of liaison committees are a couple of possibilities.

Social work ought to develop internal caucuses within its own professional associations (and unions). There are members of all subordinate groups within social work. A caucus of those with alternative sexual orientations could be established within each branch of the professional association and/or union branch, as could caucuses of social workers with disabilities, social workers of colour, unemployed social workers, older social workers, social work students, resource-poor (presently or in the past) social workers, female social workers, those of non-English speaking backgrounds, and so on.

BOX 12.1 TWELVE-STEP RECOVERY PROGRAM FOR PROFESSIONALS

My name is _____ and I am a recovering professional.
                (fill in name)

1. I admit to believing that I had no useful skills or knowledge—unlesss I called myself a 'professional'.
2. I came to believe that professionalism was not a way to distance myself from my clients.
3. I came to believe that as a 'professional', I could fix people and solve their problems.
4. I admit to calling myself a 'professional' in an attempt to cover up my insecurities and self-doubt.
5. I came to believe that the the professional relationship is not hierarchical. Just because I am the expert doesn't mean that we are not equals—right?
6. I came to believe that aspiring to a 'professional image' by wearing dress clothes, carrying a briefcase, distributing business cards, and driving a car of recent vintage did not separate me from the resource-poor people with whom I work.
7. I admit to signing my name and adding my professional credentials to everything I write.
8. I admit to using my voice-mail to screen out certain difficult people.
9. I admit to sending a memo (with my name and credentials) to people rather than bothering to talk to them.
10. I admit to saying, 'Call me and we'll do lunch.'
11. I admit to using professional jargon, acronyms, and my prolific propensity for vocabulary to impress, overpower, and distance people.
12. I admit to embracing professionalism without taking into account its effects on my stated beliefs in social justice, egalitarianism, and other social work values and ideals.

These internal caucuses serve two purposes: (1) to keep the larger membership sensitive to and informed about issues of oppression from their own colleagues; and (2) to communicate and interact with various outside organizations and groups of subordinate persons, which effectively ensures that social work is linked to the network of oppressed groups. With respect to the latter, the women's caucus of a professional social work association could establish communication links with women's groups in the community, for example, and the visible minority caucus could interact with visible minority groups in the community. In this way, the likelihood of social work becoming ethnocentric is reduced and, conversely, it is more likely to develop a more meaningful anti-sexist, anti-racist, and anti-homophobic social work practice.

A progressive professional association should also have liaison committees as linkages to other social movement groups that seek the transformation of society—the peace movement, the environmental movement, the human rights movement. One other necessary committee, if a professional association is to avoid becoming a self-serving, status quo organization, is an active social action committee led by members who have a structural (as opposed to a reformist) outlook. This committee must be supported by the membership and the executive in carrying out analyses of social programs, policies, legislation, government actions, and corporate interests. In sum, the various caucuses and the social action committee can preserve the social conscience of social work in the face of its professionalization.

Electoral Politics

Little social work literature addresses electoral politics as an arena for struggle for social workers. A great deal has been written on advocacy and on lobbying and influencing governments, but almost nothing exists on supporting a particular political party as a way of dealing with social problems, let alone as a way of transforming our current neo-conservative/liberal society.

The reasons for this lack of attention to electoral politics are partly historical and partly methodological. Historically, social work has perceived involvement in party politics as unprofessional. To become involved in politics was to meddle in the preserve of the politicians. Not only is conventional social work emotionally neutral, it is also politically neutral. Involvement in party politics was considered to be a personal choice, certainly not a professional choice. Methodologically, conventional models of social work practice, such as systems theory and the ecological approach, preclude electoral political activity. One might assess the negative impact of government policy on people, but the social worker is limited to helping people adapt to the policy or to lobby government to ameliorate the policy. In view of the fact that governments ultimately decide on the nature, shape, size, and quality of social programs, it hardly makes sense for social work not to involve itself in attempting to get the political party most sympathetic to a progressive welfare state elected. If political decisions determine the fate of the welfare state and the nature of our social relationships, social work must involve itself in the political arena.

BOX 12.2 ALL SOCIAL WORK IS POLITICAL—THERE IS NO ESCAPE

I remember a number of years ago attending a meeting of the Canadian Association of Deans and Directors of Schools of Social Work. This group met (and continues to meet) on a semi-annual basis to discuss common interests and concerns with respect to social work education in Canada. At this particular meeting someone raised a concern about a proposed piece of federal legislation that, if passed, would result in further cutbacks to welfare programs. Discussion ensued and a motion was made to send a letter from the Deans and Directors to the Canadian government protesting the legislation. One Dean who was new to the group and to Canada, as he had just recently arrived from the United States to take up his position, said that he did not think that the group should do anything of a political nature because that was not our job. Well, you could have heard a pin drop as others in the room looked at each other in disbelief. After a relatively long and uncomfortable silence, the newly arrived Dean said, 'I seem to have said something wrong.'

This is not necessarily a Canadian–American difference as, unfortunately, I have heard many, many social workers in Canada adopt this same position, arguing that social work is about people and should not be about politics. Such a position indicates a lack of awareness that social work, by its very nature, is and must be a highly political activity. That is, if I decide to do nothing to challenge the current situation, in effect, I am supporting it because there is no resistance or protest coming from me. And *this is a political choice*. My intention may not be political, but the outcome or result of my decision to do nothing is political. I have, unwittingly perhaps, actually supported the status quo by not challenging, protesting, resisting, or trying to change it. *There is no neutral political ground in social work*. I would much rather adopt the political position of trying to change the current system of dominant–subordinate relations than support it by claiming that social work is above politics and doing nothing.

In political democracies, political parties constitute an important means by which social classes or social groups organize to pursue their collective interests (Wolfe, 1989). In other countries, such as the Scandinavian nations, the working classes have been able to offset the greater power resources of capital by electing social democratic governments. These governments, in turn, have implemented policies favourable to the working class, such as full employment and the pursuit of a welfare state that promotes an equality of the highest standards (Esping-Andersen, 1989). Conversely, those countries that have elected mostly liberal or conservative governments, such as the United States and Canada, have developed political economies favouring the interests of capital over the working class, as evidenced by policies that accept high unemployment and a residual welfare state. Clearly, then, social work cannot remain at arm's length from electoral politics. Social work is not politically neutral; it is a political act or practice. If it does nothing politically, it has removed itself as a force for change, which in effect supports the status quo. Given the inherent political nature of social work, it must organize and declare its political hand.

It must align itself with other groups and organizations that share similar goals. This includes supporting political parties committed to social, political, and economic justice for all and not just for a privileged minority.

American social workers committed to social transformation do not have a national socialist party to work with. In fact, the majority of Americans do not have the background and experience to allow them to discuss the nature of capitalism and socialism objectively and critically. Many people espouse an uncritical and unexamined commitment to the 'free enterprise system' and to the 'American way' (Galper, 1980: 90). In the absence of a national socialist or radical party, Wineman (1984: 224) advocates radical activity at the local level as a means of building a 'bottom-up approach to constructing a national radical presence in electoral politics'. Such activity not only pushes mainstream politicians to the left as they scramble for the votes of women, minorities, the poor, and so on; it also helps to mobilize and consolidate multi-constituency and multi-issue coalitions as 'they begin to create a foundation for the eventual emergence of a national third party' (Wineman, 1984: 225).

In Canada there is a social democratic national party, the New Democratic Party. However, it is seldom mentioned in most Canadian social work and social welfare text books,[2] even in those books with a leftist perspective.[3] In Shankar Yelaja's widely used Canadian social policy text there is passing reference to the NDP being 'the unequivocal advocate of social welfare ideals' (Yelaja, 1987: 17) among Canada's political parties, but the potential relationship between social work and the NDP is not explored. Only Andrew Armitage pays tribute to the contributions made to the Canadian welfare state by the NDP and its predecessor, the Co-operative Commonwealth Federation.

> The New Democratic Party has been the most consistent advocate of social welfare in the Canadian political spectrum. The party's political statements, more clearly than those of other parties, have committed it to the welfare ideal of the redistribution of income, wealth, and power. When elected to office (in British Columbia, Saskatchewan, Yukon, Manitoba, and Ontario), New Democratic governments have shown a willingness to introduce social welfare programs not legislated anywhere else in Canada or, indeed, in North America. . . . Long before Liberal or Progressive Conservative governments have introduced social welfare legislation, members of Parliament from the New Democratic Party and its predecessor, the Co-operative Commonwealth Federation, have brought the need of Canadians for such programs as pensions, medicare, housing, and income guarantees before the House of Commons. (Armitage, 1996: 141–2)

However, NDP governments have also been criticized for behaving more like bourgeois (conservative and liberal) governments once elected to office (in British Columbia, Saskatchewan, and Ontario at least) in that although there were small improvements with respect to the living conditions for the poor, the NDP governments failed to make good on their promises to challenge inequality and poverty and seemed to capitulate to the 'corporate agenda' (Armitage, 2003; Ralph, 1993).

During the twentieth century, very few major policy differences existed between Canada's two major national political parties, the Liberals and the Progressive Conservatives.[4] Both parties were located near the centre of the political spectrum, with the Conservatives leaning more to the right. The Progressive Conservative Party had a tendency to disavow the progressive rhetoric of some of it leaders (Armitage, 1988: 93), and the Mulroney Conservative government systematically retrenched the Canadian welfare state during its term in power (1984–93) through a policy of gradualism (Mishra, 1990). It remains to be seen what the newly elected (23 January 2006) Conservative minority government under Stephen Harper will do to Canada's social programs, although the recent dumping of 'Progressive' from its official name should be some indication. Most of Canada's social programs have been legislated under Liberal governments, yet the motivation has often been to undermine the popularity of the NDP, to avert labour unrest, or, in the event of a minority government (such as that in 2004), to agree to NDP demands for social reform and/or improved social programs to avoid being unseated as government. There have been periods of neglect and disinterest on the part of Liberal governments, and on occasion Liberal spokespersons have appealed to the alienating aspects of welfare transfers in their quest for political support (Armitage, 1988: 92). Both the Liberal and (Progressive) Conservative parties accept the free market as the preferred socio-economic system, and both have a history of being more responsive to the needs of capital than to the needs of subordinate groups. This is the major reason for the persistence of residualism with respect to Canada's welfare state.

Given the history, ideology, and approaches of Canada's political parties to the welfare state, it makes no sense for structural social workers to support either the Liberals or the Conservatives. To do so would be the same as supporting an arsonist's bid to become fire chief. Social work is not above politics—it is a political activity. If it does not have a progressive agenda then it will automatically become part of the conservative forces in society. The warped professional notion of political neutrality must be rejected and replaced with the knowledge that electoral politics is a major arena where the struggle for social justice and social transformation occurs.

A Revitalized Public Sector

The above call for involvement in electoral politics was one of the strategies of the old social movements—to win state power and to use that power to transform society. However, postmodernists and others have expressed a legitimate concern with any proposal that the state provide the leadership, structure, and resources to meet the common (and culturally relevant) needs of people. After all, the modern nation-state was originally established as the collective expression of ideals of universal reason and order and resulted in structures of domination, control, exclusion, homogenization, and discipline (Leonard, 1997). In spite of these criticisms, more and more writers (e.g., Fisher and Karger, 1997; Fisher and Kling, 1994; Leonard, 1997; Mullaly, 2001, 2002) have argued that at some point we must turn our attention to the state and attempt to relegitimize it.

Contrary to neo-conservative dogma, the demands of a global economy require more rather than less government involvement in human, social, and economic affairs. The resources, structure, and legislation needed to ensure that people's common needs are met can only be provided, at this point in our history, by the state. Neither the market nor the voluntary sector can guarantee rights—only the state, with its ability to formulate and implement legislation, is in a position to do so. Despite its relative weakening in the face of globalization, no other institution has the capacity or the resources to rebuild our neglected social and public infrastructure. The promised benefits of a global economy have not been delivered. 'Without a legitimate public sector there are no public citizens, only private consumers' (Fisher and Karger, 1997: 177). Government policies of privatization have undermined government legitimacy and responsibility, which has resulted in fewer public servives and a loss of access to a potentially accountable and responsible public sector. Fisher and Kling (1997) point to the cynicism citizens now have for the political system, but contend that beneath voter cynicism is a genuine desire for the state to assume moral leadership that transcends elite self-interest. They believe that the answer to relegitimizing the public sector lies:

> Not in stitching inequality and oppression back together again . . . but in discovering and addressing what causes the social fabric to fray and what promotes social change—never a simple project. However, it is more feasible in a society where public life is rich, where public discourse regarding social problems is expansive and open to diverse opinions, and where society is committed to the improvement of conditions for all its members, not just the rich and powerful. (Fisher and Karger, 1997: 178–9)

Contradictions of globalization continue to grow (e.g., increasing disparities of wealth) at the same time it appears to be collapsing. In Canada, at least, the national deficit has been eliminated, the debt is being paid down, and we are now experiencing record government surpluses, which could be used to revitalize the public sector. In Canada, and elsewhere, pressure is increasing to explore new forms of politics as the existing ones become discredited (Leonard, 1997). Although there is no guarantee that the current critical situation will lead to a formation of political parties committed to solidarity in defence of diversity, social justice, and equality, Peter Leonard (1997: 178) reminds us that the future is determined by acts of human will. '[H]uman subjects act, "but not in circumstances of their own choosing".' It is worth noting that the current world situation came about by the actions of the corporate elite, not because of some law of economic determinism or principle of social evolution. What was made by a small elite group of people can be unmade and remade.

CHALLENGING AND RESISTING THE DOMINANT ORDER

The dominant discourse today is that the existing social, economic, and political order is both rational and inevitable (Agger, 1991). We are taught to accept the world as it is, and, thus, we unthinkingly reinforce and reproduce it, but we can challenge this discourse of economic determinism. Marx argued that we enter a social world not of our own making, but we are able to act upon it provided we understand how it is made, and in doing so we can develop a revolutionary 'praxis' to free ourselves, at least to some degree, from the hegemony of ruling discourses. Foucault, in his later writings, argued that power is never exercised without resistance, insubordinancy, and obstinacy. How, then, can structural social work challenge and resist the current order? This is one of the key questions that I have attempted to answer throughout this book.

Resistance and challenge can occur at all levels of social work activity. At the political or societal level Leonard (1997) argues that there is a need to develop a fully articulated alternative discourse, one that provides a powerful critique of the' globalization thesis' and the current ruling discourse that says no one has control over the determining effects of global market forces because they are the products of impersonal economic relations, new technologies, and new means of communication. Writers such as John Ralston Saul (2004, 2005) and Manfred Steger (2002, 2003) have developed powerful critiques of the globalization thesis and exposed it for what it is—an ideological social construction rather than some economic law of inevitability. Based on such critiques, the counter-discourse to the globalization thesis is that economies are the results of acts of will, and the will of capitalists has become increasingly dominant since the mid-1970s. Reisch (1995) argues that we need to become 'responsible extremists' (such as Saul and Steger) by vilifying those who espouse the dominant discourse, not by engaging in character assassination but through the targeted use of facts to counter their use of the dominant discourse.

An example of a counter-discourse that has challenged and significantly altered the dominant discourse of patriarchy is feminism. Although more than a discourse, feminism is regarded as an alternative discourse that resists and challenges the hegemony of male domination. Similarly, the dominant discourse of white supremacy has been challenged by black nationalists, black liberation philosophers and theologians, black academics, and anti-racist social workers. The dominant discourse of heterosexuality has been confronted by the discourse of the gay and lesbian movement. O'Donnell (2000) gives a wonderful example of a counter-discourse to welfare dependency and its gendered nature (Box 12.3).

BOX 12.3 WHO ARE THE REAL 'FREELOADERS'?

A dominant discourse about welfare dependency is perpetrated and perpetuated mainly by white, bourgeois males who enjoy economic and political power. Its essence is that people in receipt of welfare, mainly lone-parent females, are freeloaders on society and that we have to do something about this kind of welfare dependency. O'Donnell points out, however, that many working men are unable to cook, wash or iron clothes, or generally carry out household chores and are dependent on women to carry out these tasks. And, O'Donnell suggests, if we are truly concerned about scroungers, perhaps it is this group of freeloaders to whom we should be directing our attention and attempt to break their dependency on 'the system of a gendered division of labour'. He goes on to make his real point that 'interdependency' is an inescapable fact of the human condition and that how we organize this interdependency requires more discussion. For starters, we can, as Leonard (1997) suggests, replace the dominant discourse of welfare (and other dependencies) with a discourse of 'interdependency'.

At the agency and individual worker levels we need to practise acts of individual and collective resistance. It has already been mentioned that several university social work programs in Canada, Australia, and the US base their curriculum on critical or progressive social work frameworks that include resistance. Faculty and students discuss how the contradictions that are part of all agencies—contradictions between their social care and social control functions—provide the opportunities for acts of resistance and challenge. Tiny efforts are sought that help us connect our everyday concerns and struggles to larger strategies and visions for social justice and social change (Baines, 1997). Studies on the experiences of many graduates from progressive social work programs in Canada show that practices and strategies of resistance (e.g., defence of the client practices, increasing the client's power in the worker–client relationship, materialization and collectivization practices) are very useful in challenging the dominant discourse that blames individuals for all their problems (LeComte, 1990; Moreau and Leonard, 1989; Moreau et al., 1993). Foucault's (1988) work on the mutual interplay of power and resistance opens up unlimited opportunities for acts and strategies to undermine discursive practices of domination. This is evidenced by Ken Moffatt's study of the micro-mechanisms of power in a social assistance office and the strategies developed by workers to oppose the controlling technologies of 'surveillance and government of the welfare recipient' (Moffatt, 1999: 219).

THE MORAL PREMISE OF SOCIAL WELFARE: UNIVERSAL HUMAN NEEDS

The attempt to define and meet human needs in the past sometimes led to domination whereby the dominant group was able to exercise its control over ideas and convince people to perceive their needs in ways that were compatible with the interests of the dominant or ruling group (Gil, 1998). As well, postmodernists have criticized notions of common needs and needs identification, given the role that mass culture plays in manufacturing desire, which is often translated into needs. They view needs as individually determined, culturally specific, and highly interpretive.

Acknowledging these criticisms of any identification of a universal set of human needs, Doyal and Gough (1991) assert that a notion of objective human need is still morally necessary and that meeting such need must take precedence over the satisfaction of wants or desires. If we lack any notion of objective human need as the basis of solidarity for political struggle for justice and equality in the distribution of welfare, Doyal and Gough contend that we are left with the neo-conservative belief that there is only one universal need, the need for the market.

Producing an impressive amount of cross-cultural indicators and measures, Doyal and Gough suggest that it is possible to identify universal, transcultural human needs. Every human being has two basic needs: the need for physical health and the need for autonomy. These are the preconditions for any individual action or interaction in any culture. When physical health and autonomy are identified as needs required for individuals to act as autonomous agents, we are provided with a sound basis for social policy and for moral judgements on our own and other societies (Doyal and Gough, 1991, cited in Leonard, 1997). We are also provided with a moral premise for progressive social welfare. The need for (and public right to) physical health requires adequate health care, nutrition, housing, non-hazardous work and physical environments, economic and physical security, basic education, and safe birth control and child-bearing. The need for (and public right to) personal autonomy consists of freedom of agency and political freedom, including self-development, mental health (e.g., a sense of self-worth), and personal opportunity (Fisher and Karger, 1997). The optimal satisfaction of health and autonomy is a fundamental right of all individuals. To pretend otherwise is morally incoherent and politically disabling.

Table 12.1 summarizes ways in which the progressive social worker can and should become involved in the larger society beyond the immediate workplace, as discussed above. Although we can lay substantial groundwork for fundamental social change in our workplaces and in our work with individuals, groups, communities, and so on, only by reaching out into the wider world can we hope to effect real change. In this regard, a slogan from the environmental movement—think globally, act locally—is a useful place to begin.

WORKING WITHIN OURSELVES

Critical Self-Reflection

Originating with Argyris and Schon (1976), critical self-reflection is referred to in the literature by various terms: self-reflexive practice, critical reflection, self-reflexivity, and critically reflective practice. In essence, structural social workers integrate theory and practice through a process of 'reflection in action', questioning their knowledge claims in an ongoing way (Allan, 2003a). Fook (1999: 199) contends that critical self-reflective practice involves 'the ability to locate oneself in a situation through the recognition of how actions and interpretations, social and cultural background and personal history, emotional aspects of experience, and personally held assumptions and values influence

TABLE 12.1 OVERVIEW OF ELEMENTS FOR WORKING OUTSIDE AND AGAINST THE SYSTEM

Locations/Factors in Working Outside and Against the System	Selected Characteristics of Practice
Alternative services and organizations	Create, develop, and/or support alternative organizations founded on different principles from those of mainstream agencies. Provide prototypes of future democratic workplaces.
Coalitions, social movements, and new social movement theory	Create, develop, and join coalitions and social movements. At the global level, support and develop transnational organizations such as Greenpeace and Amnesty International.
Progressive unions	Adopt a class-conflict union perspective and approach to social justice issues. Use the union to promote and negotiate such workplace conditions as caseload sizes, more worker participation in developing agency policies and practice, etc.
Professional associations	Avoid the traditional trappings of professionalization, such as elitism, conservatism, and self-serving. Politicize the association from within. Encourage the association to join coalitions and social movements.
Electoral politics	Support progressive political parties (not bourgeois parties such as the Canadian Liberal and Conservative parties) by providing them with your vote, money, and inside work. Provide information to progressive parties that they can use for political purposes and to improve their social welfare policies.

(continued)

TABLE 12.1 (CONTINUED)

Locations/Factors in Working Outside and Against the System	Selected Characteristics of Practice
The public sector	Challenge such fatalistic ideas as that today's situation is evolutionary, inevitable, and irreversible. What was made by an elite few can be unmade and remade.
	Expose 'Third Way' politics as an excuse for individualism and blaming victims.
	Develop counter-discourse of why we need government.
The dominant social order	Develop counter-discourses to victim-blaming, free-market glorification, welfare dependency, etc. (e.g., wouldn't the rich feel better about themselves if they had to work for their money?).
	Become more aware of the micro-mechanisms of power that can be used to minimize the harm, surveillance, and degradation that many service users feel because of agency policies and practice.
Human need	Although needs are largely individually determined, culturally relevant, and highly interpretive, everyone has the need for (and right to) physical health and personal autonomy.

the situation'. Its use prevents us from taking things for granted and encourages us to reanalyze situations in ways that provide for new actions and changes in power relations. As a way of knowing, critical reflection allows marginalized aspects of experience, such as emotions and personal histories, to be valued. As a process, it focuses attention on on the social worker's influence on situations and how this might affect power relations or how it might perpetuate existing structures and beliefs.

Critical self-reflection is an element of the tradition of critical social theory, which Leonard (1997) argues provides a link to postmodern critique. Because we all internalize in varying degrees parts of the dominant ideology, it is important to develop reflexive knowledge of the dominant ideology to see how it constrains us and limits our freedom. Reflexive knowledge, which is derived through critical reflection, is knowledge about ourselves. It helps us understand how our identities are largely determined by the dominant ideology. It tells us where we are within the social order in terms of our positions of domination and subordination, and how we may exercise power in our professional and personal lives to either reproduce or resist social features that limit the freedoms or agency of others. Reflexive knowledge is also knowledge about the source and substance of our social beliefs, attitudes, and values. This kind of knowledge has the potential of helping us to free ourselves from self-imposed constraints that are derived from the massive power of the dominant ideology. Schon (1983) has developed a social work practice whereby the social worker carries out a reflective conversation with the situation. This technique can be used to identify oppressive features of the dominant ideology that may be in our minds and our social work practice. Critical self-reflection is a form of internal criticism, an ongoing questioning of our social, economic, political, and cultural beliefs, assumptions, and actions. It is also a political practice (Leonard, 1997) that allows for greater sensitivity to issues relating to power, oppression, and injustice and avoids dogma, orthodoxy, and stereotypes (Thompson, 1998).

David Gil (1998) provides a checklist of areas for critical self-reflection:

- the images of social reality that we presently hold;
- the ideas, beliefs, and assumptions we now take for granted about people, society, and the relationship between the two;
- the perceptions we hold of individual and collective needs and wants that underpin the actions, thoughts, and social relations of most people;
- our values and ideologies, which derive from our perceptions of needs and interests, and affect our choices, actions, thoughts, and social relations.

Anne Bishop (2002) discusses the importance of anyone who wishes to become an ally of oppressed groups to reflect critically on his or her own experiences as both a member of an oppressed group and as a member of an oppressor group. She argues that learning about one's oppression is much different and less difficult than learning about oneself as an oppressor, because the process of becoming an oppressor is hidden from the person. This is so because the oppressor role is equated with normalcy, universal standards and values, and political and cultural neutrality. Nothing adverse is perpetrated on the person to make him or her aware of the role of oppressor. Understanding one's position as an oppressor requires an understanding that one is a member of a particular social group and not just an individual member of society. Structural social workers will engage in ongoing critical self-reflection of their roles as oppressor and oppressed in both their personal lives and in their social work practice.

Self-Care

Structural social work is one form of struggle against oppression and in pursuit of liberation. This struggle can be painful and discouraging at times; it can become even more so because structural social work is marginalized within our own profession. Mainstream social workers will often write us off as 'out of touch' and 'unrealistic radicals'. Anyone who has lived or worked on the edge or outside the mainstream will know all about marginalization, isolation, ridicule, and defamation on a personal level. In addition, social work today is fraught with pressures that can lead to incredible stress, particularly where staff are not adequately supported in meeting the complex and demanding challenges of social problems and societal dysfunction. In turn, the stress can become so overwhelming that we function below the level of our competence to the point where our practice becomes dangerous work (Thompson, 1998). Prolonged exposure to stress can lead to burnout—a psychological condition in which the worker 'functions "on automatic pilot"—that is, in an unthinking, unfeeling way, cut off from the sensitive issues involved in his or her work' (Thompson, 1998: 226). Consequently, strategies to promote self-care and staff care are crucial. Thompson outlines a few policies and practices geared towards supporting staff:

- preventing pressures from becoming excessive, to the point where they lead to burnout;
- being responsive to staff when they experience high levels of stress;
- dealing constructively with the aftermath of stress, for example through debriefing.

It has already been emphasized that mutual support and co-operation among structural social workers is crucial if we are to avoid being co-opted by the system or agency or if we are to cope with the negative attitudes and behaviours that supervisors and mainstream colleagues may possess and exhibit. There is consensus in the literature and with people's experience of structural social work that the most important element in carrying out acts of resistance and in protecting oneself from the risks inherent in structural social work practice is to establish and work with caucuses or support groups of like-minded colleagues. Gil (1998) outlines several functions that such groups carry out for their members with respect to support and care. First, they can serve as settings for non-hierarchical, co-operative, mutually caring relationships among structural social workers who feel isolated and alienated because their views, values, beliefs, theory, and practice differ from those of their co-workers. Second, they can confirm the realism and sanity of structural social workers, which are sometimes questioned by co-workers and administrators. Third, they can serve as settings for co-operative and critical study of the structural practice and activism of members. Finally, members of such study and support groups can recruit new members, initiate the establishment of new groups, and organize networks of such groups.

Realistic Expectations

A question I am frequently asked by students when I am discussing the ultimate goal of structural social work—social transformation—is if I think it will happen. Of course, the subtext of this question is whether or not I think that structural social work will bring about some kind of social transformation in the foreseeable future. My short answer is no, I do not believe structural social work will, by itself, bring about social transformation. My longer answer is to suggest that some social workers equate social transformation with overnight revolution and believe that the absence of militant or cataclysmic, large-scale changes is proof that fundamental structural change is unrealistic. Gil (1998) reminds us that oppressive institutions have evolved over many centuries and, therefore, are often perceived to be natural, normal, legitimate, and unchangeable. There are no quick and easy strategies for eliminating oppression.

BOX 12.4 MY EXPECTATIONS FOR SOCIAL WORK GRADUATES

When I used to discuss 'realistic expectations' with my students, I would often give as a personal example that my expectation of students who graduated was that if two or three out of the whole class actually practised structural social work beyond two years, I would consider it to be a success. Of course, I was implicitly challenging the students to commit themselves to structural social work practice after graduation. One student at Victoria University in Melbourne, Australia, where I taught for several years, recently sent me an e-mail in which he commented on my stated expectation with respect to himself and a couple of his classmates. The following is an edited version of part of his e-mail.

> As for my anti-oppressive [structural] practice, well, it's something I'm always conscious of and reflective about. It's something I'm known for now, and despite having comments thrown at me like 'You're so politically correct' (like as if that's a bad thing???—if that were what it was really even about) when I refuse to engage in degrading, disrespectful conversation about service users, for instance, I stand strong. I have been able to afford this (along with the occasional refusal to implement policy which I see as oppressive) because I am good at what I do, and they know it. I've got a lot of work still to do, and inconsistency constantly knocks, but I critically reflect and deflect that too. I know two other students in my class who are still practising progressive/structural social work. So I remember your saying once that you were realistic and would only expect/hope that two students of any graduating year would still be conducting themselves that way, in five years I think. Well, I think you might get at least three out of our year.

—Reproduced with thanks to Jason Smith

Life might be a whole lot simpler if we just accepted the way things are, but I think that mainstream social workers are more susceptible to burnout than structural social workers. Their analysis and explanations of social problems do not explain the persistence of problems, nor does their analysis explain why their interventions and practices seem so ineffectual. Over time, with limited successful outcomes from their interventions, they will naturally begin to question themselves and their competencies. At least, structural social workers have an analysis that explains why mainstream interventions and 'solutions' to social problems do not work. Poor people did not invent poverty. People of colour did not create racism. Gay, lesbian, bisexual, and transexual persons did not invent homophobia. Women did not ask to be treated in a sexist way. These are structural problems that can only be satisfactorily resolved by structural change (recognizing that some personal change may be associated with structural interventions). The struggle against oppression can be painful and discouraging at times, but anyone who has ever participated in it knows that it also brings great comradeship, which is deeply rewarding. If we do nothing about oppression, we lose our basic humanity and, I suggest, we will have difficulty living with ourselves.

The social transformation of a society characterized by relations of domination and subordination will require a lengthy and difficult process, one that could take decades or centuries. This does not mean that we have to accept the status quo. It merely means that we have to be realistic about the outcomes of structural social work. The question is not, 'How I can start the revolution to end oppression?' Rather, it is, 'How can I can contribute to undermining and resisting oppression in my everyday practice?' Our task is to contribute to social transformation in any way we can—in our professional practices and in our personal lives. Although complete social transformation may not occur in the lifetimes of most of us, we will see some fundamental changes. The women's movement has brought about fundamental change in the relations between males and females. Part of this change is the common usage today of gender-inclusive language as opposed to the male-dominated discourse of a couple of decades ago. This change, of course, is much greater than a simple vocabulary alteration. It has both symbolic and real effects. Language is part of culture. It both reflects and contributes to dominant–subordinate relationships. One way of helping to change the culture (such as patriarchy) is to change the language.

Everyone in his or her day-to-day living experiences can contribute to language changes. For example, instead of using the term 'client', which denotes a relationship of inequality between the social worker (the helper) and the 'helpee', many social workers today (including myself) use the term 'service user'. An example of where a structural social worker can make a contribution to undermining some of the oppressive aspects of social work practice is in the area of case recordings and agency files. Traditionally, case recordings were written in a diagnostic discourse that tended to pathologize the service user by attributing problems to deficiencies within the individual, the family, the culture, and so on. These recordings were guarded like Fort Knox and could only be seen by selected agency personnel. The anti-oppressive social worker could help to de-pathologize the experiences of service users by identifying problems for what they are—outcomes of racism, sexism, classism, and/or other forms of oppression rather than using some victim-blaming explanation. Today, because of 'freedom of information' legislation, service users do have access to their files, which provides them with the opportunity to disagree with what is written and to offer their own stories. However, not all service users are informed about their right to look at their files. Structural social workers would ensure that this right is made known. Some agencies have a policy of co-authorship of a joint narrative about problems, needs, and claims (Leonard, 1997). This practice recognizes that narratives are open to interpretation and that the service user's knowledge is just as valuable as is some piece of universal expert knowledge, which by itself has a tendency to homogenize people within a professional discourse.

BOX 12.5 MAKING WAVES IN THE BILLABONG

In the late nineties and early part of the new century I was head of a structural social work program at Victoria University in Australia. One day in class we were discussing the nature of social transformation and what we could do as individual social workers to bring it about. I attempted to make the point that it was unrealistic to think that we could bring about some kind of overnight revolution, that we had to join with other groups who were also seeking fundamental transformation of our current society, and that it would take a long time and a lot of effort by many people before we would realize substantial structural changes. One student, much more creative than I, said that she viewed social transformation in a similar vein to making big waves in a billabong (i.e., a large pool of water). She said that if one or two people threw pebbles into the billabong, you would hardly see any movement, but if you had many, many people throwing pebbles you would see considerable turbulence in the billabong. Her point, of course, was that as more and more people practise structural social work and contribute to fundamental structural changes, social transformation will occur.

The Constructive Use of Anger [5]

Obviously, structural social work practice will not be easy. It requires an examination and deconstruction of social work's most cherished assumptions so that we can learn and become part of the resurgence of social critique in the newer forms of political movements that challenge the dominant order in the name of equality and diversity (Leonard, 1997). It requires a view of the reality of oppression, not as a closed world from which there is no exit, but as a limited situation that can be transformed (Freire, cited in Rees, 1991). It also requires an understanding of the nature and causes of the new social, economic, and political conditions of globalization and the current worldwide reactionary political climate. We cannot theorize and analyze from a distance, however, because most of all, strctural social work requires a personal and collective commitment to social justice. It is not enough to know that we should involve ourselves in struggle or even to want to become involved in social struggle.

But what is it that would drive a person to take on such an onerous commitment to literally take on the world as we now know it and attempt to transform it? The answer, I think, is to capitalize on a feeling that most social workers concerned about social injustice (at least the ones I know) possess—anger at the degrading material and social conditions experienced on a daily basis by millions of people in the less-developed countries and in capitalist countries; anger at governments that cater to the wishes of the wealthy at the expense of women, children, visible minorities, and other marginalized groups; anger at a social welfare system that homogenizes, controls, and monitors people who are forced to go to it for assistance and that has turned its workers into bureaucratic ciphers; and anger at the discrimination, exploitation, and blocked opportunities that so many people experience today, not because of anything they might have done or who they are as individuals, but simply because they belong to particular social groups, which for the most part they did not choose.

Feminists have used the construction of anger as a catalyst to attack sexism and patriarchy. According to feminist therapy, women need to get in touch with their anger and turn it outward rather than inward (Goldhor-Lerner, 1985), as the latter results in depression, despair, and anxiety, which, in turn, reproduce women's traditional roles of passivity and submission under patriarchy (Baines, 1997). A similar dynamic is experienced by social workers who internalize their anger caused by social and workplace injustice. Leonard (1997: 162) contends that anger can be mobilized from internalization as anxiety and depression into externalization as collective resistance: 'Collectively, anger emerges as a moral protest at injustice.' Herman (1992: 189) argues that anger has been the driving force behind all great social movements. It can move oppressed people and their allies from feelings of 'helpless fury' to 'righteous indignation'. Bishop (1994: 84) identifies anger as a source of power if it is used as 'an expression of our will directed against injustice'.

Peter Leonard argues that a sense of moral outrage at the structures of domination and oppression manufactured and reproduced within the current set of oppressive social arrangements provides the basis for progressive discourses and practices. 'Not intellectual detachment but anger is the human attribute which has the most possibility of generating the kind of individual and collective resistance which is a necessary precondition of emancipation' (Leonard, 1997: 162). Thompson (1998) issues an important caution about anger, however. He asserts that anger can be a positive force for change if it is channelled constructively, but if it gets out of control or is misdirected or used as a blanket approach to struggles for liberation, it can be used ideologically by the dominant group to pathologize and stigmatize subordinate group members and their anti-oppressive allies.

Anger is a gift (Lim, 1996, cited in Leonard, 1997). It is what will enable those of us who are committed to anti-oppressive social work to translate our social justice ideals into practice and to continue the struggle for liberation. If, in our personal lives and in our social work practice, we assist in making oppression acceptable by helping people to cope with it or adjust to it, we not only fail them, we fail ourselves and we become part of the problem. Social workers who are committed to social justice must join the struggle against oppression in all its forms and at all levels at which it occurs. There is no choice.

MAKING THE POLITICAL PERSONAL IN OUR OWN LIVES

The most important arena for radical change is ourselves. Moreau and Leonard (1989: 238) contend that one of the central factors conducive to the practice of structural social work is to attain congruence between our personal/political beliefs and the way we live our lives. Withorn (1984: 82) states that socially committed social workers will need 'to achieve harmony among their politics, their work, and their personal lives'. In other words, it is not enough to espouse structural ideology and to carry it out in our professional work—we must live it. To do otherwise is not only contradictory and hypocritical, it is self-defeating.

It was argued in the previous chapter that to avoid reproducing dominant–subordinate social relationships and oppressive behaviours that are part of our society, a structural social work practice must be carried out. So, too, in our personal lives must we avoid reproducing social relationships and behaviours at the root of so many of our social problems—inequality, excessive competition, exploitation of people and resources, profit-driven production, distribution, and consumption, sexism, racism, homophobia, ageism, individualism, militarism, and so on. By carrying out our ideological beliefs in our daily lives we supplement our structural work by contributing to social transformation outside of our professional practice.

Our personal relationships represent one area for personal and social transformation. Just as we strive for egalitarian and participatory relationships in the workplace, so should we practice equality in all our relationships. We must work at eliminating traditional roles and divisions based on gender in our homes and in our associations with others. Structural social workers must examine their own lives and interactions with others to determine whether or not they are contributing to a social atmosphere of oppression, aggression, and even violence. Are sexist, racist, or homophobic jokes and slurs condoned or tolerated? Does violence in any form occur? Are environmentally harmful products purchased and used? Are war toys purchased for children or do we allow them to watch violent television shows? Structural social work requires more than a nine-to-five workplace effort; it requires a commitment to personal evaluation, challenge, and change.

Do our consumer patterns support capitalism or do we take advantage of the collective, more democratic, and non-exploitative alternatives that exist in the midst of our capitalist society? With respect to our personal finances, do we use private banks that make enormous profits for a few people, often have investments in countries that violate human rights, have oppressive labour policies, and often exploit their own workers, most of whom are women? Or do we join credit unions, which are collectively owned and operated by their memberships and invest their money in the local community? Do we purchase goods and services made or delivered by non-unionized companies, or do we support the trade union movement by purchasing union-produced goods and services? Do we patronize profit-driven businesses when there are opportunities to support the development and expansion of the co-operative movement where, as with credit unions, the enterprises are membership-owned and operated in the best interests of its members and not for a few shareholders? Do we purchase environmentally friendly products and boycott products from establishments with poor environmental track records? North Americans consume billions of dollars of goods and services yearly. The market is the heart of capitalism, but it is also an arena where the traditional capitalist principles of production, distribution, and consumption can be altered.

To live structurally in our hierarchical society is not easy, however. Most of the rewards—promotions, acceptance, respect—are given to those who conform to our present social order. By engaging in structural social work we run the risk of retaliation from the status quo. This retaliation can range from persons being nervous in our presence to overt efforts to discredit us by applying labels such as 'troublemaker'. Galper (1989) and Withorn (1984) have written about the risks involved in radical work and some of the ways of coping with and reducing the risks—avoid adventurism and martyrdom; be competent in your work; work collectively; realize that all radicals experience some degree of ambivalence about their radicalism by virtue of having been socialized into a society marked by dominant–subordinate realtions. The greater risk, however, is to capitulate to the status quo and not carry out our structural ideology in our work and in our personal lives. The risk in this case is that we do nothing to bring about progressive structural change and, thus, fail the people we serve. Thereby we fail ourselves. We become part of the problem and not the solution as we join the conventional social work group delivering services and practising in ways that blame victims for their troubles. And we run the risk of cynicism, despair, and burnout because we know that in the long run what we are doing is simply perpetuating the system that causes people troubles in the first place.

In sum, to be effective as structural social workers we need a political analysis that distinguishes the causes and the consequences of social problems. We need a vision of a humanized society to give us direction in our efforts. We need knowledge to enable us to work effectively both inside and outside of our social agencies. We need to have harmony between our political beliefs and our personal lives. And we need a commitment to carry out the difficult task of social transformation. Structural social work is more than a theory or a technique or a practice modality. It is a way of life.

CRITICAL QUESTIONS

1. We are all socialized into social institutions and organizations that are characterized by hierarchy and top-down management. What would an

alternative organization characterized by collective or horizontal management look like? How would decisions be made? Who would speak for the organization? And how would other organizations relate to It, I.e., who would they communicate with?

2. Unions are concerned with the working conditions of their members. Caseload size is often an issue in social work settings and one that unions should address at the bargaining table (i.e., bargain for a reasonable ceiling on the number of cases a social worker should carry). Can you identify other workplace issues that social work unions should address?

3. Examine the official policies of each of the federal political parties in the areas of income taxation, public health care, social housing, daycare, and Aboriginal self-government. Which party has policies closest to those of progressive or structural social work? Which political party in your province has the most social workers (past or present) among its members? How can we as a profession use or influence political parties to pursue progressive social policies?

4. Do you have any rules for yourself that help you deal with any anger you might experience in the workplace? For example, earlier in my career I often reacted immediately to my anger by writing a letter or e-mail or telephoning the person (and sometimes others) responsible for my anger. This often got me in trouble as my communiqué tended to be knee-jerk and confrontational rather than thoughtful and strategic. Now, I have a rule that I wait at least one day to respond. I ask myself before acting—is my anger in check?

5. What are some of the ways you look after yourself? Can you think of other forms of self-care or strategies you might consider adopting on an individual level and on a collective level with people inside your workplace and outside?

Appendix:
Structural Analysis of
Agency/Field Placement

Almost all social agencies in our present society contain an inherent contradiction. On the one hand, they work towards and, in part, achieve greater degrees of well-being by providing resources or services to people who would otherwise have less. On the other hand, the services provided by social agencies are organized and delivered in a manner that supports and reinforces 'conformity' among users and workers to the very social institutions, beliefs, and values that generate the problems that agencies were established to deal with in the first place. Make a list of contradictions that you have identified within your agency/placement (e.g., the Mission Statement talks about respecting the dignity of people it serves, but some of the activities it asks social workers to do are social control functions).

In order for us to function effectively as structural social workers we must be aware of the social control and people-denying functions of our agency/placement and the methods used to carry out this social control and/or function of preserving the system (society). Are the social control functions of social agencies and services accidental, or do they serve a purpose? Who do they benefit?

The following series of questions focuses on gaining a better structural understanding of any particular social service agency—its origin and mandate; its definition of and focus on problems; the interventions used by its personnel; its relationship with service users; and its relationship with its employees.

1. ORIGIN AND MANDATE OF AGENCY (FIELD SETTING)

Origin: Why was the agency established in the first place, i.e., what problem(s) existed, who defined them as problems, and how were they dealt with before the agency (or service) was established?

Mandate: Where does the agency get its mandate to exist? Where does it get its funding? Is there enabling legislation and, if so, to what extent is it prescriptive and to what extent does it circumscribe work within the agency?

Purpose: Does the agency have a stated purpose, a Mission Statement? If so, what is it? If unstated, what is it and how is it communicated? Is there a philosophical statement of purpose that is supposed to guide agency practices? If so, is it consistent with the 2005 CASW *Code of Ethics*? Is it consistent with the 1994 *Code*?

2. PROBLEM DEFINITION AND FOCUS

- How are problems defined by the agency, i.e., what are the causes or sources of the problems as perceived by the agency? What is the agency's explanation for the problems?
- Are there limitations or false assumptions in the agency's definition or explanation of the problems it deals with?
- What are the agency's solutions for the problems?
- What is the prevailing thought of workers towards the problems and the people they are dealing with? What is their explanation for the problems? Is it consistent with the agency's views?
- If the problems the agency deals with were left unattended, what would be the impact on service users and on society as a whole?

3. INTERVENTIONS USED BY AGENCY PERSONNEL

- What type of social work interventions are used in your agency?
- Are they the most appropriate for resolving problems or do they simply keep a lid on the situation and the service users?
- What is the rationale behind each type of intervention used? That is, are they consistent with the way the agency has defined the problems? (For example, if the problems are basically ones of poverty, counselling for relationship problems may be inappropriate.)
- In your opinion is the service or benefit adequate to deal with the problems? If not, what kind of message do you think this gives the service users?

4. RELATIONSHIP BETWEEN AGENCY AND USERS

- Are there any conditions of eligibility for receiving services other than need? If so, what are they and why do they exist?
- Does the agency promote conformity on the part of the service user in any way?
- What are the conditions and expectations that users must carry out and/or meet in order to continue to receive services? What are the reasons for disqualifying or terminating a person from receiving service?
- Are there any connections between eligibility for receipt of services and the labour market? If so, what are they and why do they exist?
- Do service users have access to their files or records? If not, why not?

- What happens if a service user is dissatisfied with the service or the treatment she or he receives? (For example, are there established appeal procedures?)
- Are there any mechanisms for service user input into the policies or operations of the agency?

5. RELATIONSHIP BETWEEN AGENCY AND EMPLOYEES

- Who decides on policy for the agency? Does the staff have any formal input into policy formulation and/or administrative decisions?
- Who defines the working conditions? Does the staff have any say?
- How are people supervised or held accountable for their work?
- What are promotions and pay raises based on? In other words what is the system of rewards and punishment and what criteria are used?
- If workers are unionized, what input does the union have on: (i) policy; (ii) administrative decisions; and (iii) conditions of work?
- How are disagreements and grievances dealt with in the agency? That is, who is involved and who usually settles them?
- What are the prevailing mood and thought of workers towards the problems they deal with and do they agree with the agency's interpretations of causes and solutions?
- What are the prevailing mood and thought of workers towards their work? That is, do they think the interventions the agency asks them to carry out are appropriate? Do they think their efforts are having an impact on reducing or resolving the problems they are dealing with?
- What is the general morale of the workers and what do you attribute it (good or bad) to?
- How have you as a student been treated generally within the agency? List the things you appreciated hearing or having been done for you as a student.
- Make an inventory of the things you appreciated and did not appreciate (e.g., hearing comments about naïveté, idealism, etc.) as a student starting your placement. What do you think lies behind any negative treatment or comments?

6. CONCLUSION

- What structural social work do you think could be carried out in this agency (with service users, with employees, other)?

Notes

CHAPTER 1

1. 'Taylorism' is a term derived from F.W. Taylor's seminal book, *The Principles of Scientific Management* (1911). This treatise described how labour productivity could be dramatically increased by breaking down each labour process into component motions and organizing fragmented work tasks according to rigorous standards of time and motion study. Assembly-line production is an example of Taylorism in the workplace.

2. 'Fordism' is consistent with but more complex and far-reaching than Taylorism. The term is derived from Henry Ford, who applied principles of scientific management to his automated automobile assembly line in 1913. He used technology and an existing division of labour in his auto plant, but his major innovation was to flow the work to a stationary worker, which resulted in radical gains in productivity. What separates Fordism from Taylorism was Ford's recognition that mass production meant mass consumption, a new system for the reproduction of labour power, a new politics of labour control and management, a new aesthetics and psychology—in short, a new kind of society, one based on mass production and mass consumption (Harvey, 1989). The name often applied to pre-World War II society is 'Fordist capitalism', as industry and the labour process were organized around Ford's ideas about a rationalized workplace and a rationalized society.

3. Keynesianism refers to the economic theory of the British economist John Maynard Keynes (1883–1946). This theory argues for a high level of government intervention into the economy to ensure a high level of economic activity and high levels of employment. It is based on the assumption that there is a direct relationship between inflation and employment, that is, there is a supposed trade-off between the two. When unemployment levels are unacceptably high governments are to cut taxes and increase public spending to stimulate the economy and increase the number of jobs. Conversely, when the economy is overstimulated and dangerous levels of inflation occur, governments are to raise taxes and reduce public spending, which in turn would reduce inflation but also employment.

4. For fuller and more elaborate explanations of the 'crisis of legitimation', see George and Wilding (1984); Mishra (1984); Gough (1979); and Riches (1986).

5. A word on terminology is necessary. 'Neo' is a prefix that means 'new' or 'different from'. It also means the reappearance of a tradition or perspective after a period of decline or abandonment (Marshall, 1998). 'Neo-liberalism' and 'neo-conservatism' are often used interchangeably in the literature, which causes some confusion to students of social work and social policy. McBride (in Burke et al., 2000) contends that either term is correct when used to describe the ideology driving the current process of globalization. 'Neo-conservatism' is the name given to the current re-emergence of conservative thought and 'neo-liberalism' is the term given to the reappearance of classical liberalism. Both ideologies are the subjects of later chapters, where they will be explained more fully. The term used in this book when discussing the ideology underpinning globalization is 'neo-conservatism'. Much of the literature on globalization and social welfare uses 'neo-liberalism' in the same way that 'neo-conservatism' is used here. Neo-conservatism (or neo-liberalism) is a loosely knit body of ideas premised on a slight rethinking and a substantial reassertion of nineteenth-century conservatism or classical liberalism. It emphasizes market solutions rather than collective decisions to solve or deal with social and economic problems and a reduced role for the state with respect to human affairs (McBride, 2001).

6. Discourse includes not only language, but the rules governing the choice and use of language and how the ideas and language will be framed. A discourse is a framework of thought, meaning, and action (Thompson, 1998) that does not reflect knowledge, reality, or truth, but creates and maintains them. 'Knowledge, according to Foucault, is produced by discourse—it is "the way in which power, language and institutional practices combine at historically specific points to produce particular ways of thinking"' (Featherstone and Fawsett, 1994, cited in Stainton and Swift, 1996: 77). Although there is always more than one discourse at any point in time, usually one discourse is dominant. The current dominant economic discourse consists of a set of assumptions about the social and economic world that largely reflect the interests of global capitalism. The concept of 'discourse' is an important tool for understanding phenomena such as globalization and for developing social work practices that deal with the negative causes and consequences of the current globalization process. By understanding a dominant discourse we can deconstruct it and expose any discriminatory or oppressive assumptions, ideas, and beliefs that may underpin it. Also, we can develop *counter-discourses* based on the ideals of equality, fairness, and social justice. These ideas will be discussed more fully in subsequent chapters.

7. Thomas Hobbes was a seventeenth-century British philosopher who assumed that human beings were by nature isolationist and greedy creatures driven by their desires and aversions, and who were inescapably engaged in a perpetual struggle for power and control over others and for resources and privilege. He viewed society as a collection of individuals who agree to surrender some natural freedoms in order to live in a formally organized state that affords people the security necessary to satisfy their needs. He viewed government as a necessary evil without which life would be 'solitary, poor, nasty, brutish, and short'. Charles Darwin was a nineteenth-century British naturalist who became famous for his theories on evolution and natural selection. Social Darwinism is a social theory in which its proponents apply Darwin's biological ideas and theories, such as 'survival of the fittest' and 'evolutionary change', to human social institutions. This school of social thought gave a false scientific credence to laissez-faire and anti-welfare policies on the part of governments.

8. International trade during the 25-year rise of globalization (1970–95) was governed by a system of international trade agreements, collectively known as GATT (the General Agreement on Tariffs and Trade). In 1995 GATT was reconceived as a new powerful body, the World Trade Organization (WTO). Saul (2004) claims that the creation of this body was the last triumph of globalization. The rules for international trade, for the most part, would be made by the WTO rather than by national governments. Saul argues that the context or the built-in assumptions behind the establishment of the WTO are especially significant in that civilization had been reconceptualized through the 'prism of economics'. That is, any international agreement that involved a commercial element would be treated as fundamentally a commercial transaction. For example, culture would be seen as a matter of industrial regulation, and food would be seen as a secondary outcome of agricultural industries. In other words, agriculture would not be seen as a food source but as an industry subject to trade rules of the WTO. Any restrictions that a country might impose on food imports concerning use of fertilizers, herbicides, pesticides, genetic manipulation, hormones, and antibiotics were regarded as protectionism by international trade rules without the hardest of hard scientific evidence.

   The International Monetary Fund (IMF) was created in 1945 with the purposes of promoting international monetary co-operation and exchange stability, fostering economic growth and high levels of employment, and providing temporary financial assistance to countries in economic difficulty (primarily developing countries). Although these goals are laudable, the (punishing) approach used by the IMF during the period of globalization was to develop and implement structural adjustment programs (SAPs) based on what Saul calls 'crucifixion economics' (i.e., free-market economics) and to impose them on poor countries to ensure debt repayment and economic restructuring. The 'crucifixion economics' that underpinned the SAPs comprised 'low wages, compliant unions, environmental deregulation, privatization of public services, and diminished role of the state in social protection and social programs (Lundy, 2004: 4).

   The G-8 (Group of 8) is a group of the eight wealthiest nations: Canada, France, Germany, Italy, Japan, Russia, the United Kingdom, and the United States. Originally the G-6 (it did not include Canada or Russia), it was created in 1975 with the aim of bringing together the leaders of the biggest national economies to examine the world through the 'prism of economics'. The core relationship of this group was organized 'around naked, commercial self-interest, without the positive and negative counterweights of social standards, human rights, political systems, dynasties, formal religions, and, at the negative extreme, supposed racial destinies' (Saul, 2004: 35). This group supported globalization and its regulatory institutions—the IMF and WTO—and over time focused on trade as the solution to every problem, both economic and social.

9. In personal correspondence (11 June 1990), Robert D. Leighninger Jr, editor of the *Journal of Sociology and Social Welfare*, stated that writers often use Kuhnian terms to give their work borrowed legitimacy, and if the concept 'paradigm' is not applied carefully the legitimacy is bogus. Kuhn was dealing with the physical world and physical sciences, not the social world and social sciences. Leighninger did admit that one can apply the concept outside of the physical sciences and talk about multiple-paradigm sciences and paradigm shifts rather than single-paradigm social sciences and revolutions. Social work is, of course, well acquainted with borrowing concepts and knowledge and with the dangers inherent in this practice.

10. I wish to thank my colleague Richard Sigurdson, Dean of Arts at the University of Manitoba, for his assistance in conceptualizing the political ideologies discussed here. Particularly helpful was his book chapter, 'Political Ideas and Ideologies', from Rand Dyck, ed., *Studying Politics: An Introduction to Political Science* (2002).

11. Dialectics is Marx's method of theorizing. In its broadest sense, it is the study of contradictions (Cornforth, 1953). It is based on the belief that all things are interconnected and that everything is in a state of continuous change (including society and theories about society). Change occurs through the interplay among these opposing or contradictory forces. According to the dialectic, there are three main elements: (1) a thesis, which is the dominant reality (e.g., modernist thought); (2) an antithesis (e.g., postmodernism), which arises to challenge the dominant thought; and (3) a synthesis, which reconciles the thesis and antithesis. The synthesis then becomes the new reality or thesis that, in turn, will be challenged by a new antithesis and so on.

CHAPTER 2

1. This is not to say that casework must be, or that all casework is, residual or victim-blaming. Jan Fook's *Radical Casework* (1993) is an example of casework practice that links the personal with the political. That is, it links public issues with personal difficulties by including social analysis as part of its practice. Nor is this to say that all community organization is radical. No area of social work is inherently mainstream or radical. More is said about these issues in subsequent chapters.

2. Of course, many perspectives, models, theories, and so on exist within social work. With respect to our present social order, however, two basic views are held by social workers. Some believe our present society is capable of righting any social wrongs that may occur. Others believe that our present society is not capable of righting social wrongs because the social order itself produces these wrongs, and, therefore, limited reform of the system will do nothing to resolve social problems. The first group of social workers, called here conventional workers, seeks to make our social order work better. The second group, called here progressive workers, seeks to transform our present social order into one that works better for larger numbers of people. Another term for progressive social work is radical social work, which is discussed in some detail in Chapter 9.

3. This is not to suggest that the conflation of the two terms in the literature is not confusing and, in some regards, misleading. According to the *Encyclopaedia of Social Sciences* (Selizam, 1984: 544–8), the doctrine of humanism espouses that the person has two natures, good and bad, and that there is constant tension between the two. Humanitarianism denies this dualism within the individual and claims that people are innately good and reasonable. Humanism is an intellectual-philosophical stance dating to the Renaissance that puts humankind at the apex of creation and presumes, if not a godless world, then a world in which God or some supernatural or divine presence is not or cannot be an active agent in human well-being. Humanitarianism, on the other hand, consists of the efforts of humans to better the life situations of those who are less fortunate and to treat others in a humane way, and many humanitarian organizations and NGOs, rather than operating outside the spiritual realm, work from within specific ethical-religious traditions. Humanists tend to explain the spiritual essence of humans through psychological and other human-centred theories; humanitarians often reflect their concept of a divine presence in their actions towards and for others and in their belief in the presence of God in all humanity.

4. For American examples, see Galper (1975); Gil (1976, 1998); Withorn (1984); and Harrington (1962). For Canadian examples, see Banting (1982); Djao (1983); McQuaig (1993, 2001); Moscovitch and Drover (1981); and Naiman (1997).

5. For example, Michael Harrington's *The Other America* (1962) is often cited as the major work that brought to the attention of affluent America the fact that poverty was real and pervasive in the United States in the early sixties and was followed by President Lyndon Johnson declaring war on poverty in 1964. In its *Fifth Annual Review* (1968) the Economic Council of Canada revealed disturbing evidence on the extent of poverty in Canada, which led to a special Senate committee chaired by David Croll to investigate poverty and make recommendations to remedy it. Biehal and Sainsbury (1991: 250) state that poverty was rediscovered in Britain in the 1960s by non-social workers.

6. The conventional social work view of egalitarianism is that of 'equal opportunity'. This notion of egalitarianism and others will be discussed in the chapters that focus on the four different paradigms. See Benn and Peters (1959) for an overview and discussion of different meanings of egalitarianism.

7. For fuller coverage of collectivism as an organizing principle for an idealized social work society, see Galper (1975: 140–52).

8. This theme will be explored in more detail in subsequent chapters. See especially Chapters 4, 9, and 11.

CHAPTER 3

1. Several conservative American writers have attributed the growth of the underclass to the welfare programs of the 1960s War on Poverty. The welfare poor supposedly were lured away from self-suffi- ciency by these programs and lost the capacity to live independently. See, for example, Butler and Kondratas (1987); Gilder (1981); Mead (1986); Murray (1984).

CHAPTER 4

1. For example, one heir of Jeremy Bentham and Adam Smith (two classical liberals) was John Stuart Mill, one of the pioneers of reform liberalism, and another was Herbert Spencer, a promoter of the ultra-conservative ideas of social Darwinism.

2. The post-war welfare state in Britain developed from an amalgam of liberal and social democratic beliefs, values, and ideals and was based on the twin liberal pillars of Keynesian economics and Beveridge social policy. The Labour (social democratic) governments were responsible for the devel- opment of much of Britain's welfare state.

3. Marsh (1943), who wrote the Canadian equivalent (*Report on Social Security for Canada*) to the Beveridge Report, was greatly influenced by Lord Beveridge's thoughts and liberal ideology.

4. The 1993 electoral successes of the federal Reform and Bloc Québécois political parties did not change the political culture of Canadian society. Although Reform was a right-wing populist party whose breakthrough in the 1993 federal election was, in part, attributable to the collapse of the federal Progressive Conservatives, the big winner with respect to this collapse (at least for the next decade) was the federal Liberal Party (MacIvor, 1996). The Bloc Québécois has as its original purpose 'to bring together in Ottawa sovereigntists of all [ideological] tendencies' (Bouchard, 1992: 255). The Reform Party became the Canadian Reform Conservative Alliance in 2000 and merged with the Progres- sive Conservative Party to become the Conservative Party of Canada in 2003. It comprises a number of right-wing former Alliance members and a number of progressive-minded 'red Tories' from the previous Progressive Conservative Party. The extent to which the former Canadian Alliance heart of the new Conservative Party has been able to suppress its ultra-conservative rhetorical beat was seen in the 2005–6 federal election campaign, which ultimately led to the election of a Conservative minority government.

5. See Djao (1983) for an overview of this shift, and see Guest (1985) for a more detailed coverage of this shift from a residual to an institutional model of social welfare in Canada.

6. See Galper (1975) for a definitive and insightful analysis of how and why the social welfare state reinforces liberal capitalism.

7. Although this is not a Canadian text, it is authored by a prominent Canadian writer and is widely used in Canadian schools of social work.

CHAPTER 5

1. At the time of this writing (2006) two provinces, Manitoba and Saskatchewan, have social democratic (NDP) governments.

2. I am indebted to M. Dickerson and T. Flanagan (1986) for their succinct chapter on 'Socialism' in their book, *An Introduction to Government and Politics: A Conceptual Approach,* which provided much of the material for my overview of some highlights of socialism.

3. This notion of a 'provisional government' caused the anarchist wing of socialism to split from the international socialist organization that existed (1864–1972) because they feared that this transitional government might become permanent.

4. This method of radical change is called 'radical structuralism'. It is discussed in detail in Chapter 7.

5. Mishra (1981) refers to this perspective as the 'Social Administration School' of social policy (welfare).

6. Even with respect to the British experience with social democracy there is disagreement as to whether or not social democracy has moved Britain closer to a socialist state. There are also some who believe social democracy was not given a fair chance. See Pritchard and Taylor (1978) for a discussion of these issues.

7. The best-known and most controversial reform is called 'the wage-earners fund', which is intended to rectify the unequal distribution of wealth and influence created by private ownership of industry. For details on how this scheme works, see Himmelstrand et al. (1981).

8. These commissions are somewhat similar to Royal Commissions in the British sense but usually comprise one member who is an acknowledged expert in the field of inquiry. These studies average two–three years' duration.

CHAPTER 6

1. For a polemic discussion and critique of both the Marxist revolutionary and Marxist evolutionary approaches to radical social and political change and social work practice, see Pritchard and Taylor (1978: esp. ch. 7).

CHAPTER 7

1. As Agger (1991) points out, a discussion of some of the main ideas of postmodernism and post-structuralism assumes that we can cleanly separate the two, but unfortunately we cannot. 'The lack of clear definition reflects the purposeful elusiveness of work that can be variously classified as post-structural and/or postmodern' (p. 112). For my purposes, I adopt Agger's (1992: 93) definitions of postmodernism and post-structuralism. 'Postmodernism . . . is a theory of cultural, intellectual and societal discontinuity that rejects the linearism of Enlightenment notions of progress.' History is no longer perceived to follow some kind of linear path towards the attainment of humanistic (or other) goals. That is, it is not going somewhere, such as from prehistory to the end of history. The present is no longer considered to be a stepping stone to something higher or better. Agger (1992: 93) describes post-structuralism as 'the theory of knowledge and language associated with the work of Jacques Derrida . . . [it] suggests that language users do not just pluck words out of thin air or a thesaurus when trying to convey meaning. . . . Instead, the meanings of words are largely imbedded in language use itself such that *how* we talk, write and read largely determines *what* we end up saying.' Derrida argues that meaning is forever elusive and incomplete because language can never convey exactly what is meant by the language user. Even though I have presented separate definitions here of postmodernism and post-structuralism, I at times will conflate the two terms, given their significant overlap and ambiguity.

CHAPTER 8

1. I am grateful to Steve Bastow and James Martin for their work, *Third Way Discourse: European Ideologies in the Twentieth Century* (2003), from which I draw heavily, although I do not arrive at the same conclusions about the Third Way possibly representing a 'radical politics' of democracy.

2. The values are from Giddens (1998: 66); interpretations in parentheses are from various writers, including Carling (1999) and Giddens (1998).

3. The late 1960s was an era of national concern and reappraisal of the perceived inevitability of

American control and takeover of the Canadian economy. Even the Liberals were calling for more government intervention in the economy and culture and the Progressive Conservatives produced a red Tory (socially progressive) approach. A number of reports called for nationalization of key industries and stricter laws to prevent foreign takeovers. During this era, the Waffle Movement was formed within the NDP, led by two academic NDP members and social activists, Mel Watkins, an economist, and Jim Laxer, a political scientist. Its members issued a Manifesto calling for fundamental social change, including the replacement of capitalism in Canada by socialism. Among other things, it called for economic independence from the United States, the revitalization of the labour movement, an extension to the welfare state, a progressive tax structure, a guaranteed annual income, the end of regional disparities, and community democracy. The Manifesto turned out to be too radical for the leadership and many members of the NDP, and the Waffle members were turfed out of the party, in large part because of pressure from conservative labour leaders from the American international trade unions. A consequence of this was the creation of many Canadian unions, such as the Canadian Auto Workers, with Canadian sensibilities, but the cost was that the NDP lost many of its young, bright, and intellectual activists of the day. Many on the left, myself included, believe that the expulsion of the Waffle members marked a shift away from the social democratic left tradition of such people as J.S. Woodsworth and Tommy Douglas to the centre of the Canadian political spectrum.

CHAPTER 9

1. As discussed in Chapters 5 and 6, both social democracy and Marxism fall within the socialist camp. Both want the same type of society, but they differ on the means to get there.

2. Professors Jim Albert, Peter Findlay, Helen Levine, Roland Lecomte, and Allan Moscovitch, as well as visiting professors from Britain, Mike Brake and Peter Leonard.

3. Professors Gisele Legault and Pierre Racine.

4. Professor Michelle Bourgon.

5. St Thomas University in Fredericton, NB, and Carleton University in Ottawa both have adopted the structural approach as their program focus; the School of Social Work at Dalhousie University in Halifax acknowledges the major influence of a structural/feminist approach on its current anti-oppressive social work focus; the University of British Columbia, the University College of the Fraser Valley, and the University of Victoria advertise their programs as based on structural/feminist/First Nations or anti-oppressive analyses; Ryerson University and York University, both in Toronto, advertise their programs to focus on anti-oppressive social work that includes structural analyses.

6. Some examples are: Allan et al. (2003); Carniol (1990, 1995); Fook (1993); Ife (1997, 2001); Langan and Lee (1989b); Lundy (2004); Moreau and Leonard (1989); Mullaly (1993); Pease and Fook (1999); Thompson (1993); Wagner (1990); Wharf (1990).

7. For an expository discussion of the commonalities and differences contained in the radical social work literature, see Mullaly and Keating (1991).

8. There have been some criticisms of Marxist theory being embedded in positivism in that Marx's theory of 'historical materialism' has been interpreted by some as a scientific world view justifying domination. S. Leonard (1990) and Miliband (1977) argue that this interpretation is a distortion of Marx's work as it overlooks Marx's own watchwords, 'Doubt all things.'

9. See S. Leonard (1990) for an excellent overview of how each of these critical theorists has addressed these questions.

10. It is recognized here that postmodernism is a very diverse rather than a homogeneous body of thought. The characteristics ascribed to postmodernism in this chapter represent some of its major broad tendencies. Even these broad tendencies, however, have their proponents and dissenters among postmodern writers.

11. Use of the term 'conflict' is problematic as it is used by different writers to refer not only to a perspective but to a theory or to a paradigm as well as to other constructs that have a critical element. The term 'perspective' is adopted here because many different conflict theories are based on the conflict perspective—structural social work being one of them—and to call the perspective a theory is to confuse the two. The position adopted in this book is that a perspective has descriptive and analytic qualities but no prescriptive component. Theory emanates from a perspective but includes a prescription.

12. For a discussion of some internal contradictions of capitalism, such as the tendency of capitalism to overproduce and the fact that the majority of people (i.e., workers) actually produce the wealth but have no control over it, see Galper (1980).

13. For a discussion of some internal contradictions of the welfare state and of social work, see Galper (1975).

14. Mullaly and Keating (1991: 66) write: 'Radical humanism is based on the ontological assumption that the human being is fundamentally set apart from everything else in existence because of its conscious and creative capacities. From this follows the epistemological assumption that the human mind does not receive objectivity from an external world. Rather it confers objectivity by imposing its own order on the world as it is perceived. What is "known" or perceived about external reality is subjectively conferred by the knower.

   Further, 'radical structuralism reflects the ontological assumption that the human person is merely one entity among many. While human conscious and creative capacities differentiate humanity, they do not set it apart from all else. From this follows the epistemological assumption that external reality is objective and as such tends to impose itself on our consciousness.'

15. As presented in Chapter 7, although feminists share the basic view that patriarchal society is oppressive, different feminist analyses exist with respect to the cause of and solutions for patriarchy. In their oft-cited work, Jaggar and Rothenberg (née Struhl) (1978, 1984) identify four feminist frameworks: liberal, Marxist, socialist, and radical. Only liberal feminism accepts liberal capitalism and believes patriarchy can be overcome by reforming our social institutions in a way that gender-based discrimination is removed. The other three perspectives seek to transform capitalism and are compatible with structural social work. Liberal feminism is compatible with conventional social work, but not with structural social work.

16. The structural approach does not deny the need for individual change. Changing social structures will naturally affect individuals, both materially and psychologically. To think otherwise is to deny the connection between the personal and the political. Unlike conventional social work, however, structural social work does not believe that the resolution of social problems lies solely or principally in individual change.

17. This particular approach to social change, called radical humanism, was discussed in the section on 'The Dialectic in Structural Social Work' and will be used as the theoretical basis for the structural social work practice described in Chapter 11.

18. This particular approach to social change, called radical structuralism, was discussed in the section on 'The Dialectic in Structural Social Work' and will be used as the theoretical basis for the structural social work practice described in Chapter 12.

19. The implications for structural social work of how we live our lives are discussed in Chapter 12.

20. I am most grateful to Dr Katrina Brown of Dalhousie University's School of Social Work, who developed an earlier version of such characteristics.

CHAPTER 10

1. I am especially indebted to Iris Marion Young for a good deal of the material in this chapter. Young's book, *Justice and the Politics of Difference* (1990), is highly recommended for all progressive-minded social workers. I am also indebted to Barry D. Adam for his insightful analysis of internalized oppression (inferiorization) in his *The Survival of Domination: Inferiorization in Everyday Life* (1978).

2. I am grateful to two American writers, Sidanius and Pratto (1999), who presented an impressive amount of empirical data and powerful evidence showing that covert structural oppression can be found in all the major areas of an individual's life in Western democratic nations. Below, I draw heavily from their work.

CHAPTER 11

1. Schools of social work have always had as one of their major curriculum streams what was called the Human Behaviour in the Social Environment (HBSE) sequence.

2. The literature is too extensive to cite here, but since 1976 when *Social Work* published a 'Special Issue on Women' a substantial literature has developed on such topics as 'feminist counselling', feminist therapy', and 'feminist social work'.

3. For an insightful and illuminating analysis of the control functions of social agencies and services, see Galper (1975: ch. 4); Thompson (1998); and Withorn (1984).

4. Most of the literature on democratic worker-run agencies focuses on alternative organizations and services. Very little has been written on democratizing the social agency as a workplace since Galper (1980) and Simpkin (1979). Most writings in the 1980s focused on stemming the tide of the deprofessionalization and/or the proletarianization of social work.

CHAPTER 12

1. In 1995 the federal Liberal government 'replaced the shared-cost programs that pay for welfare and social services under the CAP and the Extended Program Financing (EPF) for health and post-secondary education with a single block transfer called the Canada Health and Social Transfer' (Brooks, 2004: 209). This change effectively has meant that there are no true national standards or expectations of equity in regard to social programs since provinces have greater leeway to do what they choose to with the CHST.

2. For example, Dennis Guest's basic text, The *Emergence of Social Security in Canada* (1980, 1985), makes no reference to the NDP or its predecessor, the Co-operative Commonwealth Federation (CCF), nor does Frank McGilly in his overview of Canadian income and health programs, *Canada's Public Social Services* (1990), except to mention that the provincial CCF government of Saskatchewan was the first socialist government in North America and the first government to enact and implement public hospital insurance. Similarly, neither Allan Moscovitch and Jim Albert, co-editors of *The Benevolent State: The Growth of Welfare in Canada* (1987), nor Brian Wharf, editor of *Social Work and Social Change in Canada* (1990), makes any substantial reference to the NDP, while Rosalie Chappell (1997) in *Social Welfare in Canadian Society* gives only brief mention of the NDP as a social democratic party that pursues some social democratic ideals in its political agenda.

3. Angela Djao, a Canadian Marxist sociologist, makes no mention of the NDP in her book on Canadian social welfare, *Inequality and Social Policy: The Sociology of Welfare* (1983). Likewise, Ben Carniol, a radical social worker, says nothing about the CCF/NDP in his *Case Critical* (1987, 1990, 1995). It is only in his fifth edition (2005) that he makes passing reference to the NDP.

4. The Reform Party, which began as a western Canada protest party, achieved significant electoral success in the West in the 1993 federal election, but it remained primarily a party with regional strength and had no presence in provincial electoral politics. It was further to the right than the Progressive Conservative Party. Subsequently, the Reform Party became the Canadian Alliance under a 'Unite the Right' movement and in December 2003 the Canadian Alliance and the Progressive Conservative Party amalgamated to form the Conservative Party of Canada. In January 2006 the Conservatives under the leadership of Stephen Harper won a minority government.

5. Earlier versions of this section appeared in my article, 'Confronting the Politics of Despair', *Social Work Education* 20, 2 (2001), and in my 2002 book, *Challenging Oppression: A Critical Social Work Approach*.

Bibliography

Adam, Barry D. 1978. *The Survival of Domination: Inferiorization and Everyday Life*. New York: Elsevier.

Agel, Jerome, ed. 1971. *The Radical Therapist*. New York: Ballantine Books.

Agger, Ben 1989. *Socio(ontology): A Disciplinary Reading*. Urbana: University of Illinois Press.

——. 1991. 'Critical Theory, Poststructuralism, Postmodernism: Their Sociological Relevance', *Annual Review of Sociology* 17: 105–31.

——. 1992. *Cultural Studies as Critical Theory*. London: Falmer Press.

——. 1998. *Critical Social Theories: An Introduction*. Boulder, Colo.: Westview Press.

Ahmad, B. 1990. *Black Perspectives in Social Work*. Birmingham: Venture.

——. 1991. 'Developing Anti-Racist Social Work Education Practice', in CD Project Steering Group, ed., *Setting the Context for Change*. London: CCETSW.

Albert, Jim. 1990. 'Foreign Aid: The Welfare Function in Imperialist Relations between North and South', paper presented at the twenty-third annual meeting of the Canadian Association of Schools of Social Work, Victoria, BC.

Albert, M., L. Cagan, N. Chomsky, R. Hahnel, M. King, L. Sargent, and H. Sklar. 1986. *Liberating Theory*. Boston: South End Press.

Alexander, Chauncey A. 1982. 'Social Work in the 80's: Issues and Strategies', Plenary Address, 1982 Biennial Conference, Canadian Association of Social Workers, Winnipeg, 18 June, in *The Social Worker/Le Travailleur Social* 50, 2: 63–7.

Alexander, David. 1987. 'Gendered Job Traits and Women's Occupations', PhD dissertation, University of Massachusetts.

Alexander, L., P. Lichtenbery, and D. Brunn. 1980. 'Social Workers in Unions: A Survey', *Social Work* 25, 3: 216–33.

Allan, June. 2003a. 'Theorizing Critical Social Work', in Allan, Pease, and Briskman (2003).

——. 2003b. 'Practicing Critical Social Work', in Allan, Pease, and Briskman (2003).

——, Bob Pease, and Linda Briskman, eds. 2003. *Critical Social Work: An Introduction to Theories and Practices*. Crows Nest, NSW: Allen & Unwin.

Argyris, C., and D. Schon. 1976. *Theory in Practice: Increasing Professional Effectiveness*. San Francisco: Jossey-Bass.

Aronson, J., and S. Sammon. 2000. 'Practice amid Social Service Cuts and Restructuring: Working with the Contradictions of "Small Victories"', *Canadian Social Work Review* 17, 2: 167–87.

Armitage, Andrew. 1975. *Social Welfare in Canada: Ideals and Realities*. Toronto: McClelland & Stewart.

——. 1988. *Social Welfare in Canada: Ideals, Realities, and Future Paths*, 2nd edn. Toronto: McClelland & Stewart.

——. 1996. *Social Welfare in Canada Revisited: Facing Up to the Future*, 3rd edn. Toronto: Oxford University Press.

——. 2003. *Social Welfare in Canada*, 4th edn. Toronto: Oxford University Press.

Ashe, Fidelma. 1999. 'The Subject', in Fidelma Ashe, Alan Finlayson, Moya Lloyd, Iain MacKenzie, James Martin, and Shane O'Neill, eds, *Contemporary Social and Political Theory*. Buckingham: Open University Press.

Bailey, Roy, and Mike Brake, eds. 1975. *Radical Social Work*. New York: Pantheon Books.

Baines, Carol, Patricia Evans, and Sheila Neysmith, eds. 1991. *Women's Caring: Feminist Perspectives on Social Welfare*. Toronto: McClelland & Stewart.

Baines, Donna. 1997. 'Feminist Social Work in the Inner City: The Challenges of Race, Class, and Gender', *Affilia* 12, 3: 297–317.

Bandopadhyay, Pradeep. 1971. 'One Sociology or Many: Some Issues in Radical Sociology', *Sociological Review* 19, 1: 5–29.

Banting, Keith G. 1982. *The Welfare State and Canadian Federalism*. Montreal and Kingston: McGill-Queen's University Press.

Barbour, Rosaline S. 1984. 'Social Work Education: Tackling the Theory-Practice Dilemma', *British Journal of Social Work* 14: 557–77.

Barker, Robert L. 1987. *The Social Work Dictionary*. Silver Spring, Md: National Association of Social Workers.

Basch, Michael. 1975. 'Toward a Theory That Encompasses Depression: A Revision of Existing Causal Hypotheses', in E. James Anthony and Theresa Benedek, eds, *Depression and Human Existence*. Boston: Little, Brown & Co.

Bastow, Steve, and James Martin. 2003. *Third Way Discourse: European Ideologies in the Twentieth Century*. Edinburgh: Edinburgh University Press.

Bawden, D. Lee, and J.L. Palmer. 1984. 'Social Policy: Challenging the Welfare State', in J.L. Palmer and I.V. Sawhill, eds, *The Reagan Record*. Washington: The Urban Institute.

Becker, Howard, and Harry Elmer Barnes. 1978. *Social Thought From Lore to Science*, II. Gloucester, Mass.: Peter Smith.

Bell, Daniel. 1965. *The End of Ideology: On the Exhaustion of Political Ideas in the Fifties*. New York: Free Press.

Bell, David, and Lorne Tepperman. 1979. *The Roots of Disunity: A Look at Canadian Political Culture*. Toronto: McClelland & Stewart.

Bella, Leslie. 1989. 'The Canadian Social Work Profession, 1985–1989: Professional Self-Interest and Public Welfare', paper presented to the Canadian Association of Schools of Social Work, Laval, Que., June.

Benn, S.I., and R.S. Peters. 1959. *Social Principles and the Democratic State*. London: Allen & Unwin.

Berger, Peter L., and Thomas Luckmann. 1966. *The Social Construction of Reality*. New York: Doubleday.

Berry, Christopher J. 1986. *Human Nature*. Atlantic Highlands, NJ: Humanities Press International.

Beveridge, W. 1942. *Social Insurance and Allied Services* (the Beveridge Report). London: HMSO, Cmnd 6404.

Bevir, M. 2000. 'New Labour: A Study in Ideology', *British Journal of Politics and International Relations* 2, 3: 277–301.

Biehal, Nina, and Eric Sainsbury. 1991. 'From Values to Rights in Social Work', *British Journal of Social Work* 21: 245–57.

Biklen, Douglas P. 1983. *Community Organizing: Theory and Practice*. Englewood Cliffs, NJ: Prentice-Hall.

Bishop, Anne. 1994, 2002. *Becoming an Ally: Breaking the Cycle of Oppression*. Halifax: Fernwood.

Blair, Peter. 1973. 'Orientation Towards Clients in a Public Welfare Agency', in Elihu Katz and Brenda Danet, eds, *Bureaucracy and the Public: A Reader in Official–Client Relations*. New York: Basic Books.

Blair, Tony. 1998. *The Third Way: New Politics for the New Century*. London: Fabian Society.

—— and Gerhard Schroder. 1999. *Europe: The Third Way/Die Neue Mitte*. London: Labour Party.

Blalock, Hubert M. 1967. *Toward a Theory of Minority Group Relations*. New York: Wiley.

Blunkett, David. 2001. 'No Hiding Place for Fraudsters', *Observer*, 14 Jan.

Bock, Scott. 1980. 'Conscientization: Paulo Freire and Class-Based Practice', *Catalyst* 2, 2: 5–26.

Bolger, Steve, Paul Corrigan, Jan Docking, and Nick Frost. 1981. *Towards Socialist Welfare Work*. London: Macmillan.

Borland, Jeff, Bob Gregory, and Peter Sheehan. 2001. 'Inequality and Economic Change', in Borland, Gregory, and Sheehan, eds, *Work Rich, Work Poor*. Melbourne: Victoria University, 1–20.

Bouchard, Lucien. 1992. *On the Record*. Toronto: Stoddart.

Bourgon, Michelle. 1988. 'How Feminism Can Take the Crazy Out of Your Head and Put It Back Into Society', in Geraldine Finn, ed., *Women's Studies: A Canadian Perspective*. Ottawa: Garamond Press.

Boyd, Susan, ed. 1997. *Challenging the Public/Private Divide: Feminism, Law and Public Policy*. Toronto: University of Toronto Press.

Bracken, Denis, and Christopher Walmsley. 1992. 'The Canadian Welfare State: Implications for the Continuing Education of Canadian Social Workers', *The Social Worker/Le Travailleur Social* 60, 1: 21–4.

Brake, Mike, and Roy Bailey. 1980. *Radical Social Work and Practice*. London: Edward Arnold.

Brooks, Stephen. 2004. *Canadian Democracy: An Introduction*, 4th edn. Toronto: Oxford University Press.

Brown, Leslie, and Susan Strega, eds. 2005. *Research as Resistance: Critical, Indigenous, and Anti-Oppressive Approaches*. Toronto: Canadian Scholars' Press.

Buchbinder, H., V. Burstyn, V. Forbes, and M. Steedman. 1987. *Who's on Top? The Politics of Heterosexuality*. Toronto: Garamond Press.

Bulhan, Hussein A. 1985. *Frantz Fanon and the Psychology of Oppression*. New York: Plenum Press.

Burghardt, Steve. 1982. *The Other Side of Organizing: Resolving the Personal Dilemmas and Political Demands of Daily Practice*. Cambridge, Mass.: Schenkman.

Burke, Mike, Colin Mooers, and John Shields, eds. 2000. *Restructuring and Resistance: Canadian Public Policy in the Age of Global Capitalism*. Halifax: Fernwood.

Burrell, G., and G. Morgan. 1979. *Sociological Paradigms and Organizational Analysis*. London: Heinemann.

Butler, Judith. 1990. *Gender Trouble: Feminism and the Subversion of Identity*. New York: Routledge.

Butler, Stuart, and Anna Kondratas. 1987. *Out of the Poverty Trap*. New York: Free Press.

Callaghan, J. 2000. *The Retreat of Social Democracy*. Manchester: Manchester University Press.

Callinicos, A. 2001. *Against the Third Way*. Cambridge: Polity Press.

Campbell, Colin, and William Christian. 1999. *Parties, Leaders, and Ideologies in Canada*. Toronto: McGraw-Hill Ryerson.

Campfens, Hubert. 1988. 'Forces Shaping the New Social Work in Latin America', *Canadian Social Work Review* 5: 9–27.

Canada. 2005. *Economic and Fiscal Update*. Ottawa: Department of Finance, 14 Nov.

Canadian Advisory Council on the Status of Women. 1990. *Women and Labour Market Poverty*. Ottawa: CACSW.

Canadian Association of Social Workers. 1983, 1994. Preamble to the Canadian Association of Social Workers *Code of Ethics*. Ottawa: CASW.

——. 2004a. *Women's Income and Poverty in Canada Revisited*. Ottawa: CASW.

——. 2004b. *Gendering the Poverty Line*. Ottawa: CASW.

——. 2005. *Code of Ethics*. Ottawa: CASW.

Canadian Business. 1985. 'Still Nursing After All These Years: A Special Report', Jan.: 69–70.

Canadian Centre for Policy Alternatives. 1995. *CCPA Monitor* (July–Aug.): 12.

Canadian Dimension. 2003. 'Manitoba: What the NDP Does When It Governs' (Mar.–Apr.).

Canadian Feminist Alliance for International Action. 2005. 'Canada's Commitment to Equality: A Gender Analysis of the Last Ten Federal Budgets (1995–2004)', prepared by A. Yalnizyan. Ottawa: Canadian Feminist Alliance for International Action.

Carling, A. 1999. 'New Labour's Polity: Tony Giddens and the "Third Way"', *Imprints: Journal of Analytical Socialism* 3, 3: 214–42.

Carniol, Ben. 1979. 'A Critical Approach in Social Work', *Canadian Journal of Social Work Education* 5, 1: 95–111.

——. 1984. 'Clash of Ideologies in Social Work Education', *Canadian Social Work Review*: 184–99.

——. 1987, 1990, 1995, 2000, 2005. *Case Critical*. Toronto: Between the Lines.

Carter, J. 1998. 'Postmodernity and Welfare: When Worlds Collide', *Social Policy and Administration* 32, 2: 101–5.

Caspary, William R. 1980. 'Psychotherapy and Radical Politics', *Catalyst: A Socialist Journal of the Social Services* no. 7: 27–36.

Catalyst: A Socialist Journal of the Social Services. 1981. Special issue on lesbian and gay issues and the social services, no. 12.

Chambon, Adrienne S., and Allan Irving, eds. 1994. *Essays on Postmodernism and Social Work*. Toronto: Canadian Scholars' Press.

——, ——, and Laura Epstein, eds. 1999. *Reading Foucault for Social Work*. New York: Columbia University Press.

Chandler, Robert G. 1995.'The Profession of Social Work', in Joanne C. Turner and Francis J. Turner, eds, *Canadian Social Welfare*. Scarborough, Ont.: Allyn & Bacon.

Chappel, Rosalie. 1997. *Social Welfare in Canadian Society*. Scarborough, Ont.: Nelson.

Chevigny, P. 1995. *Edge of the Knife: Police Violence in the Americas*. New York: New Press.

Christian, William, and Colin Campbell. 1974. *Political Parties and Ideologies in Canada: Liberals, Conservatives, Socialists and Nationalists*. Toronto: McGraw-Hill Ryerson.

Clark, C.L., and A. Asquith. 1985. *Social Work and Social Philosophy*. London: Routledge & Kegan Paul.

Clarke, Michelle. 1991. *Fighting Poverty through Programs: Social and Health Programs for Canada's Poor Children and Youth*. Ottawa: Children*Enfants*Jeunesse*Youth (CEJY).

Cloward, Richard A., and Frances Fox Piven. 1975. 'Notes toward a Radical Social Work', in Bailey and Brake (1975: xxiii–xxiv).

Coates, John. 1991. 'Putting Knowledge for Practice into Perspective', *Canadian Social Work Review* 8, 1: 82–96.

——. 2003. *Ecology and Social Work: Toward a New Paradigm*. Halifax: Fernwood.

Cole, Thomas R. 1986. 'Putting Off the Old: Middle Class Morality, Antebellum Protestantism, and the Origins of Ageism', in David Van Tassel and Peter N. Stearns, eds, *Old Age in a Bureaucratic Society*. New York: Greenwood.

Collins, Barbara G. 1986. 'Defining Feminist Social Work', *Social Work* 31, 3: 214–19.

Cornforth, M. 1953. *Materialism and the Dialectical Method*. New York: International Publishers.

Corrigan, Paul, and Peter Leonard. 1978. *Social Work Practice under Capitalism: A Marxist Approach*. London: Macmillan.

Cummings, Joan E. 1980. 'Sexism in Social Work: Some Thoughts on Strategy for Structural Change', *Catalyst* 8: 7–34.

Curtis, James, Edward Grabb, Neil Guppy, and Sid Gilbert. 1988. *Social Inequality in Canada: Patterns, Problems, Policies*. Scarborough, Ont.: Prentice-Hall Canada.

Dalrymple, J., and B. Burke. 1995. *Anti-Oppressive Practice: Social Care and the Law*. Buckingham: Open University Press.

Davis, A. 1981. *Women, Race and Class*. London: Women's Press.

Davis, Ann. 1991. 'A Structural Approach to Social Work', in Joyce Lishman, ed., *Handbook of Theory for Practice Teachers in Social Work*. London: Jessica Kingsley.

DeKeseredy, Walter S., and Ronald Hinch. 1991. *Woman Abuse: Sociological Perspectives*. Toronto: Thompson Educational Publishing.

De Maria, William. 1982. 'Fumbling with the Kaleidoscope: World View Clashes in Social Work', *Canadian Journal of Social Work Education* 8, 1–2: 31–44.

De Schweinitz, Karl. 1943. *England's Road to Social Security*. Philadelphia: University of Pennsylvania Press.

Dickason, Olive Patricia. 2006. *A Concise History of Canada's First Nations*. Toronto: Oxford University Press.

Dickerson, Mark O., and Thomas Flanagan. 1986. *An Introduction to Government and Politics: A Conceptual Approach*. Agincourt, Ont.: Methuen.

Djao, Angela. 1983. *Inequality and Social Policy*. Toronto: John Wiley & Sons.

Dluhy, Milan J. 1990. *Building Coalitions in the Human Services*. Newbury Park, Calif.: Sage.

Dominelli, Lena. 1996. 'Deprofessionalizing Social Work: Anti-Oppressive Practice, Competencies and Postmodernism', *British Journal of Social Work* 26: 153–75.

——. 1997. *Anti-Racist Social Work*, 2nd edn. London: Macmillan.

—— and Eileen McLeod. 1989. *Feminist Social Work*. Hampshire, UK: Macmillan Education.

Doyal, L., and I. Gough. 1991. *A Theory of Human Need*. New York: Guilford Press.

Driver, S., and L. Martell. 2000. 'Left, Right and the Third Way', *Policy and Politics* 28, 2: 147–61.

Drover, Glen, and David Woodsworth. 1978. 'Social Welfare Theory and Social Policy', *Canadian Journal of Social Work Education* 4, 1: 19–41.

Dyck, Rand, ed. 2002. *Studying Politics: An Introduction to Political Science*. Toronto: Thompson/Nelson.

Dykema, C.R. 1977. 'The Political Economy of Social Welfare: A Perspective', *Journal of Sociology and Social Welfare* 4, 3–4: 439–69.

Eagleton, T. 1996. *The Illusions of Postmodernism*. Oxford: Blackwell.

Economic Council of Canada. 1968. *Fifth Annual Review*. Ottawa.

Eichlcr, M. 1988. *Families in Canada Today*. Toronto: Gage.

Esping-Andersen, Gosta. 1989. 'The Three Political Economies of the Welfare State', *Canadian Review of Sociology and Anthropology* 26, 11: 10–36.

———. 1990. *The Three Worlds of Welfare Capitalism*. Princeton, NJ: Princeton University Press.

Fabricant, Michael, and Stephen Burghardt. 1992. *The Welfare State Crisis and the Transformation of Social Service Work*. Armonk, NY: M.E. Sharpe.

Fairclough, N. 1992. 'Discourse and Text: Linguistic and Intertextual Analysis within Discourse Analysis', *Discourse and Society* 3, 2: 193–217.

Fanon, Frantz. 1968. *The Wretched of the Earth*. London: Temple Smith.

Ferguson, Iain, and Michael Lavalette. 1999. 'Social Work, Postmodernism and Marxism', *European Journal of Social Work* 2, 1: 27–40.

—— and ——. 2005. 'Another World Is Possible', in Ferguson, Lavalette, and Whitmore (2005: 207–23).

——, ——, and Gerry Mooney. 2002. *Rethinking Welfare: A Critical Perspective*. London: Sage.

——, ——, and Elizabeth Whitmore. 2005. *Globalisation, Global Justice and Social Work*. London: Routledge.

Festinger, Leon. 1957. *A Theory of Cognitive Dissonance*. Stanford, Calif.: Stanford University Press.

Financial Times (London), 4 Feb. 2000, 5.

Findlay, P.G. 1978. 'Theories of the State and Social Welfare in Canada', *Canadian Journal of Social Work Education* 14, 1: 109–28.

Finn, Ed. 1979. 'Ontario's Bill 70 a Major Step in Workplace Safety: Unionist', *Toronto Star*, 19 Feb.

Finn, Janet L., and Maxine Jacobson. 2003. 'Just Practice: Steps toward a New Social Work Paradigm', *Journal of Social Work Education* 39, 1: 57–76.

Firestone, Shulamith. 1970. *The Dialectic of Sex: The Case for Feminist Revolution*. New York: Bantam Books.

———. 1984. 'The Dialectic of Sex', in Alison M. Jaggar and Paula S. Rothenberg, eds, *Feminist Frameworks*. New York: McGraw-Hill.

Fischer, Joel. 1978. *Effective Casework Practice*. New York: McGraw-Hill.

Fisher, Robert, and J. Kling. 1994. 'Community Organization and New Social Movement Theory', *Journal of Progressive Human Services* 5: 5–24.

—— and Howard J. Karger. 1997. *Social Work and Community in a Private World: Getting Out in Public*. White Plains, NY: Longman.

Fitzpatrick, Tony. 2002. 'In Search of a Welfare Democracy', *Social Policy and Society* 1, 1: 11–20.

Flora, Peter, and Arnold Heidenheimer, eds. 1981. *The Development of Welfare States in Europe and America*. New Brunswick, NJ: Transaction Books.

Fook, Jan. 1986. 'Feminist Contributions to Casework Practice', in H. Marchant and B. Wearing, eds, *Gender Reclaimed: Women and Social Work*. Sydney: Hale & Iremonger, 54–63.

———. 1993. *Radical Casework: A Theory of Practice*. St Leonards, NSW: Allen & Unwin.

———. 1999. 'Critical Reflectivity in Education and Practice', in Pease and Fook (1999).

———. 2000. 'Critical Perspectives on Social Work Practice', in I. O'Connor, P. Smyth, and J. Warburton, eds, *Contemporary Perspectives on Social Work and the Human Services: Challenges and Change*. St Leonards, NSW: Pearson Education, 128–38.

Forbes, David. 1986. 'Counselling in Crisis', *Catalyst* 20: 53–84.

Ford, Julienne. 1975. *Paradigms and Fairy Tales: An Introduction to the Science of Meanings*. London: Routledge & Kegan Paul.

Foucault, Michel. 1977. *Discipline and Punish*. New York: Pantheon.

———. 1980. *Power/Knowledge: Selected Interviews and Other Writings 1972–1977*, ed. Colin Gordon. New York: Pantheon.

Fox, D.R., and Isaac Prilleltensky, eds. 1997. *Critical Psychology: An Introduction*. London: Sage.

Frankel, B. 1979. 'On the State of the State: Marxist Theories of the State after Leninism', *Theory and Society* 7: 199–242.

Franklin, R. 1989. 'Wimps and Bullies: Press Reporting of Child Abuse', in P. Carter, T. Jeffs, and M. Smith, eds, *Social Work and Social Welfare Yearbook*. Philadelphia: Open University Press, 1–14.

Fraser, Heather, and Linda Briskman. 2005. 'Through the Eye of a Needle: The Challenge of Getting Justice in Australia If You're Indigenous or Seeking Asylum', in Ferguson, Lavalette, and Whitmore (2005: 109–23).

—— and Desma Strong. 2000. 'Teaching Structural Social Work Skills to Beginning Students', *Advances in Social Work Education* (Nov.): 24–32.

Fraser, Neil. 1979. 'The Labor Movement in the Explanation of Social Service Growth: The United States and Britain', *Administration in Social Work* 3, 3: 301–12.

——. 1985. 'Michel Foucault: A Young Conservative?', *Ethics* 96: 165–84.

Frayne, G. 1987. 'Tape-Analysis Grid for the Action Research on the Structural Approach to Social Work', unpublished material, Montréal, Université de Montréal, École de service social.

Freedberg, Sharon. 1989. 'Self-Determination: Historical Perspectives on Current Practice', *Social Work* 34, 1: 33–8.

Freeden, M. 1978. *The New Liberalism: An Ideology of Social Reform*. Oxford: Clarendon.

Freeman, E.M. 1990. 'Theoretical Perspectives for Practice with Black Families', in S.M.L. Logan, E.M. Freeman, and R.B. McRoy, eds, *Social Work Practice with Black Families: A Culturally Specific Perspective*. White Plains, NY: Longman, 38–52.

Freire, Paulo. 1970, 1994. *Pedagogy of the Oppressed*. New York: Continuum Publishing.

Friedman, M. 1962. *Capitalism and Freedom*. Chicago: University of Chicago Press.

Friedmann, John. 1973. 'The Public Interest and Community Participation: Toward a Reconstruction of Public Philosophy', *Journal of the American Institute of Planners* 39, 1: 2–12.

Frye, Marilyn. 1983. *The Politics of Reality: Essays in Feminist Theory*. Trumansburg, NY: Crossing Press.

Fukuyama, Francis. 1992. *The End of History and the Last Man*. New York: Free Press.

Furniss, Norman, and Timothy Tilton. 1977. *The Case for the Welfare State*. Bloomington: Indiana University Press.

Galper, Jeffry. 1975. *The Politics of Social Services*. Englewood Cliffs, NJ: Prentice-Hall.

——. 1980. *Social Work Practice: A Radical Perspective*. Englewood Cliffs, NJ: Prentice-Hall.

Gandhi, Leela. 1998. *Postcolonial Theory: A Critical Introduction*. St Leonards, NSW: Allen & Unwin.

Garrett, P. 1999. 'Mapping Child-care Social Work in the Final Years of the Twentieth Century: A Critical Response to the "Looking after Children" System', *British Journal of Social Work* 29: 27–47.

Geertz, C. 1986. 'The Uses of Diversity', *Michigan Quarterly Review* 25, 1: 105–23.

George, Vic, and Paul Wilding. 1976. *Ideology and Social Welfare*. London: Routledge & Kegan Paul.

—— and ——. 1984. *The Impact of Social Policy*. London: Routledge & Kegan Paul.

—— and ——. 1985. *Ideology and Social Welfare*, 2nd edn. London: Routledge & Kegan Paul.

—— and ——. 1994. *Welfare and Ideology*. London: Harvester Wheatsheaf.

—— and ——. 2002. *Globalization and Human Welfare*. Basingstoke: Palgrave.

Germain, Carol, ed. 1979. *Social Work Practice: People and Environment, An Ecological Perspective*. New York: Columbia University Press.

Giddens, Anthony. 1994. *Beyond Left and Right: The Future of Radical Politics*. Cambridge: Polity.

——. 1998. *The Third Way: The Renewal of Social Democracy*. Cambridge: Polity.

——. 2000. *The Third Way and Its Critics*. Cambridge: Polity.

Gil, David G. 1973. *Unravelling Social Policy*. Cambridge, Mass.: Schenkman.

——. 1976a. 'Social Policies and Social Development: A Humanistic-Egalitarian Perspective', *Journal of Sociology and Social Welfare* 3, 3: 242–63.

——. 1976b. *The Challenge of Social Equality*. Cambridge, Mass.: Schenkman.

——. 1990. 'Implications of Conservative Tendencies for Practice and Education in Social Welfare', *Journal of Sociology and Social Welfare* 17, 2: 20–1.

——. 1998. *Confronting Injustice and Oppression: Concepts and Strategies for Social Workers*. New York: Columbia University Press.

—— and Eva Gil, eds. 1985. *Toward Social and Economic Justice*. Cambridge, Mass.: Schenkman.

Gilder, George. 1981. *Wealth and Poverty*. New York: Basic Books.

Goldberg-Ward, Gale, and Ruth R. Middleman. 1974. *The Structural Approach to Direct Practice in Social Work*. New York: Columbia University Press.

Goldhor-Lerner, H. 1985. *The Dance of Anger*. New York: Harper & Row.

Gordon, D. 1978. *Therapeutic Metaphors*. Cupertino, Calif.: Meta Publications.

Goroff, Norman. 1981. 'Humanism and Social Work Paradoxes, Problems, and Promises', *Journal of Sociology and Social Welfare* 8, 1: 1–9.

Gough, Ian. 1979. *The Political Economy of the Welfare State*. London: Macmillan.

Gould, K. 1987. 'Life Model versus Conflict Model: A Feminist Perspective', *Social Work* 32, 4 (May–June): 346–51.

Gray, John. 1998. *False Dawn: The Delusions of Global Capitalism*. London: Granta Books.

Gray, M., C. Van Rooyen, G. Rennie, and J. Gaha. 2002. 'The Political Participation of Social Workers: A Comparative Study', *International Journal of Social Welfare* 11, 2: 99–110.

Green, Joyce. 2000. 'Neoliberalism and Neoconservatism', in Lorraine Code, ed., *The Encyclopedia of Feminist Theories*. New York: Routledge, 364

Guest, Dennis. 1980, 1985, 1997. *The Emergence of Social Security in Canada*. Vancouver: University of British Columbia Press.

Gutierrez, L., R. Parsons, and E. Cox. 1998. *Empowerment in Social Work Practice: A Sourcebook*. Pacific Grove, Calif.: Brooks/Cole.

Habermas, Jurgen. 1983. 'Modernity: An Incomplete Project', in Hal Foster, ed., *The Anti-Aesthetic: Essays on Postmodern Culture*. Port Townsend, Wash.: Bay Press, 3–15.

Hall, S., C. Critcher, T. Jefferson, J. Clarke, and B. Roberts. 1978. *Policing the Crisis: Muggings, the State and Law and Order*. London: Macmillan.

Haney, Eleanor H. 1989. *Vision and Struggle: Meditations on Feminist Spirituality and Politics*. Portland, Maine: Astarte Shell Press.

Hardy, Jean. 1981a. *Values in Social Work*. London: Routledge & Kegan Paul.

——. 1981b. *Values in Social Policy: Nine Contradictions*. London: Routledge & Kegan Paul.

Harmes, Adam. 2004. *The Return of the State: Protestors, Power-brokers and the New Global Compromise*. Vancouver: Douglas & McIntyre.

Harrington, Michael. 1962. *The Other America*. New York: Macmillan.

Hart, Michael Anthony. 2002. *Seeking Mino-Pimatisawin: An Aboriginal Approach to Helping*. Halifax: Fernwood.

Hartmann, Heidi. 1986. 'The Unhappy Marriage of Marxism and Feminism: Towards a More Progressive Union', in Lynda Sargent, ed., *The Unhappy Marriage of Marxism and Feminism: A Debate on Class and Patriarchy*. London: Pluto.

Harvey, David. 1989. *The Condition of Postmodernity: An Enquiry into the Origins of Cultural Change*. Cambridge: Basil Blackwell.

Hasenfeld, Yeheskel. 1987. 'Power in Social Work Practice', *Social Service Review* 61, 3: 469–83.

Hattersley, R. 2001. 'It's No Longer My Party', *The Guardian*, 24 June.

Hay, C. 1999. *The Political Economy of New Labour: Labouring under False Pretences?* Manchester: Manchester University Press.

Haynes, Karen, and James S. Mickelson. 1992. 'Social Work and the Reagan Era: Challenges to the Profession', *Journal of Sociology and Social Welfare* 19, 1: 169–83.

—— and ——. 2003. *Affecting Change: Social Workers in the Political Arena*, 5th edn. White Plains, NY: Longman.

Head, S. 1996. 'The New Ruthless Economy', *The New York Review* 43, 4 (29 Feb.).

Health Canada. 1989. *Issues: Drug Abuse by the Elderly*. Ottawa: Health Protection Branch, 20 Sept.

——. 1994. *Suicide in Canada: Update on the Report of the Task Force on Suicide in Canada*. Ottawa: Health Canada.

Health and Welfare Canada. 1991a. *Health Status of Canadian Indians and Inuit*. Ottawa: Minister of Supply and Services Canada.

——. 1991b. *Services to Elderly Patients with Mental Health Problems in General Hospitals: Guidelines*. Ottawa: Health and Welfare Canada.

——. 1992. *Aboriginal Health in Canada*. Ottawa: Health and Welfare Canada.

Healy, Karen. 1999. 'Power and Activist Social Work', in Pease and Fook (1999).

Heller, Agnes. 1987. *Beyond Justice*. New York: Basic Books.

Herald (Glasgow). 2000. 28 Nov.

Herbert, M. 2003. *Canadian Association of Social Workers Child Welfare Project: Creating Conditions for Good Practice*. Ottawa: Canadian Association of Social Workers.

Heron, Craig. 1996. *The Canadian Labour Movement: A Brief History*, 2nd edn. Toronto: James Lorimer.

Hick, Steven. 2002. *Social Work in Canada: An Introduction*. Toronto: Thompson Educational Publishing.

———. 2004. *Social Welfare in Canada: Understanding Income Security*. Toronto: Thompson Educational Publishing.

———, Jan Fook, and Richard Pozzuto, eds. 2005. *Social Work: A Critical Turn*. Toronto: Thompson Educational Publishing.

Himmelstrand, Ulf, et al. 1981. *Beyond Welfare Capitalism*. London: Heinemann.

Hobbes, Thomas. 1981 [1651]. *Leviathan*, ed., C.B. MacPherson. Harmondsworth: Penguin English Library.

Hobhouse, L.T. 1994. *Liberalism and Other Writings*, ed. J. Meadowcroft. Cambridge: Cambridge University Press.

hooks, bell. 1991. *Yearning: Race, Gender and Cultural Politics*. London: Turnaround.

———. 1993. *Sisters of the Yam: Black Women and Self-Recovery*. Boston: South End Press.

Horowitz, Gad. 1966. 'Conservatism, Liberalism and Socialism in Canada: An Interpretation', *Canadian Journal of Economics and Political Science* 32, 2: 143–71.

———. 1968. *Canadian Labour in Politics*. Toronto: University of Toronto Press.

Horton, John. 1966. 'Order and Conflict Theories of Social Problems as Competing Ideologies', *American Journal of Sociology* 72 (May): 701–13.

Howe, David. 1987. *An Introduction to Social Work Theory*. Aldershot, UK: Wildwood House.

———. 1994. 'Modernity, Postmodernity and Social Work', *British Journal of Social Work* 24: 513–32.

Hughes, J. 1973. 'Nationalization and the Private Sector', in J. Urry and J. Wakeford, eds, *Power in Britain*. London: Heinemann.

Hugman, Richard. 1998. *Social Welfare and Social Value: The Role of Caring Professions*. Basingstoke: Macmillan.

Hunsley, Terry. 1987. 'Future Directions and Challenges in Social Development', discussion paper. Ottawa: Canadian Council on Social Development.

Hutchison-Reis, M. 1989. '"And For Those of Us Who are Black?" Black Politics in Social Work', in Langan and Lee (1989b: 165–77).

Huyssens, A. 1984. 'Mapping the Postmodern', *New German Critique* 33: 5–52.

Iatridis, Demetrius. 1983. 'Neo-conservatism Reviewed', *Social Work* 28, 2: 101–7.

Ife, Jim. 1995. *Community Development: Creating Community Alternatives—Vision, Analysis and Practice*. Melbourne: Longman.

———. 1997. *Rethinking Social Work: Towards Critical Practice*. Lance Cove, NSW: Addison-Wesley Longman.

———. 1999. 'Postmodernism, Critical Theory and Social Work', in Pease and Fook (1999).

———. 2001. *Human Rights and Social Work: Towards Rights-Based Practice*. Cambridge: Cambridge University Press.

Jacques, Martin. 1990. 'After Capitalism: What Now?', *Social Policy* 21, 2: 12–16.

Jaggar, A., and P. Rothenberg. 1984. *Feminist Frameworks*, 2nd edn. New York: McGraw-Hill.

——— and P. Struhl. 1978. *Feminist Frameworks*. New York: McGraw-Hill.

Jay, M. 1973. *The Dialectical Imagination: A History of the Frankfurt School and the Institute for Social Research, 1932–50*. Boston: Little, Brown.

Jeffreys, S. 1986. *The Spinster and Her Enemies*. London: Pandora Press.

Jenson, Jane. 1989. 'Different but Not "Exceptional": Canada's Permeable Fordism', *Canadian Review of Sociology and Anthropology* 20, 1: 69–94.

Jones, Chris. 1983. *State Social Work and the Working Class*. London: Macmillan.

Jones, Howard, ed. 1975. *Towards a New Social Work*. London: Routledge & Kegan Paul.

Jordan, Bill, with Charlie Jordan. 2000. *Social Work and the Third Way: Tough Love as Social Policy*. London: Sage.

Karger, Howard Jacob. 1987. 'Ideology and the Crisis of the Welfare State', *Quarterly Journal of Ideology: A Critique of Conventional Wisdom* 11, 1: 3–11.

Keefe, Thomas. 1980. 'Empathy Skill and Critical Consciousness', *Social Casework* 61, 7: 387–93.

Kellner, Douglas. 1989. *Critical Theory, Marxism, and Modernity*. Baltimore: Johns Hopkins University Press.

Kellough, Gail. 1980. 'From Colonialism to Economic Imperialism: The Experience of the Canadian Indian', in John Harp and John R. Hofley, eds, *Structured Inequality in Canada*. Scarborough, Ont.: Prentice-Hall, 343–77.

Kerans, Patrick. 1978. 'Social Science and Ideology in Policy Analysis', *Canadian Journal of Social Work Education* 4, 1: 129–41.

Knisel, Henry S. 1968. 'Pluralism', in Sills (1968, vol. 12: 124–69).

Knuttila, Murray. 2002. *Introducing Sociology: A Critical Perspective*, 2nd edn. Toronto: Oxford University Press.

—— and Wendee Kubik. 2000. *State Theories: Classical, Global and Feminist Perspectives*, 3rd edn. Halifax: Fernwood.

Kovel, Joel. 1984. *White Racism: A Psychohistory*, 2nd edn. New York: Columbia University Press.

Krieger, N., and S. Sidney. 1996. 'Racial Discrimination and Blood Pressure: The CARDIA Study of Young Black and White Adults', *American Journal of Public Health* 86: 1370–8.

Kuhn, Thomas S. 1962, 1970. *The Structure of Scientific Revolutions*. Chicago: University of Chicago Press.

Laclau, Ernesto, and Chantal Mouffe. 2001. *Hegemony and Socialist Strategy: Toward a Radical Democratic Politics*, 2nd edn. London: Verso.

Lane, B. 1997. 'A Question of Justice', *Australian Social Work* 50, 4: 37–9.

Langan, Mary, and Phil Lee. 1989a. 'Whatever Happened to Radical Social Work', in Langan and Lee (1989b: 1–18).

—— and ——, eds. 1989b. *Radical Social Work Today*. London: Unwin Hyman.

Laski, H. 1925. *A Grammar of Politics*. London: Allen & Unwin.

Laursen, Kay. 1975. 'Professionalism', in Harold Throssell, ed., *Social Work: Radical Essays*. St Lucia, Queensland: University of Queensland Press, 47–71.

Lavalette, Michael, and Gerry Mooney. 1999. 'New Labour, New Moralism: The Welfare Politics and Ideology of New Labour under Blair', *International Socialism*, 2: 27–47.

—— and Alan Pratt. 1997. *Social Policy: A Conceptual and Theoretical Introduction*. London: Sage.

—— and ——. 2001. *Social Policy: A Conceptual and Theoretical Introduction*, 2nd edn. London: Sage.

Lecomte, Roland. 1990. 'Connecting Private Troubles and Public Issues in Social Work Education', in Wharf (1990: 31–51).

Lee, Bill. 1986. *Pragmatics of Community Organization*. Mississauga, Ont.: Common Act Press.

Lees, Ray. 1972. *Politics and Social Work*. London: Routledge & Kegan Paul.

Lemert, Charles. 1994. 'Post-structuralism and Sociology', in Steven Seidman, ed., *The Postmodern Turn: New Perspectives on Social Theory*. Cambridge: Cambridge University Press.

Leonard, Peter. 1975. 'Towards a Paradigm for Radical Practice', in Bailey and Brake (1975: 46–61).

——. 1984. *Personality and Ideology: Towards a Materialist Understanding of the Individual*. London: Macmillan.

——. 1990. 'Contesting the Welfare State in a Neo-Conservative Era', *Journal of Progressive Human Services* 1, 1: 1–25.

——. 1994. 'Knowledge/Power and Postmodernism', *Canadian Social Work Review* 11, 1: 11–26.

——. 1995. 'Postmodernism, Socialism and Social Welfare', *Journal of Progressive Human Services* 6, 2: 3–19.

——. 1997. *Postmodern Welfare: Reconstructing an Emancipatory Project*. London: Sage.

Leonard, Stephen T. 1990. *Critical Theory in Political Practice*. Princeton, NJ: Princeton University Press.

Lerner, Gerda. 1979. *The Majority Finds Its Past: Placing Women in History*. New York: Oxford University Press.

Lightman, Ernie. 1982. 'Professionalization, Bureaucratization, and Unionization in Social Work', *Social Service Review* 56, 1: 130–43.

——. 2003. *Social Policy in Canada*. Toronto: Oxford University Press.

—— and A. Irving. 1991. 'Restructuring Canada's Welfare State', *Journal of Social Policy* 20, 1: 65–86.

Lim, O. 1996. 'Anger is a Gift', unpublished research paper, McGill University.

Lloyd, Moya. 1999. 'The Body', in F. Ashe, A. Finlayson, M. Lloyd, I. MacKenzie, J. Martin, and S. O'Neill, eds, *Contemporary Social and Political Theory: An Introduction*. Buckingham: Open University Press.

Longres, John. 1986. 'Marxian Theory and Social Work Practice', *Catalyst* 5, 4: 13–34.

—— and Eileen McLeod. 1980. 'Consciousness Raising and Social Work Practice', *Social Casework* 61, 5: 267–76.

Lorde, A. 1984. *Sister Outsider: Essays and Speeches*. New York: Crossing Press.

Lowenberg, Frank M. 1984. 'Professional Ideology, Middle Range Theories and Knowledge Building for Social Work Practice', *British Journal of Social Work* 14: 309–22.

Lundy, Colleen. 2004. *Social Work and Social Justice: A Structural Approach to Practice*. Peterborough, Ont.: Broadview Press.

—— and Larry Gauthier. 1989. 'Social Work Practice and the Master–Servant Relationship', *The Social Worker/Le Travailleur Social* 57, 4: 190–4.

Lyotard, J.F. 1984. *The Postmodern Condition: A Report on Knowledge*. Manchester: Manchester University Press.

McBride, S. 2001. *Paradigm Shift: Globalization and the Canadian State*. Halifax: Fernwood.

McCready, John. 1980. *The Context for Canadian Social Policy*. Toronto: University of Toronto Faculty of Social Work, Working Papers on Social Welfare in Canada Series.

McDaniel, Susan A., and Ben Agger. 1984. *Social Problems through Conflict and Order*. Don Mills, Ont.: Addison-Wesley.

Macey, David. 2000. *The Penguin Dictionary of Critical Theory*. London: Penguin Books.

Macey, Marie, and Eileen Moxon. 1996. 'An Examination of Anti-Racist and Anti-Oppressive Theory and Practice in Social Work Education', *British Journal of Social Work* 26: 297–314.

McGilly, Frank 1990. *An Introduction to Canada's Public Social Services*. Toronto: McClelland & Stewart.

——. 1998. *An Introduction to Canada's Public Social Services: Understanding Income and Health Programs*, 2nd edn. Toronto: Oxford University Press.

McKenna, Francis. 1985. 'Corporate Welfare–Alive and Well in the 1980s', *Perception* 8, 5: 25–6.

McKenzie, Brad, and Peter Hudson. 1985. 'Native Children, Child Welfare, and the Colonization of Native People', in K.L. Levitte and B. Wharf, eds, *The Challenge of Child Welfare*. Vancouver: University of British Columbia Press.

McNally, David. 2002. *Another World Is Possible: Globalization and Anti-capitalism*. Winnipeg: Arbeiter Ring.

McQuaig, Linda. 1993. *The Wealthy Banker's Wife: The Assault on Equality in Canada*. Toronto: Penguin Books.

——. 2001. *All You Can Eat: Greed, Lust and the New Capitalism*. Toronto: Viking.

Manchester Guardian Weekly. 1985. 'Jobless Figure a Record Again', 17 Mar., cited in Mishra (1990: 29).

——. 1988. 'The NHS: A Suitable Case for Much Better Treatment', 31 Jan., cited in Mishra (1990: 24).

——. 1988. 'The Starving of the NHS', 13 Mar., 12.

Marchak, M. Patricia. 1981. *Ideological Perspectives on Canada*, 2nd edn. Toronto: McGraw-Hill Ryerson.

——. 1988. *Ideological Perspectives on Canada*, 3rd edn. Toronto: McGraw-Hill Ryerson.

Marchant, H. 1986. 'Gender, Systems Thinking and Radical Social Work', in H. Marchant and B. Wearing, eds, *Gender Reclaimed: Women in Social Work*. Sydney: Hale & Iremonger, 14–32.

Marquand, D. 1999. 'Premature Obsequies: Social Democracy Comes in from the Cold', in A. Gamble and T. Wright, eds, *The New Social Democracy*. Oxford: Blackwell.

Marsh, Leonard C. 1943. *Report on Social Security for Canada*. Ottawa: King's Printer.

——. 1950. 'The Welfare State: Is It a Threat to Canada?', in *Proceedings of the Canadian Conference on Social Work*. Ottawa: Canadian Conference on Social Work.

Marshall, Gordon, ed. 1998. *A Dictionary of Sociology*. Oxford Reference Online <www.oxfordreference.com>. Oxford: Oxford University Press.

Martin, George. 1990. *Social Policy in the Welfare State*. Englewood Cliffs, NJ: Prentice-Hall.

Marx, Karl. 1975 [1845]. 'Theses on Feuerbach', in *K. Marx, Early Writings*. Harmondsworth: Penguin.

——. 1970 [1875]. 'Critique of the Gotha Program', in K. Marx and F. Engels, *Selected Works*, vol. 3. Moscow: Progress Publishers, 13–30.

Masterman, M. 1970. 'The Nature of a Paradigm', in I. Lakatos and A. Musgrave, eds, *Criticism and the Growth of Knowledge*. Cambridge: Cambridge University Press, 59–89.

Meacher, Michael. 1977. 'The Socialist Alternative', in K. Coates and F. Singleton, eds, *The Just Society*. Nottingham: Spokesman Books, 135–48.

Mead, L. 1986. *Beyond Entitlement*. New York: Free Press.

Mendes, Philip. 2003. *Australia's Welfare Wars: The Players, the Politics and the Ideologies*. Sydney: University of New South Wales Press.

Merchant, Carolyn. 1978. *The Death of Nature*. New York: Harper & Row.

Mercier, Lucy R., and Raymond M. Berger. 1989. 'Social Service Needs of Lesbian and Gay Adolescents: Telling It Their Way', *Journal of Social Work and Human Sexuality* 8, 1: 75–95.

Middleman, Ruth R., and Gale Goldberg. 1974. *Social Service Delivery: A Structural Approach to Social Work Practice*. New York: Columbia University Press.

Midgely, J. 1982. *Professional Imperialism: Social Work in the Third World*. London: Heinemann.

———. 1992. 'Introduction: American Social Policy and the Reagan Legacy', Special Issue on the Reagan Legacy and the American Welfare State, *Journal of Sociology and Social Welfare* 19, 1: 3–11.

Miliband, Ralph. 1977. *Marxism and Politics*. Oxford: Oxford University Press.

Millett, K. 1970. *Sexual Politics*. New York: Avon Books.

Mills, C. Wright. 1959. *The Sociological Imagination*. New York: Oxford University Press.

Mishra, Ramesh. 1977. *Society and Social Policy: Theories and Practice of Welfare*. Atlantic Heights, NJ: Humanities Press.

———. 1981. *Society and Social Policy*, 2nd rev. edn. London: Macmillan.

———. 1984. *The Welfare State in Crisis*. New York: St Martin's Press.

———. 1989. 'Riding the New Wave: Social Work and the Neo-Conservative Challenge', *International Social Work* 32, 3: 171–82.

———. 1990. *The Welfare State in Capitalist Society*. Toronto: University of Toronto Press.

———. 1999. *Globalization and the Welfare State*. Cheltenham: Edward Elgar.

Moane, Geraldine. 1999. *Gender and Colonialism: A Psychological Analysis of Oppression and Liberation*. New York: St Martin's Press.

Moffatt, K. 1999. 'Surveillance and Government of the Welfare Recipient', in Chambon, Irving, and Epstein (1999).

Moosa-Mitha, Mehmoona. 2005. 'Situating Anti-oppressive Theories within Critical and Difference-Centered Perspectives', in Brown and Strega (2005).

Moraga, C., and G. Anzaldua, eds. 1983. *This Bridge Called My Back: Writings by Radical Women of Color*. New York: Kitchen Table Press.

Moreau, Maurice (n.d.). 'Practice Implications of a Structural Approach to Social Work', unpublished paper, University of Montreal.

———. 1979. 'A Structural Approach to Social Work Practice', *Canadian Journal of Social Work Education* 5, 1: 78–94.

———. 1990. 'Empowerment through Advocacy and Consciousness-Raising: Implications of a Structural Approach to Social Work', *Journal of Sociology and Social Welfare* 17, 2: 53–67.

———, Sandra Frosst, Gwyn Frayne, Mary Hlywa, Lynn Leonard, and Marilyn Rowell. 1993. *Empowerment II: Snapshots of the Structural Approach in Action*. Ottawa: Health and Welfare Canada.

——— and Lynn Leonard. 1989. *Empowerment through a Structural Approach to Social Work*. Ottawa and Montreal: Carleton University School of Social Work and Ecole de Service Social, Université de Montréal.

Moscovitch, Allan. 1996. 'Canada Health and Social Transfer: What Was Lost?', *Canadian Review of Social Policy* 37: 66–74.

——— and Jim Albert, eds. 1987. *The Benevolent State: The Growth of Welfare in Canada*. Toronto: Garamond Press.

——— and Glen Drover, eds. 1981. *Inequality: Essays on the Political Economy of Social Welfare*. Toronto: University of Toronto Press.

Mosse, George. 1985. *Nationalism and Sexuality*. New York: Fertig.

Mouffe, Chantal. 2000. *The Democratic Paradox*. London: Verso.

Mullaly, Robert (Bob). 1980. 'A Calculus for Social Planning: Rawls' Theory of Justice', Working Papers on Social Welfare in Canada. Toronto: University of Toronto Faculty of Social Work Occasional Papers Series.

———. 1984. 'Social Welfare: Vigilante Style', *Perception* 8, 2: 23–5.

———. 1994. 'Social Welfare and the New Right: A Class Mobilization Perspective', in Andrew F. Johnson, Stephen McBride, and Patrick J. Smith, eds, *Continuities and Discontinuities: The Political Economy of Social Welfare and Labour Market Policy in Canada*. Toronto: University of Toronto Press, 76–94.

———. 2001. 'Confronting the Politics of Despair: Towards the Reconstruction of Progressive Social Work in a Global Economy and Postmodern Age', *Social Work Education* 20, 3: 303–20.

——. 2002. *Challenging Oppression: A Critical Social Work Approach.* Toronto: Oxford University Press.

—— and Eric F. Keating. 1991. 'Similarities, Differences and Dialectics of Radical Social Work', *Journal of Progressive Human Services* 2, 2: 49–78.

Murray, Charles. 1984. *Losing Ground: American Social Policy 1950–1980.* New York: Basic Books.

Naiman, Joanne. 1997. *How Societies Work: Class, Power and Change in a Canadian Context.* Toronto: Irwin.

National Council of Welfare. 1975. *The Hidden Welfare System.* Ottawa: Minister of Supply and Services.

——. 1979. *The Hidden Welfare System Revisited.* Ottawa: Minister of Supply and Services.

——. 1996. *Poverty Profile 1994.* Ottawa: Minister of Supply and Services.

——. 1997. *Poverty Profile 1995.* Ottawa: Minister of Supply and Services.

Nevitte, Neil, and Roger Gibbins. 1990. *New Elites in Old States: Ideologies in the Anglo-American Democracies.* Toronto: Oxford University Press.

New York Times. 2004. 'Corporate Kleptocracy', 2 Sept., A22.

Neysmith, Sheila M. 1991. 'From Community Care to a Social Model of Care', in Baines, Evans, and Neysmith (1991).

Nove, A. 1989. 'Socialism—Why?', in H.B. McCullough, ed., *Political Ideologies and Political Philosophies.* Toronto: Thompson Educational Publishing.

Oberle, Peter. 1993. *The Incidence of Family Poverty on Canadian Indian Reserves.* Ottawa: Indian and Northern Affairs Canada.

O'Brien, Martin, and Sue Penna. 1998. *Theorising Welfare: Enlightenment and Modern Society.* London: Sage.

O'Connor, Ian, Jill Wilson, and Deborah Setterlund. 1999. *Social Work and Welfare Practice.* Sydney: Pearson Education.

O'Connor, James. 1973. *The Fiscal Crisis of the State.* New York: St Martin's Press.

Panitch, Leo, and Donald Swartz. 1988. *The Assault on Trade Union Freedoms: From Consent to Coercion Revisited.* Toronto: Garamond Press.

Parton, Nigel. 1994. 'Problematics of Government, (Post)modernity and Social Work', *British Journal of Social Work* 24: 9–32.

——. 1999. 'Reconfiguring Child Welfare Practices: Risk, Advanced Liberalism, and the Government of Freedom', in Chambon, Irving, and Epstein (1999).

Pateman, Carol. 1970. *Participation and Democratic Theory.* Cambridge: Cambridge University Press.

Patti, Rino J., and Herman Resnick. 1972. 'Changing the Agency from Within', *Social Work* 17, 4: 48–57.

Pease, Bob. 2003. 'Rethinking the Relationship between Self and Society', in Allan, Pease, and Briskman (2003: 187–201).

—— and Janis Fook, eds. 1999. *Transforming Social Work Practice: Postmodern Critical Perspectives.* St Leonards, NSW: Allen & Unwin.

Pelton, Leroy H. 1978. 'Child Abuse and Neglect: The Myth of Classlessness', *American Journal of Orthopsychiatry* 48, 4: 617.

Penkith, Laura, and Yasmin Ali. 1997. 'Racism and Social Welfare', in Lavalette and Pratt (1997).

Perception. 1991. 'Editorial: A Bleak Year for Social Progress', 15, 2: 4–6.

Philo, G., and D. Miller, eds. 2000. *Market Killing.* London: Longman.

Pilalis, Jennie. 1986. 'The Integration of Theory and Practice: A Re-examination of a Paradoxical Expectation', *British Journal of Social Work* 16: 79–96.

Pincus, Allen, and Anne Minahan. 1973. *Social Work Practice: Model and Method.* Itasca, Ill.: F.E. Peacock.

Pinderhughes, Elaine B. 1983. 'Empowerment for Our Clients and for Ourselves', *Social Casework* 64, 6: 331–8.

Piven, Frances Fox, and Richard A. Cloward. 1972. *Regulating the Poor: The Public Functions of Welfare.* New York: Random House.

—— and ——. 1977. *Poor People's Movements.* New York: Pantheon.

Pond, C. 1989. 'The Changing Distribution of Income, Wealth and Poverty', in C. Hammet, ed., *The Changing Social Structure.* London: Sage.

Powell, M. 2000. 'New Labour and the Third Way in the British Welfare State: A New and Distinctive Approach?', *Critical Social Policy* 20, 1: 39–60.

Pritchard, Colin, and Richard Taylor. 1978. *Social Work: Reform or Revolution?* London: Routledge & Kegan Paul.

Rachlin, Allan. 1991. 'Rehumanizing Dialectic: Toward an Understanding of the Interpenetration of Structure and Subjectivity', *Current Perspectives in Social Theory* 11.

Ralph, Diana. 1993. 'Anti-poverty Policy under NDP Governments', *Canadian Review of Social Policy* 31: 63.

Razack, S. 1998. *Looking White People in the Eye: Gender, Race, and Culture in Courtrooms and Classrooms*. Toronto: University of Toronto Press.

Reasons, Charles E., and William D. Perdue. 1981. *Ideology of Social Problems*. Scarborough, Ont.: Nelson Canada.

Reay, Ruth. 1986. 'Bridging the Gap: A Model for Integrating Theory and Practice', *British Journal of Social Work* 16: 49–64.

Rees, S. 1991. *Achieving Power: Practice and Policy in Social Welfare*. North Sydney: Allen & Unwin.

—— and G. Rodley, eds. 1995. *The Human Costs of Managerialism: Advocating the Recovery of Humanity*. Leichardt, NSW: Pluto Press.

Reeser, Linda C., and Irwin Epstein. 1990. *Professionalization and Activism in Social Work: The Sixties, the Eighties, and the Future*. New York: Columbia University Press.

Reisch, Michael. 1995. 'If You Think You're Not Political, Guess Again: The 1994 Elections', Keynote Address, NASW California Legislative Days Conference, 12 Feb., Sacramento, cited in Fisher and Karger (1997).

—— and Stanley Wenocur. 1983. 'Introduction', *Journal of Sociology and Social Welfare* 10, 4: 546–9.

Resnick, P. 1984. 'The Ideology of Neo-Conservatism', in Warren Magnussen et al., eds, *The New Reality: The Politics of Restraint in British Columbia*. Vancouver: New Star Books.

Reynolds, Paul Davidson. 1971. *A Primer in Theory Construction*. New York: Bobbs-Merrill.

Rice, James J., and Michael J. Prince. 2000. *Changing Politics of Canadian Social Policy*. Toronto: University of Toronto Press.

Rich, Adrienne. 1977. *Of Woman Born: Motherhood as Experience and Institution*. London: Women's Press.

——. 1980. 'Compulsory Heterosexuality and Lesbian Existence', *Signs* 5, 4 (Summer): 389–417.

Riches, Graham. 1986. *Food Banks in Canada*. Ottawa: Canadian Council on Social Development.

Riddell, P. 1985. *The Thatcher Government*. Oxford: Blackwell.

Robbins, Susan P., Pranab Chatterjee, and Edward R. Canda. 1998. *Contemporary Human Behavior Theory: A Critical Perspective for Social Work*. Boston: Allyn & Bacon.

Roberts, Geoffrey K. 1971. *A Dictionary of Political Analysis*. New York: St Martin's Press.

Roberts, J. 1992. 'Introduction', in J. Roberts and J. Vorst, eds, *Socialism in Crisis? Canadian Perspectives*. Halifax and Winnipeg: Fernwood Publishing and Society for Socialist Studies.

Rodger, John J. 2000. *From a Welfare State to a Welfare Society: The Changing Context of Social Policy in a Postmodern Era*. London: Macmillan.

Rojek, C., G. Peacock, and S. Collins. 1988. *Social Work and Received Ideas*. London: Routledge & Kegan Paul.

Rondeau, Gilles. 2000. 'Reflection—Empowerment and Social Practice, Or the Issue of Power in Social Work', *Social Work and Globalization* (Special Issue) (July): 216–20.

Room, G. 1979. *The Sociology of Welfare*. London: Palgrave Macmillan.

Rorty, Richard. 1999. *Philosophy and Social Hope*. New York: Penguin.

Rose, Stephen M., and Bruce L. Black. 1985. *Advocacy and Empowerment: Mental Health Care in the Community*. Boston: Routledge & Kegan Paul.

Rosen, S., ed. 1982. *My Voice Will Go With You: The Teaching Tales of Milton H. Erickson, M.D.* New York: Norton.

Ross, Murray. 1967. *Community Organization: Theory, Principles, and Practice*. New York: Harper & Row.

Rossiter, Amy. 1996. 'A Perspective on Critical Social Work', *Journal of Progressive Human Services* 7, 2: 23–41.

Rossiter, Clinton. 1968. 'Conservatism', in Sills (1968, vol. 3: 290–4).

Rowbotham, Sheila. 1989. *The Past Is Before Us: Feminism in Action Since the 1960s*. London: Pandora.

Rubington, Earl, and Martin S. Weinberg, eds. 1989, 1995. *The Study of Social Problems*, 2nd and 3rd edns. New York: Oxford University Press.

Rule, J.B. 1971. 'The Problem with Social Problems', *Politics and Society* 2, 1: 47–56.

Rundle, G. 1999. 'Break-out from the Giggle Palace: Social Democracy, the Postmodern Economy and the Prospects for Political Renewal', in G. Patmore and D. Glover, eds, *New Voices for Social Democracy: Labor Essays 1999–2000*. Annandale, NSW: Pluto Press, 159–72.

Rushton, J. Philippe. 1988. 'Race Differences in Behaviour: A Review and Evolutionary Analysis', *Person-ality and Individual Differences* 9, 6: 1009–24.

Ryan, W. 1976. *Blaming the Victim*, 2nd edn. New York: Vintage.

Sabia, David R., Jr, and Jerald Wallulis. 1983. *Changing Social Science: Critical Theory and Other Critical Perspectives*. Albany: State University of New York Press.

Said, Edward. 1978. *Orientalism*. New York: Pantheon.

Saiflin, Murad, and Richard W. Dixon, eds. 1984. *Dictionary of Philosophy*. New York: International Publishers.

Saul, John Ralston. 2004. 'The Collapse of Globalism and the Rebirth of Nationalism', *Harper's Magazine* (Mar.): 33–43.

——. 2005. *The Collapse of Globalism and the Reinvention of the World*. Toronto: Viking Canada.

Schneider, Robert L., and Lori Lester. 2001. *Social Work Advocacy: A New Framework for Advocacy*. Belmont, Calif.: Brooks/Cole.

Schoenberg, R., and D. Goldberg, eds. 1984. *Homosexuality and Social Work*. New York: Haworth Press.

Schon, Donald A. 1983. *The Reflective Practitioner*. London: Temple Smith.

Scott, Joan. 1988. 'Deconstructing Equality-versus-Difference: Or the Uses of Post-Structuralist Theory for Feminism', *Feminist Studies* 14: 33–50.

Scruton, Richard. 1982. *A Dictionary of Political Thought*. London: Macmillan.

Scurfield, Raymond. 1980. 'An Integrated Approach to Case Services and Social Reform', *Social Casework* 61, 10: 610–18.

Seidman, Steven. 1998. *Contested Knowledge: Social Theory in the Postmodern Era*, 2nd edn. Malden, Mass.: Blackwell.

Selizam, E., ed. 1944. *Encyclopaedia of Social Sciences*, vol. 7. New York: Macmillan.

Sennett, Richard, and Jonathan Cobb. 1972. *The Hidden Injuries of Class*. New York: Vintage.

Shaffer, G.L. 1979. 'Labor Relations and the Unionization of Professional Social Workers: A Neglected Area in Social Work Education', *Journal of Education for Social Work* 15, 1: 80–6.

Shah, H. 1989. 'It's Up to You Sisters: Black Women and Radical Social Work', in Langan and Lee (1989b: 178–91).

Sherman, Wendy Ruth, and Stanley Wenocur. 1983. 'Empowering Public Welfare Workers through Mutual Support', *Social Work* 28, 5: 375–9.

Shulman, Lawrence. 1979. *The Skills of Helping Individuals and Groups*. Itasca, Ill.: F.E. Peacock.

Sidanius, Jim, and Felicia Pratto. 1999. *Social Dominance: An Intergroup Theory of Social Hierarchy and Oppression*. Cambridge: Cambridge University Press.

Sigurdson, Richard. 2002. 'Political Ideas and Ideologies,' in Dyck (2002: 97–121).

Sills, David, ed. 1968. *International Encyclopaedia of the Social Sciences*, vols 3, 12, 14. New York: Macmillan and Free Press.

Simon, Barbara Levy. 1990. 'Rethinking Empowerment', *Journal of Progressive Human Services* 1, 1: 27–39.

Simons, Ronald L. 1982. 'Strategies for Exercising Influence', *Social Work* 27, 3: 268–73.

Simpkin, Mike. 1979. *Trapped within Welfare: Surviving Social Work*. London: Macmillan.

Sklar, H., M. Albert, L. Cagan, N. Chomsky, R. Hahnel, M. King, and L. Sargent. 1986. *Liberating Theory*. Boston: South End Press.

Small, J. 1989. 'Towards a Black Perspective in Social Work: A Transformational Exploration', in Langan and Lee (1989b: 279–91).

Smid, G., and R. van Krieken. 1984. 'Notes on Theory and Practice in Social Work: A Comparative View', *British Journal of Social Work* 14: 11–27.

Smith, C., and S. White. 1997. 'Parton, Howe and Postmodernity: A Critical Comment on Mistaken Iden-tity', *British Journal of Social Work* 27: 275–95.

Smith, David G. (1968). 'Liberalism', in Sills (1968, vol. 3: 276–92).

Smith, T. 1993. 'Postmodernism: Theory and Politics', *The Activist* 3, 7: 31–4.

Statham, Daphne. 1978. *Radicals in Social Work*. London: Routledge & Kegan Paul.

Statistics Canada. 1993. *The Violence against Women Survey*. Ottawa: Ministry of Industry, Science and Technology.

Steger, Manfred B. 2002. *Globalism: The New Market Ideology*. Lanham, Md: Rowman & Littlefield.

——. 2003. *Globalization: A Very Short Introduction*. New York: Oxford University Press.

Stephenson, M., G. Rondeau, J.C. Michaud, and S. Fiddler. 2000. *In Critical Demand: Social Work in Canada*, vol. 1, *Final Report*. Ottawa: Canadian Association of Social Workers and Canadian Association of Schools of Social Work.

Stoez, D., and H. Karger. 1990. 'Welfare Reform: From Illusion to Reality', *Social Work* 35, 2: 141–7.

Strachey, J. 1936. *The Theory and Practice of Socialism*. London: Gollancz.

Swift, Karen. 1995. *Manufacturing 'Bad Mothers': A Critical Perspective on Child Neglect*. Toronto: University of Toronto Press.

Taylor, Charles. 1985. *Philosophy and the Human Sciences*. Cambridge: Cambridge University Press.

Taylor-Gooby, P. 1987. 'The Future of the British Welfare State', mimeo. Canterbury: University of Kent.

———. 1994. 'Postmodernism and Social Policy: A Great Leap Backwards?', *Journal of Social Policy* 23, 3: 385–404.

Teeple, Gary. 2000. *Globalization and the Decline of Social Reform: Into the Twenty-First Century*, 2nd edn. Aurora, Ont.: Garamond Press.

Thompson, Neil. 1993, 1997. *Anti-Discriminatory Practice*. London: Macmillan.

———. 1998. *Promoting Equality: Challenging Discrimination and Oppression in the Human Services*. London: Macmillan.

Throssell, Harold, ed. 1975. *Social Work: Radical Essays*. St Lucia, Queensland: University of Queensland Press.

Titmuss, Richard. 1958. *Essays on the Welfare State*. London: Allen & Unwin.

Tornebohm, Håkan. 1977. *Paradigms in Fields of Research*. Gothenburg: University of Gothenburg, Dept. of Theory of Science, Report No. 93.

Townsend, Joseph. 1817 [1786]. *A Dissertation on the Poor Laws by a Well-Wisher to Mankind*. London.

Trainor, Brian T. 1996. *Radicalism, Feminism and Fanaticism: Social Work in the Nineties*. Aldershot, UK: Avebury

Van Den Bergh, N., and L.B. Cooper, eds. 1986. *Feminist Visions for Social Work*. Silver Spring, Md: National Association of Social Workers.

van Houton, Gerry. 1992. 'Socialism Today: Renewal or Retreat?', in J. Roberts and J. Vorst, eds, *Socialism in Crisis? Canadian Perspectives*. Halifax and Winnipeg: Fernwood Publishing and Society for Socialist Studies, 117–46.

Vazala-Martinez, Iris. 1985. 'Toward an Emancipatory Clinical Practice in Human Services', in Gil and Gil (1985: 55–62).

Vincent, A. 1998. 'New Ideologies for Old?', *Political Quarterly* 69, 1: 48–58.

Wachholz, Sandra, and Robert Mullaly. 2000. 'The Politics of the Textbook: A Content Analysis of Feminist, Radical and Anti-Racist Social Work Scholarship in American Introductory Social Work Textbooks Published Between 1988 and 1997', *Journal of Progressive Human Services* 11, 2: 51–75.

Wagner, David. 1990. *The Quest for a Radical Profession*. Lanham, Md: University Press of America.

——— and Marcia B. Cohen. 1978. 'Social Workers, Class and Professionalism', *Catalyst* 1, 1: 25–55.

Walker, Gillian. 1977. 'The Status of Women in Social Work Education', a brief prepared for the Canadian Association of Schools of Social Work Task Force on the Status of Women in Social Work Education. Ottawa: CASSW.

Walters, M., B. Carter, P. Papp, and O. Silverstein. 1988. *The Invisible Web: Gender Patterns in Family Relationships*. New York: Guilford.

Wardell, M.L., and K.J. Benson. 1978. 'A Dialectical View: Foundation for an Alternative Sociological Method', paper presented at the annual convention of the Midwest Sociological Society, Omaha.

Warren, Roland L., Stephen Rose, and Ann Bergunder. 1974. *The Structure of Urban Reform*. Lexington, Mass.: D.C. Heath.

Wasserton, Richard. 1980. *Philosophy and Social Issues*. South Bend, Ind.: Notre Dame University Press.

Webster's New Collegiate Dictionary. 1980. Springfield, Mass.: G. & C. Merriam.

Weeks, Wendy. 1992. 'Gender in the Social and Community Services: Implications for Management', paper presented at Human Services Management Network Conference. Brisbane: Queensland University of Technology, Apr.

West, Cornel. 1982. *Prophesy Deliverance! An Afro-American Revolutionary Christianity*. Philadelphia: Westminster.

Wharf, Brian, ed. 1990. *Social Work and Social Change in Canada*. Toronto: McClelland & Stewart.

——. 1992. *Communities and Social Policy in Canada*. Toronto: McClelland & Stewart.

—— and John Cossom. 1987. 'Citizen Participation and Social Policy', in Yelaja (1987: 266–87).

White, S. 2001. 'The Ambiguities of the Third Way', in White, ed., *New Labour: The Progressive Future?* Basingstoke: Palgrave.

Wiggins, Cindy. 1996. 'Dismantling Unemployment Insurance: The Changes, the Impacts, the Reasons', *Canadian Review of Social Policy* 37: 75–84.

Wilding, P. 1982. *Professional Power and Social Welfare*. London: Routledge & Kegan Paul.

Wilensky, Harold L. 1975. *The Welfare State and Equality*. Berkeley: University of California Press.

—— and Charles N. Lebeaux. 1958, 1965. *Industrial Society and Social Welfare*. New York: Russell Sage Foundation.

Williams, Fiona. 1989. *Social Policy: A Critical Introduction—Issues of Race, Gender and Class*. New York: Blackwell.

Williams, Frank P., and Marilyn D. McShane. 1988. *Criminological Theory*. Englewood Cliffs, NJ: Prentice-Hall.

Wineman, Steven. 1984. *The Politics of Human Services*. Montreal: Black Rose Books.

Withorn, Ann. 1984. *Serving the People: Social Services and Social Change*. New York: Columbia University Press.

Wolfe, David. 1989. 'The Canadian State in Comparative Perspective', *Canadian Review of Sociology and Anthropology* 26, 1: 95–126.

Woodsworth, D.E. 1984. 'Social Work Forum: Dialogue on Ethics', *The Social Worker/Le Travailleur Social* 52, 2: 63–5.

Woodward, K. 1997. 'Concepts of Identity and Difference', in Woodward, ed., *Identity and Difference*. Milton Keynes: Open University.

Yalnizyan, A. 2005. *Canada's Commitment to Equality: A Gender Analysis of the Last Ten Federal Budgets (1995–2004)*. Ottawa: Canadian Feminist Alliance for International Action.

Yelaja, Shankar A. 1985. *An Introduction to Social Work Practice in Canada*. Scarborough, Ont.: Prentice-Hall Canada.

——, ed. 1987. *Canadian Social Policy*, 2nd edn. Waterloo, Ont.: Wilfrid Laurier University Press.

Young, Iris Marion. 1990. *Justice and the Politics of Difference*. Princeton, NJ: Princeton University Press.

Index